GO MATH!
FLORIDA

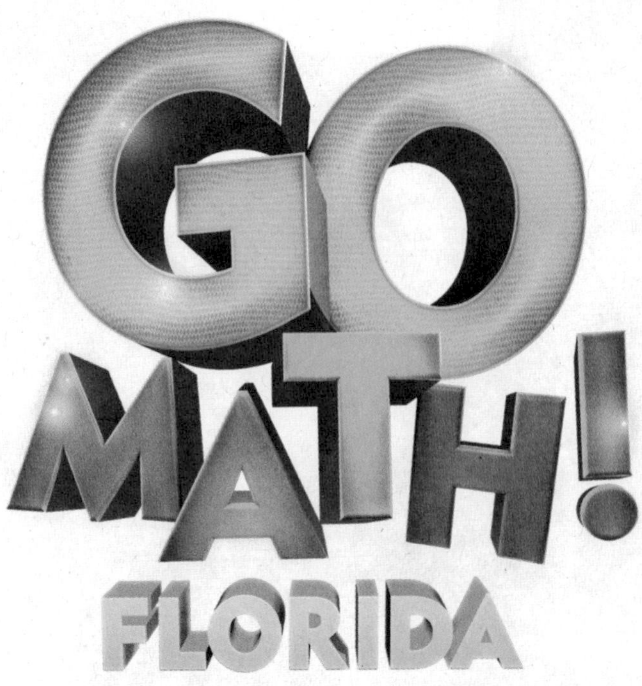

Printed in the U.S.A.

ISBN 13: 978-0-15-380264-5
ISBN 10: 0-15-380264-2

3 4 5 6 7 8 9 10 1421 19 18 17 16 15 14 13 12 11 10

4500236770

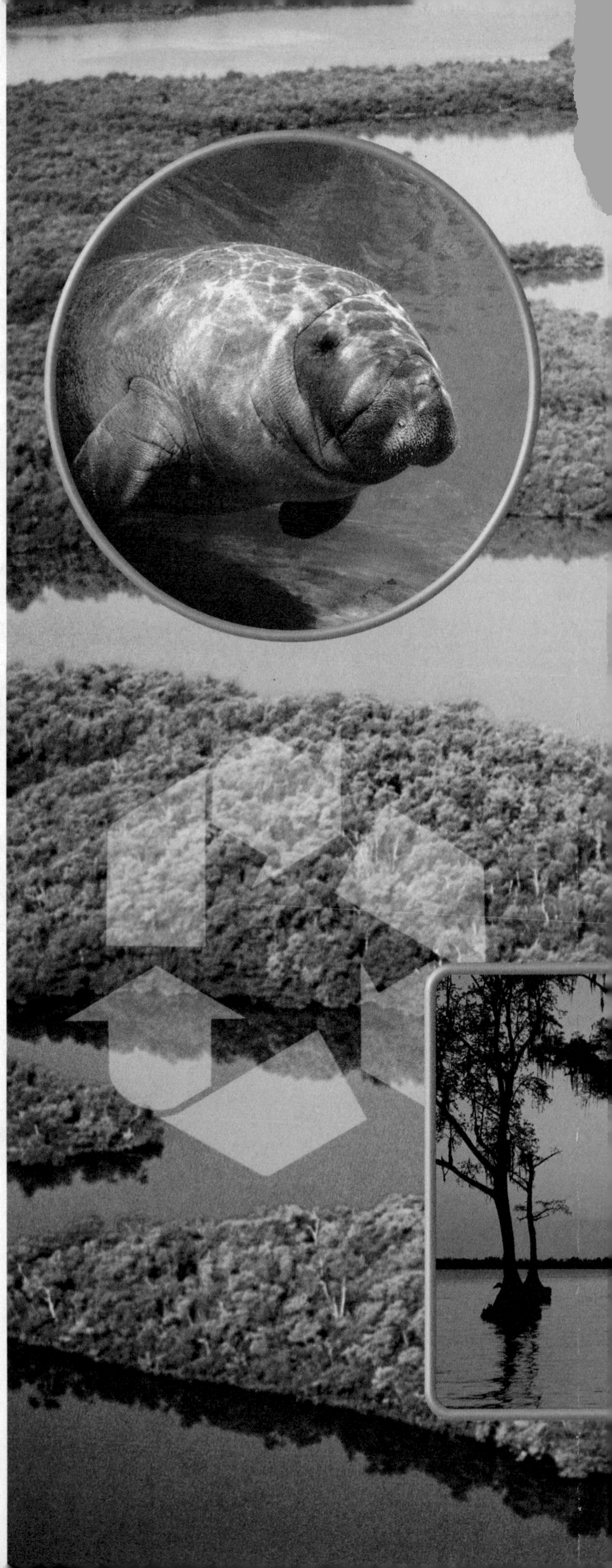

Dear Students and Families,

Welcome to **Go Math! Florida**, Grade 3! In this exciting mathematics program, there are hands-on activities to do and real-world problems to solve. Best of all, you will write your ideas and answers right in your book. In **Go Math! Florida**, writing and drawing on the pages helps you think deeply about what you are learning, and you will really understand math!

By the way, all of the pages in your **Go Math! Florida** book are made using recycled paper. We wanted you to know that you can Go Green with **Go Math! Florida.**

Sincerely,

The Authors

Planet Friendly Publishing*
Made in the United States
Printed on recycled paper, pages: 100% cover: 10%
By using this paper in a typical print run, we achieved the following environmental benefits:

- Trees Saved: 1,768
- Air Emissions Eliminated: 168,072 pounds
- Water Saved: 809,469 gallons
- Solid Waste Eliminated: 49,146 pounds

GREEN EDITION

** Learn more about our Planet Friendly Publishing efforts at greenedition.org*

** Environmental impact estimates calculated using the Environmental Defense Fund Paper Calculator. For more information, visit www.papercalculator.org*

Authors

Thomasenia Lott Adams
Professor of Mathematics Education
University of Florida
Gainesville, Florida

Juli K. Dixon
Professor of Mathematics Education
University of Central Florida
Orlando, Florida

Matt Larson
Curriculum Specialist for Mathematics
Lincoln Public Schools
Lincoln, Nebraska

Joyce C. McLeod
Visiting Professor, Retired
Rollins College, Hamilton Holt School
Winter Park, Florida

Miriam A. Leiva
Founding President, TODOS: Mathematics for All
Distinguished Professor of Mathematics Emerita
University of North Carolina
Charlotte, North Carolina

Consulting Author

Jean M. Shaw
Professor Emerita of Curriculum and Instruction
University of Mississippi
Oxford, Mississippi

Number and Operations

Develop understandings of multiplication and division and strategies for basic multiplication facts and related division facts.

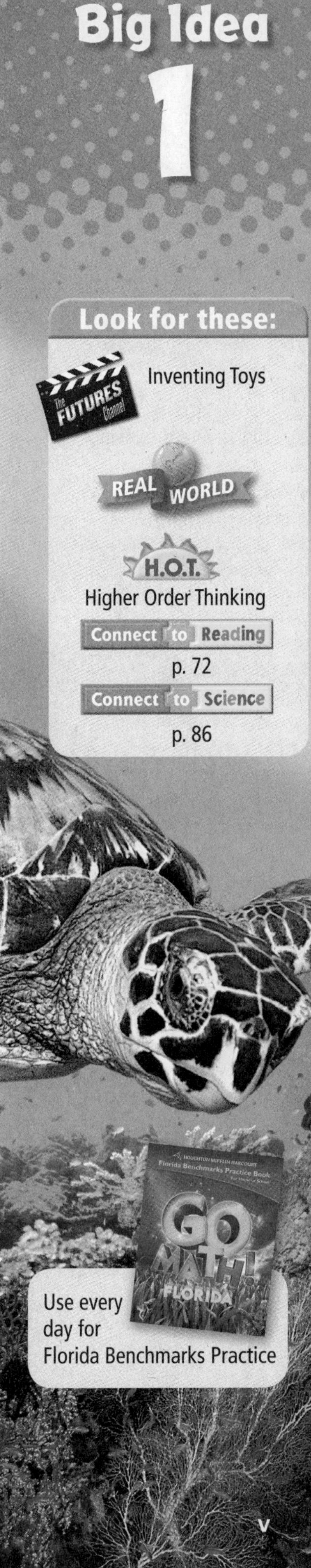

1 Teaching Benchmarks for Depth — PACING School Days: 12–14

MA.3.A.6.1: Lessons 1.2, 1.3, 1.4, 1.5, 1.6, 1.7, 1.8, 1.9, 1.10, 1.11, 1.12
MA.3.A.6.2: Lesson 1.1

2 Teaching Benchmarks for Depth — PACING School Days: 10–12

MA.3.S.7.1: Lessons 2.1, 2.3, 2.4, 2.5, 2.6, 2.7, 2.8, 2.9, 2.10
MA.3.A.6.2: Lesson 2.2

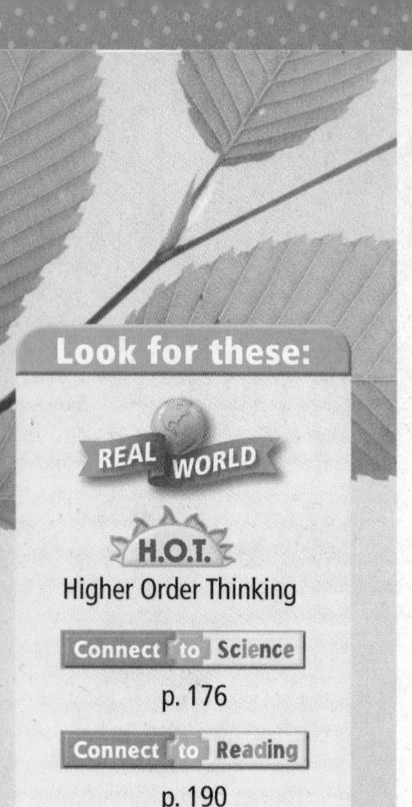

Look for these:

REAL WORLD

H.O.T. Higher Order Thinking

Connect to Science p. 176

Connect to Reading p. 190

Use every day for Florida Benchmarks Practice

3

Teaching Benchmarks for Depth — PACING School Days: 8–10

MA.3.A.1.1: Lessons 3.1, 3.2, 3.3, 3.4, 3.5, 3.6, 3.9
MA.3.A.1.2: Lessons 3.7, 3.8

Understand Multiplication 107

4

Teaching Benchmarks for Depth — PACING School Days: 12–13

MA.3.A.1.1: Lessons 4.1, 4.2, 4.4, 4.10
MA.3.A.1.2: Lessons 4.3, 4.5, 4.6, 4.8, 4.9, 4.11
MA.3.A.6.2: Lesson 4.7

Multiplication Facts and Strategies 151

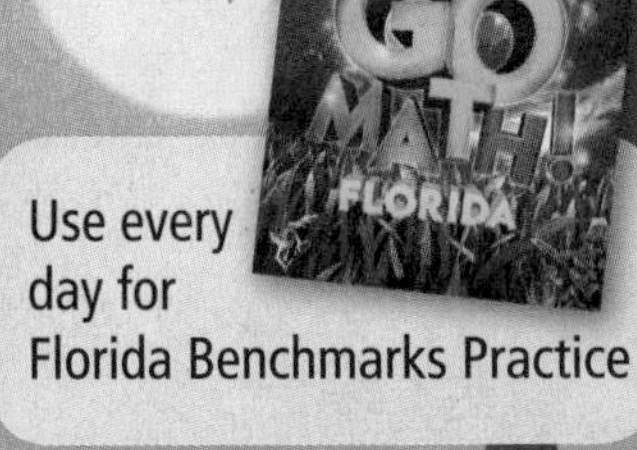

Use every day for Florida Benchmarks Practice

Big Idea 2

Look for these:

The First American Coins

Higher Order Thinking

Connect to Reading

p. 364

Use every day for Florida Benchmarks Practice

Fractions

Develop an understanding of fractions and fraction equivalence.

7

Teaching Benchmarks for Depth — PACING School Days: 10–11

MA.3.A.2.1: Lessons 7.1, 7.2, 7.3, 7.4, 7.5, 7.6, 7.7, 7.8, 7.9, 7.10

8

Teaching Benchmarks for Depth — PACING School Days: 8–9

MA.3.A.2.2: Lesson 8.3
MA.3.A.2.3: Lessons 8.1, 8.2, 8.4, 8.5
MA.3.A.2.4: Lessons 8.6, 8.7

Two-Dimensional Shapes

Describe and analyze properties of two-dimensional shapes.

9 Teaching Benchmarks for Depth — PACING School Days: 8–10

MA.3.G.3.1: Lessons 9.1, 9.2, 9.3, 9.4, 9.5, 9.6, 9.7
MA.3.A.6.2: Lesson 9.8

10 Teaching Benchmarks for Depth — PACING School Days: 10–12

MA.3.G.3.2: Lessons 10.1, 10.2, 10.4
MA.3.A.4.1: Lesson 10.3
MA.3.G.3.3: Lessons 10.5, 10.6, 10.7, 10.8, 10.9, 10.10

11 Teaching Benchmarks for Depth — Pacing School Days: 8–10

MA.3.G.5.2: Lessons 11.1, 11.2, 11.3, 11.4, 11.5
MA.3.G.5.1: Lessons 11.6, 11.7, 11.8
MA.3.A.6.2: Lesson 11.9

Length and Perimeter 463

12 Teaching Benchmarks for Depth — Pacing School Days: 8–9

MA.3.G.5.3: Lessons 12.1, 12.2, 12.3, 12.4, 12.5, 12.6, 12.7

Time 507

Big Idea 1

Number and Operations

BIG IDEA Develop understandings of multiplication and division and strategies for basic multiplication facts and related division facts.

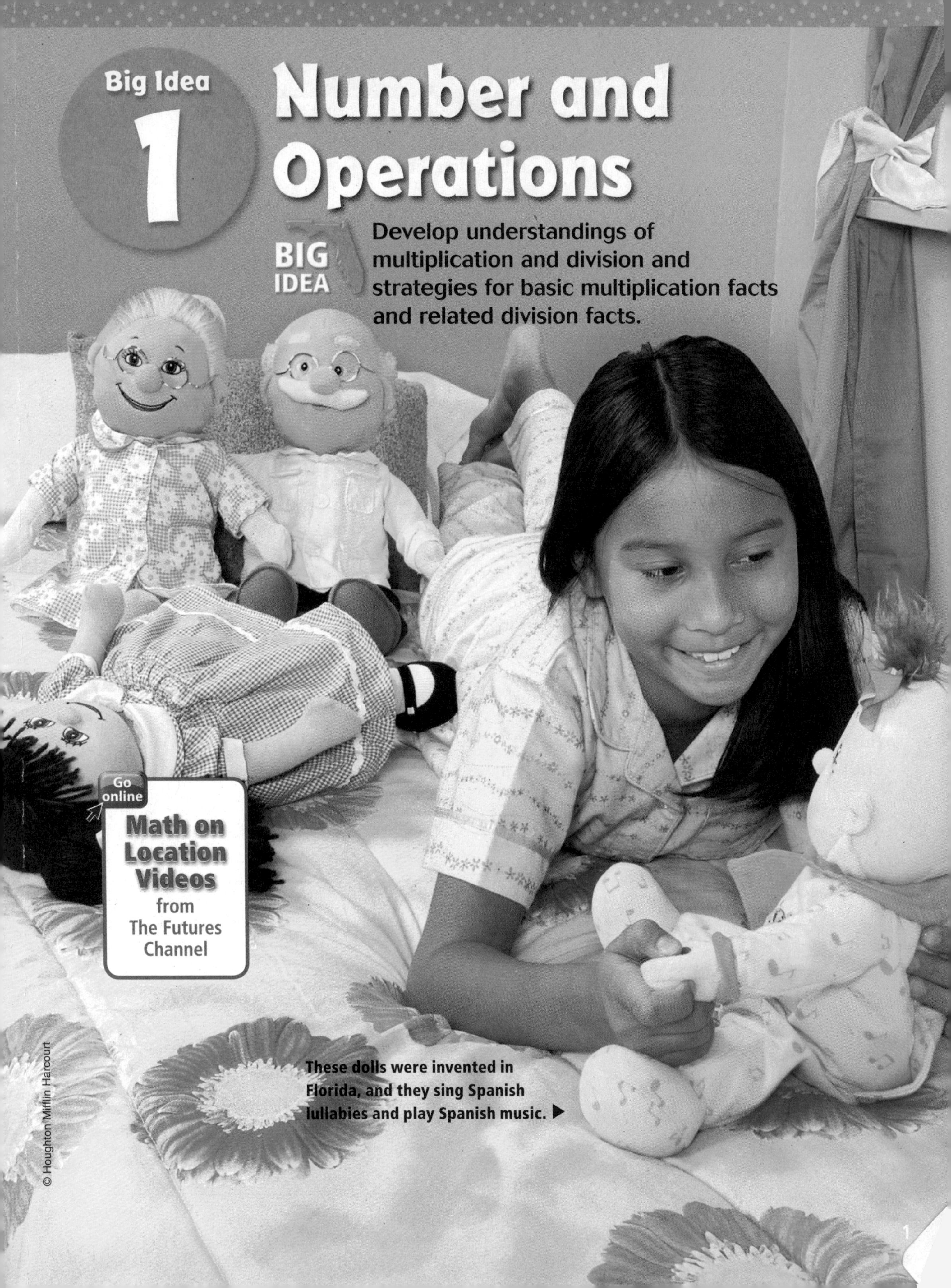

Go online

Math on Location Videos from The Futures Channel

These dolls were invented in Florida, and they sing Spanish lullabies and play Spanish music. ▶

with Math on Location Videos

Inventing Toys

The dolls in the picture are called Abuelitos. Some of them are grandmother and grandfather dolls that were invented to sing lullabies. They and the grandchildren dolls have music boxes inside them. You squeeze their hands to start them singing!

Project

You will begin to learn about the big idea when you work on this project.

Suppose you and a partner work in a toy store. You want to order enough dolls to fill two shelves in the store. Each shelf is 3 yards, or 108 inches, long. The dolls are sold in cartons of 4. Decide how many cartons you need to order so you will have enough doll boxes to fill the two shelves. Use the Important Facts to help.

Important Facts

- Each Abuelito doll is packaged in a box that is 15 inches tall by 8 inches wide by 7 inches deep.

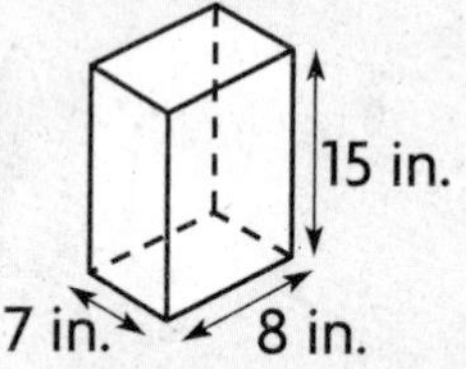

- Number of boxes in 1 carton: 4
- Abuelita Rosa sings 6 songs.
- Abuelito Pancho sings 4 songs.
- Baby Andrea and Baby Tita each sing 5 songs.
- Baby Mimi plays music but does not sing.

____

____

____

8 inches

____

____

____

____

Completed by _______________

Chapter 1

Place Value, Addition, and Subtraction

Show What You Know

Check your understanding of important skills.

Name ______________________________

Tens and Ones Regroup. Write the missing numbers.

1. 30 ones = _____ tens
2. 54 ones = _____ tens _____ ones

Regroup Tens as Hundreds Regroup. Write the missing numbers.

3. 53 tens = _____ hundreds _____ tens

Add.

4. $\begin{array}{r} 75 \\ +\ 42 \\ \hline \end{array}$
5. $\begin{array}{r} 266 \\ +\ 553 \\ \hline \end{array}$
6. $\begin{array}{r} 832 \\ +\ 795 \\ \hline \end{array}$

Regroup Hundreds as Tens Regroup. Write the missing numbers.

7. 4 hundreds 3 tens = _____ tens

Subtract.

8. $\begin{array}{r} 236 \\ -\ 72 \\ \hline \end{array}$
9. $\begin{array}{r} 438 \\ -\ 241 \\ \hline \end{array}$
10. $\begin{array}{r} 506 \\ -\ 353 \\ \hline \end{array}$

Florida FUN FACT

The Loggerhead Marinelife Center in Palm Beach County cares for 40 to 50 sick or injured sea turtles each year.

Vocabulary Power

▶ Visualize It

Sort the review words into the Venn diagram.

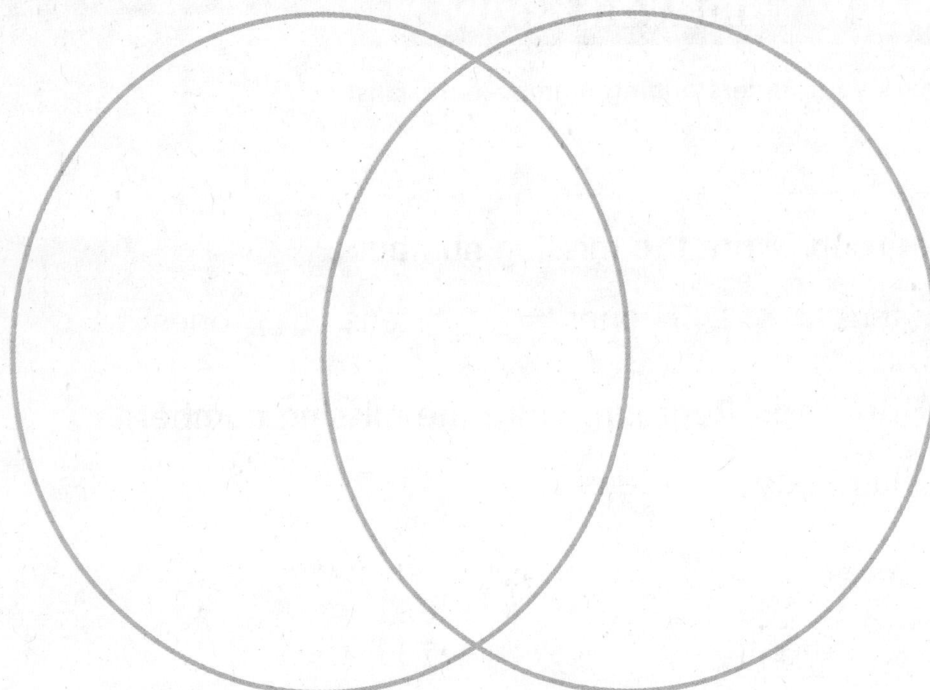

Review Words
add
difference
hundreds
ones
regroup
subtract
sum
tens

Preview Words
compatible numbers
estimate
expanded form
round
standard form
word form

▶ Understand Vocabulary

Complete the sentences by using the preview words.

1. A number close to an exact number is called an ____________________.

2. The ____________________ of a number is a way to write numbers by using words.

3. The ____________________ of a number is a way to write numbers by showing the value of each digit.

4. The ____________________ of a number is a way to write numbers by using the digits 0 to 9, with each digit having a place value.

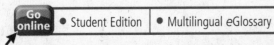

• Student Edition • Multilingual eGlossary

Name ____________________

Make a List · Place Value

Essential Question How can making a list help you solve a problem?

MA.3.A.6.2 Solve non-routine problems by making a table, chart, or list and searching for patterns.

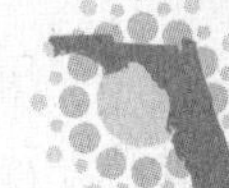

Josh wrote the numbers from 1 through 200. How many times did he write the digit 9 in the ones place? What pattern do you see?

Read the Problem

What do I need to find?

How many times did Josh write the digit ________ in the ________ place in the numbers from 1 through ________?

What information do I need to use?

all of the numbers from 1 through ________ that have the digit 9 in the ones place

How will I use the information?

I will make a list of the numbers and look for a pattern.

Solve the Problem

First, make a list of all the numbers from 1 through 100 that have a 9 in the ones place.

9	19	29		

Then, make a list of the numbers from 101 through 200 that have a 9 in the ones place.

109				

What pattern do you see? ____________________

____

____

____

1. How many times does the digit 9 appear from 1 through 100? ____________________

From 101 through 200? ____________________

Math Talk How can you find how many times the digit 9 appears in the ones place from 1 through 1,000? **Explain** your answer.

Try Another Problem

Abbie used a hundred chart to find all the 2-digit numbers in which the sum of the digits equals 10. How many numbers did she write? What pattern do you see?

1	2	3	4	5	6	7	8	9	10
11	12	13	14	15	16	17	18	19	20
21	22	23	24	25	26	27	28	29	30
31	32	33	34	35	36	37	38	39	40
41	42	43	44	45	46	47	48	49	50
51	52	53	54	55	56	57	58	59	60
61	62	63	64	65	66	67	68	69	70
71	72	73	74	75	76	77	78	79	80
81	82	83	84	85	86	87	88	89	90
91	92	93	94	95	96	97	98	99	100

Read the Problem	Solve the Problem
What do I need to find?	
What information do I need to use?	
How will I use the information?	

2. In how many 2-digit numbers does the sum of the digits equal 10? ______

3. What pattern helped you to complete the list?

______

Name ___________________________

Share and Show 

Tips

UNLOCK the Problem

- √ Circle the question.
- √ Underline important facts.
- √ Put the problem in your own words.
- √ Choose a strategy you know.

1. Julie is thinking of an even number between 12 and 29. The sum of the digits is the same as the digit in the tens place. What is Julie's number?

   First, make a list of all of the even numbers

   between _______ and _______.

   Next, _______ the digits of each number.

Even Numbers	12	14							
Sum of Digits	3								

   Then, use the last clue to find Julie's number.

   What is Julie's number? _______

SHOW YOUR WORK

2. H.O.T. **What if** Julie is thinking of an even number between 12 and 29 with digits whose difference is 7? What is the number?

   ____

3. Tami wrote the even numbers between 325 and 337. The sum of the hundreds digit and tens digit equals the ones digit. What is Tami's number?

   ____

4. Cary is thinking of an odd number between 32 and 48. The sum of the digits is 5. What is Cary's number?

   ____

5. Bryan wrote an odd number between 411 and 423. The sum of the digits is 12. What is the number?

   ____

On Your Own

6. Hillary saves 2 nickels each day. She starts saving on Monday. How many nickels will she have on Friday?

7. There are 3 rows of trumpet players in the marching band. There are 5 trumpet players in each row. How many trumpet players in all are in the marching band?

8. Sofia has 31 postcards. Adam has 7 fewer postcards than Sofia has. How many postcards does Adam have?

9. H.O.T. Write Math Tim, Matt, Valerie, and Lisa ran in a race. Lisa finished first. Matt did not finish second. Tim finished last. **Explain** how you can tell in which place Valerie finished.

10. **Test Prep** Peter wrote an even number between 32 and 54. The sum of the digits is 7. The tens digit is greater than the ones digit. What number did Peter write?

Ⓐ 25 Ⓒ 43

Ⓑ 34 Ⓓ 52

Choose a STRATEGY

- Act It Out
- Use Manipulatives
- Draw a Diagram
- Make a Table, Chart, or List
- Search for Patterns

SHOW YOUR WORK

FOR MORE PRACTICE:
Florida Benchmarks Practice Book, pp. P5–P6

Name ______________________________

Numbers Through Hundreds

Essential Question How can you represent 3-digit numbers in different ways?

MA.3.A.6.1 Represent, compute, estimate and solve problems using numbers through hundred thousands.

UNLOCK the Problem REAL WORLD

Emily needs 235 toy blocks to build a castle. The Hobbies and Toys store sells blocks in boxes of 100, in stacks of 10, and as individual pieces. How can Emily buy 235 blocks using the fewest boxes, stacks, and individual pieces?

- What does the *fewest* boxes, stacks, and individual pieces mean?

____

____

Use base-ten blocks to represent the toy blocks.

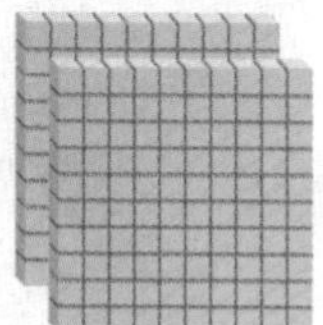

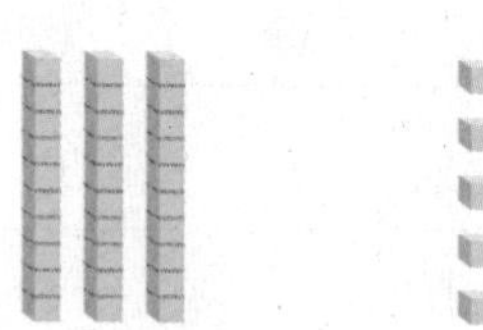

235 = _____ hundreds _____ tens _____ ones

So, Emily can buy _____ boxes of 100, _____ stacks of 10,

and _____ individual blocks.

Try This! Use a quick picture.

Suppose the toy store has no boxes of 100 blocks. What is another way Emily can buy 235 blocks? Look at the quick picture.

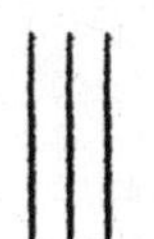

235 = _____ tens _____ ones

Think: 1 hundred = 10 tens

Math Talk **Explain** how Emily can buy 235 blocks if the toy store has only boxes of 100 and individual pieces.

More Examples

Elton needs 123 blocks to build a tower. The Toy Chest store sells blocks in boxes of 100, in stacks of 10, and as individual pieces. Find all the ways Elton can buy 123 blocks.

Make a list of all of the boxes, stacks, and individual pieces that equal 123.

BOXES OF 100	STACKS OF 10	INDIVIDUAL PIECES
	2	3
1	1	
1		23
	12	3
0	11	
0	10	
0		33
0	8	
0		53
0		63
0	5	
0	4	
0		93
0		103
0		113
0	0	

Math Talk **Explain** how you know the table lists all the ways.

• What pattern do you see in the list? ______________________

____

Name ___________________________

Share and Show 

1. Andy needs 157 blocks to build a house. He has 14 stacks of 10 blocks. Draw blocks to show how many more he needs.

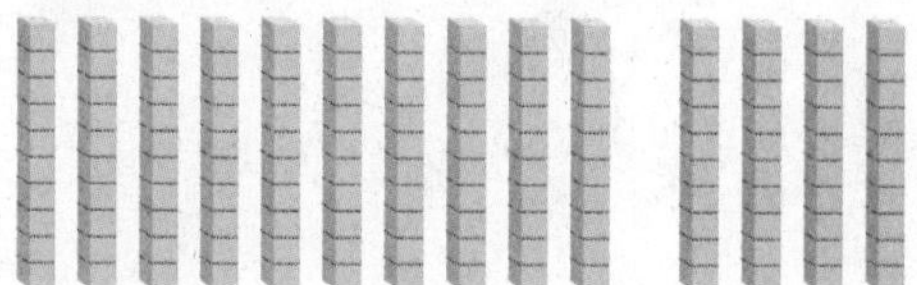

Math Talk Explain one way you can show the number 157 without tens blocks.

2. Write the number the blocks show. Draw a quick picture that shows the number another way.

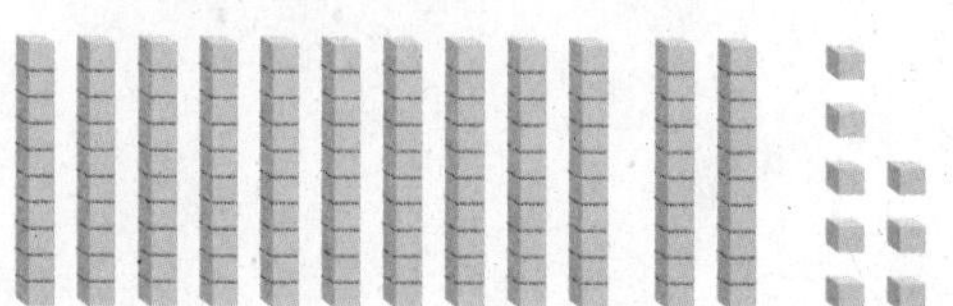

______

3. Complete the chart to show other ways to model the number 214.

HUNDREDS	TENS	ONES
2	1	
2		14
	11	4
1		14
1	9	

On Your Own

4. Write the number the blocks show. Draw a quick picture that shows the number another way.

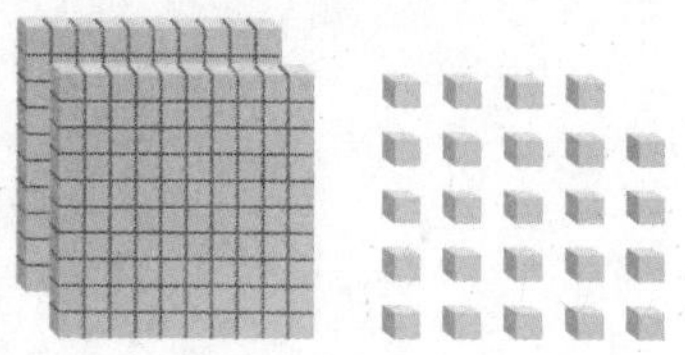

______

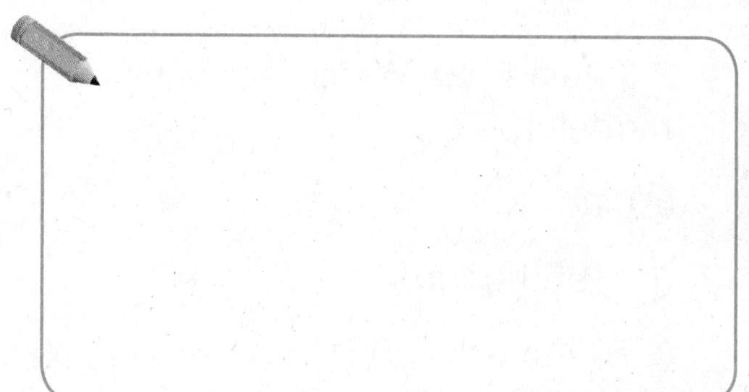

Problem Solving REAL WORLD

SHOW YOUR WORK

5. Taylor needs 270 toy blocks to build a train. The toy store sells boxes of 100 and stacks of 10. Taylor wants to buy the fewest boxes and stacks. Draw a model of the blocks he will buy.

6. If you buy 4 boxes of 100 blocks and 86 stacks of 10 blocks, do you have 486 blocks? **Explain.**

____

____

7. Write Math **What's the Error?** Brian drew this model and said it was the number 5024. **Explain** his error.

| | | | | | o o o o
| | | | | | o o o o o
| | | | | | o o o o o
| | | | | | o o o o o
| | | | | | o o o o o

____

____

8. H.O.T. Eve has 24 stacks of 10 blocks. Dan has 2 boxes of 100 blocks and 38 individual pieces. Who has more blocks? **Explain.**

____

____

9. **Test Prep** Which is a way to model 496?

Ⓐ 496 tens

Ⓑ 496 hundreds

Ⓒ 4 hundreds 96 ones

Ⓓ 49 tens 16 ones

FOR MORE PRACTICE:
Florida Benchmarks Practice Book, pp. P7–P8

Name ____________________

Numbers Through Thousands

Essential Question How can you represent 4-digit numbers in different ways?

MA.3.A.6.1 Represent, compute, estimate and solve problems using numbers through hundred thousands.

UNLOCK the Problem REAL WORLD

A toy store sells blocks in crates of 1,000. The ABC Blocks factory uses boxes of 100 blocks to pack a crate of 1,000. How many boxes of 100 blocks are in each crate of 1,000?

- Underline what the problem is asking you to find.
- Circle the number you will count by to find the answer.

Count the total number of boxes of 100 blocks that will go into each crate.

[1] [2] 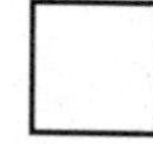 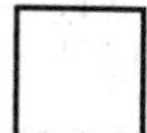  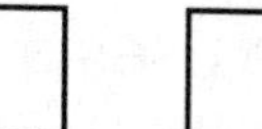  [ ] [ ] [ ]

100 200 ______ ______ ______ ______ ______ ______ ______ ______

So, there are ______ boxes of 100 blocks in each crate of 1,000.

Example

ABC Blocks has an order for 2,640 blocks. Suppose the factory has no crates. How many boxes of 100 will it pack?

You know there are 10 boxes of 100 in 1,000,

so there are ______ boxes of 100 in 2,000.

There are ______ hundreds in 640.

Add the hundreds. 20 + 6 = ______

In 2,640 there are ______ hundreds.

So, the factory will pack ______ boxes of 100.

Math Talk What if the factory had crates and stacks, but no boxes? **Explain** how it could pack the order.

Try This! **Show numbers in different ways.**

A When George packs orders at ABC Blocks, he likes to use the fewest crates, boxes, stacks, and pieces. George's packing list is shown below. Complete the chart.

Number of Blocks Ordered	Crates (Thousands)	Boxes (Hundreds)	Stacks (Tens)	Pieces (Ones)
1,479		4		9
5,084	5			4

B When there are not enough crates, boxes, or stacks to pack the orders, George uses a package that is the next smaller size. The list below shows what packages George cannot use. Complete the packing chart.

Number of Blocks Ordered	Crates (Thousands)	Boxes (Hundreds)	Stacks (Tens)	Pieces (Ones)
1,479	0			9
5,084		0	0	

C George drew a quick picture to show 1,479 blocks a different way. Use a symbol to tell if the models are equal or not equal.

Math Idea

= is equal to

≠ is not equal to

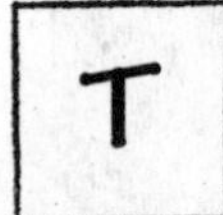

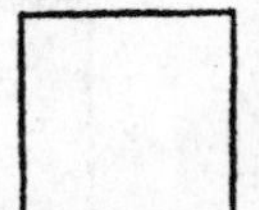

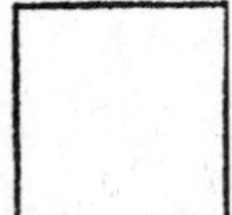

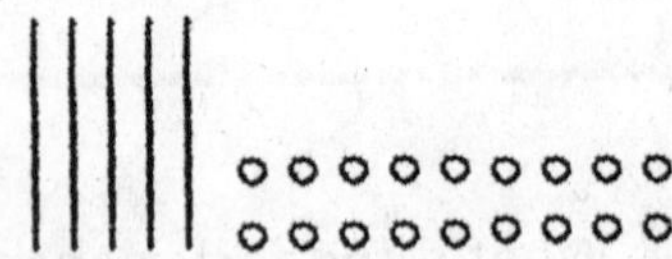

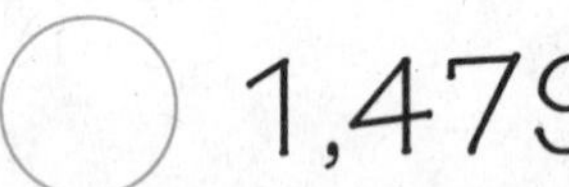

1,479

Name ____________________

Share and Show 

1. The block factory has an order for 2,140 blocks. How can it pack the blocks using the fewest crates, boxes, and stacks?

____

Remember

Crate = 1,000 blocks

Box = 100 blocks

Stack = 10 blocks

2. Suppose the block factory has only boxes and stacks? How can it pack the order for 2,140 blocks?

____

3. Suppose the block factory has only crates and stacks? How can it pack the order for 2,140 blocks?

____

Math Talk If the block factory has only 1 crate, some boxes, and some stacks, **explain** how it can pack the order.

On Your Own

Complete the packing chart. Use the fewest crates, boxes, stacks, and pieces.

	Number of Blocks Ordered	Crates (Thousands)	Boxes (Hundreds)	Stacks (Tens)	Pieces (Ones)
4.	3,287	3			7
5.	4,609		6	0	
6.	2,715				

Complete the packing chart. When there is a zero, use the next smaller size package.

	Number of Blocks Ordered	Crates (Thousands)	Boxes (Hundreds)	Stacks (Tens)	Pieces (Ones)
7.	2,418	0		1	8
8.	5,123	5	0		
9.	4,967	0		0	

Problem Solving REAL WORLD

Think: 1 crate = 1,000; 1 box = 100; 1 stack = 10

10. The block factory packed 2 crates, 6 boxes, and 9 stacks of blocks. How many blocks were packed in all?

____

SHOW YOUR WORK

11. The block factory packed 3 crates, 6 boxes, and 5 stacks of blocks. Then they packed 3 crates, 7 boxes, and 4 stacks of blocks. Are the orders equal or not equal? Write = or ≠.

____

12. H.O.T. Suppose you model the number 1,400 with base-ten blocks. You use 41 base-ten blocks. Which blocks do you use?

____

13. **Write Math** The block factory packed orders for 1,575 blocks and 1,725 blocks. Which order is larger? **Explain**

____

____

____

14. **Test Prep** Which is NOT a way to model 1,257 with base-ten blocks?

Ⓐ 1 thousand 2 hundreds 5 tens 7 ones

Ⓑ 1 thousand 25 hundreds 7 ones

Ⓒ 12 hundreds 57 ones

Ⓓ 1 thousand 257 ones

FOR MORE PRACTICE:
Florida Benchmarks Practice Book, pp. P9–P10

Name ___________________________

Read and Write Numbers Through Thousands

MA.3.A.6.1 Represent, compute, estimate and solve problems using numbers through hundred thousands.

Essential Question What are some ways you can read and write numbers?

UNLOCK the Problem REAL WORLD

When ABC Blocks receives an order, it is given to a team of workers. Each worker on the team checks the order by expressing the number in a different form. A new order for 4,365 blocks has come in. What form does each team member use?

- How many blocks were ordered?

____

Word form is a way to write numbers the way you say them.

Sam gets the order and reads the number to Mary.

four thousand, three hundred sixty-five

Expanded form is a way to write numbers by showing the value of each digit.

Mary records the total number of blocks that will be in each type of package.

4,000 + 300 + 60 + 5

Math Idea

The location of a digit in a number tells its value.

Standard form is a way to write numbers by using the digits 0–9, with each digit having a place value.

When the order is complete, Kyle writes the total number of blocks on the packing slip.

4,365

So, Sam says the number using _____________ form, Mary uses _____________ form, and Kyle uses _____________ form.

Math Talk What is the least number of crates, boxes, stacks, and individual pieces needed for the order for 4,365 blocks? **Think:** 1 crate = 1,000; 1 box = 100; 1 stack = 10

Try This! Complete the chart to show each number in three ways.

Standard Form	Expanded Form	Word Form
5,702		five thousand, ________ hundred ________
		two thousand, four hundred ninety-one
	3,000 + 600 + 80 + 7	________ thousand, ________ hundred eighty-seven

Share and Show 

1. Complete the expanded form for 6,295.

________ + 200 + 90 + ________

Math Talk **Explain** how you can tell the number of each type of package by looking at the expanded form of a number.

Write the number in standard form.

2. 8,000 + 200 + 40 + 9

____

3. five thousand, two hundred sixteen

____

4. 6,000 + 80 + 7

____

5. three thousand, four hundred two

____

Complete the chart to show the number in three ways.

	Standard Form	Expanded Form	Word Form
6.		7,000 + 500 + 60 + 2	________ thousand, ________ hundred sixty-two
7.			eight thousand, ninety
8.	4,103		________ thousand, one hundred ________
9.			six thousand, forty-nine

Name ____________________

On Your Own

Write the number in standard form.

10. seven thousand, eighty-one ____________________

11. $4{,}000 + 600 + 90 + 8$ ____________________

Complete the chart to show the number in three ways.

	Standard Form	Expanded Form	Word Form
12.	1,307		one thousand, ________ hundred ________
13.		6,000 + 10 + 4	six thousand, fourteen
14.			seven thousand, three hundred twenty-one

Write the value of the underlined digit.

15. $\underline{9},427$ ________

16. $5,\underline{0}84$ ________

17. $2,3\underline{2}0$ ________

18. $4,69\underline{8}$ ________

19. $3,00\underline{2}$ ________

20. $6,1\underline{3}5$ ________

21. $\underline{4},573$ ________

22. $8,\underline{7}90$ ________

Complete the expanded form.

23. 1,000 + ____________ + 40 + 6 = 1,746

24. ____________ + 200 + ____________ + 3 = 5,273

25. 7,000 + ____________ + ____________ = 7,081

26. ____________ + ____________ + ____________ = 4,309

Problem Solving REAL WORLD

27. Unscramble the place values. Write the number two ways.
4 tens + 8 thousands + 6 ones + 5 hundreds

____

____

28. Write Math Neal wrote a 4-digit number. One digit was zero. The other digits were even numbers. Neal did not use the same digit twice. What is the least number he could have written? **Explain** how you know.

____

____

____

____

29. **Sense or Nonsense** Is 3,000 + 650 + 2 equal or not equal to 3,000 + 400 + 200 + 52? Write = or ≠. **Explain.**

____

____

30. H.O.T. Write all the possible odd 4-digit numbers using the digits 1, 4, 7, and 0.

____

____

31. **Test Prep** The block factory received an order for 3,870 blocks. Which of the following is equal to 3,870?

Ⓐ 3,000 + 80 + 7
Ⓑ 3,000 + 800 + 7
Ⓒ 3,000 + 700 + 8
Ⓓ 3,000 + 800 + 70

FOR MORE PRACTICE:
Florida Benchmarks Practice Book, pp. P11–P12

Name ______________________________

Numbers Through Hundred Thousands

MA.3.A.6.1 Represent, compute, estimate and solve problems using numbers through hundred thousands.

Essential Question What patterns can you use with place value?

CONNECT You have learned how to find the value of a digit in a 4-digit number. You can use a pattern to find the value of a digit in any number.

UNLOCK the Problem

Look at the patterns in the table.

ones	1
tens	10 ones = 10
hundreds	10 tens = 100
thousands	10 hundreds = 1,000
ten thousands	10 thousands = 10,000
hundred thousands	10 ten thousands = 100,000

What patterns do you see? ______________________________

____

____

Try This! Use the place-value chart below to answer the questions.

Hundred Thousands	Ten Thousands	Thousands	Hundreds	Tens	Ones
	6	0,	0	0	0
5	0	0,	0	0	0

In 60,000,

- how many ten thousands in all? ______
- how many thousands in all? ______
- how many hundreds in all? ______

In 500,000,

- how many ten thousands in all? ______
- how many thousands in all? ______
- how many hundred thousands in all? ______

Example

Jacksonville is the largest city in Florida. Recently there were 852,460 people living in Jacksonville. How many thousands of people in all lived there?

Jacksonville

_____ is in the hundred thousands place

and has a value of ____________________.

_____ is in the ten thousands place and has a

value of ____________________.

_____ is in the thousands place and has a value of ____________________.

_____ is in the hundreds place and has a value of ____________________.

_____ is in the tens place and has a value of ____________________.

_____ is in the ones place and has a value of ____________________.

Write the number 852,460 in expanded form.

____________________ + 50,000 + ____________________ + 400 + ____________

Think: To find the total number of thousands, you have to add the numbers of thousands, ten thousands, and hundred thousands.
800 + 50 + 2 = 852

So, there are 852 thousand people in all.

Try This! **Use a place-value chart to compare two numbers.**

There were 155,315 people living in Port St. Lucie and 164,523 people living in Cape Coral. In which city did more people live?

Hundred Thousands	Ten Thousands	Thousands	Hundreds	Tens	Ones
1	5	5,	3	1	5
1	6	4,	5	2	3

Start at the left. The hundred thousands are the same.
Compare the ten thousands. They are not the same.
6 > 5, so 164,523 > 155,315. So, there were more people living in Cape Coral.

Name ______________________

Share and Show 

Use the place-value chart.

Ten Thousands	Thousands	Hundreds	Tens	Ones
4	0,	0	0	0

Math Talk Describe the pattern you see in the chart.

In 40,000,

1. how many ten thousands in all? ______

2. how many thousands in all? ______

3. how many hundreds in all? ______

On Your Own

Use the place-value chart.

Hundred Thousands	Ten Thousands	Thousands	Hundreds	Tens	Ones
7	0	0,	0	0	0

In 700,000,

4. how many hundred thousands in all? ______

5. how many thousands in all? ______

Complete the sentences.

The capital of Florida is Tallahassee. In a recent year, there were 176,429 people living in Tallahassee.

6. The digit ______ is in the ten thousands place and has a value of ______.

7. The digit ______ is in the hundreds place and has a value of ______.

8. Write the number 176,429 in expanded form.

______

9. Fort Lauderdale, Florida, has 179,971 people. Is that more or fewer people than Tallahassee has? ______

Problem Solving REAL WORLD

Use the table for 10–12.

Population	
City	**Number of People**
Hialeah	228,528
Miami	395,434
Orlando	228,765
St. Petersburg	253,369
Tampa	336,264

10. How many thousands of people live in Miami?

11. Which city has more people—Hialeah or Orlando?

12. Which cities have more than 25 ten thousands of people?

SHOW YOUR WORK

13. The Tampa Bay Rays baseball team plays its home games in Tropicana Field in St. Petersburg, Florida. The stadium holds 45,000 people. How many hundreds of people in all can the stadium hold?

14. H.O.T. Unscramble the place values. Write the number in standard form. 3 tens + 4 ten thousands + 9 ones + 8 thousands + 2 hundred thousands + 6 hundreds

15. **Test Prep** On one day, a theme park in Central Florida had 26,572 visitors. How many thousands of people visited the theme park?

Ⓐ 26

Ⓑ 2

Ⓒ 265

Ⓓ 65

FOR MORE PRACTICE:
Florida Benchmarks Practice Book, pp. P13–P14

Name ________________________

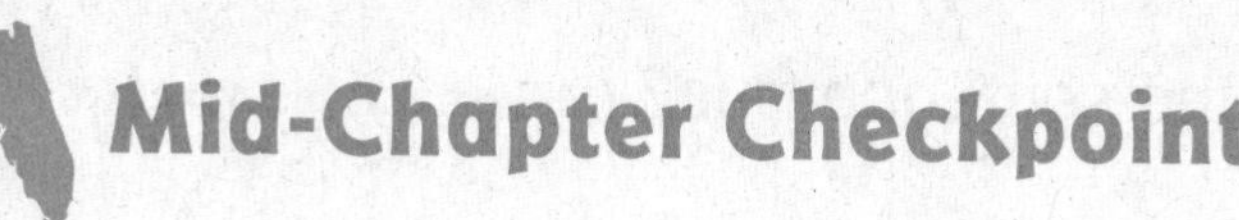

▶ Check Vocabulary

Choose the best term from the box.

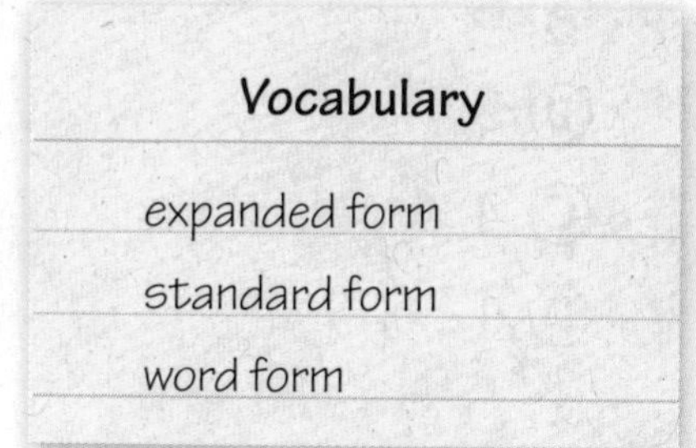

1. The ________________ of a number is a way to write numbers by using words. (MA.3.A.6.1; p. 17)
2. A way to write numbers by showing the value of each digit is called ________________. (MA.3.A.6.1; p. 17)

▶ Check Concepts

3. Write the number the blocks show. Draw a quick picture that shows the number another way. (MA.3.A.6.1; pp. 9–12)

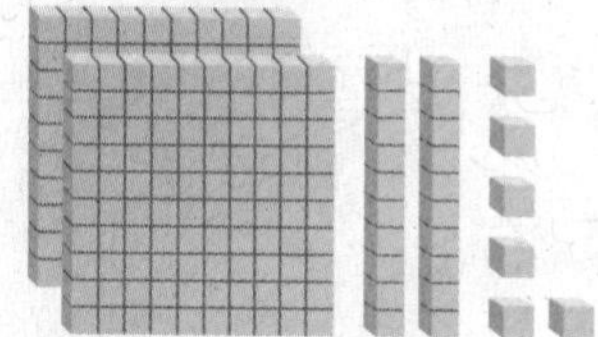

____

Write the number in standard form. (MA.3.A.6.1; pp. 17–20)

4. $8{,}000 + 500 + 90 + 3$ ________________
5. six thousand, seventeen ________________
6. nine thousand, eighty ________________
7. $7{,}000 + 400 + 9$ ________________

Complete the packing chart. Use the fewest crates, boxes, stacks, and pieces. (MA.3.A.6.1; pp. 13–16)

	Number of Blocks Ordered	Crates (Thousands)	Boxes (Hundreds)	Stacks (Tens)	Pieces (Ones)
8.	8,635	8		3	
9.	4,702		7		2

Fill in the bubble for the correct answer choice.

10. Which digit makes the sentence true? (MA.3.A.6.1; pp. 13–16)

8,▢14 < 8,395

Ⓐ 6

Ⓑ 5

Ⓒ 4

Ⓓ 1

11. What is NOT a way to model 1,428? (MA.3.A.6.1; pp. 13–16)

Ⓕ 142 hundreds 8 ones

Ⓖ 14 hundreds 2 tens 8 ones

Ⓗ 1 thousand 4 hundreds 2 tens 8 ones

Ⓘ 14 hundreds 28 ones

12. In 2007, there were fifty-one thousand, seven hundred twenty-five students enrolled at the University of Florida, in Gainesville. What is another way to write this number? (MA.3.A.6.1; pp. 21–24)

Ⓐ 50,000 + 1,000 + 700 + 20 + 5

Ⓑ 51,275

Ⓒ 50,000 + 7,000 + 100 + 20 + 5

Ⓓ 50,725

13. One dolphin at the Sea Center weighed 104 pounds. Which is a way to model 104? (MA.3.A.6.1; pp. 9–12)

Ⓕ 10 hundreds 4 ones

Ⓖ 104 tens

Ⓗ 10 tens 4 ones

Ⓘ 104 hundreds

Name ____________________

Estimate Sums

Essential Question How can you estimate sums using rounding and compatible numbers?

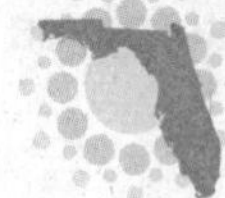

MA.3.A.6.1 Represent, compute, estimate and solve problems using numbers through hundred thousands.

The table shows how many dogs went to the park during the summer months. About how many dogs went to the park during June and August?

Pine Lake Dog Park

Month	Number of Dogs
June	1,632
July	617
August	489

You can estimate to find *about* how many. An **estimate** is a number close to an exact amount.

One Way Use compatible numbers.

Compatible numbers are numbers that are easy to compute mentally and are close to the real numbers.

$$\begin{array}{r} 1{,}632 \\ +\ \ 489 \\ \hline \end{array} \rightarrow \begin{array}{r} 1{,}500 \\ +\ \ \ \ \ 5\ \square \\ \hline \end{array}$$

So, about __________ dogs went to Pine Lake Dog Park in June and August.

Math Talk Will the sum of the compatible numbers 1,500 and 500 be greater than or less than the exact sum? **Explain.**

- What other compatible numbers could you have used?

____

- About how many dogs went to the park during July and August? What compatible numbers could you use to estimate?

____

Another Way Use place value to round.

1,632 + 489 = ■

When you **round** a number, you find a number that tells about how much or about how many.

Rounding

- Find the place to which you want to round. Round both numbers to the same place value.
- Look at the digit to its right.
- If the digit is less than 5, the digit in the rounding place stays the same.
- If the digit is 5 or more, the digit in the rounding place increases by one.
- Write zeros for the digits to the right.

STEP 1 Round 1,632 to the nearest hundred.

- Record the 1 in the thousands place.
- Since $3 < 5$, the digit 6 stays the same.
- Write zeros for the tens and ones places.

```
  1,632  →  ■
+   489     + ___
```

STEP 2 Round 489 to the nearest hundred.

- Since $8 > 5$, the digit 4 increases by one.
- Write zeros for the tens and ones places.

```
  1,632  →    1,600
+   489  →  + ■
```

STEP 3 Find the sum.

```
  1,632  →    1,600
+   489  →  +   500
                ■
```

Math Talk **Explain** how rounding and using compatible numbers are alike.

Try This! Find an estimate.

A Use compatible numbers.

```
  847  →    ■
+ 462  →  + 450
            ■
```

B Use rounding.

```
  5,304  →    5,000
+ 3,941  →  + ■
              ■
```

Name ______________________________

Share and Show 

1. Use compatible numbers to complete the problem. Then estimate the sum.

$$\begin{array}{r} 3{,}428 \\ +\ 432 \\ \hline \end{array} \qquad \begin{array}{r} 3,\square \\ +\ \square \\ \hline \square \end{array}$$

Math Talk What other compatible numbers could you use for 3,428 and 432?

Estimate the sum.

2. $\begin{array}{r} 3{,}697 \\ +\ 4{,}805 \\ \hline \end{array}$ $\begin{array}{r} \square \\ +\ \square \\ \hline \square \end{array}$

✓3. $\begin{array}{r} 421 \\ +\ 218 \\ \hline \end{array}$ $\begin{array}{r} \square \\ +\ \square \\ \hline \square \end{array}$

✓4. $\begin{array}{r} 1{,}492 \\ +\ 847 \\ \hline \end{array}$ $\begin{array}{r} \square \\ +\ \square \\ \hline \square \end{array}$

On Your Own

Estimate the sum.

5. $\begin{array}{r} 319 \\ +\ 54 \\ \hline \end{array}$ $\begin{array}{r} \square \\ +\ \square \\ \hline \square \end{array}$

6. $\begin{array}{r} 271 \\ +\ 430 \\ \hline \end{array}$ $\begin{array}{r} \square \\ +\ \square \\ \hline \square \end{array}$

7. $\begin{array}{r} 327 \\ +\ 581 \\ \hline \end{array}$ $\begin{array}{r} \square \\ +\ \square \\ \hline \square \end{array}$

8. $\begin{array}{r} 5{,}328 \\ +\ 893 \\ \hline \end{array}$ $\begin{array}{r} \square \\ +\ \square \\ \hline \square \end{array}$

9. $\begin{array}{r} 1{,}037 \\ +\ 517 \\ \hline \end{array}$ $\begin{array}{r} \square \\ +\ \square \\ \hline \square \end{array}$

10. $\begin{array}{r} 1{,}057 \\ +\ 478 \\ \hline \end{array}$ $\begin{array}{r} \square \\ +\ \square \\ \hline \square \end{array}$

11. $\begin{array}{r} 3{,}806 \\ +\ 2{,}460 \\ \hline \end{array}$ $\begin{array}{r} \square \\ +\ \square \\ \hline \square \end{array}$

12. $\begin{array}{r} 2{,}217 \\ +\ 1{,}148 \\ \hline \end{array}$ $\begin{array}{r} \square \\ +\ \square \\ \hline \square \end{array}$

13. $\begin{array}{r} 6{,}732 \\ +\ 3{,}244 \\ \hline \end{array}$ $\begin{array}{r} \square \\ +\ \square \\ \hline \square \end{array}$

Problem Solving REAL WORLD

Use the table for 14–15.

Dan's Pet Supplies Sold		
Month	**Bags of Pet Food**	**Toys**
June	619	2,210
July	970	3,032
August	728	2,540

SHOW YOUR WORK

14. Dan is looking at the list of supplies he sold. About how many bags of pet food did Dan sell in June and July?

____

15. Hank estimated the number of toys sold for three months and said the estimate was 7,000. Karl estimated the number of toys sold and said the estimate was 8,000. **Explain** how Karl found his estimate. _______________

____

____

____

____

16. Pete's Pets ordered 2,047 bags of cat food and 1,429 bags of dog food. About how many bags of food did Pete's Pets order? **Explain** how you estimated.

____

____

____

17. **Test Prep** For her new pet store, Tracy ordered 325 pet toys, 165 bags of dog food and 1,442 cans of cat food. About how many total items did Tracy order?

Ⓐ 1,500 Ⓒ 2,500

Ⓑ 1,900 Ⓓ 3,000

FOR MORE PRACTICE:
Florida Benchmarks Practice Book, pp. P15–P16

Name ____________________

Add 4-Digit Numbers

Essential Question How can you use different strategies to add 4-digit numbers?

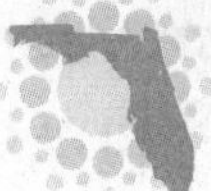

MA.3.A.6.1 Represent, compute, estimate and solve problems using numbers through hundred thousands.

UNLOCK the Problem REAL WORLD

Amy's family members are planning a car trip from Minneapolis, Minnesota, to Orlando, Florida. They will first travel 1,120 miles to Atlanta, Georgia. Then they will travel 480 miles to Orlando.

How many miles will Amy's family travel in all?

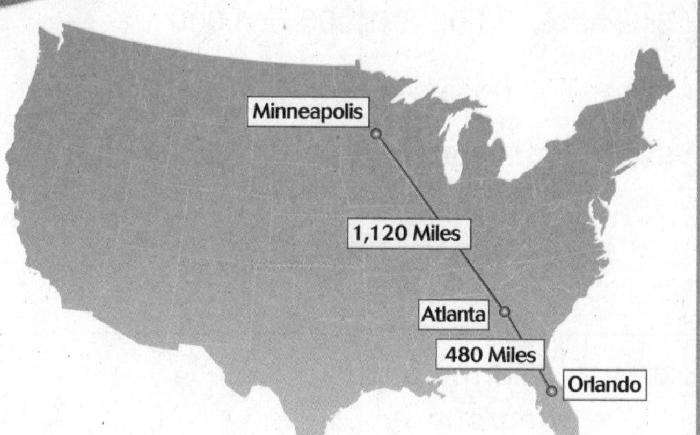

One Way Use the Break Apart strategy. 1,120 + 480

STEP 1 Estimate.

1,120	→		1,000
+ 480	→	+	500
			1,500

Estimating before you find the exact answer helps you know if your exact answer is reasonable.

STEP 2 Break apart the addends. Start with the thousands. Then add each place.

1,120	=	1,000 +	____	+	20	
+ 480	=		400	+	____	
		1,000 +	500	+	____	

Find the total sum. ____________

So, Amy's family will travel ____________ miles in all.

Since 1,600 is close to the estimate of 1,500, the answer is reasonable.

Math Talk What is another way to break apart 1,120 + 480?

Try This! **Use the Break Apart strategy to find 1,643 + 432.**

1,643	=	1,000 +	____	+	____	+	____
+ 432	=		400	+	____	+	____
		1,000 +	____	+	70	+	5

1,643 + 432 = ____________

Marc traveled 2,645 miles from Los Angeles, California, to Portland, Maine. Then he traveled 1,378 miles from Portland to Biloxi, Mississippi. How many miles did he travel in all?

Another Way Use place value. 2,645 + 1,378

Estimate. 2,600 + 1,400 = 4,000

THINK	RECORD
STEP 1 Add the ones. Regroup. 13 ones = 1 ten ____ ones	1 2,645 + 1,378
STEP 2 Add the tens. Regroup. 12 tens = 1 hundred ____ tens	1 1 2,645 + 1,378 3
STEP 3 Add the hundreds. Regroup. 10 hundreds = 1 thousand ____ hundreds	1 1 1 2,645 + 1,378 23
STEP 4 Add the thousands.	1 1 1 2,645 + 1,378 ,023

Math Talk How do you know whether your answer is reasonable?

So, Marc traveled ________ miles in all.

Share and Show

1. Find the sum. Use the break apart strategy.

$$\begin{array}{rcl} 5{,}374 & = & 5{,}000 + \square + 70 + \square \\ +\ 3{,}195 & = & \square + 100 + \square + 5 \\ \hline & & \square + \square + \square + \square = \square \end{array}$$

Name ____________________

Find the sum.

2. 5,041 + 283

3. 2,833 + 175

4. 1,805 + 4,607

5. 1,479 + 4,506

Math Talk Explain how you regrouped in exercise 4.

On Your Own

Find the sum.

6. 836 + 391

7. 4,007 + 2,504

8. 413 + 145

9. 6,073 + 798

10. 643 + 167

11. 7,514 + 2,450

12. 3,847 + 2,091

13. 4,704 + 966

14. 3,026 + 474

15. 8,719 + 1,246

16. 2,575 + 3,850

17. 3,308 + 5,648

H.O.T. Find the missing digits.

18. 5,▢6▢ + ▢,7▢8 = 9,741

19. ▢,3▢1 + 1,▢8▢ = 6,980

20. 4,▢▢6 + ▢,10▢ = 7,910

UNLOCK the Problem REAL WORLD

TEST PREP

21. Zoey traveled from Denver to Atlanta. Her plane flew 1,750 miles from Denver to Boston. It then flew 945 miles from Boston to Atlanta. Zoey's plane flew the same distance to return home. How far did Zoey travel?

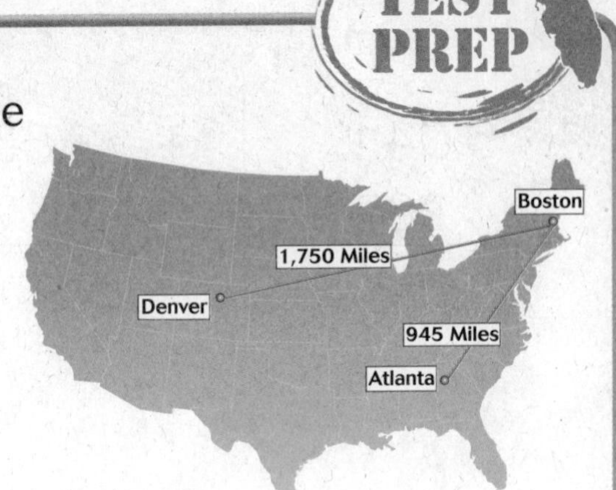

Ⓐ 2,695 miles　　Ⓒ 5,390 miles

Ⓑ 4,380 miles　　Ⓓ 6,380 miles

a. What do you need to find? ______________________

b. What is the estimate of the total distance Zoey travels?

____

c. Show the steps you use to solve the problem.

d. Complete the sentences.

Zoey travels __________ miles from Denver to Boston.

Then she travels __________ miles from Boston to Atlanta.

Zoey travels __________ miles from Denver to Atlanta.

Zoey travels a total of __________ miles round trip.

e. Fill in the bubble for the correct answer choice above.

22. The Mississippi River is 898 miles longer than the Colorado River. The Colorado River is 1,450 miles long. How many miles long is the Mississippi River?

Ⓕ 2,038 miles　　Ⓗ 2,348 miles

Ⓖ 2,238 miles　　Ⓘ 2,538 miles

23. The Millers spent $4,568 on airline tickets in 2008. They spent $5,308 in 2009. What was the total amount they spent on tickets in those two years?

Ⓐ $9,865　　Ⓒ $9,987

Ⓑ $9,876　　Ⓓ $9,988

FOR MORE PRACTICE:
Florida Benchmarks Practice Book, pp. P17–P18

Name ____________________

Add Greater Numbers

Essential Question How is adding 5- and 6-digit numbers like adding 4-digit numbers?

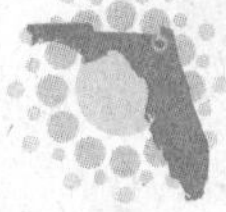

MA.3.A.6.1 Represent, compute, estimate and solve problems using numbers through hundred thousands.

CONNECT You know how to add 4-digit numbers. You can use this skill to add greater numbers.

Florida oranges are shipped on trucks. Suppose the oranges on one truck weigh 38,448 pounds. The oranges on another truck weigh 40,952 pounds. How many pounds of oranges are carried on both trucks?

- What do you need to find?

  ____

  ____

- Circle the numbers you need to use.

One Way Use place value. 38,448 + 40,952.

Estimate. 38,000 + 41,000 = 79,000

THINK	RECORD
STEP 1 Add the ones. Regroup. 10 ones = 1 ten ______ ones	¹ 38,448 + 40,952 ____
STEP 2 Add the tens. Regroup. 10 tens = 1 hundred ______ tens	¹ ¹ 38,448 + 40,952 ____0
STEP 3 Add the hundreds. Regroup. 14 hundreds = 1 thousand ______ hundreds	¹ ¹ ¹ 38,448 + 40,952 ____00
STEP 4 Add the thousands. Add the ten thousands.	¹ ¹ ¹ 38,448 + 40,952 ____,400

So, there are ______ pounds of oranges on both trucks.

Math Talk Is your answer reasonable? **Explain.**

Other Ways

A Use the Break Apart strategy.

38,448	=	30,000	+	8,000	+	400	+	40	+	8
+ 40,952	=	+ 40,000			+	900	+	50	+	2

The sum is ______________.

B Use a calculator to find 95,721 + 106,935.

202656.

The sum is ______________.

Try This! Find the sum two ways. Show your work.

$$\begin{array}{r} 14{,}759 \\ +\ 2{,}683 \\ \hline \end{array}$$

Share and Show

1. In which problem do you need to regroup? Find that sum.

   ____

   a. $\begin{array}{r} 76{,}563 \\ +\ 2{,}400 \\ \hline \end{array}$ **b.** $\begin{array}{r} 56{,}867 \\ +\ 89{,}473 \\ \hline \end{array}$

Math Talk In Example **a**, **explain** how you know you don't need to regroup.

Name ___________________________

Find the sum.

2. $\begin{array}{r} 56{,}304 \\ +\ 3{,}295 \\ \hline \end{array}$

3. $\begin{array}{r} 15{,}784 \\ +\ 12{,}257 \\ \hline \end{array}$

4. $\begin{array}{r} 125{,}342 \\ +\ 236{,}415 \\ \hline \end{array}$

On Your Own

Find the sum.

5. $\begin{array}{r} 58{,}309 \\ +\ 97{,}824 \\ \hline \end{array}$

6. $\begin{array}{r} 353{,}042 \\ +\ 43{,}645 \\ \hline \end{array}$

7. $\begin{array}{r} 35{,}340 \\ +\ 27{,}015 \\ \hline \end{array}$

8. $\begin{array}{r} 110{,}352 \\ +\ 82{,}416 \\ \hline \end{array}$

9. $\begin{array}{r} 28{,}460 \\ +\ 12{,}359 \\ \hline \end{array}$

10. $\begin{array}{r} 807{,}235 \\ +\ 45{,}218 \\ \hline \end{array}$

11. $\begin{array}{r} 417{,}904 \\ +\ 28{,}722 \\ \hline \end{array}$

12. $\begin{array}{r} 97{,}723 \\ +\ 19{,}231 \\ \hline \end{array}$

13. $\begin{array}{r} 617{,}583 \\ +\ 34{,}019 \\ \hline \end{array}$

H.O.T. Find the missing digits.

14. $\begin{array}{r} 2\ \square\ 5{,}369 \\ +\ 34\square{,}2\square1 \\ \hline \square 53{,}640 \end{array}$

15. $\begin{array}{r} 48\square{,}084 \\ +\ 5\square5{,}7\square5 \\ \hline 995{,}\square49 \end{array}$

Problem Solving REAL WORLD

Use the table for 16–18.

Greene County School District Orders

Item	Number
Fruit bars	65,430
Yogurt	32,825
Fruit juice	145,700

16. Mr. Walker ordered 14,790 more fruit bars after he sent the district order. What is the total number of fruit bars Greene County schools will receive?

____

17. Write Math **What's the Error?** Darcy said the total number of fruit bars and yogurts ordered was 97,255. Is Darcy correct? **Explain.**

____

____

____

18. H.O.T. Suppose Greene County ordered 10,000 more fruit bars and 10,000 more yogurts. **Explain** how you can estimate the total number of fruit bars and yogurts the school district ordered in all.

____

____

____

19. Dylan chose two numbers. The numbers were 58,914 and 58,723. What is the greatest place-value position in which the digits are different? ______________________

20. **Test Prep** In 1850, the population of Florida was 87,445. In 1900, the population was 441,097 greater. What was the population in 1900?

Ⓐ 525,432 Ⓒ 528,542

Ⓑ 528,441 Ⓓ 628,442

SHOW YOUR WORK

FOR MORE PRACTICE:
Florida Benchmarks Practice Book, pp. P19–P20

Name ______________________________

Estimate Differences

Essential Question How can you estimate differences by using rounding and compatible numbers?

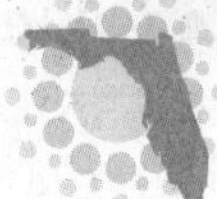

MA.3.A.6.1 Represent, compute, estimate and solve problems using numbers through hundred thousands.

UNLOCK the Problem REAL WORLD

In 1962, John Glenn was the first American to orbit Earth in the *Friendship 7* capsule. In 2007, space shuttle *Endeavour* carried the first teacher, Barbara Morgan, to the International Space Station. About how many years after Glenn's orbit did the first teacher go to the Space Station?

- Does the problem ask for an exact answer? How do you know?

____

____

____

- Circle the numbers you need to use.

To find *about* how many years later, you can estimate.

One Way Use compatible numbers.

2,007 → 2,000
− 1,962 → − 1,9 ___

Count up by tens from 1960 to 2000.

_______ _______ _______ _______

I counted _____ tens, or _____ years.

So, about _____ years after Glenn's orbit, the first teacher went to the Space Station.

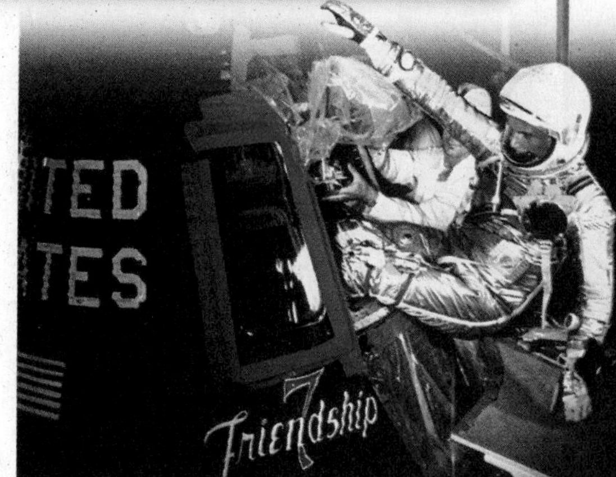

▲ ***Friendship 7*** **made 3 orbits around Earth. The flight lasted almost 5 hours.**

Math Talk Since the compatible numbers 2,000 and 1,960 are close to the real numbers, 2,007 and 1,962, what will the real difference be close to?

Try This! **Use compatible numbers.**

A 2,632 → 2,500
− 1,450 → − ______

B 7,855 → ______
− 2,268 → − 2,000

Example Use place value to round.

3,468 − 1,635 = ▢

Remember

- If the digit to the right of the rounding place is less than 5, the digit in the rounding place stays the same.
- If the digit to the right is 5 or more, the digit in the rounding place increases by one.

STEP 1 **Round 3,468 to the nearest thousand.**

Think: If the digit to the right is less than 5, the digit in the rounding place stays the same.

Look at the hundreds digit.
4 < 5, so the thousands digit stays the same. Write a zero for each digit to the right.

```
  3,468 →  ____
− 1,635    − ____
```

So, 3,468 rounds to ________.

STEP 2 **Round 1,635 to the nearest thousand.**

Think: If the digit to the right is more than 5, the digit in the rounding place increases by one.

Look at the hundreds digit.
6 > 5, so the thousands digit increases by one.
Write a zero for each digit to the right.

```
  3,468 →   3,000
− 1,635 → − ____
```

So, 1,635 rounds to ________.

STEP 3 **Find the difference.**

```
  3,468 →   3,000
− 1,635 → − 2,000
            ____
```

Try This! Use place value to round.

A

```
  1,478 →   1,500
−   521 → − ____
            ____
```

Think: Round both numbers to the same place value.

Math Talk Explain a different way you can round each number in B to find the estimate.

B

```
  6,042 →   ____
− 4,218 → − ____
            ____
```

Name ______________________

Share and Show 

1. Write compatible numbers for the problem at the right. Then estimate the difference.

   7,426 → ______
   − 509 → − ______
   ______

Math Talk Explain another way you can estimate 7,426 – 509.

Estimate the difference.

2. 9,257 − 5,821

3. 7,642 − 1,137

4. 7,364 − 3,252

On Your Own

Estimate the difference.

5. 936 − 421

6. 8,804 − 1,259

7. 2,937 − 2,048

8. 6,442 − 436

9. 584 − 208

10. 8,396 − 4,471

11. 4,796 − 1,263

12. 9,528 − 3,274

13. 5,361 − 2,489

Problem Solving REAL WORLD

Use the table for 14–16.

Space Shuttle Data	
Shuttle	**Number of Orbits**
Discovery	4,671
Atlantis	3,873
Endeavour	3,461

14. Greg's science class is reading about the space shuttles. About how many more orbits did *Discovery* make than *Endeavour?* **Explain.**

15. Sean said the 3 shuttles made about 13,000 orbits. **Explain** why you agree or disagree.

16. Write Math ► About how many more orbits did *Atlantis* make than *Endeavour?* **Explain** how you can use compatible numbers to estimate.

17. H.O.T. I am a 4-digit number. All of my digits are even numbers. The sum of my ones and tens digits is 8. My hundreds and ones digits are both 4. The sum of my digits is 18. What number am I? ____

18. **Test Prep** A total of 1,253 people went to the science fair. Of these people, 906 arrived before noon. About how many people arrived in the afternoon?

Ⓐ 150 Ⓒ 300

Ⓑ 250 Ⓓ 500

SHOW YOUR WORK

FOR MORE PRACTICE:
Florida Benchmarks Practice Book, pp. P21–P22

Name ______________________________

Subtract 4-Digit Numbers

Essential Question How can you use different strategies to subtract 4-digit numbers?

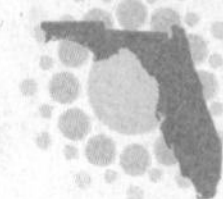

MA.3.A.6.1 Represent, compute, estimate and solve problems using numbers through hundred thousands.

UNLOCK the Problem REAL WORLD

Owls Stadium has 5,136 seats. For Saturday's game, 4,821 tickets for the seats have been sold. How many tickets are left?

- Underline what you need to find.
- Circle numbers you will use.

One Way Combine place values to subtract. 5,136 − 4,821

STEP 1

Subtract the ones.
Subtract the tens.

```
  5, 1 3 6
− 4, 8 2 1
```

STEP 2

Look at the hundreds place.
Since 8 > 1, combine place values.
Combine the hundreds and the thousands places.

There are 51 hundreds and 48 hundreds.
Subtract the hundreds.

```
  5, 1 3 6
− 4, 8 2 1
        1 5
```

Think: 51 – 48

So, there are ______ tickets left.

Other Ways

A **Use the Break Apart strategy. 3,000 − 1,475**

Remember
Since you cannot subtract from zero, regroup the next greater place value.

- First, break apart 3,000 as 2,000 + 1,000.

```
             2,000    1,000
  3,000  =   3,000 +    0   +  0 + 0
− 1,475  =  −1,000 +  400   + 70 + 5
```

- Then, break apart 1,000 as 900 + 90 + 10. Subtract each column.

```
             2,000     900     90   10
  3,000  =   3,000 +    0   +  0 +  0
− 1,475  =  −1,000 +  400   + 70 +  5
             1,000 +        + 20 +  5
```

- Add the differences. 1,000 + 500 + 20 + 5 = ____________

3,000 − 1,475 = ____________

B **Use place value to subtract. 2,377 − 1,849**

STEP 1 Since 9 > 7, regroup the tens.
7 tens = 6 tens 10 ones

_____ ones − _____ ones = _____ ones

```
    6 17   Think:
 2, 3 7 7  (10 + 7)
−1, 8 4 9
```

STEP 2 Subtract the tens.

_____ tens − _____ tens = _____ tens

```
    6 17
 2, 3 7 7
−1, 8 4 9
        8
```

STEP 3 Since 8 > 3, regroup the thousands.
2 thousands 3 hundreds = 1 thousand 13 hundreds

_____ hundreds − _____ hundreds = _____ hundreds

```
 1 13 6 17
 2, 3 7 7
−1, 8 4 9
      2 8
```

STEP 4 Subtract the thousands.

_____ thousand − _____ thousand = _____ thousands

```
 1 13 6 17
 2, 3 7 7
−1, 8 4 9
    5 2 8
```

Try This! Combine place values to subtract.

STEP 1 Subtract the ones.

```
  7, 2 1 5
− 3, 1 9 4
```

STEP 2 Since 9 > 1, combine place values.
Combine the tens and hundreds.

21 tens − 19 tens = _____ tens

```
  7, 2 1 5
− 3, 1 9 4
         1
```

STEP 3 Subtract the thousands.

```
  7, 2 1 5
− 3, 1 9 4
   , 0 2 1
```

Math Talk In Step 2, what does the zero in the hundreds place in the answer represent?

Name ______________________________

Share and Show 

Combine place values and subtract. Circle the place values you combined.

1. 8,403
− 4,251

Subtract.

2. 5,648
− 3,256

3. 8,347
− 7,527

4. 6,904
− 4,635

Math Talk Which place values can you combine in Exercise 3?

On Your Own

Subtract.

5. 8,319
− 3,276

6. 4,502
− 251

7. 8,004
− 7,952

8. 7,572
− 4,850

9. 5,821
− 4,245

10. 9,621
− 7,557

H.O.T. **Algebra** Find the missing number.

11. 879
− ____
240

12. 8,285
− ____
1,374

13. 4,036
− ____
1,472

UNLOCK the Problem REAL WORLD

14. All unsold tickets for seats at the Owls games are donated to the Youth Center. Last week, the Owls donated 70 tickets. This week, the Owls sold 5,027 tickets. The Owls Stadium has 5,136 seats. What is the difference between the number of tickets donated this week and last week?

a. What do you need to find? ______________________________

____

b. How can you find how many tickets were donated this week?

____

c. How can you find the difference between the number of tickets donated this week and the number donated last week?

____

d. How can you check your answer? ______________________________

____

e. Show the steps you use to find your answer.

f. Complete the sentences.

Last week, the Owls donated ______ tickets.

This week, the Owls donated ______ tickets.

The difference between the number of tickets donated this week and last week is ______.

15. At the Owls game, 1,023 people bought Owls game programs. The stadium sold 658 Owls caps. How many more game programs than caps were sold?

____

16. **Test Prep** Owls Stadium has 5,136 seats. How many seats would the stadium need to add to have exactly 6,000 seats?

Ⓐ 964 Ⓒ 864

Ⓑ 954 Ⓓ 854

FOR MORE PRACTICE:
Florida Benchmarks Practice Book, pp. P23–P24

Name ______________________________

Subtract Greater Numbers

Essential Question How is subtracting 5- and 6-digit numbers like subtracting 4-digit numbers?

MA.3.A.6.1 Represent, compute, estimate and solve problems using numbers through hundred thousands.

UNLOCK the Problem REAL WORLD

Katie's class is reading about mountains in Alaska. She learned that Mt. Blackburn is 16,390 feet tall. Mt. Bear is 14,831 feet tall. How many feet taller is Mt. Blackburn than Mt. Bear?

- What words tell you what operation you will use?

____

- Circle the numbers you need to use.

Use place value to subtract. 16,390 − 14,831

Estimate. 16,500 − 15,000 = 1,500

STEP 1 Subtract the ones.
0 < 1, so regroup.

9 tens 0 ones = 8 tens ______ ones

```
      8 10
16, 3 9 0
−14, 8 3 1
```

STEP 2 Subtract the tens.

```
      8 10
16, 3 9 0
−14, 8 3 1
          9
```

STEP 3 Subtract the hundreds.
3 < 8, so regroup.
6 thousands 3 hundreds =

5 thousands ______ hundreds

```
  5 13 8 10
1 6, 3 9 0
−14, 8 3 1
        5 9
```

STEP 4 Subtract the thousands.
Subtract the ten thousands.

```
  5 13 8 10
1 6, 3 9 0
−14, 8 3 1
    , 5 5 9
```

So, Mt. Blackburn is ____________ feet taller than Mt. Bear.

Math Talk Why don't you write a zero in the ten thousands place?

Subtract 6-digit Numbers **Use place value or a calculator to subtract.**

Pearl Printers sold 237,508 hiking books to the school book fairs. Emerald Printers sold 108,945 fewer hiking books to the fairs. How many hiking books did Emerald Printers sell?

One Way

Use place value to subtract. 237,508 − 108,945

STEP 1 Subtract the ones.
Subtract the tens. Regroup.

5 hundreds 0 tens =

4 hundreds ______ tens

```
        4 10
  237,5 0 8
− 108,9 4 5
```

STEP 2 Subtract the hundreds. Regroup.

7 thousands 4 hundreds =

6 thousands ______ hundreds

```
      14
    6  4 10
  237,5 0 8
− 108,9 4 5
        6 3
```

STEP 3 Subtract the thousands.
Regroup.

3 ten thousands 6 thousands =
2 ten thousands 16 thousands

```
   16 14
  2 6  4 10
  237,5 0 8
− 108,9 4 5
     ,5 6 3
```

STEP 4 Subtract the ten thousands
Subtract the hundred thousands.

```
   16 14
  2 6  4 10
  237,5 0 8
− 108,9 4 5
    8,5 6 3
```

So, Emerald Printers sold ____________ hiking books.

Another Way Use a calculator to find 237,508 − 108,945.

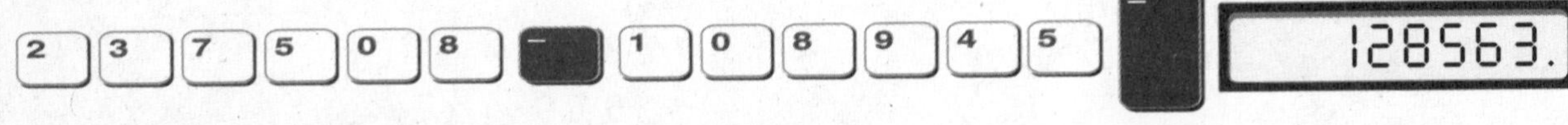

The difference is ____________.

Name ______________________

Share and Show 

1. Look at the problem. Combine place values to subtract. Find the difference.

$$\begin{array}{r} 176{,}382 \\ -\ 145{,}960 \\ \hline \end{array}$$

Find the difference.

2. $\begin{array}{r} 87{,}046 \\ -\ 31{,}728 \\ \hline \end{array}$

3. $\begin{array}{r} 50{,}739 \\ -\ 42{,}691 \\ \hline \end{array}$

4. $\begin{array}{r} 438{,}046 \\ -\ 326{,}587 \\ \hline \end{array}$

Math Talk **Explain** how you can combine place values to help you solve Exercise 3.

On Your Own

Find the difference.

5. $\begin{array}{r} 48{,}009 \\ -\ 17{,}945 \\ \hline \end{array}$

6. $\begin{array}{r} 90{,}014 \\ -\ 86{,}728 \\ \hline \end{array}$

7. $\begin{array}{r} 983{,}368 \\ -\ 261{,}125 \\ \hline \end{array}$

8. $\begin{array}{r} 35{,}276 \\ -\ 7{,}459 \\ \hline \end{array}$

9. $\begin{array}{r} 63{,}200 \\ -\ 33{,}070 \\ \hline \end{array}$

10. $\begin{array}{r} 205{,}710 \\ -\ 34{,}982 \\ \hline \end{array}$

11. $\begin{array}{r} 80{,}702 \\ -\ 60{,}698 \\ \hline \end{array}$

12. $\begin{array}{r} 51{,}238 \\ -\ 6{,}504 \\ \hline \end{array}$

13. $\begin{array}{r} 584{,}201 \\ -\ 493{,}557 \\ \hline \end{array}$

Algebra **Find the missing number.**

14. $\begin{array}{r} 28{,}019 \\ -\ \square \\ \hline 22{,}673 \end{array}$

15. $\begin{array}{r} 89{,}494 \\ -\ \square \\ \hline 71{,}192 \end{array}$

16. $\begin{array}{r} 54{,}308 \\ -\ \square \\ \hline 26{,}895 \end{array}$

Problem Solving REAL WORLD

Use the table for 17–19.

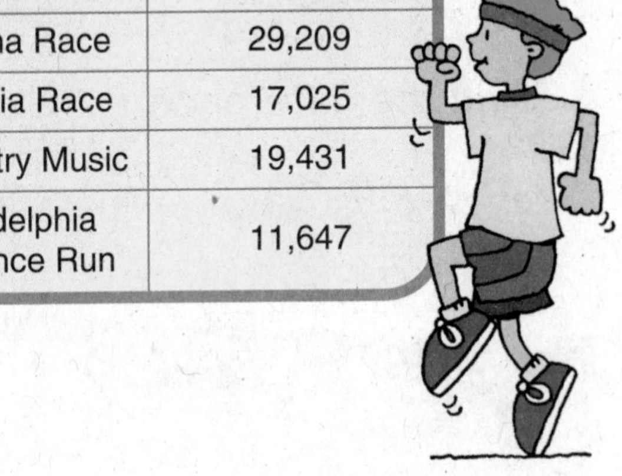

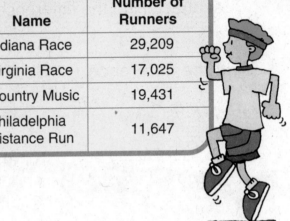

2007 Half-Marathons	
Name	**Number of Runners**
Indiana Race	29,209
Virginia Race	17,025
Country Music	19,431
Philadelphia Distance Run	11,647

17. How many more runners were in the Country Music Half-Marathon than in the Philadelphia Distance Run?

____

18. There were 765 more runners in a Florida race than in the Philadelphia Distance Run. How many runners were in the Florida race?

____

19. Write Math ▸ **Explain** how to find the difference between the number of runners in the Indiana Race and the number of runners in the Virginia Race. What place values did you combine?

____

____

____

SHOW YOUR WORK

20. H.O.T. This year, there were 48,750 people watching a race. This is 21,895 fewer people than the number who watched last year. How many people watched the race last year?

____

21. **Test Prep** In 1513, Ponce de Leon landed in what is now the state of Florida. If the year is 2010, how many years ago did Ponce de Leon land in Florida?

Ⓐ 485 Ⓒ 497

Ⓑ 496 Ⓓ 498

FOR MORE PRACTICE:
Florida Benchmarks Practice Book, pp. P25–P26

Name ______________________

Choose the Operation

Essential Question How can you recognize which operation to choose to solve a problem?

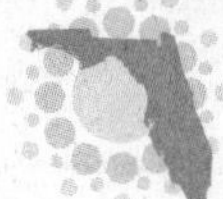

MA.3.A.6.1 Represent, compute, estimate and solve problems using numbers through hundred thousands.

UNLOCK the Problem

You are the detective! For the mini-mystery below, write a problem to explain what happened. Solve the problem.

Mini-Mystery What's the question?

Facts: Danny's Downloads has 5,787 online movies.

Movies 2-Go has 4,216 online movies.

Result: There are 10,003 online movies to choose from.

STEP 1 Round. 5,787 → 6,000

4,216 → 4,000

10,003 → 10,000

STEP 2 Estimate the sum and difference. Compare them to the result.

Sum:

$$\begin{array}{r} 6{,}000 \\ +\ 4{,}000 \\ \hline \end{array}$$

Difference:

$$\begin{array}{r} 6{,}000 \\ -\ 4{,}000 \\ \hline \end{array}$$

STEP 3 Which estimate is closer to the result? ____________

STEP 4 What's the question?

____

____

STEP 5 Solve the problem.

5,787 ◯ 4,216 = 10,003

Math Talk Explain how you can check to see if the answer to this mini-mystery is correct.

Try This! **For this mini-mystery, find the error. Then solve the problem.**

Mini-Mystery **What's the error?**

Facts: The male rhino weighs 7,153 pounds.
The female rhino weighs 5,547 pounds.

Result: Jorge found that the two rhinos together weigh 12,600 pounds.

STEP 1 Round.

7,153 → ______

5,547 → ______

12,600 → ______

STEP 2 Estimate the sum and difference. Compare them to the result.

Sum:

$$\begin{array}{r} 7,000 \\ +\ 6,000 \\ \hline \end{array}$$

Difference:

$$\begin{array}{r} 7,000 \\ -\ 6,000 \\ \hline \end{array}$$

STEP 3 Which estimate is closer to the result? ______

STEP 4 Solve the problem.

$$\begin{array}{r} 7,153 \\ +\ 5,547 \\ \hline \end{array}$$

STEP 5 What is Jorge's error?

______

______

Math Talk Explain how you know 12,700 is the correct answer.

Name ______________________

Share and Show 

Write a problem and solve the mini-mystery.

Facts: Rita scored 1,028 points in basketball last year. Joanne scored 935 points.

Result: 93 points

1. Round each number.

   1,028 → ________

   935 → ________

   93 → ________

2. Estimate the sum and difference. Compare them to the result.

   $$\begin{array}{r} 1{,}000 \\ +\ 900 \\ \hline \end{array} \qquad \begin{array}{r} 1{,}000 \\ -\ 900 \\ \hline \end{array}$$

3. Which estimate is closer to the result? ________

4. Write a problem.

   ____

   ____

5. Solve the problem you wrote.

   ____

On Your Own

Write a problem and solve the mini-mystery.

Facts: Jacob received 18,736 votes in the election. Martin received 16,888 votes.

Result: 35,624 votes

6. Write a problem.

   ____

   ____

   ____

7. Solve the problem you wrote.

   ____

   ____

   ____

Problem Solving REAL WORLD

Use and complete the table for 8–11.

8. Two south Florida counties, Palm Beach and Broward, have a total of 3,179 square miles. How many square miles are in Broward County?

9. H.O.T. If you doubled the size of Monroe County, it would still be 33 square miles less than the size of Collier County. How many square miles are in Collier County?

10. Which two counties combined are greater in square miles than Miami-Dade County but smaller than Palm Beach County?

11. Which county in the table has the greatest area in square miles? The smallest area? What is the difference?

12. Test Prep Lee County has a population of 440,888. Collier County's population is 251,377. How much greater is the population of Lee County?

    Ⓐ 190,511

    Ⓑ 189,511

    Ⓒ 89,511

    Ⓓ 18,511

South Florida Counties

County	Area (in square miles)
Palm Beach	1,974
Broward	
Miami-Dade	1,946
Monroe	997
Collier	
Hendry	1,153
Lee	804
Total	**10,106**

SHOW YOUR WORK

FOR MORE PRACTICE:
Florida Benchmarks Practice Book, pp. P27–P28

Name ____________________

Chapter Review/Test

▶ Check Vocabulary

Choose the best term from the box to complete the sentence.

Vocabulary
compatible numbers
estimate
expanded form
standard form

1. A number close to an exact number is called an ____________________. (MA.3.A.6.1; p. 27)

2. The ____________________ of a number is a way to write numbers by showing the value of each digit. (MA.3.A.6.1; p. 17)

3. ____________________ are numbers that are easy to compute mentally. (MA.3.A.6.1; p. 27)

▶ Check Concepts and Skills

Complete the chart to show the number in three ways. (MA.3.A.6.1; pp.17–20)

	Standard Form	Expanded Form	Word Form
4.	2,716	2,000 +	___ thousand, ___ hundred ___
5.		8,000 + 30 + 4	___ thousand, ___
6.			five thousand, nine hundred one

Estimate the sum or difference. (MA.3.A.6.1; pp 27–30 , 39–42)

7. 7,106 + 2,348 → ___ + ___

8. 32,472 − 4,851 → ___ − ___

Go online Assessment Options Chapter Test

Fill in the bubble for the correct answer choice.

9. In 1883, the building of the Brooklyn Bridge was finished. At that time, the bridge was the world's largest bridge with the roadway suspended between two towers.

   In 2015, how old will the Brooklyn Bridge be? (MA.3.A.6.1; pp. 43–46)

   Ⓐ 117 years
   Ⓑ 132 years
   Ⓒ 207 years
   Ⓓ 227 years

10. The table below shows the Florida population of three age groups in the year 2005.

Florida Population 8- to 10-year-olds 2005	
8-year-olds	215,597
9-year-olds	219,349
10-year-olds	222,902

   In 2005, how many more 10-year-olds than 9-year-olds lived in Florida? (MA.3.A.6.1; pp. 47–50)

   Ⓕ 2,553 Ⓗ 3,543
   Ⓖ 3,443 Ⓘ 3,553

11. Rachel and Natalie collect stamps. Rachel has 1,068 stamps. Natalie has 1,429 stamps. Which is the best estimate of the number of stamps they have in all? (MA.3.A.6.1; pp. 27–30)

   Ⓐ 1,000
   Ⓑ 2,500
   Ⓒ 3,000
   Ⓓ 3,500

Name ______________________________

12. Annie's Apple Farm is open on Saturdays and Sundays during the fall months.

Annie's Apple Farm	
Month	**Number of Visitors**
October	1,207
November	582

What is the number of people who visited the farm in October, written in expanded form? **(MA.3.A.6.1; pp. 17–20)**

Ⓕ 1,000 + 200 + 70
Ⓖ 100 + 200 + 0 + 7
Ⓗ 1,000 + 200 + 7
Ⓘ 1,000 + 20 + 7

13. Bill Bradley, known as "Dollar Bill," retired from the New York Knicks basketball team in 1977. During his basketball career, he scored 9,217 points.

Which is NOT a way to represent 9,217 with base-ten blocks? **(MA.3.A.6.1; pp. 13–16)**

Ⓐ 9 thousands 2 hundreds 1 ten 7 ones
Ⓑ 92 hundreds 17 ones
Ⓒ 8 thousands 12 hundreds 17 ones
Ⓓ 8 thousands 2 hundreds 11 tens 7 ones

14. The table below shows two bicycle trails in Florida.

Florida Bicycle Trails	
Name	**Distance (in feet)**
Pinellas Trail	184,800
Withlacoochee State Trail	242,880

What is the total distance of both trails? **(MA.3.A.6.1; pp. 35–38)**

Ⓕ 417,680 ft
Ⓖ 427,680 ft
Ⓗ 428,680 ft
Ⓘ 437,680 ft

15. A citrus grower shipped 375,480 boxes of oranges and 198,260 boxes of grapefruit. Which of the following is true? **(MA.3.A.6.1; pp. 21–24)**

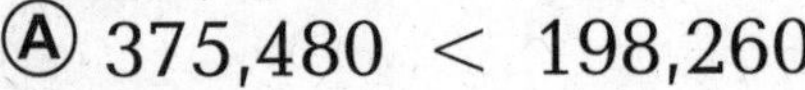

Ⓐ 375,480 < 198,260

Ⓑ 375,480 = 198,260

Ⓒ 198,260 > 375,480

Ⓓ 375,480 > 198,260

16. Sunrise Elementary is having its annual Read-a-thon. The third graders have read 468 books so far.

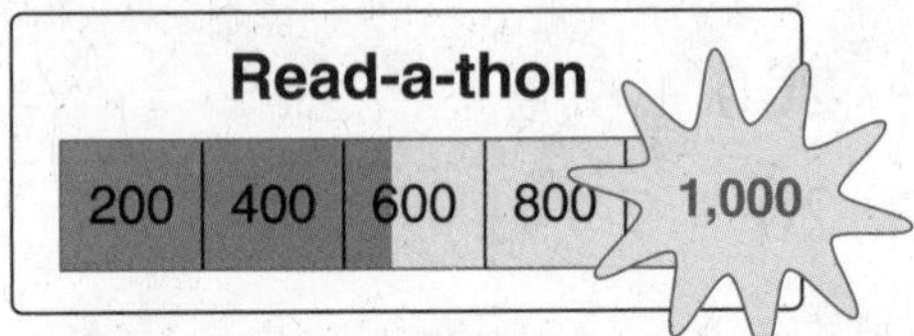

Third Grade: 468 books read so far!

How many more books do the third graders need to read to reach their goal?
(MA.3.A.6.1; pp. 43–46)

Ⓕ 522 Ⓗ 632

Ⓖ 532 Ⓘ 1,468

17. Lincoln Zoo keeps track of the number of its visitors each summer. How many people visited the zoo in June and July?
(MA.3.A.6.1; pp. 31–34)

Lincoln Zoo Attendance

Month	Number of Visitors
June	1,484
July	2,607
August	3,703

Ⓐ 4,091 Ⓒ 3,911

Ⓑ 3,991 Ⓓ 2,291

18. James is thinking of a number. The ones digit is 7. The tens digit is 4. The ten thousands digit is 8. The rest of the digits are zeros. What number is James thinking of?
(MA.3.A.6.1; pp. 21–24)

Ⓕ 8,407

Ⓖ 8,074

Ⓗ 80,047

Ⓘ 80,740

Chapter 2 Collect and Analyze Data

Show What You Know 

Check your understanding of important skills.

Name ______________________________

▶ Numbers to 20 **Circle the number word. Write the number.**

1. 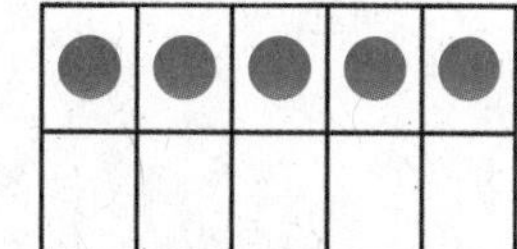

fourteen

fifteen

____

2. 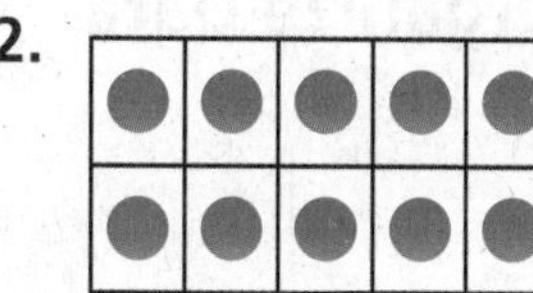 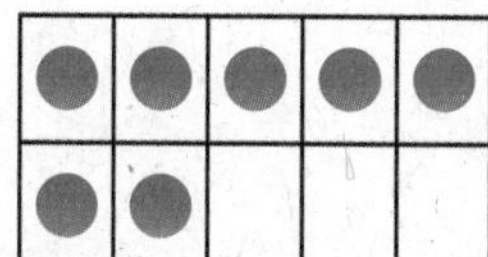

seventeen

eighteen

____

▶ Skip Count **Skip count to find the missing numbers.**

3. Count by 2s. 2, 4, ____, ____, 10, ____, ____, 16

4. Count by 5s. 5, 10, ____, ____, ____, 30, ____

▶ Addition and Subtraction Facts **Find the sum or difference.**

5. $12 - 4 =$ ____

6. $9 + 8 =$ ____

7. $11 - 7 =$ ____

Florida FUN FACT

You can see and feed giraffes at the Brevard Zoo in Melbourne, Florida. A baby giraffe was born at the zoo. She was 6 feet tall and could stand up and walk one hour after being born.

Assessment Options

Soar to Success: Math

Vocabulary Power

▶ Visualize It

Complete the bubble map, using preview words.

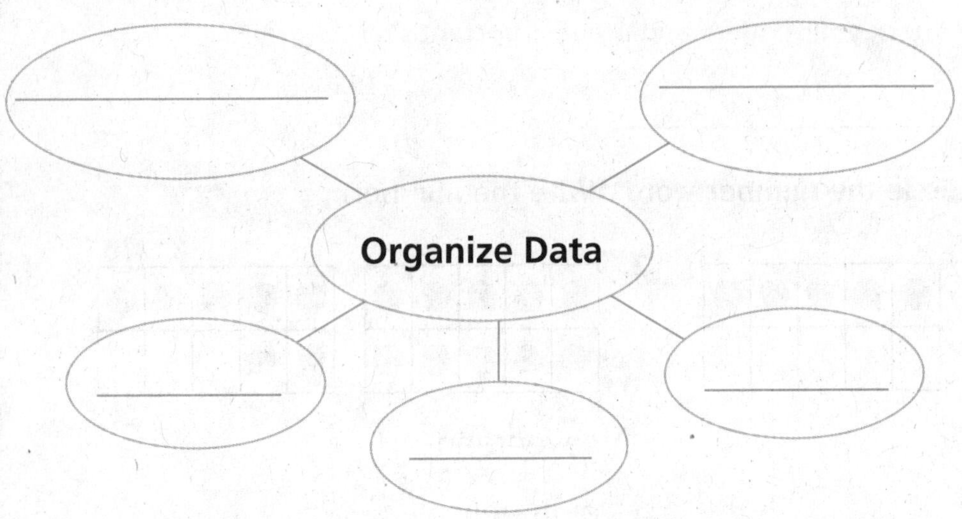

Review Words

compare
count
fewer
more
skip count

Preview Words

experiment
frequency table
horizontal bar graph
key
line plot
pictograph
results
scale
survey
tally mark
tally table
vertical bar graph

▶ Understand Vocabulary

Write the review word or preview word that answers the riddle.

1. I am a test that is done in order to find out something. ________
2. I am the numbers that are placed at fixed distances on a graph to help label the graph. ________
3. I am the part of a map or graph that explains the symbols. ________
4. I am a method of gathering information. ________
5. When you do this, you decide whether numbers are equal to, less than, or greater than each other. ________

Go online • Student Edition • Multilingual eGlossary

Name ______________________________

Collect Data

Essential Question What are ways you can collect and organize information?

MA.3.S.7.1 Construct and analyze frequency tables, bar graphs, pictographs, and line plots from data, including data collected through observations, surveys, and experiments.

UNLOCK the Problem REAL WORLD

Data is information that is collected about people or things.

You can collect data by taking a **survey**. The answers collected are the **results** of the survey.

The students in Alicia's class voted for their favorite ice cream flavors. Which flavor got the most votes? Which got the fewest votes?

- What do you need to find?

____

____

____

You can record data in a **tally table** by making tally marks as you gather data. Each tally mark | stands for 1 vote. 𝍸 stands for 5 votes.

Ice Cream Flavors	
Flavor	**Tally**
Vanilla	𝍸 II
Chocolate	𝍸 III
Strawberry	IIII

You can show the number of tally marks in a **frequency table** to make the data easier to read.

Ice Cream Flavors	
Flavor	**Number**
Vanilla	7
Chocolate	8
Strawberry	4

The number of votes for each flavor from greatest to least is 8, 7, and 4.

So, ________________ got the most votes.

________________ got the fewest votes.

Try This! Take a survey.

Make a tally table like the one above. Have each classmate vote for one flavor of ice cream. Then record your data in a frequency table. Share your results with the class.

Example

A You can collect data by observing, or watching things that happen.

Carl studied three manatees during June, July, and August. He recorded how many times he saw each of the manatees each month.

	Bandit	Midnight	Owen
June	||||	|||	𝍸
July	||	𝍸 |	𝍸 |||
August	|	||||	𝍸 |||

1. How many times did Carl see any of the three manatees during June? ____________

2. Which manatee did Carl see most often? ____________

3. During which month did Carl see the most manatees? ____________

Math Talk How might the manatee data be used?

B You can collect data from an experiment. An experiment is a test you do to find out something.

Toss a coin 25 times. Record the results in a tally table. Then show the data in the frequency table at the right.

Coin Toss Results	
Heads	
Tails	

4. **Explain** what the result of the 26th toss might be.

____

____

Name ____________________

Share and Show 

1. What number would you write in a frequency table to show 卌 卌 |||? _____

Use the Favorite Sports table for 2–4.

2. How many more students voted for soccer than for basketball? _____

✓ 3. How many students in all voted for football or baseball? _____

✓ 4. How many students voted in all? _____

Favorite Sports	
Sport	**Tally**
Basketball	卌 ||
Soccer	卌 ||||
Baseball	卌 |
Football	||||

Math Talk **Explain** why the fifth tally mark is drawn differently than the first 4 marks.

On Your Own

Use the Shirt Colors list for 5–6.

5. Kelly made a list of the colors of shirts that the students in her class were wearing. Use the tables below to organize her data into a tally table and a frequency table.

Shirt Colors			
Jen	white	Kim	blue
Patty	red	Lee	red
Matt	blue	Pam	white
Jared	white	Brad	red
Carl	green	Jake	blue

6. How many more students are wearing white or red shirts than blue or green shirts? _____

Problem Solving REAL WORLD

Use the Tile Experiment table for 7–9.

Tile Experiment	
Color	**Tally**
Red	𝍸
Blue	𝍸 𝍸 𝍸 ||
Green	𝍸 ||

7. Caitlin pulled color tiles from a bag one at a time and then put them back. How many times did she pull a blue tile?

8. How many more times did Caitlin pull a blue tile than a red or green tile?

9. H.O.T. What does the data tell about the number of tiles in the bag?

10. **Sense or Nonsense?** Greg used a tally table to record the number of cards he has in his sports card collection. Then he used a frequency table to show his data. Does Greg's frequency table make sense? **Explain.**

Greg's Sports Cards	
Sport	**Tally**
Hockey	𝍸 |
Baseball	𝍸 𝍸 |||
Football	𝍸 𝍸 ||
Basketball	𝍸 ||||

Greg's Sports Cards	
Sport	**Number**
Hockey	6
Baseball	8
Football	12
Basketball	10

11. **Test Prep** Jen made a tally table to record her friends' choices of favorite kind of pet. Her table shows

Dog 𝍸 𝍸 ||

How many people chose Dog?

Ⓐ 7 Ⓑ 10 Ⓒ 12 Ⓓ 15

 FOR MORE PRACTICE:
Florida Benchmarks Practice Book, pp. P35–P36

Name ______________________________

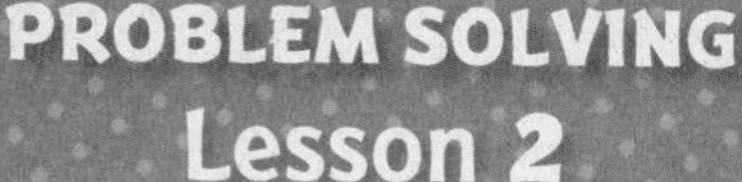

Make a Table · Data

Essential Question How can making a table help you solve a problem?

MA.3.A.6.2 Solve non-routine problems by making a table, chart, or list and searching for patterns.

UNLOCK the Problem REAL WORLD

Mrs. Bishop asked the students in her art classes to vote for their favorite paint colors. The list at the right shows how they voted. Use the list to find how many students voted in all.

- Six students voted for green.
- Twice as many students who voted for green voted for yellow.
- Twice as many students who voted for yellow voted for red.
- Twice as many students who voted for red voted for blue.

Read the Problem

What do I need to find?

how many students in Mrs. Bishop's art classes voted for their ____________ ____________

What information do I need to use?

the information in ____________ that tells how the students voted

How will I use the information?

I will put the information in a table.

Then I will ____________ to find the total number of students.

Solve the Problem

Favorite Paint Colors	
Green	6
Yellow	
Red	
Blue	

Record _____ for green.

_____ + _____ = _____, so _____ students voted for yellow.

_____ + _____ = _____, so _____ students voted for red.

_____ + _____ = _____, so _____ students voted for blue.

_____ the votes for green, yellow, red, and blue to find the total in all.

_____ + _____ + _____ + _____ = _____

Try Another Problem

Mr. Garcia gives music lessons to some students in Bree's school. The list at the right shows how many students take lessons. How many students in all take music lessons?

- 16 students take piano lessons.
- 4 fewer students take guitar lessons than take piano lessons.
- 4 fewer students take violin lessons than take guitar lessons.
- 4 fewer students take flute lessons than violin lessons.

Read the Problem	Solve the Problem
What do I need to find?	**Record the steps you used to solve the problem.**
What information do I need to use?	
How will I use the information?	

2. Describe the pattern you see in the table. ____________________

____

Name ______________________________

Share and Show 

1. Derek's grandfather put $50 into a savings account for him. At the end of the first week, he added $5. Each week, he added another $5. If his grandfather continues the pattern, how much money will Derek have at the end of the eighth week?

You can put the information in a table and look for a pattern to solve the problem.

First, add $50 + __________ = __________ to find the amount at the end of the first week.

Add __________ + $5 = __________ to find the amount at the end of the second week.

Add __________ + $5 = __________ to find the amount at the end of the third week.

Record the amounts in the table.

Week	1	2	3	4	5	6	7	8
Amount								

Then, count by __________ to complete the table.

So, Derek will have __________ at the end of the eighth week.

2. What pattern did you use to complete the table?

____

3. How much more money did Derek have in week 8 than in week 3? __________

4. H.O.T. What if Derek's grandfather added $10 to his savings account at the end of each even week? How much would Derek have at the end of eighth week?

____

On Your Own

Choose a STRATEGY

- Act It Out
- Use Manipulatives
- Draw a Diagram
- Make a Table, Chart, or List
- Search for Patterns

5. Isabel is thinking of a number between 234 and 250. The sum of the digits is twice the digit in the ones place. What is Isabel's number?

____

SHOW YOUR WORK

6. Ben needs 4,000 points to win a puzzle at the arcade. He has 2,947 points. How many more points does he need?

____

7. The pet show had 1,436 visitors on Saturday and 2,075 visitors on Sunday. How many visitors did the pet show have in all?

____

8. **Write Math** Heather has 6 dimes and 10 pennies. Jason has 3 quarters. Who has more money? **Explain** your answer.

____

9. **H.O.T.** Andrew has 10 more goldfish than Todd. Together, they own 50 goldfish. How many goldfish does each have?

____

10. **Test Prep** If the pattern continues, how much will 8 T-shirts cost?

T-shirts	1	2	3	4	5
Cost	\$5	\$10		\$20	

Ⓐ \$24 Ⓑ \$28 Ⓒ \$35 Ⓓ \$40

FOR MORE PRACTICE:
Florida Benchmarks Practice Book, pp. P37–P38

Name ____________________

Understand Pictographs

Essential Question How do you read a pictograph in which each symbol equals 1?

MA.3.S.7.1 Construct and analyze frequency tables, bar graphs, pictographs, and line plots from data, including data collected through observations, surveys, and experiments.

UNLOCK the Problem REAL WORLD

A **pictograph** uses small pictures or symbols to show information.

Nick made a pictograph to show how the students in his class get to school. How many students ride a bike?

- Underline the word that tells you where to find the information to answer the problem.
- What does the ☺ stand for?

____

Each row has a label that names one way students get to school.

How We Get to School

Walk	☺ ☺ ☺
Bike	☺ ☺ ☺ ☺
Bus	☺ ☺ ☺ ☺ ☺ ☺ ☺ ☺
Car	☺ ☺ ☺ ☺ ☺ ☺

Key: Each ☺ = 1 student.

The title says that the pictograph is about how students get to school.

The **key** tells that each picture or symbol stands for the way 1 student gets to school.

To find the number of students who ride a bike, count the number of ☺ after the Bike label.

☺, ☺, ☺, ☺

So, _____ students ride a bike to school.

- How many more students get to school by bus than by car? _____
- How many students in all are in Nick's class? _____

Share and Show 

Use the Number of Books Students Read pictograph for 1–3.

Number of Books Students Read	
September	
October	
November	
Key: Each = 1 book.	

1. What does each stand for?

2. How many books did the students read in September?

3. How many more books did the students read in October than in November?

Math Talk Explain how to find how many books the students read in all.

On Your Own

Use the Favorite Games pictograph for 4–8.

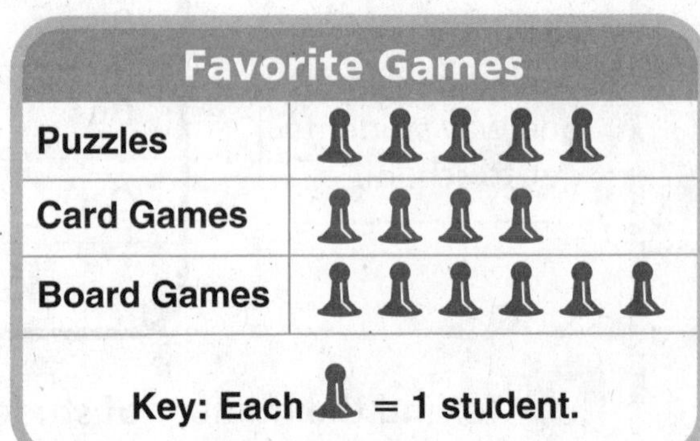

Favorite Games	
Puzzles	
Card Games	
Board Games	
Key: Each = 1 student.	

4. How many students chose puzzles?

5. Which game did the fewest students choose?

6. Which two games did a total of 9 students choose?

7. How many more students chose board games than card games?

8. Computer Games was added to the Favorite Games choices. Twice as many students chose computer games as card games. How many students chose computer games?

Name ___________________________________

Use the Favorite Lunch pictograph for 9–14.

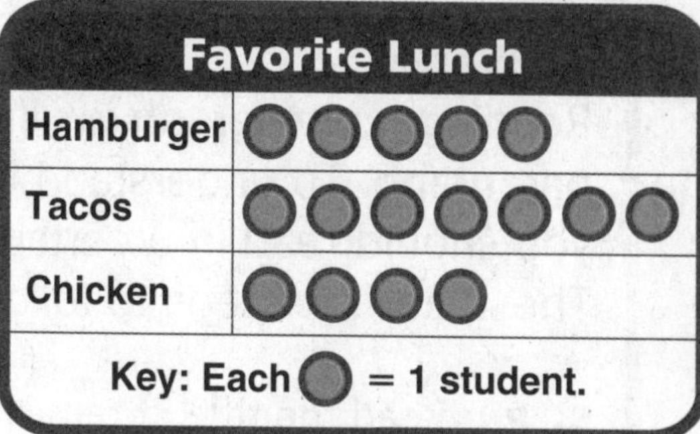

Favorite Lunch
Hamburger
Tacos
Chicken
Key: Each = 1 student.

9. The students in Jill's class voted for their favorite lunch food. How many students chose tacos?

____

10. Did more students choose hamburger and chicken, or did more choose tacos?

____

11. How many students in all were surveyed?

____

12. Write Math **Explain** what you can tell just by comparing the different numbers of symbols in the pictograph.

____

____

____

13. H.O.T. Pizza was added to the Favorite Lunch choices. Twice as many students chose pizza as hamburger. How many students chose pizza? **Explain** your answer.

____

____

14. **Test Prep** In the Favorite Lunch pictograph, how many students did NOT choose tacos?

Ⓐ 7 Ⓒ 11

Ⓑ 9 Ⓓ 12

SHOW YOUR WORK

Connect to Reading

Sequence

Reading a pictograph is different from reading a paragraph. To understand the data in a pictograph, you should read in a certain order, or in *sequence*. These are the steps to follow.

STEP 1 Read the title. It tells what the pictograph is about.

STEP 2 Read the key. It tells what the symbol stands for.

STEP 3 Look at each row of symbols. Count the number of symbols in the row.

STEP 4 Compare the numbers of symbols in the rows.

STEP 5 Draw conclusions about what the data show.

Our Favorite Subjects

Math	웃웃웃웃웃웃
Reading	웃웃웃웃웃웃웃웃
Science	웃웃웃웃
Social Studies	웃웃웃웃
Key: Each 웃 = 1 student.	

Use the pictograph to answer the questions.

1. Why is it important to read the title first?

____

2. How many students in all were surveyed? _____
3. How many more students chose reading than social studies? _____
4. Which two subjects received the same number of votes?

____

5. Explain why it is important to read the key before you count and compare the numbers of symbols for different choices.

____

FOR MORE PRACTICE:
Florida Benchmarks Practice Book, pp. P39–P40

Name ______________________________

Use a Pictograph

Essential Question How do you read a pictograph in which each symbol equals more than 1?

MA.3.S.7.1 Construct and analyze frequency tables, bar graphs, pictographs, and line plots from data, including data collected through observations, surveys, and experiments.

UNLOCK the Problem REAL WORLD

Areas that are part of the national park system are good places to vacation and to learn about plants and animals.

The pictograph shows the number of national park areas some states have. How many does Florida have?

- What does each 🌲 represent?

____

- How many 🌲 are shown for Florida?

____

National Park Areas	
Florida	🌲 🌲 🌲 🌲 🌲 half-🌲
Georgia	🌲 🌲 🌲 🌲 🌲 🌲 🌲
Louisiana	🌲 🌲 🌲
South Carolina	🌲 🌲 🌲 🌲 half-🌲
Tennessee	🌲 🌲 🌲 🌲 🌲 🌲
Key: Each 🌲 = 2 national park areas.	

Math Idea

Half of the picture has half of the value of the whole picture.

🌲 = 2 park areas

half-🌲 = 1 park area

A symbol in a pictograph can stand for more than one.

To find the number of national park areas in Florida, count each tree as 2 parks. So, the first tree is 2 parks, the second tree is 4 parks, and so on. Then add 1 more park when you get to the half-🌲.

2, 4, _____, _____, _____ _____ + _____ = 11

So, there are _____ national park areas in Florida.

Everglades National Park, in Florida, is the largest subtropical wilderness in the United States.

- Which state listed in the pictograph has the most national park areas? _______________

- How many park areas does it have? _______________

Share and Show 

Use the pictograph for 1–7.

National Park Areas

State	
Florida	🌲🌲🌲🌲🌲 half tree
Georgia	🌲🌲🌲🌲🌲🌲🌲
Louisiana	🌲🌲🌲
South Carolina	🌲🌲🌲🌲 half tree
Tennessee	🌲🌲🌲🌲🌲🌲

Key: Each 🌲 = 2 national park areas.

1. How many national park areas are found in Tennessee? Use the symbols. Fill in the blanks.

   🌲 🌲 🌲 🌲 🌲 🌲

   2, 4, ____, ____, ____, ____

2. Which state listed in the pictograph has the fewest national park areas? How many does it have?

   ______

3. How many more national park areas are there in Tennessee than in South Carolina?

   ______

4. Which state has 5 fewer national park areas than Georgia?

   ______

5. Which states combined have 19 national park areas?

   ______

6. Suppose Florida had 5 more national park areas. How many tree symbols in all would there be for Florida's national park areas?

   ______

7. Is the number of national park areas in Louisiana and South Carolina combined greater than or less than the number of park areas in Georgia?

   ______

Math Talk Explain how a key helps you read a pictograph.

▲ The Blue Ridge Mountain chain stretches from Georgia to Pennsylvania.

Name ________________________________

On Your Own

Use the pictograph for 8–13.

8. What does each 🌲 stand for?

____

9. Kyle has visited every national park area in New York. How many national park areas has he visited?

____

10. How many more national park areas are there in Texas than in Minnesota?

____

11. Which two states combined have the same number of national park areas as Texas?

____

____

12. H.O.T. Are there more national park areas in New York alone or in Texas, Kansas, and Minnesota combined? **Explain.**

____

____

____

____

____

13. Which states have an even number of national park areas?

____

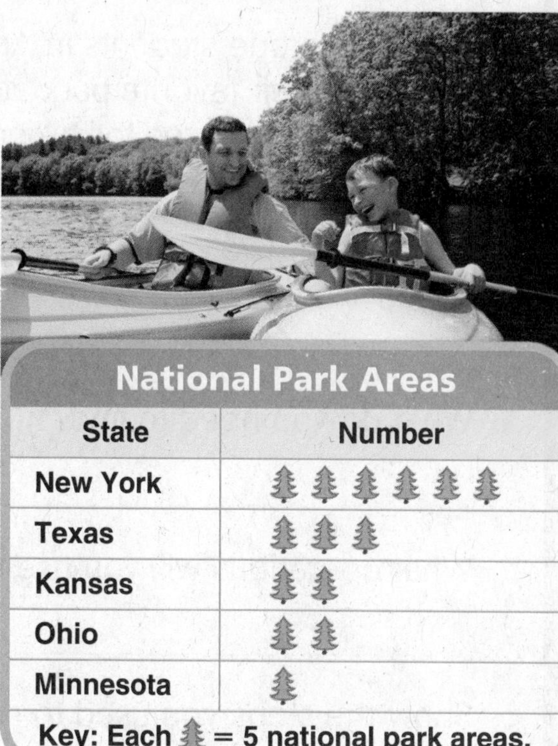

National Park Areas

State	Number
New York	🌲🌲🌲🌲🌲🌲
Texas	🌲🌲🌲
Kansas	🌲🌲
Ohio	🌲🌲
Minnesota	🌲

Key: Each 🌲 = 5 national park areas.

UNLOCK the Problem

14. The third-grade students in Amanda's school voted for their favorite park activity. How many more students voted for biking than for fishing?

Ⓐ 15 Ⓑ 20 Ⓒ 25 Ⓓ 35

Park Activities	
Activity	**Number**
Biking	☀ ☀ ☀ ◐
Hiking	☀ ☀ ☀ ☀
Boating	☀ ☀ ☀
Fishing	☀ ◐
Key: Each ☀ = 10 students	

a. What do you need to find?

____

b. What operations will you use to solve the problem?

____

c. Show the steps you used to solve the problem.

d. Complete the sentences.

Each ☀ = _____ students.

_____ students voted for biking.

_____ students voted for fishing.

_____ more students voted for biking than for fishing.

e. Fill in the bubble for the correct answer.

15. How many students in all voted for their favorite park activity?

Ⓕ 12

Ⓖ 110

Ⓗ 120

Ⓘ 125

16. Lester made a pictograph to show how many fish he caught. This is his key.

Each 🐟 = 10 fish.

How many fish does

stand for?

Ⓐ 3 Ⓑ 4 Ⓒ 35 Ⓓ 40

FOR MORE PRACTICE:
Florida Benchmarks Practice Book, pp. P41–P42

Name ______________________

Make a Pictograph

Essential Question How do you make a pictograph?

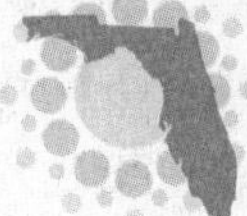

MA.3.S.7.1 Construct and analyze frequency tables, bar graphs, pictographs, and line plots from data, including data collected through observations, surveys, and experiments.

UNLOCK the Problem REAL WORLD

The students in Delia's class made the table at the right. They used it to record the places they would like to go during a field trip. How can you show the data in a pictograph?

Field Trip Choices

Place	Number
Museum	4
Science center	10
Aquarium	8
Zoo	6

Make a pictograph.

STEP 1

Write the title at the top of the pictograph. Write the name of a place in each row.

STEP 2

Look at the numbers in the table. Choose a picture for the key, and tell how many each picture represents. Write the key at the bottom of the graph.

STEP 3

Draw the correct number of pictures for each field trip choice.

Museum	

Key: Each ___ = ___ students.

- How did you decide how many pictures to draw for the science center?

____

____

Share and Show 

Jeremy pulled marbles from a bag one at a time and then put them back. He recorded the results each time. Make a pictograph of the data.
Use this key:

Each ◯ = 2 marbles.

Jeremy's Marble Experiment	
Color	**Number**
Blue	4
Green	11
Red	8
Yellow	2

Key:	

Use your pictograph above for 1–3.

1. Which color marble did Jeremy pull most often?

   Think: which color has the most pictures?

   ____

2. How many more times did Jeremy pull out a red marble than a yellow marble?

   ____

3. Which color marble did Jeremy pull out more often than blue but less often than green?

   ____

Math Talk **Explain** how you knew how many pictures to draw for green.

Name ______________________________

On Your Own

4. Two classes from Delia's school visited the science center. They recorded their favorite exhibits in the tally table. Use the data in the table to make a pictograph. Use this key:

   Each ☼ = 5 votes.

Favorite Exhibits

Exhibit	Tallies
Nature	卌
Solar System	卌 卌
Light and Sound	卌 卌 卌
Human Body	卌 卌

Use the Favorite Exhibits pictograph for 5–7.

5. Which exhibits received the same number of votes?

____

6. What if a weather exhibit received 25 votes? **Explain** how many pictures you would draw.

____

7. H.O.T. What if the Solar System exhibit received 12 votes? Would it make sense to use the key Each ☼ = 5 votes? **Explain**.

____

____

Problem Solving REAL WORLD

8. While at the science center, Delia's classmates learned how many teeth some mammals have. Use the data in the table to make a pictograph. Use this key:

   Each Δ = 2 teeth.

Teeth in Mammals

Animal	Number
Beaver	20
Cat	30
Raccoon	40
Squirrel	22

Key: ____________________

Use your pictograph for 9–11.

9. **Pose a Problem** Write a question and its answer by using the data in your pictograph.

   ____

   ____

10. Write Math ▸ If the data in the table included only the beaver, cat, and raccoon, explain how many teeth the Δ could stand for.

    ____

11. **Test Prep** How many pictures would you draw for Cat if each Δ = 5 teeth?

    (A) 4 (B) 5 (C) 6 (D) 8

FOR MORE PRACTICE:
Florida Benchmarks Practice Book, pp. P43–P44

Name ______________________________

Mid-Chapter Checkpoint

▶ Check Vocabulary

Choose the best term from the box to complete the sentence.

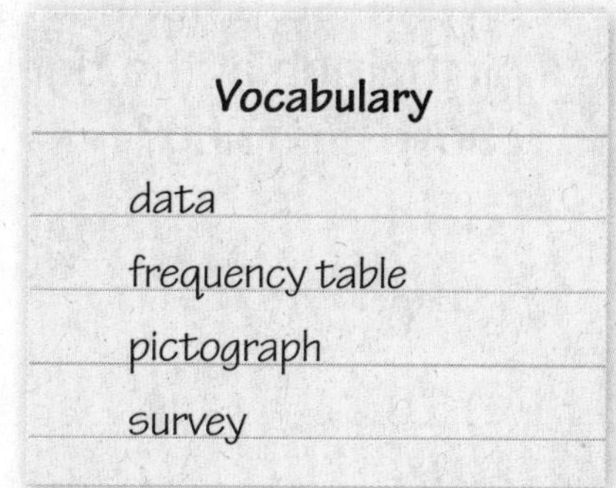

Vocabulary

data
frequency table
pictograph
survey

1. ________________ is information that is collected about people or things. (MA.3.S.7.1; p. 61)

2. A ________________ uses small pictures or symbols to show information. (MA.3.S.7.1; p. 69)

▶ Check Concepts

Use the Favorite Seasons table. (MA.3.S.7.1; pp. 61–64)

Favorite Seasons

Season	Tally
Spring	𝍸
Summer	𝍸 |||
Fall	||||
Winter	𝍸	

3. Which season got the most votes?

____

4. Which season got 1 less vote than winter?

____

5. How many more students chose summer than fall?

____

6. How many students were surveyed in all?

____

Use the Our Pets pictograph. (MA.3.S.7.1; pp. 69–72)

Our Pets

Bird	🐾 🐾 🐾 🐾
Cat	🐾 🐾 🐾 🐾 🐾
Dog	🐾 🐾 🐾 🐾 🐾 🐾 🐾
Fish	🐾 🐾 🐾

Key: Each 🐾 = 1 student.

7. How many students have cats as pets?

____

8. Three more students have dogs than which other pet? ________________

9. How many students in all answered the survey?

____

Fill in the bubble for the correct answer choice.

Use the Summer Activities pictograph for 10–14.

Summer Activities	
Camping	☀ ☀ ☀ ☀ ☀
Biking	☀ ☀ ☀ ☀
Swimming	☀ ☀ ☀ ☀ ☀ ☀
Canoeing	☀ ☀ ☀

Key: Each ☀ = 5 students.

10. Some students in Brooke's school chose their favorite summer activities. The results are in the pictograph at the right. How many students chose camping? **(MA.3.S.7.1; pp. 73–76)**

Ⓐ 5
Ⓑ 10
Ⓒ 20
Ⓓ 25

11. How many more students chose swimming than canoeing? **(MA.3.S.7.1; pp. 73–76)**

Ⓕ 3
Ⓖ 10
Ⓗ 15
Ⓘ 20

12. Which activity did 10 fewer students choose than camping? **(MA.3.S.7.1; pp. 73–76)**

Ⓐ canoeing
Ⓑ biking
Ⓒ swimming
Ⓓ hiking

13. How many students were surveyed in all? **(MA.3.S.7.1; pp. 73–76)**

Ⓕ 25
Ⓖ 45
Ⓗ 75
Ⓘ 90

14. How many more students chose biking or canoeing than swimming? **(MA.3.S.7.1; pp. 73–76)**

Ⓐ 3 Ⓑ 4 Ⓒ 5 Ⓓ 7

Name ______________________________

Understand Bar Graphs

Essential Question How do you read data in a bar graph?

MA.3.S.7.1 Construct and analyze frequency tables, bar graphs, pictographs, and line plots from data, including data collected through observations, surveys, and experiments.

UNLOCK the Problem REAL WORLD

A **bar graph** uses bars to show data. A **scale** of equally spaced numbers helps you read the number each bar shows.

The students in the reading group made a bar graph to record the number of books they read in October. How many books did Amy read?

- Underline the words that tell you where to find the information to answer the question.
- How many students are in the reading group?

____

The title tells what the bar graph is about.

Each bar is labeled with a student's name.

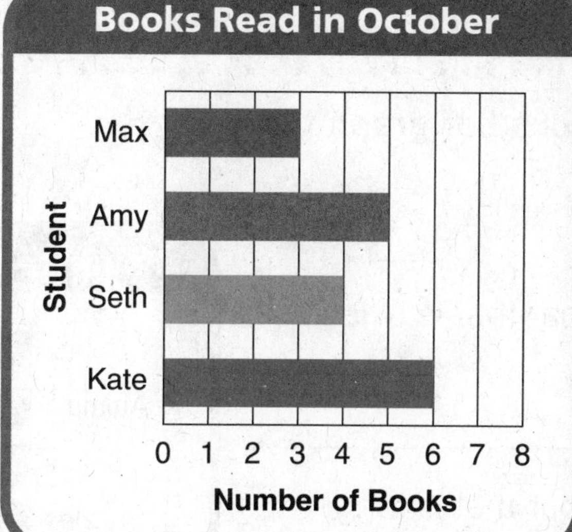

The length of a bar tells how many books each student read.

Find the bar for Amy. It ends at ______.

So, Amy read ______ books in October.

Math Talk **Explain** why it is important for the space between the numbers to be the same.

1. How many books did Max read? ______

2. How many more books did Kate read than Seth? ______

3. Suppose Amy read 2 more books. How many books did Amy read? ______ Shade the graph to show how many she read.

Share and Show 

Use the Favorite Ways to Exercise bar graph for 1–3.

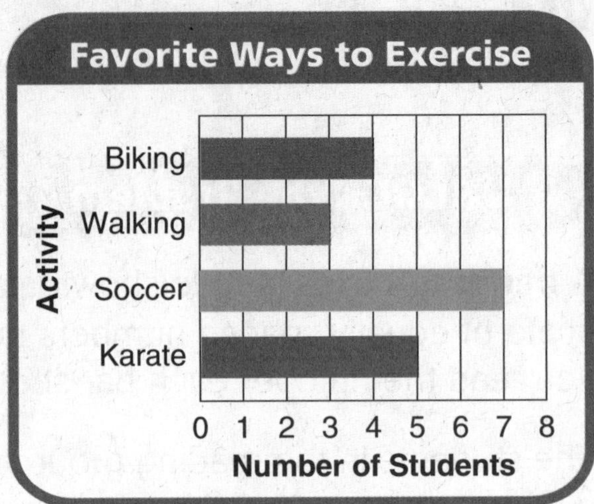

1. Which activity did the most students choose?

   Think: which bar is the longest?

   ____

2. How many students answered the survey? ______

3. Which activity received 3 fewer votes than soccer? ______

Math Talk What can you tell just by comparing the lengths of the bars in the graph? **Explain.**

On Your Own

Use the Favorite Kinds of Books bar graph for 4–8.

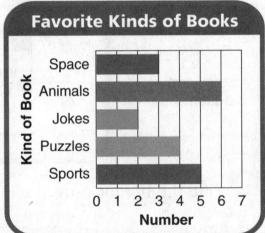

Favorite Kinds of Books

Kind of Book: Space, Animals, Jokes, Puzzles, Sports

0 1 2 3 4 5 6 7

Number

4. Which kind of book did the fewest students choose? ______

5. Which kind of book has a bar that is twice as long as the bar for space?

   ____

6. Which kind of book has a bar that is longer than puzzles but not as long as animals?

   ____

7. Did more students like books about animals or books about space and jokes?

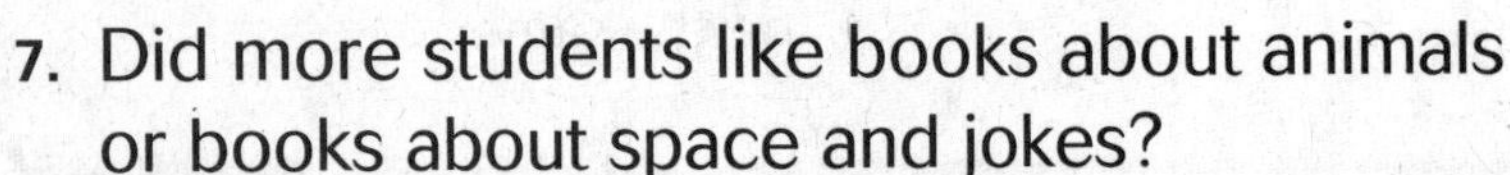

   ____

8. **What if** 7 more students were asked and they choose books about computers? **Describe** what the bar graph would look like.

   ____

   ____

Name ______________________________

Problem Solving REAL WORLD

Use the bar graph for 9–14.

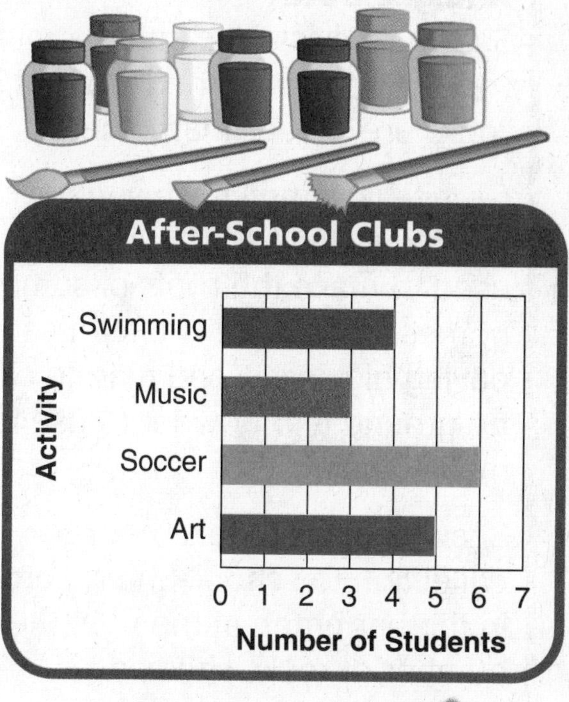

9. The most students are in the

   ____________ club.

10. There are ______________ more students in the soccer club than in the music club.

11. There are more students in the swimming

    and ____________ clubs than in the

    music and ____________ clubs.

12. Which club has more members than the swimming club, but fewer members than the soccer club? ______________

13. There are ______ members in the four clubs altogether.

14. Write Math ▶ **Pose a Problem** Write a question and its answer by using the data in the After-School Clubs bar graph.

    ____

    ____

    ____

SHOW YOUR WORK

15. **Test Prep** Jason is making a bar graph to show how many pets his friends have. Which pet will have the shortest bar?

    Ⓐ 8 dogs
    Ⓑ 3 hamsters
    Ⓒ 6 cats
    Ⓓ 4 birds

Connect to Science

Analyze Data

Shawna's class is learning about rocks. She has learned that some rocks are harder than others.

Granite is sometimes used for making statues. Slate can be used to make the roofs of some homes. Sandstone is often used for paving highways, and marble can be ground into powder to use for making paint.

Shawna plans to take her rock collection to school. She recorded in the bar graph at the right the number of rocks she has.

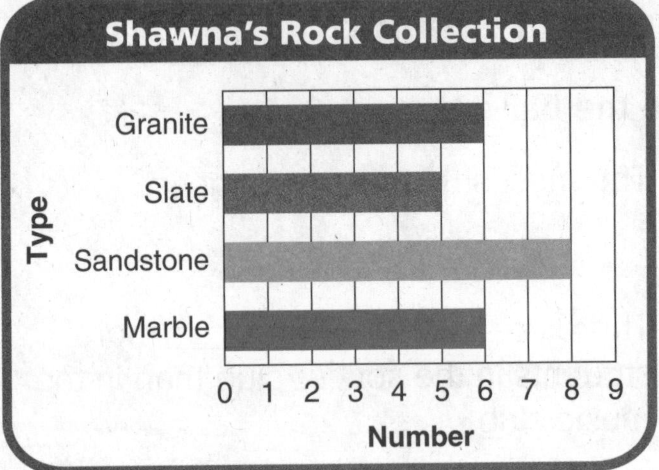

Use the bar graph for 1–5.

1. Shawna has the most of which kind of rock?

   ______

2. How many pieces of slate does Shawna have?

   ______

3. Which two kinds of rock does she have in equal numbers?

   ______

4. Shawna has 2 fewer pieces of marble than which other rock?

   ______

5. How many rocks does Shawna have in all?

   ______

FOR MORE PRACTICE:
Florida Benchmarks Practice Book, pp. P45–P46

Name ____________________________

Use a Bar Graph

Essential Question How do you read data in a bar graph in which the space between the numbers equals more than 1?

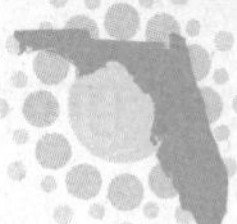

MA.3.S.7.1 Construct and analyze frequency tables, bar graphs, pictographs, and line plots from data, including data collected through observations, surveys, and experiments.

UNLOCK the Problem REAL WORLD

Erin's family wants to ride as many roller coasters as possible. Which amusement park in the graph has the greatest number of roller coasters?

- Underline the sentence that tells what Erin's family wants to do.
- How many amusement parks are shown? ______

On the bar graphs below, the scale shows the numbers 0, 2, 4, 6, 8, 10, 12, 14, and 16. Each space between the numbers represents 2 roller coasters.

These bar graphs show the same data.

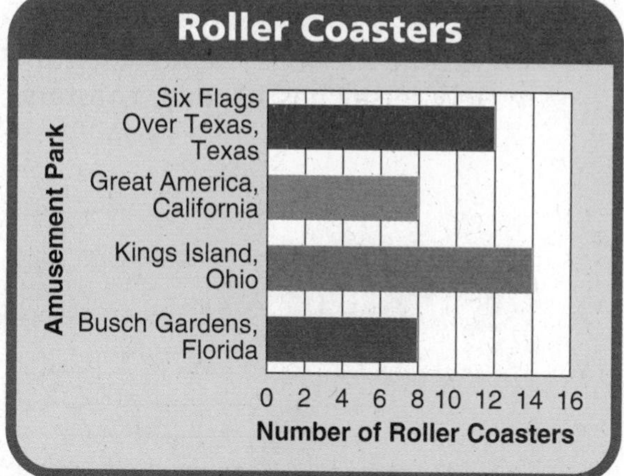

In a **horizontal bar graph**, the bars go across from left to right. The length of the bar shows the number.

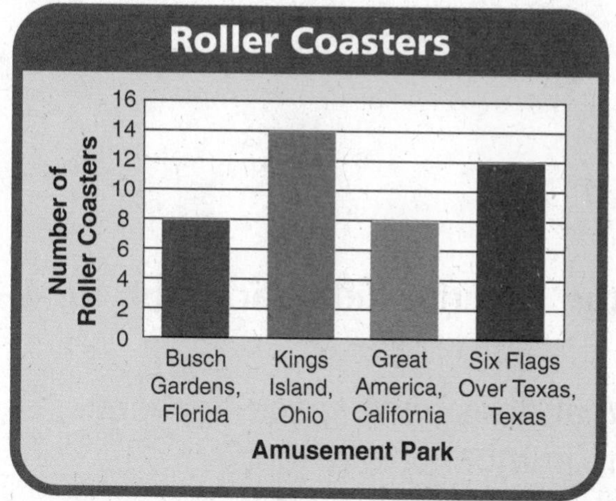

In a **vertical bar graph**, the bars go up from the bottom. The height of the bar shows the number.

The longest bar ends at ______. It is for ______________.

So, ______________ has the greatest number of roller coasters.

Math Talk What if the bar for Busch Gardens ended halfway between 8 and 10? How many roller coasters would Busch Gardens have? **Explain** how you know.

Share and Show 

Use the Roller Coasters bar graph for 1–3.

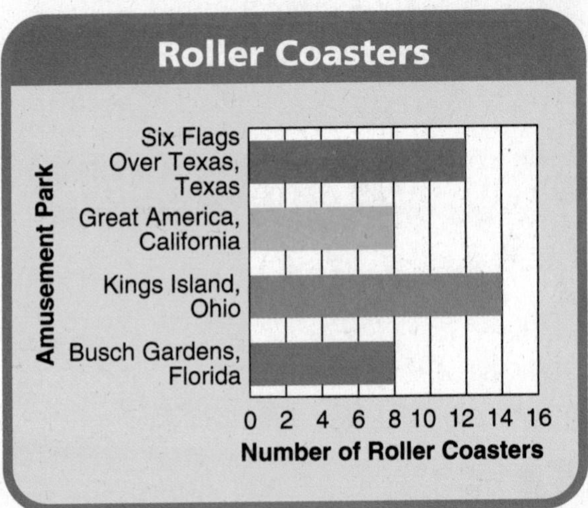

1. Which amusement parks have the same number of roller coasters?

   Think: Which bars have the same length?

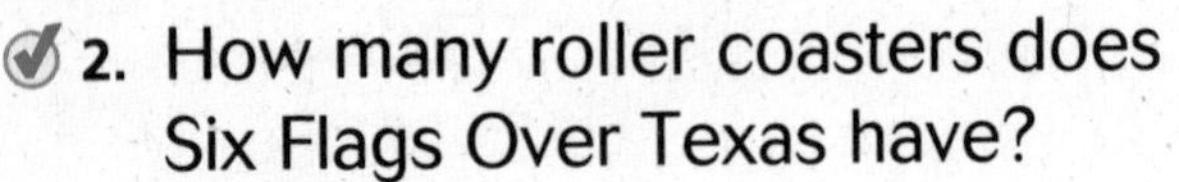

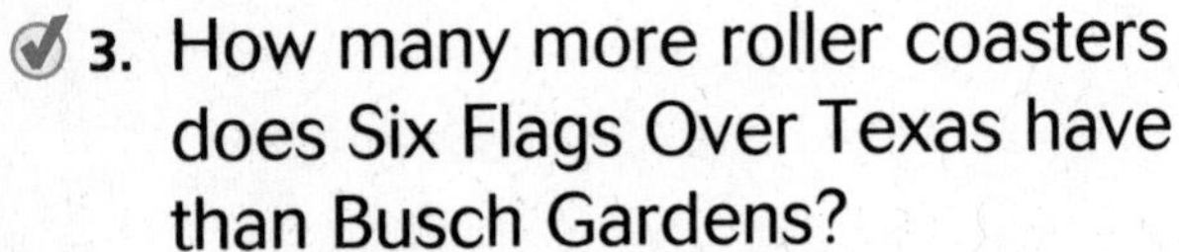

2. How many roller coasters does Six Flags Over Texas have? ______

3. How many more roller coasters does Six Flags Over Texas have than Busch Gardens? ______

Math Talk Explain how you would show that Six Flags Great Adventure in New Jersey has 13 roller coasters.

On Your Own

Use the Favorite Ride bar graph for 4–7.

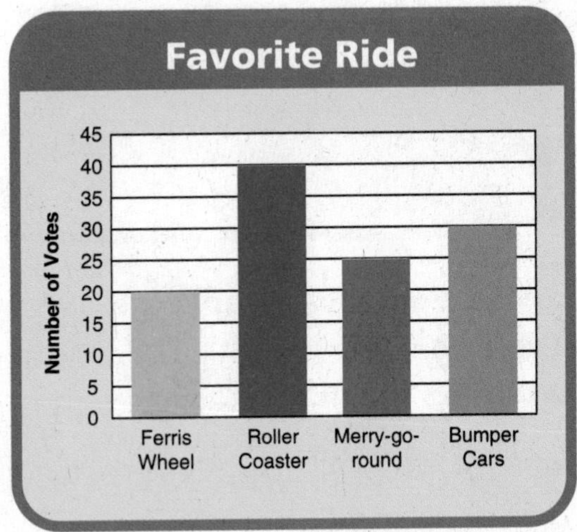

4. What does each space between the numbers represent? ______

5. How many students voted for roller coaster? ______

6. How many students voted in all? ______

7. Which two rides are the students' favorites? Explain how you know.

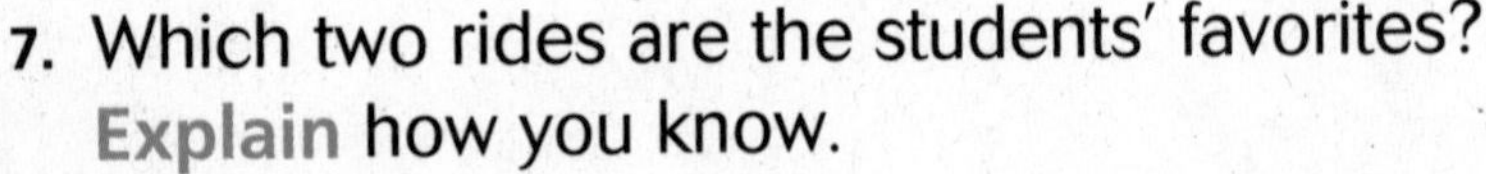

Name ____________________

Use the bar graph for 8–11 and 13.

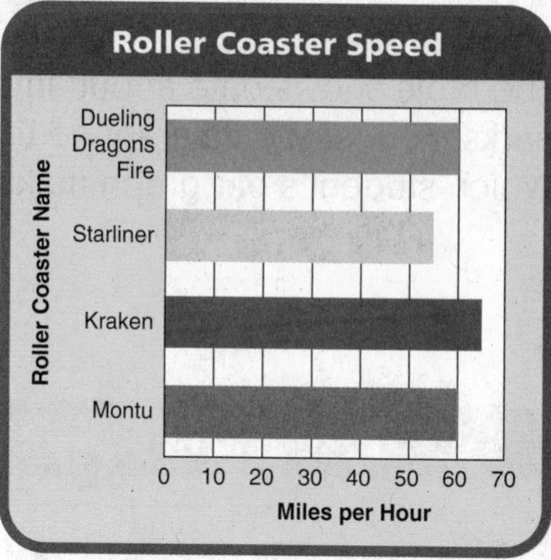

8. Which roller coasters have the same speed?

____

9. How much faster is Kraken than Starliner?

____

10. Write Math Write a question that could be answered by using the data in the Roller Coaster Speed bar graph.

____

____

11. H.O.T. **Explain** how the bar graph would change if the space between the numbers represented 2 miles per hour.

____

____

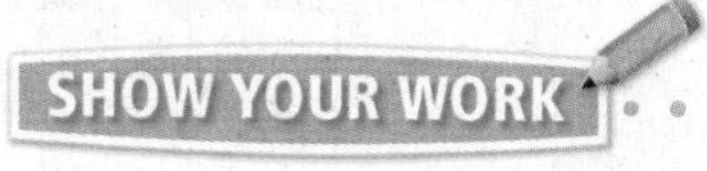

12. The first amusement park in the United States was built in Bristol, Connecticut in 1846. In 2011, how many years ago did it open?

____

13. **Test Prep** Which roller coaster has a speed that is 5 miles per hour faster than the speed of Dueling Dragons Fire?

Ⓐ Dueling Dragons Fire

Ⓑ Starliner

Ⓒ Kraken

Ⓓ Montu

Problem Solving REAL WORLD

Sense or Nonsense?

The table shows data about amusement parks. Four students graphed the data. Which student's bar graph makes sense?

____

Amusement Parks

State	Number
Florida	18
New York	20
Ohio	11
Texas	12

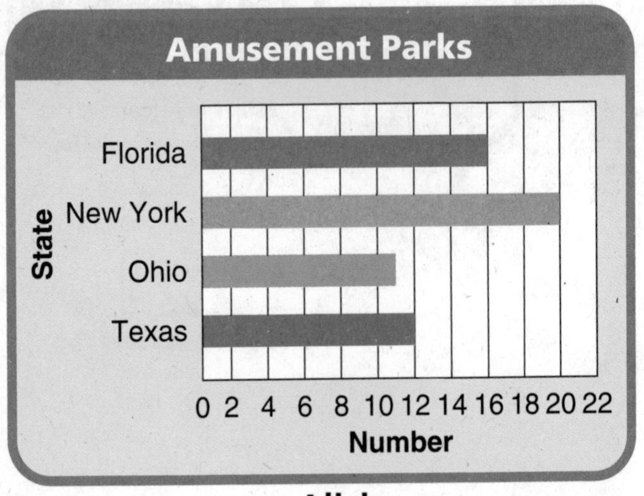

Alicia

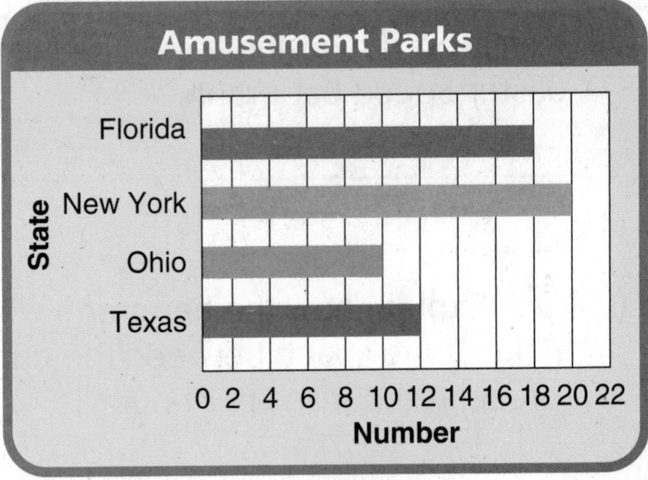

Spencer

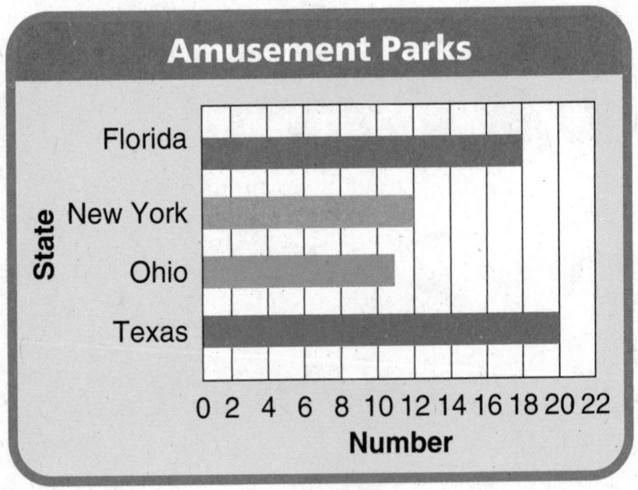

Tyler

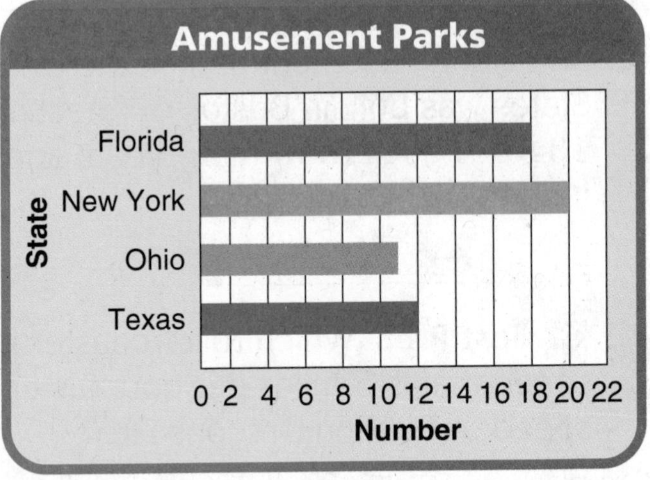

Kate

Explain why the other bar graphs do not make sense.

____

____

FOR MORE PRACTICE:
Florida Benchmarks Practice Book, pp. P47–P48

Name ____________________

Make a Bar Graph

Essential Question How can you make a bar graph to show data?

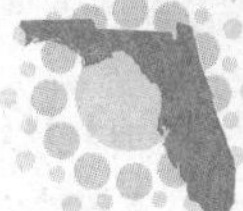

MA.3.S.7.1 Construct and analyze frequency tables, bar graphs, pictographs, and line plots from data, including data collected through observations, surveys, and experiments.

UNLOCK the Problem REAL WORLD

Jordan took a survey of his classmates' favorite team sports. He recorded the results in the table at the right. How can he show the results in a bar graph?

Favorite Team Sports

Sport	Number
Soccer	12
Basketball	4
Baseball	14
Football	9

Make a bar graph.

STEP 1

Write a title at the top to tell what the graph is about. Label the side of the graph to tell about the bars. Label the bottom of the graph to explain what the numbers tell.

STEP 2

Choose numbers for the bottom of the graph so that most of the bars will end on a line. Since the least number is 4 and the greatest number is 14, make the scale 0–16. Mark the scale by twos.

STEP 3

Draw and shade a bar to show the number for each sport.

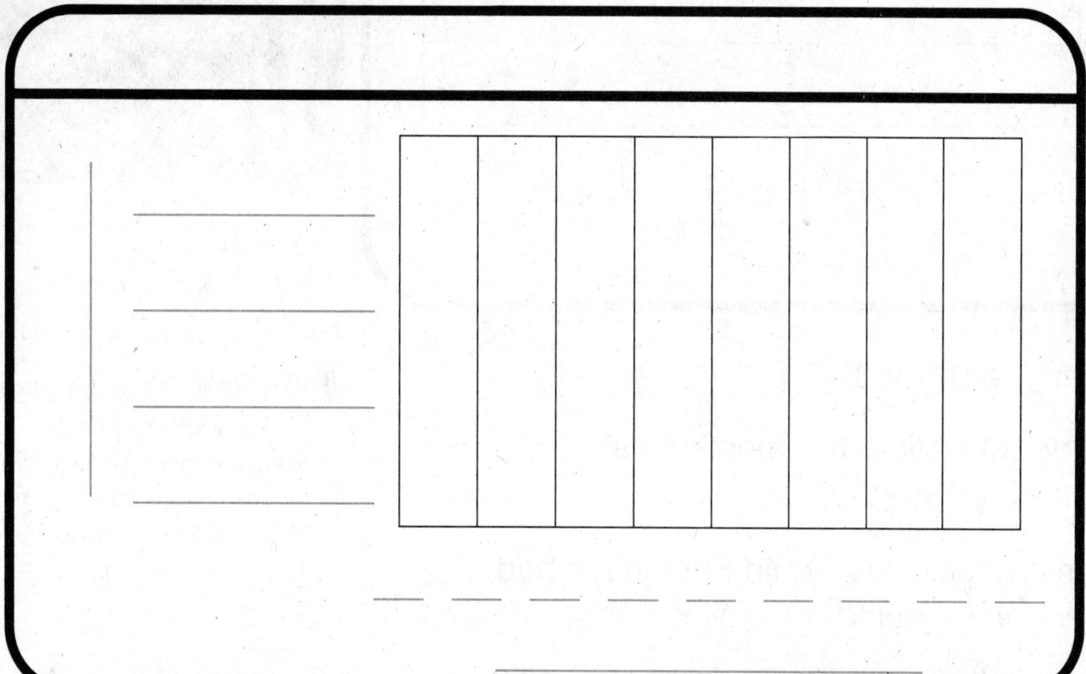

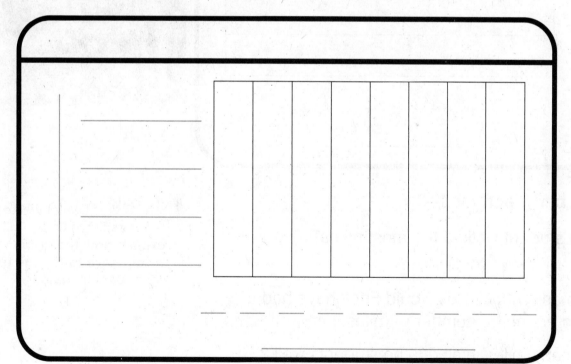

Math Talk How did you know how long to draw the bar for football?

Share and Show 

Matt's school is having a walk-a-thon to raise money for the school library. Matt made a pictograph to show the number of miles some students walked. Make a bar graph of Matt's data. Use a scale of 0–12, and mark the scale by 2s.

School Walk-a-Thon	
Sam	👕 👕 👕 👕 👕
Matt	👕 👕 👕
Ben	👕
Erica	👕 👕 👕 👕
Key: Each 👕 = 2 miles.	

Use your bar graph for 1–3.

1. Which student walked the most miles? ______

   Think: which student's bar is the longest?

2. How many more miles would Erica have had to walk to equal the number of miles Sam walked? ______

3. How many miles in all did the students walk? ______

Math Talk If Daniel walked twice as far as Erica, explain how the graph would have to change to show Daniel's data.

Name ___

On Your Own

4. Lydia and Joey did an experiment with a spinner. Lydia recorded the result of each spin in the table at the right. Use the data in the table to make a bar graph. Use a scale of 0–25, and mark it by 5s.

Spinner Results

Color	Tally
Red	卌 卌 卌 卌
Yellow	卌 卌
Blue	卌 卌 卌

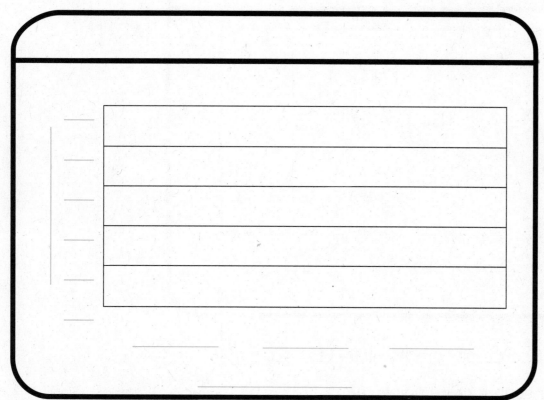

Use the Spinner Results graph for 5–7.

5. The pointer landed on ___ twice as many times as it landed on ___.

6. The spinner landed on blue ___ fewer times than it landed on red.

7. **Explain** why the scale is 0–25 by 5s.

___

___

Problem Solving REAL WORLD

8. Susie recorded the number of points some basketball players scored. Use the data in the table to make a bar graph. Choose numbers so that most of the numbers will end on a line.

Points Scored	
Raul	10
James	30
Dwight	15
Sean	25
Billy	10

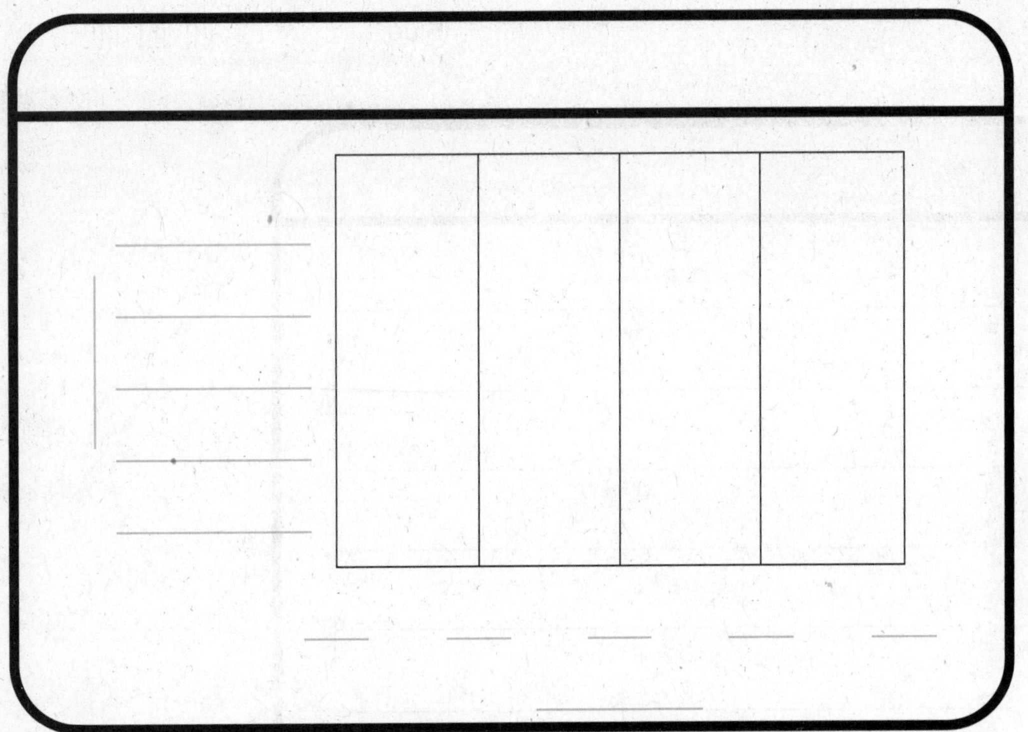

Use the Points Scored bar graph for 9–11.

9. Which player scored more points than Dwight but fewer points than James? ______

10. H.O.T. Write a question that could be answered by using the data in your bar graph.

______

______

11. Test Prep Which player scored the most points?

(A) Sean (B) Dwight (C) James (D) Billy

FOR MORE PRACTICE:
Florida Benchmarks Practice Book, pp. P49–P50

Name ______________________

Understand Line Plots

Essential Question How do you read data shown in a line plot?

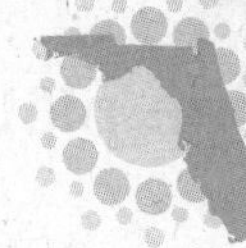

MA.3.S.7.1 Construct and analyze frequency tables, bar graphs, pictographs, and line plots from data, including data collected through observations, surveys, and experiments.

UNLOCK the Problem REAL WORLD

A **line plot** shows data on a number line.

Some students took a survey of the number of letters in their first names. Then they recorded the data in a line plot.

How many students have 6 letters in their first names?

Letters in Our First Names					
3	4	5	6	7	8
||	|||	~~||||~~ |	||||		|||

Each *x* stands for 1 student. →

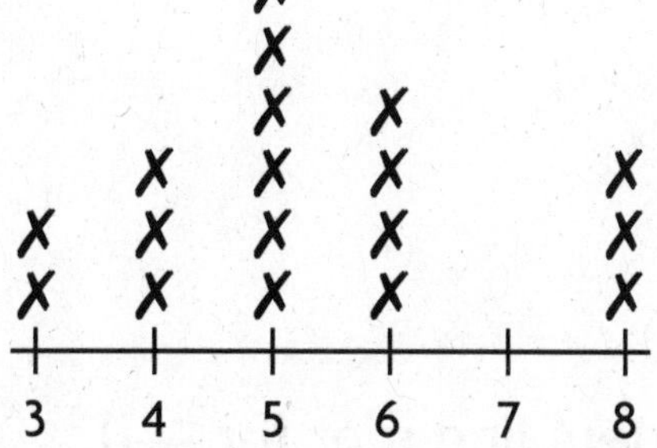

Number of Letters in Our First Names

← The numbers show the number of letters in a name.

Find 6 on the number line. The 6 stands for 6 __________.

There are ______ *x*s above the 6.

So, ______ students have 6 letters in their first names.

1. Which number of letters was found most often? ______
2. How many letters are in your first name? ____________
3. Put an *X* above the number of letters in your first name.

Math Talk There are no *x*s above 7. Explain what you think that means.

Share and Show 

Use the Number of Pets line plot for 1–3.

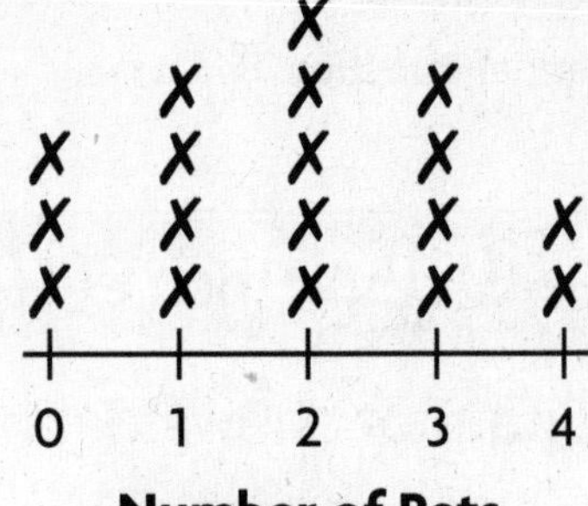

1. How many students have 1 pet?

   Think: how many *x*s are above 1?

   ____

2. How many pets do the fewest students have?

   ____

3. What is the difference between the greatest number of pets and the least number of pets?

   ____

Math Talk Explain how you can find the number of students who have 2 pets.

On Your Own

Use the Heights of Third Graders line plot for 4–8.

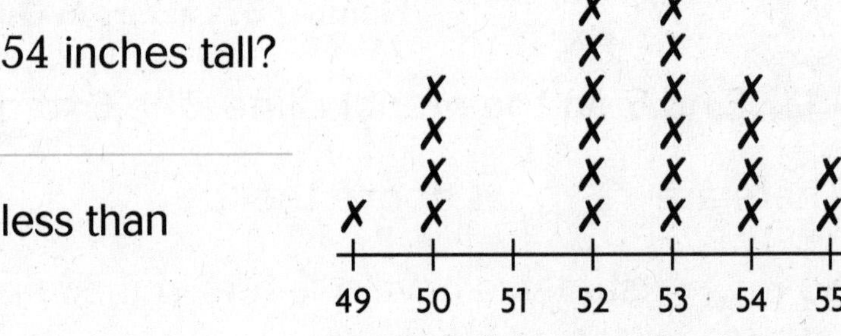

4. How many of the third graders are 54 inches tall?

   ____

5. How many of the third graders are less than 52 inches tall?

   ____

6. Complete the sentence. Most of the third-grade students are ______ inches or taller.

7. What is the difference between the greatest height and the least height?

   ____

8. **Explain** why there are no *x*s above the 51 inches mark on the line plot.

   ____

Name ______________________

Problem Solving REAL WORLD

Use the line plot for 9–14.

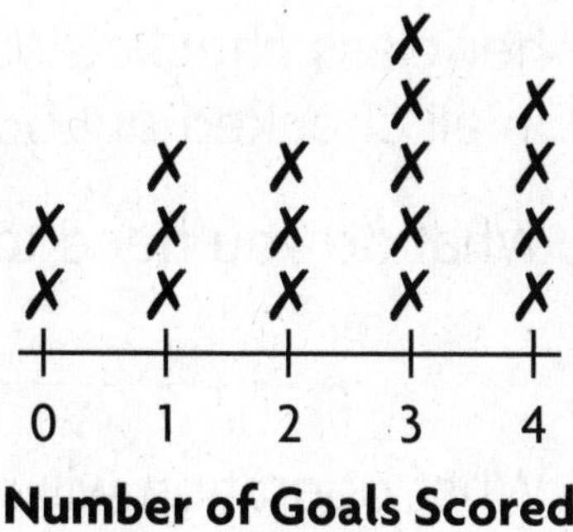

9. Alex recorded in a line plot the number of goals some soccer players scored. How many players scored 4 goals?

____

10. Which number of goals was scored by the most players?

____

11. Which number of goals was scored by the fewest players?

____

12. Write Math **Explain** how to find the difference between the most goals scored and the fewest goals scored.

____

____

13. H.O.T. Suppose 3 additional students had scored 1 goal each. Explain how the line plot would be different.

____

____

____

14. How many more soccer players scored 3 goals than 2 goals?

____

UNLOCK the Problem

REAL WORLD

15. Addison made this line plot to show the number of library books some students in her class checked out. How many students in all checked out books?

	X				
	X	X			
	X	X			
X	X	X	X		
X	X	X	X		X
X	X	X	X		X
1	2	3	4	5	6

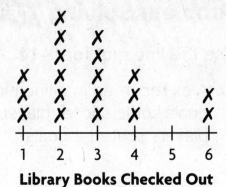

Library Books Checked Out

a. What do you need to find? ____________________

____

b. What operation will you use to find the answer? ____________________

c. Show the steps you used to find the answer.

d. Complete the sentences.

1 book _____ students

2 books _____ students

3 books _____ students

4 books _____ students

5 books _____ students

6 books _____ students

So, _____ students in all checked out books.

16. What is the difference between the fewest books checked out and the most books checked out?

____

17. **Test Prep** How many students checked out fewer than 3 books?

Ⓐ 1

Ⓑ 2

Ⓒ 3

Ⓓ 9

FOR MORE PRACTICE:
Florida Benchmarks Practice Book, pp. P51–P52

Name ____________________

Make a Line Plot

Essential Question How do you make a line plot from data in a table?

MA.3.S.7.1 Construct and analyze frequency tables, bar graphs, pictographs, and line plots from data, including data collected through observations, surveys, and experiments.

UNLOCK the Problem REAL WORLD

Sarah rolled a number cube 20 times. She used a tally table to record each number rolled. Make a line plot to show the data Sarah collected.

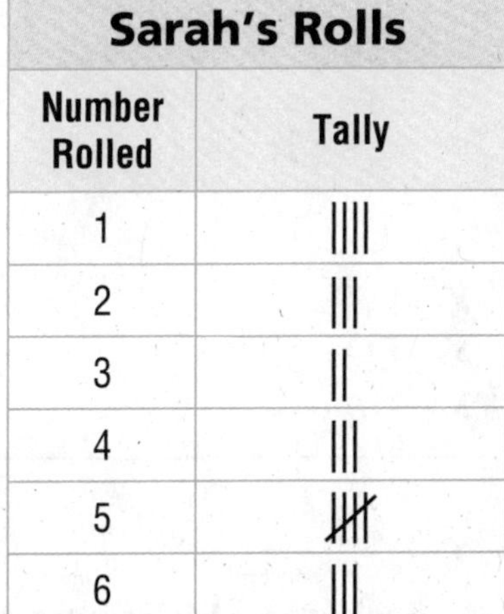

Sarah's Rolls	
Number Rolled	Tally
1					
2				
3			
4				
5	𝍸 (5)
6				

Make a line plot by completing the number line below.

STEP 1 Write a title below the numbers to describe what the line plot shows.

STEP 2 Label the numbers from 1 to 6 to show the numbers on the number cube.

STEP 3 Draw an *x* above the number line to show how many times Sarah rolled each number.

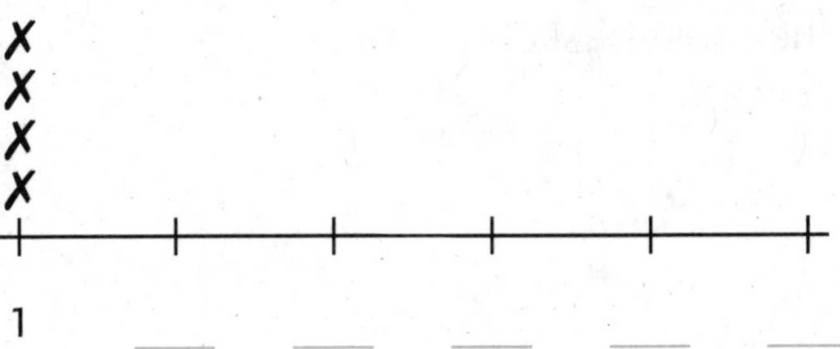

1 ____ ____ ____ ____ ____

____

Math Talk **Explain** what the data in the line plot tells you about the experiment.

- Which number did Sarah roll most often? ______

Share and Show 

Jeremy invited some friends to pick strawberries in Plant City. He used a table to record the number of baskets picked. Complete the line plot of the data.

Baskets of Strawberries Picked	
5	𝍷𝍷𝍷
6	𝍸 𝍷
7	𝍸
8	𝍷
9	𝍷𝍷

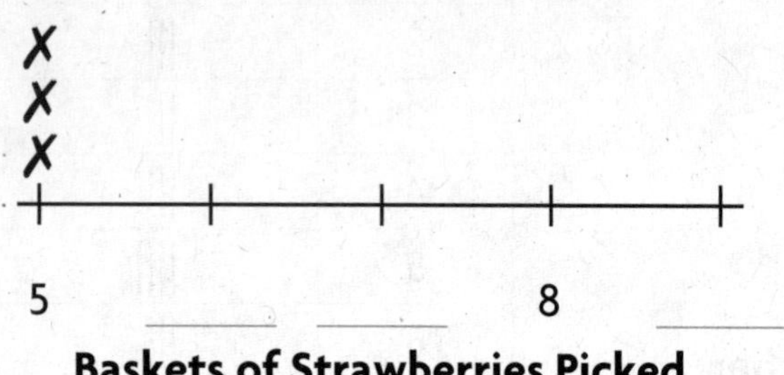

Use your line plot for 1–5.

1. How many people picked 6 baskets of strawberries?

   ____

2. What number of baskets did the fewest people pick?

   ____

3. What is the difference between the most baskets picked and the fewest baskets picked?

   ____

4. How many more people picked 7 baskets than 9 baskets?

   ____

5. Did more people pick 7 or more baskets or fewer than 7 baskets?

   ____

Name ___________________________

On Your Own

6. The frequency table shows the number of brothers and sisters the students in Mrs. Riley's class have. Use the data in the table to complete the line plot.

Numbers of Brothers and Sisters	
0	5
1	6
2	5
3	3

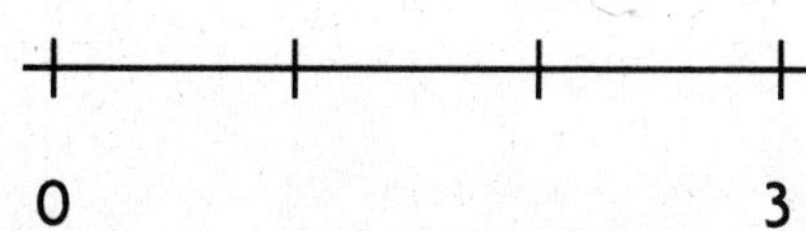

Numbers of Brothers and Sisters

Use your line plot for 7–13.

7. How many students have zero brothers or sisters? ______

8. How many more students have 2 brothers and sisters than have 3 brothers and sisters? ______

9. Which number of brothers and sisters is found most often? ______

10. What is the difference between the most brothers and sisters and the fewest brothers and sisters? ______

11. How many students have 2 or more brothers and sisters? ______

12. Which number of brothers and sisters is found least often? ______

13. Do more students have 2 or more brothers or sisters or fewer than 2 brothers or sisters? ______

Problem Solving REAL WORLD

Ages of Campers	
Age	**Number**
8	1
9	0
10	5
11	3
12	7
13	4
14	3

14. During her summer vacation, Kira participated in the NASA Space Camp for Kids at Kennedy Space Center. She recorded the ages of some of the campers in the table at the right. Use the data in the table to make a line plot.

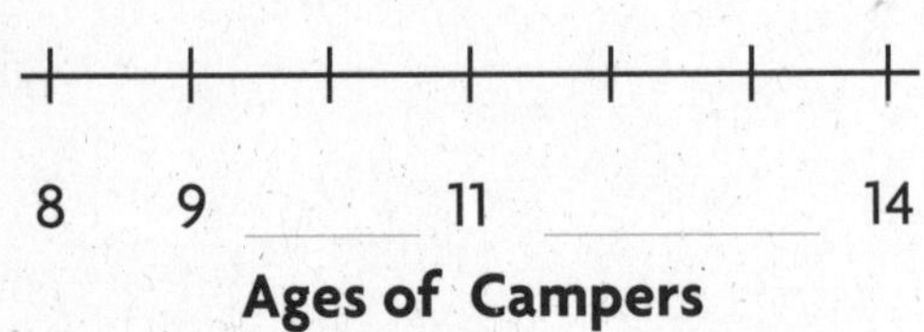

Use your line plot for 15–18.

15. What age were the most campers? ______

16. How many campers were 11 years old or older? ______

17. H.O.T. Suppose Kira recorded the ages of 7 more campers. If 4 more campers were 13 years old and 3 more were 10 years old, **explain** how the line plot would be different.

____

____

18. **Test Prep** What is the difference between the ages of the youngest camper and the oldest camper?

Ⓐ 2 years Ⓒ 8 years

Ⓑ 6 years Ⓓ 14 years

 FOR MORE PRACTICE:
Florida Benchmarks Practice Book, pp. P53–P54

Name ____________________

Chapter Review/Test

▶ Check Vocabulary

Choose the best term from the box.

Vocabulary
bar graph
frequency table
line plot
pictograph

1. In a ______________, each piece of data is recorded on a number line. (MA.3.S.7.1; p. 95)
2. A ______________ uses pictures to show information. (MA.3.S.7.1; p. 69)
3. A ______________ uses bars to show data. (MA.3.S.7.1; p. 83)

▶ Check Concepts

Use the Dolphins Max Saw table for 4–6. (MA.3.S.7.1; pp. 61–64)

Dolphins Max Saw

Day	Number
Friday	12
Saturday	15
Sunday	19

4. Max recorded in a table the number of dolphins he saw. How many dolphins did he see on Saturday?

____

5. How many more dolphins did Max see on Sunday than on Friday? ______________
6. If you made a bar graph of the data in the table, what labels would you use? ______________

Use the Number of Goals Scored line plot for 7–9. (MA.3.S.7.1; pp. 95–98)

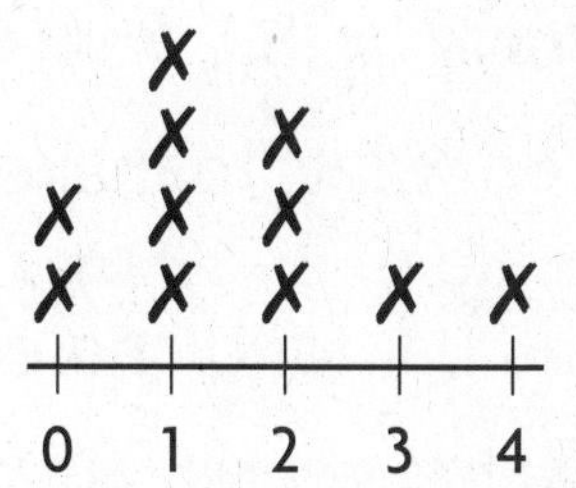

7. Katie recorded the goals the players on her soccer team scored. How many players scored 2 goals?

____

8. What does each *x* stand for? ______________
9. Did more players score fewer than 2 goals or 2 or more goals? ______________

Go online Assessment Options Chapter Test

Fill in the bubble for the correct answer choice.

Use the bar graph for 10–14. (MA.3.S.7.1; pp. 83–90)

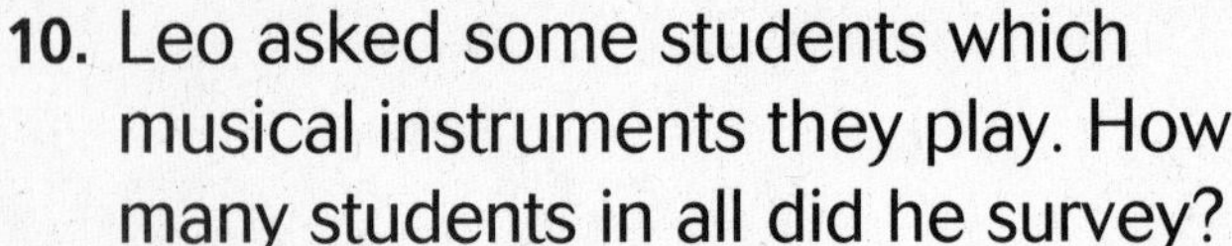

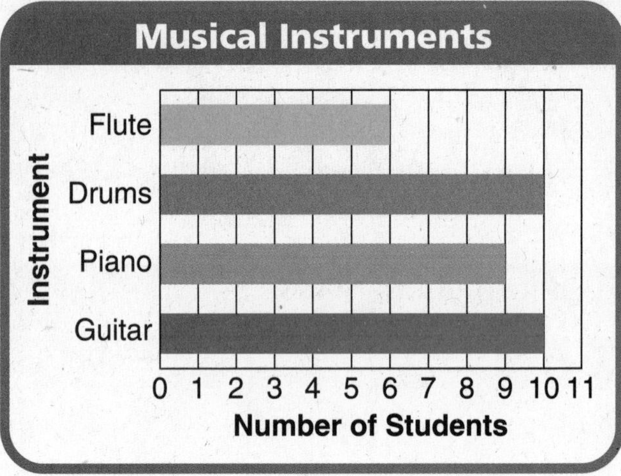

10. Leo asked some students which musical instruments they play. How many students in all did he survey? (MA.3.S.7.1; pp. 83–86)

Ⓐ 15 Ⓒ 35

Ⓑ 25 Ⓓ 45

11. Three more students play piano than which other instrument? (MA.3.S.7.1; pp. 83–86)

Ⓕ flute Ⓗ violin

Ⓖ drums Ⓘ guitar

12. The same number of students play which two instruments? (MA.3.S.7.1; pp. 83–86)

Ⓐ guitar and drums

Ⓑ piano and drums

Ⓒ drums and flute

Ⓓ flute and piano

13. How many more students play drums than play flute? (MA.3.S.7.1; pp. 83–86)

Ⓕ 2 Ⓗ 4

Ⓖ 3 Ⓘ 5

14. Leo wants to make a new graph with a scale of 0–12 by 2s. Where should the bar for piano end? (MA.3.S.7.1; pp. 87–90)

Ⓐ between 6 and 8

Ⓑ on 8

Ⓒ between 8 and 10

Ⓓ on 10

Name ______________________________

Use the pictograph for 15–18.

Jim's Books	
Animal	
Puzzle	
Sports	
Key: Each = 2 books.	

15. Jim made a pictograph to show the types of books he has. Which part of the pictograph tells you what each symbol stands for? **(MA.3.S.7.1; pp. 73–76)**

Ⓕ label Ⓗ title

Ⓖ key Ⓘ scale

16. How many puzzle books does Jim have? **(MA.3.S.7.1; pp. 73–76)**

Ⓐ 3

Ⓑ $3\frac{1}{2}$

Ⓒ 7

Ⓓ 8

17. How many more sports books than animal books does Jim have? **(MA.3.S.7.1; pp. 73–76)**

Ⓕ 2

Ⓖ 3

Ⓗ 4

Ⓘ 24

18. Which statement is true about the books Jim has? **(MA.3.S.7.1; pp. 73–76)**

Ⓐ There are more puzzle books than animal books.

Ⓑ There are fewer sports books than puzzle books.

Ⓒ There are more sports books than animal books and puzzle books combined.

Ⓓ Jim has 31 books in all.

Use the Baskets of Blueberries Picked line plot for 19–22.

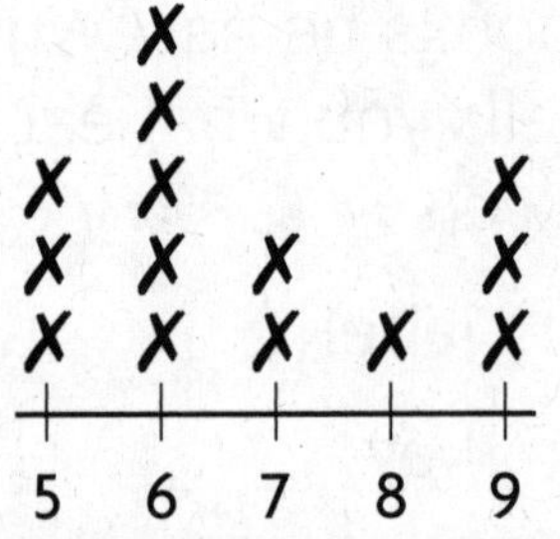

19. The largest blueberry festival in Florida is held in June in the city of Wellborn. How many people picked 9 baskets of blueberries? (MA.3.S.7.1; pp. 95–98)

Ⓕ 2

Ⓖ 3

Ⓗ 5

Ⓘ 9

20. Which number of baskets of blueberries was picked by the most people? (MA.3.S.7.1; pp. 95–98)

Ⓐ 9

Ⓑ 7

Ⓒ 6

Ⓓ 5

21. How many people picked more than 6 baskets of blueberries? (MA.3.S.7.1; pp. 95–98)

Ⓕ 6

Ⓖ 7

Ⓗ 8

Ⓘ 11

22. What is the difference between the most baskets of blueberries picked and the fewest baskets of blueberries picked? (MA.3.S.7.1; pp. 95–98)

Ⓐ 9

Ⓑ 5

Ⓒ 4

Ⓓ 3

Chapter 3

Understand Multiplication

Show What You Know

Check your understanding of important skills.

Name ______________________

Skip Counting Skip count. Write how many in all.

1.   

____ ____ ____ ____

____ apples

2. 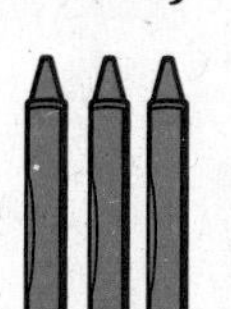  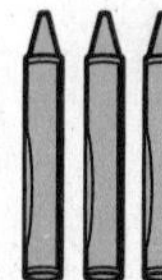

____ ____ ____

____ crayons

Skip Count by Twos and Fives Skip count. Write the missing numbers.

3. 2, 4, 6, ____, ____, ____

4. 5, 10, 15, ____, ____, ____

Equal Groups Complete.

5. 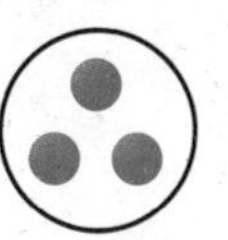 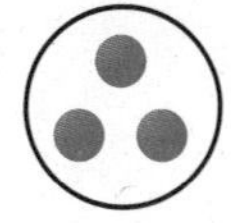

____ + ____ + ____ + ____

____ groups of ____

____ in all

6.     

____ + ____ + ____ + ____ + ____

____ groups of ____

____ in all

Florida FUN FACT

In 1982, students chose the Florida panther to be the Florida state animal. The Florida panther is endangered.

Vocabulary Power

▶ Visualize It

Complete the tree map by using the review words.

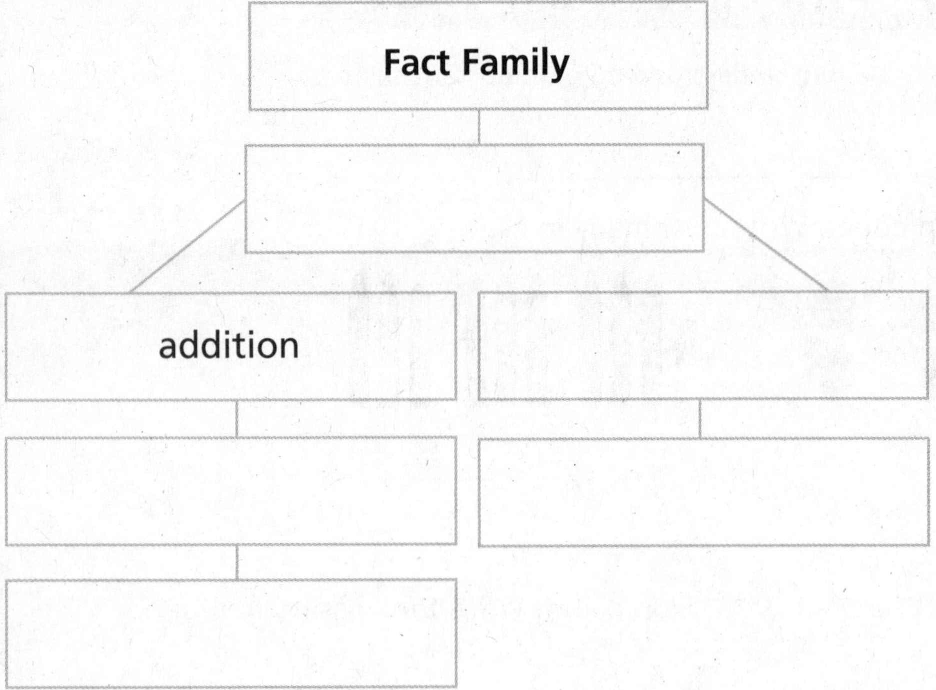

Review Words

- addend
- addition
- difference
- fact family
- number sentences
- subtraction
- sum

Preview Words

- array
- equal groups
- factor
- multiply
- product

▶ Understand Vocabulary

Read the definition. Write the preview word that matches it.

1. An arrangement of objects or numbers in rows and columns ____________

2. The answer in a multiplication problem ____________

3. When you combine equal groups to find how many in all ____________

4. A number that is multiplied by another number to find a product ____________

Go online • Student Edition • Multilingual eGlossary

Name ___

Count Equal Groups

Essential Question How can you use equal groups to find how many in all?

MA.3.A.1.1 Model multiplication and division including problems presented in context: repeated addition, multiplicative comparison, array, how many combinations, measurement, and partitioning.

UNLOCK the Problem REAL WORLD

Equal groups have the same number of objects in each group.

Tim likes to play with marbles. He makes 8 equal groups with 2 marbles in each group. How many marbles does Tim have in all?

- How many equal groups did Tim make?

___

- How many marbles are in each group?

___

- How can you find how many in all?

___

Use counters to model the equal groups.

Materials ■ counters

STEP 1 Draw 2 counters in each group.

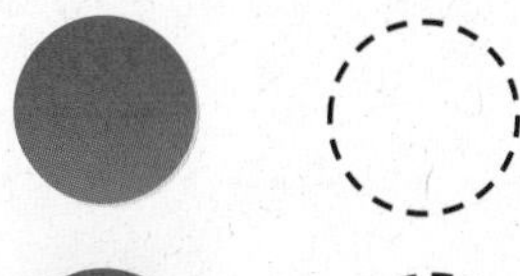

1 2 3 4 5 6 7 8

STEP 2 Skip count to find how many marbles Tim has in all.

2, ___, 6, ___, ___, ___, ___, ___

There are ___ groups with ___ marbles in each group.

So, Tim has ___ marbles in all.

Example

Erin has a collection of toy cats. She puts the cats in 6 equal groups. There are 3 cats in each group. How many toy cats does Erin have in all?

You can use a number line to skip count equal groups.

How many cats are in each group? ______

How many equal groups of cats are there? ______

Begin at 0. Draw jumps on the number line to skip count by 3s.

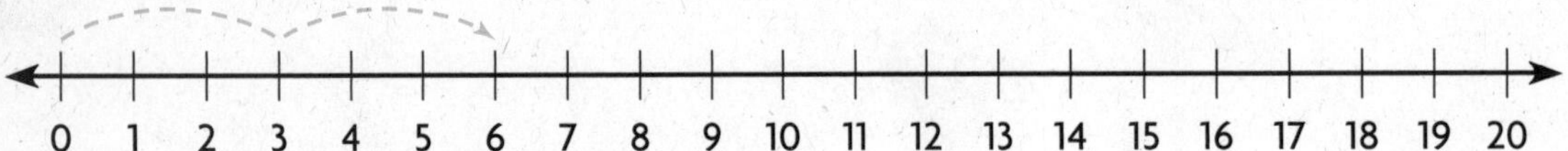

How many jumps did you make? ______

So, Erin has ______ toy cats in all.

- Why did you jump by 3s on the number line? ______

Share and Show

1. Skip count to find how many counters in all.

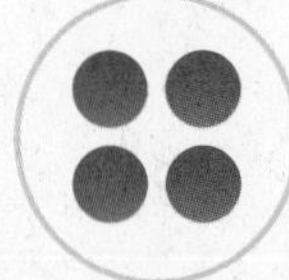 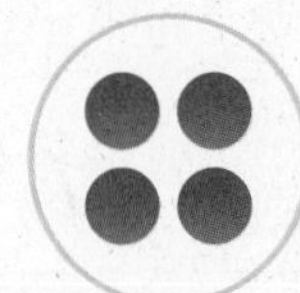 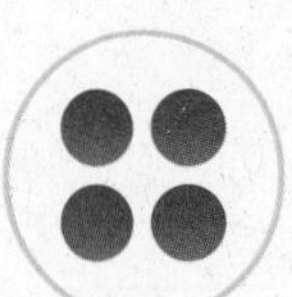 ______

2. Skip count by drawing the jumps on the number line. Find how many in 3 jumps of 5.

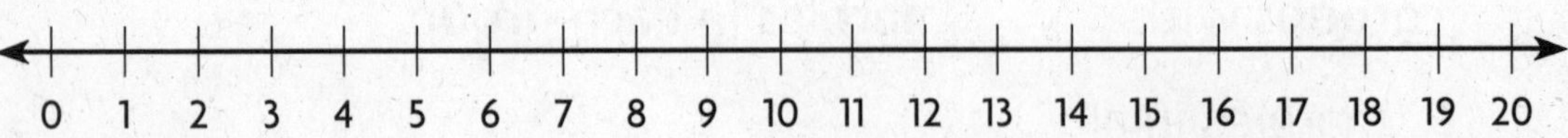

______

Math Talk **Explain** how you could use a number line to skip count to find how many are in 3 groups of 4.

Name ___

Draw equal groups. Skip count to find how many in all.

3. 2 groups of 6 ___

4. 5 groups of 2 ___

5. 4 groups of 4 ___

6. 3 groups of 7 ___

On Your Own

Draw equal groups. Skip count to find how many in all.

7. 3 groups of 5 ___

8. 4 groups of 3 ___

Draw jumps on the number line. Skip count to find how many in all.

9. 5 groups of 4 ___

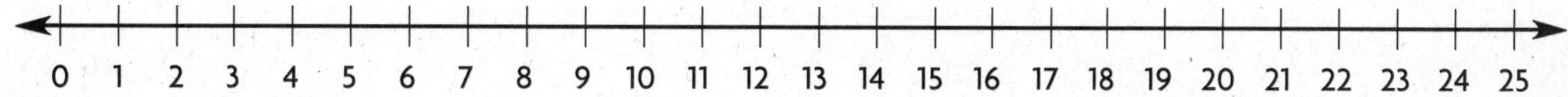

10. 4 groups of 6 ___

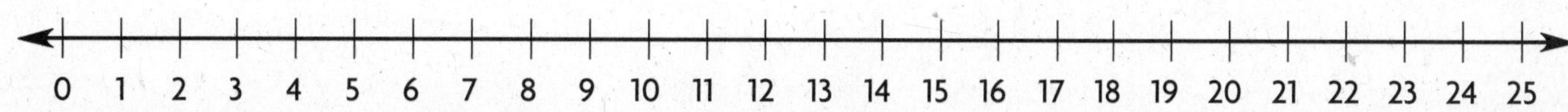

Problem Solving 

SHOW YOUR WORK

11. James has 3 bags of apples. There are 8 apples in each bag. How many apples does James have in all?

____

12. Lois peeled apples to make 4 apple pies. She used 6 apples for each pie. How many apples did she peel?

____

13. H.O.T. Caleb has 2 quarters, 3 dimes, and 4 nickels. Avery has 1 quarter, 5 dimes, and 5 nickels. How much money does each child have? Who has more money?

____

____

14. Write Math ▸ Write a problem that can be solved by finding 8 groups of 5. Solve the problem.

____

____

____

____

____

15. Test Prep Brooke put 5 stuffed animals on each of 4 chairs. How many animals are on the chairs?

Ⓐ 4 Ⓒ 9

Ⓑ 5 Ⓓ 20

FOR MORE PRACTICE:
Florida Benchmarks Practice Book, pp. P61–P62

Name ___________________________

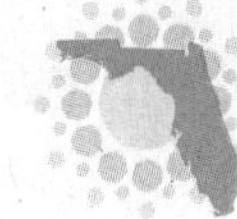

ALGEBRA
Lesson 2

Relate Addition and Multiplication

Essential Question How is multiplication like addition? How is it different?

MA.3.A.1.1 Model multiplication and division including problems presented in context: repeated addition, multiplicative comparison, array, how many combinations, measurement, and partitioning.

UNLOCK the Problem REAL WORLD

Jasmine needs 3 bananas to make one loaf of banana bread. The same numbers of bananas are in each loaf. How many bananas does Jasmine need to make 4 loaves?

- How many loaves is Jasmine making? _____
- How many bananas are in each loaf? _____
- How can you solve the problem?

____

One Way Add equal groups.

Use the 4 circles to show the 4 loaves.

Draw 3 counters in each circle to show the bananas Jasmine needs for each loaf.

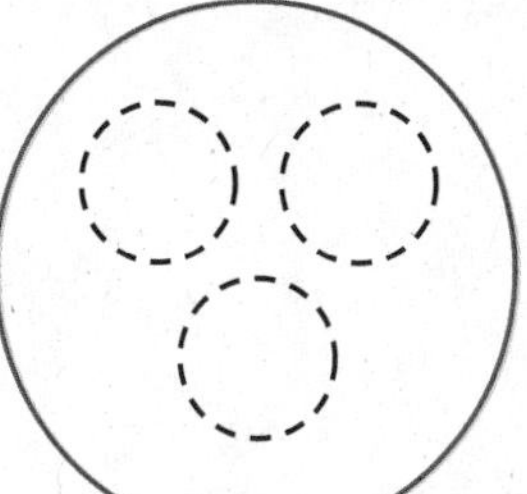 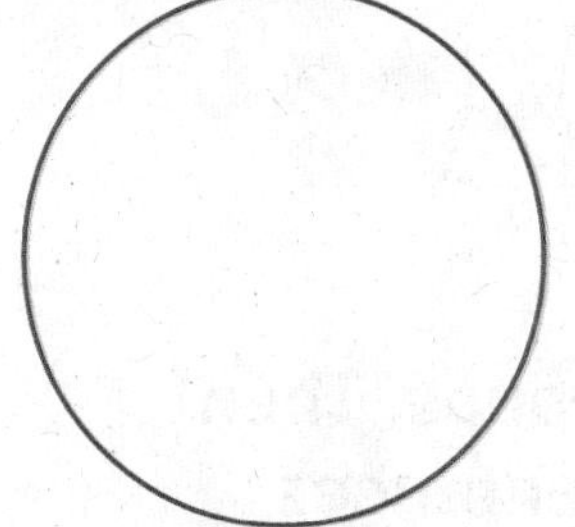 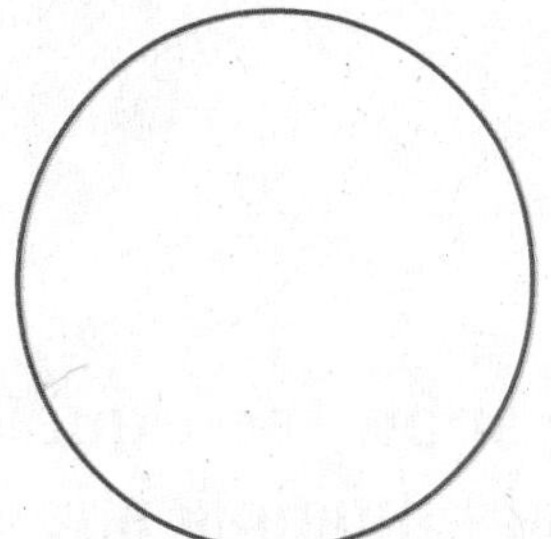 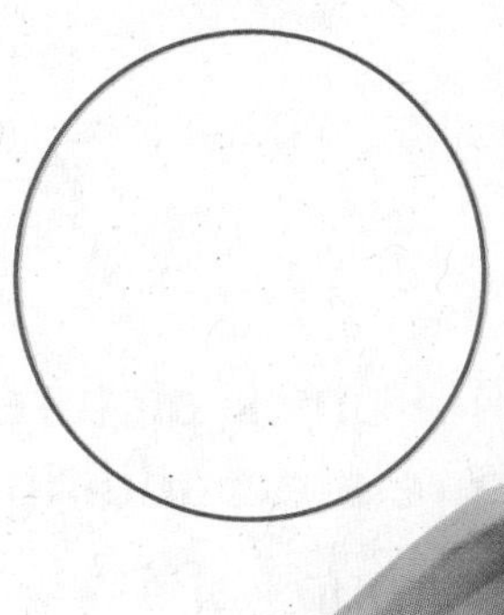

Find the number of counters in all.
Complete the addition sentence.

3 + _____ + _____ + _____ = _____

So, Jasmine needs _____ bananas to make _____ loaves.

Math Talk How is the picture you drew like the addition sentence you wrote?

Another Way Multiply.

When you **multiply**, you combine equal groups to find how many in all.

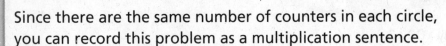

Think: 4 groups of 3

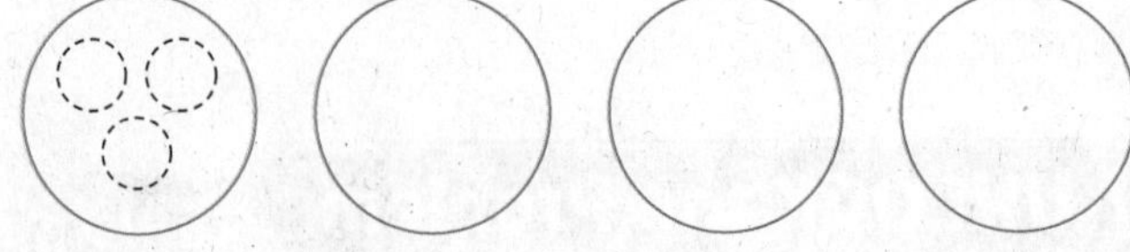

Draw 3 counters in each circle.

Since there are the same number of counters in each circle, you can record this problem as a multiplication sentence.

Write: $4 \times 3 = 12$
Read: 4 times 3 equals 12.

Multiplication is another way to find how many there are altogether in equal groups.

Share and Show

1. Write related addition and multiplication sentences for the model.

_____ + _____ = _____

_____ × _____ = _____

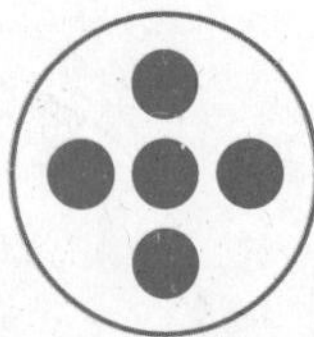

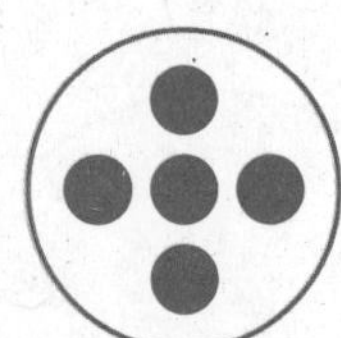

Draw a quick picture to show the equal groups. Then write related addition and multiplication sentences.

2. 2 groups of 4

_____ + _____ = _____

_____ × _____ = _____

3. 3 groups of 5

_____ + _____ + _____ = _____

_____ × _____ = _____

Math Talk **Explain** why you can write only an addition sentence for this model.

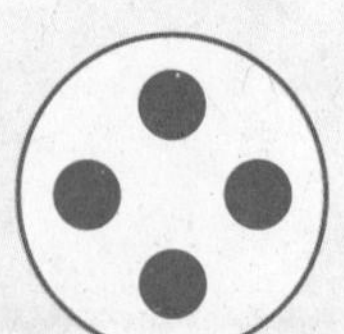

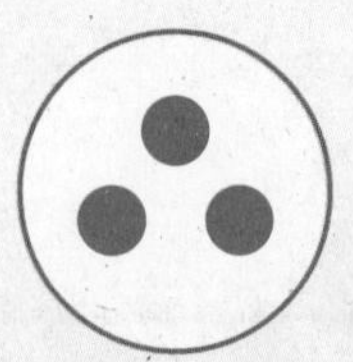

Name ________________________________

On Your Own

Draw a quick picture to show the equal groups. Then write related addition and multiplication sentences.

4. 2 groups of 6

_____ + _____ = _____

_____ × _____ = _____

5. 4 groups of 5

_____ + _____ + _____ + _____ = _____

_____ × _____ = _____

Draw a quick picture on your MathBoard. Then write related addition and multiplication sentences.

6. 3 groups of 4

_____ + _____ + _____ = _____

_____ × _____ = _____

7. 2 groups of 5

_____ + _____ = _____

_____ × _____ = _____

8. 4 groups of 6

_____ + _____ + _____ + _____ = _____

_____ × _____ = _____

9. 3 groups of 7

_____ + _____ + _____ = _____

_____ × _____ = _____

Write a multiplication sentence.

10. 

_____ × _____ = _____

11. 

_____ × _____ = _____

12. 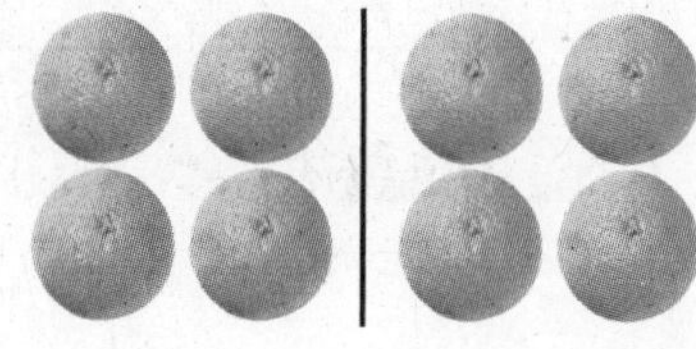

_____ × _____ = _____

13. $2 + 2 + 2 + 2 = 8$

_____ × _____ = _____

14. $4 + 4 + 4 + 4 = 16$

_____ × _____ = _____

15. $9 + 9 + 9 = 27$

_____ × _____ = _____

Complete.

16. $6 + 6 + 6 =$ _____ × _____ = _____

17. $8 + 8 + 8 + 8 =$ _____ × _____ = _____

Problem Solving REAL WORLD

Use the table for 18–19.

Average Weight of Fruits	
Fruit	**Weight in Ounces**
Apple	6
Orange	5
Peach	3
Banana	4

18. John bought 3 oranges. How much do the oranges weigh in all? Write a multiplication sentence to find the answer.

    ______ $\times$ ______ $=$ ______ ounces

19. Thomas bought 3 apples. Sydney bought 4 bananas. Which weighed more–the 3 apples or the 4 bananas? How much more?

    Explain how you know. ____________________

    ____

    ____

    ____

SHOW YOUR WORK

20. H.O.T. **Sense or Nonsense?** Jared said that he could write related multiplication and addition sentences for $5 + 4 + 4$. Does Jared's statement make sense? **Explain.**

    ____

    ____

    ____

21. Write Math Write a word problem that can be solved using 3×4. Solve the problem. ____________________

    ____

    ____

22. **Test Prep** Which is another way to show $2 + 2 + 2 + 2$?

    Ⓐ 2×2 Ⓒ 4×2

    Ⓑ 6×2 Ⓓ 2×8

FOR MORE PRACTICE:
Florida Benchmarks Practice Book, pp. P63–P64

Name ______________________________

Multiply with 2

Essential Question How is multiplying by 2 related to addition?

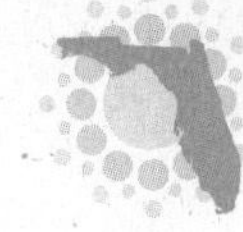

MA.3.A.1.1 Model multiplication and division including problems presented in context: repeated addition, multiplicative comparison, array, how many combinations, measurement, and partitioning.

UNLOCK the Problem — REAL WORLD

Four students are putting on a play. Each of the 4 students has 2 costumes. How many costumes do they have in all?

- What does the word "each" tell you?

____

- How can you find the number of costumes the 4 students have?

____

 **Find 4 × 2.**

MODEL

Draw counters to show the costumes.

THINK

4 groups of 2

$2 + 2 + 2 + 2$

2, 4, 6, 8

RECORD

$4 \times 2 = 8$

4 ↓ factor ↓ how many groups

2 ↓ factor ↓ how many in each group

8 ↓ product

$$\begin{array}{r} 2 \\ \times\, 4 \\ \hline 8 \end{array}$$

2 ← factor
4 ← factor
8 ← product

The **factors** are the numbers multiplied.

The **product** is the answer to a multiplication problem.

So, the 4 students have ______ costumes in all.

Math Talk How would your model change if there were 2 students in the play and they each wore 4 costumes?

Use Doubles Multiplying with 2 is the same as adding doubles.

 2 × 3 = 3 + 3 = 6

2 × 4 = 4 + 4 = 8

2 × _____ = 5 + _____ = _____

2 × _____ = 6 + _____ = _____

2 × _____ = 7 + _____ = _____

Math Talk How could you use doubles to find 2 × 14?

Share and Show 

1. Complete the multiplication sentence the model shows.

   2 × _____ = _____

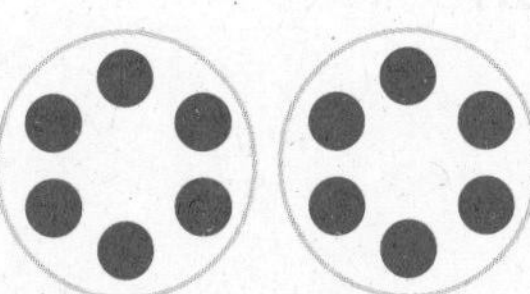

Write the multiplication sentence for the model.

2. 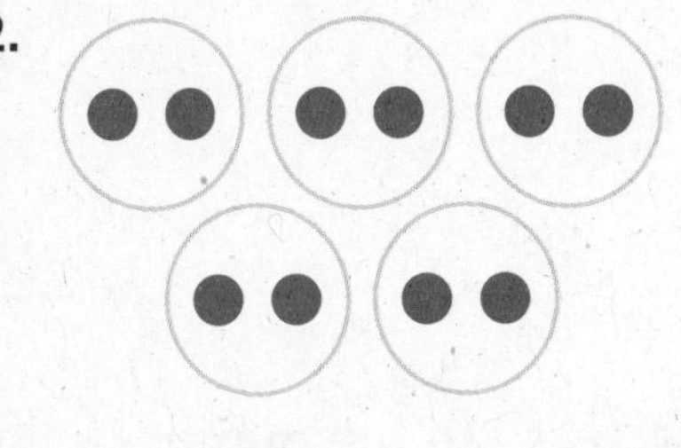

   _____ × _____ = _____

3. 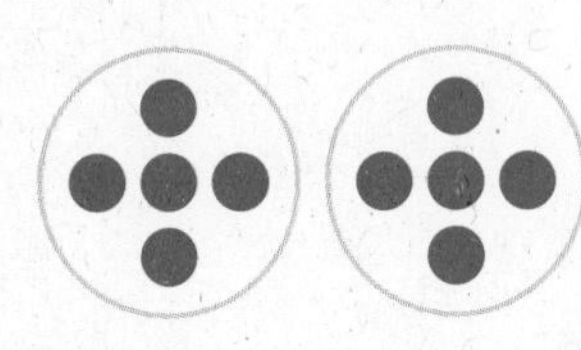

   _____ × _____ = _____

Draw a quick picture. Write the product.

4. $\begin{array}{r} 2 \\ \times 4 \\ \hline \end{array}$

5. $\begin{array}{r} 8 \\ \times 2 \\ \hline \end{array}$

Name ____________________

On Your Own

Write the multiplication sentence for the model.

6. 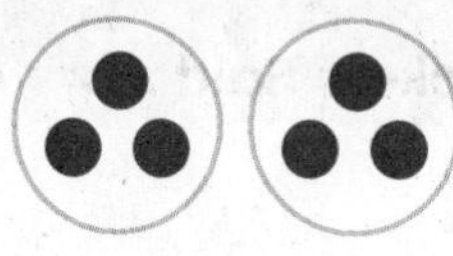

____ × ____ = ____

7. 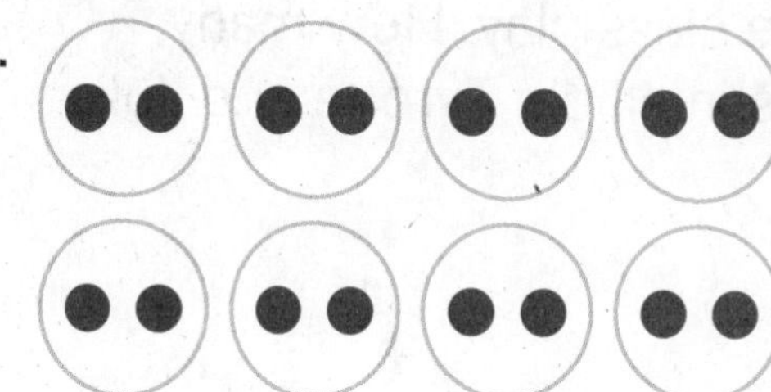

____ × ____ = ____

Find the product.

8. $\begin{array}{r} 4 \\ \times 2 \\ \hline \end{array}$

9. $\begin{array}{r} 9 \\ \times 2 \\ \hline \end{array}$

10. $\begin{array}{r} 6 \\ \times 2 \\ \hline \end{array}$

11. $\begin{array}{r} 7 \\ \times 2 \\ \hline \end{array}$

12. $\begin{array}{r} 3 \\ \times 2 \\ \hline \end{array}$

13. $\begin{array}{r} 8 \\ \times 2 \\ \hline \end{array}$

14. $\begin{array}{r} 2 \\ \times 2 \\ \hline \end{array}$

15. $\begin{array}{r} 5 \\ \times 2 \\ \hline \end{array}$

Algebra Complete the table.

16.

×	1	2	3	4	5	6	7	8	9
2									

Complete.

17. ____ × 2 = 10

18. ____ × 2 = 18

19. 7 × ____ = 14

UNLOCK the Problem REAL WORLD

20. Ms. Williams' class sold tickets for the class play. How many tickets in all did Tyrone and Julia sell?

Play Tickets	
Name	**Tickets Sold**
Tyrone	🎟🎟🎟🎟
Julia	🎟🎟🎟🎟🎟🎟🎟
Lee	🎟🎟🎟🎟🎟🎟🎟🎟

Key: Each 🎟 = 2 tickets sold.

a. What do you need to find? ______________________________

____

b. What operations will you use to solve the problem? **Explain.** ______________________________

____

____

c. Show the steps you use to solve the problem.

d. Complete the sentences.

Tyrone sold ______ tickets.

Julia sold ______ tickets.

Together, Tyrone and Julia sold ______ tickets.

21. H.O.T. Suppose Sam sold 20 tickets to the school play. How many tickets would you draw on the pictograph above to show his sales?

____

____

____

22. **Test Prep** Lindsey and Matt each brought 5 guests to the school play. Which number sentence shows their total number of guests?

Ⓐ $2 + 5 = 7$

Ⓑ $5 + 2 = 7$

Ⓒ $2 \times 2 = 4$

Ⓓ $2 \times 5 = 10$

Name ______________________________

Multiply with 4

Essential Question How does multiplying with 2 help you multiply with 4?

MA.3.A.1.1 Model multiplication and division including problems presented in context: repeated addition, multiplicative comparison, array, how many combinations, measurement, and partitioning.

UNLOCK the Problem REAL WORLD

Matchbox® cars were invented by Jack Odell in 1952. Caleb has 3 Matchbox cars. Each car has 4 wheels. What is the total number of wheels on Caleb's cars?

- Circle the number of cars that Caleb has.
- What do you need to find?

____

____

One Way Draw a picture.

MODEL

Draw a quick picture to show the wheels on each car.

THINK

3 groups of 4

_____ + _____ + _____ = _____

RECORD

_____ × _____ = _____

So, Caleb's cars have a total of _____ wheels.

Another Way Use a number line.

MODEL

Finish the jumps on the number line.

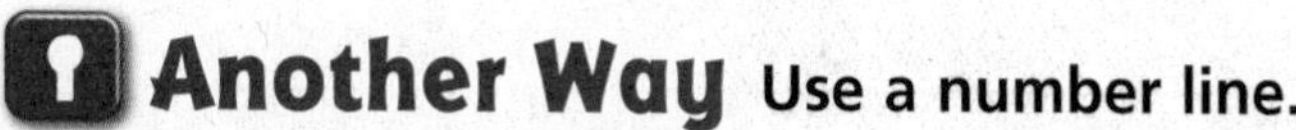

THINK

Skip count by 4s.

_____, _____, _____

RECORD

_____ × _____ = _____

Math Talk How is making jumps on the number line like skip counting?

Use doubles to multiply with 4.

When you multiply with 4, you can multiply with 2 and then double the product.

	MULTIPLY WITH 2	DOUBLE THE PRODUCT
$4 \times 3 =$ _____	$2 \times 3 = 6$ 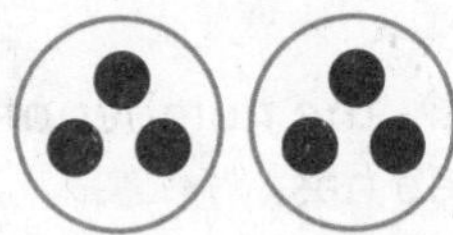	$6 + 6 = 12$, so $4 \times 3 =$ _____. 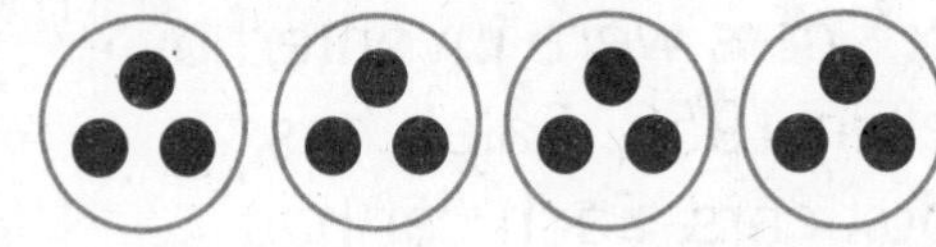
$4 \times 5 =$ _____	$2 \times 5 = 10$ 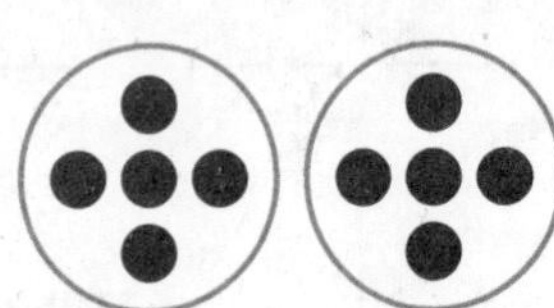	$10 + 10 = 20$, so $4 \times 5 =$ _____. 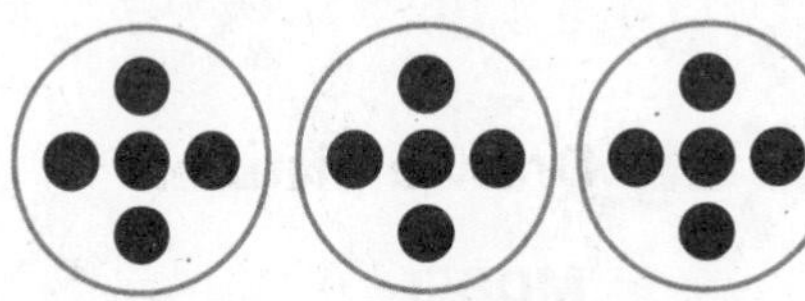 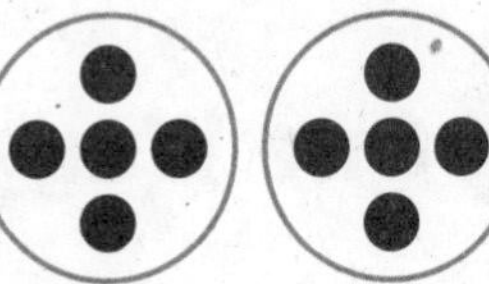

Math Talk Explain how knowing the product for 2×8 helps you find the product for 4×8.

Share and Show 

1. Draw the jumps on this number line to find 4×5.

$4 \times 5 =$ _____

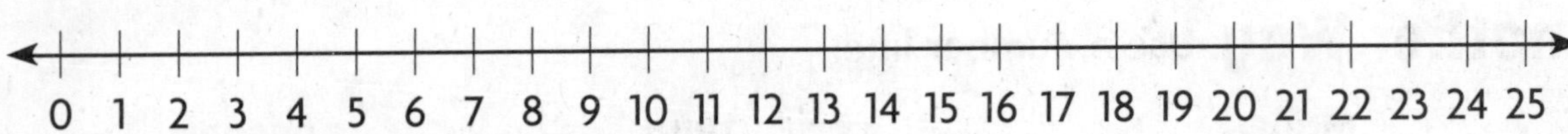

Find the product. Use your MathBoard.

2. $\begin{array}{r} 6 \\ \times 4 \\ \hline \end{array}$

3. $\begin{array}{r} 3 \\ \times 4 \\ \hline \end{array}$

✓4. $\begin{array}{r} 5 \\ \times 4 \\ \hline \end{array}$

✓5. $\begin{array}{r} 8 \\ \times 4 \\ \hline \end{array}$

6. $4 \times 7 =$ _____
7. $1 \times 4 =$ _____
8. $4 \times 4 =$ _____
9. $4 \times 2 =$ _____
10. $3 \times 4 =$ _____
11. $4 \times 6 =$ _____
12. $5 \times 4 =$ _____
13. $4 \times 1 =$ _____

Name ______________________________

On Your Own

Find the product.

14. $\begin{array}{r} 2 \\ \times 4 \\ \hline \end{array}$
15. $\begin{array}{r} 7 \\ \times 4 \\ \hline \end{array}$
16. $\begin{array}{r} 6 \\ \times 4 \\ \hline \end{array}$
17. $\begin{array}{r} 1 \\ \times 4 \\ \hline \end{array}$
18. $\begin{array}{r} 5 \\ \times 4 \\ \hline \end{array}$
19. $\begin{array}{r} 8 \\ \times 4 \\ \hline \end{array}$
20. $\begin{array}{r} 4 \\ \times 4 \\ \hline \end{array}$
21. $\begin{array}{r} 3 \\ \times 4 \\ \hline \end{array}$
22. $\begin{array}{r} 9 \\ \times 4 \\ \hline \end{array}$
23. $\begin{array}{r} 2 \\ \times 7 \\ \hline \end{array}$
24. $\begin{array}{r} 8 \\ \times 2 \\ \hline \end{array}$
25. $\begin{array}{r} 4 \\ \times 9 \\ \hline \end{array}$
26. $\begin{array}{r} 2 \\ \times 6 \\ \hline \end{array}$
27. $\begin{array}{r} 9 \\ \times 2 \\ \hline \end{array}$
28. $\begin{array}{r} 2 \\ \times 3 \\ \hline \end{array}$

Complete the multiplication table for the factors 2 and 4.

	×	1	2	3	4	5	6	7	8	9
29.	2									
30.	4									

H.O.T. **Algebra** Write the missing number.

31. $4 \times 8 = 8 +$ ____ $+$ ____ $+$ ____

32. $4 \times 3 = 3 +$ ____ $+$ ____ $+$ ____

33. $6 \times 4 =$ ____ $+ 4$

34. $4 \times 9 =$ ____ $+ 6$

35. $7 \times 4 = 20 +$ ____

36. $1 + 1 + 1 + 1 =$ ____ $\times 4$

37. $9 =$ ____ $\times 9$

38. $5 +$ ____ $+$ ____ $+$ ____ $= 4 \times 5$

Problem Solving 

Use the bar graph for 39–40.

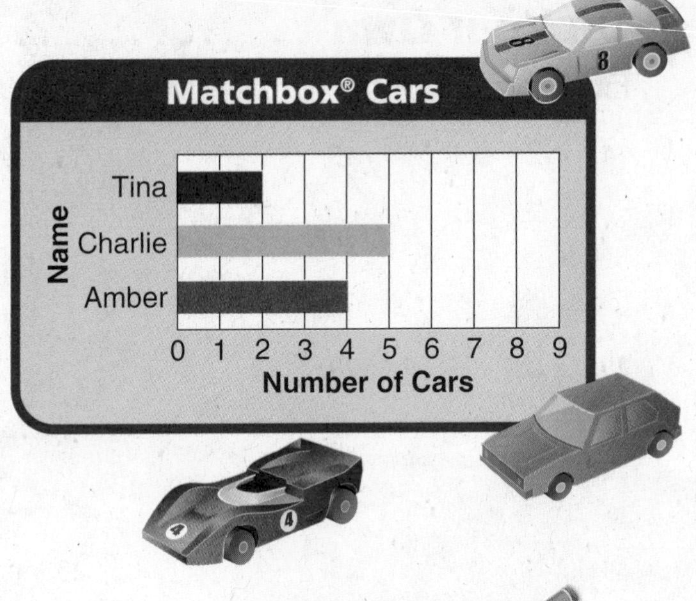

39. Tina, Charlie, and Amber have Matchbox® cars. How many wheels do their cars have altogether?

____

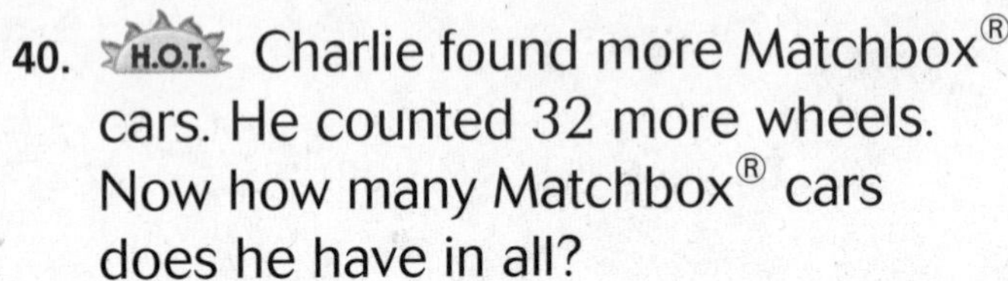

40. H.O.T. Charlie found more Matchbox® cars. He counted 32 more wheels. Now how many Matchbox® cars does he have in all?

____

41. Write Math **Explain** how you can use doubles to find 4×7.

____

____

____

42. The toy store ordered 1,200 Matchbox® cars. It received 955. How many cars were missing?

____

43. **Test Prep** There are 4 groups of 5 cars on the toy shelf. How many cars are there in all?

Ⓐ $4 + 5 = 9$

Ⓑ $4 \times 5 = 20$

Ⓒ $4 \times 4 = 16$

Ⓓ $5 \times 5 = 25$

SHOW YOUR WORK

 FOR MORE PRACTICE:
Florida Benchmarks Practice Book, pp. P67–P68

Name ______________________________

Mid-Chapter Checkpoint

▶ Check Vocabulary

Choose the best term from the box to complete the sentence.

Vocabulary
factors
multiply
product
skip count

1. You ________________ when you combine equal groups to find how many in all. (MA.3.A.1.1; p. 114)
2. The answer in a multiplication problem is called the ________________. (MA.3.A.1.1; p. 117)
3. The numbers you multiply are called the ________________. (MA.3.A.1.1; p. 117)

▶ Check Concepts and Skills

Use the number line to skip count. Find how many in all. (MA.3.A.1.1; pp. 109–112)

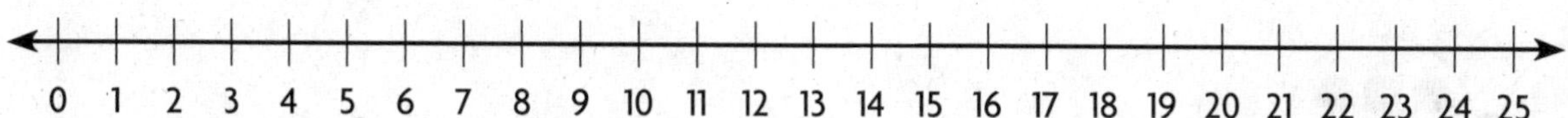

4. 3 groups of 4 ______
5. 6 groups of 2 ______
6. 5 groups of 3 ______
7. 4 groups of 6 ______

Write a multiplication sentence for each. (MA.3.A.1.1; pp. 113–116)

8. 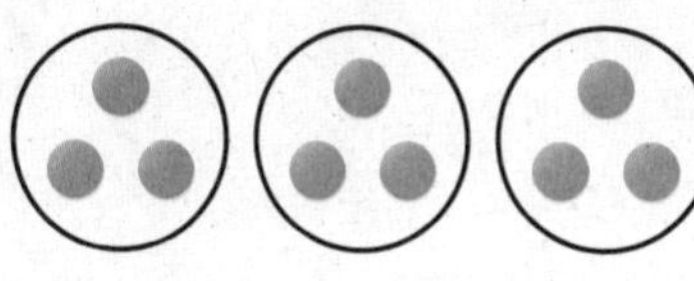

____

9. 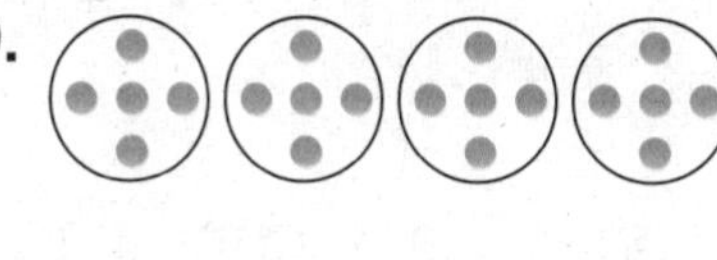

____

10. 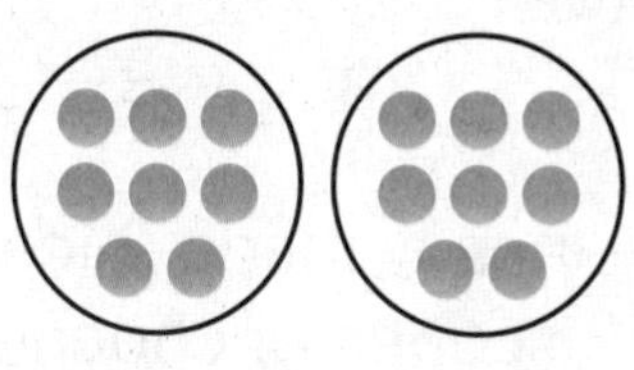

____

Find the product. (MA.3.A.1.1; pp. 117–120, 121–124)

11. $\begin{array}{r} 4 \\ \times 2 \\ \hline \end{array}$

12. $\begin{array}{r} 6 \\ \times 2 \\ \hline \end{array}$

13. $\begin{array}{r} 3 \\ \times 2 \\ \hline \end{array}$

14. $\begin{array}{r} 5 \\ \times 2 \\ \hline \end{array}$

15. $\begin{array}{r} 7 \\ \times 2 \\ \hline \end{array}$

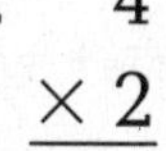

Fill in the bubble for the correct answer choice.

16. Beth's mother is making cookies. She put 4 cookies on each of 8 plates. How many cookies did she make? (MA.3.A.1.1; pp. 121–124)

Ⓐ 8 Ⓒ 24

Ⓑ 12 Ⓓ 32

17. Avery gave 5 animal stickers to each of her 4 best friends. Which number sentence can be used to find the number of stickers she gave away in all? (MA.3.A.1.1; pp. 109–112)

Ⓕ $4 + 5 = ■$

Ⓖ $5 - 4 = ■$

Ⓗ $4 \times 5 = ■$

Ⓘ $5 \times 5 = ■$

18. Matt put his marbles into two equal groups. Which multiplication sentence shows his groups of marbles? (MA.3.A.1.1; pp. 113–116)

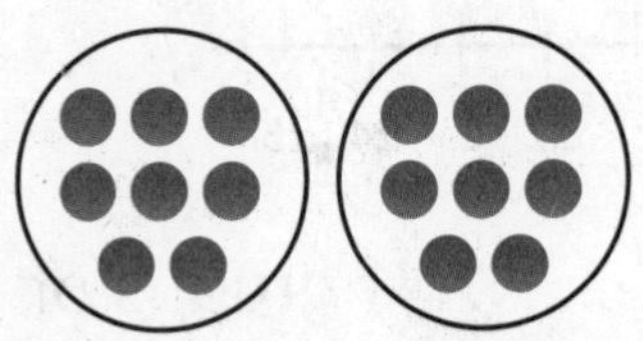

Ⓐ $8 + 8 = 16$

Ⓑ $2 \times 8 = 16$

Ⓒ $16 - 8 = 8$

Ⓓ $8 \times 8 = 64$

19. Lindsey made 3 ice cream cones. Each cone had 2 scoops of chocolate ice cream. How many scoops did Lindsey use in all? (MA.3.A.1.1; pp. 117–120)

Ⓕ 5

Ⓖ 6

Ⓗ 7

Ⓘ 8

Name ______________________________

Draw a Diagram · Multiplication

Essential Question How can drawing a diagram help you solve a problem?

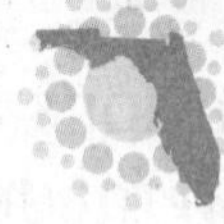

MA.3.A.1.1 Model multiplication and division including problems presented in context: repeated addition, multiplicative comparison, array, how many combinations, measurement, and partitioning.

UNLOCK the Problem REAL WORLD

There are 4 rows of 6 trumpet players and 2 rows of 6 drummers in the marching band. How many trumpet players and drummers are there in all?

Draw a diagram to help you solve the problem.

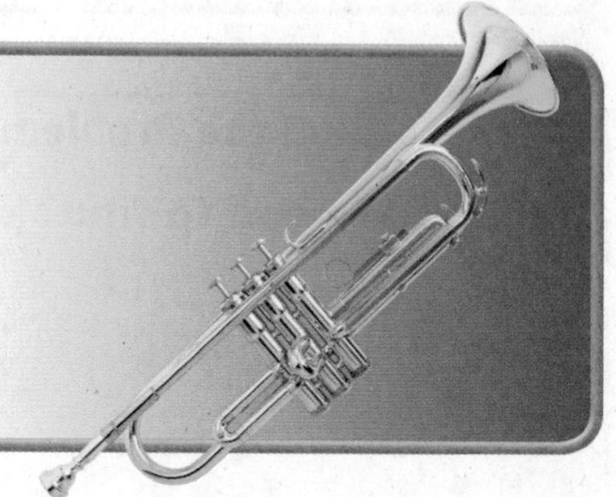

Read the Problem	Solve the Problem
What do I need to find? I need to find how many ____________ and __________ there are in all. **What information do I need to use?** There are ____ rows of ____________ and 2 rows of __________ in the marching band. There are _____ in each row. **How will I use the information?** I will draw a diagram. Then I will ____________ to find the number of trumpet players and drummers. Last, I will add the two numbers to find how many there are in all.	Draw a diagram to show the trumpet players and drummers. Draw 4 rows of 6 smiley faces for the trumpet players. Then draw 2 more rows of 6 for the drummers. Multiply to find the number of drummers and trumpet players. _____ × _____ = _____ _____ × _____ = _____ Then add to find how many in all. _____ + _____ = _____ So, there are _____ trumpet players and drummers in all.

Try Another Problem

Twelve students in Mrs. Taylor's class want to start a band. Seven students each made a drum. The rest made 2 maracas each. How many maracas in all were made?

Read the Problem	Solve the Problem
What do I need to find?	**Record the steps you used to solve the problem.**
What information do I need to use?	
How will I use the information?	

- How many maracas in all did the students make? ______
- How do you know your answer is correct? ______

______

Math Talk Why wouldn't you draw 2 circles with 5 counters in each to represent this problem?

Name ______________________

Share and Show 

1. There are 6 groups of 4 students who play the trumpet in the marching band. There are 3 groups of 2 students who play the trombone. How many students play the trumpet or trombone?

   First, draw a diagram to show the players.

   Draw _____ circles with _____ counters in each for the trumpet players. Draw _____ circles with _____ counters in each for the trombone players.

   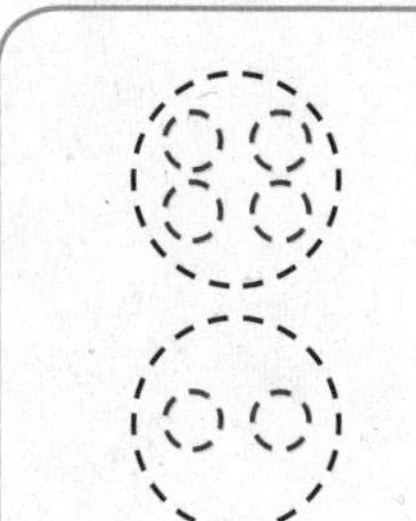

   Then, multiply to find the total for each instrument.

   $6 \times 4 =$ _____ $\quad 3 \times 2 =$ _____

   Add to find the number in all. _____ + _____ = _____

   So, _____ students play the trumpet or trombone.

2. H.O.T. **What if** there are 4 groups of 7 saxophone players? How many saxophone and trumpet players in all are there? _____

3. Suppose there are 5 groups of trumpet players instead of 6 groups. In front of the trumpet players are 18 saxophone players. How many students play the trumpet or saxophone? _____

4. There are 3 rows of flute players in the marching band. There are 7 students in each row. How many flute players are in the marching band? _____

Choose a STRATEGY

- Act It Out
- Use Manipulatives
- Draw a Diagram
- Make a Table, Chart, or List
- Search for Patterns

SHOW YOUR WORK

On Your Own

Use the pictograph for 5–7.

Favorite Instrument Survey	
Instrument	**Number of Votes**
Flute	2 drum symbols
Trumpet	3 drum symbols
Guitar	5 drum symbols
Drum	4 drum symbols
Key: Each drum symbol = 2 votes.	

5. **Write Math** The pictograph shows how students in Jillian's class voted for their favorite instruments. How many students voted for the guitar? **Explain** how you got your answer.

____

____

____

SHOW YOUR WORK

6. On the day of the survey, two students were absent. The pictograph shows the votes of all the other students in the class including Jillian. How many students in all are in the class?

____

7. **H.O.T.** Jillian added the number of votes for two instruments and got a total of 12 votes. For which two instruments did she add the votes?

__________ and __________

8. The electric guitar was invented in 1931. This was 110 years after the harmonica was invented. In what year was the harmonica invented?

____

9. **Test Prep** After music class, the students filled 4 cabinets with their instruments. Each cabinet has space for 8 instruments. How many instruments did the students put away?

Ⓐ 12 Ⓒ 24

Ⓑ 16 Ⓓ 32

 FOR MORE PRACTICE:
Florida Benchmarks Practice Book, pp. P69–P70

Name ___________________________

Model with Arrays

Essential Question How can I use arrays to model multiplication?

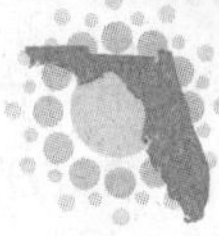

MA.3.A.1.1 Model multiplication and division including problems presented in context: repeated addition, multiplicative comparison, array, how many combinations, measurement, and partitioning.

UNLOCK the Problem REAL WORLD

Tomatoes are the most popular garden vegetable grown in Florida. Lee plants 3 rows of tomato plants with 6 plants in each row. How many tomato plants are there in all?

▲ Tomatoes are a great source of vitamins.

Activity 1

Materials ■ square tiles ■ workmat

- Show the tomato plants in an array. An **array** is a set of objects or numbers arranged in rows and columns. Make an array with 3 rows of 6 tiles.
- Now draw the array you made.

- Find the total number of tiles.

Multiply. 3 × 6 = _____

3 ↓ number of rows

6 ↓ number in each row

So, there are _____ tomato plants in all.

Math Talk Does the number of tiles change if you turn the array to show 6 rows of 3? **Explain.**

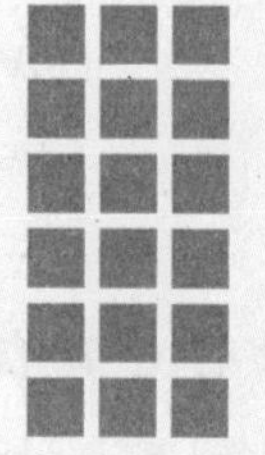

Activity 2 **Materials** ■ square tiles

Use 8 tiles. Make as many different arrays as you can using all 8 of the tiles. Draw the arrays. The first one is done for you.

A 

1 row of 8

$1 \times 8 = 8$

B

8 rows of ____

$8 \times$ ____ $= 8$

C

____ rows of ____

____ $\times$ ____ $= 8$

D

____ rows of ____

____ $\times$ ____ $= 8$

You can make ____ different arrays using 8 tiles.

Share and Show 

1. Complete. Use the array.

____ rows of ____ = ____

____ $\times$ ____ = ____

Write the multiplication sentence for the array.

2.  ____________

3.  ____________

Math Talk Suppose you make an array with 12 tiles and you want to put 3 tiles in each row. How do you decide how many rows you need to make?

Name ___________________________

On Your Own

Write the multiplication sentence for the array.

4. 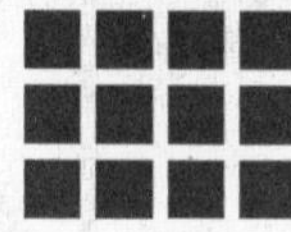

____

5. 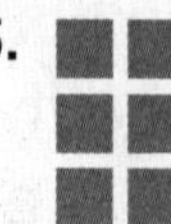

____

Draw an array to find the product.

6.

$2 \times 6 =$ ______

7.

$1 \times 3 =$ ______

8.

$3 \times 5 =$ ______

9.

$4 \times 4 =$ ______

10.

$2 \times 3 =$ ______

11.

$2 \times 7 =$ ______

Problem Solving 

Use the table to solve 12–14.

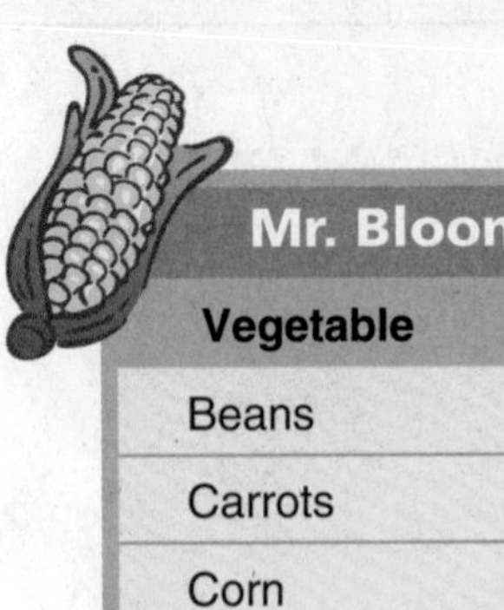

Mr. Bloom's Garden	
Vegetable	**Number**
Beans	4 rows of 6
Carrots	2 rows of 8
Corn	5 rows of 9
Beets	4 rows of 7

12. Mr. Bloom grows vegetables in his garden. Draw an array and write the multiplication sentence to show how many corn plants Mr. Bloom has in his garden.

____

SHOW YOUR WORK

13. H.O.T. Mr. Bloom has 12 strawberry plants. Describe all of the possible arrays that Mr. Bloom could make with his strawberry plants. The first one is done for you.

2 rows of 6; ______________________

____

____

14. List the vegetables in order by the number of plants. Put the names in order from the greatest to least.

____

____

15. **Test Prep** What multiplication sentence does this array show?

Ⓐ $2 \times 3 = 6$

Ⓑ $4 \times 1 = 4$

Ⓒ $2 \times 5 = 10$

Ⓓ $2 \times 4 = 8$

 FOR MORE PRACTICE:
Florida Benchmarks Practice Book, pp. P71–P72

Name ___________________________________

Commutative Property

Essential Question How can you use the Commutative Property to find products?

MA.3.A.1.2 Solve multiplication and division fact problems by using strategies that result from applying number properties.

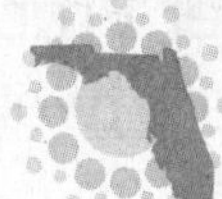

UNLOCK the Problem REAL WORLD

Dave works at the Bird Store. He arranges 15 boxes of birdseed in rows on the shelf. What are two ways he can arrange the boxes in equal rows on the shelf?

- Circle the number you need to use.

Activity Make an array. Arrange 15 tiles in 5 rows.

Materials ■ color tiles

Draw a quick picture of your array.

How many tiles are in each row? __________

What multiplication sentence does your array show? __________

Suppose Dave arranges the boxes in 3 rows.

How many boxes are in each row? __________

Draw a quick picture of your array.

What multiplication sentence does your array show? __________

So, two ways Dave can arrange the 15 boxes are in

__________ rows of 3 or in 3 rows of __________.

Math Talk Why do 5 rows of 3 and 3 rows of 5 both equal the same number?

Multiplication Property The **Commutative Property of Multiplication**, or Order Property of Multiplication, states that you can multiply two factors in either order and get the same product.

2 × ______ = ______ 3 × ______ = ______

So, 2 × ______ = 3 × ______.

Math Idea

You can think of facts that show the Commutative Property of Multiplication, such as 2 × 3 = 6 and 3 × 2 = 6, as "turn-around facts." They have the same factors, but the factors are in a different order.

- Explain how the problem looks different if there are 6 birds in 2 cages or 6 birds in 3 cages.

____

____

Try This! **Find the product. Then draw a quick picture on the right that shows the turn-around fact. Complete the multiplication sentences.**

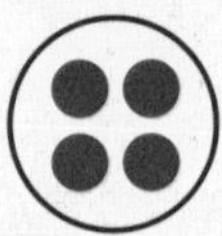
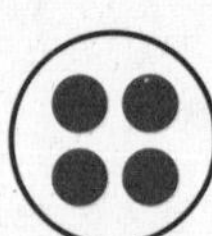
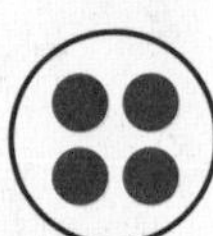

______ × 4 = ______ ______ × 3 = ______

B

2 × ______ = ______ 5 × ______ = ______

Name ______________________________

Share and Show 

1. Write the multiplication sentence for the array.

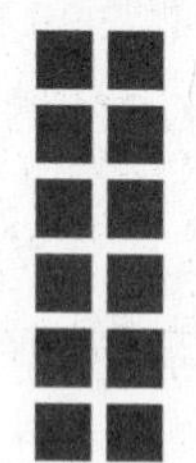

______________ ______________

Math Talk Explain what the factor 2 means in each multiplication sentence.

Write the multiplication sentence for the model. Then use the Commutative Property to write another multiplication sentence.

2. 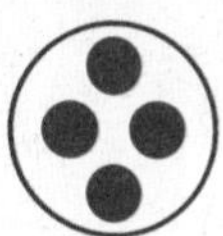 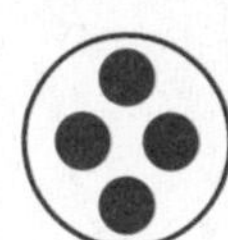

____ × ____ = ____

____ × ____ = ____

 3. 

____ × ____ = ____

____ × ____ = ____

4. 

____ × ____ = ____

____ × ____ = ____

On Your Own

Write the multiplication sentence for the model. Then use the Commutative Property to write another multiplication sentence.

5. 

____ × ____ = ____

____ × ____ = ____

6. 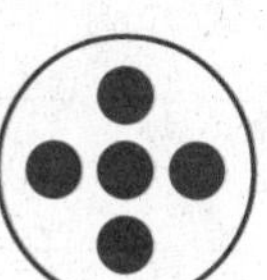

____ × ____ = ____

____ × ____ = ____

7. 

____ × ____ = ____

____ × ____ = ____

H.O.T. Algebra Write the missing factor.

8. $2 \times 6 =$ ______ $\times 2$

9. $4 \times 3 =$ ______ $\times 4$

10. $3 \times 5 =$ ______ $\times 3$

11. $4 \times 1 =$ ______ $\times 4$

12. $2 \times 5 =$ ______ $\times 2$

13. $6 \times 1 =$ ______ $\times 6$

Problem Solving

14. Jenna used 18 pinecones to make peanut butter bird feeders. She hung the same number of feeders in each of 6 trees. Draw an array to show how many feeders she put in each tree.

    She put ______ bird feeders in each tree.

15. What if Jenna hung the same number of feeders in each of 9 trees? How many feeders did she put in each tree? ______

SHOW YOUR WORK

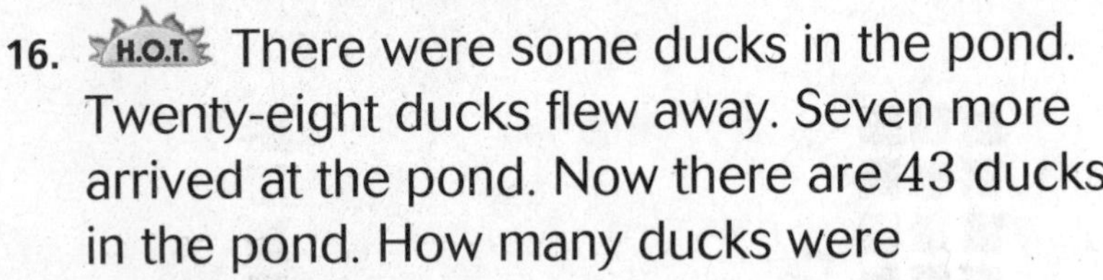

16. H.O.T. There were some ducks in the pond. Twenty-eight ducks flew away. Seven more arrived at the pond. Now there are 43 ducks in the pond. How many ducks were in the pond to start? ______

17. Write Math Write 2 different word problems about 12 birds to show 2×6 and 6×2. You can draw bird cages to show the groups.

    ____

    ____

    ____

    ____

    ____

18. **Test Prep** Which is an example of the Commutative Property of Multiplication shown by the arrays at the right?

    Ⓐ $2 + 3 = 3 \times 2$ Ⓒ $2 \times 4 = 4 \times 2$

    Ⓑ $4 \times 1 = 4 + 1$ Ⓓ $2 \times 6 = 3 \times 4$

FOR MORE PRACTICE:
Florida Benchmarks Practice Book, pp. P73–P74

Name ______________________

Multiply with 1 and 0

Essential Question What happens when you multiply a number by 0?

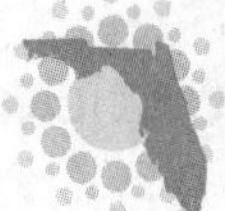

MA.3.A.1.2 Solve multiplication and division fact problems by using strategies that result from applying number properties.

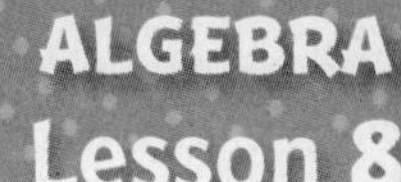

UNLOCK the Problem REAL WORLD

Luke sees 4 doghouses. Each doghouse has 2 dogs in it. What multiplication sentence tells how many dogs there are?

- How many doghouses are there? _____
- How many dogs are in each doghouse to start? _____

Draw a quick picture to show the dogs in the doghouses.

_____ × _____ = _____

One dog walks away from each doghouse. Cross out 1 dog in each doghouse above. How many dogs are there now? What multiplication sentence shows what you drew?

_____ × _____ = _____
↓ doghouses ↓ dogs left in each house ↓ total number of dogs

So, there are _____ dogs left in the doghouses.

What if one more dog walks away from each doghouse? How could you use multiplication to find the total number of dogs left in the doghouses?

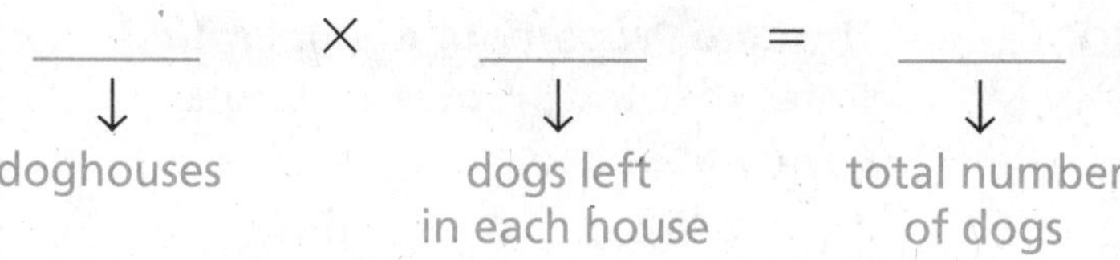

_____ × _____ = _____
↓ doghouses ↓ dogs left in each house ↓ total number of dogs

- How do the doghouses look now? _____________________

Example

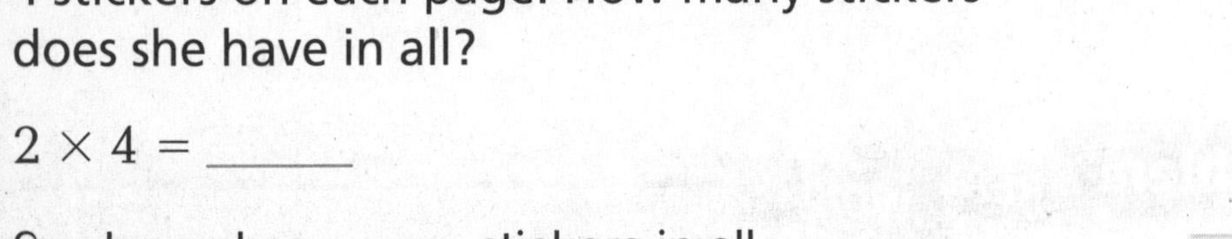

Jenny has 2 pages of dog stickers. There are 4 stickers on each page. How many stickers does she have in all?

$2 \times 4 =$ ______

So, Jenny has ______ stickers in all.

Suppose Jenny uses 1 page of the stickers. What multiplication sentence shows how many stickers she has left?

______ $\times$ ______ $=$ ______

So, Jenny has ______ stickers left.

Now, Jenny uses the rest of the stickers. What multiplication sentence shows how many stickers Jenny has left?

______ $\times$ ______ $=$ ______

So, Jenny has ______ stickers left.

- What number tells that Jenny does not have any stickers left? ______

1. What pattern do you see when you multiply numbers with 1 as a factor?

Think: $1 \times 2 = 2$ $1 \times 3 = 3$ $1 \times 4 = 4$

____

____

The **Identity Property of Multiplication** states that the product of any number and 1 is that number.

$7 \times 1 = 7$ $6 \times 1 = 6$

$1 \times 7 = 7$ $1 \times 6 = 6$

2. What pattern do you see when you multiply numbers with 0 as a factor?

Think: $0 \times 1 = 0$ $0 \times 2 = 0$ $0 \times 5 = 0$

____

____

The **Zero Property of Multiplication** states that the product of zero and any number is zero.

$0 \times 5 = 0$ $5 \times 0 = 0$

$0 \times 8 = 0$ $8 \times 0 = 0$

Name ______________________

Share and Show 

1. What multiplication sentence could you write for this picture? Find the product.

____

Find the product.

2. $3 \times 1 =$ ____ 3. $0 \times 2 =$ ____ ✓4. $4 \times 0 =$ ____ ✓5. $1 \times 6 =$ ____

Math Talk Explain how 3×1 and $3 + 1$ are different.

On Your Own

Find the product.

6. $5 \times 1 =$ ____ 7. $8 \times 0 =$ ____ 8. $1 \times 9 =$ ____ 9. $0 \times 7 =$ ____

10. $0 \times 4 =$ ____ 11. $1 \times 1 =$ ____ 12. $1 \times 3 =$ ____ 13. $6 \times 1 =$ ____

14. 1×0 15. 1×7 16. 0×6 17. 2×1 18. 8×1 19. 0×5

Practice: Copy and Solve

20. 8×0 21. 1×4 22. 0×9 23. 9×1 24. 5×1 25. 0×1

26. 3×4 27. 2×6 28. 3×8 29. 4×4 30. 7×3 31. 3×3

Algebra Complete the multiplication sentence.

32. $12 \times 0 =$ ____ 33. ____ $\times 1 = 5$ 34. $1 \times 28 =$ ____ 35. $0 \times 46 =$ ____

Problem Solving 

Use the table for 36–38.

Vehicle	Number of Wheels
Car	4
Tricycle	3
Bicycle	2
Unicycle	1

36. At the circus Jon saw 5 unicycles. How many wheels are on the unicycles in all? Write a multiplication sentence.

_____ × _____ = _____

37. 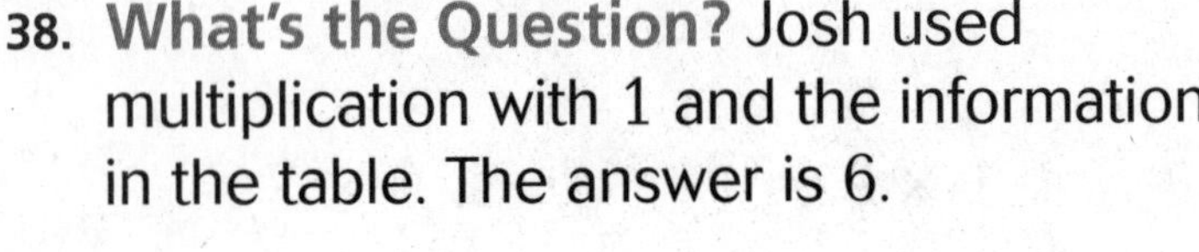

Brian's family's vehicles have a total of 17 wheels. If 2 of the vehicles are cars, how many vehicles are bicycles and tricycles?

____

SHOW YOUR WORK

38. **What's the Question?** Josh used multiplication with 1 and the information in the table. The answer is 6.

____

____

39. **Write Math** Write a word problem that uses multiplying with 1 or 0. Show how to solve your problem.

____

____

____

40. **Test Prep** Eric has 1 pencil box at school. He has 6 pencils in the box. Which number sentence shows how many pencils Eric has in all?

Ⓐ $6 + 1 = 7$

Ⓑ $0 \times 6 = 0$

Ⓒ $6 - 1 = 5$

Ⓓ $1 \times 6 = 6$

FOR MORE PRACTICE:
Florida Benchmarks Practice Book, pp. P75–P76

Name ________________________________

Multiply with 5

Essential Question How can you multiply with 5 as a factor?

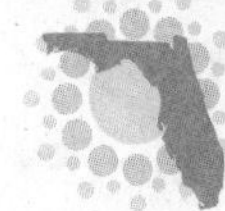

MA.3.A.1.1 Model multiplication and division including problems presented in context: repeated addition, multiplicative comparison, array, how many combinations, measurement, and partitioning.

UNLOCK the Problem REAL WORLD

The school chorus is having a concert. For the first song, there are 3 rows with 5 students in each row. How many students sing the first song?

- How many rows of students sing the first song? _____
- How many are in each row? _____

One Way Make an array.

Use tiles to make an array with 3 rows of 5. Then draw your array.

Find the number of tiles.

$3 \times 5 =$ _____. So, _____ students sing the first song.

Other Ways A Use a number line.

Start at 0. Complete 3 jumps of 5 spaces each.

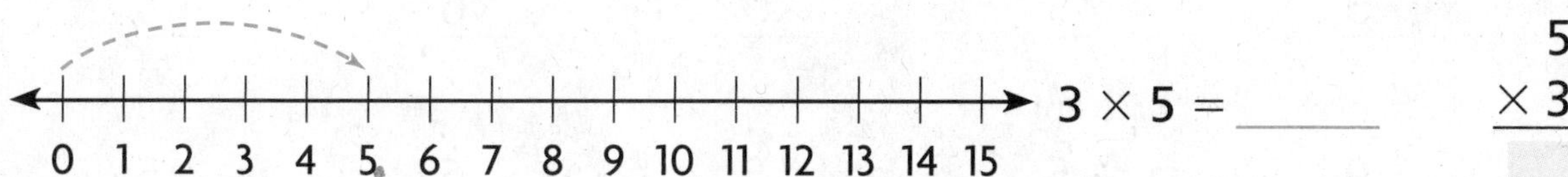

$3 \times 5 =$ _____

$$\begin{array}{r} 5 \\ \times\ 3 \\ \hline \end{array}$$

B Use skip counting.

For the last song, there are 6 rows with 5 students in each row. How many students sing the last song?

Skip count by 5s until you say 6 numbers.

5, 10, _____, 20, _____, _____

$6 \times 5 =$ _____

So, _____ students sing the last song.

Math Talk How can knowing $3 \times 5 = 15$, help you find 6×5?

Name ______________________________

Share and Show 

1. How can you use this number line to find 8×5?

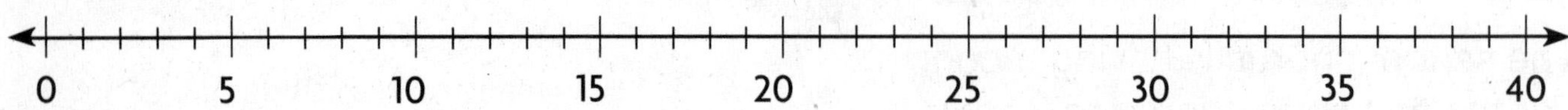

Math Talk Explain how knowing 4×5 can help you find 8×5.

Find the product.

2. $2 \times 5 =$ ____
3. ____ $= 4 \times 5$
4. ____ $= 5 \times 5$
5. $7 \times 5 =$ ____

On Your Own

Find the product.

6. $5 \times 2 =$ ____
7. ____ $= 5 \times 3$
8. ____ $= 1 \times 5$
9. $6 \times 5 =$ ____
10. $0 \times 5 =$ ____
11. $9 \times 5 =$ ____
12. ____ $= 2 \times 5$
13. ____ $= 5 \times 7$
14. $\begin{array}{r} 4 \\ \times 0 \\ \hline \end{array}$
15. $\begin{array}{r} 7 \\ \times 5 \\ \hline \end{array}$
16. $\begin{array}{r} 5 \\ \times 8 \\ \hline \end{array}$
17. $\begin{array}{r} 1 \\ \times 9 \\ \hline \end{array}$
18. $\begin{array}{r} 5 \\ \times 6 \\ \hline \end{array}$
19. $\begin{array}{r} 5 \\ \times 5 \\ \hline \end{array}$
20. $\begin{array}{r} 1 \\ \times 5 \\ \hline \end{array}$
21. $\begin{array}{r} 9 \\ \times 5 \\ \hline \end{array}$
22. $\begin{array}{r} 5 \\ \times 3 \\ \hline \end{array}$
23. $\begin{array}{r} 5 \\ \times 9 \\ \hline \end{array}$
24. $\begin{array}{r} 5 \\ \times 2 \\ \hline \end{array}$
25. $\begin{array}{r} 5 \\ \times 7 \\ \hline \end{array}$

H.O.T. **Algebra** **Use the pictures to find the missing numbers.**

26. $3 \times$ ______ $=$ ______

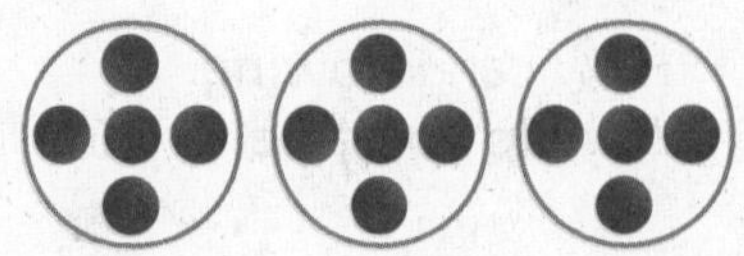

27. ______ $\times 3 =$ ______

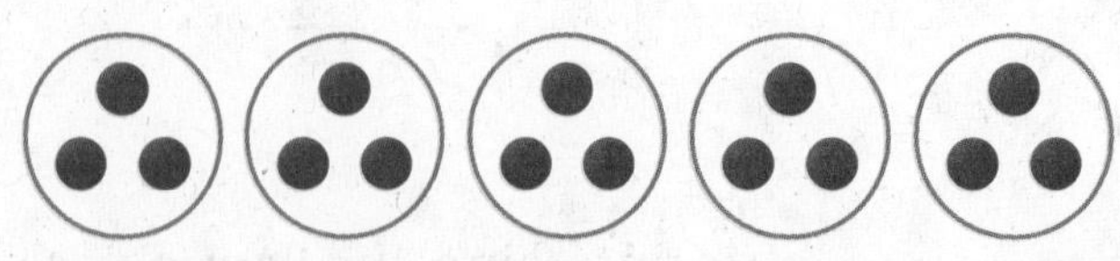

Name ________________________________

UNLOCK the Problem

28. Kevin needs to set up chairs for 42 people to watch the school chorus. So far he has set up 5 rows with 5 chairs in each row. How many more chairs does he need to set up?

Ⓐ 11 Ⓑ 12 Ⓒ 17 Ⓓ 25

a. What do you need to find? ________________________________

b. What operations will you use to find how many more chairs Kevin needs to set up? ________________________________

c. Show the steps you used to solve the problem.

d. Complete the sentences.

Kevin needs to set up ______ chairs for people to watch the chorus.

He has set up ______ rows with ______ chairs in each row.

Kevin needs to set up ______ more chairs.

e. Fill in the bubble for the correct answer above.

29. A music store sold 1,586 guitar books and 1,297 piano books. How many more guitar books than piano books were sold?

Ⓕ 179 more books

Ⓖ 189 more books

Ⓗ 279 more books

Ⓘ 289 more books

30. The school chorus sings 5 songs. If each song lasts 3 minutes, for how many minutes does the chorus sing?

Ⓐ 2 minutes

Ⓑ 8 minutes

Ⓒ 15 minutes

Ⓓ 35 minutes

Problem Solving REAL WORLD

Use the table for 31–33.

Stringed Instruments	
Instrument	**Strings**
Guitar	6
Banjo	5
Mandolin	8
Violin	4

31. John and his dad own 4 banjos. They want to replace the strings on all of them. How many strings should they buy? Write a multiplication sentence to solve.

____

32. H.O.T. Mr. Case has 2 guitars, 4 banjos, and 1 mandolin. What is the total number of strings on Mr. Case's instruments?

____

33. Mr. James has 3 banjos. Mr. Lewis has 5 times as many. How many banjos does Mr. Lewis have?

____

34. Write Math When you multiply by 5, the ones digit in the product is one of these two numbers. Name the numbers. **Explain** how you know.

____

____

____

35. **Test Prep** A music store has guitars displayed on 5 shelves. There are 5 guitars on each shelf. How many guitars are there in all?

Ⓐ 10 guitars

Ⓑ 20 guitars

Ⓒ 15 guitars

Ⓓ 25 guitars

SHOW YOUR WORK

FOR MORE PRACTICE:
Florida Benchmarks Practice Book, pp. P77–P78

Name ___________________________________

Chapter Review/Test

▶ Check Vocabulary

Choose the best term from the box to complete the sentence.

Vocabulary
array
Commutative Property of Multiplication
Identity Property of Multiplication
product
Zero Property of Multiplication

1. The ______________________________ states that the product of any number and 1 is that number. **(MA.3.A.1.2; p. 139)**

2. An ______________ is a group of objects in rows and columns. **(MA.3.A.1.1; p. 131)**

3. The ______________________________ states that the product of zero and any number is zero. **(MA.3.A.1.2; p. 139)**

4. The ______________________________ states that factors can be multiplied in any order and their product is the same. **(MA.3.A.1.2; p. 135)**

▶ Check Concepts and Skills

Write the multiplication sentence for the array. **(MA.3.A.1.1; pp. 131–134)**

5. 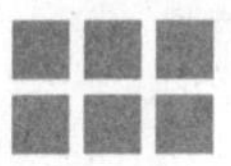

_____ × _____ = _____

6. 

_____ × _____ = _____

7. 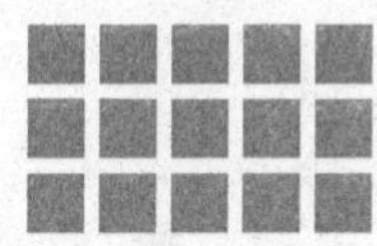

_____ × _____ = _____

Find the product. **(MA.3.A.1.1; MA.3.A.1.2; pp. 117–120, 121–124, 139–141, 143–146)**

8. $\begin{array}{r} 4 \\ \times 2 \\ \hline \end{array}$

9. $\begin{array}{r} 4 \\ \times 6 \\ \hline \end{array}$

10. $\begin{array}{r} 9 \\ \times 1 \\ \hline \end{array}$

11. $\begin{array}{r} 6 \\ \times 3 \\ \hline \end{array}$

12. $\begin{array}{r} 5 \\ \times 0 \\ \hline \end{array}$

13. $\begin{array}{r} 4 \\ \times 4 \\ \hline \end{array}$

14. $\begin{array}{r} 2 \\ \times 7 \\ \hline \end{array}$

15. $\begin{array}{r} 3 \\ \times 5 \\ \hline \end{array}$

16. $\begin{array}{r} 0 \\ \times 2 \\ \hline \end{array}$

17. $\begin{array}{r} 9 \\ \times 1 \\ \hline \end{array}$

18. $\begin{array}{r} 4 \\ \times 8 \\ \hline \end{array}$

19. $\begin{array}{r} 5 \\ \times 7 \\ \hline \end{array}$

Go online Assessment Options
Chapter Test

Fill in the bubble for the correct answer choice.

20. John bought a model car. The cashier gave him 4 nickels as change. How much change did he receive in all? (MA.3.A.1.1; pp. 143–146)

    Ⓐ 4 cents
    Ⓑ 10 cents
    Ⓒ 12 cents
    Ⓓ 20 cents

21. Lucy and her mother made tacos. They put 2 tacos on each of 5 plates. How many tacos did they make? (MA.3.A.1.1; pp. 117–120)

    Ⓕ 2
    Ⓖ 5
    Ⓗ 10
    Ⓘ 25

22. Morgan has 6 toy cars. Each car has 4 wheels. How many wheels do the cars have in all? (MA.3.A.1.1; pp. 121–124)

    Ⓐ 4
    Ⓑ 10
    Ⓒ 12
    Ⓓ 24

23. Terry put her vacation photos in an album. She put 6 photos on each of 5 pages. How many photos did Terry put in her album in all? (MA.3.A.1.1; pp. 143–146)

    Ⓕ 5
    Ⓖ 6
    Ⓗ 30
    Ⓘ 36

Name ______________________________

TEST PREP

24. Skip count to find how many are in 4 groups of 3.
(MA.3.A.1.1; pp. 109–112)

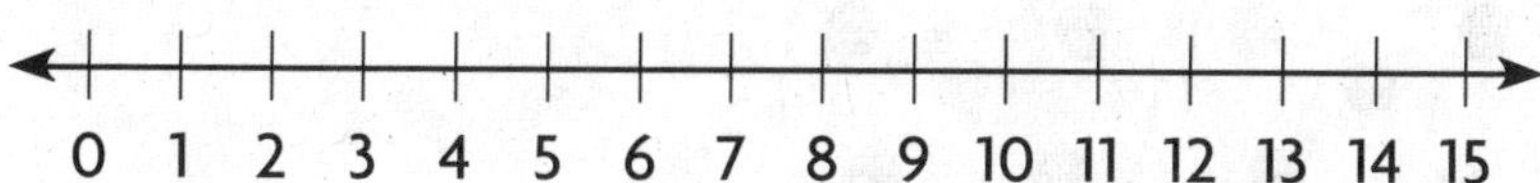

Ⓐ 3
Ⓑ 6
Ⓒ 12
Ⓓ 15

25. Caleb and his dad baked some cookies. They put 5 cookies on each of 4 plates. Which number sentence shows how many cookies they made in all? (MA.3.A.1.1; pp. 121–124)

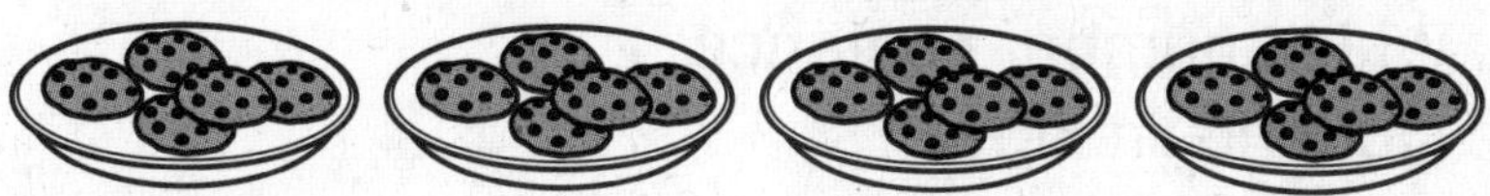

Ⓕ $2 \times 5 = 10$
Ⓖ $3 \times 4 = 12$
Ⓗ $4 \times 4 = 16$
Ⓘ $4 \times 5 = 20$

26. Josh has 4 dogs. Each dog gets 2 dog biscuits every day. How many biscuits will Josh need for all of his dogs for Saturday and Sunday? (MA.3.A.1.1; pp. 117–120)

Ⓐ 4
Ⓑ 8
Ⓒ 12
Ⓓ 16

27. Lacy made a design with 4 groups of 7 buttons. How many buttons did she use? (MA.3.A.1.1; pp. 121–124)

Ⓕ 28 Ⓗ 24
Ⓖ 26 Ⓘ 14

28. Susan made a model with counters. What multiplication sentence does her model show?
(MA.3.A.1.1; pp. 121–124)

Ⓐ $2 \times 6 = 12$

Ⓑ $3 \times 6 = 18$

Ⓒ $4 \times 6 = 24$

Ⓓ $6 \times 6 = 36$

29. The students in Steven's class took a survey about their pets. Twelve students in the class each have 1 dog for a pet. Which number sentence shows how many dogs the students in Steven's class have in all? (MA.3.A.1.2; pp. 139–142)

Ⓕ $12 + 1 = 13$

Ⓖ $12 \times 1 = 12$

Ⓗ $12 - 1 = 11$

Ⓘ $1 + 1 = 2$

30. James made arrays with square tiles to show the Commutative Property of Multiplication. Which multiplication sentences are shown by his arrays?
(MA.3.A.1.2; pp. 135–138)

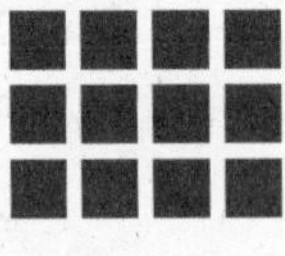
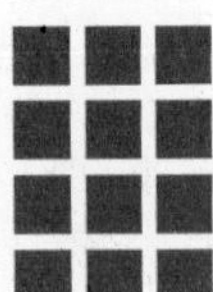

Ⓐ $3 \times 2 = 6$ and $2 \times 3 = 6$

Ⓑ $3 \times 4 = 12$ and $4 \times 3 = 12$

Ⓒ $3 \times 3 = 9$ and $4 \times 4 = 16$

Ⓓ $3 \times 7 = 21$ and $7 \times 3 = 21$

Chapter 4 Multiplication Facts and Strategies

Show What You Know 

Check your understanding of important skills.

Name ______________________

Repeated Addition Use repeated addition to find how many in all.

1. 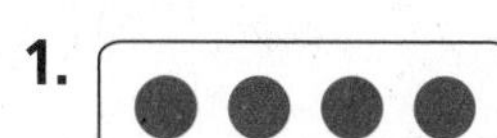 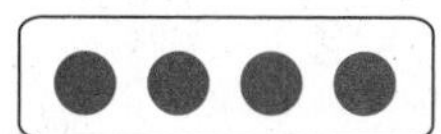

____ + ____ = ____

2. 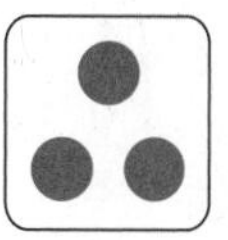 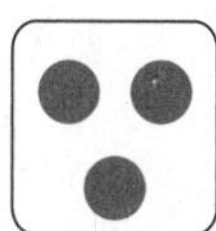 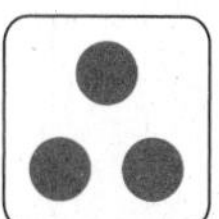

____ + ____ + ____ + ____ = ____

Model with Arrays Use the array. Complete.

3. 3 rows of 2

____ × ____ = ____

4.  2 rows of 4

____ × ____ = ____

Multiply with 0, 1, 2, and 4 Multiply.

5. $4 \times 2 =$ ____
6. $6 \times 0 =$ ____
7. $1 \times 7 =$ ____
8. $4 \times 5 =$ ____
9. $3 \times 1 =$ ____
10. $4 \times 4 =$ ____

Florida FUN FACT

The orange blossom was named the Florida state flower in 1909. Most of the honey that is produced in Florida is made by bees that gather nectar from the orange blossoms.

FLORIDA BENCHMARKS

Vocabulary Power

▶ Visualize It

Complete the tree map by using the review words.

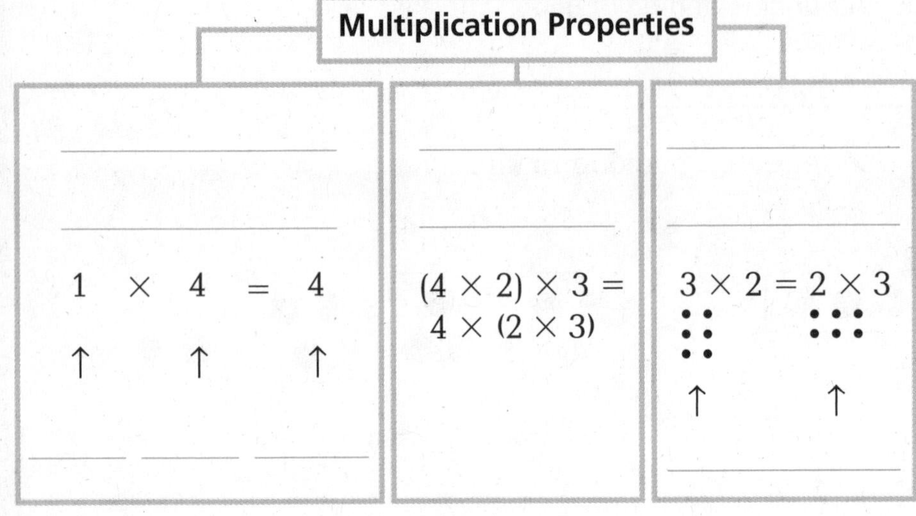

Review Words

arrays
Associative Property
Commutative Property
factor
Identity Property
product

Preview Words

combination
Distributive Property of Multiplication
multiple
tree diagram
variable

▶ Understand Vocabulary

Complete the sentences by using the preview words.

1. The property that states that multiplying a sum by a number is the same as multiplying each addend by the number and then adding the products is the ______________________.

2. A ______________ is a symbol or a letter that stands for an unknown number.

3. A ______________ is a result of joining two or more things.

4. A ______________ of 5 is any product that has 5 as one of its factors.

Go online • Student Edition • Multilingual eGlossary

Name ______________________

Multiply with 6

Essential Question What are some ways to model multiplying with 6?

MA.3.A.1.1 Model multiplication and division including problems presented in context: repeated addition, multiplicative comparison, array, how many combinations, measurement, and partitioning.

UNLOCK the Problem REAL WORLD

Jessica arranged insect stickers in her sticker book in rows of 6. She has 5 rows of stickers. How many stickers does she have in all?

One Way Use an array.

- Complete the array of 5 rows with 6 tiles in each row.

- Find the number of tiles. $5 \times 6 =$ ______ $\begin{array}{r} 6 \\ \times 5 \\ \hline \end{array}$

So, Jessica has ______ stickers in all.

Other Ways

A Use a number line.

- Make 5 jumps for the 5 rows of stickers. Jump 6 spaces at a time for the number in each row.
- You land on 6, ______, ______, ______, and ______. These numbers are multiples of 6.

$5 \times 6 =$ ______

A **multiple** of 6 is any product that has 6 as one of its factors.

B Use doubles.

When multiplying an even number, $6 \times 5 = \blacksquare$

first multiply by half the number. $3 \times 5 =$ ______

Then, double the product. ______ $+ 15 =$ ______

$6 \times 5 =$ ______.

Math Talk Why do you multiply 3×5 when using doubles to find 6×5?

C **Use a multiplication table.**

Find the product for 5 × 6 where row 5 and column 6 meet.

5 × 6 = _____

- Look at the columns for 3 and 6 in the table. What do you notice about their products?

____

____

×	0	1	2	3	4	5	6	7	8	9
0	0	0	0	0	0	0	0	0	0	0
1	0	1	2	3	4	5	6	7	8	9
2	0	2	4	6	8	10	12	14	16	18
3	0	3	6	9	12	15	18	21	24	27
4	0	4	8	12	16	20	24	28	32	36
5	0	5	10	15	20	25	30	35	40	45
6	0	6	12	18	24	30	36	42	48	54
7	0	7	14	21	28	35	42	49	56	63
8	0	8	16	24	32	40	48	56	64	72
9	0	9	18	27	36	45	54	63	72	81

Share and Show

1. Use the array to find 6 × 3.

   6 × 3 = _____

Find the product.

2. 6 × 1 = _____
3. _____ = 3 × 6
4. _____ = 6 × 4
5. 6 × 8 = _____

Math Talk How can you use the product of 5 × 6 to find the product of 6 × 6?

On Your Own

Find the product.

6. 6 × 5 = _____
7. _____ = 8 × 6
8. _____ = 6 × 6
9. 0 × 6 = _____
10. 7 × 6 = _____
11. 4 × 5 = _____
12. _____ = 1 × 6
13. _____ = 5 × 5

14. 6 × 5
15. 3 × 5
16. 9 × 6
17. 6 × 7
18. 6 × 6
19. 6 × 3

Name ______________________________

Algebra Complete the table.

	Multiply by 3.	
	Factor	Product
20.	6	
21.		24

	Multiply by 6.	
	Factor	Product
22.	3	
23.	7	

	Multiply by ___.	
24.	Factor	Product
	6	30
25.	5	

Problem Solving REAL WORLD

Use the table for 26–28.

Winged Insects	
Insect	Wings
Fly	2
Beetle	4
Honeybee	4

26. How many wings do 6 honeybees have?

____

27. H.O.T. How many more wings do 6 beetles have than 6 flies?

____

28. Write Math Write a number sentence that shows how many wings 3 flies have. **Explain** how this fact can help you find the number of wings 6 flies have.

____

____

____

29. Sean saw 8 ladybugs while he was camping. A ladybug has 6 legs. How many legs do 8 ladybugs have in all?

____

UNLOCK the Problem REAL WORLD

30. Jamal is studying about ants. He has learned that an ant is an insect, so it has 6 legs and 2 antennae. These antennae, or feelers, allow the ant to smell, touch, taste, and hear. How many legs and antennae do 8 ants have?

a. What do you need to find?

____

b. How can you use multiplication to solve the problem?

____

____

c. Draw arrays to find how many legs and antennae 8 ants have.

d. Complete the sentences.

One ant has ______ legs.

Eight ants have 8 × ______ legs.

8 × ______ = ______

One ant has ______ antennae.

Eight ants have 8 × ______ antennae.

8 × ______ = ______

I need to ______ to find the total number of legs and antennae.

______ + ______ = ______

So, 8 ants have ______ legs and antennae in all.

31. All insects have 6 legs and all spiders have 8 legs. Which has more legs, 5 insects or 4 spiders?

____

32. **Test Prep** How many legs do 6 ants have?

Ⓕ 8

Ⓖ 24

Ⓗ 36

Ⓘ 48

FOR MORE PRACTICE:
Florida Benchmarks Practice Book, pp. P87–P88

Name ______________________________

Associative Property

Essential Question Why is the Associative Property also called the Grouping Property?

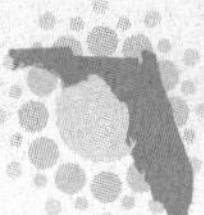

MA.3.A.1.2 Solve multiplication and division fact problems by using strategies that result from applying number properties.

CONNECT You have learned the Associative Property of Addition. When the grouping of addends is changed, the sum stays the same.

$$(2 + 3) + 4 = 2 + (3 + 4)$$

Math Idea

Always multiply the numbers in parentheses first.

The **Associative Property of Multiplication** says that when the grouping of the factors is changed, the product is the same. It is also called the Grouping Property.

UNLOCK the Problem REAL WORLD

Each car on the roller coaster has 2 rows of seats. Each row has 2 seats. There are 3 cars in each train. How many seats in all are on each train?

- Read the first two sentences. How can you find the number of seats in each car?

____

- Underline what you need to find.

Use an array.

You can use an array to show $3 \times (2 \times 2)$.

$3 \times (2 \times 2) = \square$

$3 \times$ _____ $=$ _____

You can change the grouping with parentheses and get the same answer.

$(3 \times 2) \times 2 = \square$

_____ $\times 2 =$ _____

So, there are 3 cars with 4 seats in each car.

There are _____ seats in all on the roller coaster train.

Math Talk Why are the products for $3 \times (2 \times 2)$ and $(3 \times 2) \times 2$ the same?

Use the Commutative and Associative Properties

You can also change the order of the factors. The product is the same.

$4 \times 3 \times 2 = \square$	$4 \times 3 \times 2 = \square$
$4 \times (3 \times 2) = \square$	$(4 \times 2) \times 3 = \square$
$4 \times$ _____ $=$ _____	_____ $\times 3 =$ _____

Math Talk Why would you group the factors 3, 2, and 8 as $(3 \times 2) \times 8$ rather than $(3 \times 8) \times 2$?

Share and Show 

1. Find the product of 1, 2, and 3. Write another way to group the factors. Is the product the same? Why?

____

____

Find the product. Write another way to group the factors.

2. $(2 \times 1) \times 7$

____

____

3. $3 \times (2 \times 2)$

____

____

✓4. $4 \times (3 \times 1)$

____

____

✓5. $(3 \times 2) \times 6$

____

____

6. $1 \times (2 \times 5)$

____

____

7. $(1 \times 3) \times 6$

____

____

Math Talk Choose one of the ways you grouped the factors in one of the problems above. **Explain** why you multiplied those factors.

Name ______________________

On Your Own

Find the product. Write another way to group the factors.

8. $(2 \times 3) \times 1$

9. $8 \times (3 \times 2)$

10. $(1 \times 3) \times 5$

11. $(3 \times 2) \times 4$

12. $(6 \times 1) \times 4$

13. $(2 \times 2) \times 6$

14. $2 \times (4 \times 2)$

15. $5 \times (2 \times 4)$

16. $9 \times (1 \times 2)$

Use parentheses. Find the product.

17. $2 \times 1 \times 9$

18. $1 \times 3 \times 5$

19. $4 \times 1 \times 6$

20. $2 \times 2 \times 6$

21. $1 \times 2 \times 6$

22. $1 \times 9 \times 4$

23. $2 \times 2 \times 2$

24. $4 \times 2 \times 2$

25. $2 \times 4 \times 5$

H.O.T. **Find the missing factor.**

26. $7 \times (2 \times$ ____ $) = 28$

27. $30 = 6 \times (5 \times$ ____ $)$

28. ____ $\times (3 \times 2) = 24$

29. $32 = 4 \times (2 \times$ ____ $)$

30. $8 \times (5 \times$ ____ $) = 40$

31. $0 =$ ____ $\times (25 \times 1)$

Problem Solving REAL WORLD

Use the graph for 32–33.

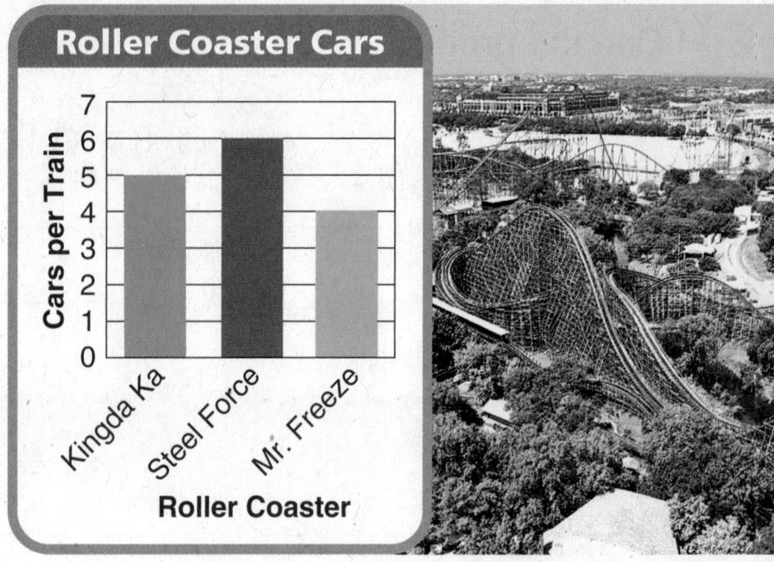

32. Each car on the Steel Force train has 3 rows with 2 seats in each row. How many seats are on the train? Draw a quick picture.

____

33. H.O.T. A Kingda Ka train has 4 seats per car, but the last car has only 2 seats. How many seats are on one Kingda Ka train?

____

34. Write Math **Sense or Nonsense?** Each week, Kelly works 2 days for 4 hours each day and earns $5 an hour. Len works 5 days for 2 hours each day and earns $4 an hour. Kelly says they both earn the same amount. Does this statement make sense? **Explain.**

____

____

35. **Test Prep** Mark has 2 rows of 3 car models on each of his 3 shelves. How many models does he have in all?

Ⓐ 8 Ⓒ 11

Ⓑ 9 Ⓓ 18

SHOW YOUR WORK

FOR MORE PRACTICE:
Florida Benchmarks Practice Book, pp. P89–P90

Name ______________________________

Combinations

Essential Question What other way besides a tree dragram can you use to find the number of combinations?

MA.3.A.1.1 Model multiplication and division including problems presented in context: repeated addition, multiplicative comparison, array, how many combinations, measurement, and partitioning.

UNLOCK the Problem REAL WORLD

Louis has the lunch choices of a sandwich and drink shown below.

Sandwich	Drink
turkey	juice
ham	milk
roast beef	

A **combination** is a result of joining two or more things. How many different combinations of 1 sandwich and 1 drink are possible?

- What are you asked to find?

  ____

  ____

  ____

- What are the 3 sandwich choices?

  ____

- What are the 2 drink choices?

  ____

One Way Use a tree diagram.

Find the possible combinations.

Sandwich	Drink	Combinations
turkey	juice	turkey sandwich with juice
	milk	turkey sandwich with ________
ham	________	ham sandwich with ________
	milk	________ sandwich with milk
roast beef	________	________ sandwich with juice
	________	roast beef sandwich with milk

So, there are _____ possible combinations of 1 sandwich and 1 drink that Louis can choose from.

Math Talk **Explain** how the number of choices would change if no ham sandwiches were served.

1. How many combinations are there of a turkey sandwich and a drink? _____

Another Way Multiply.

You can multiply to find possible combinations. There are 3 sandwich choices and 2 drink choices.

Sandwich	Drink
turkey	juice
ham	milk
roast beef	

$3 \times 2 =$ _____

So, there are _____ possible combinations of 1 sandwich and 1 drink.

2. How many combinations of 1 sandwich and 1 drink would be possible if cheese was added to the sandwich choices? _______________

3. How can you use multiplication to find the answer? _______________

Share and Show 

1. What are the possible combinations of yogurt and 1 topping? Use the tree diagram.

____

____

____

Yogurt	Topping
vanilla	strawberry
	cherry
chocolate	strawberry
	cherry

Math Talk **Explain** how you can use multiplication to find the number of yogurt and topping combinations.

2. Find the number of combinations of a soup and a fruit. Use multiplication.

Soup	Fruit
tomato	banana
chicken noodle	apple
vegetable	

_____ combinations

3. Find the number of combinations of a kind of shoe and a color. Use multiplication.

Shoes	Colors
sneakers	red
sandals	black
boots	white

_____ combinations

Name ______________________________

On Your Own

Find the number of combinations. Complete the tree diagram.

4. peanut butter: smooth, crunchy
jelly: grape, strawberry, raspberry

_____ combinations

5. shirts: yellow, green, striped
pants: jeans, shorts

_____ combinations

Find the number of combinations. Use multiplication.

6. snacks: pretzels, popcorn, chips
drinks: water, juice, milk

_____ × _____ = _____

_____ combinations

7. T-shirts: blue, red, white, black
hats: purple, blue, green

_____ × _____ = _____

_____ combinations

8. crackers: round, square
spread: butter, cheese, jelly

_____ × _____ = _____

_____ combinations

9. Shoes: white, black, brown, red
Socks: red, blue, white, green

_____ × _____ = _____

_____ combinations

10. H.O.T. Write a combination problem that has 12 as the number of combinations. Show how to solve the problem.

____

____

____

Problem Solving REAL WORLD

Use the table for 11–12. Make a tree diagram or use multiplication.

John's Money	
Bills	**Coins**
$1	1¢
$5	5¢
	10¢
	25¢
	50¢

11. John has bills and coins in his pocket. If he reaches in and pulls out 1 coin and 1 bill, how many combinations of 1 coin and 1 bill could he make?

____

____

____

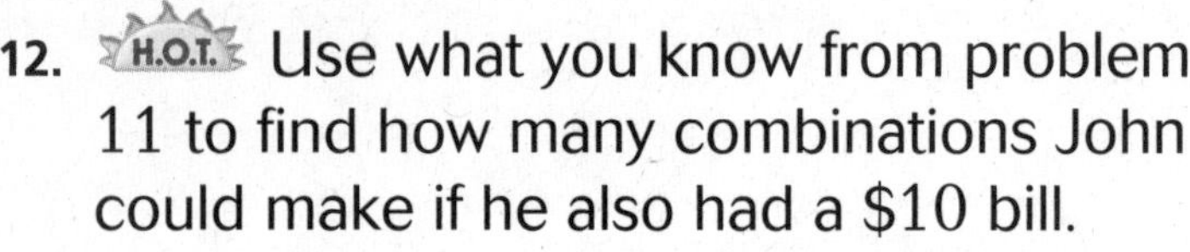

12. H.O.T. Use what you know from problem 11 to find how many combinations John could make if he also had a $10 bill.

____

____

____

SHOW YOUR WORK

13. Write Math **What's the Error?** Oliver has 2 hats and 4 jackets. He says he has 6 combinations of 1 hat and 1 jacket. Is he correct? How could you help Oliver understand the problem?

____

____

____

14. **Test Prep** Zach's printer has 3 colors of paper and 3 colors of ink. How many combinations of paper color and ink color are possible?

   Ⓐ 1   Ⓒ 6

   Ⓑ 5   Ⓓ 9

FOR MORE PRACTICE:
Florida Benchmarks Practice Book, pp. P91–P92

Name ______________________________

Distributive Property

Essential Question How can you use the Distributive Property to find products?

MA.3.A.1.2 Solve multiplication and division fact problems by using strategies that result from applying number properties.

UNLOCK the Problem REAL WORLD

Mark bought 6 new fish for his aquarium. He paid $7 for each fish. How much did he spend in all?

Find $6 \times \$7$.

- What are you asked to find?

____

____

- Circle the numbers you will use to solve the problem.

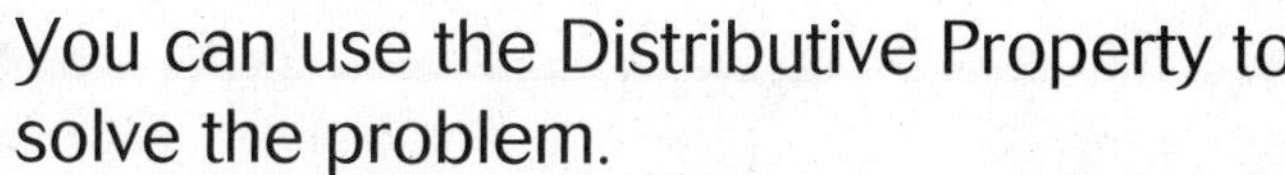

You can use the Distributive Property to solve the problem.

The **Distributive Property of Multiplication** states that multiplying a sum by a number is the same as multiplying each addend by the number and then adding the products.

Remember

sum—the answer to an addition problem

addends—the numbers being added

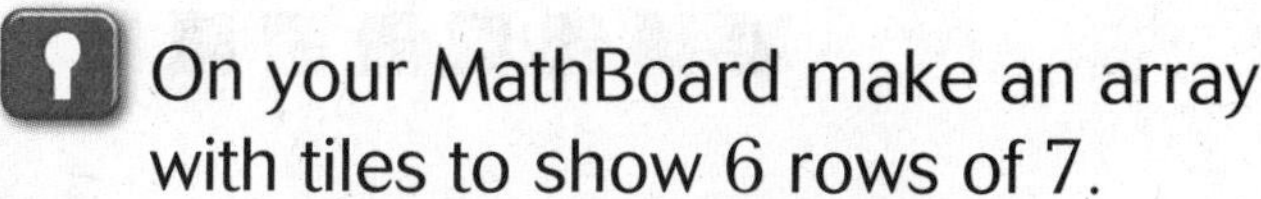

On your MathBoard make an array with tiles to show 6 rows of 7.

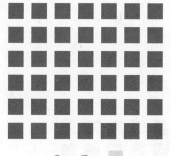

$6 \times 7 = \blacksquare$

Break apart the array to make two smaller arrays for products you know.

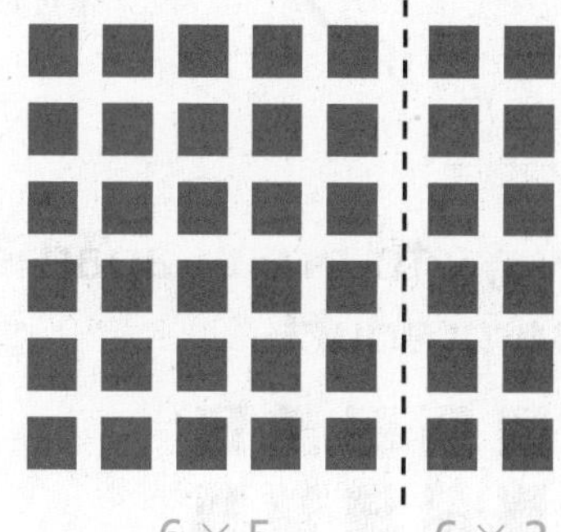

6×5 6×2

$6 \times 7 = \blacksquare$

$6 \times 7 = 6 \times (5 + 2)$ Think of 7 as 5 + 2.

$6 \times 7 = (6 \times 5) + (6 \times 2)$ Multiply each addend by 6.

$6 \times 7 =$ ______ + ______ Add the products.

$6 \times 7 =$ ______

So, Mark spent $ ______ for his new fish.

Math Talk What other ways could you break apart the 6×7 array?

Try This!

Suppose Mark bought 9 fish for \$6 each. One way to break apart a 9×6 array is 5×6 and 4×6. Draw a quick picture to show another way you can break apart a 9×6 array to make two smaller arrays for products you know.

So, Mark spent \$ _____ for 7 fish.

Share and Show

1. Draw a line to show how you could break apart this 6×8 array into two smaller arrays for products you know.

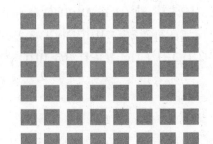

- What numbers do you multiply? _____ and _____
- What numbers do you add? _____ + _____

$6 \times 8 =$ _____ $\times$ _____ $+$ _____ $\times$ _____

$6 \times 8 =$ _____ $+$ _____

$6 \times 8 =$ _____

Name two ways to break apart each array. Then find the product.

2.

____

____

3.

____

____

Math Talk Why do you have to add to find the total product using the Distributive Property?

Name ________________________

On Your Own

Name two ways to break apart the array. Then find the product.

4. 

____

____

5. 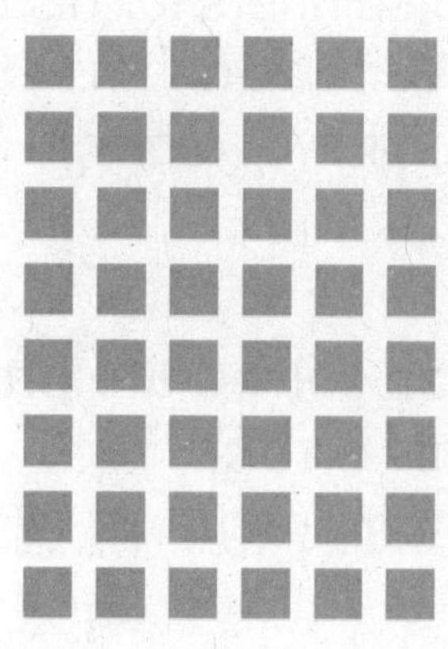

____

____

6. Choose a multiplication fact with 7, 8, or 9 as one of the factors. Draw and label its array. Then write two ways to break apart your array to find the product.

7. H.O.T. **Sense or Nonsense?** Robin says, "I can find 8×7 by multiplying 3×7 and doubling it." Does her statement make sense? **Explain** your answer.

8. **Test Prep** Which number sentence below is an example of the Distributive Property of Multiplication?

Ⓐ $6 \times 8 = 48$

Ⓑ $8 \times 6 = 48$

Ⓒ $6 \times 8 = 8 \times 6$

Ⓓ $6 \times 8 = (6 \times 2) + (6 \times 6)$

Problem Solving 

What's the Error?

9. Brandon needs 8 spinners for his tackle box. The cost of each spinner is \$9. How much will Brandon have to pay in all?

   $8 \times \$9 = ■$

Look at how Brandon solved the problem. Find and describe his error.

$8 \times 9 = (4 \times 9) + (5 \times 9)$

$8 \times 9 = 36 + 45$

$8 \times 9 = 81$

____

____

____

Use the array to help. Solve the problem and correct his error.

$8 \times 9 =$ _____ $\times$ _____ $+$ _____ $\times$ _____

$8 \times 9 =$ _____ $+$ _____

$8 \times 9 =$ _____

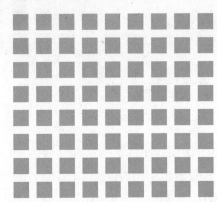

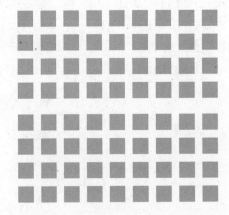

So, Brandon will have to pay \$ _____ for the spinners.

 FOR MORE PRACTICE:
Florida Benchmarks Practice Book, pp. P93–P94

Name ______________________________

Multiply with 8

Essential Question What strategies can you use to multiply with the factor 8?

MA.3.A.1.2 Solve multiplication and division fact problems by using strategies that result from applying number properties.

UNLOCK the Problem REAL WORLD

A scorpion has 8 legs. How many legs do 5 scorpions have?

- How many legs does one scorpion have? _____
- What are you asked to find?

____

____

Find 5×8.

One Way Use doubles.

$5 \times 8 = \blacksquare$

↙ ↘

$4 + 4$

Think: The factor 8 is an even number. $4 + 4 = 8$

$5 \times 4 =$ _____

20 doubled is _____

$5 \times 8 =$ _____

So, 5 scorpions have _____ legs.

▲ **Scorpions are most often found in hot places, such as Arizona and Texas.**

Other Ways

A Use the Commutative Property.

Use facts you know to find 5×8.

You know that $8 \times 5 =$ _____, so $5 \times 8 =$ _____.

8 rows of 5 = 40

5 rows of 8 = 40

Math Talk Describe two different ways you can use doubles to find 4×8.

B **Use a number line.**

Use the number line to show 5 jumps of 8.

So, 5 scorpions have _____ legs.

Share and Show

1. **Explain** one way you could find 6×8.

____

____

Find the product.

2. $3 \times 8 =$ _____
3. _____ $= 2 \times 8$
4. _____ $= 7 \times 8$
5. $9 \times 8 =$ _____

Math Talk **Explain** why using doubles is a good strategy for finding 8×8.

On Your Own

Find the product.

6. $1 \times 8 =$ _____
7. $4 \times 8 =$ _____
8. _____ $= 3 \times 8$
9. _____ $= 8 \times 7$

10. 8×8
11. 6×3
12. 9×8
13. 1×8
14. 8×2
15. 5×7

Practice: Copy and Solve **Find the product.**

16. 8×4
17. 6×8
18. 0×8
19. 5×8

20. 6×4
21. 7×3
22. 5×5
23. 3×8
24. 6×5
25. 7×8

Name ______________________________

 **Algebra** Complete the table.

	Multiply by 4.	
26.	9	
27.	3	
28.	5	

	Multiply by 8.	
29.	4	
30.	2	
31.	7	

32.	Multiply by ___.	
	3	18
	6	36
33.	9	

Problem Solving REAL WORLD

Use the table for 34–37.

Average Yearly Rainfall in North American Deserts	
Desert	**Inches**
Chihuahuan	8
Great Basin	9
Mojave	4
Sonoran	9

34. About how much rain falls in the Chihuahuan Desert in 4 years? **Explain** how you can use doubles to find the answer.

____

____

35. In 2 years, how many more inches of rain fall in the Sonoran Desert than in the Mojave Desert?

____

____

36. Write Math **Pose a Problem** Look back at Problem 35. Write a similar problem by comparing two different deserts.

____

____

____

37. How can you find how many inches of rain fall in the Chihuahuan Desert in 5 years?

____

38. Test Prep A black widow spider has 8 legs. How many legs do 7 black widow spiders have?

Ⓐ 1 Ⓒ 48

Ⓑ 15 Ⓓ 56

Connect to Science

There are 90 species of scorpions that live in the United States. Only 3 species of scorpions live in Florida. They are the Florida bark scorpion, the Guiana striped scorpion, and the Hentz striped scorpion.

Facts About Scorpions

Scorpions:

- are between 1 and 4 inches long.
- mostly eat insects.
- glow under ultraviolet light.

They have:

- 8 legs for walking.
- 2 long, claw-like pincers used to hold their food.
- a curled tail held over their body with a stinger on the tip.

▲ Scorpions glow under ultraviolet light.

39. How many species of scorpions do *not* live in Florida? ______

40. Students saw 8 scorpions. What multiplication sentences can you write to find how many pincers and legs they saw on the 8 scorpions in all?

____

41. Three scorpions were in a display with ultraviolet light. Eight groups of 4 students saw the display. How many students saw the glowing scorpions? ______

 FOR MORE PRACTICE:
Florida Benchmarks Book, pp. P95–P96

Name ______________________________

Mid-Chapter Checkpoint

▶ Check Vocabulary

Choose the best term from the box to complete the sentence.

Vocabulary
Associative Property of Multiplication
combination
Distributive Property of Multiplication
multiple

1. A ______________________ of 6 is any product that has 6 as one of its factors. (MA.3.A.1.1; p. 157)

2. A ______________________ is a result of joining two or more things. (MA.3.A.1.1; p. 165)

3. A property that states when the grouping of factors is changed, the product remains the same is the called the ______________________. (MA.3.A.1.2; p. 161)

▶ Check Concepts and Skills

Find the number of combinations. Make a tree diagram or use multiplication. (MA.3.A.1.1; pp. 165–168)

4. 1 Pet and 1 Color

Pet	Color
dog	brown
cat	black
	white

_____ combinations

5. 1 Flavor of Ice Cream and 1 Topping

Ice Cream	Topping
vanilla	caramel
chocolate	fudge
strawberry	fruit

_____ combinations

Find the product. (MA.3.A.1.1, MA.3.A.1.2; pp. 153–156, 157–160, 173–176)

6. 6×3

7. 3×4

8. 5×3

9. 3×3

10. 6×2

11. 8×6

12. 6×6

13. 6×8

14. 6×4

15. 9×8

Fill in the bubble for the correct answer choice.

TEST PREP

16. Lori saw 6 lightning bugs. They each had 6 legs. How many legs did the lightning bugs have in all?

(MA.3.A.1.1; pp. 157–160)

Ⓐ 6
Ⓑ 12
Ⓒ 24
Ⓓ 36

17. Zach gave each of his three dogs 2 dog biscuits a day, for 5 days. How many biscuits did Zach give to his dogs in all? (MA.3.A.1.2; pp. 161–164)

Ⓕ 6
Ⓖ 7
Ⓗ 10
Ⓘ 30

18. John owns a fish store. Last week he sold 6 times as many mollies as he did goldfish. He sold 8 goldfish. How many mollies did he sell? (MA.3.A.1.2; pp. 173–176)

Ⓐ 8
Ⓑ 14
Ⓒ 48
Ⓓ 54

19. Mark put all of his shirts in 4 equal stacks. There are 6 shirts in each stack. How many shirts does Mark have altogether? (MA.3.A.1.1; pp. 157–160)

Ⓕ 6
Ⓖ 10
Ⓗ 24
Ⓘ 36

Name ______________________

Make a Table · Multiplication

Essential Question How does making a table help you solve problems?

MA.3.A.6.2 Solve non-routine problems by making a table, chart, or list and searching for patterns.

UNLOCK the Problem REAL WORLD

Scott has a stamp album. Some pages have one stamp on them, and other pages have two stamps on them. If Scott has 18 stamps, how many different ways could he put them in the album? Use the graphic organizer below to solve the problem.

Read the Problem

What do I need to find?

____

____

____

What information do I need to use?

Scott has _____ stamps. Some of the pages have _____ stamp on them, and the other pages have _____ stamps.

How will I use the information?

I will make a ______ showing all the different ways of organizing the stamps in the album.

Solve the Problem

Make a table to show the number of pages with one stamp and with two stamps. Each row must equal _____, the total number of stamps.

Pages with 1 Stamp	Pages with 2 Stamps	Total Stamps
2	8	18
4	7	18
6	6	18
	5	18
10		18
12	3	
	2	

1. What number patterns do you see in the table?

____

____

Try Another Problem

What if Scott got 3 more stamps and now has 21 stamps? How many pages in his album could have one stamp on them? How many pages could have two stamps? How many different ways could he put the odd number of stamps in the album?

Read the Problem	Solve the Problem
What do I need to find? __________ __________	
What information do I need to use? __________ __________ __________	
How will I use the information? __________ __________	

2. What patterns do you see in this table? __________

____

3. How are these patterns different from the patterns in the table on page 179? __________

____

____

Name ______________________________

Share and Show 

1. Aaron's mother is making lemonade for the students in his class. For each pitcher, she uses 1 cup of lemon juice, 1 cup of sugar, and 6 cups of water. How many total cups of ingredients will she need to make 5 pitchers of lemonade?

   First, make a table to show how many cups of lemon juice, sugar, and water are in 1 pitcher of lemonade.

   Next, multiply to find the number of cups of water needed for each pitcher of lemonade.

   Last, use the table to solve the problem.

Think: For every pitcher, the number of cups of water increases by 6.

Number of Pitchers	1	2	3		5
Cups of Lemon Juice	1		3		
Cups of Sugar	1	2			
Cups of Water	6	12		24	
Total Cups of Ingredients	8				

So, in 5 pitchers of lemonade, there are _____ cups of lemon juice, _____ cups of sugar, and _____ cups of water.

2. H.O.T. **What if** it takes 20 lemons to make 5 cups of lemon juice? How many lemons would it take to make 8 cups of lemon juice? Explain your answer.

____

____

3. What pattern do you see in the total number of cups of lemon juice, sugar, and water used in each pitcher?

____

____

On Your Own

4. The mockingbird is the state bird of Florida. Julie saw 3 mockingbirds each day she went bird-watching. How many mockingbirds did Julie see in 6 days?

____

5. Greg wants to make $1.75 using dollars, half dollars and quarters. How many ways can he do this?

Name the ways. _______________

6. H.O.T. Carter collects old coins. He has 6 dimes, 4 quarters, and 6 nickels. How many coins does he have? How much money does he have in all?

____

7. Write Math Cammi needs 36 postcards. She buys 4 packages of 10 postcards. How many postcards does Cammi have left over? **Explain.**

____

8. The orange blossom is the state flower of Florida. Suppose there are 3 flowers on each of 7 clusters of blossoms. How many flowers are there in all?

____

9. **Test Prep** Each year for 3 years, the Williams family has made 3 trips to Wekiwa Springs State Park. How many times did the family visit Wekiwa Springs in all?

Ⓐ 3 Ⓒ 9

Ⓑ 6 Ⓓ 12

Choose a STRATEGY

- Act It Out
- Use Manipulatives
- Draw a Diagram
- Make a Table, Chart, or List
- Search for Patterns

SHOW YOUR WORK

 FOR MORE PRACTICE:
Florida Benchmarks Practice Book, pp. P97–P98

Name ______________________________

Multiply with 9

Essential Question What pattern helps you multiply with the factor 9?

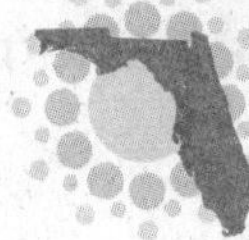

MA.3.A.1.2 Solve multiplication and division fact problems by using strategies that result from applying number properties.

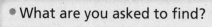

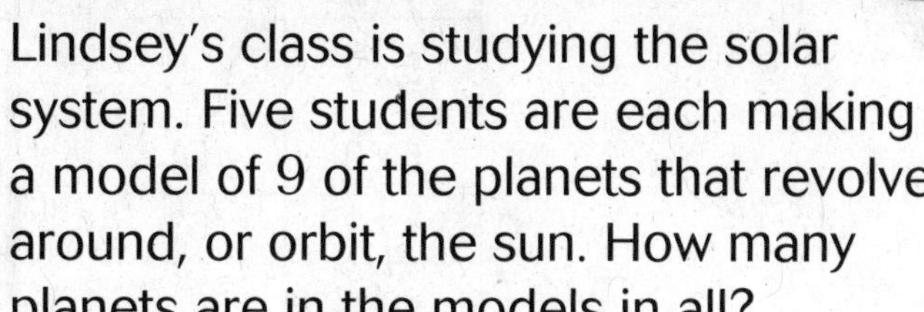

Lindsey's class is studying the solar system. Five students are each making a model of 9 of the planets that revolve around, or orbit, the sun. How many planets are in the models in all?

Find 5×9.

- What are you asked to find?

____

____

- How many students are making models? ______

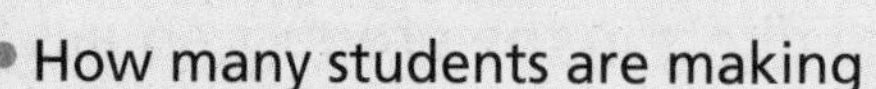

One Way Use the Distributive Property to multiply with 9.

A With multiplication and addition

$5 \times 9 = \blacksquare$

Think of 9 as 3 + 6. $5 \times 9 = 5 \times (3 + 6)$

Multiply each addend by 5. $5 \times 9 = (5 \times 3) + (5 \times 6)$

Add the products. $5 \times 9 =$ ______ + ______

$5 \times 9 =$ ______

B With ten and subtraction

$5 \times 9 = \blacksquare$

Think of 9 as 10 − 1. $5 \times 9 = 5 \times (10 - 1)$

Multiply each addend by 5. $5 \times 9 = (5 \times 10) - (5 \times 1)$

Think: Count by 10.

Subtract. $5 \times 9 = 50 - 5$

$5 \times 9 =$ ______

So, there are ______ planets in the 5 solar system models.

Another Way Use patterns of 9 to find 5 × 9.

The table shows the 9s facts.

- First, look at each row in the table. The tens digit in the product is 1 less than the factor that is multiplied by 9.

$5 \times 9 = 4\square$

↓

$5 - 1$

- Then, look at each product in the table. The sum of the digits in the product equals 9.

$5 \times 9 = \_\_\_\_$

↓

$4 + 5 = 9$

Table of 9s	
Factor	Product
1 x 9	9
2 x 9	18
3 x 9	27
4 x 9	36
5 x 9	
6 x 9	54
7 x 9	63
8 x 9	
9 x 9	

Try This! Complete the 9s table for 8 × 9.
Use the patterns to find 9 × 9.

Math Talk What two digits are in the product for 6 × 9?

Share and Show

1. What is the tens digit in the product of 3 × 9? ____

   Think: What number is 1 less than 3?

Find the product.

2. $9 \times 8 =$ ____ 3. ____ $= 2 \times 9$ 4. ____ $= 9 \times 6$ 5. $9 \times 1 =$ ____

On Your Own

Practice: Copy and Solve Find the product.

6. 9×0 7. 5×9 8. 6×9 9. 1×9

10. 9×2 11. 9×9 12. 9×4 13. 3×9

14. 9×5 15. 8×4 16. 6×9 17. 9×7 18. 7×8

Name ___________________________

H.O.T. **Algebra** **Compare. Write <, >, or =.**

19. 2×9 ◯ 3×6 **20.** 5×9 ◯ 6×7 **21.** 1×9 ◯ 3×3

22. 9×4 ◯ 7×5 **23.** 9×0 ◯ 2×3 **24.** 5×8 ◯ 3×9

Problem Solving REAL WORLD

For 25–28, use the table.

Moons

Planet	Number of Moons
Earth	1
Mars	2
Jupiter	63
Saturn	47
Uranus	27
Neptune	13

25. The number of moons for one of the planets can be found by multiplying 7×9. Which planet is it?

____

26. Describe a multiplication fact with 9 that could have been used to find the number of moons Uranus has.

____

____

____

27. H.O.T. This planet has 9 times as many moons as Mars and Earth have together. Which planet is it? **Explain** your answer.

____

____

____

28. Write Math Nine groups of students made models of Mars and its moons. How many moons were made in all? **Explain** how to find the answer.

____

____

UNLOCK the Problem REAL WORLD

TEST PREP

29. The school library has 97 books about space. John and eight of his friends each check out 9 books. How many space books are still in the school library?

Ⓐ 6 Ⓑ 16 Ⓒ 81 Ⓓ 97

a. What do you need to know? ________________________________

____

b. Describe one way you can find the answer. ________________________________

____

c. Show the steps you use to solve the problem.

d. Complete the sentences.

The library has ______ space books.

John and ______ friends each check out ______ books.

Multiply ______ × ______ to find how many books they checked out in all.

What else must you do to solve the problem? ________________

So, there are ______ space books left in the library.

e. Fill in the bubble for the answer choice above.

30. Mark read 5 pages of a space book every day for a week. How many pages did he read in all?

Ⓕ 5 Ⓗ 35

Ⓖ 15 Ⓘ 40

31. Joel has 4 shelves of model airplanes. He has 9 airplanes on each shelf. How many model airplanes does he have in all?

Ⓐ 36 Ⓒ 9

Ⓑ 27 Ⓓ 4

FOR MORE PRACTICE:
Florida Benchmarks Practice Book, pp. P99–P100

Name ______________________________

Multiply with 7

Essential Question How can you multiply with the factor 7?

MA.3.A.1.2 Solve multiplication and division fact problems by using strategies that result from applying number properties.

UNLOCK the Problem REAL WORLD

Jason's family has a new puppy. Jason walks the puppy once a day. How many times will Jason walk the puppy in 4 weeks?

Find 4×7.

- How often does Jason walk the puppy?

  ____

- How many days are in 1 week?

  ____

One Way Use the Commutative Property.

If you know 7×4, you can use that fact to find 4×7.

$7 \times 4 =$ _____,

so $4 \times 7 =$ _____.

So, Jason will walk the puppy _____ times in 4 weeks.

Other Ways

A **Use the Distributive Property.**

STEP 1 Complete the array to show 4 rows of 7.

STEP 2 Draw the dashed line to break the array into two smaller arrays for facts you know.

STEP 3 Multiply the smaller arrays. Add the products.

$4 \times$ _____ $=$ _____ $4 \times$ _____ $=$ _____

_____ $+$ _____ $=$ _____

So, $4 \times 7 =$ _____.

Math Talk **Explain** two other ways you can break apart the 4×7 array.

B **Look for a pattern. Write a rule.**

Weeks	1	2	3	4
Number of Walks	7	14	21	

Pattern: The number of walks equals the number of weeks times 7.

Rule: Multiply the number of weeks by 7.
To find how many times Jason walks the puppy in 4 weeks, multiply 4×7.

So, $4 \times 7 =$ _____

Share and Show

1. **Explain** how you could break apart an array to find 8×7. Use a quick picture of an array to help.

____

Math Talk How could you use doubles to find 8×7?

Find the product.

2. $9 \times 7 =$ _____ 3. _____ $= 5 \times 7$ ✓4. _____ $= 3 \times 7$ ✓5. $7 \times 1 =$ _____

On Your Own

Find the product.

6. _____ $= 7 \times 7$ 7. $7 \times 6 =$ _____ 8. _____ $= 1 \times 7$ 9. _____ $= 7 \times 2$

10. $\begin{array}{r} 7 \\ \times 3 \\ \hline \end{array}$ 11. $\begin{array}{r} 5 \\ \times 6 \\ \hline \end{array}$ 12. $\begin{array}{r} 9 \\ \times 7 \\ \hline \end{array}$ 13. $\begin{array}{r} 5 \\ \times 7 \\ \hline \end{array}$ 14. $\begin{array}{r} 6 \\ \times 8 \\ \hline \end{array}$ 15. $\begin{array}{r} 7 \\ \times 6 \\ \hline \end{array}$

16. $\begin{array}{r} 8 \\ \times 9 \\ \hline \end{array}$ 17. $\begin{array}{r} 0 \\ \times 7 \\ \hline \end{array}$ 18. $\begin{array}{r} 8 \\ \times 8 \\ \hline \end{array}$ 19. $\begin{array}{r} 7 \\ \times 4 \\ \hline \end{array}$ 20. $\begin{array}{r} 3 \\ \times 6 \\ \hline \end{array}$ 21. $\begin{array}{r} 8 \\ \times 7 \\ \hline \end{array}$

Problem Solving REAL WORLD

Use the table for 22–24.

Midnight's Care	
Food	3 cups a day
Water	4 cups a day
Bath	2 times a month

22. Lori has a dog named Midnight. How many baths will Midnight have in 7 months? ______

23. How many more cups of water than food will Midnight get in 1 week?

______

SHOW YOUR WORK

24. H.O.T. Write Math José's dog, Rusty, eats 4 cups of food a day. In one week, does Midnight eat more or less food than Rusty eats? **Explain.**

______

______

______

______

25. *Ruff* dog food costs 9¢ for each ounce. How much does an 8-ounce can of food cost? ______

26. Dave takes Zoey, his golden retriever, for a 3-mile walk twice a day. How many miles do they walk in one week?

______

27. **Test Prep** Sam walks his dog 5 miles a day. How many miles does he walk in one week?

Ⓐ 5 miles
Ⓑ 25 miles
Ⓒ 35 miles
Ⓓ 40 miles

Connect to Reading

Summarize

To help you stay healthy, you should eat a balanced diet and exercise every day.

The table shows the recommended daily servings for third graders. You should eat the right amounts of each food group.

Suppose you want to share with your friends what you learned about healthy eating. How could you summarize what you learned?

When you **summarize**, you restate the most important information in a shorter way to help you understand what you have read.

Recommended Daily Servings

Food Group	Servings
Whole grains (bread, cereal)	6 ounces
Vegetables (beans, corn)	2 cups
Fruits (apples, oranges)	1 cup
Dairy products (milk, cheese)	3 cups
Meat, beans, fish eggs, nuts	5 ounces
8 ounces = 1 cup	

- To stay healthy, you should eat a balanced ________________ and ________________ every day.

- A third grader should eat 3 cups of ________________, such as milk and cheese, each day.
- A third grader should eat ________________ of vegetables and fruits each day.

  How many cups of vegetables and fruits should a third grader eat in 1 week? ________________

  Remember: 1 week = 7 days

- A third grader should eat ________________ ounces of whole grains, such as bread and cereal, in 1 week.

 FOR MORE PRACTICE:
Florida Benchmarks Practice Book, pp. P101–P102

Name ______________________________

Missing Factors

Essential Question How can you use an array or a multiplication table to find missing factors?

MA.3.A.1.1 Model multiplication and division including problems presented in context: repeated addition, multiplicative comparison, array, how many combinations, measurement, and partitioning.

UNLOCK the Problem REAL WORLD

Brandy plans to invite 24 people to a picnic. The invitations come in packs of 8. How many packs of invitations does Brandy need to buy?

$$a \times 8 = 24$$

A **variable** is a letter or symbol that stands for an unknown number. Find the number the a stands for.

- How many people is Brandy inviting?

  ____

- How many invitations are in 1 package?

  ____

One Way Make an array.

- Make an array with 24 tiles. Use 8 tiles in each row.

a	$\times$	8	$=$	24
↑		↑		↑
factor		factor		product
number of rows		number in each row		total

- Count how many rows of 8 tiles.

There are ______ rows of 8 tiles. The missing factor is ______.

$a =$ ______

______ $\times 8 = 24$

So, Brandy needs ______ packs of invitations.

Another Way Use a multiplication table.

$f \times 8 = 24$

Start at the column for the factor 8, since 8 is the second factor.

Look down to the product, 24.

Look left across the row from 24.

The missing factor is ____.

$f =$ ____

____ $\times 8 = 24$

Think: In this multiplication sentence, the variable *f* stands for the missing factor.

×	0	1	2	3	4	5	6	7	8	9
0	0	0	0	0	0	0	0	0	0	0
1	0	1	2	3	4	5	6	7	8	9
2	0	2	4	6	8	10	12	14	16	18
3	0	3	6	9	12	15	18	21	24	27
4	0	4	8	12	16	20	24	28	32	36
5	0	5	10	15	20	25	30	35	40	45
6	0	6	12	18	24	30	36	42	48	54
7	0	7	14	21	28	35	42	49	56	63
8	0	8	16	24	32	40	48	56	64	72
9	0	9	18	27	36	45	54	63	72	81

Math Talk How can you use the Commutative Property to check your answer?

Share and Show

1. What is the missing factor shown by this array?

$5 \times$ ____ $= 35$

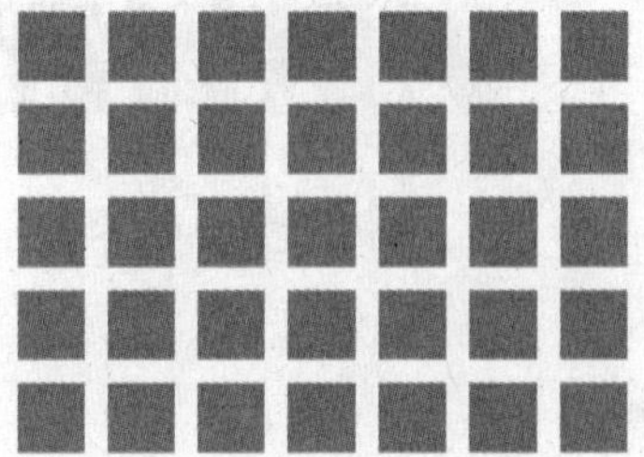

Find the missing factor.

2. $d \times 3 = 27$

   $d =$ ____

3. $6 \times b = 30$

   $b =$ ____

4. $20 = c \times 5$

   $c =$ ____

5. ■ $\times 2 = 14$

   ■ $=$ ____

6. $36 = b \times 9$

   $b =$ ____

7. $8 \times e = 64$

   $e =$ ____

8. $7 \times t = 42$

   $t =$ ____

9. $z \times 9 = 72$

   $z =$ ____

Math Talk **Explain** how to use the multiplication table to find the missing factor in ■ $\times 6 = 42$.

Name ______________________

On Your Own

Find the missing factor.

10. ■ $\times 2 = 18$

■ = ____

11. $28 = 4 \times m$

m = ____

12. $y \times 3 = 9$

y = ____

13. $7 \times g = 63$

g = ____

14. $5 \times p = 40$

p = ____

15. $8 \times w = 56$

w = ____

16. $36 = s \times 6$

s = ____

17. $e \times 9 = 72$

e = ____

18. $3 \times$ ■ $= 27$

■ = ____

19. $6 \times a = 42$

a = ____

20. $d \times 5 = 35$

d = ____

21. $32 = 8 \times n$

n = ____

22. $a \times 4 = 24$

a = ____

23. $7 = 7 \times n$

n = ____

24. $w \times 3 = 15$

w = ____

25. $z \times 8 = 48$

z = ____

26. $35 = h \times 5$

h = ____

27. $54 = c \times 6$

c = ____

28. $7 \times p = 49$

p = ____

29. $y \times 9 = 36$

y = ____

H.O.T. **Algebra** Find the missing factor.

30. $3 \times 6 = k \times 9$

k = ____

31. $4 \times y = 2 \times 6$

y = ____

32. $5 \times g = 36 - 6$

g = ____

33. $6 \times 4 = a \times 3$

a = ____

34. $9 \times d = 70 + 2$

d = ____

35. $8 \times h = 60 - 4$

h = ____

Problem Solving REAL WORLD

Use the table for 36–40.

Item	Number in a pack	Cost
Bowls	6	$10
Cups	8	$3
Tablecloth	1	$2
Napkins	36	$2
Forks	50	$3

Picnic Supplies

36. Brandy needs 40 cups for the picnic. How many packs of cups should she buy?

37. Write Math Suppose Brandy needs 40 bowls for the picnic. How many packs should she buy?

38. Brandy's mother bought 3 tablecloths and 2 packs of napkins. How much did she spend in all?

39. H.O.T. Suppose Brandy needs an equal number of bowls and cups for the picnic. How many packs of each will she need to buy?

40. H.O.T. Lori buys 200 forks. She gives the cashier $20. How much change should she get?

41. Test Prep What is the missing factor?

$$\blacksquare \times 6 = 42$$

Ⓐ 8 Ⓑ 7 Ⓒ 6 Ⓓ 5

SHOW YOUR WORK

FOR MORE PRACTICE:
Florida Benchmarks Practice Book, pp. P103–P104

Name ______________________

Multiplication Properties

Essential Question How can you use the Identity, Zero, Commutative, Associative, and Distributive Properties to find products?

MA.3.A.1.2 Solve multiplication and division fact problems by using strategies that result from applying number properties.

CONNECT You have learned that multiplication properties can help you find products.

UNLOCK the Problem REAL WORLD

Identity Property The product of 1 and any number equals that number.

5 × 1 = _____

What kind of picture would show 5 × 1? Complete the quick picture to show the multiplication sentence.

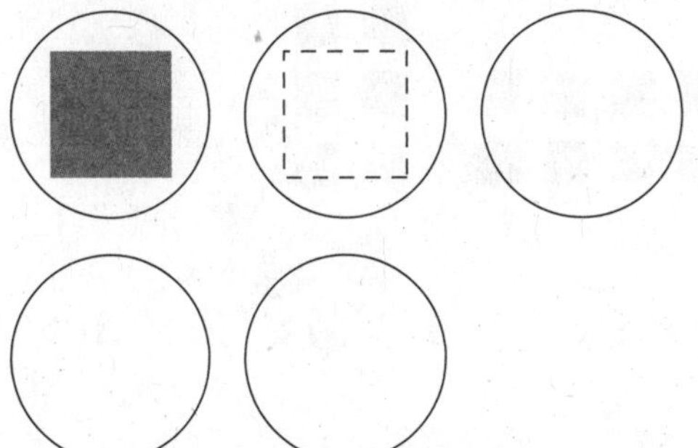

Zero Property The product of zero and any number equals zero.

6 × 0 = _____

What kind of picture would show 6 × 0? Complete the quick picture.

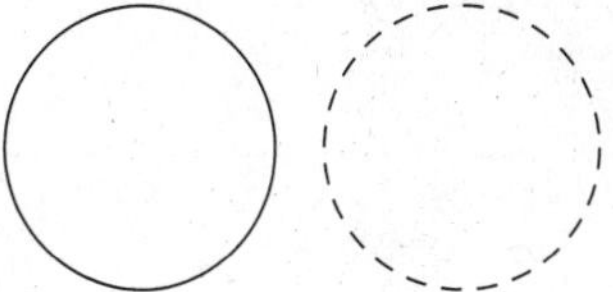

Commutative Property When you multiply two factors in any order, the product is the same.

Complete the quick pictures to show the arrays for the multiplication sentences.

3 × _____ = _____   _____ × 3 = _____

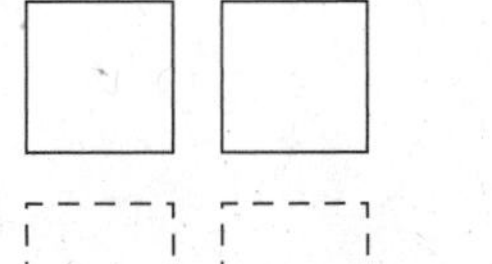

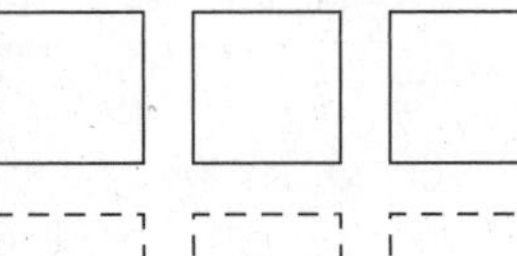

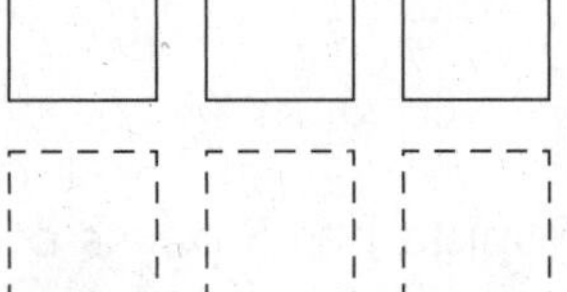

Associative Property When you group factors in different ways, the product is the same.

Circle each group of 4 twos.

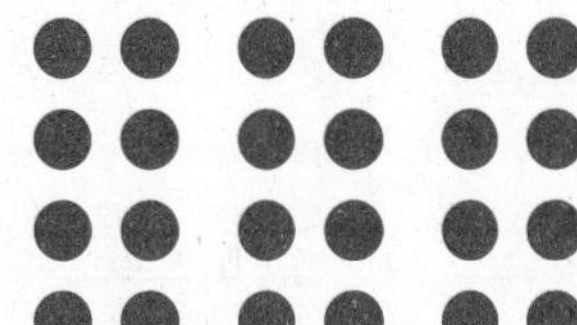

(4 × 2) × 3 = _____

8 × 3 = _____

Circle each group of 2 threes.

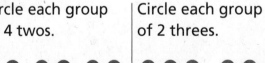

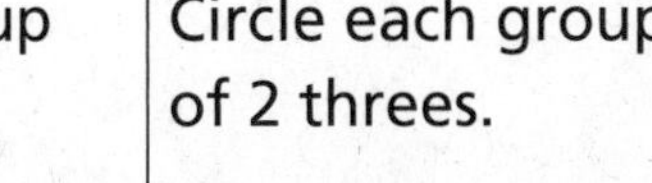

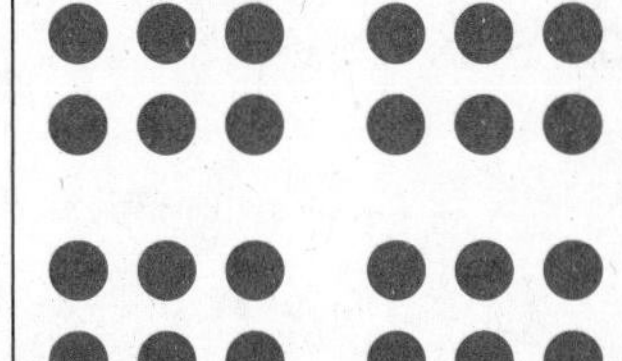

4 × (2 × 3) = _____

4 × 6 = _____

Distributive Property Multiplying a sum by a number is the same as multiplying each addend by the number and then adding the products.

$5 \times 6 = \blacksquare$

Think: $5 \times 6 = 5 \times (3 + 3)$

$5 \times 6 = (5 \times 3) + (5 \times 3)$

$5 \times 6 =$ _____ + _____

$5 \times 6 =$ _____

You can use the Distributive Property to find 9s facts with subtraction.

$7 \times 9 = \blacksquare$

$7 \times 9 = 7 \times (10 - 1)$

$7 \times 9 = (7 \times 10) - (7 \times 1)$

Think: Count by 10.

Subtract. $7 \times 9 =$ _____ − _____

$7 \times 9 =$ _____

Share and Show

1. Which property do these arrays show?

____

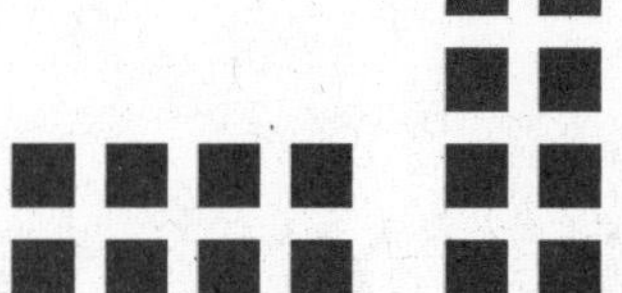

Find the product.

2. 5×1 _____

3. 8×4 _____

4. 0×9 _____

5. $(3 \times 3) \times 7$ _____

6. 0×7 _____

7. $8 \times (1 \times 2)$ _____

8. 9×2 _____

9. 7×6 _____

10. 9×7 _____

11. 9×9 _____

12. 6×9 _____

13. $(4 \times 2) \times 7$ _____

Math Talk Sophia has 5 packs of 8 cards. John has 8 packs of 5 cards. Who has more cards? **Explain** how you can tell if they have the same number of cards without multiplying.

Name ____________________

On Your Own

Find the product.

14. $(4 \times 2) \times 7$ ______

15. 9×3 ______

16. 6×0 ______

17. $(3 \times 3) \times 8$ ______

18. $(2 \times 3) \times 4$ ______

19. 6×8 ______

20. 0×9 ______

21. 1×1 ______

22. $5 \times (0 \times 9)$ ______

23. $(9 \times 1) \times 9$ ______

24. 7×7 ______

25. 8×9 ______

H.O.T. **Algebra** **Find the missing factor.**

26. $5 \times ■ = 6 \times 5$ ______

27. $3 \times (2 \times 4) = (■ \times 2) \times 4$ ______

28. $■ \times 3 = 3 \times 9$ ______

29. $9 \times a = 49 + 5$

$a =$ ______

30. $7 \times b = (8 \times 3) + 4$

$b =$ ______

31. $(8 \times c) \times 5 = 34 + 6$

$c =$ ______

Write <, >, or =.

32. 4×2 ◯ $5 + 2$

33. 7×7 ◯ 50

34. 3×8 ◯ 6×4

35. 7×4 ◯ $30 - 4$

36. 4×9 ◯ 6×6

37. 5×9 ◯ 6×8

Problem Solving REAL WORLD

Use the pictograph for 38–40.

Knitting Supplies
Needles
Knitting Book
Yarn
Key: Each = $2.

38. Amy bought 3 balls of yarn to knit a hat How much did she spend in all?

____

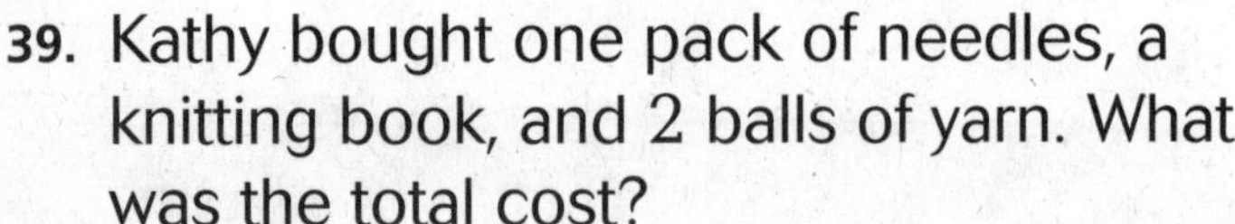

39. Kathy bought one pack of needles, a knitting book, and 2 balls of yarn. What was the total cost?

____

40. Write Math Sandy bought 8 balls of yarn. **Explain** how you can use the Commutative Property to find the cost.

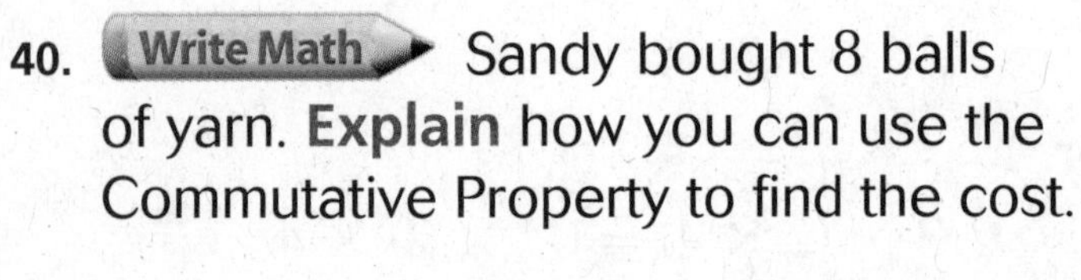

____

____

41. H.O.T. What is the missing factor? **Explain** your answer.

$$\blacksquare \times 0 = 0$$

____

____

____

42. **Test Prep** Which of the number sentences below is an example of the Identity Property?

Ⓐ $5 \times 3 = 3 \times 5$

Ⓑ $0 \times 6 = 6 \times 0$

Ⓒ $7 \times 1 = 7$

Ⓓ $(8 \times 2) \times 4 = 8 \times (2 \times 4)$

SHOW YOUR WORK

FOR MORE PRACTICE:
Florida Benchmarks Practice Book, pp. P105–P106

Name ___________________________________

Chapter Review/Test

▶ Check Vocabulary

Choose the best term from the box to complete the sentence.

Vocabulary
Associative Property of Multiplication
Distributive Property of Multiplication
multiple
variable

1. The ___________________________ states that when the grouping of factors is changed, the product remains the same. (MA.3.A.1.2; p. 161)

2. A ______________ is a symbol or letter that stands for an unknown number. (MA.3.A.1.1; p. 191)

3. The ___________________________ states that multiplying a sum by a number is the same as multiplying each addend by the number and then adding the products. (MA.3.A.1.2; p. 169)

▶ Check Concepts and Skills

Write one way to break apart the array to find the product. (MA.3.A.1.2; pp. 169–172)

4. 

$5 \times 7 =$ ________ $+$ ________

$5 \times 7 =$ _____ $+$ _____ $=$ _____

5. 

$4 \times 9 =$ ________ $+$ ________

$4 \times 9 =$ _____ $+$ _____ $=$ _____

Find the product. (MA.3.A.1.1, MA.3.A.1.2; pp. 153–156, 157–160, 173–176, 183–186, 187–190)

6. 6×8

7. 7×9

8. 9×5

9. 6×3

10. 5×8

11. 7×7

Go online Assessment Options Chapter Test

Fill in the bubble for the correct answer choice.

TEST PREP

12. Vicky went to the store and bought 3 pairs of shorts. They each cost \$8. How much did she spend in all?

(MA.3.A.1.2; pp. 173–176)

Ⓐ \$3

Ⓑ \$8

Ⓒ \$21

Ⓓ \$24

13. A honeybee is an insect. It has 6 legs. How many more legs do 7 honeybees have than 5 honeybees?

(MA.3.A.1.1; pp. 157–160)

Ⓕ 5

Ⓖ 6

Ⓗ 12

Ⓘ 30

14. Jody has bags of shells. Each bag has 6 shells. She gives 3 bags to each of 2 friends. How many shells did Jody give away? (MA.3.A.1.2; pp. 161–164)

Ⓐ 36

Ⓑ 18

Ⓒ 12

Ⓓ 6

15. Mark has a red shirt, a blue shirt, and a green shirt. He has blue shorts, tan shorts, and black shorts. Draw a tree diagram or use multiplication to find how many combinations of shirts and shorts are possible.

(MA.3.A.1.1; pp. 165–168)

Ⓕ 3

Ⓖ 6

Ⓗ 9

Ⓘ 12

Name ______________________________

16. James made an array with 6 rows of 8 blocks. Which number sentence shows one way to break apart his array to find the product? **(MA.3.A.1.2; pp. 169–172)**

Ⓐ $6 \times 8 = (6 + 4) + (6 + 4)$

Ⓑ $6 \times 8 = (6 \times 4) + (6 \times 4)$

Ⓒ $6 \times 8 = (3 \times 4) + (3 \times 4)$

Ⓓ $6 \times 8 = (6 \times 8) + (6 \times 8)$

17. Zach and his dad baked some cupcakes for his class. They put 6 cupcakes on each of 8 plates. How many cupcakes did they make in all? **(MA.3.A.1.2; pp. 173–176)**

Ⓕ 12

Ⓖ 14

Ⓗ 24

Ⓘ 48

18. Sydnee's class is studying animals that hibernate, or go into a sleep-like state during the winter. A black bear's heartbeat slows to about 9 beats per minute. About how many times will a black bear's heart beat in 5 minutes? **(MA.3.A.1.2; pp. 183–186)**

Ⓐ 45

Ⓑ 36

Ⓒ 18

Ⓓ 9

19. Shayla was on vacation for 7 weeks. She spent 3 weeks at band camp and the rest of the time at home. How many days did she spend at home? (MA.3.A.1.2; pp. 187–190)

Ⓕ 7

Ⓖ 14

Ⓗ 21

Ⓘ 28

20. Summer thought of a number riddle. "The product of 4 and another factor is 32. What is the other factor?" What number would you use to solve Summer's riddle? (MA.3.A.1.1; pp. 191–194)

Ⓐ 4

Ⓑ 8

Ⓒ 12

Ⓓ 16

21. Rusty is a large dog. He eats 2 cups of dog food twice a day. How many cups of dog food does Rusty eat in one week? Which multiplication property can help you solve the problem? (MA.3.A.1.2; pp. 161–164)

$2 \times 2 \times 7 = \blacksquare$ cups

Ⓕ Associative Property of Multiplication

Ⓖ Identity Property of Multiplication

Ⓗ Zero Property of Multiplication

Ⓘ Commutative Property of Multiplication

Chapter

5 Understand Division

Show What You Know

Check your understanding of important skills.

Name ______________________________

▶ Make Equal Groups **Circle equal groups. Complete the sentence.**

1. Separate into groups of 3.

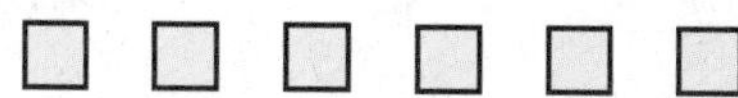

There are _____ equal groups.

2. Separate into groups of 2.

There are _____ equal groups.

▶ Count Equal Groups **Complete.**

3.   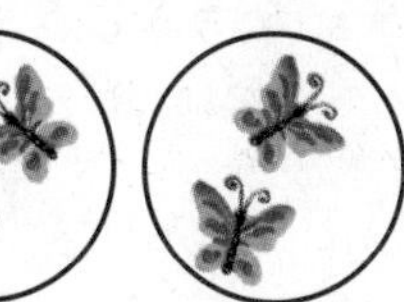

_____ groups

_____ in each group

4. 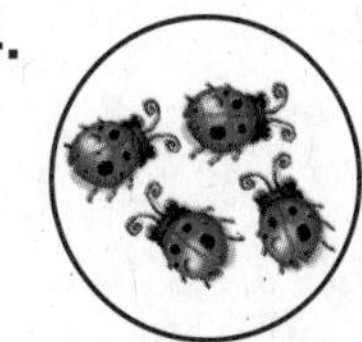 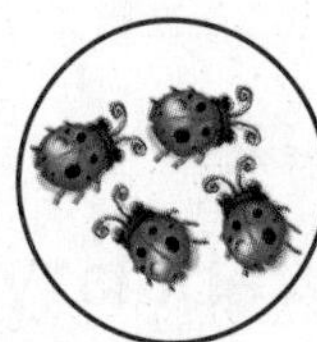

_____ groups

_____ in each group

▶ Multiplication Facts Through 9 **Find the product.**

5. $8 \times 5 =$ _____

6. _____ $= 7 \times 7$

7. $3 \times 9 =$ _____

Florida FUN FACT

The ruby-throated hummingbird is the most common hummingbird in Florida. It is about 3 inches long and weighs only as much as a penny. It can fly right, left, up, down, forward, backward, and upside down!

FLORIDA BENCHMARKS

Vocabulary Power

▶ Visualize It

Complete the Bubble Map by using the review words.

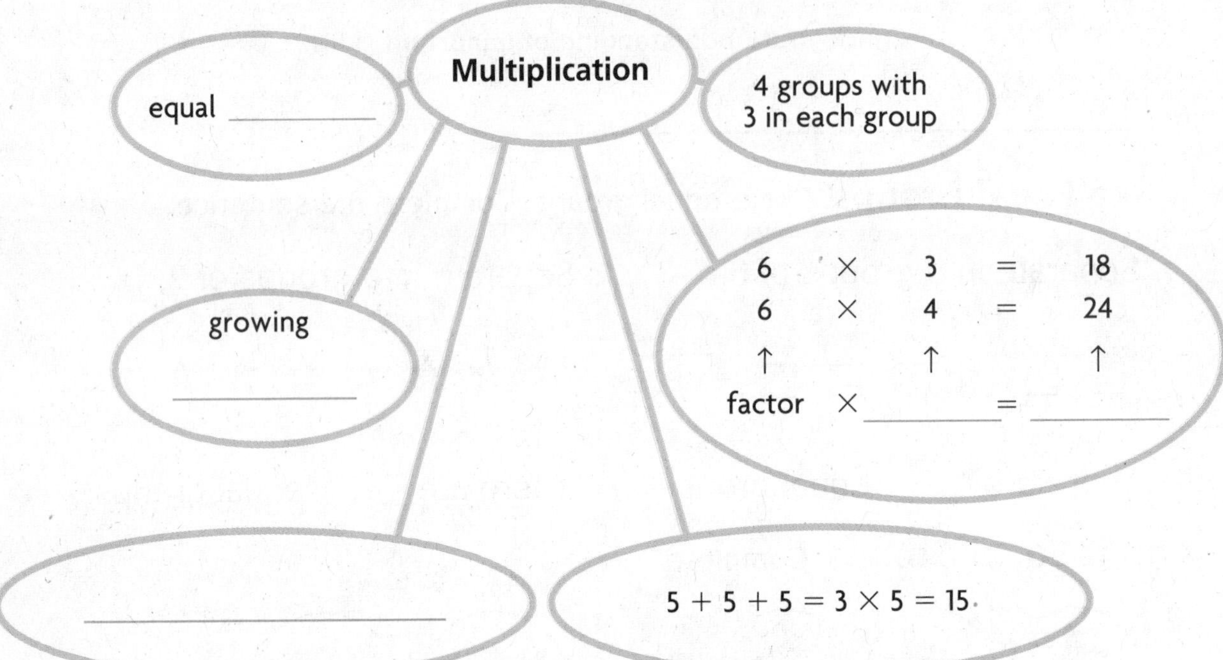

▶ Understand Vocabulary

Draw a line to match each word or term with its definition.

Preview Words	Definitions
1. dividend	A set of related multiplication and division number sentences
2. fact family	The number, not including the remainder, that results from division
3. quotient	The number that is to be divided in a division problem

Review Words

- equal groups
- factor
- patterns
- product
- repeated addition

Preview Words

- dividend
- fact family
- quotient

Name ______________________

Size of Equal Groups

Essential Question How can you model a division problem to find how many in each group?

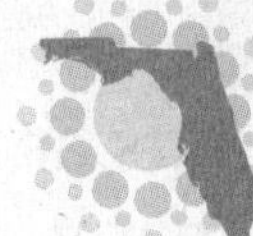

MA.3.A.1.1 Model multiplication and division including problems presented in context: repeated addition, multiplicative comparison, array, how many combinations, measurement, and partitioning.

UNLOCK the Problem REAL WORLD

William has 12 shells from Sanibel Island. He puts an equal number of his shells in each of 3 boxes. How many shells are in each box?

- What do you need to find?

____

- Circle the numbers you need to use.

When you multiply, you put equal groups together. When you **divide**, you separate into equal groups.

You can divide to find the number in each group.

Activity Use counters to model the problem.

Materials ■ counters ■ MathBoard

STEP 1

Use 12 counters.

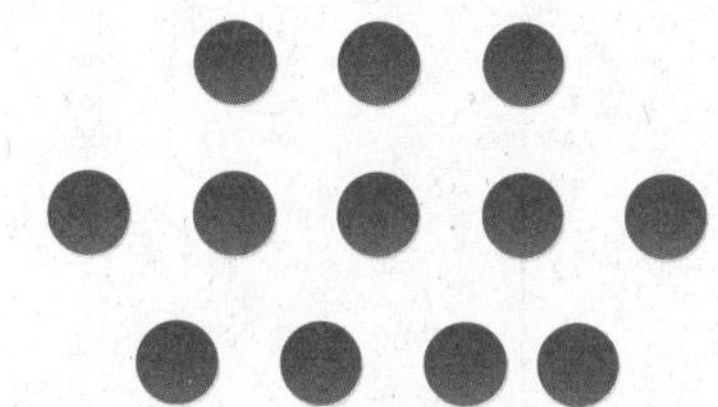

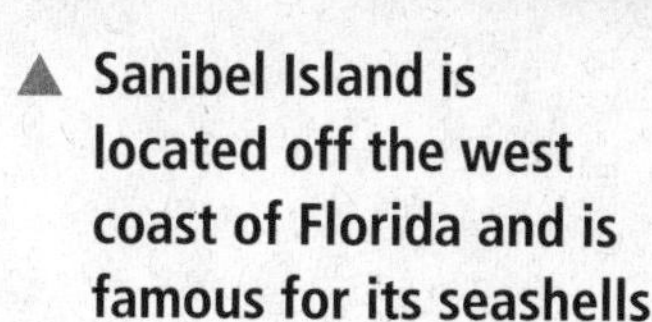

▲ Sanibel Island is located off the west coast of Florida and is famous for its seashells.

STEP 2

Draw 3 circles on your MathBoard. Place 1 counter at a time in each circle until all 12 counters are used. Draw the rest of the counters to show your work.

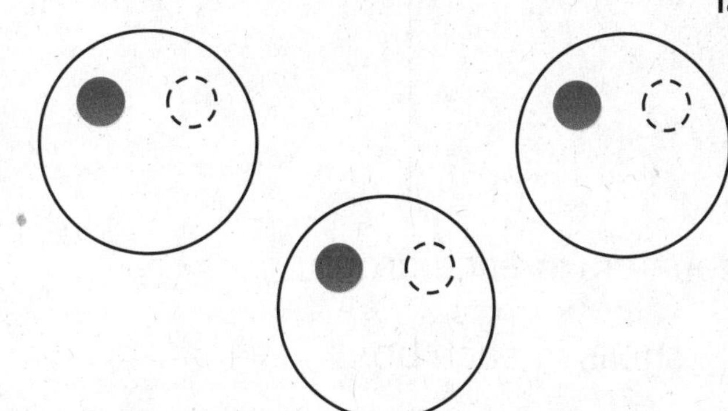

There are ______ counters in each group.

So, there are ______ shells in each box.

Try This!

Sarah has 15 shells. She puts an equal number of shells in each of 5 boxes. How many shells are in each box?

STEP 1

Draw 5 squares to show 5 boxes.

STEP 2

Draw 1 counter in each square to show the shells. Continue drawing 1 counter at a time until all 15 counters are drawn.

There are _____ counters in each group.

So, there are _____ shells in each box.

1. How many counters did you draw? _____
2. How many equal groups did you make? _____
3. How many counters are in each group? _____

Name ___________________________

Share and Show MATH BOARD

1. Jon has 8 counters. He makes 4 equal groups. Draw a picture to show the number of counters in each group.

Math Talk Explain how you know the groups are equal.

Use counters or draw a quick picture on your MathBoard. Make equal groups. Complete the table.

	Counters	Number of Equal Groups	Number in Each Group
✓ 2.	10	2	
✓ 3.	24	6	
4.	12	4	

On Your Own

Use counters or draw a quick picture on your MathBoard. Make equal groups. Complete the table.

	Counters	Number of Equal Groups	Number in Each Group
5.	14	7	
6.	21	3	
7.	20	5	
8.	12	6	
9.	36	9	

Problem Solving REAL WORLD

Use the table for 10–11.

Beach Photos	
Name	**Number of Photos**
Madison	28
Joe	25
Ella	15

10. Madison puts all of her photos in a photo album. She puts an equal number of photos on each of 4 pages in her album. How many photos are on each page?

____

11. H.O.T. Joe and Ella combine their photos. Then they put an equal number on each page of an 8-page photo album. How many photos are on each page?

____

12. Write Math Rebekah's family found 30 sand dollars. **Explain** how to divide the sand dollars equally among the 6 people in her family.

____

____

____

____

____

13. **Test Prep** Zana has 9 rocks from a trip. She puts an equal number of rocks in each of 3 bags. How many rocks are in each bag?

Ⓐ 27 Ⓒ 6

Ⓑ 12 Ⓓ 3

SHOW YOUR WORK

 FOR MORE PRACTICE: Florida Benchmarks Practice Book, pp. P113–P114

Name ______________________________

Number of Equal Groups

Essential Question How can you model a division problem to find how many equal groups?

MA.3.A.1.1 Model multiplication and division including problems presented in context: repeated addition, multiplicative comparison, array, how many combinations, measurement, and partitioning.

CONNECT You have learned how to divide to find the number in each group. Now you will learn how to divide to find the number of equal groups.

UNLOCK the Problem REAL WORLD

William has 12 shells and some boxes. He wants to put his shells in groups of 3. How many boxes does he need for his shells?

- Underline what you need to find.
- How many shells does William want in each group? ______

Draw to model the problem.

- Look at the 12 counters.
- Circle a group of 3 counters.
- Continue circling groups of 3 until all 12 counters are in groups.

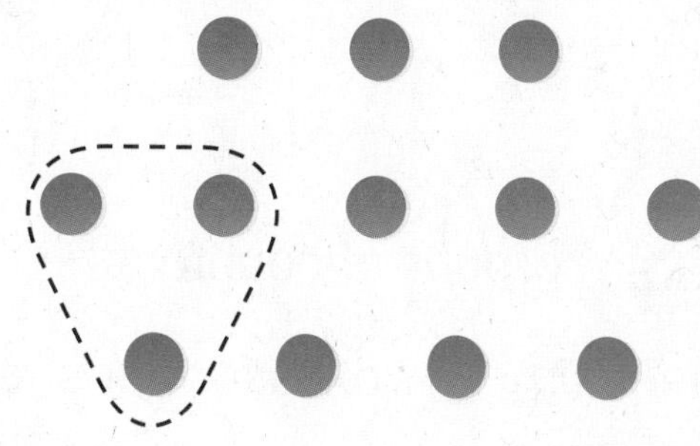

There are _____ groups of counters.

So, William needs _____ boxes for his shells.

Math Talk **Explain** how your drawing would look if William wanted to put his shells in groups of 4.

▲ The Florida horse conch can grow to a length of 24 inches!

Try This!

Sarah has 15 shells. She wants to put them in groups of 5. How many boxes does she need for her shells?

STEP 1

Draw 15 counters.

STEP 2

Make a group of 5 counters by drawing a circle around them. Continue circling groups of 5 until all 15 counters are in groups.

There are _____ groups of counters.

So, Sarah needs _____ boxes for her shells.

- **What if** Sarah wants to put her 15 shells in groups of 3?

How many boxes does she need? _____
Draw a quick picture to show your work.

Name ______________________________

Share and Show 

1. Emily has 12 counters. She puts them in groups of 2. Draw a picture to show the number of groups.

Math Talk **Explain** how you find the number of equal groups when you divide.

Draw counters on your MathBoard. Then circle equal groups. Complete the table.

	Counters	Number of Equal Groups	Number in Each Group
2.	20		4
3.	24		3
4.	18		2

On Your Own

Draw counters on your MathBoard. Then circle equal groups. Complete the table.

	Counters	Number of Equal Groups	Number in Each Group
5.	16		8
6.	25		5
7.	27		9
8.	32		4

UNLOCK the Problem

9. A store has 24 beach towels in stacks of 6 towels each. How many stacks of beach towels are at the store?

a. What do you need to find? ______________________

____

b. How will you use what you know about making equal groups to solve the problem? ______________________

____

c. Draw counters in groups to find how many towels are in each stack.

d. Complete the sentences.

The store has _____ beach towels.

There are _____ towels in each stack.

So, there are _____ stacks of beach towels at the store.

10. Some friends share 35 beach toys equally. If each friend gets 5 beach toys, how many friends are there?

____

11. **Test Prep** Dan puts 27 pebbles into groups of 3. How many groups of pebbles are there?

Ⓐ 9 Ⓒ 7

Ⓑ 8 Ⓓ 6

 FOR MORE PRACTICE: Florida Benchmarks Practice Book, pp. P115–P116

Name ____________________

Divide by 2

Essential Question What does dividing by 2 mean?

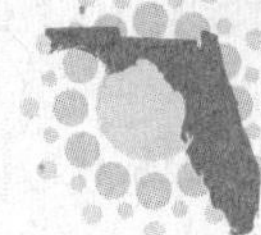

MA.3.A.1.1 Model multiplication and division including problems presented in context: repeated addition, multiplicative comparison, array, how many combinations, measurement, and partitioning.

UNLOCK the Problem — REAL WORLD

There are 10 hummingbirds and 2 feeders in Marissa's backyard. If there are an equal number of birds at each feeder, how many birds are at each one?

- What do you need to find?
  ____
- Circle the numbers you need to use.
- What can you use to help solve the problem? ____________________

Activity 1 Use counters to find how many in each group.

Materials ■ counters ■ MathBoard

- Use 10 counters.
- Draw 2 circles on your Math Board.
- Place 1 counter at a time in each circle until all 10 counters are used.
- Draw the rest of the counters to show your work.

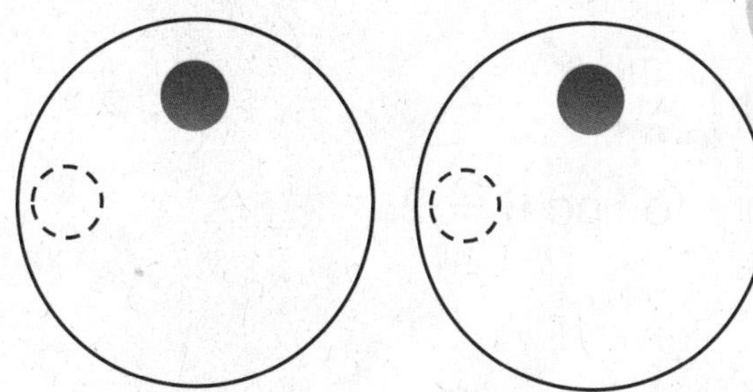

▲ **A hummingbird can beat its wings as many as 80 times per second and can fly at a speed of 25 miles per hour!**

There are _____ counters in each of the 2 groups.

So, there are _____ hummingbirds at each feeder.

Here are two ways to record dividing by 2.

10	÷	2	=	5
↑		↑		↑
dividend		**divisor**		**quotient**

$$\begin{array}{r} 5 \leftarrow \text{quotient} \\ \text{divisor} \rightarrow 2\overline{)10} \\ \uparrow \\ \text{dividend} \end{array}$$

Math Talk Is the number of hummingbirds at each feeder the dividend, the divisor, or the quotient?

Activity 2 Draw to find how many equal groups.

There are 10 hummingbirds in Tyler's backyard. If there are 2 hummingbirds at each feeder, how many feeders are there?

Math Idea

You can divide to find the number in each group or to find the number of equal groups.

- Look at the 10 counters.
- Circle a group of 2 counters.
- Continue circling groups of 2 until all 10 counters are in groups.

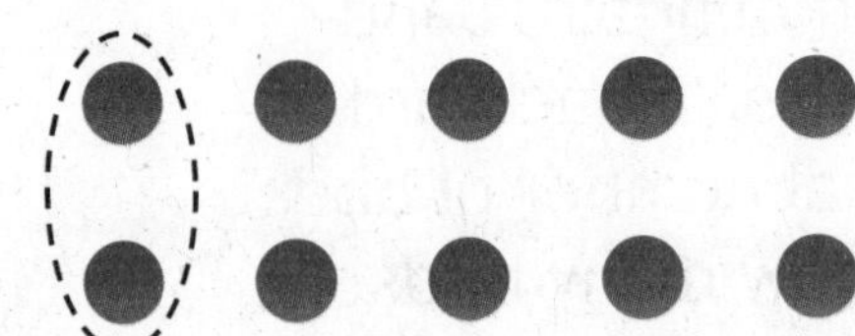

There are _____ groups of 2 counters.

So, there are _____ feeders.

Write: $10 \div 2 = 5$ or $2\overline{)10}$ with quotient 5

Read: Ten divided by two equals five.

Share and Show

1. Complete the picture to find $6 \div 2$. _____

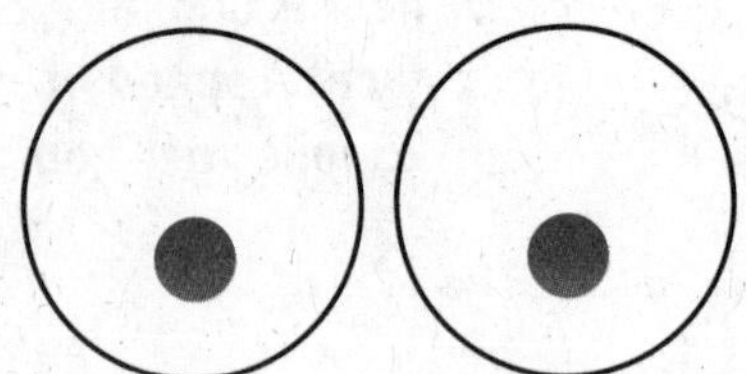

Math Talk Describe another division sentence that could be written for the picture you drew.

Write a division sentence for the picture.

2. 

_____

3. 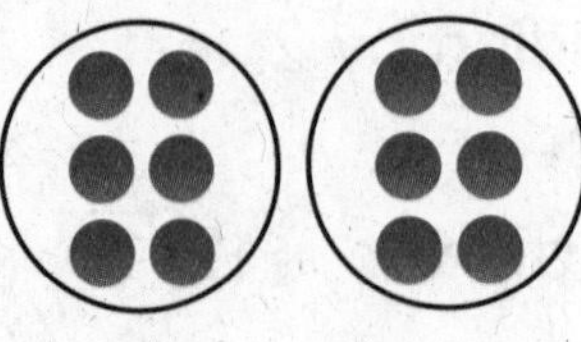

_____

4. 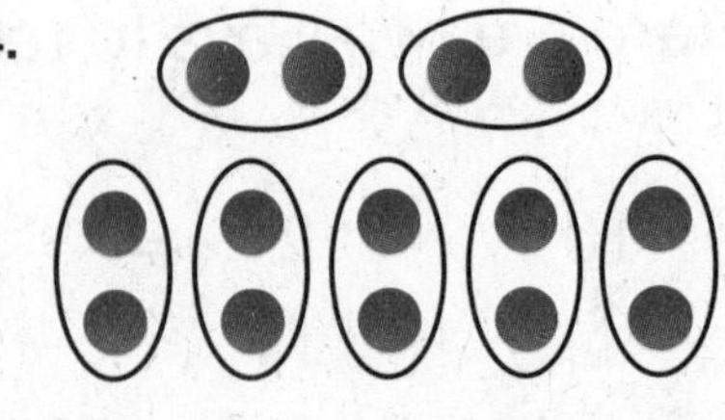

_____

Name ______________________

On Your Own

Write a division sentence for the picture.

5. 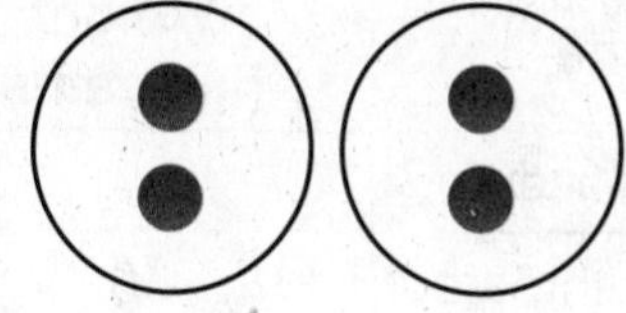

____

6. 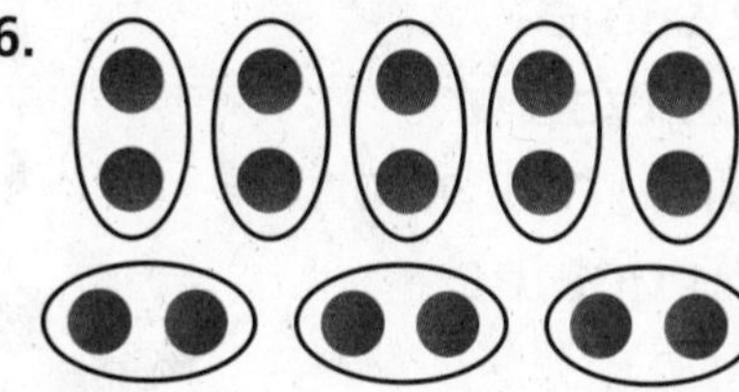

____

7. 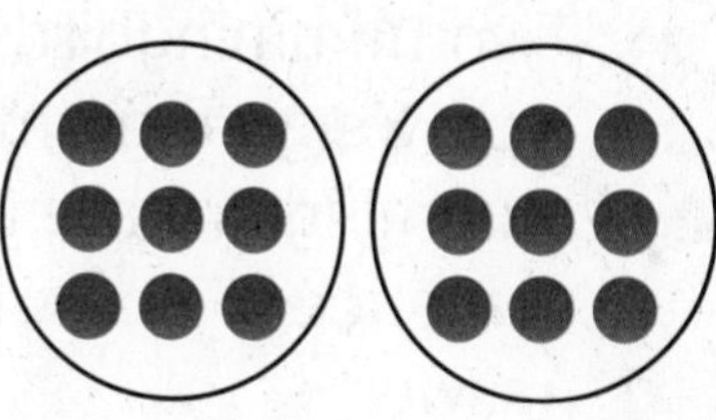

____

Find the quotient. You may want to draw a quick picture to help.

8. $6 \div 2 =$ ____

9. ____ $= 10 \div 2$

10. $2 \div 2 =$ ____

11. ____ $= 14 \div 2$

12. ____ $= 12 \div 2$

13. $16 \div 2 =$ ____

14. ____ $= 8 \div 2$

15. $4 \div 2 =$ ____

16. $2\overline{)8}$

17. $2\overline{)12}$

18. $2\overline{)18}$

19. $2\overline{)4}$

Algebra Complete.

20. ____ $\div 2 = 5$

21. ____ $\div 2 = 7$

22. ____ $\div 2 = 3$

23. ____ $\div 2 = 8$

Problem Solving REAL WORLD

Use the table for 24–25.

Type	Weight (in Grams)
Magnificent	7
Ruby-throated	3
Anna's	4

Hummingbirds

24. Two hummingbirds of the same type weigh 8 grams. Which type of hummingbird are they? Write a division sentence to show how you got the answer.

____

25. H.O.T. There are 3 Anna's hummingbirds and 2 of another type of hummingbird at a feeder. The birds have a weight of 26 grams in all. What other type of hummingbird is at the feeder? **Explain**.

____

SHOW YOUR WORK

26. Write Math ▸ There are 12 hummingbird eggs in all. If there are 2 eggs in each nest, how many nests are there? **Explain** how you found your answer.

____

27. **Test Prep** Jo sees the same number of birds each hour for 2 hours. She sees 16 birds in all. How many birds does Jo see each hour?

Ⓐ 6 Ⓑ 7  Ⓒ 8 Ⓓ 9

Name ________________________________

Divide by 5

Essential Question What does dividing by 5 mean?

MA.3.A.1.1 Model multiplication and division including problems presented in context: repeated addition, multiplicative comparison, array, how many combinations, measurement, and partitioning.

UNLOCK the Problem REAL WORLD

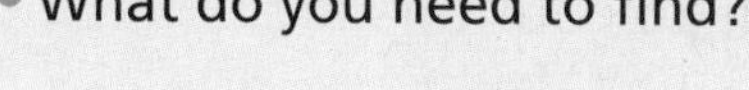

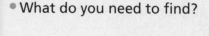

A dog trainer has 20 dog treats for 5 dogs in his class. If each dog gets the same number of treats, how many treats will each dog get?

- What do you need to find?

____

____

- Circle the numbers you need to use.

Activity 1 Use counters to find how many in each group.

Materials ■ counters ■ MathBoard

- Use 20 counters.
- Draw 5 circles on your Math Board.
- Place 1 counter at a time in each circle until all 20 counters are used.
- Draw the rest of the counters to show your work.

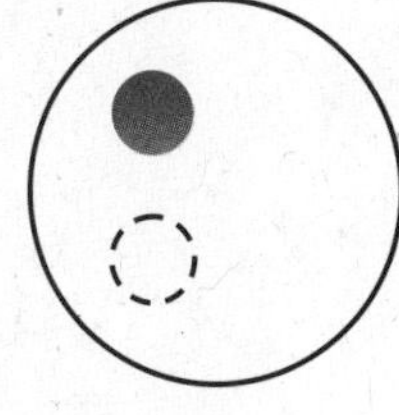 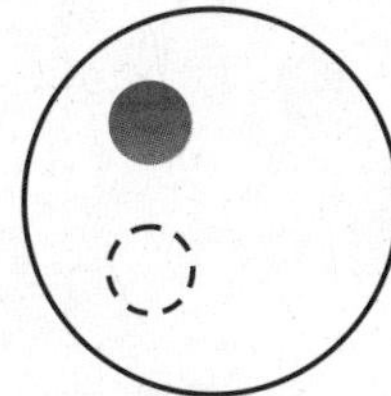 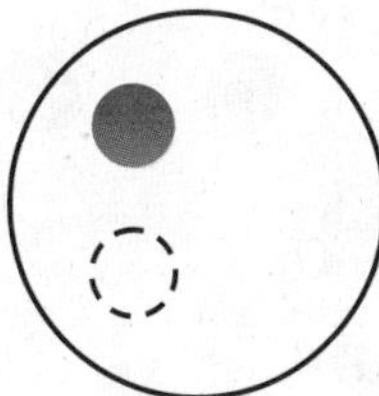 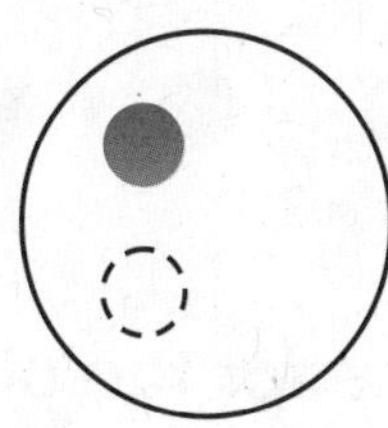 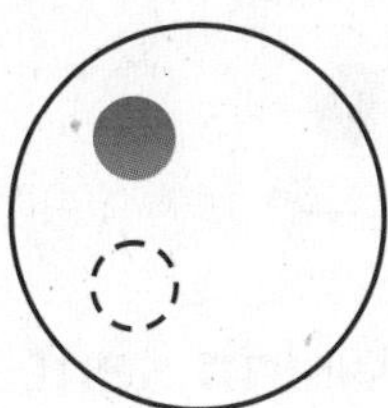

There are _____ counters in each of the 5 groups.

So, each dog will get _____ treats.

20	÷	5	=	4
↑		↑		↑
dividend		divisor		quotient

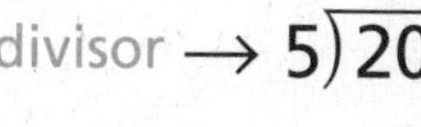

$$\begin{array}{r} 4 \\ 5\overline{)20} \end{array}$$

4 ← quotient

divisor → 5)20

↑

dividend

Activity 2 Draw to find how many equal groups.

A dog trainer has 20 dog treats. If he gives 5 treats to each dog in his class, how many dogs are in the class?

- Look at the 20 counters.
- Circle a group of 5 counters.
- Continue circling groups of 5 until all 20 counters are in groups.

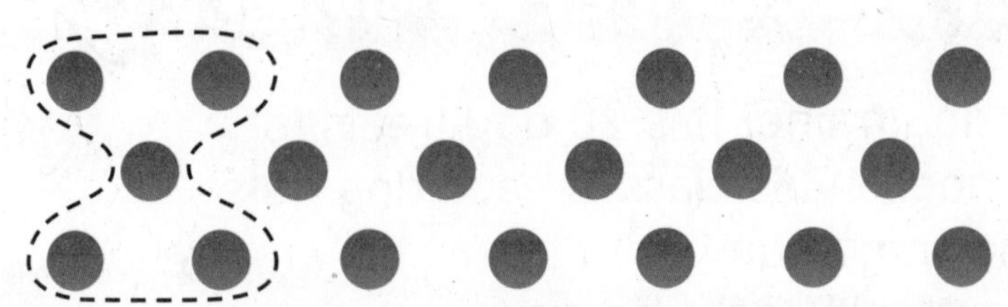

There are _____ groups of 5 counters.

So, there are _____ dogs in the class.

Share and Show

1. Complete the picture to find $25 \div 5$. _____

Math Talk Explain how you know how many groups to make.

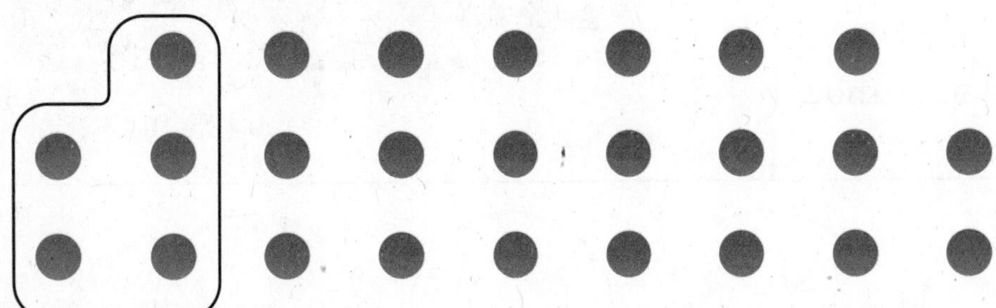

Write a division sentence for the picture.

2.

_____

3.

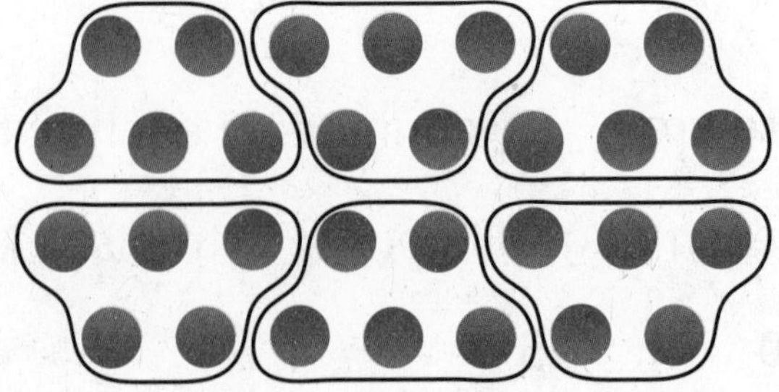

_____

Name ________________________________

On Your Own

Write a division sentence for the picture.

4. 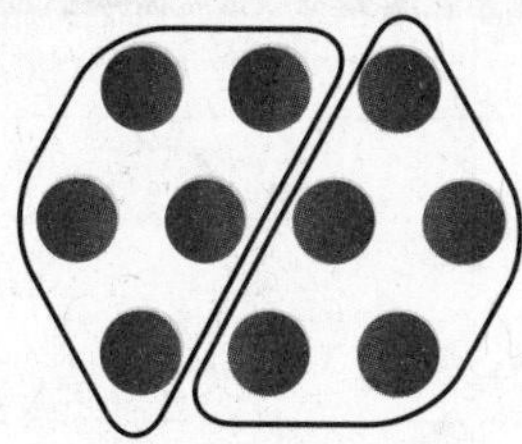

____

5. 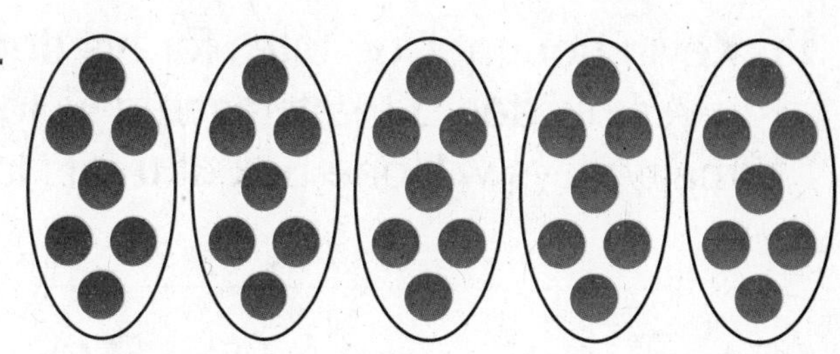

____

Find the quotient. You may want to draw a quick picture to help.

6. ____ $= 20 \div 5$

7. $5 \div 5 =$ ____

8. ____ $= 18 \div 2$

9. $45 \div 5 =$ ____

10. $35 \div 5 =$ ____

11. ____ $= 10 \div 5$

12. $40 \div 5 =$ ____

13. ____ $= 4 \div 2$

14. $5\overline{)30}$

15. $2\overline{)16}$

16. $5\overline{)45}$

17. $5\overline{)15}$

H.O.T. **Algebra** Complete the table.

18.

÷	6	8	10	12
2				

19.

÷	25	30	35	40
5				

Problem Solving REAL WORLD

Use the table for 20–22.

Dog Treats	
Type	**Number in Box**
Chew Sticks	14
Chewies	25
Dog Bites	30
Puppy Chips	45

20. Kevin bought Dog Bites for his dog. If he gives his dog 5 treats each day, for how many days will one box of treats last?

____

21. H.O.T. Pat bought one box of Chew Sticks for his 2 dogs. Mia bought one box of Chewies for her 5 dogs. How many more treats will each of Pat's dogs get than each of Mia's dogs? **Explain.**

____

____

____

____

____

22. Write Math ▶ Beth bought Puppy Chips and wants to give them all to the puppies she trains. If there are 5 puppies in her class, how many treats will each one get? **Explain** how you know.

____

____

____

____

23. **Test Prep** A pet store employee puts 15 dog leashes on hooks. If she puts 5 leashes on each hook, how many hooks does she use?

Ⓐ 2 Ⓑ 3 Ⓒ 4 Ⓓ 5

SHOW YOUR WORK

 FOR MORE PRACTICE:
Florida Benchmarks Practice Book, pp. P119–P120

Name ___________________________________

Mid-Chapter Checkpoint

▶ Check Vocabulary

Choose the best term from the box.

Vocabulary
divide
divisor
quotient

1. You __________ when you separate into equal groups. **(MA.3.A.1.1; p. 205)**

2. The number, not including the remainder, that results from division is the __________. **(MA.3.A.1.1; p. 213)**

▶ Check Concepts

Use counters or draw a quick picture on your MathBoard. Make equal groups. Complete the table.
(MA.3.A.1.1; pp. 205–208, 209–212)

	Counters	Number of Equal Groups	Number in Each Group
3.	6	2	
4.	30		5
5.	28	7	

Write a division sentence for the picture.
(MA.3.A.1.1; pp. 213–216, 217–220)

6. 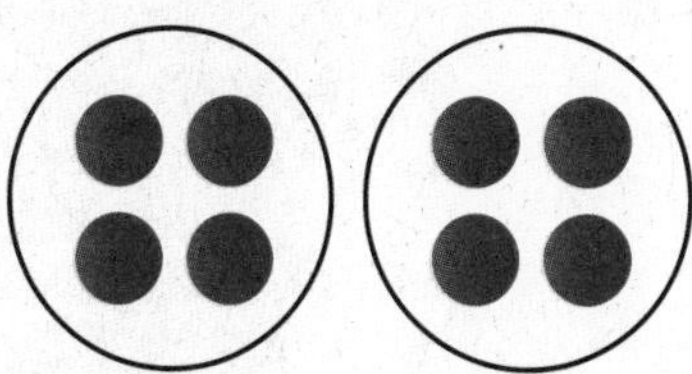

____

7. 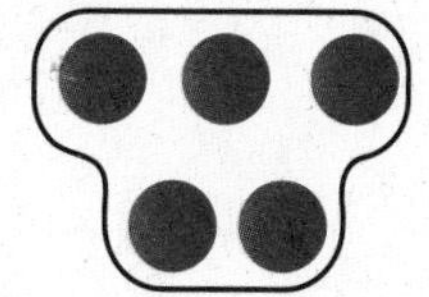 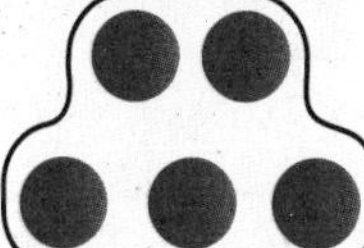 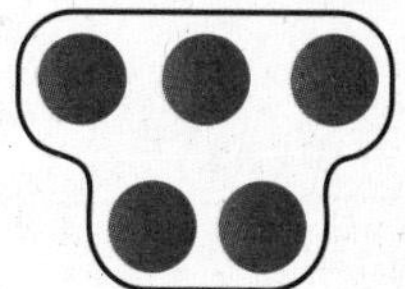

____

Find the quotient. You may want to draw a quick picture to help.

8. $12 \div 2 =$ _____

9. $2\overline{)16}$

10. _____ $= 45 \div 5$

11. $5\overline{)25}$

Fill in the bubble for the correct answer choice.

12. Adam plants 14 seeds in some flowerpots. If he puts 2 seeds in each pot, how many flowerpots does he use? **(MA.3.A.1.1; pp. 209–212)**

Ⓐ 7 Ⓒ 12

Ⓑ 8 Ⓓ 16

13. Desiree has 20 stickers. She gives them to 5 friends. If she gives the same number of stickers to each friend, which number sentence can be used to find the number of stickers each friend received? **(MA.3.A.1.1; pp. 217–220)**

Ⓕ $20 + 5 = \blacksquare$

Ⓖ $20 - 5 = \blacksquare$

Ⓗ $20 \times 5 = \blacksquare$

Ⓘ $20 \div 5 = \blacksquare$

14. Jayden modeled a division sentence with some counters. Which division sentence could he have modeled? **(MA.3.A.1.1; pp. 213–216)**

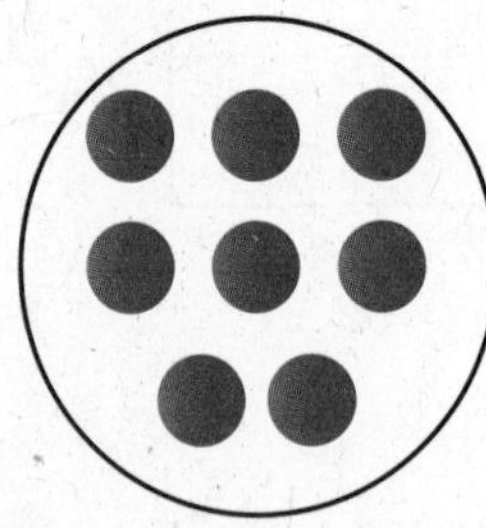
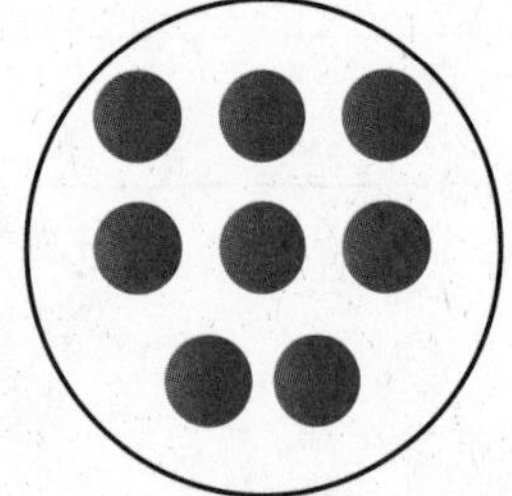

Ⓐ $12 \div 2 = 6$

Ⓑ $14 \div 2 = 7$

Ⓒ $16 \div 2 = 8$

Ⓓ $18 \div 2 = 9$

15. Lillian bought 24 cans of cat food. They came in packs of 4. How many packs of cat food did Lillian buy? **(MA.3.A.1.1; pp. 209–212)**

Ⓕ 5 Ⓗ 7

Ⓖ 6 Ⓘ 8

Name ______________________________

Division and Subtraction

Essential Question How is division related to subtraction?

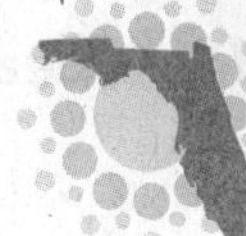

MA.3.A.1.1 Model multiplication and division including problems presented in context: repeated addition, multiplicative comparison, array, how many combinations, measurement, and partitioning.

UNLOCK the Problem REAL WORLD

Sarah and Mandy brought a total of 12 newspapers to school for the recycling program. Each girl brought in one newspaper each day. For how many days did the girls bring in newspapers?

- How many newspapers were brought in altogether? _____
- How many newspapers did the two girls bring in altogether each day? _____

One Way Count back on a number line.

- Start at 12.
- Count back by 2s as many times as you can. Draw the rest of the jumps on the number line.
- Count the number of times you jumped back by 2.

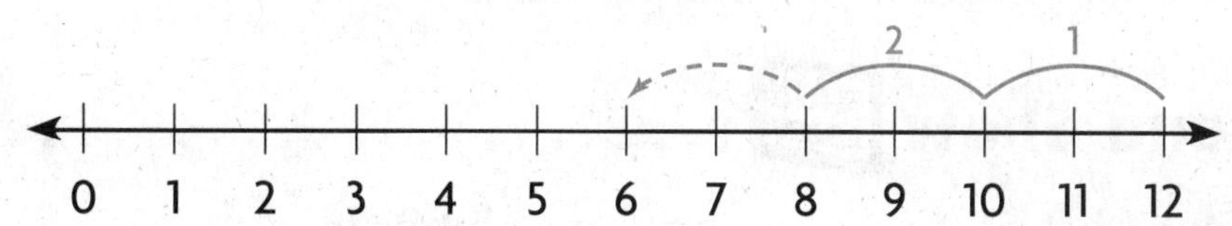

You jumped back by two 6 times, so Sarah and Mandy brought in newspapers for _____ days. $12 \div 2 =$ _____

Math Talk **Explain** in your own words how you found the answer.

- What do your jumps of 2 represent? ______________________________

____

Another Way Use repeated subtraction.

- Start with 12.
- Subtract 2 until you reach 0.
- Count the number of times you subtract 2.

12 − 2 = 10	10 − 2 = 8	8 − 2 = ___	6 − 2 = ___	4 − 2 = ___	2 − 2 = ___
Number of times you subtract 2: 1	2	3	4	5	6

Since you subtract two 6 times, there are ____ groups of 2 in 12.

ERROR Alert
Be sure to keep subtracting 2 until you are unable to subtract 2 anymore.

Write: $12 \div 2 = 6$ or $2\overline{)12}$ with 6 as the quotient

Read: Twelve divided by two equals six.

Share and Show

1. Draw the rest of the jumps on the number line to complete the division sentence. $12 \div 4 =$ ____

Math Talk **Explain** how to count back on a number line to divide.

Write a division sentence.

2.

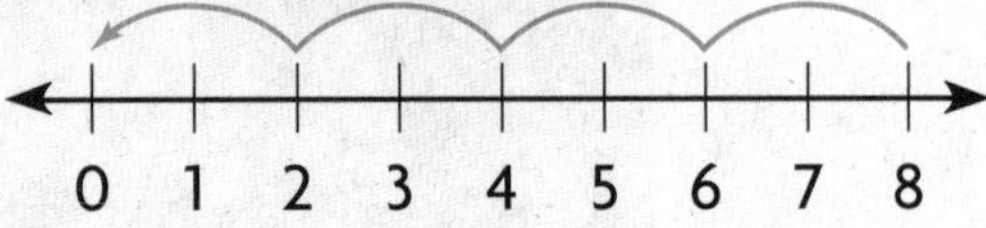

____

✓3. 10 − 5 = 5; 5 − 5 = 0

____

Use a number line or repeated subtraction to solve.

4. $16 \div 4 =$ ____

5. $3\overline{)21}$

6. $18 \div 9 =$ ____

✓7. $6\overline{)24}$

Name ______________________________

On Your Own

Write a division sentence.

8. 
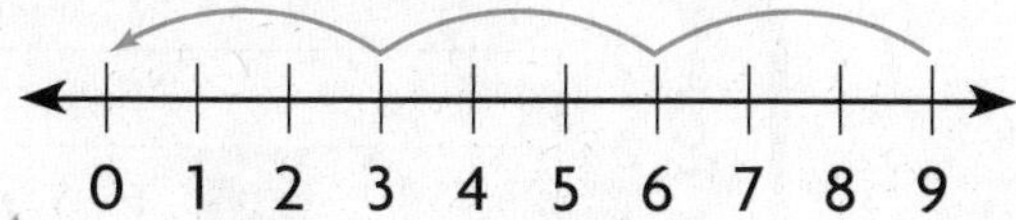

____

9. $\begin{array}{r} 28 \\ -\ 7 \\ \hline 21 \end{array} \rightarrow \begin{array}{r} 21 \\ -\ 7 \\ \hline 14 \end{array} \rightarrow \begin{array}{r} 14 \\ -\ 7 \\ \hline 7 \end{array} \rightarrow \begin{array}{r} 7 \\ -\ 7 \\ \hline 0 \end{array}$

____

10. 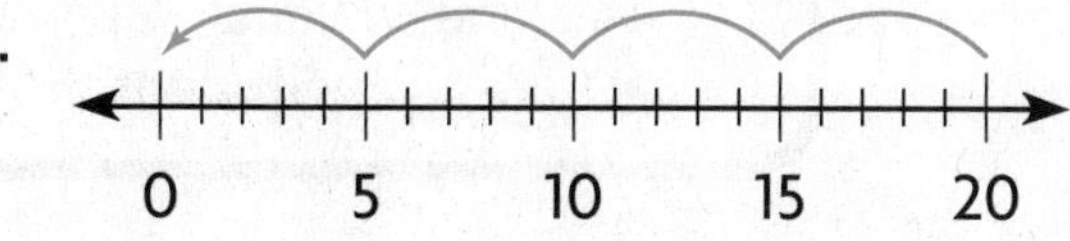

____

11. $\begin{array}{r} 24 \\ -\ 8 \\ \hline 16 \end{array} \rightarrow \begin{array}{r} 16 \\ -\ 8 \\ \hline 8 \end{array} \rightarrow \begin{array}{r} 8 \\ -\ 8 \\ \hline 0 \end{array}$

____

12. H.O.T. Write a word problem that can be solved by using one of the division problems above.

____

____

Use a number line or repeated subtraction to solve.

13. $18 \div 6 =$ ____

14. $14 \div 7 =$ ____

15. ____ $= 27 \div 9$

16. ____ $= 24 \div 3$

17. ____ $= 35 \div 5$

18. ____ $= 20 \div 4$

19. $16 \div 8 =$ ____

20. $6 \div 2 =$ ____

21. $3\overline{)12}$

22. $6\overline{)36}$

23. $2\overline{)18}$

24. $8\overline{)32}$

Problem Solving REAL WORLD

Use the graph for 25–27.

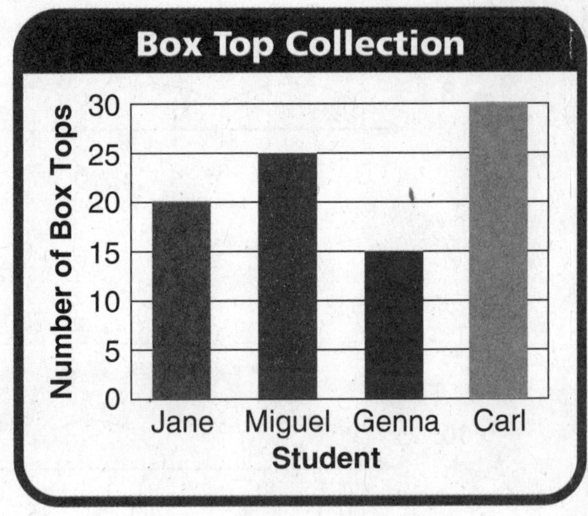

25. Carl puts his box tops in 6 equal piles. How many box tops are in each pile?

____

26. H.O.T. Miguel brought an equal number of box tops to school each day for 5 days. Jane also brought an equal number of box tops each day for 5 days. How many box tops did the two students bring in altogether each day? **Explain.**

____

____

____

____

27. Write Math ▶ **What's the Question?** Genna put an equal number of her box tops in each of 3 bins. The answer is 5. What's the question?

____

____

28. **Test Prep** Maya collected 7 shells each day. She collected 21 shells in all. For how many days did Maya collect shells?

Ⓐ 2 days Ⓒ 4 days

Ⓑ 3 days Ⓓ 6 days

SHOW YOUR WORK

FOR MORE PRACTICE:
Florida Benchmarks Practice Book, pp. P121–P122

Name ___

Model with Arrays

Essential Question How can you use arrays to solve division problems?

MA.3.A.1.1 Model multiplication and division including problems presented in context: repeated addition, multiplicative comparison, array, how many combinations, measurement, and partitioning.

Investigate

Materials ■ square tiles

You can use arrays to model division and find equal groups.

A. Count out 30 tiles. Make an array to find how many groups of 5 are in 30.

B. Make a row of 5 tiles.

C. Continue to make as many rows of 5 tiles as you can.

How many rows of 5 did you make? ___

Draw Conclusions

1. **Explain** how you used the tiles to find the number of rows of 5 in 30.

___

___

2. H.O.T. **Apply** Tell how to use an array to find how many rows of 6 are in 30.

___

___

Connect

You can write a division sentence to show how many rows of 5 are in 30. First, use your tiles to complete the array below.

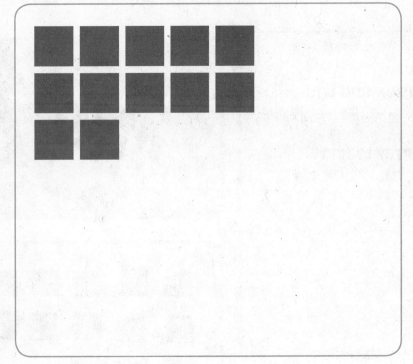

Math Talk **Explain** how making an array helps you divide.

There are ______ rows of 5 tiles in 30.

So, $30 \div 5 =$ ______.

Try This! Count out 24 tiles. Make an array by placing 6 tiles in each row until all of the tiles have been used. Draw your array below.

- How many rows of 6 are in 24? ______________
- What division sentence can you write for your array? ______________

Name ____________________

Share and Show 

Use square tiles to make an array. Solve.

1. How many rows of 3 are in 18? ____

✓2. How many rows of 6 are in 12? ____

3. How many rows of 7 are in 21? ____

4. How many rows of 8 are in 32? ____

Make an array. Then write a division sentence.

5. 25 tiles in 5 rows ____________

✓6. 14 tiles in 2 rows ____________

7. 24 tiles in 4 rows ____________

8. 27 tiles in 9 rows ____________

9. 15 tiles in 3 rows ____________

10. 24 tiles in 8 rows ____________

Math Talk **Explain** when you count the number of rows to get the answer and when you count the number of tiles in each row to get the answer.

11. **Write Math** ▶ **Explain** two ways you could make an array with tiles for 18 ÷ 6.

____

____

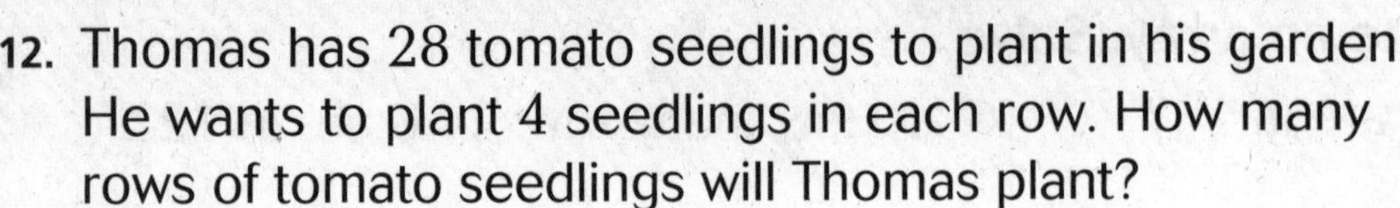

TEST PREP

12. Thomas has 28 tomato seedlings to plant in his garden. He wants to plant 4 seedlings in each row. How many rows of tomato seedlings will Thomas plant?

Ⓐ 5 Ⓑ 6 Ⓒ 7 Ⓓ 8

a. What do you need to find? ____________________

____

b. How will you use an array to solve the problem? ____________________

____

c. Draw an array to find the number of rows of tomato seedlings.

d. What is another way you could have solved the problem?

____

____

e. Complete the sentences.

Thomas has __________ tomato seedlings.

He wants to plant __________

seedlings in each __________.

So, Thomas will plant __________ rows of tomato seedlings.

f. Fill in the bubble for the correct answer choice above.

13. Faith plants 12 flowers in groups of 3. How many groups of flowers does she plant?

Ⓕ 15 Ⓖ 9 Ⓗ 5 Ⓘ 4

14. A store sold 20 red flowerpots on Saturday. The customers bought 5 pots each. How many customers bought the red flowerpots?

Ⓐ 3 Ⓑ 4 Ⓒ 5 Ⓓ 6

FOR MORE PRACTICE:
Florida Benchmarks Practice Book, pp. P123–P124

Name ______________________________

Use Manipulatives · Division

Essential Question How can you use manipulatives to solve problems?

MA.3.A.1.1 Model multiplication and division including problems presented in context: repeated addition, multiplicative comparison, array, how many combinations, measurement, and partitioning.

UNLOCK the Problem — REAL WORLD

Stacy has 16 flowers. She puts an equal number of flowers in each of 4 vases. How many flowers does Stacy put in each vase?

Use the graphic organizer below to solve the problem.

Read the Problem

What do I need to find?

I need to find the number of ________ Stacy puts in each ________.

What information do I need to use?

Stacy has ______ flowers. She puts an equal number of flowers in each of ______ vases.

How will I use the information?

I will use manipulatives and act out the problem by making equal ________ with counters.

Solve the Problem

Describe how to use manipulatives to solve.

First, count out ______ counters.

Next, make ______ groups. Place 1 counter in each group until all 16 counters are used.

Last, draw the equal groups by completing the picture below.

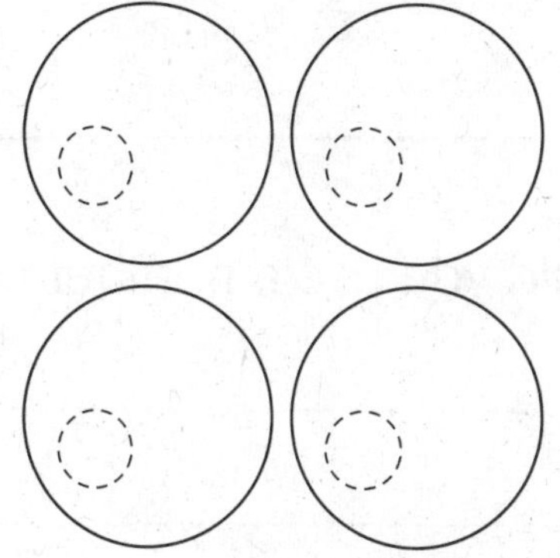

Stacy puts ______ flowers in each vase.

Try Another Problem

Hayden is planning a party. He bakes 21 cookies. If he plans to give each person 3 cookies, how many people will be at his party?

Read the Problem	Solve the Problem
What do I need to find?	**Describe how to use manipulatives to solve the problem.**
What information do I need to use?	
How will I use the information?	

- How could you use a number line to solve the problem? ______________________________

____

____

Math Talk **Explain** another way you could solve the problem.

Name ______________________________

Share and Show 

1. Jamie is having a party. She has 16 cups. She puts them in 2 equal stacks. How many cups are in each stack?

   First, decide which manipulatives to use to solve the problem.

   You can use counters to represent the ________.

   You can draw ________ to represent the stacks.

   Then, draw to find the number of ________ in each stack.

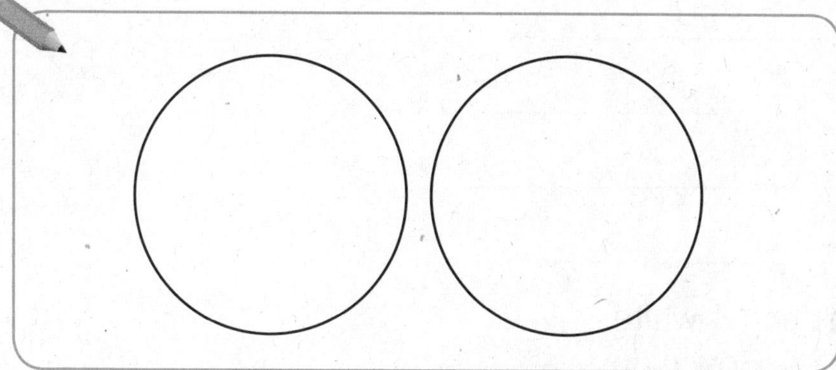

$16 \div 2 =$ ______

So, there are ______ cups in each stack.

2. **H.O.T. What if** Jamie makes 8 equal stacks of cups? How many cups would be in each stack? Use what you know from Problem 1 to solve.

   ____

3. At Luke's school party, the children get into teams to play a game. If there are 35 children and they make teams of 5, how many teams are there?

   ____

4. Anne put 20 cupcakes on 4 plates. If she put the same number of cupcakes on each one, how many cupcakes did she put on each plate?

   ____

Choose a STRATEGY

- Act It Out
- Use Manipulatives
- Draw a Diagram
- Make a Table, Chart, or List
- Search for Patterns

SHOW YOUR WORK

On Your Own

Use the table for 5–6.

Sadie's Party Supplies	
Item	**Number**
Plates	26
Napkins	28
Cups	24

5. Sadie's plates came in packages of 5. How many packages of plates did she have to buy so she would have 26 plates?

6. Write Math Sadie bought 4 packages of napkins and 3 packages of cups. She did not have any of these items left over. Which item had more in each package? How many more? **Explain** how you found your answer.

SHOW YOUR WORK

7. Megan put 3 red balloons and 4 white balloons at each of 4 tables. How many balloons are at the tables altogether?

8. H.O.T. There are 12 cookies on a plate. How many different numbers of students could share them equally without breaking any of the cookies?

9. **Test Prep** Miguel bought 18 party favors. He gave 2 party favors to each of the children at his party. How many children were at Miguel's party?

Ⓐ 20 Ⓑ 16 Ⓒ 9 Ⓓ 8

FOR MORE PRACTICE:
Florida Benchmarks Practice Book, pp. P125–P126

Name ____________________

Multiplication and Division

Essential Question How can you use multiplication to divide?

MA.3.A.1.3 Identify, describe, and apply division and multiplication as inverse operations.

UNLOCK the Problem REAL WORLD

Mark went to a carnival. He went on the same ride 4 times and used 12 tickets. How many tickets did he use each time he went on the ride?

- What do you need to find?

____

____

- Circle the numbers you need to use.

One Way Use arrays.

You can use arrays to understand how multiplication and division are related.

- Show an array with 12 counters in 4 equal rows by completing the drawing.
- Find how many counters are in each row.

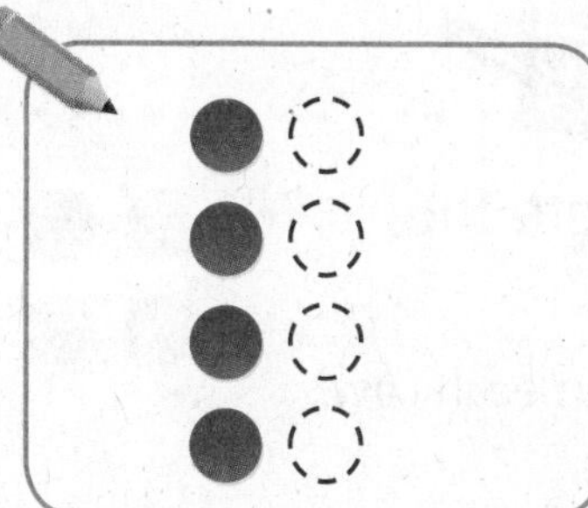

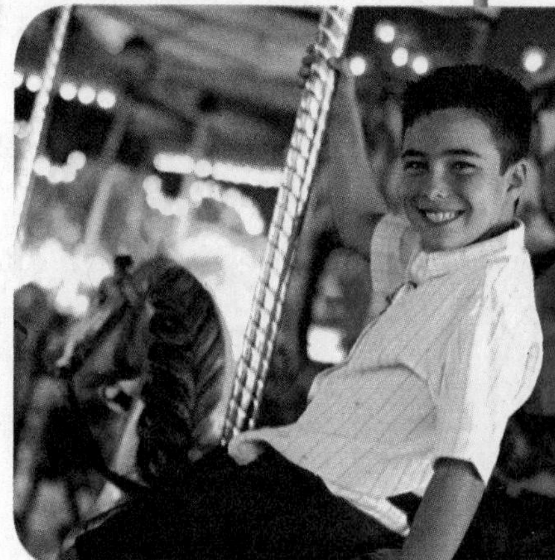

There are ______ counters in each row.

So, Mark used ______ tickets each time he went on the ride.

Since $4 \times 3 = 12$, then $12 \div 4 = 3$.

Multiplication and division are opposite operations, or **inverse operations**.

Try This! Draw an array with 8 counters in 2 equal rows. Then use your array to find $8 \div 2$.

$8 \div 2 =$ ______

Another Way Use a multiplication table.

Since division is the opposite of multiplication, you can use a multiplication table to find a quotient.

Think of a related multiplication fact.

Think: $4 \times \blacksquare = 12$

- Find the row for the factor, 4.
- Look right to find the product, 12.
- Look up to find the missing factor, _____.

Since $4 \times$ _____ $= 12$, then $12 \div 4 =$ _____.

×	0	1	2	3	4	5	6	7	8	9
0	0	0	0	0	0	0	0	0	0	0
1	0	1	2	3	4	5	6	7	8	9
2	0	2	4	6	8	10	12	14	16	18
3	0	3	6	9	12	15	18	21	24	27
4	0	4	8	12	16	20	24	28	32	36
5	0	5	10	15	20	25	30	35	40	45
6	0	6	12	18	24	30	36	42	48	54
7	0	7	14	21	28	35	42	49	56	63
8	0	8	16	24	32	40	48	56	64	72
9	0	9	18	27	36	45	54	63	72	81

Share and Show

1. Use the array to complete the number sentence.

Think: There are 3 counters in each row.

$6 \div 2 =$ _____

Math Talk **Explain** how you could use a multiplication table to find the quotient for $6 \div 2$.

Complete.

2.

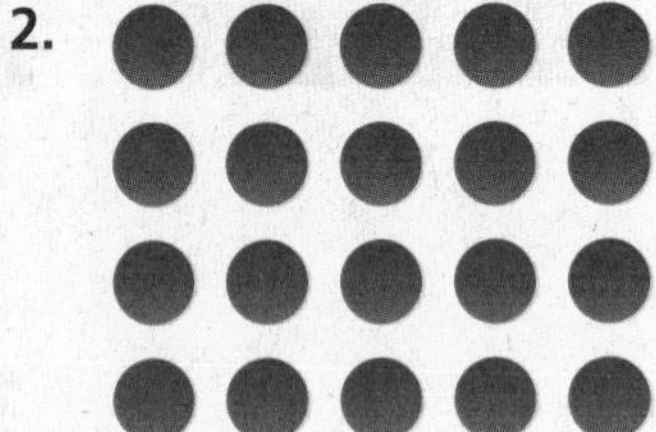

4 rows of _____ $= 20$

$20 \div 4 =$ _____

3.

2 rows of _____ $= 12$

$12 \div 2 =$ _____

✓ 4.

3 rows of _____ $= 21$

$21 \div 3 =$ _____

Complete the number sentences. Use a multiplication table or draw an array to help.

5. $5 \times$ _____ $= 40$ $40 \div 5 =$ _____

✓ 6. $6 \times$ _____ $= 18$ $18 \div 6 =$ _____

Name ____________________

On Your Own

Complete.

7. ●●●●●● / ●●●●●● / ●●●●●● / ●●●●●● / ●●●●●●

5 rows of _____ = 30

30 ÷ 5 = _____

8. ●●●●● / ●●●●● / ●●●●●

3 rows of _____ = 15

15 ÷ 3 = _____

9. ●●●●●●● / ●●●●●●● / ●●●●●●● / ●●●●●●●

4 rows of _____ = 28

28 ÷ 4 = _____

Complete the number sentences. Use a multiplication table or draw an array to help.

10. $7 \times$ _____ $= 21$ $21 \div 7 =$ _____

11. $8 \times$ _____ $= 16$ $16 \div 8 =$ _____

12. $4 \times$ _____ $= 32$ $32 \div 4 =$ _____

13. $6 \times$ _____ $= 24$ $24 \div 6 =$ _____

14. $9 \times$ _____ $= 18$ $18 \div 9 =$ _____

15. $5 \times$ _____ $= 25$ $25 \div 5 =$ _____

16. $6 \times$ _____ $= 42$ $42 \div 6 =$ _____

17. $7 \times$ _____ $= 35$ $35 \div 7 =$ _____

Algebra Complete.

18. $3 \times 3 = 27 \div$ _____

19. $16 \div 2 =$ _____ $\times 2$

20. $30 \div$ _____ $= 2 \times 3$

Problem Solving REAL WORLD

Use the signs for 21–23.

21. Garrett bought 8 tickets for the Wildcat ride 3 different times. How many times did Garrett ride the Wildcat?

____

22. Jack rode the Scooter 3 times, and Kate rode the Crazy Sub 4 times. Who used more tickets? How many more?

____

23. H.O.T. **Sense or Nonsense?** Scott has 13 tickets. He says that to ride the Scooter 4 times, he needs more tickets. Is he correct? **Explain.**

____

24. H.O.T. **Pose a Problem** Ms. Summers bought 7 tickets for each of her 2 children. How many tickets did she buy in all? Write a related word problem to represent the inverse operation.

____

25. **Test Prep** At a game booth, there are 35 prizes in 5 equal rows. How many prizes are in each row?

Ⓐ 6 Ⓑ 7 Ⓒ 8 Ⓓ 9

SHOW YOUR WORK

FOR MORE PRACTICE: Florida Benchmarks Practice Book, pp. P127–P128

Name ___________________________

Fact Families

Essential Question How do fact families relate multiplication and division?

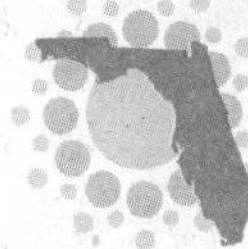

MA.3.A.1.3 Identify, describe, and apply division and multiplication as inverse operations.

UNLOCK the Problem

A set of related multiplication and division number sentences is called a **fact family**. What related number sentences can you write for 2, 5, and 10?

- What do you need to find?

  ____

- What can you make to model a fact family?

  ____

Activity

Materials ■ square tiles

STEP 1

Make an array with 2 rows of 5 tiles. Draw the rest of the tiles. Then count the total number of tiles.

There are _____ tiles.

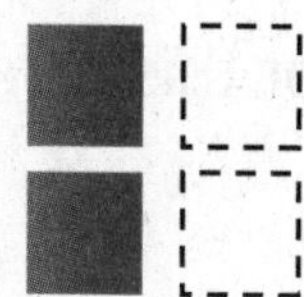

STEP 2

Now make an array with 5 rows of 2 tiles.

Draw the rest of the tiles.

Then count the total number of tiles.

There are _____ tiles.

STEP 3

Write two multiplication sentences and two division sentences that describe the arrays.

$2 \times 5 =$ _____ $10 \div 5 =$ _____

$5 \times 2 =$ _____ $10 \div 2 =$ _____

So, these related number sentences make up a fact family.

Try This! **Draw an array with 4 rows of 4 tiles.**

Your array shows the fact family for 4, 4, and 16.

$4 \times 4 =$ ______ $16 \div 4 =$ ______

Since both factors are the same, there are only two number sentences in this fact family.

- Write another fact family that has only two number sentences.

____

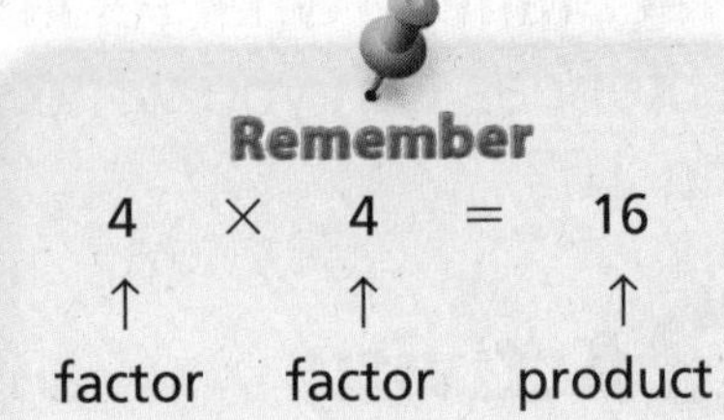

Share and Show

1. Complete the fact family for this array.

$2 \times 8 = 16$ $16 \div 2 = 8$

______ ______

Math Talk Do fact families always include inverse operations? **Explain.**

Write the fact family for the array.

2. 

______
______
______
______

3. 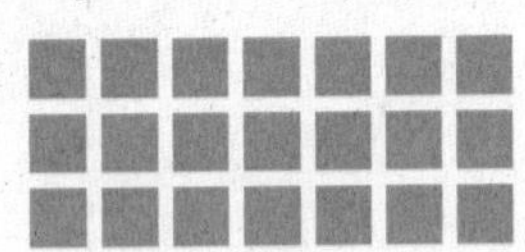

______
______
______
______

4. 

______
______
______
______

5. Why does the fact family for the array in Problem 2 have only two number sentences?

____

Name ______________________________

On Your Own

Write the fact family for the array.

6. 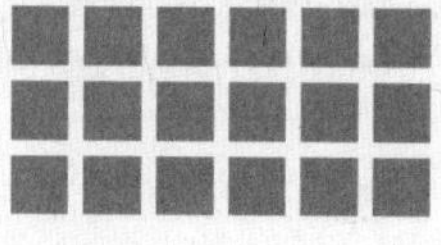

____

____

____

____

7. 

____

____

____

____

8. 

____

____

____

____

Complete the fact family.

9. 4 × 7 = ____

7 × ____ = 28

28 ÷ ____ = 4

28 ÷ 4 = ____

10. 5 × ____ = 30

6 × ____ = 30

30 ÷ 6 = ____

30 ÷ 5 = ____

11. ____ × 9 = 27

____ × 3 = 27

____ ÷ 9 = 3

27 ÷ ____ = 9

Write the fact family for the set of numbers.

12. 2, 4, 8

____

____

____

____

13. 3, 8, 24

____

____

____

____

14. 6, 6, 36

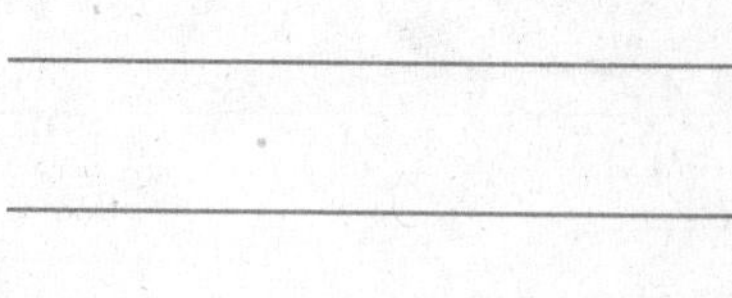

____

____

____

____

15. 4, 5, 20

____

____

____

____

16. 2, 6, 12

____

____

____

____

17. 5, 8, 40

____

____

____

____

Problem Solving REAL WORLD

Use the table for 18–19.

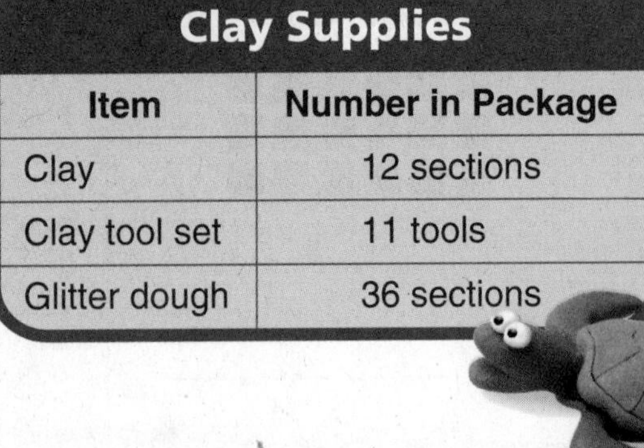

Clay Supplies

Item	Number in Package
Clay	12 sections
Clay tool set	11 tools
Glitter dough	36 sections

18. Mr. Lee divides 1 package of clay and 1 package of glitter dough equally among 4 students. How many more glitter dough sections than clay sections does each student get?

SHOW YOUR WORK

19. H.O.T. **What's the Error?** Ty has a package of glitter dough. He says he can give 9 friends 5 equal sections. Describe his error.

20. H.O.T. **Pose a Problem** Write a word problem that can be solved by using $35 \div 5$. Solve your problem.

21. **Test Prep** Which number sentence is NOT included in the same fact family as $9 \times 4 = 36$?

Ⓐ $4 \times 9 = 36$

Ⓑ $36 \div 6 = 6$

Ⓒ $36 \div 4 = 9$

Ⓓ $36 \div 9 = 4$

FOR MORE PRACTICE:
Florida Benchmarks Practice Book, pp. P129–P130

Name ______________________________

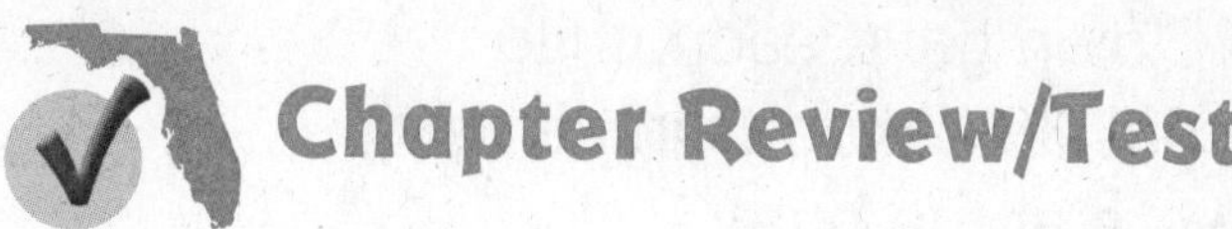

Check Vocabulary

Choose the best term from the box.

Vocabulary
dividend
fact family
inverse operations

1. Multiplication and division are opposite operations, or ______________. (MA.3.A.1.3; p. 235)
2. A set of related multiplication and division number sentences is called a ______________. (MA.3.A.1.3; p. 239)

Check Concepts

Find the quotient. You may want to draw a quick picture to help. (MA.3.A.1.1; pp. 213–216, 217–220)

3. $4 \div 2 =$ ____

4. $2\overline{)18}$

5. ____ $= 35 \div 5$

6. $5\overline{)10}$

Complete the number sentences. Use a multiplication table or draw an array to help. (MA.3.A.1.3; pp. 235–238)

7. $3 \times$ ____ $= 24$ $24 \div 3 =$ ____

8. $5 \times$ ____ $= 15$ $15 \div 5 =$ ____

Write the fact family for the set of numbers. (MA.3.A.1.3; pp. 239–242)

9. 4, 8, 32
____
____
____
____

10. 3, 3, 9
____
____
____
____

11. 6, 7, 42
____
____
____
____

Go online Assessment Options
Chapter Test

Fill in the bubble for the correct answer choice.

12. At a party, Claire the Clown gave each child 4 balloons. She gave out 36 balloons in all. How many children were at the party? (MA.3.A.1.1; pp. 209–212)

Ⓐ 6

Ⓑ 7

Ⓒ 8

Ⓓ 9

13. Leo divided 20 cookies equally among 5 friends. How many cookies did each friend get? (MA.3.A.1.1; pp. 217–220)

Ⓕ 4

Ⓖ 5

Ⓗ 15

Ⓘ 25

14. Caroline has 27 books. She put an equal number of her books on each of 3 shelves. How many books are on each shelf? (MA.3.A.1.1; pp. 227–230)

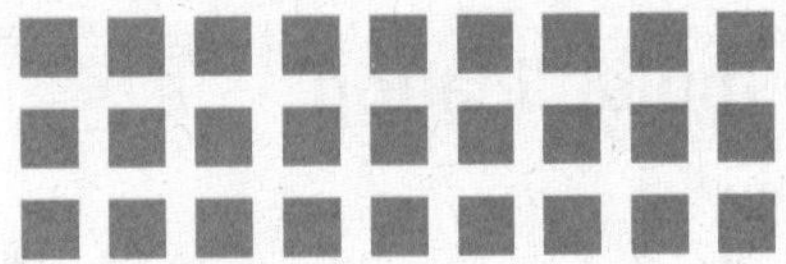

Ⓐ 7 Ⓒ 9

Ⓑ 8 Ⓓ 10

15. Aidan bought 12 goldfish and 2 fishbowls. He put an equal number of fish in each bowl. Which number sentence can be used to find how many goldfish are in each fishbowl? (MA.3.A.1.1; pp. 213–216)

Ⓕ $12 - 2 = \blacksquare$

Ⓖ $2 + \blacksquare = 12$

Ⓗ $12 \div 2 = \blacksquare$

Ⓘ $2 \times 12 = \blacksquare$

Name ______________________________

Fill in the bubble for the correct answer choice.

16. Which division sentence belongs to this fact family? **(MA.3.A.1.3; pp. 239–242)**

$4 \times 6 = 24$ $6 \times 4 = 24$

Ⓐ $20 \div 4 = 5$

Ⓑ $24 \div 6 = 4$

Ⓒ $18 \div 6 = 3$

Ⓓ $24 \div 3 = 8$

17. Jasmine made some cards for her family. She used 16 stickers and put 4 of them on each card. How many cards did Jasmine make? **(MA.3.A.1.1; pp. 223–226)**

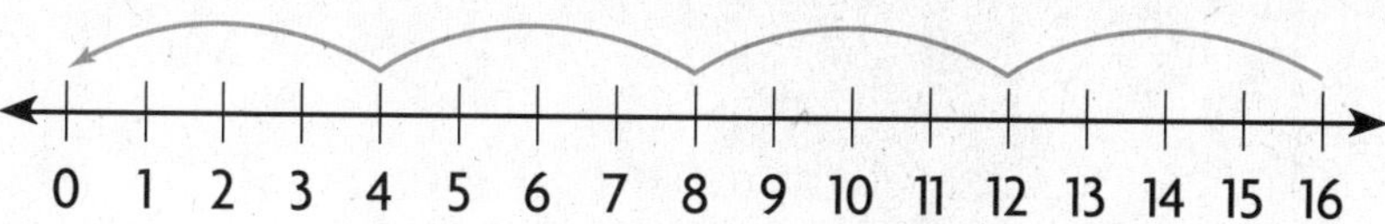

Ⓕ 2 Ⓗ 4

Ⓖ 3 Ⓘ 5

18. Which of the following multiplication sentences can be used to find $42 \div 7$? **(MA.3.A.1.3; pp. 235–238)**

Ⓐ $6 \times 6 = 36$

Ⓑ $5 \times 8 = 40$

Ⓒ $8 \times 6 = 48$

Ⓓ $7 \times 6 = 42$

19. Mr. Jacobs gave 32 summer reading books to 8 students. He divided them equally among the students. How many books did each student get? **(MA.3.A.1.1; pp. 205–208)**

Ⓕ 4

Ⓖ 5

Ⓗ 24

Ⓘ 40

20. Brendan bought 30 baseball cards. They came in packs of 6. How many packs of baseball cards did Brendan buy? **(MA.3.A.1.1; pp. 209–212)**

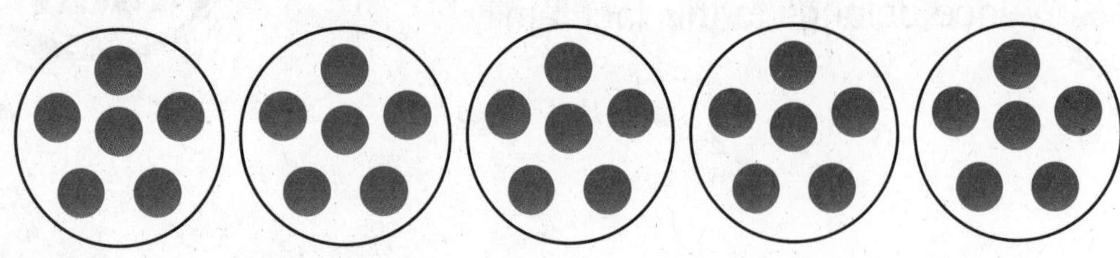

Ⓐ 3

Ⓑ 4

Ⓒ 5

Ⓓ 6

21. Which multiplication fact is related to this division fact? **(MA.3.A.1.3; pp. 235–238)**

$$18 \div 9 = 2$$

Ⓕ $9 \times 2 = 18$

Ⓖ $2 \times 8 = 16$

Ⓗ $9 \times 3 = 27$

Ⓘ $3 \times 6 = 18$

22. Amelia made 3 pizzas. She has 21 mushrooms to put on the pizzas. She wants to put the same number of mushrooms on each pizza. Which number sentence shows how many mushrooms will go on each pizza?

(MA.3.A.1.1; pp. 205–208)

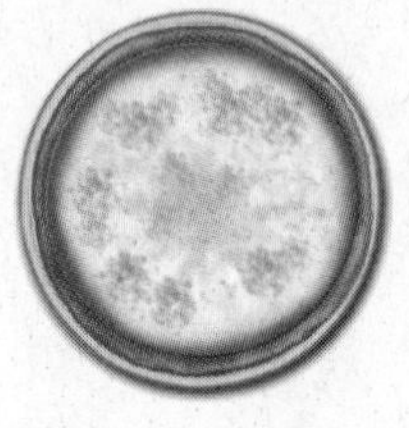 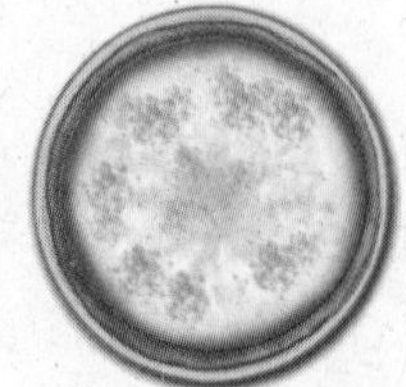 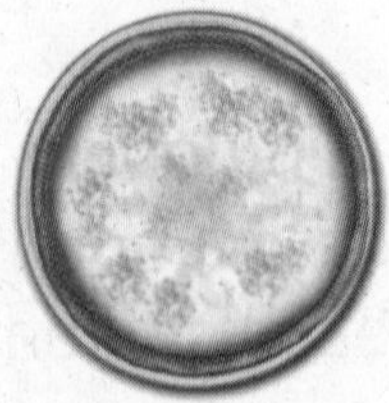

Ⓐ $21 - 3 = 18$

Ⓑ $21 + 3 = 24$

Ⓒ $21 \times 3 = 63$

Ⓓ $21 \div 3 = 7$

Chapter 6

Division Facts and Strategies

Show What You Know

Check your understanding of important skills.

Name ______________________________

▶ Equal Groups **Draw to make equal groups. Complete.**

1. Divide 6 counters into 2 equal groups.

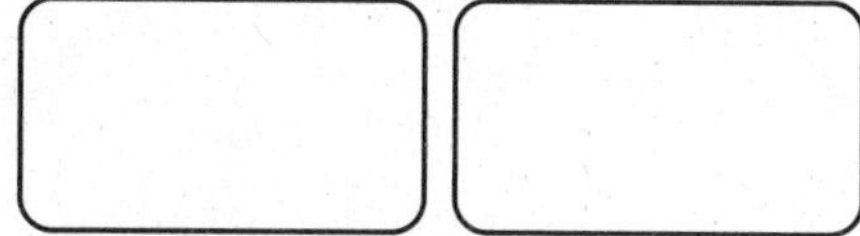

_____ in all

_____ equal groups

_____ in each group

2. Divide 12 counters into groups of 4.

_____ in all

_____ equal groups

_____ in each group

▶ Missing Factors **Write the missing factor.**

3. $2 \times$ _____ $= 10$

4. $42 =$ _____ $\times 7$

5. _____ $\times 6 = 18$

▶ Multiplication Facts Through 9 **Find the product.**

6. _____ $= 6 \times 9$

7. $3 \times 8 =$ _____

8. $4 \times 4 =$ _____

Florida FUN FACT

The zebra longwing butterfly was named the Florida state insect in 1996. Zebra butterflies are unusual in that they come together at night and sleep in groups, returning again and again to the same place.

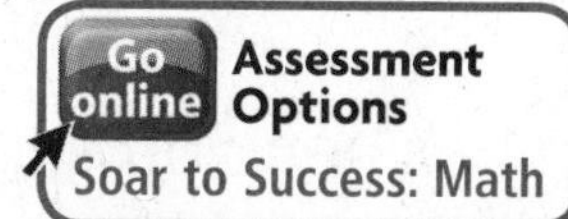

FLORIDA BENCHMARKS

Vocabulary Power

▶ Visualize It

Sort the review words into the Venn diagram.

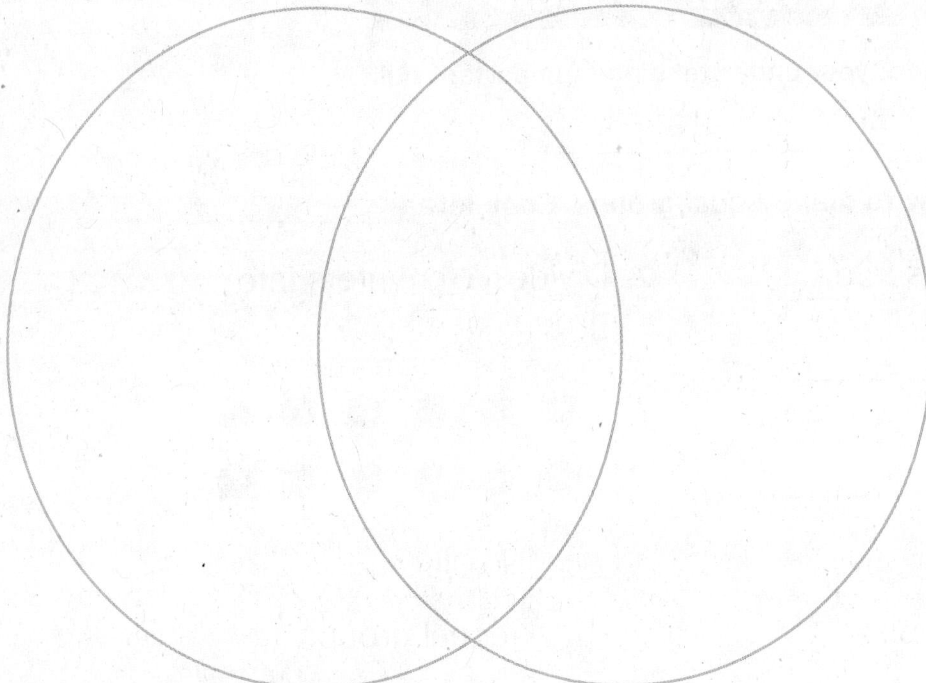

Review Words

- divide
- dividend
- divisor
- fact family
- factor
- inverse operations
- multiply
- product
- quotient

Preview Words

- array
- division sentence
- equal groups
- remainder
- variable

▶ Understand Vocabulary

Complete the sentences by using the preview words.

1. A ________________ is a symbol or a letter that stands for an unknown number.
2. An ________________ is an arrangement of objects in rows and columns.
3. The amount left over when a number cannot be divided evenly is the ________________.
4. When you separate into ________________, you are dividing.

Go online • Student Edition • Multilingual eGlossary

Name ______________________________

Divide by 3

Essential Question What strategies can you use to divide by 3?

MA.3.A.1.1 Model multiplication and division including problems presented in context: repeated addition, multiplicative comparison, array, how many combinations, measurement, and partitioning.

UNLOCK the Problem REAL WORLD

For field day, 18 students have signed up for the relay race. Each relay team needs 3 students. How many teams can be made?

- What do you need to find?

____

____

- Circle the numbers you need to use.

One Way Make equal groups.

- Look at the 18 counters below.
- Circle as many groups of 3 as you can.
- Count the number of groups.

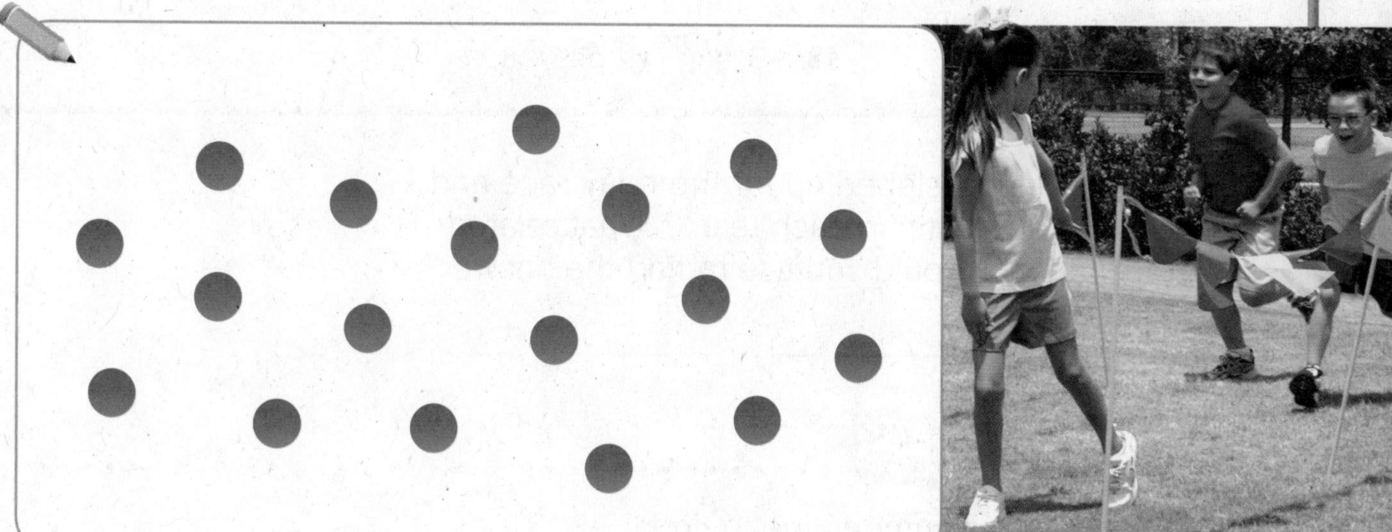

There are ______ groups of 3.

So, ______ teams can be made.

You can write $18 \div 3 = 6$ or $3\overline{)18}$ with quotient 6.

Math Talk Explain how you know your answer is correct.

Other Ways

A Count back on a number line.

- Start at 18.
- Count back by 3s as many times as you can. Complete the jumps on the number line.
- Count the number of times you jumped back by 3.

ERROR Alert

Be sure to count back the same number of spaces each time you jump back on the number line.

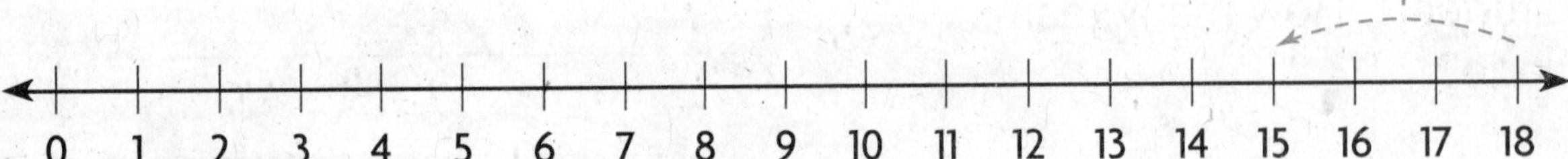

You jumped back by three _____ times.

B Use a related multiplication fact.

Since division is the opposite of multiplication, think of a related multiplication fact to find $18 \div 3$.

$\blacksquare \times 3 = 18$
$6 \times 3 = 18$

Think: What number completes the multiplication fact?

$18 \div 3 =$ _____ or $3\overline{)18}$

- What if 24 students signed up for the relay race and there were 3 students on each team? What related multiplication fact would you use to find the answer?

____

Share and Show

1. Count back on the number line to find $12 \div 3$. _____

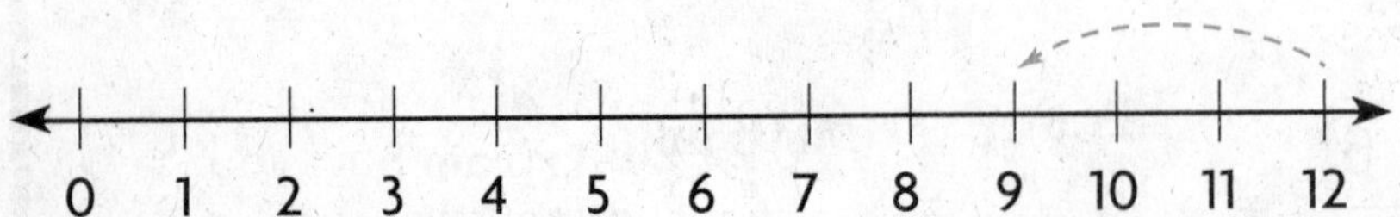

Math Talk **Explain** what the number of times you jump back on a number line tells you.

Find the quotient.

2. $6 \div 3 =$ ___ | 3. ___ $= 14 \div 2$ | 4. $21 \div 3 =$ ___ | 5. ___ $= 30 \div 5$

Name ___________________________

On Your Own

Find the quotient.

6. $10 \div 5 =$ ___

7. $9 \div 3 =$ ___

8. ___ $= 18 \div 2$

9. $24 \div 3 =$ ___

10. ___ $= 12 \div 2$

11. $40 \div 5 =$ ___

12. $15 \div 3 =$ ___

13. ___ $= 6 \div 3$

14. $27 \div 3 =$ ___

15. ___ $= 45 \div 5$

16. $3 \div 3 =$ ___

17. ___ $= 8 \div 2$

18. $3\overline{)15}$

19. $2\overline{)4}$

20. $5\overline{)20}$

21. $3\overline{)18}$

22. $2\overline{)16}$

23. $3\overline{)12}$

24. $3\overline{)6}$

25. $5\overline{)35}$

Algebra Write +, −, ×, or ÷.

26. $25 \bigcirc 5 = 10 \div 2$

27. $3 \times 3 = 6 \bigcirc 3$

28. $16 \bigcirc 2 = 24 - 16$

29. $13 + 19 = 8 \bigcirc 4$

30. $14 \bigcirc 2 = 6 \times 2$

31. $21 \div 3 = 5 \bigcirc 2$

Problem Solving REAL WORLD

Use the table for 32–33.

Field Day Events

Activity	Number of Students
Relay race	25
Beanbag toss	18
Jump-rope race	27

32. The students run the relay race in teams of 5. How many teams compete? Write the number sentence that shows the number of teams.

____

33. H.O.T. Students doing the jump-rope race and the beanbag toss compete in teams of 3. How many more teams participate in the jump-rope race than in the beanbag toss? **Explain** how you know.

____

____

____

34. Write Math **What's the Question?** Michael puts 21 sports cards into stacks of 3. The answer is 7 stacks.

____

____

35. **Test Prep** Olivia buys 24 beanbags for field day. They come in packs of 3. How many packs of beanbags does Olivia buy?

Ⓐ 6 Ⓒ 8

Ⓑ 7 Ⓓ 9

SHOW YOUR WORK

FOR MORE PRACTICE:
Florida Benchmarks Practice Book, pp. P137–P138

Name ______________________________

Divide by 4

Essential Question What strategies can you use to divide by 4?

MA.3.A.1.1 Model multiplication and division including problems presented in context: repeated addition, multiplicative comparison, array, how many combinations, measurement, and partitioning.

A tree farmer plants 12 sabal palm trees in 4 equal rows. How many trees are in each row?

- What do you need to find?

  ____

  ____

- Circle the number that tells you how many rows of palm trees the tree farmer planted.

One Way Make an array.

- Look at the array.
- Continue the array by drawing 1 tile in each of the 4 rows until all 12 tiles are shown.
- Count the number of tiles in each row.

There are ______ tiles in each row.

So, there are ______ trees in each row.

You can write $12 \div 4 = 3$ or $4\overline{)12}$ with quotient 3.

▲ Florida's state tree is the sabal palm.

Other Ways

A **Make equal groups.**

- Draw 1 counter in each group.
- Continue drawing 1 counter at a time until all 12 counters are drawn.

There are ______ counters in each group.

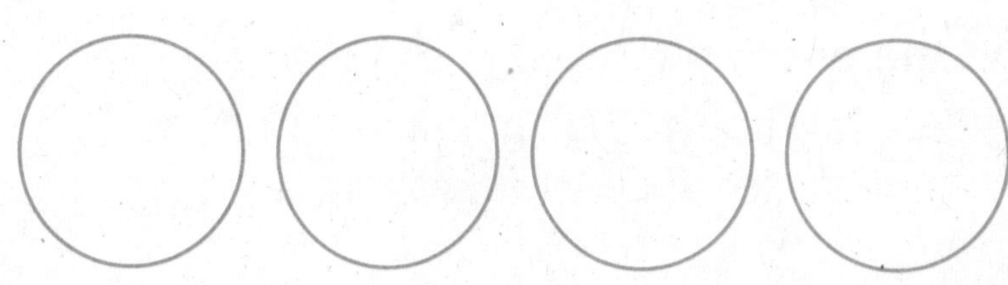

B **Use factors to find 12 ÷ 4.**

The factors of 4 are 2 and 2.

$2 \times 2 = 4$

factors ↖ ↗ ↑ product

To divide by 4, use the factors.

$12 \div 4 = ■$

Divide by 2. $12 \div 2 = 6$

Then divide by 2 again. $6 \div 2 = 3$

$12 \div 4 =$ _____

C **Use a related multiplication fact.**

$12 \div 4 = ■$

$4 \times ■ = 12$

$4 \times 3 = 12$

Think: What number completes the multiplication fact?

$12 \div 4 =$ _____ or $4\overline{)12}$

Remember

A variable is a letter or symbol that stands for an unknown number.

Try This! **Use factors of 4 to find 16 ÷ 4.**

Factors of 4 are 2 and 2. $16 \div 4 = ■$

- Divide by 2. $16 \div 2 =$ _____
- Then divide by 2 again. $8 \div 2 =$ _____

So, $16 \div 4 =$ _____.

Share and Show

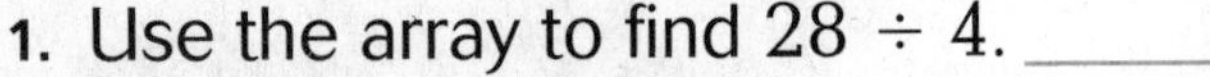

1. Use the array to find $28 \div 4$. _____

Math Talk Explain how you used the array to find the quotient.

Find the quotient.

2. _____ $= 21 \div 3$
3. $8 \div 4 =$ _____
4. _____ $= 40 \div 5$
5. $24 \div 4 =$ _____
6. $20 \div 4 = a$ $a =$ _____
7. $12 \div 2 = p$ $p =$ _____
8. $27 \div 3 = g$ $g =$ _____
9. $12 \div 4 = t$ $t =$ _____

Name ______________________

On Your Own

Find the quotient.

10. $32 \div 4 =$ ___

11. ___ $= 15 \div 5$

12. $20 \div 4 =$ ___

13. ___ $= 16 \div 2$

14. $12 \div 3 =$ ___

15. $4 \div 4 =$ ___

16. ___ $= 6 \div 2$

17. ___ $= 36 \div 4$

18. $45 \div 5 = b$

$b =$ ___

19. $24 \div 4 = e$

$e =$ ___

20. $8 \div 2 = z$

$z =$ ___

21. $24 \div 3 = h$

$h =$ ___

22. $4\overline{)28}$

23. $2\overline{)18}$

24. $4\overline{)16}$

25. $5\overline{)25}$

Algebra **Complete the table.**

26.

÷	9	12	15	18
3				

27.

÷	20	24	28	32
4				

Algebra **Find the missing number.**

28. $14 \div$ ___ $= 7$

29. $30 \div$ ___ $= 6$

30. $8 \div$ ___ $= 2$

31. $24 \div$ ___ $= 8$

Problem Solving REAL WORLD

Use the table for 32–33.

Palm Trees Planted	
Type	**Number Planted**
Royal palm	24
Coconut palm	28
Queen palm	16

32. Douglas planted the queen palm trees in 4 equal rows. Then he added 2 more trees to each row. How many palm trees did he plant in each row?

____

33. H.O.T. Mr. Banks planted the coconut palm trees in 4 equal rows. Mr. Webb planted the royal palm trees in 3 equal rows. Who planted more trees in each row? How many more? **Explain** how you know.

____

____

____

SHOW YOUR WORK

34. Write Math ▸ Ms. Bryan spent $36 on 4 bags of fertilizer. Each bag cost the same amount. How much did each bag cost? **Explain** how you found your answer.

____

____

____

35. **Test Prep** Eric planted 20 flowers in 4 equal groups. How many flowers did he plant in each group?

Ⓐ 4 Ⓒ 6

Ⓑ 5 Ⓓ 7

FOR MORE PRACTICE:
Florida Benchmarks Practice Book, pp. P139–P140

Name ____________________

Division Rules for 1 and 0

Essential Question What are the rules for dividing with 1 and 0?

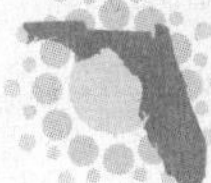

MA.3.A.1.2 Solve multiplication and division fact problems by using strategies that result from applying number properties.

UNLOCK the Problem REAL WORLD

What rules for division can help you divide with 1 and 0?

If there is only 1 cage, then all the birds must go in that cage.

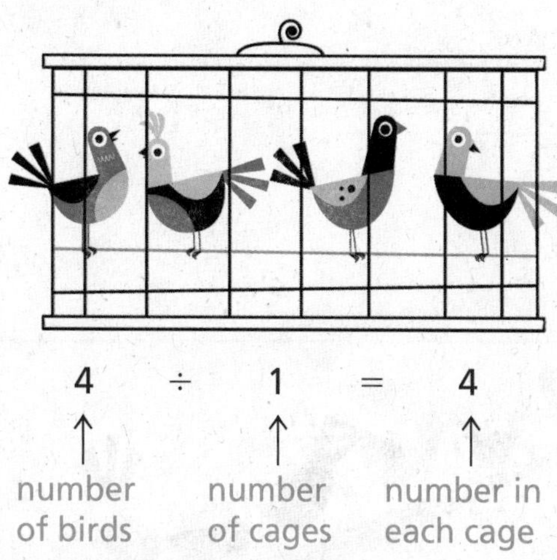

4 ÷ 1 = 4

↑ number of birds ↑ number of cages ↑ number in each cage

Rule A: Any number divided by 1 equals that number.

Try This! There are 3 fish and 1 fishbowl. Draw a quick picture to show the fish in the fishbowl.

Write the number sentence your picture shows.

_____ ÷ _____ = _____

If there are the same numbers of birds and cages, then 1 bird goes in each cage.

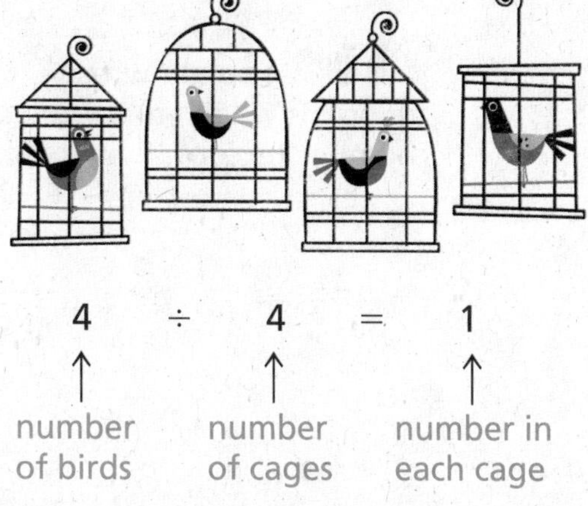

4 ÷ 4 = 1

↑ number of birds ↑ number of cages ↑ number in each cage

Rule B: Any number (except 0) divided by itself equals 1.

Try This! There are 3 fish and 3 fishbowls. Draw a quick picture to show the fish divided equally among the fishbowls.

Write the number sentence your picture shows.

_____ ÷ _____ = _____

If there are 0 birds and 4 cages, there will not be any birds in the cages.

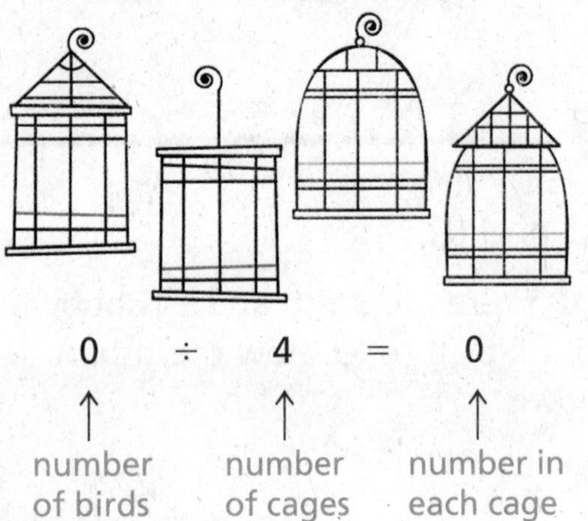

$0 \div 4 = 0$

↑ number of birds ↑ number of cages ↑ number in each cage

Try This! There are 0 fish and 3 fishbowls. Draw a quick picture to show the fishbowls.

Write the number sentence your picture shows.

_____ ÷ _____ = _____

Rule C: Zero divided by any number (except 0) equals 0.

If there are 0 cages, then you cannot separate the birds equally into cages. Dividing by 0 is not possible.

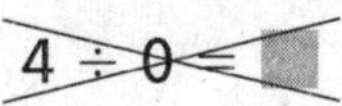

Rule D: You cannot divide by 0.

Share and Show

1. Use the picture to find $2 \div 2$. _____

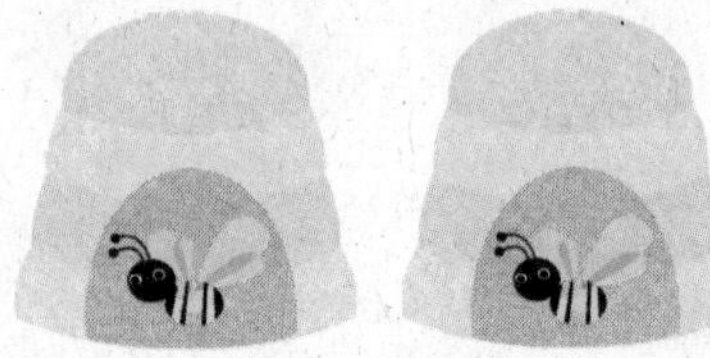

Math Talk **Explain** what happens when you divide a number (except 0) by itself.

Find the quotient.

2. $7 \div 1 =$ _____

3. $8 \div 8 =$ _____

✓4. $0 \div 5 =$ _____

✓5. $6 \div 6 =$ _____

Name ______________________________

On Your Own

Practice: Copy and Solve Find the quotient.

6. $0 \div 8$
7. $5 \div 5$
8. $2 \div 1$
9. $0 \div 7$
10. $6 \div 1$
11. $25 \div 5$
12. $0 \div 6$
13. $18 \div 3$
14. $14 \div 2$
15. $9 \div 9$
16. $28 \div 4$
17. $8 \div 1$
18. $3\overline{)27}$
19. $5\overline{)10}$
20. $3\overline{)0}$
21. $4\overline{)4}$

H.O.T. **Algebra** Compare. Write <, >, or =.

22. $7 \div 7 \bigcirc 7 \div 1$
23. $9 \times 1 \bigcirc 9 \div 1$
24. $2 \div 2 \bigcirc 0 \div 2$

Problem Solving REAL WORLD

25. Angie has 7 parakeets. She puts 4 in a cage. She divides the other parakeets equally among 3 friends. How many parakeets does each friend get to hold?

____

26. Mary has some parrots. She gives each parrot 1 grape. If Mary gives out 5 grapes, how many parrots does she have?

____

27. H.O.T. Write Math ▶ Suppose a zoo has 59 birds that are in 59 cages. Use what you know about division rules to find the number of birds in each cage. **Explain** your answer.

____

____

28. Test Prep Joe has 4 horses. He puts each horse in its own stall. How many stalls does Joe use?

Ⓐ 0 Ⓒ 2

Ⓑ 1 Ⓓ 4

Connect to Reading

Compare and Contrast

You have learned the rules for division with 1. Compare and contrast them to help you learn how to use the rules to solve problems.

Compare the rules. Think about how they are *alike*. Contrast the rules. Think about how they are *different*.

Read: Rule A: Any number divided by 1 equals that number.

Rule B: Any number (except 0) divided by itself equals 1.

Compare: How are the rules alike?

- Both rules are about dividing with 1.

Contrast: How are the rules different?

- Rule A is about dividing a number by 1. The quotient is that number.
- Rule B is about dividing a number (except 0) by itself. The quotient is always 1.

Read the problem. Write a number sentence. Solve. Circle *Rule A* or *Rule B* to tell which rule you used.

29. Jamal bought 7 goldfish at the pet store. He put them in 1 fishbowl. How many goldfish did he put in the bowl?

____

Rule A Rule B

30. Ava has 6 turtles. She divides them equally among 6 aquariums. How many turtles does she put in each aquarium?

____

Rule A Rule B

FOR MORE PRACTICE:
Florida Benchmarks Practice Book, pp. P141–P142

Name ______________________

Divide by 6

Essential Question What strategies can you use to divide by 6?

MA.3.A.1.1 Model multiplication and division including problems presented in context: repeated addition, multiplicative comparison, array, how many combinations, measurement, and partitioning.

UNLOCK the Problem REAL WORLD

Ms. Moore needs to buy 24 juice boxes for the class picnic. Juice boxes come in packs of 6. How many packs does Ms. Moore need to buy?

- What do you need to find?

____

____

- Circle the number that tells you how many juice boxes come in a pack.

One Way Make equal groups.

- Draw 24 counters.
- Circle as many groups of 6 as you can.
- Count the number of groups.

There are _____ groups of 6.

So, Ms. Moore needs to buy _____ packs of juice.

You can write $24 \div 6 = 4$ or $6\overline{)24}$ with quotient 4.

Math Talk If you divided the 24 counters into groups of 4, how many groups would there be? **Explain** how you know.

Other Ways

A Use a related multiplication fact.

$24 \div 6 = \blacksquare$

$\blacksquare \times 6 = 24$

$4 \times 6 = 24$

Think: What number completes the multiplication fact?

$24 \div 6 = \_\_\_\_$ or $6\overline{)24}$

B Use factors.

The factors of 6 are 3 and 2.

$3 \times 2 = 6$

factors   product

To divide by 6, use the factors.

$24 \div 6 = \blacksquare$

Divide by 3. $24 \div 3 = 8$

Then divide by 2. $8 \div 2 = 4$

$24 \div 6 = \_\_\_\_$

- How does knowing $9 \times 6 = 54$ help you find $54 \div 6$?

____

____

Share and Show

1. Continue making equal groups to find $18 \div 6$. ____

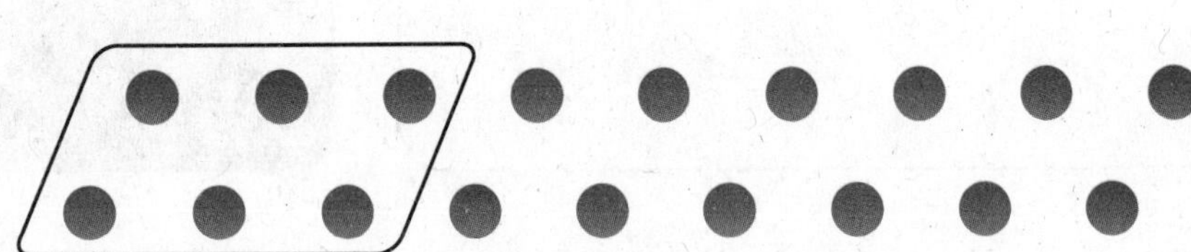

Math Talk Explain how you could use factors to find $18 \div 6$.

Find the missing factor and quotient.

2. $6 \times \_\_\_ = 36$ $36 \div 6 = \_\_\_$

3. $6 \times \_\_\_ = 12$ $12 \div 6 = \_\_\_$

Find the quotient.

4. $\_\_\_ = 0 \div 2$

5. $6 \div 6 = \_\_\_$

6. $\_\_\_ = 28 \div 4$

7. $42 \div 6 = \_\_\_$

Name ______________________

On Your Own

Find the missing factor and quotient.

8. $6 \times$ ____ $= 30$ $30 \div 6 =$ ____

9. $5 \times$ ____ $= 45$ ____ $= 45 \div 5$

10. $2 \times$ ____ $= 16$ ____ $= 16 \div 2$

11. $6 \times$ ____ $= 48$ $48 \div 6 =$ ____

Find the quotient.

12. $18 \div 6 =$ ____

13. ____ $= 7 \div 1$

14. ____ $= 24 \div 6$

15. $27 \div 3 =$ ____

16. $k = 54 \div 6$
$k =$ ____

17. $20 \div 4 = w$
$w =$ ____

18. $0 \div 8 = s$
$s =$ ____

19. $d = 36 \div 6$
$d =$ ____

20. $5\overline{)35}$

21. $6\overline{)42}$

22. $6\overline{)6}$

23. $2\overline{)10}$

Algebra **Find the missing number.**

24. $48 \div$ ____ $= 8$

25. $21 \div$ ____ $= 7$

26. $16 \div$ ____ $= 4$

27. $3 \div$ ____ $= 3$

Problem Solving REAL WORLD

28. There are 30 students in a relay race at the picnic. They are divided into teams of 6 students. How many teams are there?

SHOW YOUR WORK

____

29. H.O.T. Cody baked 24 muffins. He ate 6 of them. How many muffins does he have left? How many can he give to each of his 6 friends if each friend gets the same number? **Explain.**

____

____

____

30. **What's the Error?** Mary has 36 stickers to give to 6 friends. She says she can give each friend only 5 stickers. Use a division sentence to describe Mary's error.

____

____

____

31. **Test Prep** Each picnic table at a park can seat up to 6 people. How many tables will 48 people fill?

Ⓐ 9 Ⓒ 7

Ⓑ 8 Ⓓ 6

FOR MORE PRACTICE:
Florida Benchmarks Practice Book, pp. P143–P144

Name ___________________________

Mid-Chapter Checkpoint

▶ Check Concepts

1. **Explain** how to find $20 \div 4$ by making an array. (MA.3.A.1.1; pp. 253–256)

____

____

____

2. **Explain** how to find $30 \div 6$ by making equal groups. (MA.3.A.1.1; pp. 261–264)

____

____

____

Find the quotient. (MA.3.A.1.1, MA.3.A.1.2; pp. 249–252, 253–256, 257–260, 261–264)

3. $24 \div 3 =$ ____

4. ____ $= 0 \div 9$

5. $16 \div 4 =$ ____

6. ____ $= 48 \div 6$

7. ____ $= 8 \div 4$

8. ____ $= 12 \div 6$

9. $5 \div 1 =$ ____

10. $15 \div 3 =$ ____

11. ____ $= 6 \div 6$

12. $21 \div 3 =$ ____

13. ____ $= 0 \div 3$

14. $36 \div 4 =$ ____

15. $1\overline{)8}$

16. $4\overline{)24}$

17. $6\overline{)54}$

18. $3\overline{)9}$

Fill in the bubble for the correct answer choice.

19. Carter has 18 new books. He plans to read 3 of them each week. For how many weeks will Carter read his new books? **(MA.3.A.1.1; pp. 249–252)**

Ⓐ 5 weeks

Ⓑ 6 weeks

Ⓒ 15 weeks

Ⓓ 21 weeks

20. Gabriella made 4 waffles for breakfast. She has 28 berries to put on top of the waffles. She will put an equal number of berries on each waffle. How many berries will Gabriella put on each waffle?

(MA.3.A.1.1; pp. 253–256)

Ⓕ 5 Ⓗ 7

Ⓖ 6 Ⓘ 8

21. There are 36 people waiting in line to ride on a train. Each car in the train can hold 6 people. Which number sentence could be used to find the number of cars needed to hold all 36 people?

(MA.3.A.1.1; pp. 261–264)

Ⓐ $36 - 6 = \blacksquare$

Ⓑ $\blacksquare + 6 = 36$

Ⓒ $36 \div 6 = \blacksquare$

Ⓓ $36 \times 6 = \blacksquare$

22. Alyssa has 4 cupcakes. She gives 1 cupcake to each of her cousins. How many cousins does Alyssa have?

(MA.3.A.1.2; pp. 257–260)

Ⓕ 0 Ⓗ 2

Ⓖ 1 Ⓘ 4

Name ______________________

Divide by 7

Essential Question What strategies can you use to divide by 7?

MA.3.A.1.1 Model multiplication and division including problems presented in context: repeated addition, multiplicative comparison, array, how many combinations, measurement, and partitioning.

UNLOCK the Problem REAL WORLD

Erin used 28 large apples to make 7 apple pies. She used the same number of apples for each pie. How many apples did Erin use for each pie?

- How many apples did Erin use altogether for her pies?

____

- How many apple pies did Erin make?

____

One Way Make an array.

- Draw 1 tile in each of 7 rows.
- Continue drawing 1 tile in each of the 7 rows until all 28 tiles are drawn.
- Count the number of tiles in each row.

There are _____ tiles in each row.

So, Erin used _____ apples for each pie.

You can write $28 \div 7 = 4$ or $7\overline{)28}$ with quotient 4.

- What if Erin cut each pie into 8 slices?

  How many slices would there be altogether? __________

Other Ways

A Use a related multiplication fact.

$28 \div 7 = \blacksquare$ $7 \times \blacksquare = 28$

$7 \times 4 = 28$

Think: What number completes the multiplication fact?

$28 \div 7 =$ _____ or $7\overline{)28}$

B Make equal groups.

- Draw 7 circles to show 7 groups.
- Draw 1 counter in each group.
- Continue drawing 1 counter at a time until all 28 counters are drawn.

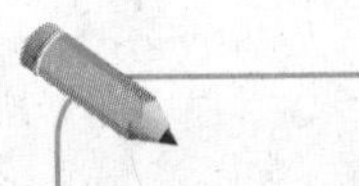

There are _____ counters in each group.

Share and Show

1. Use the related multiplication fact to find $42 \div 7$. _____
   $7 \times 6 = 42$

Math Talk Explain why you can use a related multiplication fact to solve a division problem.

Find the missing factor and quotient.

2. $7 \times$ _____ $= 7$ $7 \div 7 =$ _____

3. $7 \times$ _____ $= 35$ $35 \div 7 =$ _____

Find the quotient.

4. $4 \div 2 =$ _____

5. $56 \div 7 =$ _____

6. _____ $= 20 \div 5$

7. _____ $= 21 \div 7$

Name ______________________

On Your Own

Find the missing factor and quotient.

8. $3 \times \_\_\_ = 9$ $\_\_\_ = 9 \div 3$

9. $7 \times \_\_\_ = 49$ $49 \div 7 = \_\_\_$

10. $7 \times \_\_\_ = 63$ $63 \div 7 = \_\_\_$

11. $4 \times \_\_\_ = 32$ $\_\_\_ = 32 \div 4$

Find the quotient.

12. $\_\_\_ = 42 \div 7$

13. $15 \div 3 = \_\_\_$

14. $0 \div 7 = \_\_\_$

15. $\_\_\_ = 25 \div 5$

16. $48 \div 6 = \_\_\_$

17. $7 \div 1 = \_\_\_$

18. $\_\_\_ = 35 \div 7$

19. $\_\_\_ = 18 \div 2$

20. $24 \div 4 = x$
$x = \_\_\_$

21. $n = 28 \div 7$
$n = \_\_\_$

22. $r = 54 \div 6$
$r = \_\_\_$

23. $14 \div 7 = j$
$j = \_\_\_$

24. $7\overline{)56}$

25. $1\overline{)9}$

26. $7\overline{)21}$

27. $2\overline{)8}$

Algebra Complete the table.

28.

÷	18	24	30	36
6				

29.

÷	35	42	49	56
7				

UNLOCK the Problem REAL WORLD

30. Gavin sold 21 pies to 7 different people. Each person bought the same number of pies. How many pies did Gavin sell to each person?

Ⓐ 3 Ⓑ 4 Ⓒ 14 Ⓓ 28

a. What do you need to find? ______________________________

____

b. How will you use division to solve the problem? ______________________________

____

c. Draw a picture or write the steps to find the number of pies Gavin sold to each person.

d. What is another way you could have solved the problem?

____

____

e. Complete the sentences.

Gavin sold _____ pies to _____ different people.

Each person bought the same number of __________.

So, Gavin sold _____ pies to each person.

f. Fill in the bubble for the correct answer choice above.

31. Clare bought 49 peaches to make peach pies for a bake sale. She used 7 peaches for each pie. How many pies did Clare make?

Ⓕ 9 Ⓖ 8 Ⓗ 7 Ⓘ 6

32. There are 35 pies in all sitting on 7 shelves at a bakery. If each shelf has the same number of pies, how many pies are on each shelf?

Ⓐ 4 Ⓑ 5 Ⓒ 6 Ⓓ 7

 FOR MORE PRACTICE:
Florida Benchmarks Practice Book, pp. P145–P146

Name ______________________________

Divide by 8

Essential Question What strategies can you use to divide by 8?

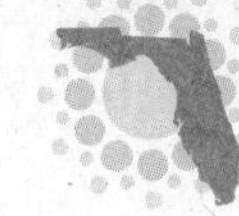

MA.3.A.1.1 Model multiplication and division including problems presented in context: repeated addition, multiplicative comparison, array, how many combinations, measurement, and partitioning.

UNLOCK the Problem REAL WORLD

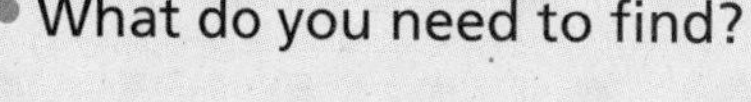

At Stephen's camping store, firewood is sold in bundles of 8 logs. He has 32 logs to put in bundles. How many bundles of firewood can he make?

- What do you need to find?

____

____

- Circle the number that tells you how many logs are in each bundle.

One Way Use repeated subtraction.

- Start with 32.
- Subtract 8 until you reach 0.
- Count and record the number of times you subtract 8.

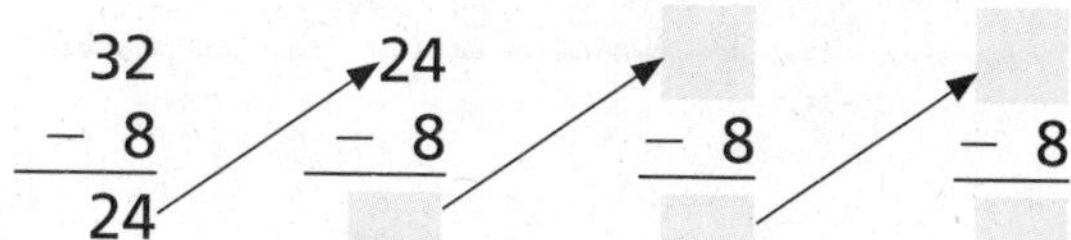

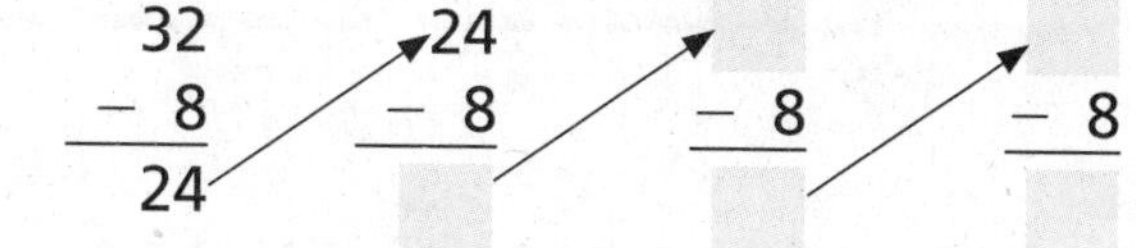

$32 - 8 = 24$ → $24 - 8 = \square$ → $\square - 8 = \square$ → $\square - 8 = \square$

Number of times you subtract 8: 1 2 ____ ____

ERROR Alert

When using repeated subtraction, continue to subtract the divisor until you are unable to subtract anymore.

You subtract eight ______ times.

So, Stephen can make ______ bundles of firewood.

You can write $32 \div 8 = 4$ or $8\overline{)32}$ with quotient 4.

Another Way Use a related multiplication fact.

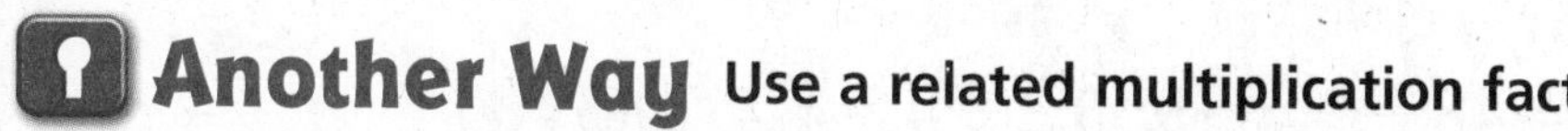

$32 \div 8 = \square$

$\square \times 8 = 32$

$4 \times 8 = 32$

Think: What number completes the multiplication fact?

$32 \div 8 =$ ______ or $8\overline{)32}$

Divide with Remainders What if Stephen has 19 logs to put in bundles of 8? How many bundles of firewood can Stephen make?

Make equal groups.

- Look at the 19 counters. Circle as many groups of 8 as you can.

There are _____ groups of 8.

There are _____ counters left over.

So, Stephen can make _____ bundles of firewood.

He will have _____ logs left over.

The amount left over when a number cannot be divided evenly is called the **remainder**.

You write 19 ÷ 8 = 2 r3.
The quotient is 2. The remainder is 3.

Read Math
2 r3 is read 2 remainder 3.

Share and Show

1. Use repeated subtraction to find 16 ÷ 8. _____

$$\begin{array}{r} 16 \\ -\ 8 \\ \hline 8 \end{array} \quad \begin{array}{r} 8 \\ -8 \\ \hline 0 \end{array}$$

Think: How many times do you subtract 8?

Math Talk Explain why you subtract 8 from 16 to find 16 ÷ 8.

Find the missing factor and quotient.

2. 8 × _____ = 56 56 ÷ 8 = _____

✓3. 8 × _____ = 40 40 ÷ 8 = _____

Find the quotient.

4. 18 ÷ 3 = _____

5. _____ = 48 ÷ 8

6. 32 ÷ 4 = _____

✓7. _____ = 24 ÷ 8

8. Complete the number sentence.

30 ÷ 8 = _____ r _____

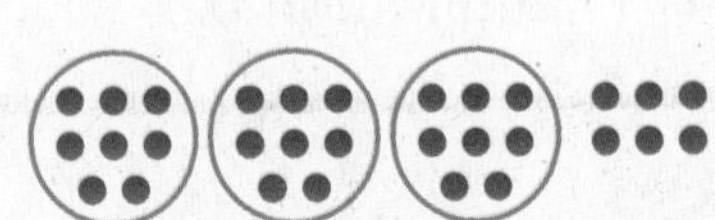

Name ______________________________

On Your Own

Find the missing factor and quotient.

9. $8 \times$ ____ $= 8$ $8 \div 8 =$ ____

10. $5 \times$ ____ $= 35$ ____ $= 35 \div 5$

11. $6 \times$ ____ $= 18$ $18 \div 6 =$ ____

12. $8 \times$ ____ $= 72$ ____ $= 72 \div 8$

Find the quotient.

13. $28 \div 4 =$ ____

14. $16 \div 8 =$ ____

15. ____ $= 3 \div 3$

16. ____ $= 21 \div 7$

17. $g = 32 \div 8$
$g =$ ____

18. $45 \div 5 = z$
$z =$ ____

19. $12 \div 2 = m$
$m =$ ____

20. $e = 48 \div 8$
$e =$ ____

21. $9\overline{)0}$

22. $6\overline{)24}$

23. $8\overline{)64}$

24. $1\overline{)8}$

25. $3\overline{)15}$

26. $8\overline{)56}$

27. $7\overline{)42}$

28. $4\overline{)36}$

Algebra Write +, −, ×, or ÷.

29. $6 \times 6 = 32 \bigcirc 4$

30. $12 \bigcirc 3 = 19 - 15$

31. $40 \div 8 = 35 \bigcirc 7$

Problem Solving REAL WORLD

Use the table for 32–33.

Tent Sizes	
Type	**Number of People**
Columbia	10
Vista	8
Condor	7

32. H.O.T. There are 58 people camping at Zoe's family reunion. They have Columbia tents and Vista tents. How many of each type of tent do they need to sleep exactly 58 people if each tent is filled? **Explain.**

SHOW YOUR WORK

33. Write Math There are 42 people who plan to camp over the weekend. What is the minimum number of Condor tents they need? **Explain.**

34. Josh is dividing 37 marshmallows equally among 8 campers. How many marshmallows will each camper get? How many will be left over?

35. **Test Prep** Grace set 8 plates at each picnic table so 24 campers could eat dinner. How many picnic tables did Grace have to set?

Ⓐ 3　　Ⓒ 5

Ⓑ 4　　Ⓓ 6

 FOR MORE PRACTICE:
Florida Benchmarks Practice Book, pp. P147–P148

Name ______________________

Divide by 9

Essential Question What strategies can you use to divide by 9?

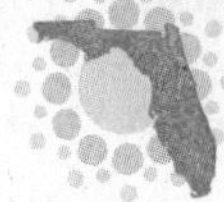

MA.3.A.1.1 Model multiplication and division including problems presented in context: repeated addition, multiplicative comparison, array, how many combinations, measurement, and partitioning.

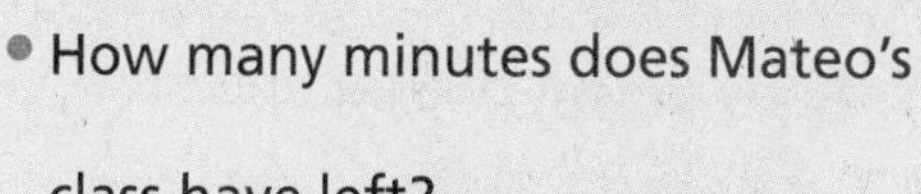

UNLOCK the Problem REAL WORLD

Mateo's class goes to The Florida Aquarium in Tampa. The students have 27 minutes left to spend equally at each of 9 small exhibits. How much time can they spend at each exhibit?

- How many minutes does Mateo's class have left? ______
- How many exhibits are there? ______

One Way Make equal groups.

- Draw 9 circles to show 9 groups.
- Draw 1 counter in each group.
- Continue drawing 1 counter at a time until all 27 counters are drawn.

▲ Swim with the Fishes has more than 2,300 fish! It is the largest exhibit at The Florida Aquarium.

There are ______ counters in each group.

So, Mateo's class can spend ______ minutes at each exhibit.

You can write $27 \div 9 = 3$ or $9\overline{)27}$ with quotient 3.

Other Ways

A Use factors to find 27 ÷ 9.

The factors of 9 are 3 and 3.

$3 \times 3 = 9$

factors — product

To divide by 9, use the factors.

27 ÷ 9 = ■

Divide by 3. 27 ÷ 3 = 9

Then divide by 3 again. 9 ÷ 3 = 3

27 ÷ 9 = ____

B Use a related multiplication fact.

27 ÷ 9 = ■

9 × ■ = 27

9 × 3 = 27

Think: What number completes the multiplication fact?

27 ÷ 9 = ____ or $9\overline{)27}$

• What multiplication fact can you use to find 63 ÷ 9? ____

Share and Show MATH BOARD

1. Draw counters in the groups to find 18 ÷ 9. ____

Math Talk Explain how you would use factors to find 18 ÷ 9.

Find the quotient.

2. ____ = 45 ÷ 9

3. 36 ÷ 6 = ____

4. 21 ÷ 3 = ____

5. ____ = 54 ÷ 9

6. $7\overline{)28}$

7. $9\overline{)9}$

8. $5\overline{)40}$

9. $9\overline{)36}$

Name ________________________

On Your Own

Find the quotient.

10. $8 \div 2 =$ _____

11. _____ $= 72 \div 9$

12. $56 \div 8 =$ _____

13. _____ $= 27 \div 9$

14. _____ $= 5 \div 1$

15. _____ $= 36 \div 4$

16. $81 \div 9 =$ _____

17. $30 \div 5 =$ _____

18. _____ $= 36 \div 9$

19. $21 \div 7 =$ _____

20. _____ $= 9 \div 3$

21. $42 \div 6 =$ _____

22. $64 \div 8 = e$

$e =$ _____

23. $0 \div 3 = g$

$g =$ _____

24. $k = 20 \div 4$

$k =$ _____

25. $s = 9 \div 9$

$s =$ _____

26. $35 \div 5 = h$

$h =$ _____

27. $p = 4 \div 1$

$p =$ _____

28. $54 \div 9 = w$

$w =$ _____

29. $a = 14 \div 2$

$a =$ _____

Practice: Copy and Solve

30. $9\overline{)18}$

31. $3\overline{)27}$

32. $6\overline{)48}$

33. $7\overline{)14}$

34. $4\overline{)12}$

35. $9\overline{)63}$

36. $2\overline{)16}$

37. $5\overline{)25}$

H.O.T. **Algebra** Complete the table.

38.

÷	24	32	40	48
8				

39.

÷	45	54	63	72
9				

UNLOCK the Problem REAL WORLD

40. Carlos has 28 blue tang fish and 17 yellow tang fish in one large fish tank. He wants to separate the fish equally into 9 smaller tanks. How many tang fish will Carlos put in each smaller tank?

a. What do you need to find? ____________________

____

b. What operations will you use to solve the problem? ____________________

____

c. Write the steps to find how many tang fish Carlos will put in each smaller tank.

d. Complete the sentences.

Carlos has _____ blue tang fish and _____ yellow tang fish in one large fish tank.

He wants to separate the fish into _____ smaller tanks.

So, Carlos will put _____ fish in each smaller tank.

41. Sophie has a new fish. She feeds it 9 fish pellets each day. If Sophie has fed her fish 72 pellets, for how many days has she had her fish?

____

42. **Test Prep** At the aquarium, Ms. Brady separates 36 students into 9 equal groups. How many students are in each group?

Ⓐ 2
Ⓑ 3
Ⓒ 4
Ⓓ 5

FOR MORE PRACTICE:
Florida Benchmarks Practice Book, pp. P149–P150

Name ______________________________

Act It Out · Division

Essential Question How can you use the strategy *act it out* to solve problems?

MA.3.A.6.1 Represent, compute, estimate and solve problems using numbers through hundred thousands.

UNLOCK the Problem REAL WORLD

Madeline cuts a ribbon into 2 equal pieces. Then she cuts 4 inches off one piece. That piece is now 5 inches long. What was the length of the original ribbon?

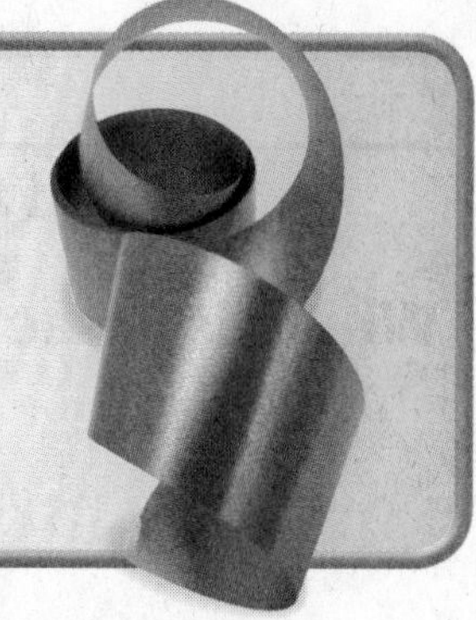

Use the graphic organizer below to solve the problem.

Read the Problem

What do I need to find?

I need to find the length of the original ________.

What information do I need to use?

Madeline cuts a ribbon into _____ equal pieces. She cuts _____ inches off one piece, making that piece _____ inches long.

How will I use the information?

I will use the information to _____ out the problem.

Solve the Problem

Describe how to act out the problem.

Start with a drawing of the ribbon.

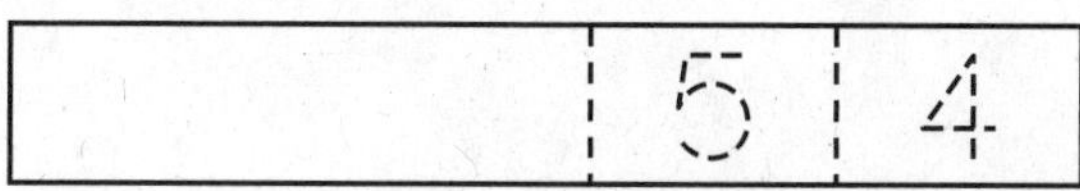

Cut it into 2 equal pieces. Then show _____ inches cut off one piece, with 5 inches left.

$5 + 4 = $ _____

5 ↑ final length; 4 ↑ inches cut off; _____ ↑ length of one piece

Now I know 1 piece is _____ inches long.

Next, multiply to find the length of the original ribbon.

$2 \times 9 = $ _____

2 ↑ number of pieces; 9 ↑ length of one piece; _____ ↑ length of ribbon

The length of the original ribbon was _____ inches.

Try Another Problem

Chad bought 4 packs of T-shirts. He gave 5 T-shirts to his brother. Now Chad has 19 shirts. How many T-shirts were in each pack?

Read the Problem	Solve the Problem
What do I need to find?	**Describe how to act out the problem.**
What information do I need to use?	
How will I use the information?	

- How can you use multiplication and subtraction to check your answer?

____

____

____

Math Talk **Explain** another strategy you could use to solve this problem.

Name ______________________________

Share and Show 

Act It Out
Use Manipulatives
Draw a Diagram
Make a Table, Chart, or List
Search for Patterns

1. Mac collects toy cars. He bought 4 packs of cars. Then his friend gave him 9 cars. Now Mac has 21 cars. How many cars were in each pack?

Act out the problem by using counters or the picture and by writing number sentences.

First, subtract the cars Mac's friend gave him.

21	−	____	=	____
↑		↑		↑
total cars		cars given to Mac		cars in 4 packs

Then, divide to find the number of cars in each pack.

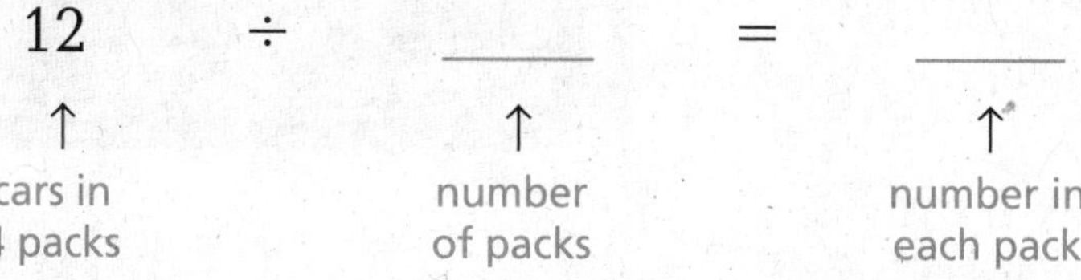

12	÷	____	=	____
↑		↑		↑
cars in 4 packs		number of packs		number in each pack

So, there were ____ cars in each pack.

2. H.O.T. **What if** Mac bought 8 packs of cars and then his friend gave him 3 cars? If Mac has 19 cars now, how many cars were in each pack?

____

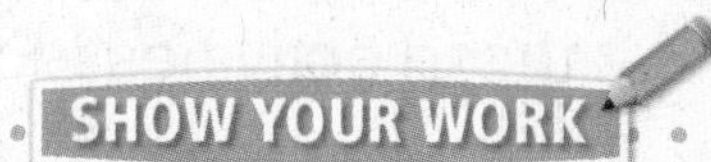

3. Ryan collects model cars. He gave 7 of his model cars to a friend. Then he bought 6 more cars. Now Ryan has 13 cars. How many cars did Ryan start with?

____

4. Chloe bought 5 sets of books. She donated 9 of her books to her school. Now she has 26 books. How many books were in each set?

____

On Your Own

Use the table for 5–6.

Mall of America Facts	
Stores	520
Restaurants	50
Food Stores	36

5. Suppose 448 of the stores at the Mall of America are NOT clothing stores. How many are clothing stores? How many clothing stores are in each section if they are divided equally among 8 sections of the mall?

____

6. Mark visited every food store. He visited the same number of food stores each day. List 2 different ways he could have done this.

____

____

7. H.O.T. Write Math Rose saw a movie, shopped, and ate at a restaurant. She did not see the movie first. She shopped right after she ate. In what order did Rose do these activities? **Explain** how you know.

____

____

____

____

____

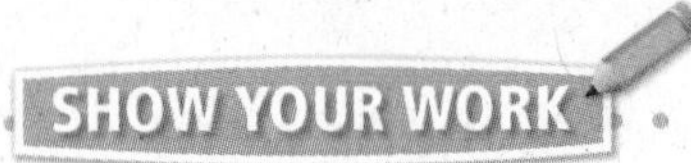

8. **Test Prep** Mr. Acosta went to the same number of stores each day for 4 days. On the fifth day, he went to 10 stores. He visited 34 stores in all. How many stores did he visit on each of the first 4 days?

Ⓐ 6 Ⓒ 14

Ⓑ 11 Ⓓ 20

FOR MORE PRACTICE:
Florida Benchmarks Practice Book, pp. P151–P152

Name ____________________

▶ Check Concepts

1. **Explain** how to find 24 ÷ 8 by using repeated subtraction. (MA.3.A.1.1; pp. 271–274)

____

____

2. **Explain** how to find 36 ÷ 9 by using a related multiplication fact. (MA.3.A.1.1; pp. 275–278)

____

____

Find the quotient. (MA.3.A.1.1, MA.3.A.1.2; pp. 249–252, 253–256, 257–260, 261–264, 267–270, 271–274, 275–278)

3. 12 ÷ 4 = ____

4. 35 ÷ 7 = ____

5. ____ = 0 ÷ 2

6. ____ = 27 ÷ 3

7. ____ = 48 ÷ 6

8. ____ = 9 ÷ 9

9. 64 ÷ 8 = ____

10. 24 ÷ 4 = ____

11. $7\overline{)49}$

12. $3\overline{)9}$

13. $1\overline{)7}$

14. $9\overline{)72}$

Find the missing factor and quotient. (MA.3.A.1.1, MA.3.A.1.3; pp. 261–264, 267–270, 271–274)

15. 6 × ______ = 42 42 ÷ 6 = ______

16. 7 × ______ = 28 ______ = 28 ÷ 7

17. 8 × ______ = 16 16 ÷ 8 = ______

18. 6 × ______ = 54 ______ = 54 ÷ 6

Go online Assessment Options
Chapter Test

Fill in the bubble for the correct answer choice.

19. Maria has 54 flower seeds and 9 pots. If she wants to put an equal number of seeds in each pot, how many seeds will Maria put in each pot? **(MA.3.A.1.1; pp. 275–278)**

Ⓐ 6

Ⓑ 7

Ⓒ 8

Ⓓ 9

20. There are 56 students at basketball camp. The coaches put 8 players on each team. Which of the following can be used to find how many teams were made? **(MA.3.A.1.3; pp. 271–274)**

Ⓕ $56 - 8 = ■$

Ⓖ $■ + 8 = 56$

Ⓗ $■ \times 8 = 56$

Ⓘ $56 + 8 = ■$

21. Tristan bought 21 tickets to go on his favorite ride at the fair. The ride costs 3 tickets. How many times can Tristan go on his favorite ride? **(MA.3.A.1.1; pp. 249–252)**

Ⓐ 7

Ⓑ 9

Ⓒ 18

Ⓓ 24

22. Mr. Mitchell bought 20 pencils for his 4 children to share equally. Which number sentence could be used to find the number of pencils each of Mr. Mitchell's children received? **(MA.3.A.1.1; pp. 253–256)**

Ⓕ $20 + 4 = ■$

Ⓖ $20 - 4 = ■$

Ⓗ $20 \times 4 = ■$

Ⓘ $20 \div 4 = ■$

Name ________________________________

Fill in the bubble for the correct answer choice.

23. Forty-two students are going on a field trip. They are riding in 7 vans. Each van holds the same number of students. How many students are riding in each van?
(MA.3.A.1.1; pp. 267–270)

Ⓐ 5

Ⓑ 6

Ⓒ 7

Ⓓ 8

24. Five people are going camping. They brought 5 tents. If an equal number of people sleep in each of the 5 tents, how many people will sleep in each one?
(MA.3.A.1.2; pp. 257–260)

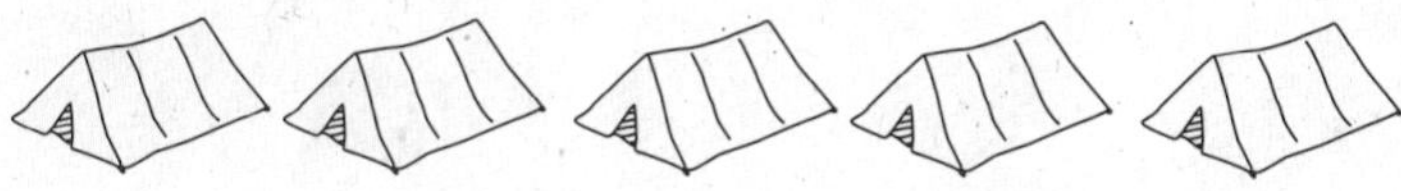

Ⓕ 1

Ⓖ 5

Ⓗ 10

Ⓘ 25

25. Kendall made 30 muffins. Each of her baking trays holds 6 muffins. Which number sentence could be used to find how many trays Kendall used to bake her muffins? **(MA.3.A.1.1; pp. 261–264)**

Ⓐ $30 - 6 = \blacksquare$

Ⓑ $6 + \blacksquare = 30$

Ⓒ $30 \div 6 = \blacksquare$

Ⓓ $6 \times 30 = \blacksquare$

26. Dominic took swimming lessons for 12 hours over 3 weeks. He swam the same number of hours each week. For how many hours did Dominic swim during each of the 3 weeks? (MA.3.A.1.1; pp. 249–252)

Ⓕ 3 hours

Ⓖ 4 hours

Ⓗ 9 hours

Ⓘ 15 hours

27. For field day, 81 third graders were separated into teams of 9 students. Which of the following can be used to find how many teams were made?
(MA.3.A.1.3; pp. 275–278)

Ⓐ $9 + ■ = 81$

Ⓑ $81 - 9 = ■$

Ⓒ $81 + 9 = ■$

Ⓓ $■ \times 9 = 81$

28. Alexandra has 6 new books, and there is 1 empty shelf left in her bookcase. She puts her books on the empty shelf. How many books are on the shelf?
(MA.3.A.1.2; pp. 257–260)

Ⓕ 0 Ⓗ 6

Ⓖ 1 Ⓘ 7

29. Mr. Jackson bought 24 bottles of water. He drank an equal number of his bottles of water on each of 6 days. How many bottles of water did Mr. Jackson drink each day? (MA.3.A.1.1; pp. 261–264)

Ⓐ 4

Ⓑ 6

Ⓒ 12

Ⓓ 18

Big Idea

2 Fractions

BIG IDEA Develop an understanding of fractions and fraction equivalence.

Go online

Math on Location Videos from The Futures Channel

The Florida quarter tells about discovery in our state—in the past and in the future. ▶

with Math on Location Videos

The First American Coins

Many years ago, a coin called a "piece of eight" was sometimes cut into 8 equal parts. Each part was equal to one eighth ($\frac{1}{8}$) of the whole. Now, U.S. coin values are based on the dollar. Four quarters are equal in value to 1 dollar. So, 1 quarter is equal to one fourth ($\frac{1}{4}$) of a dollar.

Project

You will begin to learn about the big idea when you work on this project.

Work with a partner. In which year were Florida's state quarters minted? Use the Important Facts to help you. Then write fractions to answer these questions:

1. 1 dime is equal to what part of a dollar?
2. 1 nickel is equal to what part of a dollar?
3. 1 penny is equal to what part of a dollar?

Important Facts

- The U.S. Government minted state quarters every year from 1999 to 2008 in the order that the states became part of the United States.
- 1999–Delaware, Pennsylvania, New Jersey, Georgia, Connecticut
- 2000–Massachusetts, Maryland, South Carolina, New Hampshire, Virginia
- 2001–New York, North Carolina, Rhode Island, Vermont, Kentucky
- 2002–Tennessee, Ohio, Louisiana, Indiana, Mississippi

2003–Illinois, Alabama, Maine, Missouri, Arkansas
2004–Michigan, Florida, Texas, Iowa, Wisconsin
2005–California, Minnesota, Oregon, Kansas, West Virginia
2006–Nevada, Nebraska, Colorado, North Dakota, South Dakota
2007–Montana, Washington, Idaho, Wyoming, Utah
2008–Oklahoma, New Mexico, Arizona, Alaska, Hawaii

____

____

____

____

Completed by ______________________

Chapter

7 Understand Fractions

Show What You Know

Check your understanding of important skills.

Name ______________________________

▶ Equal Parts Circle the shape that has equal parts.

1. 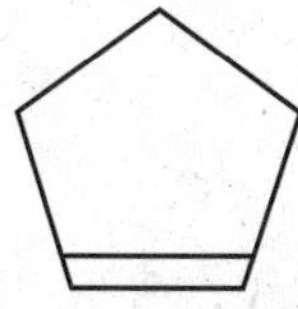 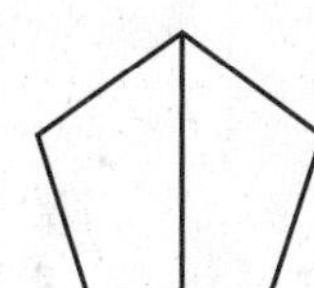

2. 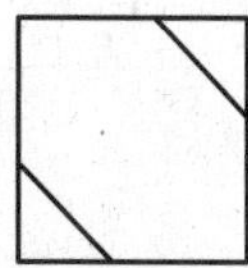 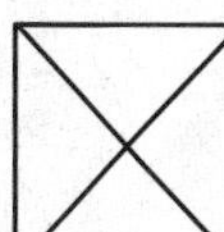 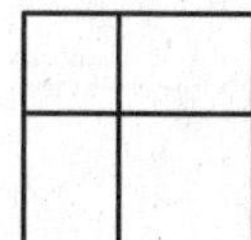

▶ Parts of a Whole Write the number of shaded parts and the number of equal parts.

3. ____ shaded parts
____ equal parts

4. 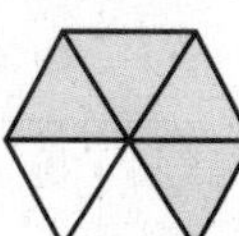 ____ shaded parts
____ equal parts

▶ Parts of a Group Write the number that are red and the number in the whole group.

5. 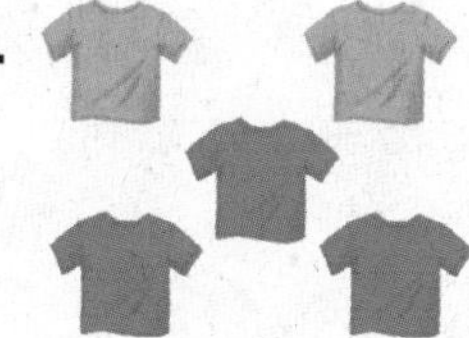 ____ red
____ in all

6.  ____ red
____ in all

Florida FUN FACT

Orlando, Florida, has several theme parks. You can ride a roller coaster, pet a dolphin, or even be splashed by a whale!

FLORIDA BENCHMARKS

Vocabulary Power

▶ Visualize It

Complete the Bubble Map by using the words with a ✓.

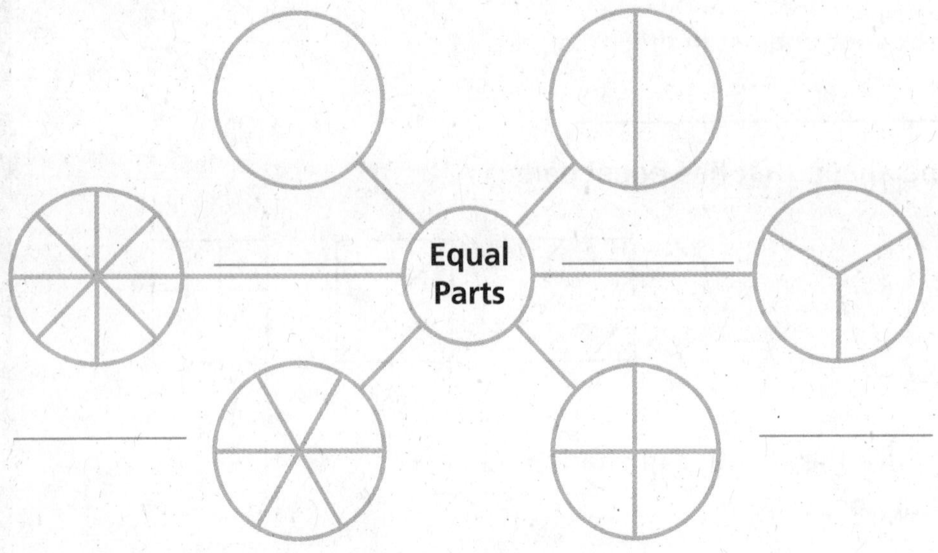

Review Word
✓ whole

Preview Words
denominator
✓ eighths
✓ fourths
fraction
✓ halves
mixed number
numerator
✓ sixths
✓ thirds

▶ Understand Vocabulary

Read the description. Write the preview word.

1. It is a number that names part of a whole or part of a group. ________________
2. It is the part of a fraction above the line, which tells how many parts are being counted.

   ____
3. It is the part of a fraction below the line, which tells how many equal parts there are in the whole or in the group. ________________
4. It is a number represented by a whole number and a fraction. ________________

Go online • Student Edition • Multilingual eGlossary

Name ___________________________

Equal Parts of a Whole

Essential Question What are equal parts of a whole?

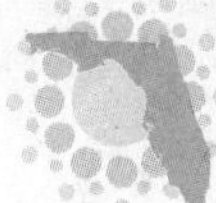

MA.3.A.2.1 Represent fractions, including fractions greater than one, using area, set and linear models.

UNLOCK the Problem REAL WORLD

Lauren shares a sandwich with her brother. They each get an equal part. How many equal parts are there?

- What do you need to find?

  ____

  ____

- How many people share the sandwich? ______________

Equal parts are exactly the same size. Each whole shape below is divided into equal parts.

2 **halves**

3 **thirds**

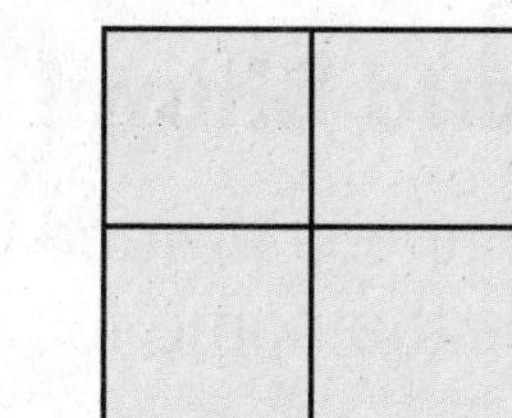

4 **fourths**

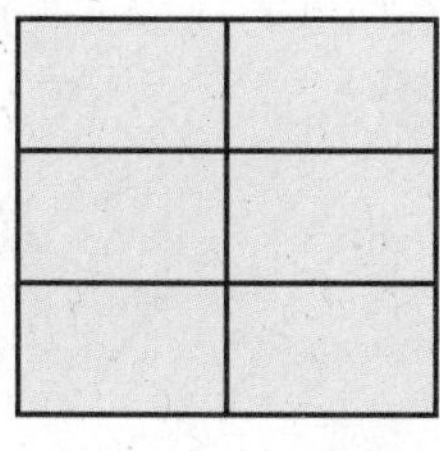

_____ **sixths**

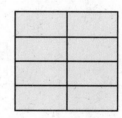

_____ **eighths**

Since Lauren's sandwich is divided equally between 2 people, there are 2 equal parts.

- Draw a picture to show a different way Lauren's sandwich could have been divided into halves.

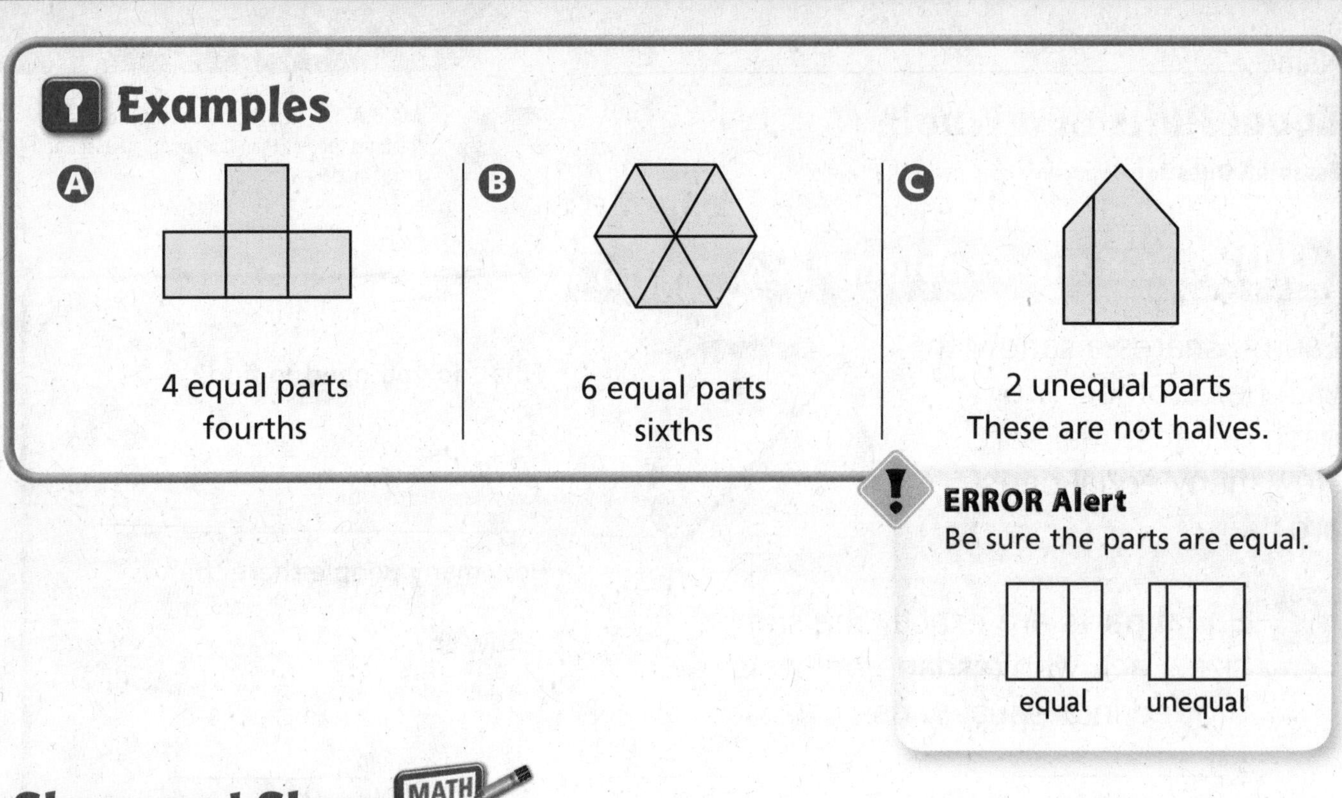

Share and Show

1. This shape is divided into 3 equal parts. What is the name for the parts?

____

Math Talk Explain how you know if parts are equal.

Write the number of equal parts. Then write the name for the parts.

2. 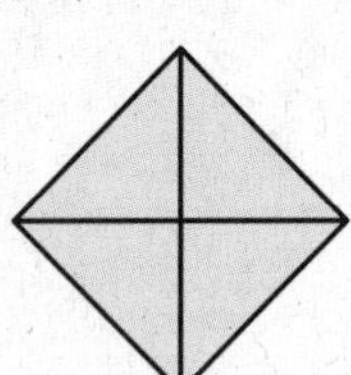

_____ equal parts

____

3. 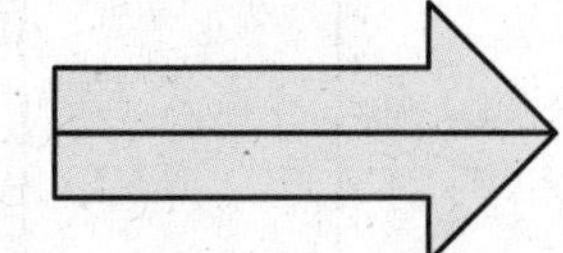

_____ equal parts

____

✓4. 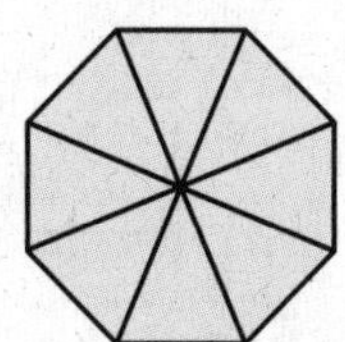

_____ equal parts

____

Write whether each shape is divided into *equal* parts or *unequal* parts.

5. 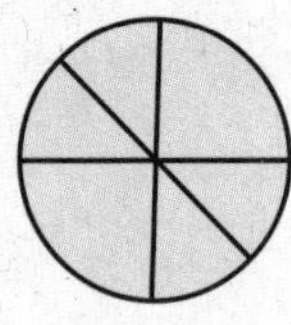

___________ parts

6. 

___________ parts

✓7. 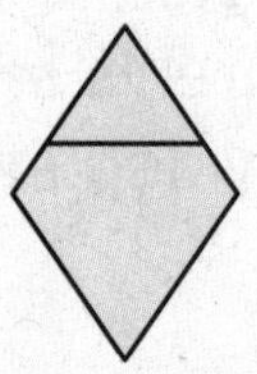

___________ parts

Name ___________________________

On Your Own

Write the number of equal parts. Then write the name for the parts.

8. 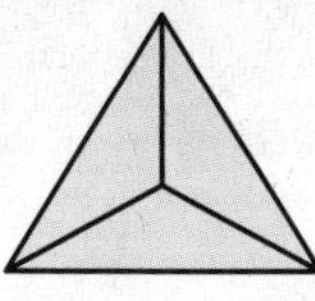

_____ equal parts

____

9. 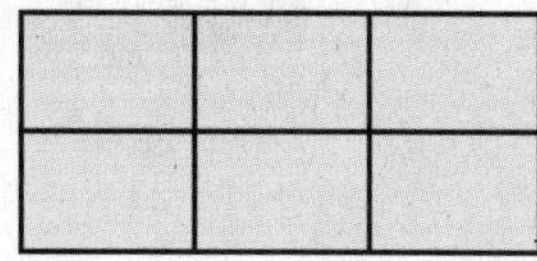

_____ equal parts

____

10. 

_____ equal parts

____

11. 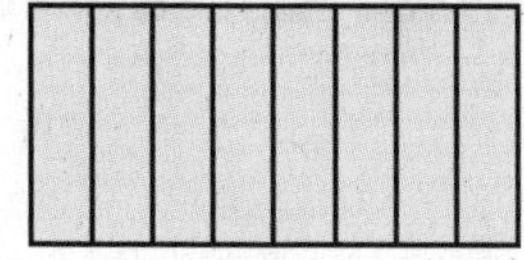

_____ equal parts

____

12. 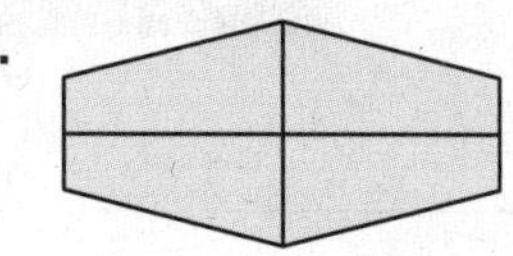

_____ equal parts

____

13. 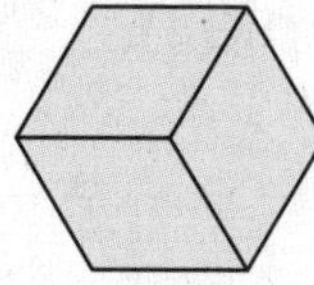

_____ equal parts

____

Write whether each shape is divided into *equal* parts or *unequal* parts.

14. 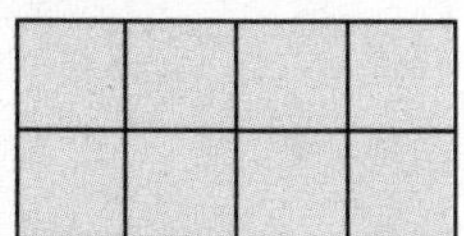

___________ parts

15. 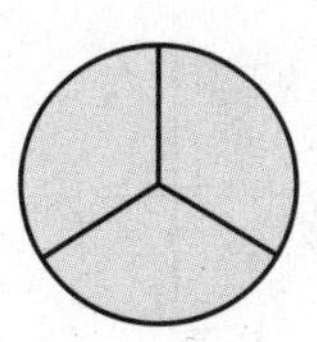

___________ parts

16. 

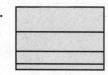

___________ parts

Draw lines to divide the circles into equal parts.

17. 2 halves

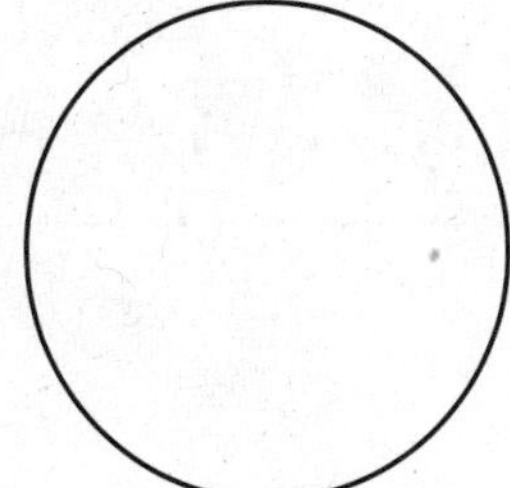

18. 4 fourths

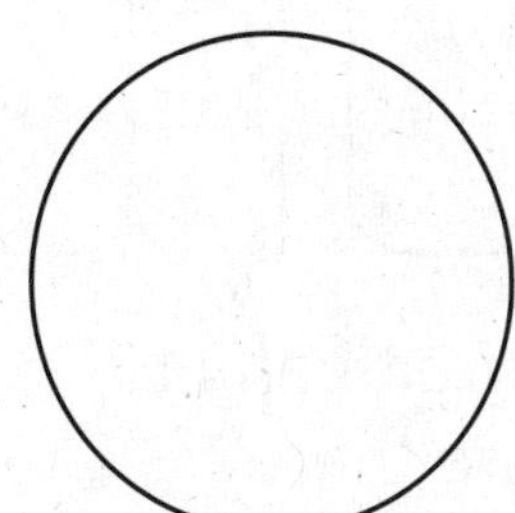

19. 8 eighths

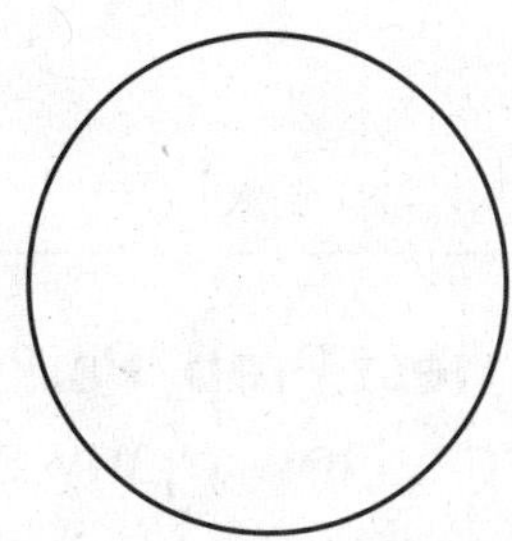

Problem Solving REAL WORLD

Use the pictures for 20–21.

20. Mrs. Rivera bought 2 sub sandwiches for Alex's party. She cut each sub into parts. What is the name of the parts for Sub A?

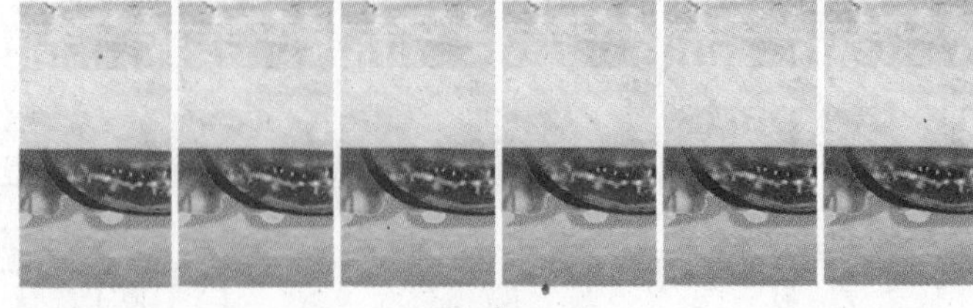

Sub A

____

21. H.O.T. **Sense or Nonsense?** Alex said his mom divided Sub B into eighths. Does his statement make sense? **Explain.**

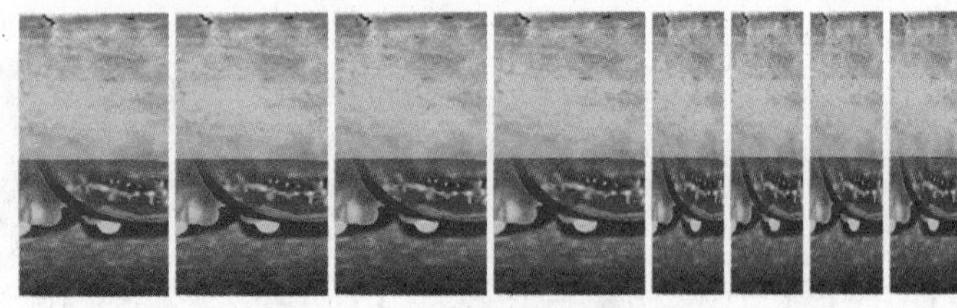

Sub B

____

____

22. Shelby cut a triangle out of paper. She wants to divide the triangle into 2 equal parts. Draw a quick picture to show what her triangle could look like.

23. Andrew wants to divide a square piece of paper into 4 equal parts. Draw two different quick pictures to show what his paper could look like.

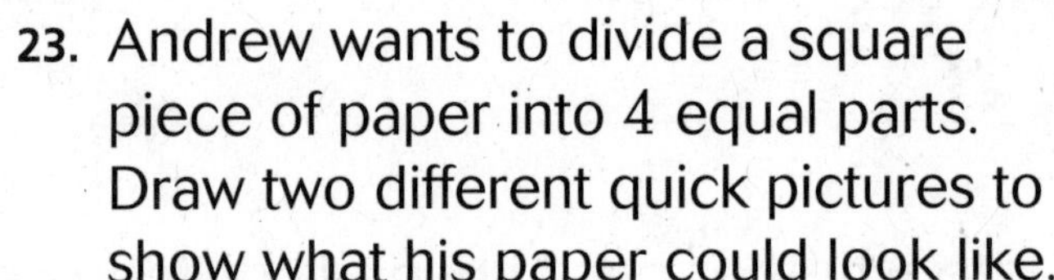

24. **Test Prep** Parker divides a fruit bar into thirds. How many equal parts are there?

Ⓐ 2 Ⓒ 4

Ⓑ 3 Ⓓ 8

FOR MORE PRACTICE:
Florida Benchmarks Practice Book, pp. P161–P162

Name ____________________

Equal Shares

Essential Question Why do you need to know how to make equal shares?

MA.3.A.2.1 Represent fractions, including fractions greater than one, using area, set and linear models.

UNLOCK the Problem REAL WORLD

Four friends share 2 pizzas equally. How much pizza does each friend get?

- What do you need to find?

____

____

Draw to model the problem.

STEP 1 Draw 2 circles to show the pizzas.

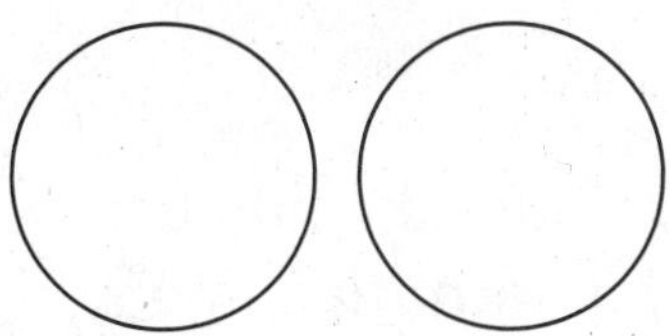

STEP 2 Draw lines to divide each pizza in half.

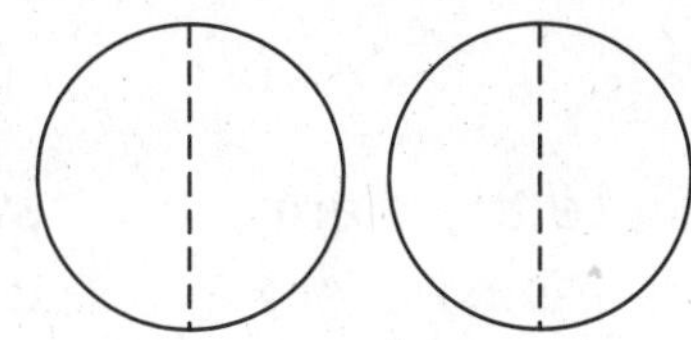

STEP 3 Find the amount of pizza each friend gets.

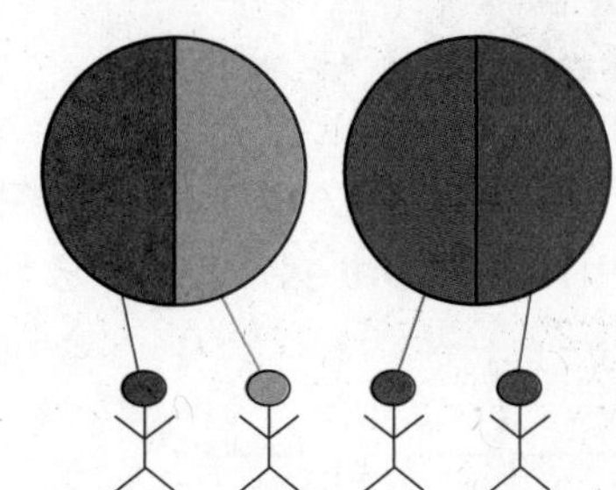

Each circle has _____ equal parts.

So, each friend gets 1 half.

Try This! Four girls share 3 oranges equally. Draw a quick picture to find out how much each girl gets.

- Draw 3 circles to show the oranges.
- Since there are 4 girls, draw lines to divide each circle into fourths.
- Count the number of fourths each girl gets.

So, each girl gets _____ fourths.

Three friends share 4 fruit squares equally. How much does each friend get?

One Way

STEP 1 Draw 4 squares to show the fruit squares.

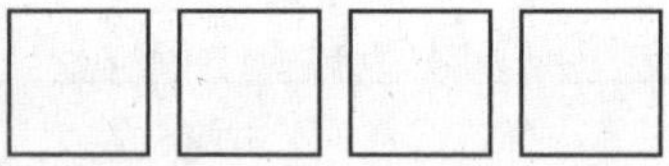

STEP 2 There are more squares than friends, so each friend gets 1 whole square.

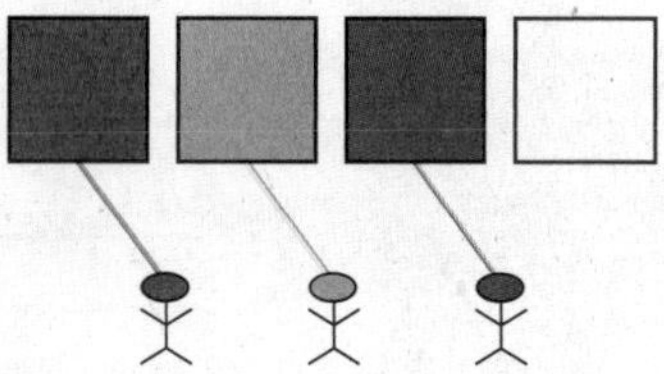

STEP 3 Divide the leftover square into thirds.

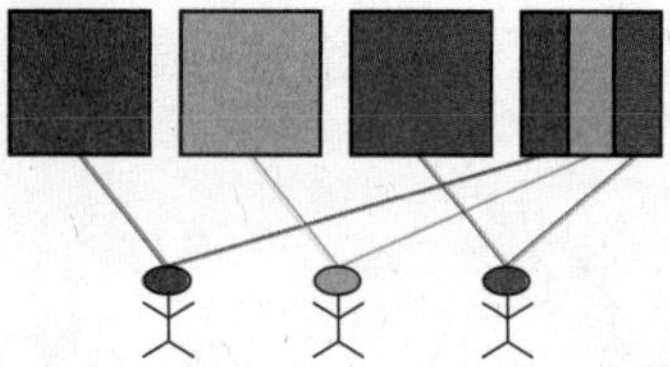

So, each friend gets 1 whole square and 1 third of another.

Another Way

STEP 1 Draw 4 squares to show the fruit squares.

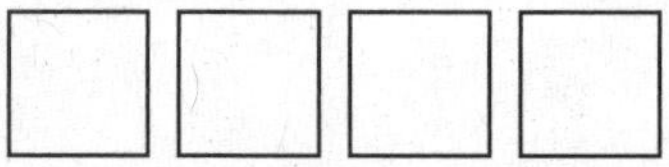

STEP 2 Since there are 3 friends, divide every square into thirds.

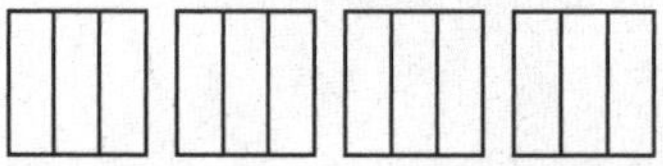

STEP 3 Count the number of thirds each friend gets.

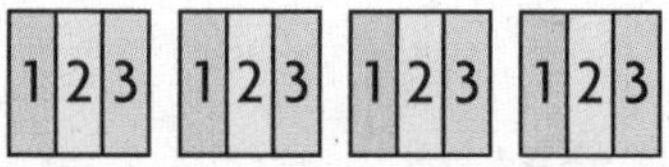

1 2 3 1 2 3 1 2 3 1 2 3

So, each friend gets 4 thirds.

Try This! Two boys share 3 veggie squares equally. Draw a quick picture to find out how much each boy gets.

- Draw 3 squares to show the veggie squares.
- Draw lines to divide the squares.
- Find the amount each boy gets.

So, each boy gets ________.

Math Talk **Explain** a different way you could have divided the veggie squares.

Name ___________________________________

Share and Show 

1. Two friends share 5 cookies equally. Use the picture to find how much each friend gets.

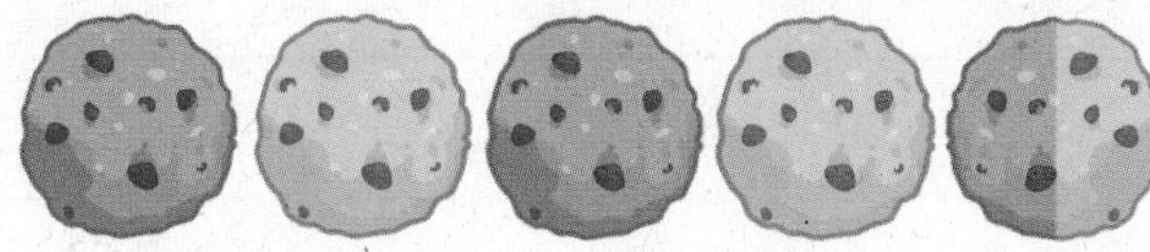

Math Talk
Explain another way the cookies could have been divided.

____

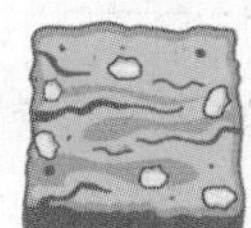 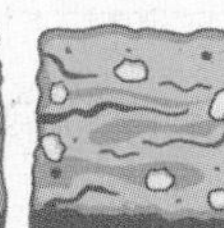 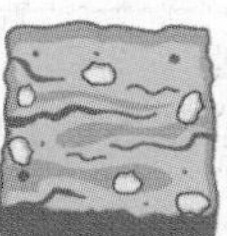 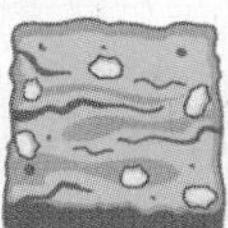 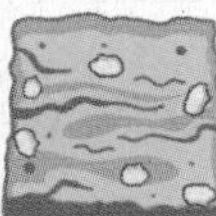

Draw lines to show how much each person gets. Write the answer.

2. 3 sisters share 5 brownies.

____

3. 6 neighbors share 4 pies.

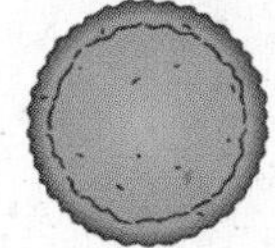 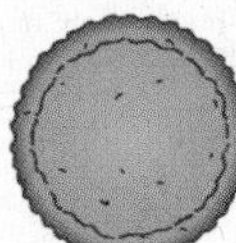 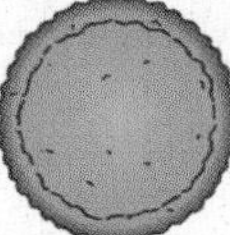 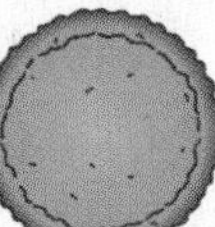

____

On Your Own

Draw lines to show how much each person gets. Write the answer.

4. 3 classmates share 2 granola bars.

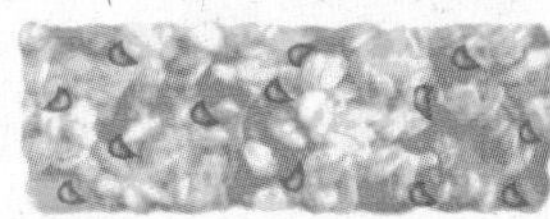 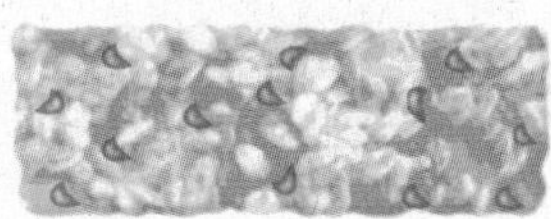

____

5. 4 brothers share 6 sandwiches.

____

UNLOCK the Problem REAL WORLD

6. Julia has 4 adults and 3 children coming over for dessert. She is going to serve 2 small blueberry pies. If she plans to give each person, including herself, an equal amount of pie, how much pie will each person get?

a. What do you need to find? ______________________

____

b. How will you use what you know about drawing equal shares to solve the problem? ______________________

____

c. Draw a quick picture to find the amount of pie each person will get.

d. Complete the sentences.

Julia has _____ adults and _____ children coming over for dessert.

She is going to serve _____ blueberry pies.

So, each person will get __________ of a blueberry pie.

7. Abby baked 5 cherry pies. She wants to share them equally among 4 of her neighbors. How much pie will each neighbor get?

____

8. **Test Prep** Six friends share 2 pizzas. How much pizza does each friend get?

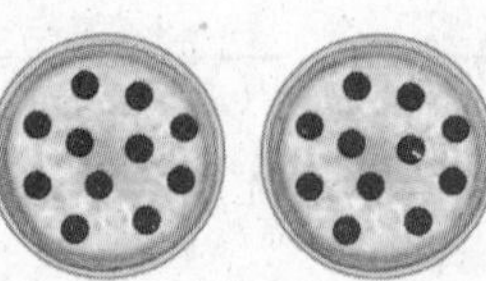

Ⓐ 2 sixths
Ⓑ 3 sixths
Ⓒ 6 halves
Ⓓ 6 thirds

FOR MORE PRACTICE:
Florida Benchmarks Book, pp. P163–164

Name ______________________________

Unit Fractions of a Whole

MA.3.A.2.1 Represent fractions, including fractions greater than one, using area, set and linear models.

Essential Question What do the top and bottom numbers of a fraction tell?

A **fraction** is a number that names part of a whole or part of a group.

A **unit fraction** has 1 as its top number. $\frac{1}{6}$ is a unit fraction.

In a fraction, the top number tells how many equal parts are being counted. $\longrightarrow$ 1

The bottom number tells how many equal parts are in the whole or in the group. $\longrightarrow$ 6

UNLOCK the Problem REAL WORLD

Luke's family picked strawberries. They used them to make a strawberry pie. They cut it into 6 equal pieces. Luke ate 1 piece. What fraction of the strawberry pie did he eat?

▲ Each year Plant City hosts the Florida Strawberry Festival, which has a parade, rides, and a strawberry shortcake-eating contest!

Find part of a whole.

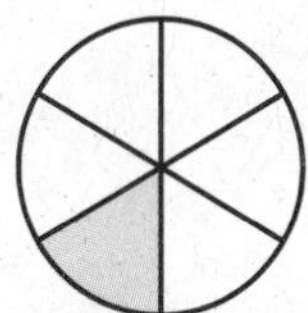

Shade 1 of the 6 equal parts.

Read: one sixth **Write:** $\frac{1}{6}$

So, Luke ate ______ of the strawberry pie.

Use a fraction to find a whole.

This shape  is $\frac{1}{4}$ of the whole.
Here are examples of what the whole could look like.

Ⓐ 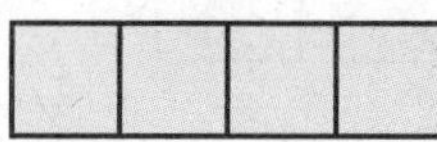

Ⓑ 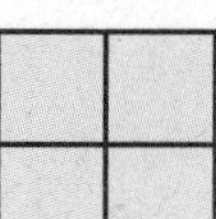

Ⓒ 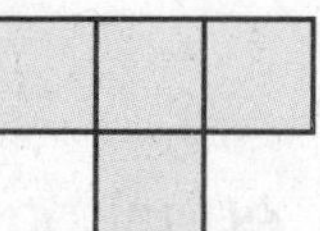

- Look again at the examples at the bottom of page 299. Draw two other pictures of what the whole could look like.

Share and Show

1. What fraction names the shaded part? ______

Think: 1 out of 10 equal parts is shaded.

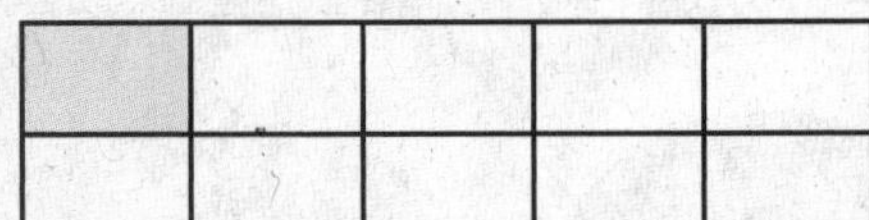

Math Talk Explain how you knew what number to write as the bottom number of the fraction in Problem 1.

Write the number of equal parts in the whole. Then write the fraction that names the shaded part.

2. 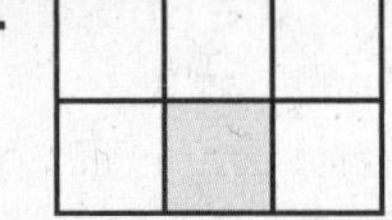

______ equal parts

______

3. 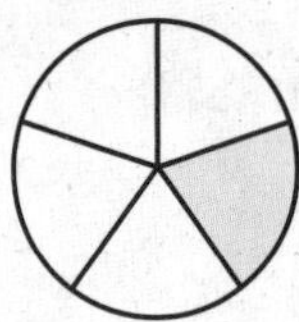

______ equal parts

______

4. 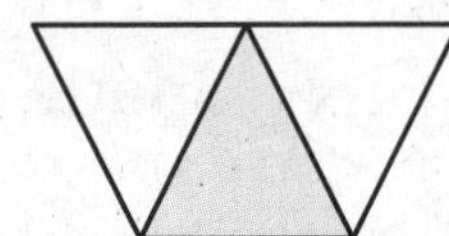

______ equal parts

______

5. 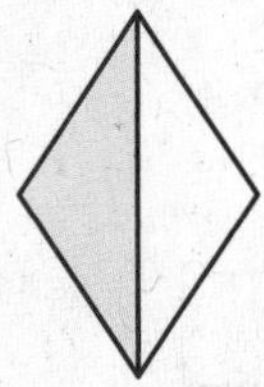

______ equal parts

______

6. 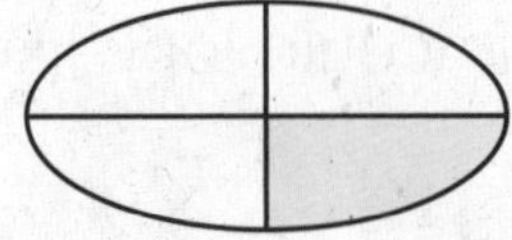

______ equal parts

______

7. 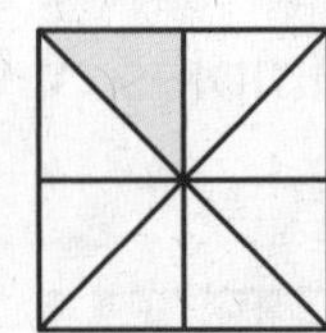

______ equal parts

______

Name ____________________

On Your Own

Write the number of equal parts in the whole. Then write the fraction that names the shaded part.

8. 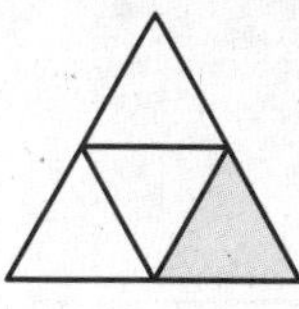

_____ equal parts

_____

9. 

_____ equal parts

_____

10. 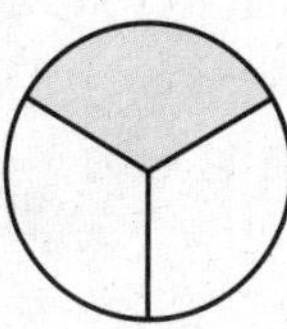

_____ equal parts

_____

11. 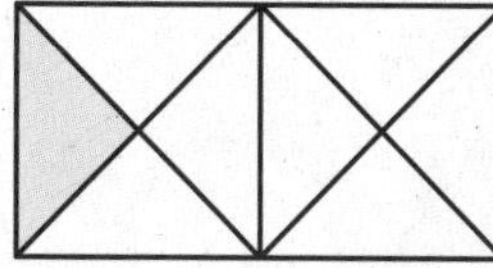

_____ equal parts

_____

12. 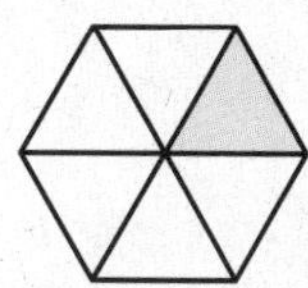

_____ equal parts

_____

13. 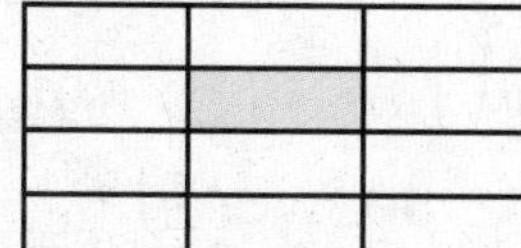

_____ equal parts

_____

H.O.T. **Draw a picture of the whole.**

14. $\frac{1}{2}$ is 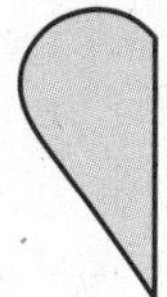

15. $\frac{1}{3}$ is 

16. $\frac{1}{5}$ is

17. $\frac{1}{4}$ is

Problem Solving REAL WORLD

Use the pictures for 18–20.

Kylie's Lunch	Dylan's Lunch
sub	pizza
cookie	fruit bar

18. The missing parts of the pictures show what Kylie and Dylan ate for lunch. What fraction of the pizza did Dylan eat?

____

19. What fraction of the cookie did Kylie eat? Write the fraction in numbers and in words.

_____ _______________

20. **Write Math** ▸ **What's the Question?** The answer is $\frac{1}{4}$.

____

____

21. **H.O.T.** Diego drew lines to divide a square into 6 pieces. Then he shaded part of the square. Diego says he shaded $\frac{1}{6}$ of the square. Is he correct? **Explain** how you know.

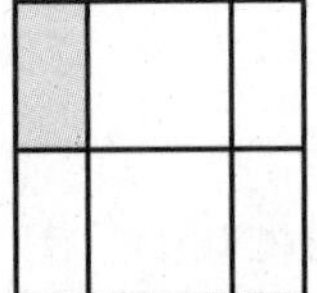

____

____

22. **H.O.T.** Riley's granola bar is broken into equal pieces. She ate one piece, which was $\frac{1}{5}$ of the bar. How many more pieces does Riley need to eat to finish the granola bar?

____

23. **Test Prep** Mary shaded part of a rectangle. What fraction names the part she shaded?

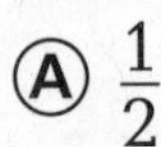

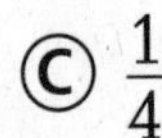

Ⓐ $\frac{1}{2}$ Ⓒ $\frac{1}{4}$

Ⓑ $\frac{1}{3}$ Ⓓ $\frac{1}{5}$

Name ______________________

Fractions of a Whole

Essential Question How can you show a fraction as part of a whole?

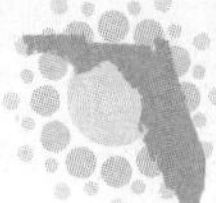

MA.3.A.2.1 Represent fractions, including fractions greater than one, using area, set and linear models.

UNLOCK the Problem REAL WORLD

The first pizzeria in America opened in New York in 1905. The pizza recipe came from Italy. Look at Italy's flag. What fraction of the flag is not red?

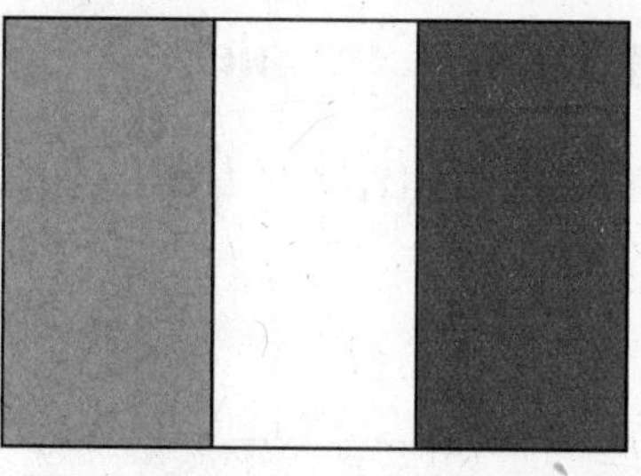

▲ The ingredients of some pizzas—basil, mozzarella, and tomato—show the colors of Italy's flag.

A fraction can name more than 1 equal part of a whole.

The flag is divided into 3 equal parts, and 2 parts are not red.

2 parts not red → 2 ← numerator
3 equal parts in all → 3 ← denominator

Read: two thirds **Write:** $\frac{2}{3}$

two parts out of three equal parts 2 divided by 3

So, _____ of the flag is not red.

The **numerator** tells how many parts are being counted.

The **denominator** tells how many equal parts are in the whole or in the group.

Try This! Write the missing word or number.

A

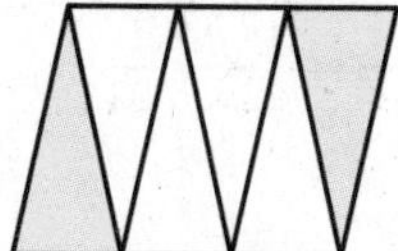

$\frac{2}{6}$

_____ sixths

B

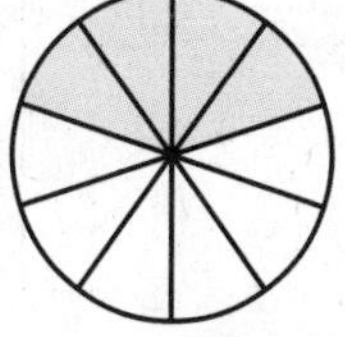

$\frac{\square}{10}$

four tenths

C

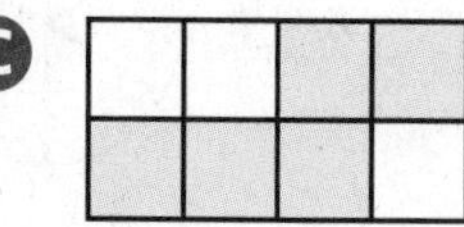

$\frac{5}{8}$

_____ eighths

D

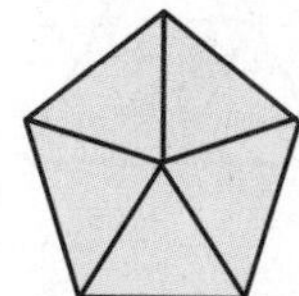

$\frac{\square}{5}$, or 1

one whole

Fractions on a Number Line

A number line can show parts of one whole. The space from one whole number to the next represents one whole. The line can be divided into any number of equal parts.

Try This! **Complete the sentence.**

A This number line shows thirds.

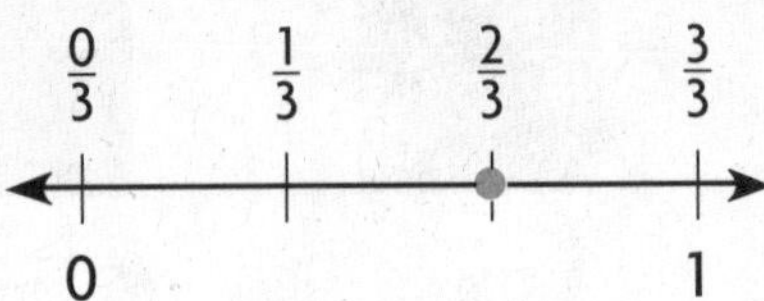

The point shows the location of ______.

B This number line shows fourths.

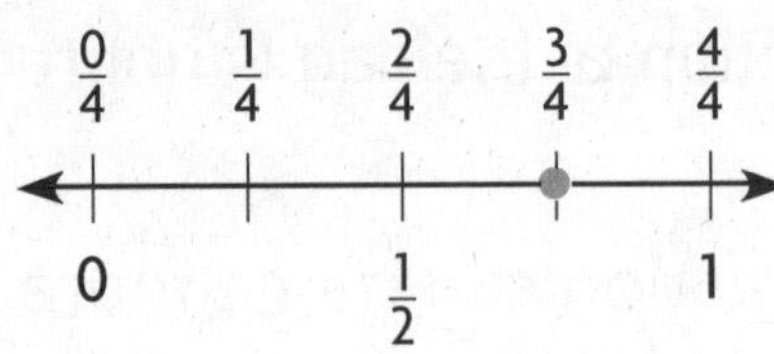

The point shows the location of ______.

Share and Show 

1. What fraction names the point? ______

Think: What number comes after 4?

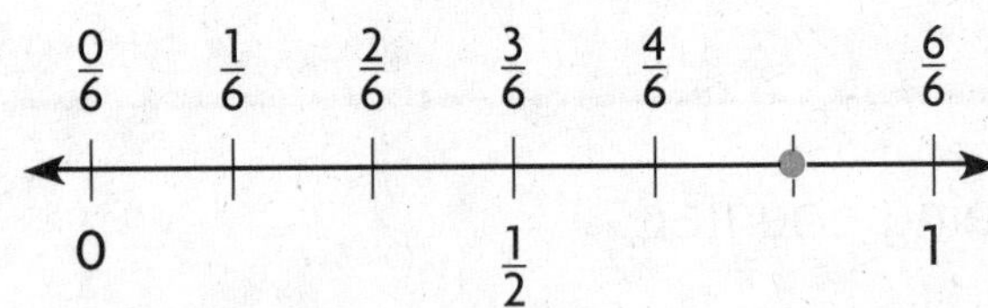

Math Talk **Explain** what the numerator and denominator of a fraction tell you.

Write a fraction in numbers and in words to name the shaded part.

2.

______

______ fourths

✓ 3.

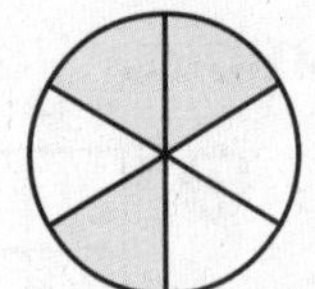

______

______ sixths

✓ 4.

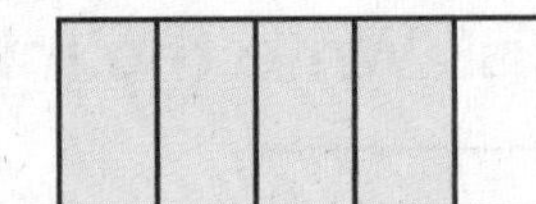

______

______ fifths

Name ________________________________

On Your Own

Write a fraction in numbers and in words to name the shaded part.

5. 

______

______ eighths

6. 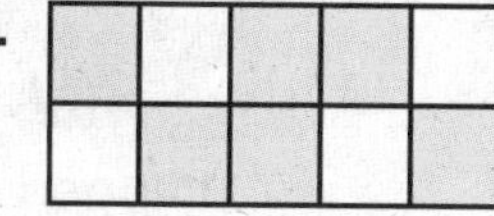

______

______ tenths

7. 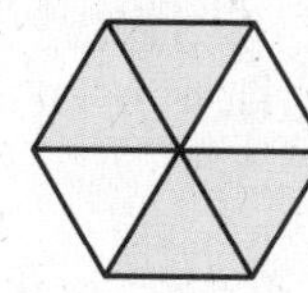

______

______ sixths

8. 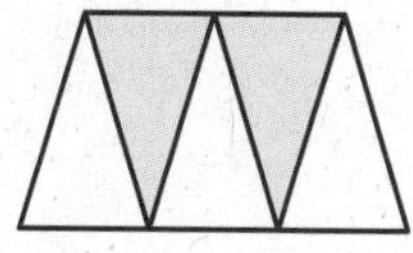

______

______ fifths

9. 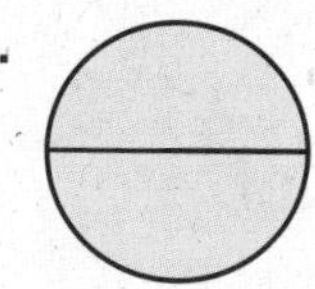

______

______ halves

10. 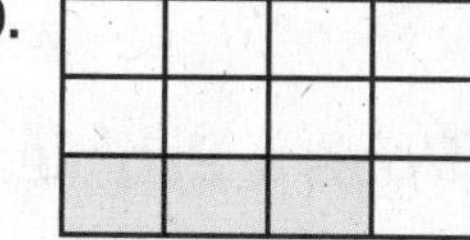

______

______ twelfths

Shade the fraction circle to model the fraction. Then write the fraction in numbers.

11. six out of eight

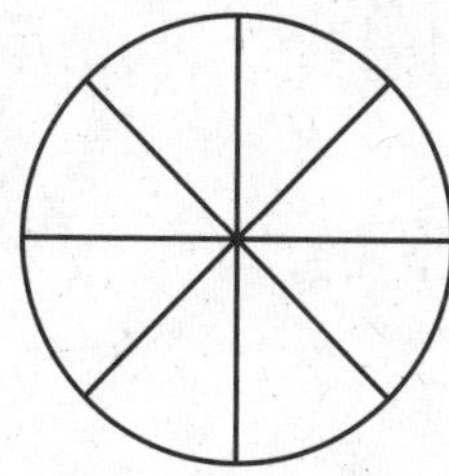

______

12. three fourths

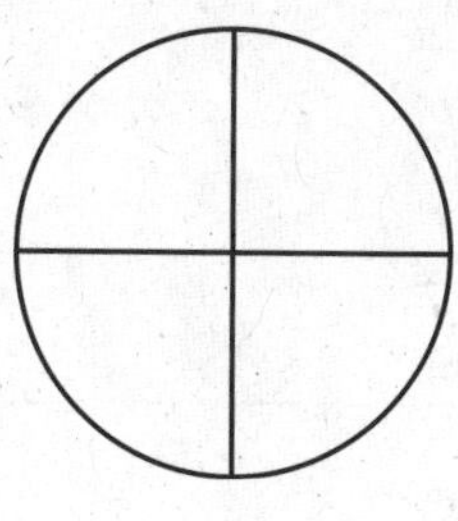

______

13. two divided by three

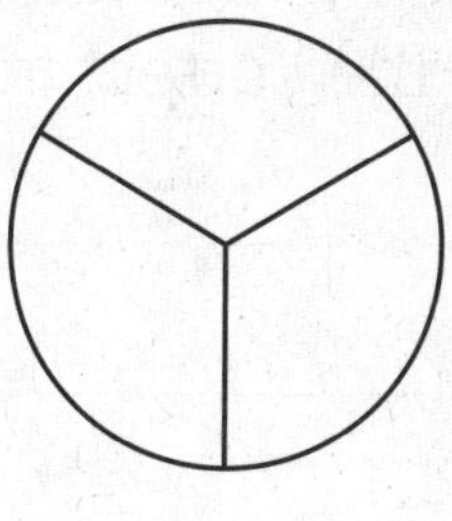

______

Write a fraction that names each point.

14. 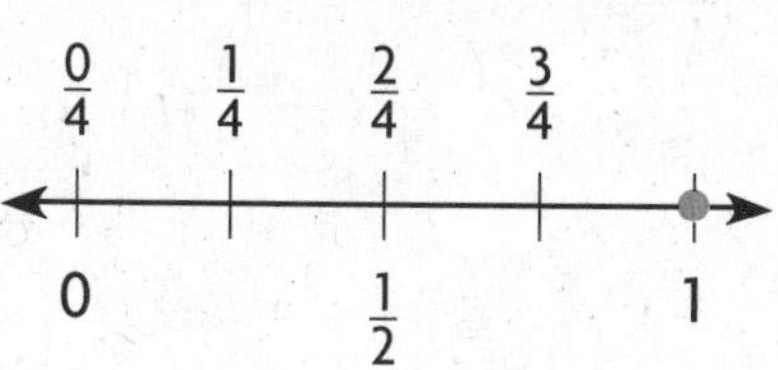

______

15. 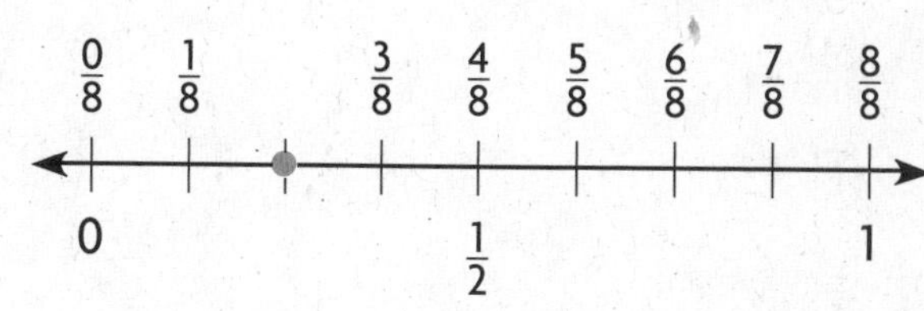

______

Problem Solving REAL WORLD

Use the pictures for 16–18.

Pepperoni

Cheese

Veggie

16. Mrs. Ormond ordered pizza. Each pizza had 8 equal slices. What fraction of the pepperoni pizza is left?

____

17. What fraction of the cheese pizza is left?

____

18. H.O.T. **Pose a Problem** Use the picture of the veggie pizza to write a problem that has a fraction as the answer. Solve your problem.

____

____

____

19. H.O.T. **What's the Error?** Kate says that $\frac{2}{3}$ names the shaded part. Describe her error. Write the correct fraction.

____

____

____

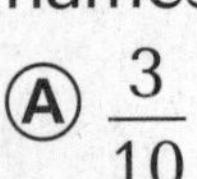

20. **Test Prep** What fraction names the shaded part?

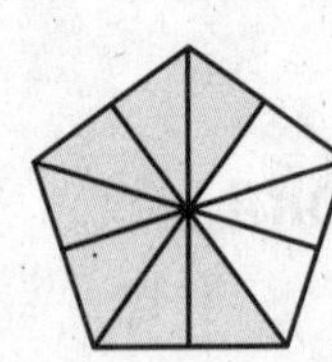

Ⓐ $\frac{3}{10}$

Ⓑ $\frac{3}{7}$

Ⓒ $\frac{7}{10}$

Ⓓ $\frac{10}{7}$

FOR MORE PRACTICE:
Florida Benchmarks Practice Book, pp. P167–P168

Name ______________________________

Mid-Chapter Checkpoint

▶ Check Vocabulary

Choose the best term from the box to complete the sentence.

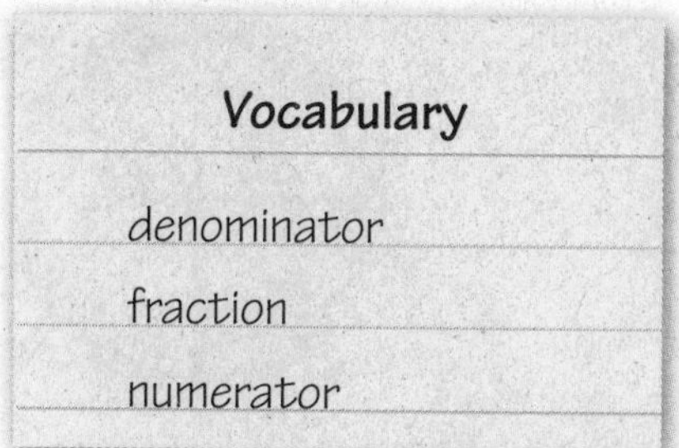

1. A ________________ is a number that names part of a whole or part of a group. **(MA.3.A.2.1; p. 299)**

2. The ________________ tells how many equal parts are in the whole or in the group. **(MA.3.A.2.1; p. 303)**

▶ Check Concepts

Write the number of equal parts. Then write the name for the parts. (MA.3.A.2.1; pp. 291–294)

3. 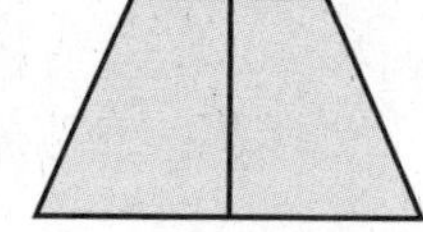

_____ equal parts

____

4. 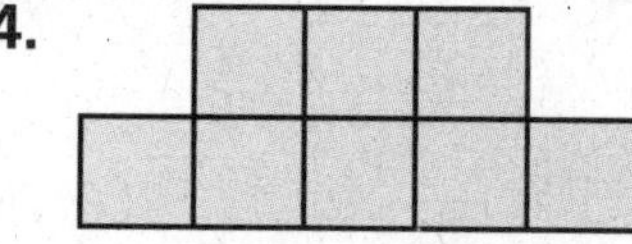

_____ equal parts

____

5. 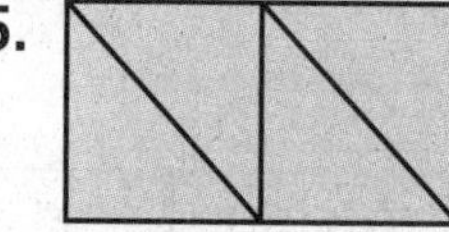

_____ equal parts

____

Write the number of equal parts in the whole. Then write the fraction that names the shaded part.
(MA.3.A.2.1; pp. 299–302)

6. 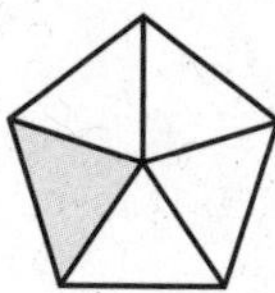

_____ equal parts

_____

7. 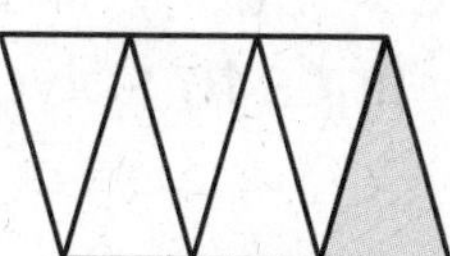

_____ equal parts

_____

8. 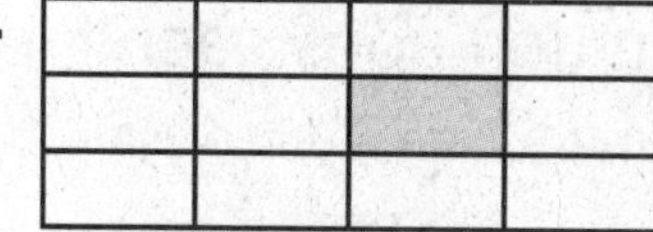

_____ equal parts

_____

Write a fraction that names the shaded part. (MA.3.A.2.1; pp. 303–306)

9. 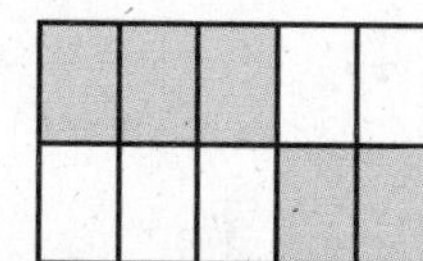 _____

10. 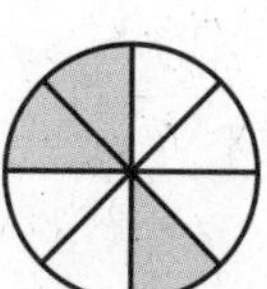 _____

11. 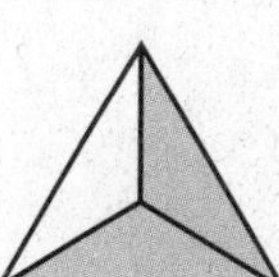 _____

Fill in the bubble for the correct answer choice.

12. Jessica ordered a pizza. What fraction of the pizza has mushrooms? **(MA.3.A.2.1; pp. 303–306)**

Ⓐ $\frac{2}{6}$

Ⓑ $\frac{2}{8}$

Ⓒ $\frac{6}{8}$

Ⓓ $\frac{8}{6}$

13. Wyatt drew the rectangle below and divided it into equal parts. What is the name for the parts?
(MA.3.A.2.1; pp. 291–294)

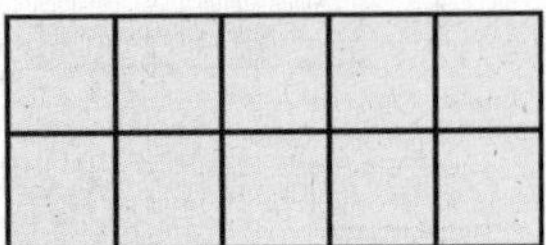

Ⓕ sixths

Ⓖ eighths

Ⓗ tenths

Ⓘ twelfths

14. Six friends share 3 oatmeal squares equally. How much does each friend get? Draw lines to solve.
(MA.3.A.2.1; pp. 295–298)

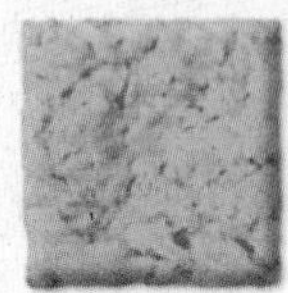 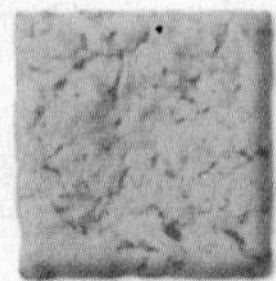 

Ⓐ 1 half

Ⓑ 1 third

Ⓒ 1 fourth

Ⓓ 1 sixth

Name ______________________________

Fractions Greater Than 1

Essential Question When do you use fractions greater than 1?

MA.3.A.2.1 Represent fractions, including fractions greater than one, using area, set and linear models.

UNLOCK the Problem REAL WORLD

Sarah volunteers at an animal shelter. She feeds each kitten $\frac{1}{3}$ can of food. How many cans of food does she give to 5 kittens?

- How much food does Sarah give to each kitten? ____________
- How many kittens does she feed? ____________

One Way Make a model.

- Shade $\frac{1}{3}$ for the amount of food Sarah gives to each of the 5 kittens.
- Then count the number of shaded pieces.

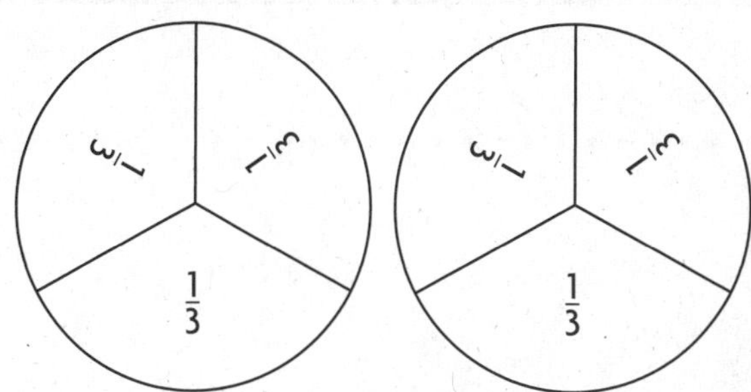

Remember: $\frac{3}{3} = 1$

______ pieces are shaded.

So, there are $\frac{5}{3}$ in all.

$\frac{5}{3} = \frac{3}{3} + \frac{2}{3}$

$\frac{5}{3} = 1 + \frac{2}{3} = 1\frac{2}{3}$

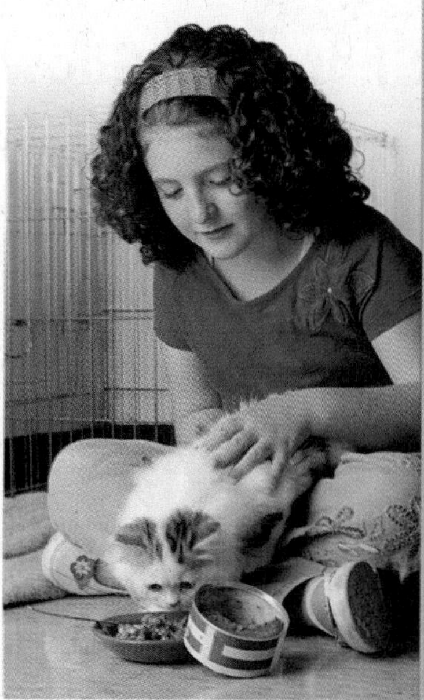

The number $\frac{5}{3}$ is a fraction greater than 1. A **fraction greater than 1** has a numerator that is greater than its denominator.

The number $1\frac{2}{3}$ is a mixed number. A **mixed number** is made up of a whole number and a fraction.

So, Sarah gives 5 kittens ______, or ______, cans of food.

Read Math

Read $1\frac{2}{3}$ as *one and two thirds.*

Another Way Use a number line.

Sarah walked to raise money for the animal shelter. She earned a prize for every $\frac{1}{3}$ mile she walked. If she earned 5 prizes, how many miles did Sarah walk?

- Continue drawing one jump for each $\frac{1}{3}$ mile Sarah walked.
- Then count the number of jumps.

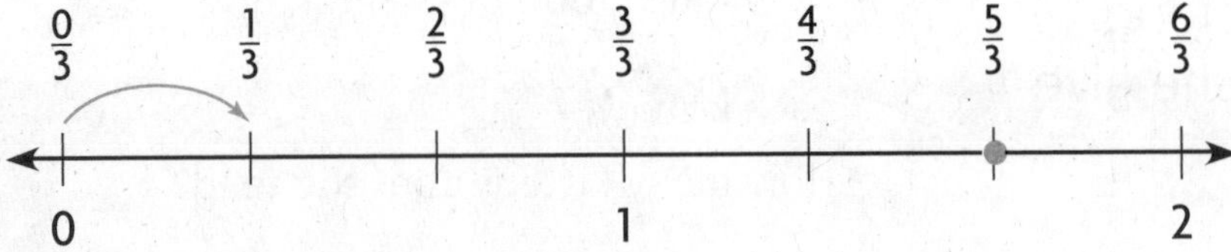

There are ______ jumps.

Five jumps on the number line is 2 thirds more than 1.

$\frac{5}{3} = 1 + \frac{2}{3} =$ ______

So, Sarah walked ______, or ______, miles.

Share and Show

1. Write a mixed number for the parts that are shaded. ______

Think: There are $\frac{7}{4}$ in all.

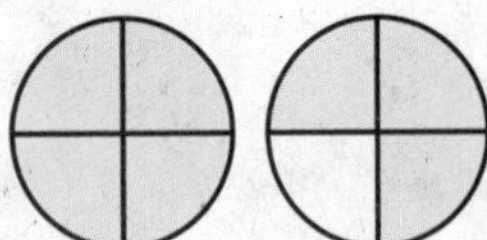

Math Talk Explain how you know whether a fraction can be renamed as a mixed number.

Write a fraction greater than 1 for the parts that are shaded.

2. 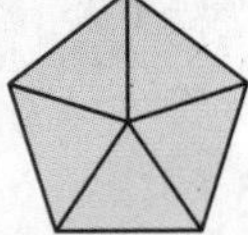 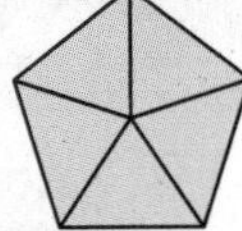 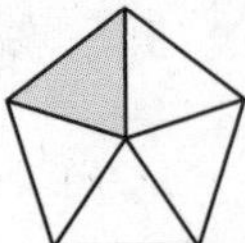  ______

3.  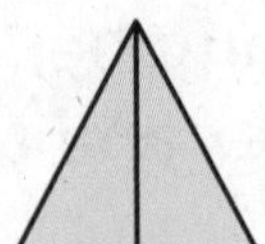 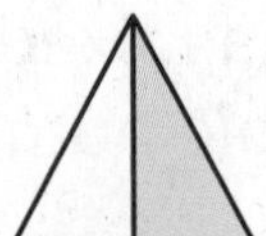 ______

4. 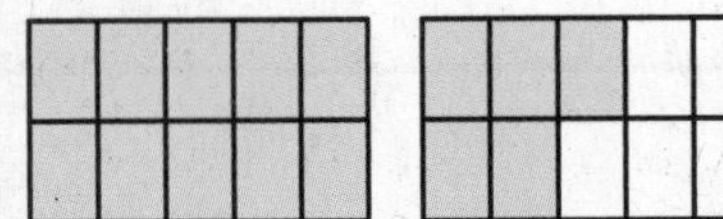 ______

5. 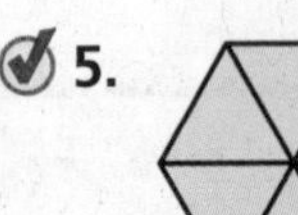 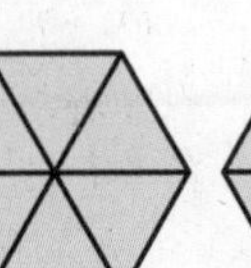 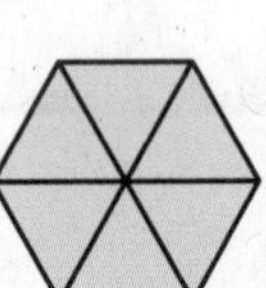 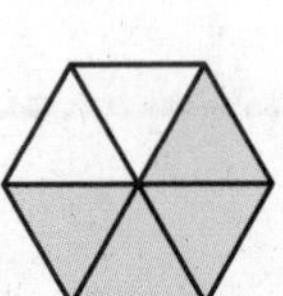 ______

Name ____________________

On Your Own

Write a fraction greater than 1 for the parts that are shaded.

6. 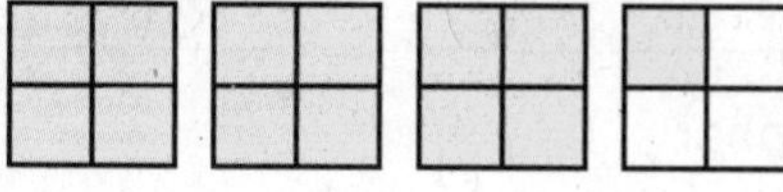 ______

7. 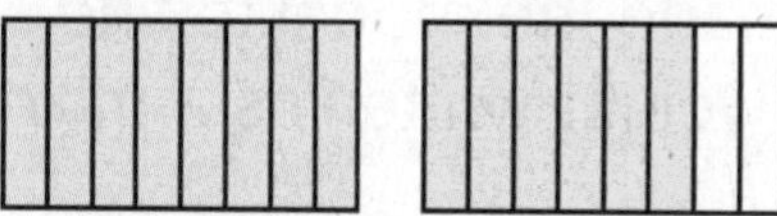 ______

8. 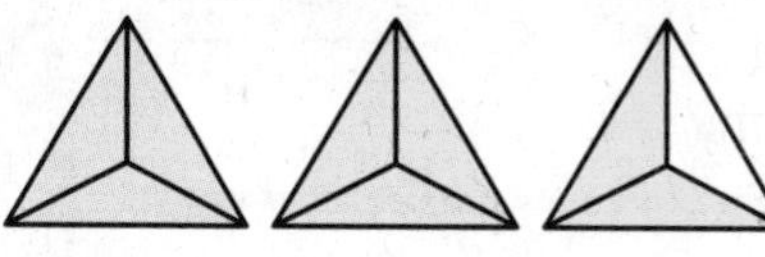 ______

9. 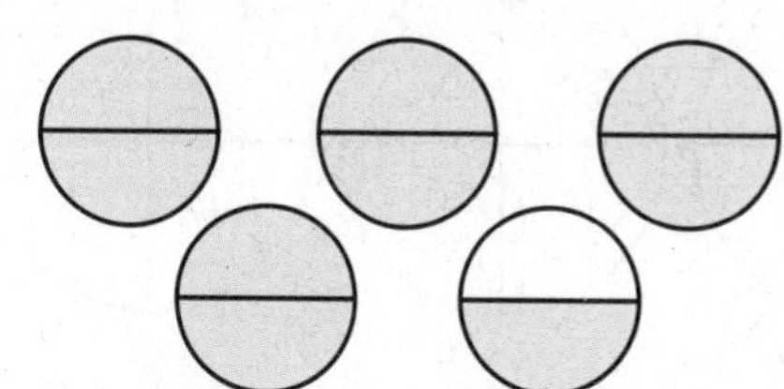 ______

For 10–13, use the number line to write the fraction greater than 1 as a mixed number.

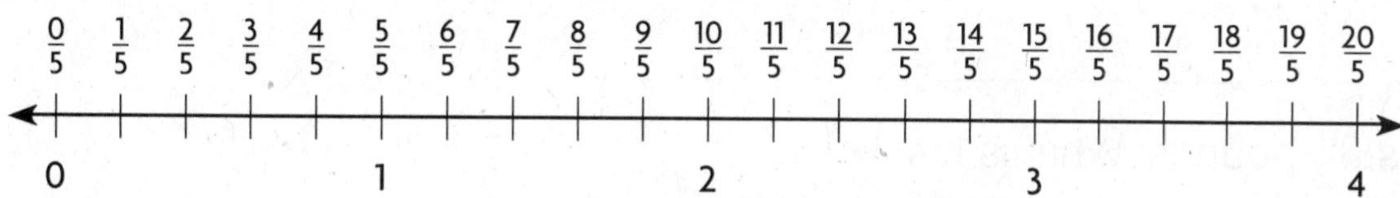

10. $\frac{6}{5}$ ______

11. $\frac{13}{5}$ ______

12. $\frac{9}{5}$ ______

13. $\frac{17}{5}$ ______

H.O.T. Draw a quick picture to show the mixed number. Then write the mixed number as a fraction greater than 1.

14. $2\frac{2}{4}$

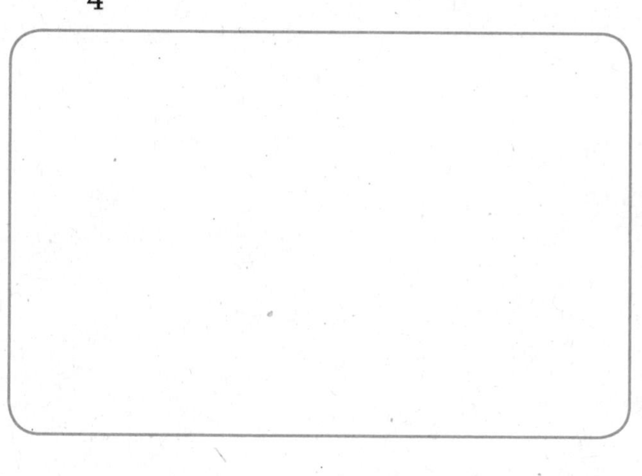

______

15. $1\frac{5}{6}$

______

Problem Solving REAL WORLD

Use the table for 16–17.

Weights of Kittens	
Name	**Weight (in pounds)**
Timber	$\frac{11}{4}$
Kally	$\frac{9}{6}$
Tabby	$\frac{10}{3}$

16. The table shows the weights of some kittens. Shade the model to find Timber's weight written as a mixed number.

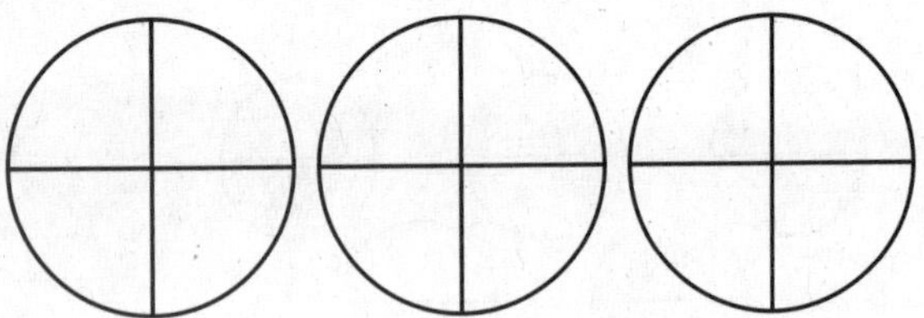

17. H.O.T. Which kitten weighs between 1 and 2 pounds?

18. Max weighs $3\frac{1}{2}$ pounds. What is his weight written as a fraction greater than 1? Draw a quick picture to solve.

19. Write Math Buttercup is a cat at the animal shelter. She weighs $2\frac{5}{8}$ pounds. Is her weight closer to 2 pounds or 3 pounds? **Explain** how you know.

20. **Test Prep** Ms. Adams gave $\frac{1}{4}$ of an apple to each of 10 children. How many apples did she give to the children in all?

Ⓐ $1\frac{4}{10}$ Ⓒ $2\frac{1}{4}$

Ⓑ $1\frac{2}{4}$ Ⓓ $2\frac{2}{4}$

SHOW YOUR WORK

FOR MORE PRACTICE:
Florida Benchmarks Practice Book, pp. P169–P170

Name ______________________________

Fractions of a Group

Essential Question How can you show a fraction as part of a group?

MA.3.A.2.1 Represent fractions, including fractions greater than one, using area, set and linear models.

UNLOCK the Problem REAL WORLD

Jake and Emma each have a collection of marbles. What fraction of each collection is blue?

You can use a fraction to name part of a group.

Jake's Marbles

number of blue marbles → ☐ ← numerator
total number of marbles → 10 ← denominator

Read: three tenths, or three out of ten

Write: $\frac{3}{10}$

So, ______ of Jake's marbles are blue.

Emma's Marbles

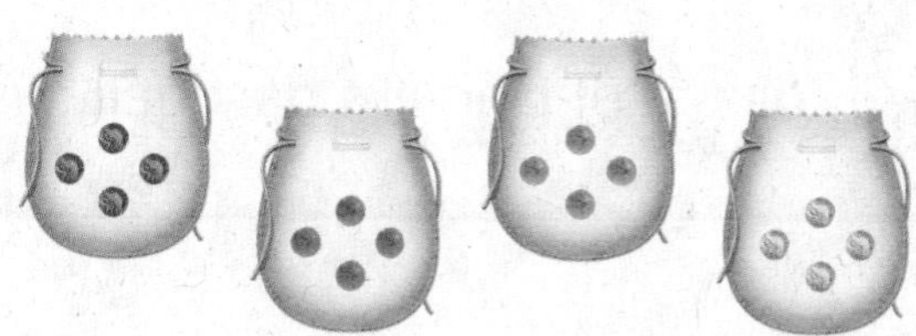

bags of blue marbles → ☐ ← numerator
total number of bags → 4 ← denominator

Read: one fourth, or one out of four

Write: $\frac{1}{4}$

So, ______ of Emma's marbles are blue.

Try This! **Name part of a group.**

Draw 2 red counters and 6 yellow counters.

Write the fraction of counters that are red.

☐ ← number of red counters
☐ ← total number of counters

Write the fraction of counters that are not red.

☐ ← number of yellow counters
☐ ← total number of counters

So, ______ of the counters are red and ______ are not red.

Fractions Greater Than 1

Sometimes a fraction can name more than a whole group.

Daniel collects baseballs. He has collected 19 so far. He puts them in cases that hold 12 baseballs each. What fraction of Daniel's baseball cases are filled?

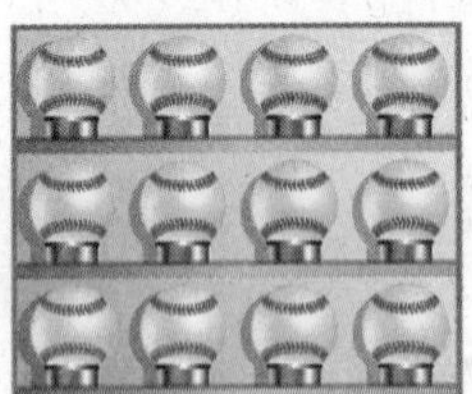 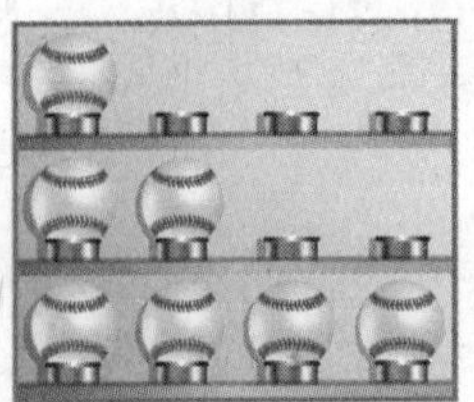

So, $1\frac{7}{12}$, or $\frac{19}{12}$, of Daniel's baseball cases are filled.

Try This! **Complete the mixed number and the fraction greater than 1 that name the part filled.**

A

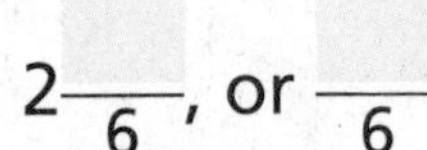

$2\frac{\square}{6}$, or $\frac{\square}{6}$

B

 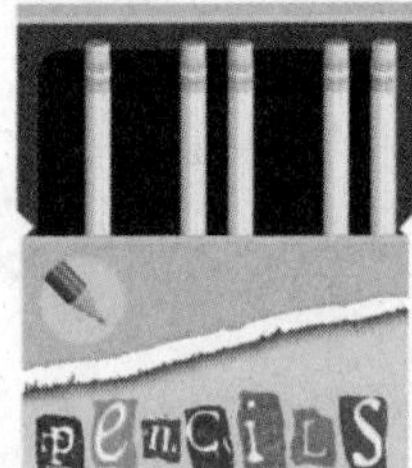

$1\frac{\square}{8}$, or $\frac{\square}{8}$

Share and Show

1. What fraction of the counters are red? ______

Think: How many red counters are there? How many total counters are there?

Math Talk Explain another way to name the fraction for Problem 3.

Write a fraction that names the red part of each group.

2.      ______

✓3. 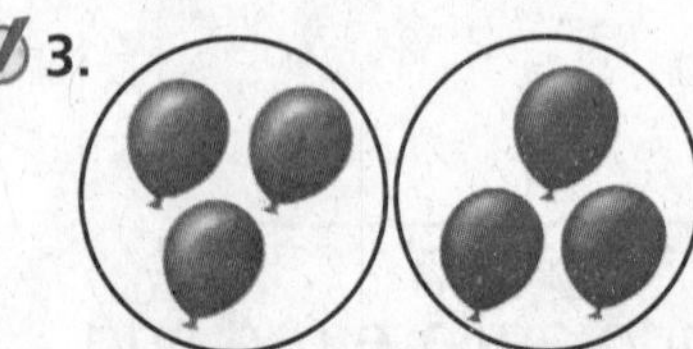 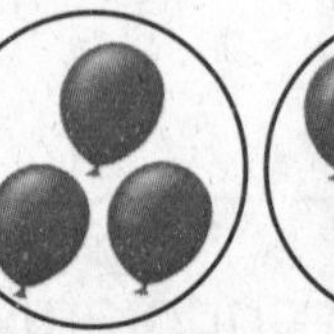  ______

Name ______________________________

Write a mixed number and a fraction greater than 1 that name the part filled.

4.   

Think: 1 carton = 1

______ ______

5.  

Think: 1 container = 1

______ ______

On Your Own

Write a fraction that names the blue part of each group.

6.  ______

7.  ______

8. 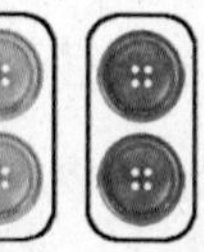 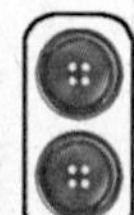 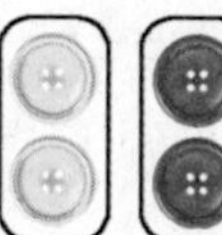 ______

9.    ______

Write a mixed number and a fraction greater than 1 that name the part filled.

10. 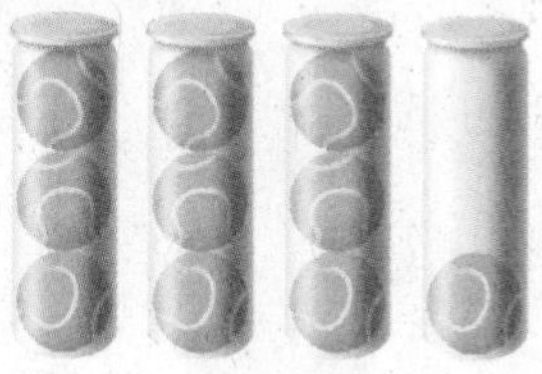

Think: 1 canister = 1

______ ______

11.  

Think: 1 carton = 1

______ ______

Draw a quick picture on your MathBoard. Then write a fraction that names the shaded part.

12. Draw 8 circles.
Shade 8 circles.

______

13. Draw 12 triangles.
Make 6 groups.
Shade 4 groups.

______

14. Draw 4 rectangles.
Shade 2 rectangles.

______

Problem Solving REAL WORLD

Use the graph for 15–16.

15. The bar graph shows the winners of the Smith Elementary School Marble Tournament. How many games were played? What fraction of the games did Scott win?

_______________ _______________

16. What fraction of the games did Robyn NOT win?

____

SHOW YOUR WORK

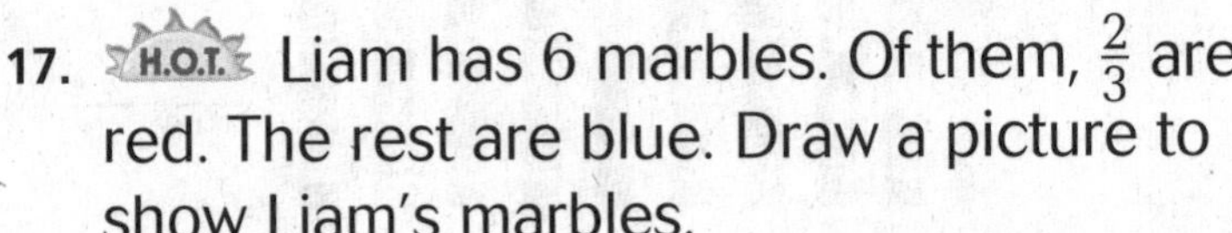

17. H.O.T. Liam has 6 marbles. Of them, $\frac{2}{3}$ are red. The rest are blue. Draw a picture to show Liam's marbles.

18. Write Math **What's the Question?** A bag has 2 yellow cubes, 3 blue cubes, and 1 white cube. The answer is $\frac{5}{6}$.

____

____

19. **Test Prep** Makayla picked some flowers. What fraction of her flowers are yellow?

Ⓐ $\frac{1}{8}$ Ⓑ $\frac{2}{8}$ Ⓒ $\frac{3}{8}$ Ⓓ $\frac{4}{8}$

FOR MORE PRACTICE:
Florida Benchmarks Practice Book, pp. P171–P172

Name ______________________________

Find Part of a Group

Essential Question How can you use a fraction to find part of a group?

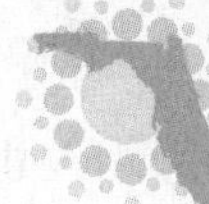

MA.3.A.2.1 Represent fractions, including fractions greater than one, using area, set and linear models.

UNLOCK the Problem REAL WORLD

Audrey bought a bouquet of 12 flowers. One third of them are purple. How many of the flowers are purple?

- How many flowers did Audrey buy in all? ______________
- What fraction of the flowers are purple? ______________

Activity 1

Materials ■ two-color counters ■ MathBoard

- Put 12 counters on your MathBoard.
- Since the denominator in $\frac{1}{3}$ is 3, divide the 12 counters into 3 equal groups. Now draw the counters below.

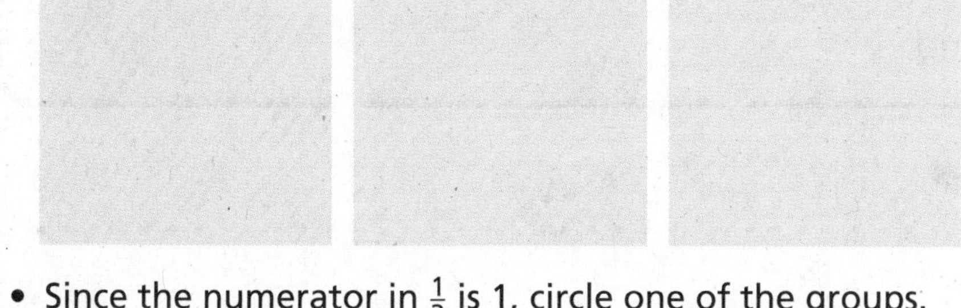

- Since the numerator in $\frac{1}{3}$ is 1, circle one of the groups. Then count the number of counters in that group.

There are _____ counters in 1 group. $\frac{1}{3}$ of 12 = _____

So, _____ of the flowers are purple.

- What if Audrey bought a bouquet of 9 flowers and one third of them are yellow? Use your MathBoard and counters to find how many of the flowers are yellow.

____

Activity 2

Materials ■ two-color counters ■ MathBoard

Joseph picked 12 flowers from his mother's garden. Three fourths of them are red. How many of the flowers are red?

- Put 12 counters on your MathBoard.
- Since the denominator in $\frac{3}{4}$ is 4, divide the 12 counters into 4 equal groups. Now draw the counters below.

- Since the numerator in $\frac{3}{4}$ is 3, circle three of the groups. Then count the number of counters in those three groups.

There are _____ counters in 3 groups. $\frac{3}{4}$ of $12 =$ _____

So, _____ of the flowers are red.

Share and Show

1. Use the model to find $\frac{1}{2}$ of 8. _____

Think: How many counters are in 1 of the 2 equal groups?

Math Talk Explain why you count the number of counters in just one of the groups in Problem 1.

Circle equal groups to solve.

2. $\frac{3}{5}$ of $10 =$ _____

3. $\frac{2}{3}$ of $6 =$ _____

4. $\frac{1}{6}$ of $12 =$ _____

Name ______________________________

On Your Own

Circle equal groups to solve.

5. $\frac{1}{4}$ of 12 = _____

6. $\frac{7}{10}$ of 10 = _____

7. $\frac{4}{5}$ of 15 = _____

8. $\frac{3}{3}$ of 9 = _____

9. $\frac{2}{6}$ of 18 = _____

10. $\frac{5}{8}$ of 8 = _____

11. $\frac{3}{4}$ of 16 = _____

12. $\frac{2}{3}$ of 12 = _____

13. $\frac{1}{2}$ of 6 = _____

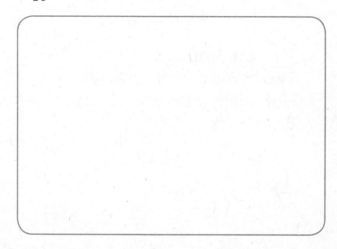

Draw counters. Then circle equal groups to solve.

14. $\frac{4}{8}$ of 16 = _____

15. $\frac{6}{10}$ of 20 = _____

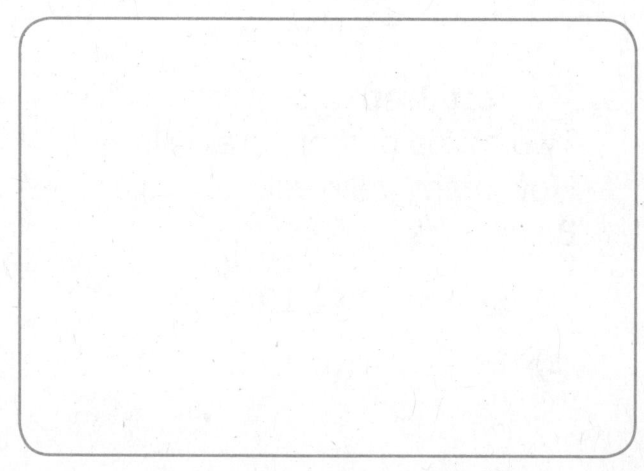

Problem Solving REAL WORLD

Use the table for 16–17.

Flower Seeds Bought	
Name	**Number of Packs**
Ryan	8
Brooke	10
Cole	20

16. Three fourths of the seed packs Ryan bought are poppy seeds. How many packs of poppy seeds did Ryan buy? Draw counters to solve.

____

17. Write Math One fifth of Brooke's seed packs and four tenths of Cole's seed packs are daisy seeds. How many packs of daisy seeds did they buy altogether? **Explain** how you know.

____

____

____

18. H.O.T. **Sense or Nonsense?** Sophia bought 12 pots. Four sixths of them are green. Sophia said she bought 8 green pots. Does her answer make sense? **Explain** how you know.

____

____

____

____

19. **Test Prep** Bailey picked 15 flowers. Two thirds of them are yellow. How many yellow flowers did Bailey pick?

Ⓐ 5 Ⓒ 10

Ⓑ 6 Ⓓ 12

SHOW YOUR WORK

Name ______________________________

Draw a Diagram · Fractions

Essential Question How can you use the strategy *draw a diagram* to solve problems?

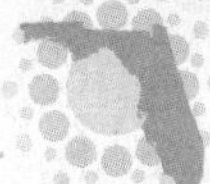

MA.3.A.2.1 Represent fractions, including fractions greater than one, using area, set and linear models.

UNLOCK the Problem REAL WORLD

Cameron has 9 fish in his fish tank. Two thirds of them are clown fish. How many of Cameron's fish are clown fish?

Use the graphic organizer below to solve the problem.

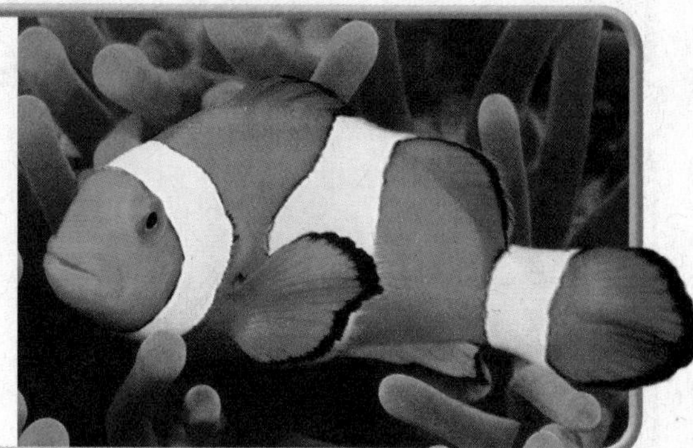

Read the Problem

What do I need to find?

I need to find how many of the fish in Cameron's fish tank are

________________.

What information do I need to use?

Cameron has _____ fish in his fish tank.

________________ of them are clown fish.

How will I use the information?

I will use the information in the problem to draw a ________________.

Solve the Problem

Describe how to draw a diagram to solve.

Use 9 counters. Since the denominator in $\frac{2}{3}$ is _____, divide the counters into _____ equal groups. Draw the counters below.

Since the numerator in $\frac{2}{3}$ is _____, circle _____ of the groups. Then count the number of counters in those groups.

Cameron has _____ clown fish.

Try Another Problem

A pet store has 16 rabbits. Three eighths of them are gray. How many of the pet store's rabbits are gray?

Read the Problem	Solve the Problem
What do I need to find?	
What information do I need to use?	
How will I use the information?	

- How did your diagram help you solve the problem? ____________

____

____

Math Talk Suppose $\frac{1}{2}$ of the rabbits are gray. **Explain** how you can find the number of gray rabbits without drawing a diagram.

Name ______________________________

Share and Show

MATH BOARD

1. Lily has 15 toys for her dogs. One fifth of them are red. How many of the dog toys are red?

First, count out _____ counters.

Since the denominator in $\frac{1}{5}$ is _____, divide the counters into _____ equal groups.

Next, draw a diagram to show the counters.

Last, since the numerator in $\frac{1}{5}$ is _____, circle and count the number of counters in _____ group. So, _____ of the dog toys are red.

2. H.O.T. **What if** three fifths of the 15 dog toys Lily has are blue? How many dog toys are blue?

____

3. Samuel has 10 lizards. One half of them are male. How many of the lizards are male?

____

4. Rachel counted 12 birds in her backyard. Five sixths of them were mourning doves. How many of the birds were mourning doves?

____

Choose a STRATEGY

- Act It Out
- Use Manipulatives
- Draw a Diagram
- Make a Table, Chart, or List
- Search for Patterns

SHOW YOUR WORK

On Your Own

Tips

UNLOCK the Problem

- √ Circle the question.
- √ Underline important facts.
- √ Choose a strategy you know.

5. H.O.T. Six friends share 5 small pizzas. Each friend first eats half of a pizza. How much more pizza does each friend need to eat to finish all the pizzas and share them equally?

SHOW YOUR WORK

6. There are 18 bottlenose dolphins at an aquarium. Four sixths of them are adults. How many of the bottlenose dolphins are adults?

7. Write Math Brayden bought 5 packs of dog treats. He gave 5 treats to his neighbor's dog. Now Brayden has 25 treats left for his dog. How many dog treats were in each pack? Explain how you know.

8. **Test Prep** There are 16 turtles at a science center. Two eighths of them are painted turtles. How many of the turtles are painted turtles?

Ⓐ 2 Ⓒ 6

Ⓑ 4 Ⓓ 10

 FOR MORE PRACTICE:
Florida Benchmarks Practice Book, pp. P175–P176

Name ______________________________

Find the Whole Group Using Unit Fractions

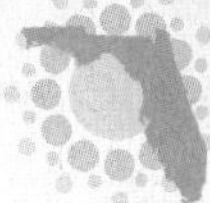

MA.3.A.2.1 Represent fractions, including fractions greater than one, using area, set and linear models.

Essential Question How can you use a unit fraction to find the whole group?

CONNECT You have learned how to find part of a group. Now you will learn how to find the whole group when you know one part.

UNLOCK the Problem REAL WORLD

Cooper has 3 yo-yos in his backpack. They are $\frac{1}{4}$ of his whole collection. How many yo-yos are in Cooper's whole collection?

- Circle the numbers you need to use to solve the problem.
- What number tells how many parts are in the whole collection?

____

Draw to model the problem.

STEP 1 The denominator in $\frac{1}{4}$ tells you there are 4 parts in the whole group. Draw 4 circles to show 4 parts.

STEP 2 Since 3 yo-yos are $\frac{1}{4}$ of the group, draw 3 counters in the first circle.

STEP 3 Since the first circle has 3 counters, draw 3 counters in each of the remaining circles also. Then count all of the counters.

So, there are ______ yo-yos in Cooper's whole collection.

Math Talk **Explain** how your drawing would change if Cooper's 3 yo-yos were $\frac{1}{6}$ of his whole collection.

Try This! Five buttons are $\frac{1}{2}$ of the group. How many buttons are in the whole group?

- The denominator in $\frac{1}{2}$ tells you there are 2 parts in the whole group. Draw

  _____ circles to show _____ parts.
- Since 5 buttons are $\frac{1}{2}$ of the group,

  draw _____ counters in the first circle.
- Since the first circle has 5 counters, draw

  _____ counters in the second circle also. Then count all of the counters.

So, there are _____ buttons in the whole group.

Share and Show 

1. Two counters are $\frac{1}{5}$ of the group. Use the picture to find how many counters are in the whole group. _____

   Think: There are 2 counters in the first part, so there are 2 counters in every part.

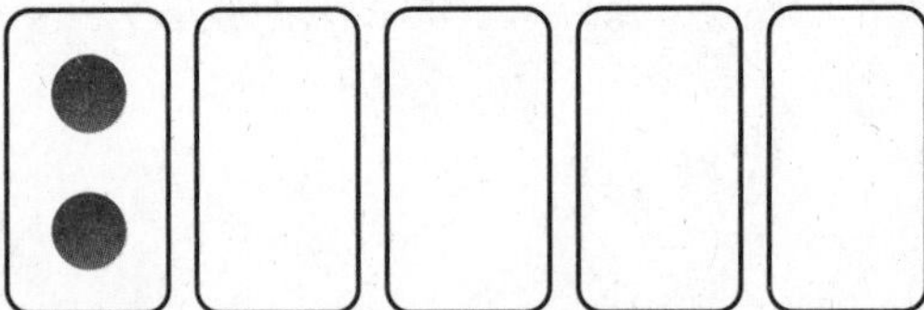

Math Talk **Explain** how the denominator helps you find the whole group.

Complete the drawing to find how many are in the whole group.

2. Three triangles are $\frac{1}{3}$ of the group.

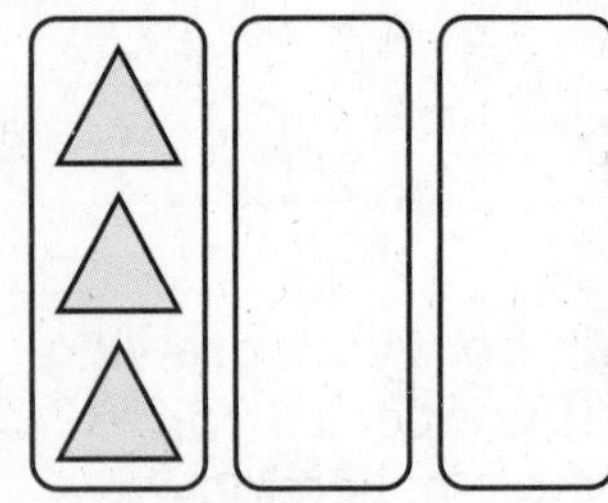

_____ are in the whole group.

3. Two squares are $\frac{1}{4}$ of the group.

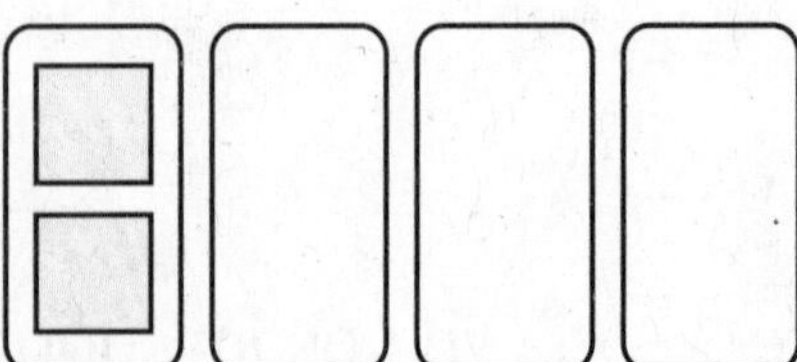

_____ are in the whole group.

Name ______________________________

On Your Own

Complete the drawing to find how many are in the whole group.

4. Three circles are $\frac{1}{5}$ of the group.

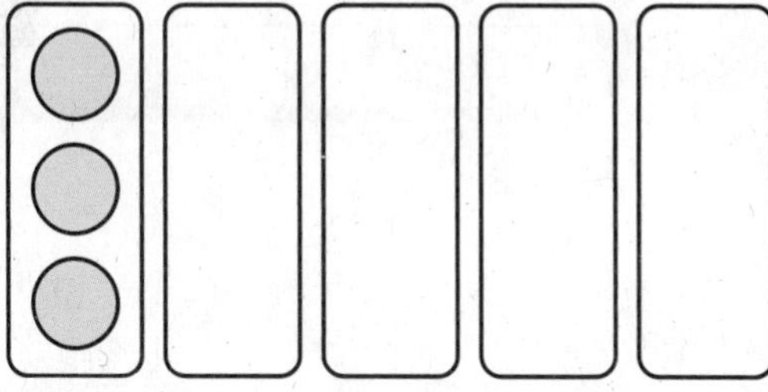

_____ are in the whole group.

5. One triangle is $\frac{1}{6}$ of the group.

_____ are in the whole group.

6. Four squares are $\frac{1}{2}$ of the group.

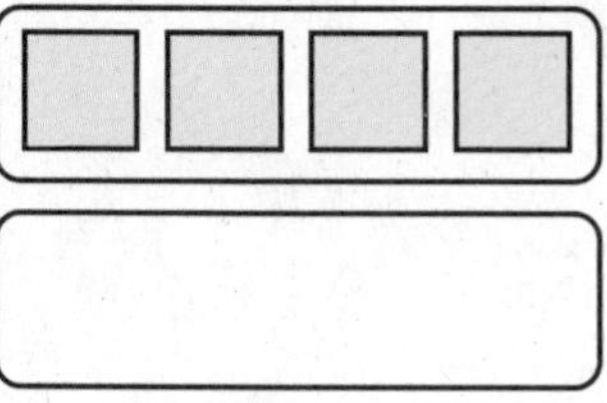

_____ are in the whole group.

7. Five circles are $\frac{1}{3}$ of the group.

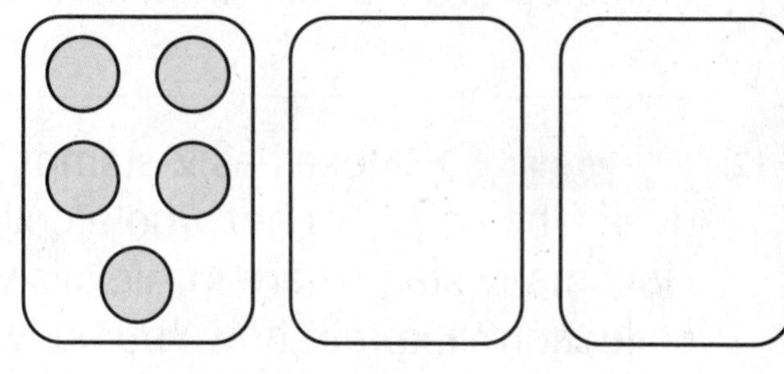

_____ are in the whole group.

H.O.T. Draw a quick picture to find how many are in the whole group.

8. Two counters are $\frac{1}{6}$ of the group.

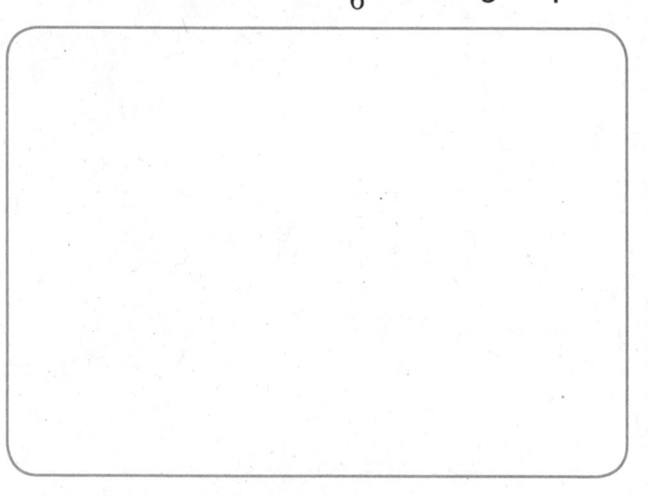

_____ are in the whole group.

9. Four counters are $\frac{1}{4}$ of the group.

_____ are in the whole group.

Problem Solving REAL WORLD

Use the table for 10–11.

Postcards Collected	
Name	**Number**
Kyle	7
Seth	4
Gracie	6

10. The table shows the number of postcards some students collected in 1 week. The postcards Kyle collected are $\frac{1}{2}$ of his whole collection. How many postcards are in his whole collection?

____

11. H.O.T. The postcards Gracie collected are $\frac{1}{3}$ of her whole collection. How many postcards are in her whole collection? How many more postcards does Gracie have than Seth if the postcards he collected are $\frac{1}{3}$ of his whole collection?

_______________ _______________

SHOW YOUR WORK

12. Write Math Alexa has 2 stamps on her desk. They are $\frac{1}{8}$ of her whole collection. How many stamps are in Alexa's whole collection? **Explain** how you know.

____

____

____

____

13. **Test Prep** Two hats are $\frac{1}{3}$ of the group. How many hats are in the whole group?

Ⓐ 4 Ⓒ 6

Ⓑ 5 Ⓓ 8

FOR MORE PRACTICE:
Florida Benchmarks Practice Book, pp. P177–P178

Name ______________________________

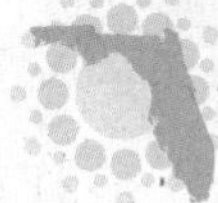

Find the Whole Group

Essential Question How can you use a fraction to find the whole group?

MA.3.A.2.1 Represent fractions, including fractions greater than one, using area, set and linear models.

CONNECT You have learned how to find the whole group by using unit fractions. Now you will learn how to find the whole group by using other fractions.

UNLOCK the Problem REAL WORLD

Alicia has 6 trophies in her room. They are $\frac{3}{4}$ of her whole collection. How many trophies are in Alicia's whole collection?

- How many parts are in the whole collection? __________
- How many parts of Alicia's whole collection are in her room? __________

Draw to model the problem.

STEP 1 The denominator in $\frac{3}{4}$ tells you there are 4 parts in the whole group. Draw 4 circles to show 4 parts. Then draw a line around $\frac{3}{4}$ of your circles.

STEP 2 Since 6 trophies are $\frac{3}{4}$ of the group, divide 6 counters equally among the 3 circles you drew a line around. Draw to show your work.

STEP 3 Since there are 2 counters in each of the first 3 circles, draw 2 counters in the fourth circle also. Then count all of the counters.

So, there are _____ trophies in Alicia's whole collection.

Math Talk Explain how you used division to find how many counters were in the first 3 circles.

Try This! Eight marbles are $\frac{2}{3}$ of the group. How many marbles are in the whole group?

- The denominator in $\frac{2}{3}$ tells you there are 3 parts in the whole group. Draw 3 circles to show _____ parts. Then draw a line around $\frac{2}{3}$ of your circles.
- Since 8 marbles are $\frac{2}{3}$ of the group, divide _____ counters equally between the 2 circles you drew a line around. Draw to show your work.
- Since there are 4 counters in each of the first 2 circles, draw _____ counters in the third circle also. Then count all of the counters.

So, there are _____ marbles in the whole group.

Share and Show

MATH BOARD

1. Four counters are $\frac{2}{5}$ of the group. Use the picture to find how many counters are in the whole group. _____

Think: There are 2 counters in each of the first two parts, so there are 2 counters in every part.

Math Talk **Explain** how you know how many parts to divide the given items into.

Complete the drawing to find how many are in the whole group.

2. Four triangles are $\frac{4}{6}$ of the group.

_____ are in the whole group.

3. Nine circles are $\frac{3}{4}$ of the group.

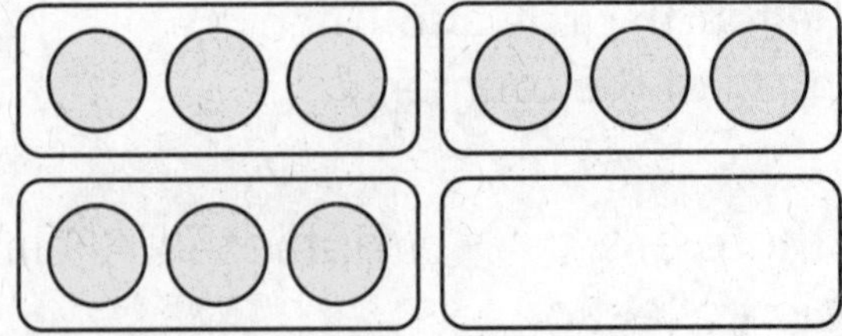

_____ are in the whole group.

Name ______________________________

On Your Own

Complete the drawing to find how many are in the whole group.

4. Ten squares are $\frac{2}{3}$ of the group.

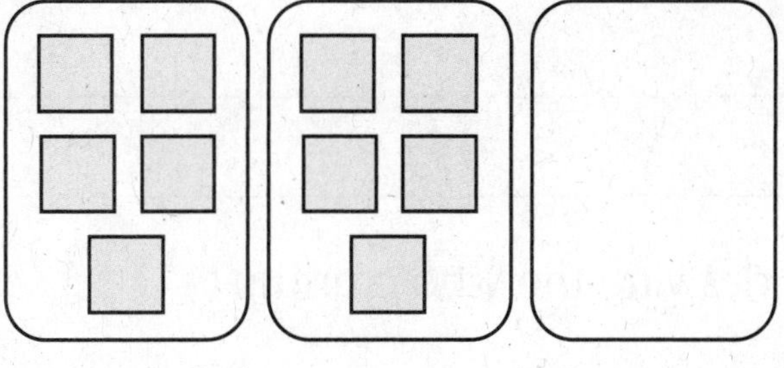

_____ are in the whole group.

5. Six triangles are $\frac{3}{6}$ of the group.

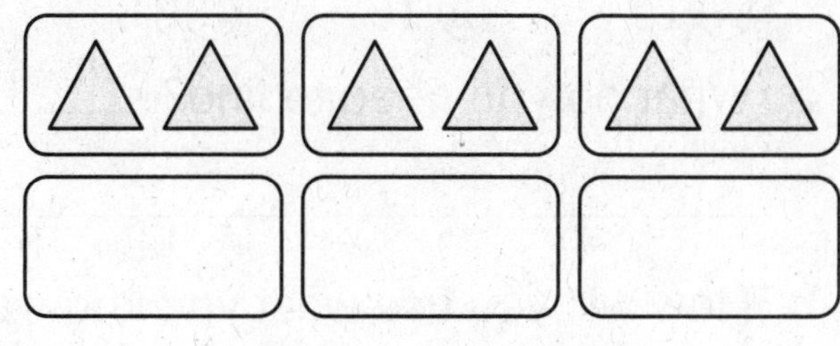

_____ are in the whole group.

6. Nine circles are $\frac{3}{5}$ of the group.

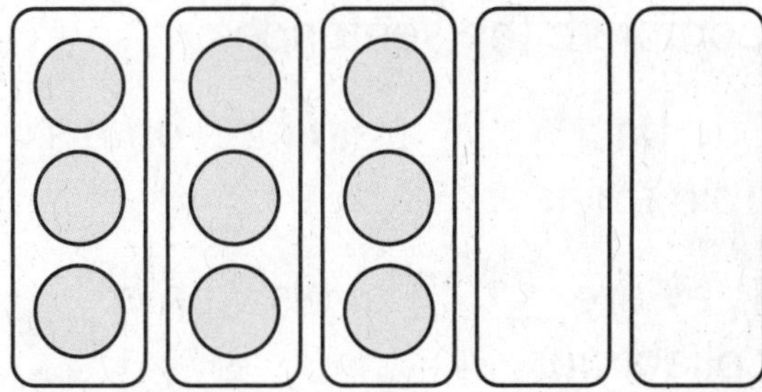

_____ are in the whole group.

7. Eight squares are $\frac{2}{4}$ of the group.

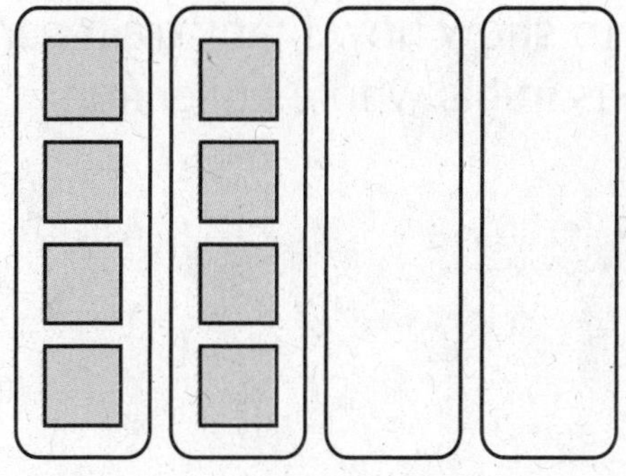

_____ are in the whole group.

H.O.T. Draw a quick picture to find how many are in the whole group.

8. Ten counters are $\frac{5}{6}$ of the group.

_____ are in the whole group.

9. Four counters are $\frac{2}{8}$ of the group.

_____ are in the whole group.

UNLOCK the Problem 

10. Eric has 12 train cars on his train track. They are $\frac{4}{5}$ of his whole collection. How many train cars are in Eric's whole collection?

Ⓐ 15 Ⓑ 16 Ⓒ 18 Ⓓ 20

a. What do you need to find? ____________________

____

b. How will you use what you know about drawing the whole group to solve the problem? ____________________

____

____

c. Draw to show how many train cars Eric has in his whole collection.

d. Complete the sentences.

Eric has ______ train cars on his train track.

They are ______ of his whole collection.

So, there are ______ train cars in Eric's whole collection.

e. Fill in the bubble for the correct answer choice above.

11. Emily has 6 books about space on her shelf. They are $\frac{2}{4}$ of her whole collection. How many space books are in Emily's whole collection?

Ⓕ 8 Ⓖ 9 Ⓗ 10 Ⓘ 12

12. Four coins are $\frac{2}{3}$ of the group. How many coins are in the whole group?

   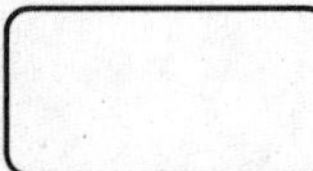

Ⓐ 5 Ⓑ 6 Ⓒ 9 Ⓓ 12

FOR MORE PRACTICE:
Florida Benchmarks Practice Book, pp. P179–P180

Name ________________________________

Chapter Review/Test

▶ Check Vocabulary

Choose the best term from the box to complete the sentence.

Vocabulary
denominator
mixed number
numerator
unit fraction

1. The ______________________ tells how many parts are being counted. (MA.3.A.2.1; p. 303)
2. A ______________________ is a number made up of a whole number and a fraction. (MA.3.A.2.1; p. 309)
3. A ______________________ has 1 as its top number. (MA.3.A.2.1; p. 299)

▶ Check Concepts

Write a fraction greater than 1 for the parts that are shaded. (MA.3.A.2.1; pp. 309–312)

4. 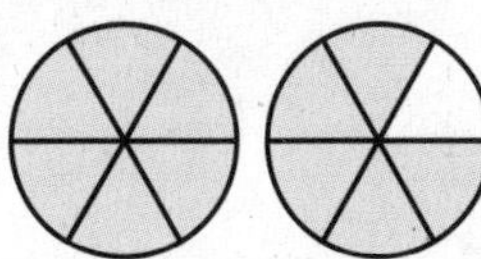 ______

5.    ______

Write a fraction that names the blue part of the group. (MA.3.A.2.1; pp. 313–316)

6. 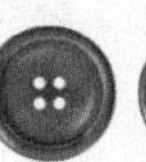    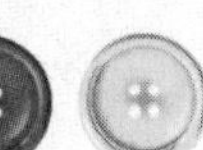 ______

7. 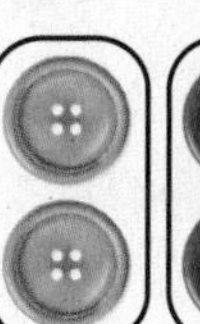  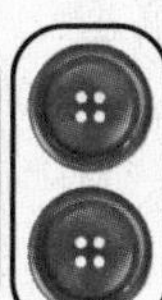 ______

Circle equal groups to solve. (MA.3.A.2.1; pp. 317–320)

8. $\frac{1}{3}$ of 6 = ______

9. $\frac{3}{4}$ of 12 = ______

10. $\frac{2}{5}$ of 10 = ______

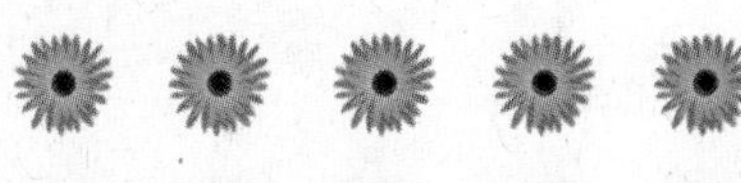

Go online Assessment Options
Chapter Test

Fill in the bubble for the correct answer choice.

11. Mason's mom bought a pumpkin pie. Mason wants to eat 1 slice for dessert. What fraction of the pie will he eat? **(MA.3.A.2.1; pp. 299–302)**

Ⓐ $\frac{1}{4}$

Ⓑ $\frac{1}{6}$

Ⓒ $\frac{1}{8}$

Ⓓ $\frac{1}{10}$

12. Jada has 10 pencils. What fraction of her pencils are green? **(MA.3.A.2.1; pp. 313–316)**

Ⓕ $\frac{2}{8}$

Ⓖ $\frac{2}{10}$

Ⓗ $\frac{8}{2}$

Ⓘ $\frac{8}{10}$

13. Ms. Kennedy gave $\frac{1}{2}$ of an orange to each of 5 children. How many oranges did she give to the children in all? **(MA.3.A.2.1; pp. 309–312)**

Ⓐ $1\frac{1}{2}$

Ⓑ $2\frac{1}{2}$

Ⓒ $1\frac{1}{5}$

Ⓓ $2\frac{2}{5}$

Name ____

Fill in the bubble for the correct answer choice.

14. Jessica has these fruits in a bowl.

 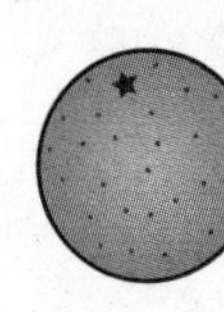  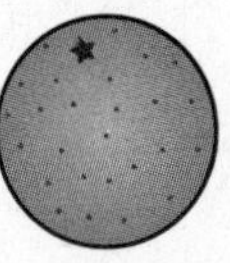  

What fraction shows the number of oranges compared to the whole group? **(MA.3.A.2.1; pp. 313–316)**

Ⓕ $\frac{1}{6}$ Ⓗ $\frac{3}{6}$

Ⓖ $\frac{2}{6}$ Ⓘ $\frac{2}{4}$

15. Max drew the shape below and divided it into equal parts. What is the name for the parts?
(MA.3.A.2.1; pp. 291–294)

Ⓐ halves

Ⓑ thirds

Ⓒ fourths

Ⓓ sixths

16. Avery has 12 marbles. Two sixths of them are blue. How many of Avery's marbles are blue?
(MA.3.A.2.1; pp. 317–320)

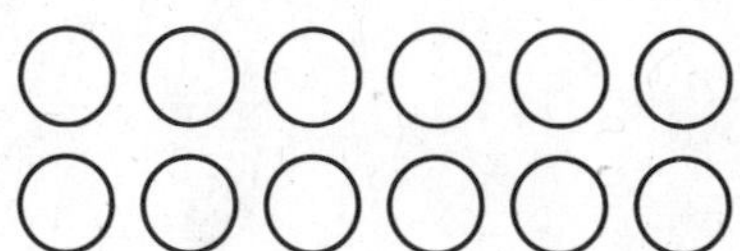

Ⓕ 4 Ⓗ 8

Ⓖ 6 Ⓘ 10

17. Destiny has 3 books on her desk. They are $\frac{1}{2}$ of the books she checked out from the library. How many books did Destiny check out from the library?

(MA.3.A.2.1; pp. 325–328)

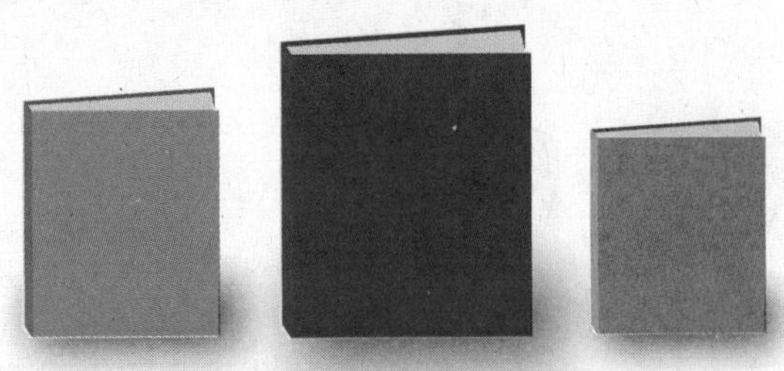

Ⓐ 4 Ⓒ 6

Ⓑ 5 Ⓓ 8

18. Julian made a flag for his clubhouse. What fraction of his flag is green? (MA.3.A.2.1; pp. 303–306)

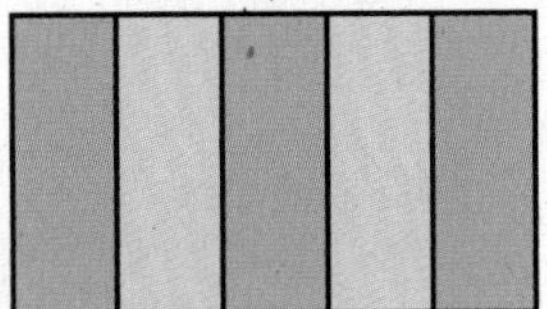

Ⓕ $\frac{5}{2}$ Ⓗ $\frac{3}{5}$

Ⓖ $\frac{2}{3}$ Ⓘ $\frac{2}{5}$

19. Seven friends each ran $\frac{1}{3}$ of a mile in a relay race. How many miles did the friends run in all?

(MA.3.A.2.1; pp. 309–312)

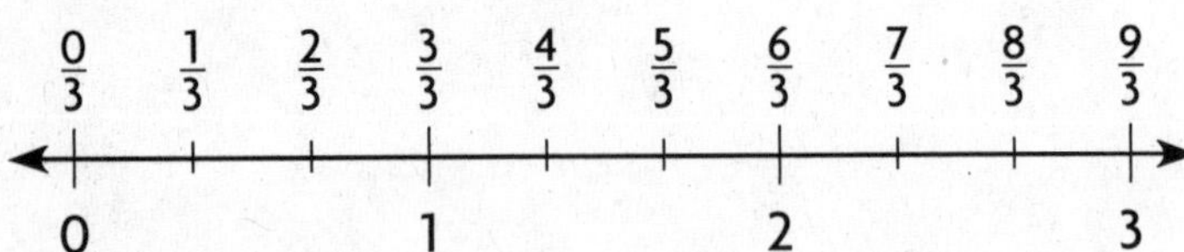

Ⓐ $\frac{4}{3}$ miles

Ⓑ $\frac{5}{3}$ miles

Ⓒ $\frac{6}{3}$ miles

Ⓓ $\frac{7}{3}$ miles

Chapter 8

Compare and Order Fractions

Show What You Know

Check your understanding of important skills.

Name ____________________

▶ Halves and Fourths

1. Find the shape that is divided into 2 equal parts. Color $\frac{1}{2}$.

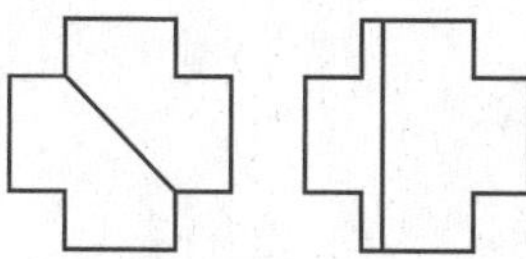

2. Find the shape that is divided into 4 equal parts. Color $\frac{1}{4}$.

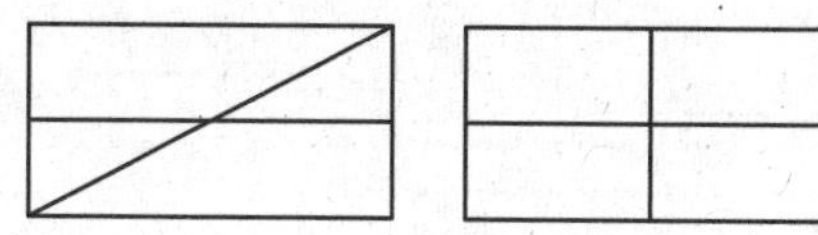

▶ Fractions of a Whole

Write the fraction that names the shaded part of each shape.

3. 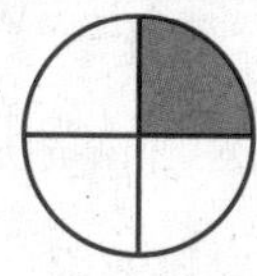 ____

4. 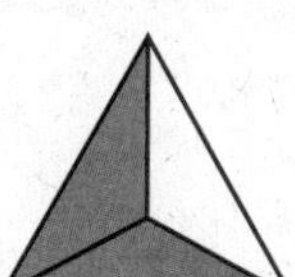 ____

5. 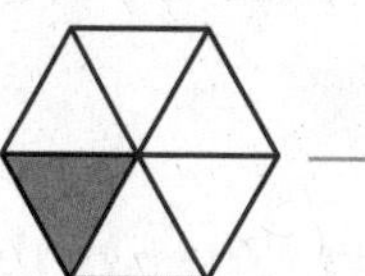 ____

▶ Fractions of a Group

Write the fraction that names the red part of each group.

6.   ____

7. 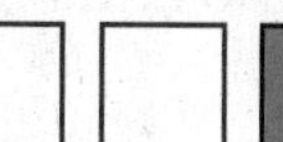    ____

At the Big Cypress Seminole Reservation, you can learn about alligators, and other creatures of the Florida Everglades.

FLORIDA BENCHMARKS

Vocabulary Power

▶ Visualize It

Use the checked words to complete the Flow Map.

Fractions and Mixed Numbers

What is it?		What are some examples?
______	→	$\frac{2}{3} > \frac{1}{3}$
______	→	$\frac{1}{4} < \frac{2}{4}$
______	→	$\frac{1}{2} = \frac{2}{4}$
______	→	$\frac{1}{3}, \frac{1}{4}$
______	→	$2\frac{1}{3}, 3\frac{1}{2}$

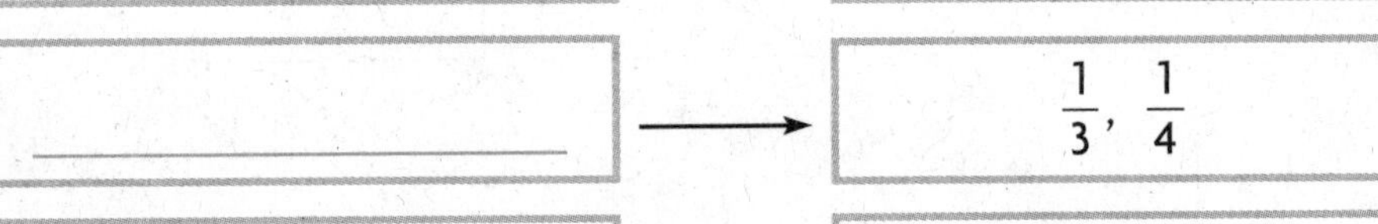

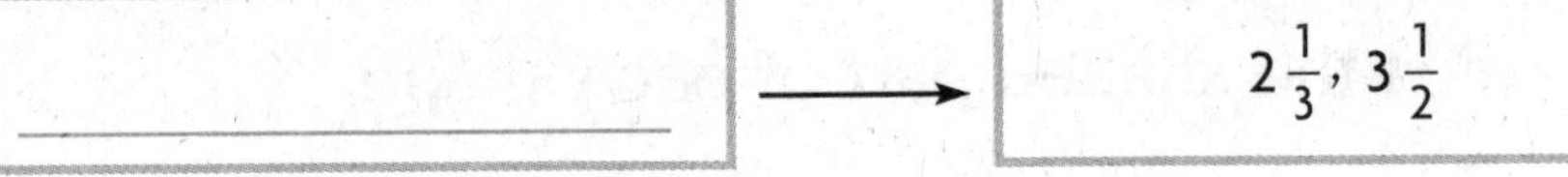

Review Words

- denominator
- eighths
- equal parts
- fourths
- fraction
- halves
- ✓ mixed numbers
- numerator
- sixths
- tenths
- thirds
- twelfths
- ✓ unit fractions

Preview Words

- benchmark
- compare
- ✓ equivalent fractions
- ✓ greater than >
- ✓ less than <

▶ Understand Vocabulary

Write the review or preview word that answers the riddle.

1. We are two fractions that name the same amount.

______

2. I am the part of a fraction above the line. I tell how many parts are being counted.

______

3. I am the part of a fraction below the line. I tell how many equal parts are in the whole or in the group.

______

Go online • Student Edition • Multilingual eGlossary

Name ______________________________

Use Manipulatives · Compare Fractions

Essential Question How can you compare fractions by using manipulatives?

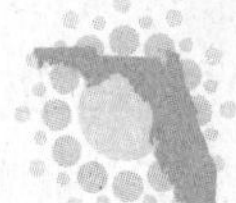

MA.3.A.2.3 Compare and order fractions, including fractions greater than one, using models and strategies.

UNLOCK the Problem REAL WORLD

Vincent and Harry climbed up a rock wall at the park. Vincent climbed $\frac{3}{5}$ of the way up the wall. Harry climbed $\frac{6}{8}$ of the way up the wall. Who climbed higher?

You can compare fractions by using manipulatives to help you solve the problem.

Remember

greater than >

less than <

Read the Problem

What do I need to find?

____

What information do I need to use?

__________ climbed ______ of the way.

__________ climbed ______ of the way.

How will I use the information?

I will use ____________________

and ______________ the lengths of

the models to find who climbed

__________.

Solve the Problem

1

$\frac{1}{5}$	$\frac{1}{5}$	$\frac{1}{5}$

$\frac{1}{8}$	$\frac{1}{8}$	$\frac{1}{8}$	$\frac{1}{8}$	$\frac{1}{8}$	$\frac{1}{8}$

Compare the lengths.

______ ◯ ______

The length of the $\frac{3}{5}$ model is less than the length of the $\frac{6}{8}$ model.

So, ____________ climbed higher on the rock wall.

Try Another Problem

The camp leader is making waffles for breakfast. Tracy ate $\frac{3}{6}$ of her waffle. Kim ate $\frac{5}{6}$ of her waffle. Who ate more of her waffle?

Read the Problem	Solve the Problem
What do I need to find out?	**Record the steps you used to solve the problem.**
What information do I need to use?	
How will I use the information?	

- How did your model help you solve the problem? ____________________

- Tracy and Kim each had a glass of milk with breakfast. Tracy drank $\frac{5}{8}$ of her milk. Kim drank $\frac{7}{8}$ of her milk. Who drank more of her milk? **Explain.**

____

Math Talk **Explain** how you know that $\frac{5}{6}$ is greater than $\frac{3}{6}$ without using models.

Name ______________________________

Share and Show 

1. At the park, people can climb a rope ladder to its top. Rosa climbed $\frac{6}{10}$ of the ladder. Justin climbed $\frac{5}{6}$ of the ladder. Who climbed higher on the rope ladder?

   First, what are you asked to find?

   ____

   Then, model each of the fractions and compare them.

   Think: Compare $\frac{6}{10}$ and $\frac{5}{6}$.

   Last, find the greater fraction.

   ______ ◯ ______

   So, ____________ climbed higher on the rope ladder.

2. **What if** Cara also tried the rope ladder and climbed $\frac{9}{10}$ of it? Who climbed highest on the rope ladder—Rosa, Justin, or Cara? How do you know?

   ____

   ____

   ____

   ____

3. Ted walked $\frac{4}{5}$ mile to his soccer game. Then he walked $\frac{3}{5}$ mile to his friend's house. Which distance is shorter? **Explain** how you know.

   ____

   ____

UNLOCK the Problem

- √ Model the problem with manipulatives.
- √ Circle the question.
- √ Underline important facts.

SHOW YOUR WORK

On Your Own

Use the table for 4–5.

4. Suri is frosting 12 cupcakes for her party. The table shows the fraction of cupcakes frosted with each frosting flavor. Which flavor did Suri use on the greatest number of cupcakes?

   Hint: Use 12 counters to model the cupcakes.

5. With which two flavors did Suri frost the same number of cupcakes?

6. H.O.T. Suppose Suri had also used peanut butter frosting on the cupcakes. She frosted $\frac{1}{4}$ of the cupcakes with vanilla, $\frac{6}{12}$ with chocolate, $\frac{1}{12}$ with strawberry, and $\frac{1}{6}$ with peanut butter. Which flavor frosting did Suri use on the fewest cupcakes?

7. Ms. Gordon has many cookie recipes. One recipe uses $\frac{2}{3}$ cup oatmeal and $\frac{3}{4}$ cup flour. Will Ms. Gordon use more oatmeal or more flour? **Explain.**

8. **Test Prep** Rick lives $\frac{4}{5}$ mile from school. Noah lives $\frac{3}{6}$ mile from school. Which correctly compares the distances?

   Ⓐ $\frac{4}{5} = \frac{3}{6}$ Ⓒ $\frac{4}{5} > \frac{3}{6}$

   Ⓑ $\frac{4}{5} < \frac{3}{6}$ Ⓓ $\frac{3}{6} > \frac{4}{5}$

Choose a STRATEGY

- Act It Out
- Use Manipulatives
- Draw a Diagram
- Make a Table, Chart, or List
- Search for Patterns

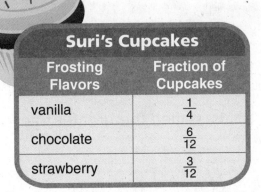

Suri's Cupcakes

Frosting Flavors	Fraction of Cupcakes
vanilla	$\frac{1}{4}$
chocolate	$\frac{6}{12}$
strawberry	$\frac{3}{12}$

SHOW YOUR WORK

FOR MORE PRACTICE:
Florida Benchmarks Practice Book, pp. P187–P188

Name ______________________________

Compare Fractions Using Benchmarks

MA.3.A.2.3 Compare and order fractions, including fractions greater than one, using models and strategies.

Essential Question How can you use models and benchmarks to compare fractions?

Benchmarks are numbers that are easy to work with. The numbers $\frac{1}{2}$ and 1 are benchmarks that make it easier for you to compare fractions.

UNLOCK the Problem REAL WORLD

Gaby ordered a pizza. She ate $\frac{5}{8}$ of it. Did Gaby eat more than or less than $\frac{1}{2}$ of her pizza?

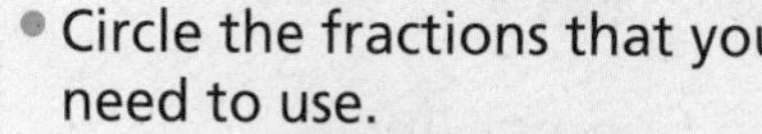

- Circle the fractions that you need to use.

Use benchmarks to compare fractions.

A **Compare $\frac{5}{8}$ and $\frac{1}{2}$.**

Gaby ate ______________ of her pizza.

Is $\frac{5}{8}$ greater than or less than $\frac{1}{2}$?

____

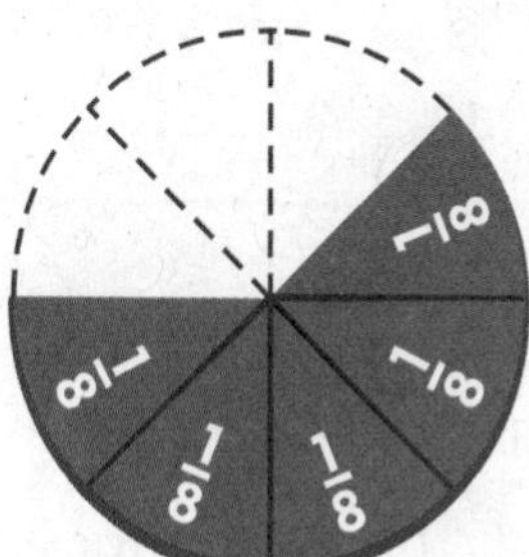

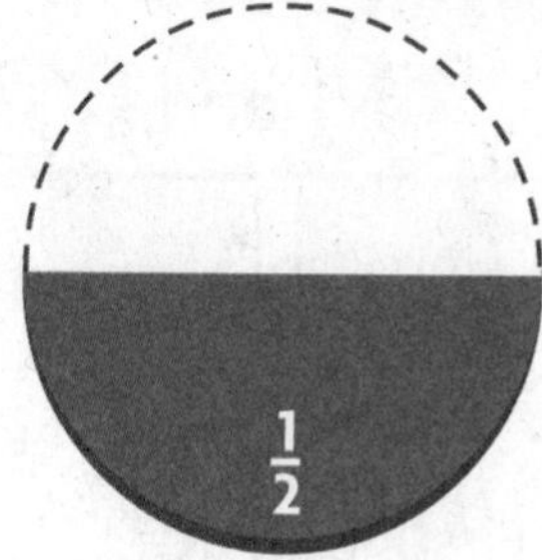

So, Gaby ate ______________ $\frac{1}{2}$ of her pizza.

Lexi ate $\frac{7}{8}$ of her pizza.

Did Lexi eat more than or less than 1 whole pizza?

B **Compare $\frac{7}{8}$ and 1.**

Lexi ate ______________ of her pizza.

Is $\frac{7}{8}$ greater than or less than 1?

____

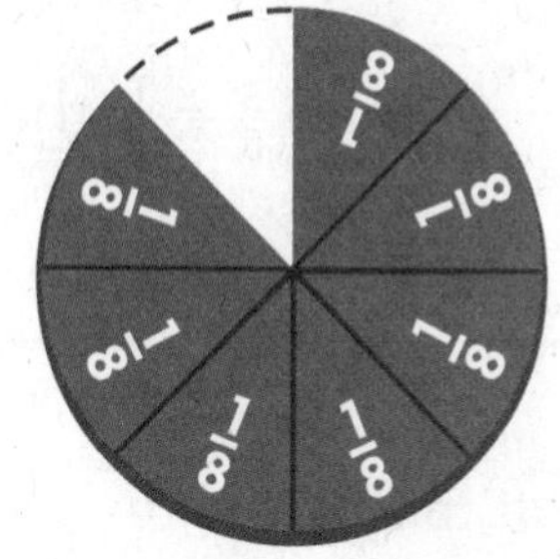

So, Lexi ate ______________ 1 whole pizza.

Use Benchmarks and Number Lines

A Compare $\frac{2}{6}$ and $\frac{3}{4}$.

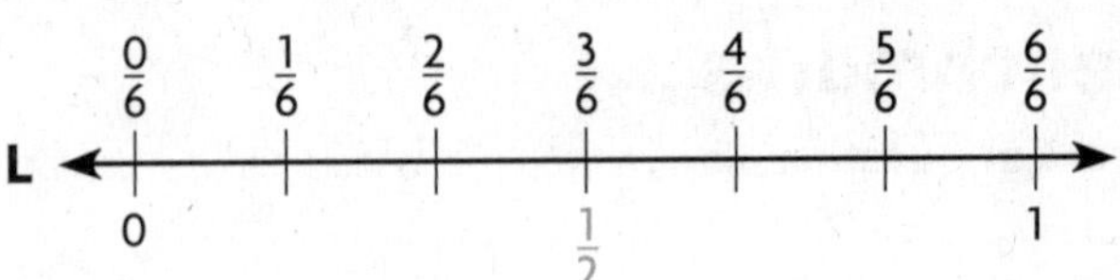

- Circle $\frac{2}{6}$ on number line **L**.

  $\frac{2}{6}$ is to the left of $\frac{1}{2}$, so $\frac{2}{6}$ ○ $\frac{1}{2}$.

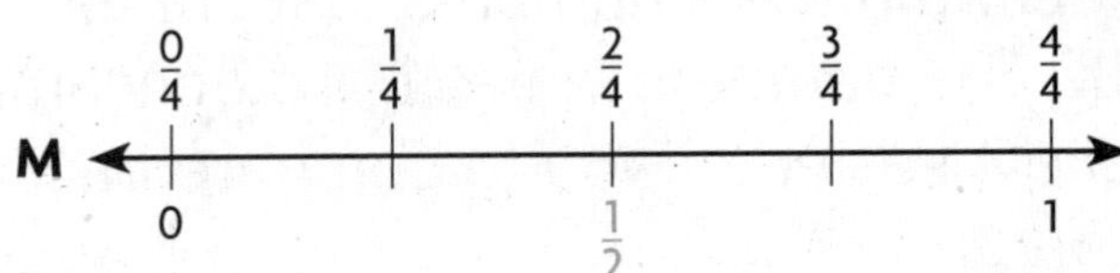

- Circle $\frac{3}{4}$ on number line **M**.

  $\frac{3}{4}$ is to the right of $\frac{1}{2}$, so $\frac{3}{4}$ ○ $\frac{1}{2}$.

  $\frac{2}{6}$ ○ $\frac{1}{2}$ and $\frac{3}{4}$ ○ $\frac{1}{2}$, so $\frac{2}{6}$ ○ $\frac{3}{4}$.

B Compare $\frac{4}{5}$ and $\frac{5}{3}$.

- Circle $\frac{4}{5}$ on number line **S**.

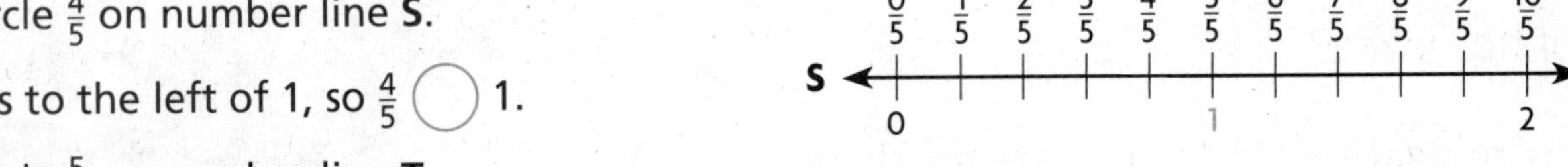

  $\frac{4}{5}$ is to the left of 1, so $\frac{4}{5}$ ○ 1.

- Circle $\frac{5}{3}$ on number line **T**.

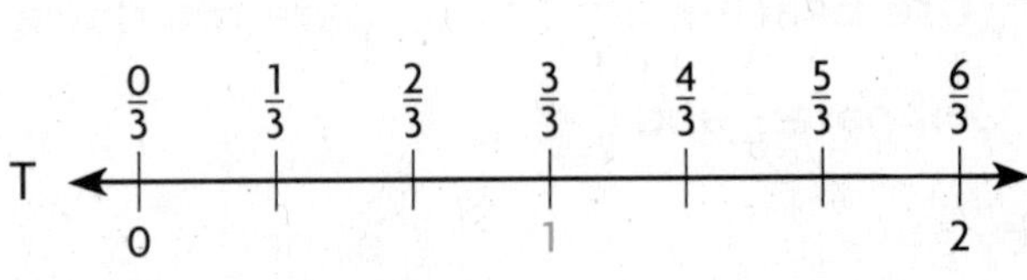

  $\frac{5}{3}$ is to the right of 1, so $\frac{5}{3}$ ○ 1.

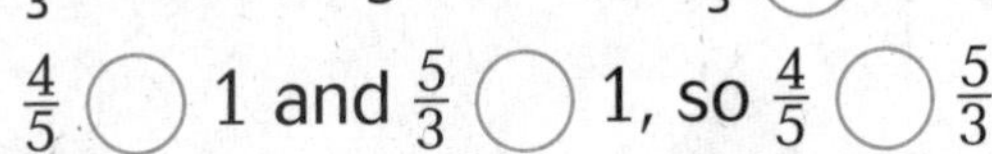

  $\frac{4}{5}$ ○ 1 and $\frac{5}{3}$ ○ 1, so $\frac{4}{5}$ ○ $\frac{5}{3}$.

Use Reasoning

C Compare $\frac{3}{8}$ and $\frac{5}{6}$.

- First, look at $\frac{3}{8}$.

  > If the numerator is *less* than half the denominator, the fraction is less than $\frac{1}{2}$.

  You know that $\frac{1}{2}$ of 8 = 4. Since $\frac{4}{8} = \frac{1}{2}$, then $\frac{3}{8}$ ○ $\frac{1}{2}$.

- Then look at $\frac{5}{6}$.

  You know that $\frac{1}{2}$ of 6 = 3. Since $\frac{3}{6} = \frac{1}{2}$, then $\frac{5}{6}$ ○ $\frac{1}{2}$.

  So, $\frac{3}{8}$ ○ $\frac{5}{6}$.

D Compare $\frac{4}{6}$ and $\frac{1}{4}$.

- First, look at $\frac{4}{6}$.

  > If the numerator is *greater* than half the denominator, the fraction is greater than $\frac{1}{2}$.

  You know that $\frac{1}{2}$ of 6 = 3. Since $\frac{3}{6} = \frac{1}{2}$, then $\frac{4}{6}$ ○ $\frac{1}{2}$.

- Then look at $\frac{1}{4}$.

  You know that $\frac{1}{2}$ of 4 = 2. Since $\frac{2}{4} = \frac{1}{2}$, then $\frac{1}{4}$ ○ $\frac{1}{2}$.

  So, $\frac{4}{6}$ ○ $\frac{1}{4}$.

Math Talk Is $\frac{4}{9}$ greater than or less than $\frac{1}{2}$? **Explain** how you know.

Name ___________________________

Share and Show 

1. Use the models to compare $\frac{8}{12}$ and $\frac{1}{2}$.

$\frac{8}{12}$ ◯ $\frac{1}{2}$

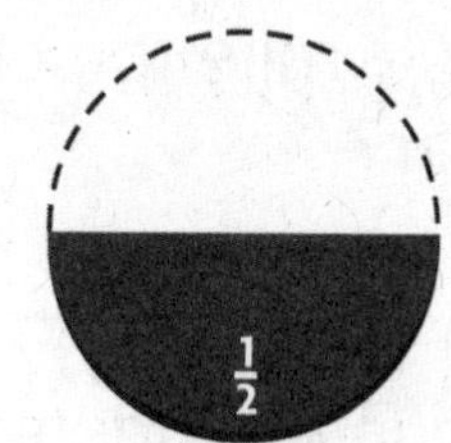

Use the benchmarks on the number line to help you compare. Write < or >.

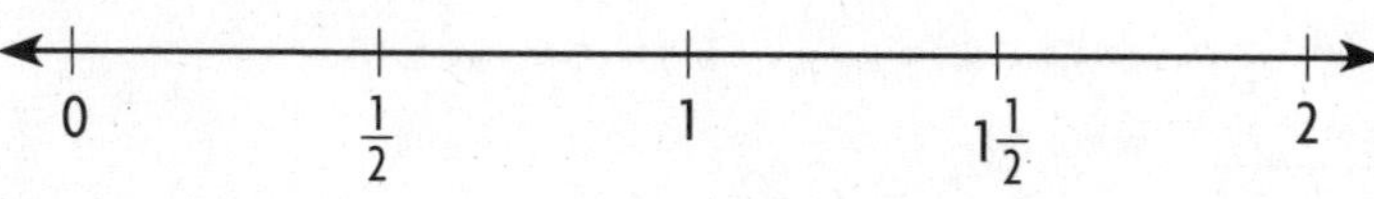

2. $\frac{1}{3}$ ◯ $\frac{3}{6}$

3. $\frac{3}{10}$ ◯ $\frac{3}{2}$

4. $\frac{11}{12}$ ◯ $\frac{4}{8}$

5. $\frac{2}{6}$ ◯ $\frac{2}{4}$

Math Talk Name one fraction greater than $\frac{1}{2}$ and one fraction less than $\frac{1}{2}$. **Explain** your choices.

On Your Own

Compare. Write < or >.

6. $\frac{7}{8}$ ◯ $\frac{2}{4}$

7. $\frac{4}{3}$ ◯ $\frac{10}{12}$

8. $\frac{8}{10}$ ◯ $\frac{6}{12}$

9. $\frac{2}{3}$ ◯ $\frac{1}{6}$

10. $\frac{3}{8}$ ◯ $\frac{11}{10}$

11. $\frac{3}{4}$ ◯ $\frac{2}{6}$

12. $\frac{3}{6}$ ◯ $\frac{2}{5}$

13. $\frac{6}{12}$ ◯ $\frac{2}{8}$

14. H.O.T. Ms. Hopper wrote the following fractions on the chalkboard.

$\frac{1}{20}, \frac{51}{100}, \frac{2}{40}, \frac{21}{20}, \frac{99}{100}, \frac{11}{20}$

Sort the fractions into three groups: less than $\frac{1}{2}$, greater than $\frac{1}{2}$, and greater than 1. Complete the chart.

less than $\frac{1}{2}$	greater than $\frac{1}{2}$	greater than 1

Problem Solving REAL WORLD

15. Julie walks $\frac{2}{3}$ mile to school. Mike walks $\frac{1}{4}$ mile to school. Who walks farther?

____

16. A group of students ate $\frac{5}{12}$ of a large pepperoni pizza, and $\frac{11}{12}$ of a large cheese pizza. Which pizza had fewer pieces left?

____

17. Tim ran $\frac{4}{8}$ mile. Lucy ran $\frac{7}{10}$ mile.

Who ran farther? _______________

18. Maggie's mother made two pies the same size. Maggie's family ate $\frac{2}{3}$ of the apple pie and $\frac{3}{4}$ of the cherry pie. Which pie had more left over?

____

19. Write Math **What's the Error?** Tom has two pieces of wood to build a birdhouse. One piece is $\frac{3}{4}$ yard long. The other piece is $\frac{4}{8}$ yard long. Tom says both pieces of wood are the same length. **Explain** his error.

____

____

20. **Test Prep** Todd and Lisa are playing a game with fraction pieces. Which statement is NOT correct?

Ⓐ $\frac{5}{6} < \frac{1}{2}$ Ⓒ $\frac{5}{6} > \frac{1}{2}$

Ⓑ $\frac{3}{6} = \frac{1}{2}$ Ⓓ $\frac{5}{6} < 1$

FOR MORE PRACTICE:
Florida Benchmarks Practice Book, pp. P189–P190

Name ___________________________

Compare Fractions with the Same Numerator

MA.3.A.2.2 Describe how the size of the fractional part is related to the number of equal sized pieces in the whole.

Essential Question How does the number of fraction parts relate to the size of each part?

UNLOCK the Problem REAL WORLD

Josh is at Enzo's Pizza. He can sit at a table with 5 of his friends or at a different table with 7 of his friends. The same size pizza is shared equally among the people at each table. At which table should Josh sit to get a larger piece of pizza?

- How can you represent as a fraction each amount of pizza Josh would get?

- Including Josh, how many friends will be sharing pizza at each table?

____

- What are you asked to find?

____

____

Model the Problem

There will be 6 friends sharing one pizza or 8 friends sharing another.

So, Josh will get either $\frac{1}{6}$ or $\frac{1}{8}$ of a pizza.

Compare $\frac{1}{6}$ and $\frac{1}{8}$.

Shade $\frac{1}{6}$ of Pizza A.

Shade $\frac{1}{8}$ of Pizza B.

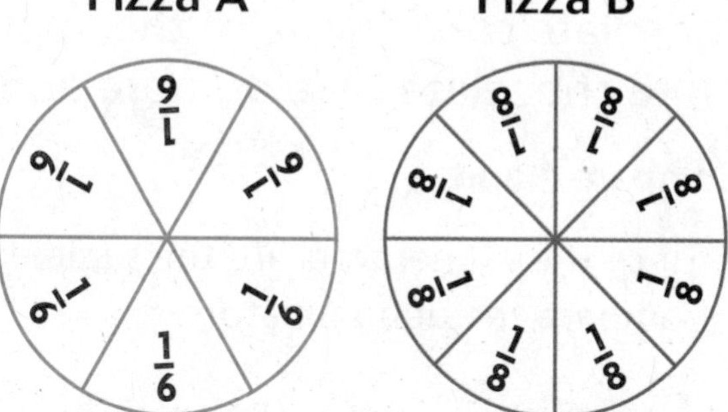

- Which piece of pizza is larger?

$\frac{1}{6} \bigcirc \frac{1}{8}$

So, Josh should sit at the table with ______ friends to get a larger piece of pizza.

1. Which pizza has more pieces? ________
The *more* pieces a whole is divided into,

the ________ the pieces.

2. Which pizza has fewer pieces? ________
The *fewer* pieces a whole is divided into,

the ________ the pieces.

Math Talk Suppose Josh wants 2 pieces of one of the pizzas above. Is $\frac{2}{6}$ or $\frac{2}{8}$ of the pizza a greater amount? **Explain** how you know.

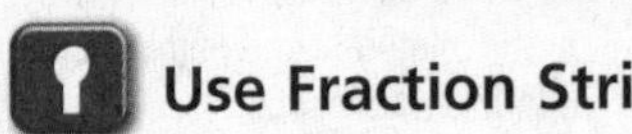

More Examples

Use Fraction Strips

On Saturday, the campers paddled $\frac{3}{12}$ mile down the Wekiva River. On Sunday, they paddled $\frac{3}{5}$ mile down the river. On which day did the campers paddle farther?

Compare $\frac{3}{12}$ and $\frac{3}{5}$.

- Place a ✓ next to the fraction strips that have more parts.
- Shade $\frac{3}{12}$. Then shade $\frac{3}{5}$. Compare the shaded parts.
- $\frac{3}{12} \bigcirc \frac{3}{5}$

1											
$\frac{1}{12}$	$\frac{1}{12}$	$\frac{1}{12}$	$\frac{1}{12}$	$\frac{1}{12}$	$\frac{1}{12}$	$\frac{1}{12}$	$\frac{1}{12}$	$\frac{1}{12}$	$\frac{1}{12}$	$\frac{1}{12}$	$\frac{1}{12}$
$\frac{1}{5}$	$\frac{1}{5}$	$\frac{1}{5}$	$\frac{1}{5}$	$\frac{1}{5}$							

Think: $\frac{1}{5}$ is greater than $\frac{1}{12}$, so $\frac{3}{5}$ is greater than $\frac{3}{12}$.

So, the campers paddled farther on __________.

Use Reasoning

For her class party, Becky baked two cakes that were the same size. After the party, she had $\frac{2}{8}$ of the chocolate cake and $\frac{2}{10}$ of the apple cake left over. Was more chocolate cake or more apple cake left over?

Compare $\frac{2}{8}$ and $\frac{2}{10}$.

- Since the numerators are the same, compare the denominators. $\frac{2}{8}$ ■ $\frac{2}{10}$

> - The *more* pieces a whole is divided into, the __________ the pieces.
> - The *fewer* pieces a whole is divided into, the __________ the pieces.

- $\frac{1}{8}$ is __________ than $\frac{1}{10}$.
- $\frac{2}{8} \bigcirc \frac{2}{10}$

So, there was more ______________ cake left over.

Try This! Write < or >.

$\frac{1}{7} \bigcirc \frac{1}{8}$ $\frac{2}{3} \bigcirc \frac{2}{4}$ $\frac{3}{9} \bigcirc \frac{3}{5}$ $\frac{1}{25} \bigcirc \frac{1}{23}$

Name ______________________________

Share and Show

1. Shade the models to show $\frac{1}{6}$ and $\frac{1}{4}$.

Then compare the fractions.

$\frac{1}{6} \bigcirc \frac{1}{4}$

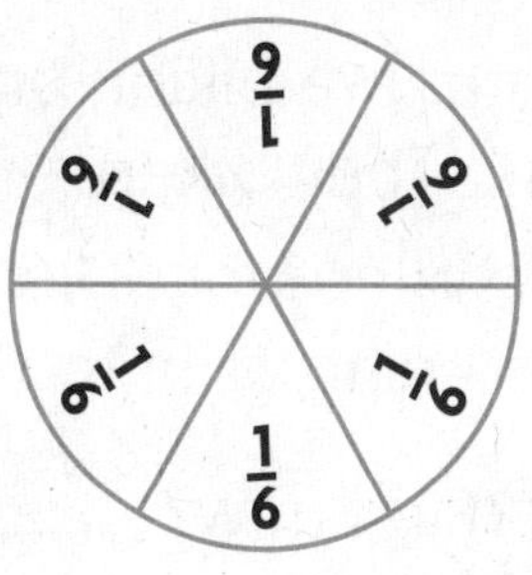

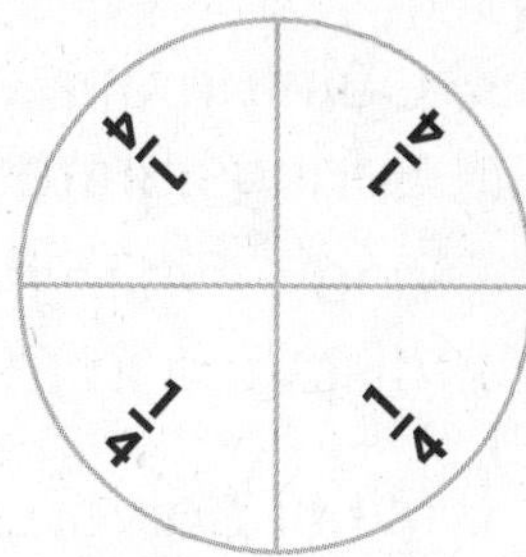

Compare. Write < or >.

2. $\frac{1}{8} \bigcirc \frac{1}{5}$

3. $\frac{2}{10} \bigcirc \frac{2}{6}$

4. $\frac{2}{6} \bigcirc \frac{2}{4}$

5. $\frac{4}{12} \bigcirc \frac{4}{6}$

6. $\frac{1}{5} \bigcirc \frac{1}{10}$

7. $\frac{7}{12} \bigcirc \frac{7}{8}$

Math Talk Explain why $\frac{6}{8}$ is greater than $\frac{6}{12}$.

On Your Own

Compare. Write < or >.

8. $\frac{1}{3} \bigcirc \frac{1}{4}$

9. $\frac{2}{5} \bigcirc \frac{2}{12}$

10. $\frac{4}{10} \bigcirc \frac{4}{5}$

11. $\frac{5}{8} \bigcirc \frac{5}{12}$

12. $\frac{1}{12} \bigcirc \frac{1}{4}$

13. $\frac{3}{10} \bigcirc \frac{3}{8}$

14. H.O.T. **Sense or Nonsense?** James ate $\frac{3}{4}$ of his pancake. David ate $\frac{2}{3}$ of his pancake. Who ate more of his pancake?

James said he knows he ate more because he looked at the amounts left. Does his answer make sense? Shade the models. **Explain.**

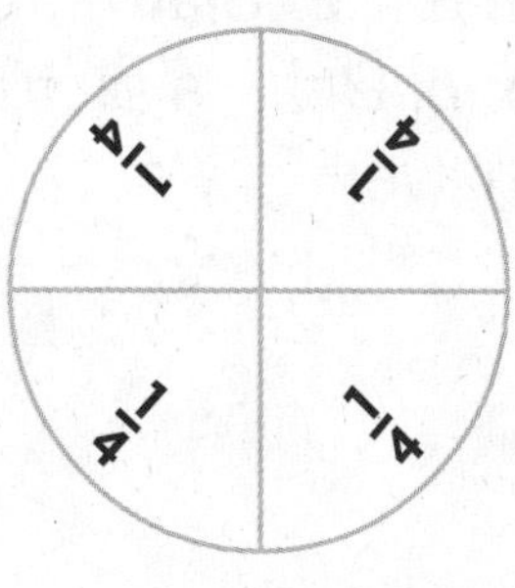

James

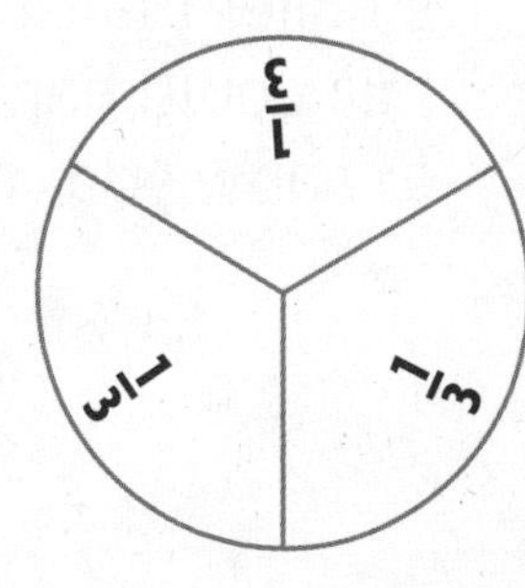

David

____

____

____

UNLOCK the Problem REAL WORLD

15. Quinton and Hunter are biking on trails in Wekiwa Springs State Park. They biked $\frac{7}{8}$ mile in the morning and $\frac{7}{10}$ mile in the afternoon. Did they bike a greater distance in the morning or in the afternoon?

a. What do you need to know? ______________________

b. How do you know which is greater, $\frac{1}{8}$ or $\frac{1}{10}$? ______________________

____

c. How can you solve the problem?

d. Complete the sentences.

In the morning, the boys biked

__________ mile.

In the afternoon, they biked

__________ mile.

The boys biked a greater distance

in the __________. $\frac{7}{8}$ ◯ $\frac{7}{10}$

16. H.O.T. Zach has a piece of pie that is $\frac{1}{4}$ of a pie. Max has a piece of pie that is $\frac{1}{2}$ of a pie. Max's piece is smaller than Zach's. **Explain** how this could happen. Draw a picture to show your answer.

____

____

____

17. **Test Prep** Before taking a hike, Kate and Dylan each ate a granola bar. Kate ate $\frac{1}{3}$ of her bar. Dylan ate $\frac{1}{2}$ of his bar. Which of the following correctly compares the amounts of granola bars that were eaten?

Ⓐ $\frac{1}{3} > \frac{1}{2}$

Ⓑ $\frac{1}{2} < \frac{1}{3}$

Ⓒ $\frac{1}{2} > \frac{1}{3}$

Ⓓ $\frac{1}{3} = \frac{1}{2}$

FOR MORE PRACTICE:
Florida Benchmarks Practice Book, pp. P191–P192

Name ______

Compare Fractions

Essential Question How do you compare fractions, including fractions greater than one, by using strategies?

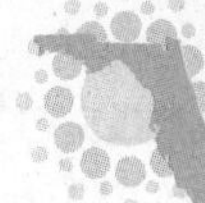

MA.3.A.2.3 Compare and order fractions, including fractions greater than one, using models and strategies.

UNLOCK the Problem REAL WORLD

Nick and Ben are fishing for largemouth bass. Ben catches one bass that weighs $2\frac{1}{4}$ pounds. Nick catches a bass that weighs $1\frac{1}{2}$ pounds. Who catches the larger fish?

- Circle the numbers you need to compare.
- What are you asked to find?

______

Compare $2\frac{1}{4}$ and $1\frac{1}{2}$.

Strategy

- When two mixed numbers have *unlike* whole numbers, you have to compare only the whole numbers.

____ > ____

____ $\frac{\square}{\square}$ > ____ $\frac{\square}{\square}$

So, ______ catches the larger fish.

- Why don't you also have to compare the fractions when the whole numbers are different?

______

Morgan ran $1\frac{2}{3}$ miles. Alexa ran $1\frac{1}{3}$ miles. Who ran farther?

Compare $1\frac{2}{3}$ and $1\frac{1}{3}$.

$1\frac{\square}{3} > 1\frac{\square}{3}$

So, ______ ran farther.

Strategy

- When two mixed numbers have the *same* whole numbers, you compare only the fractions.
- When the denominators are the same, you compare only the number of pieces, or the numerators.

Math Talk **Explain** how to compare $2\frac{6}{10}$ and $2\frac{3}{10}$.

More Examples

Ms. Davis bought $2\frac{2}{3}$ pounds of cherries and $2\frac{1}{4}$ pounds of strawberries. Did the cherries or the strawberries weigh more?

 **Compare $2\frac{2}{3}$ and $2\frac{1}{4}$.**

Strategy

- Since the whole numbers are the same, compare the fractions $\frac{2}{3}$ and $\frac{1}{4}$.

- Think about the benchmark $\frac{1}{2}$.
  Is $\frac{2}{3}$ greater than or less than $\frac{1}{2}$? ______________________
- Is $\frac{1}{4}$ greater than or less than $\frac{1}{2}$? ______________________
- $\frac{2}{3}$ ◯ _____  2 — ◯ 2 — 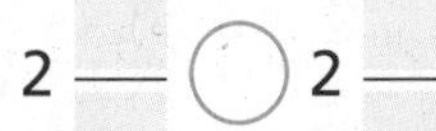

So, the __________ weighed more.

José and Leah are eating small pizzas. One plate has $\frac{4}{5}$ of José's cheese pizza. Another plate has $\frac{5}{6}$ of Leah's pepperoni pizza. Whose pizza has the larger piece missing?

 **Compare $\frac{4}{5}$ and $\frac{5}{6}$.**

Strategy

- You can compare fractions by comparing missing pieces of a whole.

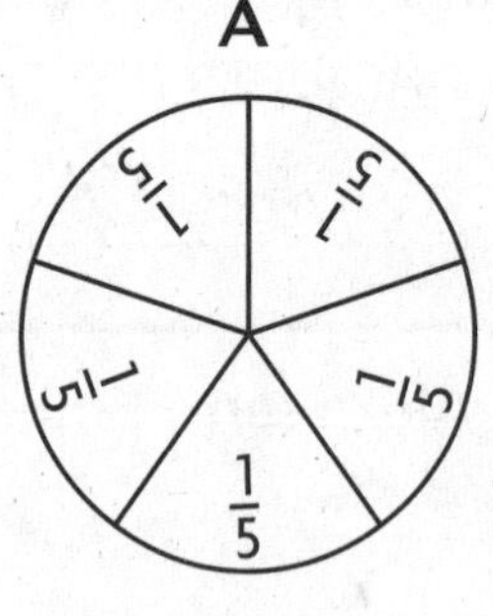

$\frac{4}{5}$
José

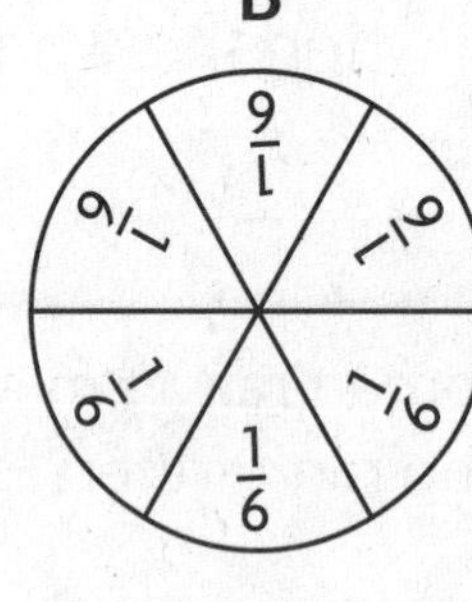

$\frac{5}{6}$
Leah

- Shade $\frac{4}{5}$ of circle **A** and $\frac{5}{6}$ of circle **B**. Each fraction represents a whole that is missing one piece.
- Which circle has a larger piece missing? _____

Since $\frac{4}{5}$ has a larger piece missing, $\frac{4}{5}$ is __________ than $\frac{5}{6}$.

 $\frac{4}{5}$ ◯ $\frac{5}{6}$

So, __________ pizza has a larger piece missing.

Math Talk Compare $\frac{3}{4}$ and $\frac{2}{3}$. How does knowing that $\frac{1}{4}$ is less than $\frac{1}{3}$ help you compare $\frac{3}{4}$ and $\frac{2}{3}$?

Name ______________________________

Share and Show 

1. Compare $\frac{9}{10}$ and $\frac{7}{8}$.

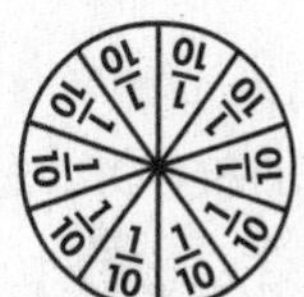
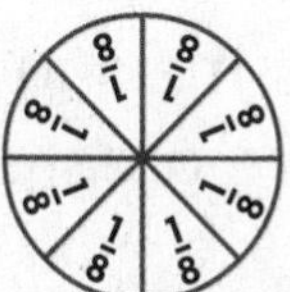

Think: What is missing from each to make one whole?

Write $<$ or $>$. $\frac{9}{10}$ ◯ $\frac{7}{8}$

Compare. Write $<$ or $>$. Write the strategy you used.

✓2. $1\frac{2}{4}$ ◯ $2\frac{1}{4}$

____

✓3. $2\frac{2}{5}$ ◯ $2\frac{4}{5}$

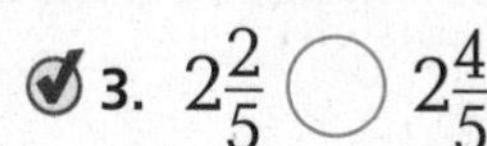

____

Math Talk **Explain** how the missing pieces in Exercise 1 help you compare $\frac{9}{10}$ and $\frac{7}{8}$.

On Your Own

Compare. Write $<$ or $>$. Write the strategy you used.

4. $1\frac{2}{6}$ ◯ $1\frac{4}{5}$

____

5. $2\frac{5}{6}$ ◯ $2\frac{7}{8}$

____

6. $1\frac{2}{8}$ ◯ $1\frac{6}{8}$

____

7. $5\frac{4}{10}$ ◯ $4\frac{5}{6}$

____

8. $2\frac{2}{3}$ ◯ $2\frac{5}{6}$

____

9. $4\frac{5}{6}$ ◯ $4\frac{3}{8}$

____

Problem Solving 

Use the table for 10–11.

Fruit Punch	
Ingredient	Cups
Orange juice	$2\frac{6}{8}$
Pineapple juice	$2\frac{1}{4}$
Lemon juice	$\frac{1}{4}$
Cranberry juice	$1\frac{2}{4}$

10. Seth's class is making fruit punch. Is the amount of orange juice greater than or less than the amount of pineapple juice? **Explain.** ________

____

____

____

____

11. Is the amount of cranberry juice greater than or less than the amount of pineapple juice? **Explain.**

SHOW YOUR WORK

____

____

____

____

12. H.O.T. **What's the Error?** Luke says that $\frac{11}{12}$ is greater than $\frac{11}{8}$ because the denominator 12 is larger than the denominator 8. Describe Luke's error. Tell which strategy you would use.

____

____

____

13. **Test Prep** Tracy is making a blueberry cake. She is using $1\frac{1}{3}$ cups of sugar and $1\frac{6}{8}$ cups of flour. Which compares the ingredients correctly?

Ⓐ $1\frac{1}{3} > 1\frac{6}{8}$ Ⓒ $1\frac{1}{3} = 1\frac{6}{8}$

Ⓑ $1\frac{6}{8} > 1\frac{1}{3}$ Ⓓ $1\frac{6}{8} < 1\frac{1}{3}$

 FOR MORE PRACTICE:
Florida Benchmarks Practice Book, pp. P193–P194

Name ______________________

Mid-Chapter Checkpoint

▶ Check Vocabulary

Choose the best term from the box to complete the sentence.

Vocabulary
benchmarks
fraction

1. Numbers that are easy to work with, such as $\frac{1}{2}$ and 1, are called ______________. **(MA.3.A.2.3; p. 343)**

▶ Check Concepts and Skills

Use the benchmarks to help you compare. Write < or >. **(MA.3.A.2.3; pp. 343–346)**

2. 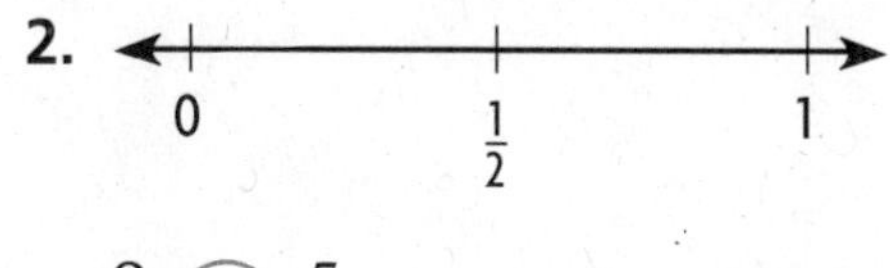

$\frac{2}{6}$ ◯ $\frac{5}{8}$

3. 0 $\frac{1}{2}$ 1

$\frac{1}{5}$ ◯ $\frac{6}{10}$

4. 0 $\frac{1}{2}$ 1

$\frac{8}{12}$ ◯ $\frac{2}{5}$

5. 0 $\frac{1}{2}$ 1

$\frac{4}{6}$ ◯ $\frac{1}{4}$

Compare. Write < or >. **(MA.3.A.2.2; pp. 347–350; MA.3.A.2.3, pp. 351–354)**

6. $\frac{1}{6}$ ◯ $\frac{1}{4}$

7. $\frac{1}{8}$ ◯ $\frac{1}{10}$

8. $\frac{2}{10}$ ◯ $\frac{2}{6}$

9. $\frac{4}{3}$ ◯ $\frac{2}{3}$

10. $\frac{7}{8}$ ◯ $\frac{3}{8}$

11. $1\frac{8}{10}$ ◯ $1\frac{3}{8}$

12. $3\frac{2}{4}$ ◯ $3\frac{3}{4}$

13. $\frac{9}{10}$ ◯ $\frac{5}{6}$

14. $\frac{5}{8}$ ◯ $\frac{5}{12}$

Fill in the bubble for the correct answer choice.

15. Two walls in Tiffany's room are the same size. Tiffany paints $\frac{1}{5}$ of one wall. Jake paints $\frac{1}{8}$ of the other wall. Which number sentence shows who painted more?

(MA.3.A.2.2; pp. 347–350)

Ⓐ $\frac{1}{5} < \frac{1}{8}$

Ⓑ $\frac{1}{8} = \frac{1}{5}$

Ⓒ $\frac{1}{5} > \frac{1}{8}$

Ⓓ $\frac{1}{8} > \frac{1}{5}$

16. Matthew ran $\frac{5}{8}$ mile during track practice. Paul ran $\frac{5}{10}$ mile. Which number sentence shows who ran the greater distance? (MA.3.A.2.2; pp. 347–350)

Ⓕ $\frac{5}{10} = \frac{5}{8}$

Ⓖ $\frac{5}{8} < \frac{5}{10}$

Ⓗ $\frac{5}{8} > \frac{5}{10}$

Ⓘ $\frac{5}{10} > \frac{5}{8}$

17. Mallory bought 6 roses for her mother. Two-sixths of the roses are red and $\frac{4}{6}$ are yellow. Which number sentence shows whether there are more red or more yellow roses? (MA.3.A.2.3; pp. 339–342)

Ⓐ $\frac{4}{6} < \frac{2}{6}$

Ⓑ $\frac{2}{6} < \frac{4}{6}$

Ⓒ $\frac{4}{6} = \frac{2}{6}$

Ⓓ $\frac{2}{6} > \frac{4}{6}$

18. Lani used $1\frac{2}{3}$ cups of flour and $1\frac{3}{4}$ cups of sugar to bake cookies. Which number sentence shows the correct comparison of the two amounts?

(MA.3.A.2.3; pp. 351–354)

Ⓕ $1\frac{2}{3} = 1\frac{3}{4}$

Ⓖ $1\frac{2}{3} > 1\frac{3}{4}$

Ⓗ $1\frac{3}{4} < 1\frac{2}{3}$

Ⓘ $1\frac{3}{4} > 1\frac{2}{3}$

Name ______________________________

Order Fractions

Essential Question How do you order fractions less than and greater than one?

MA.3.A.2.3 Compare and order fractions, including fractions greater than one, using models and strategies.

UNLOCK the Problem REAL WORLD

Harrison, Tad, and Dale ride their bikes to school. Harrison rides $\frac{4}{8}$ mile, Tad rides $\frac{1}{3}$ mile, and Dale rides $\frac{4}{5}$ mile. Order the distances the boys ride from greatest to least.

- Circle the fractions you need to use.
- Underline the sentence that tells you what you need to do.

Use the strategies you know to order the fractions from greatest to least.

- **Think:** I know that $\frac{4}{8}$ is equal to ______.
- I know that $\frac{1}{3}$ is less than ______.
- I know that $\frac{4}{5}$ is greater than ______ and close to 1.

Write the fractions on the number line.

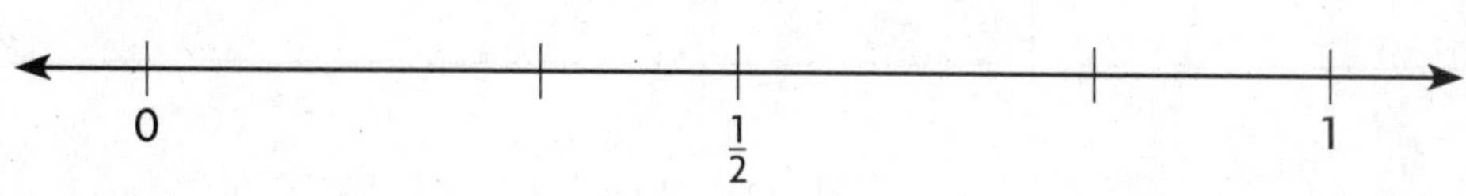

So, the distances in order from greatest to least

are ______ > ______ > ______.

Try This! Order $2\frac{4}{9}$, $1\frac{1}{6}$, and $1\frac{3}{4}$ from greatest to least.

- First, compare the whole numbers. Since 2 > 1, $2\frac{4}{9}$ is the greatest number.
- Then compare $1\frac{1}{6}$ and $1\frac{3}{4}$. Since they both have 1 as the whole number, compare only the fractions.
- Compare $\frac{1}{6}$ and $\frac{3}{4}$. Use a strategy you know. ______ > ______

So, the order from greatest to least is ______ > ______ > ______.

Math Idea

To order mixed numbers, compare the whole numbers first. Then compare the fractions.

Share and Show 

1. Use the number lines to order $\frac{3}{4}$, $\frac{5}{8}$, and $\frac{1}{6}$ from least to greatest. Circle $\frac{3}{4}$, $\frac{5}{8}$, and $\frac{1}{6}$ on the number lines.

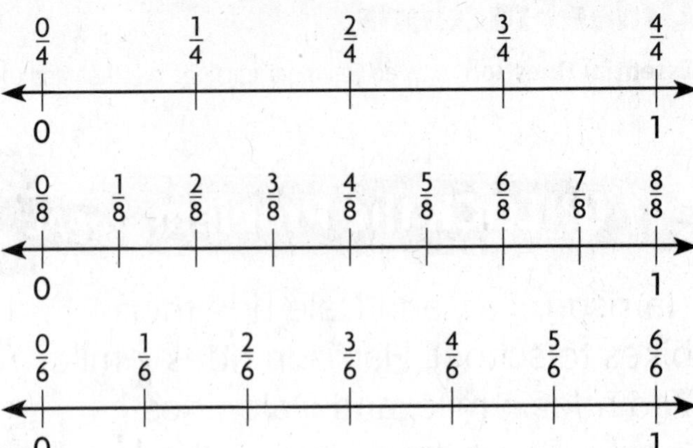

____ < ____ < ____

Order from *greatest* to *least*.
Use the strategies you know.

2. $\frac{6}{8}$, $\frac{1}{2}$, $\frac{1}{4}$, $\frac{2}{6}$

____ ○ ____ ○ ____ ○ ____

3. $1\frac{5}{6}$, $1\frac{2}{10}$, $2\frac{8}{10}$

____ ○ ____ ○ ____

4. $3\frac{2}{7}$, $2\frac{2}{5}$, $2\frac{2}{3}$

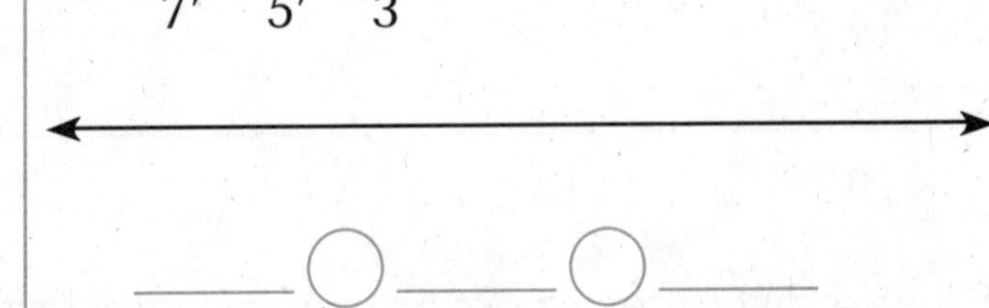

____ ○ ____ ○ ____

5. $\frac{3}{7}$, $\frac{1}{9}$, $\frac{1}{7}$

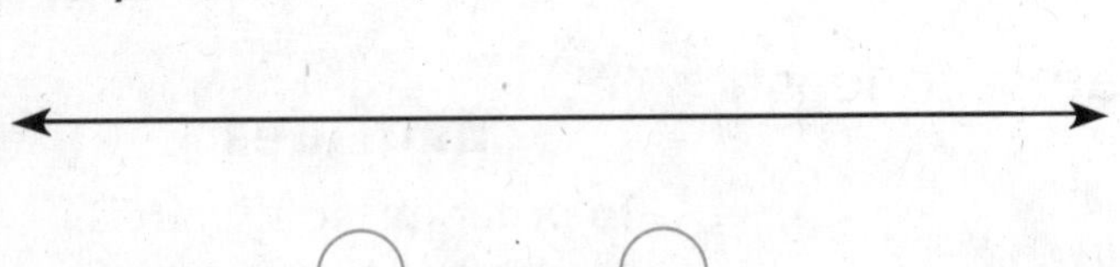

____ ○ ____ ○ ____

6. $1\frac{7}{8}$, $\frac{5}{4}$, $1\frac{2}{4}$

____ ○ ____ ○ ____

7. $\frac{5}{4}$, $\frac{4}{3}$, $\frac{3}{2}$

____ ○ ____ ○ ____

Math Talk Explain how you would order the fractions $\frac{1}{2}$, $\frac{1}{8}$, and $\frac{1}{4}$ from least to greatest. What strategy would you use?

Name ____________________

On Your Own

Order from *least* to *greatest*.
Use the strategies you know.

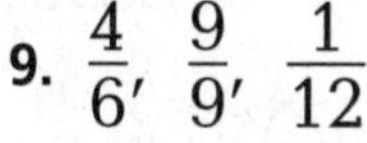

8. $\frac{1}{4}, \frac{4}{5}, \frac{1}{8}$

9. $\frac{4}{6}, \frac{9}{9}, \frac{1}{12}$

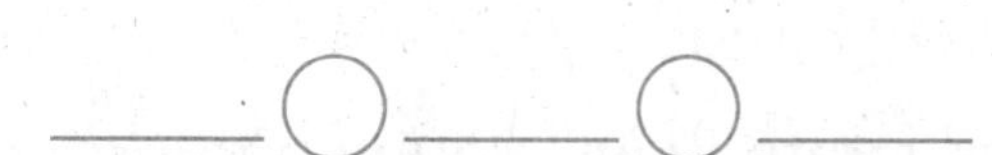

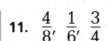

10. $2\frac{7}{8}, 2\frac{5}{12}, 2\frac{1}{10}$

11. $\frac{4}{8}, \frac{1}{6}, \frac{3}{4}$

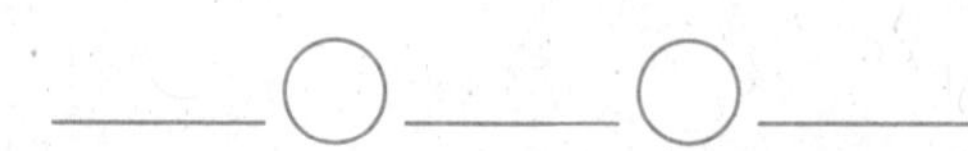

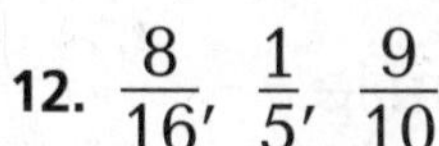

12. $\frac{8}{16}, \frac{1}{5}, \frac{9}{10}$

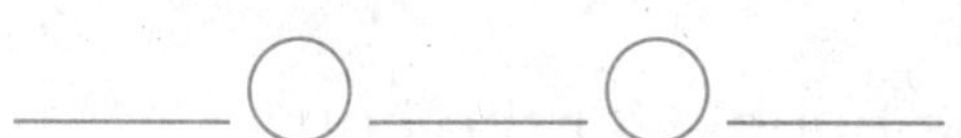

13. $1\frac{4}{5}, \frac{4}{5}, 2\frac{4}{5}$

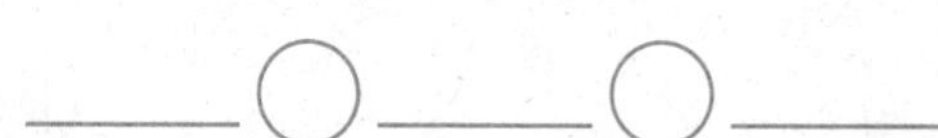

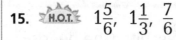

14. H.O.T. $1\frac{3}{4}, 1\frac{7}{8}, 1\frac{2}{3}$

Hint: Which fraction has the greatest piece missing needed to complete the whole?

15. H.O.T. $1\frac{5}{6}, 1\frac{1}{3}, \frac{7}{6}$

Hint: How many sixths are in one whole?

Math Talk Explain how you know that $\frac{2}{6}$ is less than $\frac{1}{2}$.

UNLOCK the Problem REAL WORLD

16. In fifteen minutes, Greg's sailboat went $\frac{9}{10}$ mile. Gina's sailboat went $\frac{5}{6}$ mile, and Stuart's sailboat went $\frac{4}{5}$ mile. Which shows the distances in order from greatest to least?

Ⓐ $\frac{5}{6}, \frac{4}{5}, \frac{9}{10}$ Ⓑ $\frac{5}{6}, \frac{9}{10}, \frac{4}{5}$ Ⓒ $\frac{4}{5}, \frac{5}{6}, \frac{9}{10}$ Ⓓ $\frac{9}{10}, \frac{5}{6}, \frac{4}{5}$

a. What do you need to know? ______________________________

____

b. What strategy will you use to order the fractions? ______________________________

____

c. Show the steps you used to solve the problem.

$\frac{1}{10}$ ◯ $\frac{1}{6}$, so $\frac{9}{10}$ ◯ $\frac{5}{6}$

$\frac{1}{6}$ ◯ $\frac{1}{5}$, so $\frac{5}{6}$ ◯ $\frac{4}{5}$

d. Complete the sentences.

Greg's sailboat went —— mile.

Gina's sailboat went —— mile.

Stuart's sailboat went —— mile.

The distances from greatest to least are ——, ——, ——.

e. Fill in the bubble for the correct answer choice above.

17. Pam is making biscuits. She needs $\frac{1}{3}$ cup of butter, $\frac{3}{4}$ cup of water, and $\frac{1}{2}$ cup of milk. Which list orders the ingredients from *least* to *greatest*?

Ⓕ $\frac{1}{2}, \frac{3}{4}, \frac{1}{3}$ Ⓗ $\frac{3}{4}, \frac{1}{2}, \frac{1}{3}$

Ⓖ $\frac{1}{3}, \frac{1}{2}, \frac{3}{4}$ Ⓘ $\frac{1}{3}, \frac{3}{4}, \frac{1}{2}$

18. Jesse ran $\frac{7}{8}$ mile on Monday, $\frac{5}{4}$ miles on Tuesday, and $\frac{1}{2}$ mile on Wednesday. Which list orders the distances from *greatest* to *least*?

Ⓐ $\frac{5}{4}, \frac{1}{2}, \frac{7}{8}$ Ⓒ $\frac{7}{8}, \frac{1}{2}, \frac{5}{4}$

Ⓑ $\frac{7}{8}, \frac{5}{4}, \frac{1}{2}$ Ⓓ $\frac{5}{4}, \frac{7}{8}, \frac{1}{2}$

FOR MORE PRACTICE:
Florida Benchmarks Practice Book, pp. P195–P196

Name ______________________________

Model Equivalent Fractions

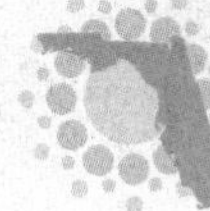

Essential Question How can you find equivalent fractions by paper folding?

MA.3.A.2.4 Use models to represent equivalent fractions, including fractions greater than one, and identify representations of equivalence.

Investigate

Materials ■ sheet of notebook paper

Two or more fractions that name the same amount are called **equivalent fractions**. You can use a sheet of paper to model fractions equivalent to $\frac{1}{2}$.

A. First, fold a sheet of paper into two equal parts. Open the paper and count the parts.

There are _____ equal parts. Each part is _____ of the paper.

Write $\frac{1}{2}$ on each of the halves.

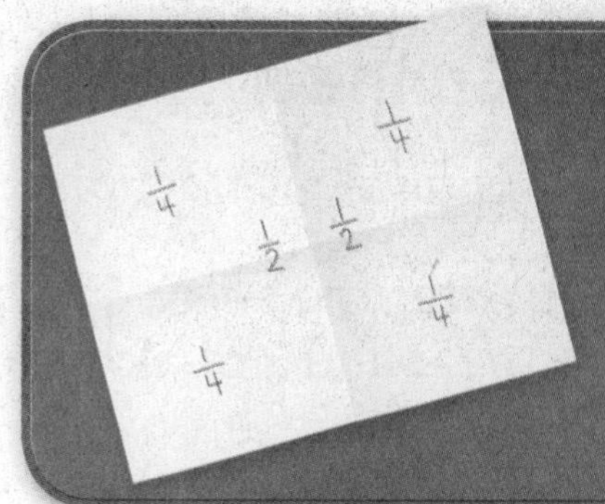

B. Next, fold the paper in half two times. Open the paper.

Now there are _____ equal parts. Each part is _____ of the paper.

Write $\frac{1}{4}$ on each of the fourths.

Look at the parts. $\frac{1}{2} = \frac{\square}{4}$

C. Last, fold the paper in half three times.

Now there are _____ equal parts. Each part is _____ of the paper.

Write $\frac{1}{8}$ on each of the eighths.

Find the equivalent fractions on your paper.

So, $\frac{1}{2}$, $\frac{\square}{\square}$, and $\frac{\square}{\square}$ are equivalent.

Draw Conclusions

1. **Explain** how many $\frac{1}{8}$ parts are equivalent to one $\frac{1}{4}$ part on your paper.

____

2. **Application What if** you folded your paper a fourth time? How many equal parts are there now?

_______ equal parts

What fraction names each part? _______
How many $\frac{1}{16}$ parts are equivalent to one $\frac{1}{2}$ part?

____

Math Talk **Explain** why the 16^{ths} are smaller than the 8^{ths} on your folded paper.

Connect

Equivalent fractions can help you compare fractions.

After the party, $\frac{3}{4}$ of an apple pie was left over and $\frac{5}{8}$ of a cherry pie was left. Which pie had more left over?

Compare $\frac{3}{4}$ and $\frac{5}{8}$.

Use your fraction pieces. Find how many $\frac{1}{8}$ pieces there are in $\frac{3}{4}$.

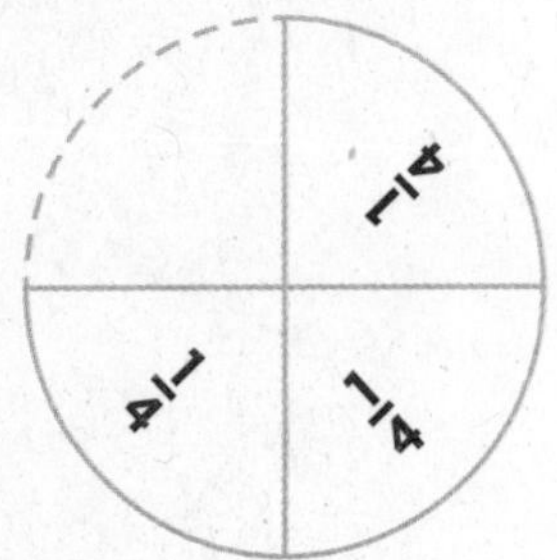

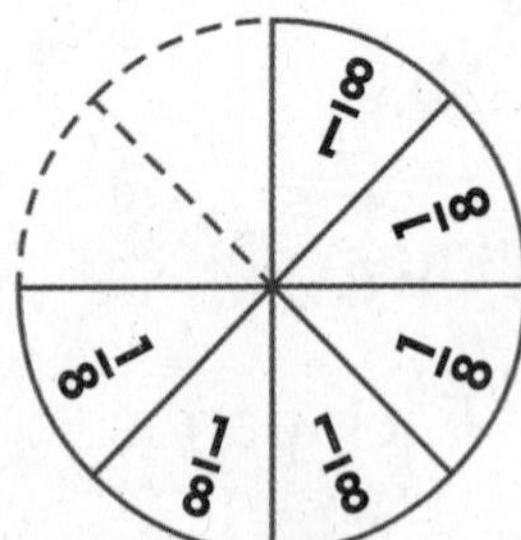

There are six $\frac{1}{8}$ pieces in $\frac{3}{4}$.

So, $\frac{6}{8}$ and $\frac{3}{4}$ both name the same amount.

Now you can compare fractions with the same denominator to solve the problem. $\frac{6}{8} \bigcirc \frac{5}{8}$

So, since $\frac{6}{8} > \frac{5}{8}$, there was more apple pie left over.

Name ______________________

Share and Show 

Shade to find the equivalent fraction.

1.

1									
$\frac{1}{5}$		$\frac{1}{5}$		$\frac{1}{5}$		$\frac{1}{5}$		$\frac{1}{5}$	
$\frac{1}{10}$	$\frac{1}{10}$	$\frac{1}{10}$	$\frac{1}{10}$	$\frac{1}{10}$	$\frac{1}{10}$	$\frac{1}{10}$	$\frac{1}{10}$	$\frac{1}{10}$	$\frac{1}{10}$

$\frac{3}{5} = \frac{\square}{10}$

2.

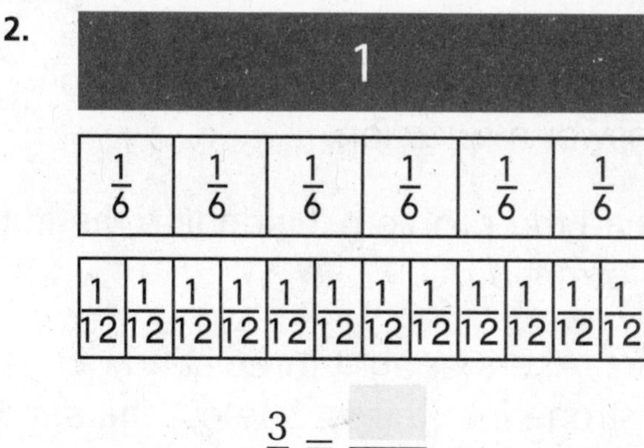

$\frac{3}{6} = \frac{\square}{12}$

3.

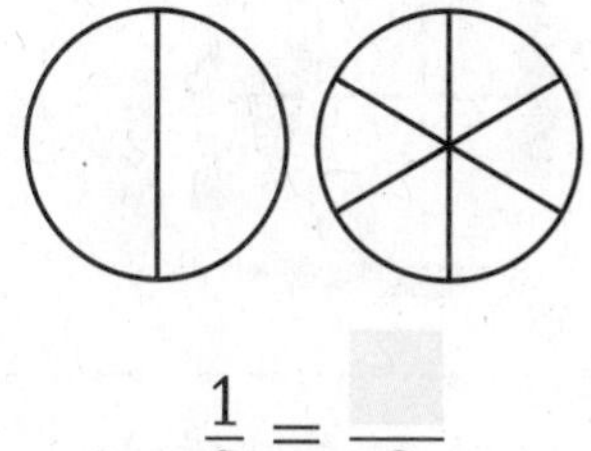

$\frac{1}{2} = \frac{\square}{6}$

4.

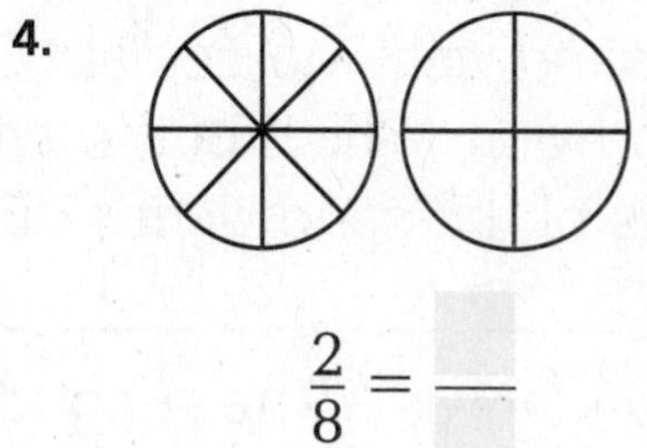

$\frac{2}{8} = \frac{\square}{\square}$

5.

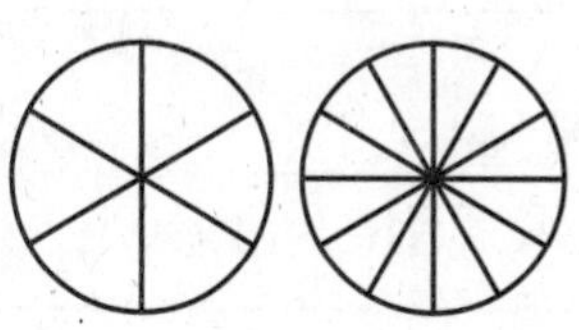

$\frac{4}{6} = \frac{\square}{\square}$

6. H.O.T. Use the model. Find a fraction equivalent to $\frac{2}{3}$.

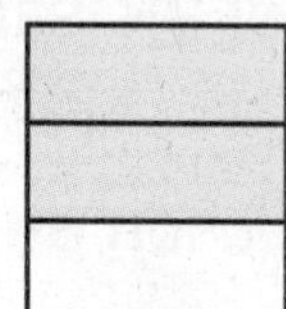

Hint: Draw a line or lines on the model to help you.

$\frac{2}{3} = \frac{\square}{\square}$

7. Write Math ▶ There are three pizzas the same size. Charles ate $\frac{1}{2}$ of the first pizza. The second pizza was cut into 6 equal pieces. Mattie ate 3 of them. The third pizza was cut into 8 equal pieces. Trudi ate 4 pieces.

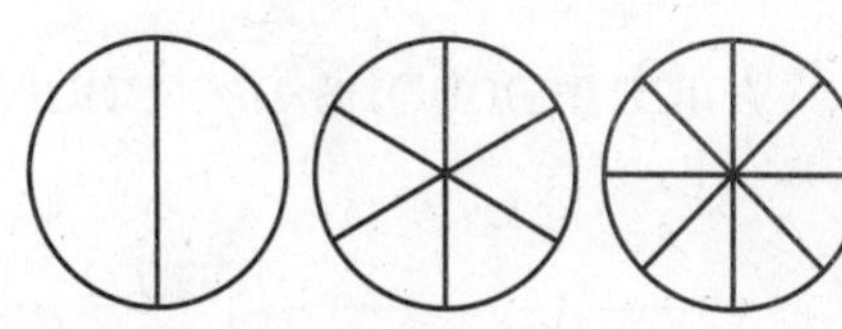

- Did everyone eat the same amount? Shade the models. **Explain.**

____

Connect to Reading

Summarize

You can *summarize* the information in a problem by underlining it or writing the information needed to answer a question.

Read the problem. Underline the important information.

Mrs. Akers bought three sandwiches. She cut the first one into thirds. She cut the second one into fourths and the third one into sixths. Marian ate 2 pieces of the first sandwich. Jason ate 2 pieces of the second sandwich. Marcos ate 3 pieces of the third sandwich. Which of the children ate equivalent parts of the sandwiches? **Explain.**

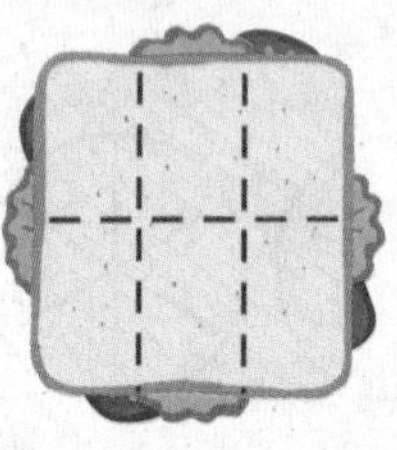

The first sandwich was cut into ________.	The second sandwich was cut into ________.	The third sandwich was cut into ________.
Marian ate ______ pieces of the sandwich.	Jason ate ______ pieces of the sandwich.	Marcos ate ______ pieces of the sandwich.
Marian ate $\frac{\square}{\square}$ of the first sandwich.	Jason ate $\frac{\square}{\square}$ of the second sandwich.	Marcos ate $\frac{\square}{\square}$ of the third sandwich.

Are all the fractions equivalent? ______

Which fractions are equivalent? $\frac{\square}{\square} = \frac{\square}{\square}$

So, __________ and __________ ate equivalent parts of the sandwiches.

 FOR MORE PRACTICE:
Florida Benchmarks Practice Book, pp. P197–P198

Name ______________________________

Equivalent Fractions

Essential Question How can you use models to name equivalent fractions, including fractions greater than one?

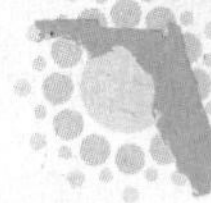

MA.3.A.2.4 Use models to represent equivalent fractions, including fractions greater than one, and identify representations of equivalence.

UNLOCK the Problem REAL WORLD

Cole brought 2 turkey sandwiches to the picnic. Each sandwich was cut into fourths. After he ate lunch, Cole had 5 pieces of sandwich left.

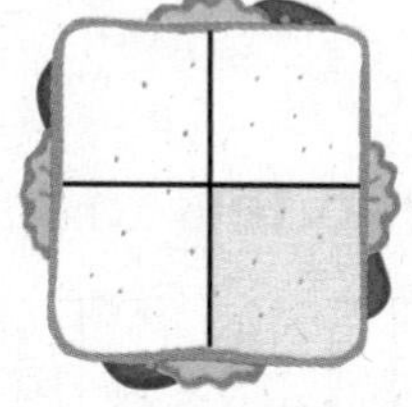

Shade the pieces to show what Cole ate.

- What fraction names the pieces that Cole ate?

  ______

- What fraction names the pieces left over? ______

Cole divided each of the leftover pieces in half. Draw a dashed line on each piece to show how Cole divided it.

After you divide each fourth-size piece into 2 equal pieces, there will be 8 pieces in a whole sandwich. The pieces are called eighths.

- What fraction names the total number of pieces Cole has? $\frac{\square}{8}$

So, $\frac{\square}{4}$ and $\frac{\square}{8}$ are equivalent since they both name the same amount of the sandwiches.

Try This! Write an equivalent fraction for the shaded part of the models.

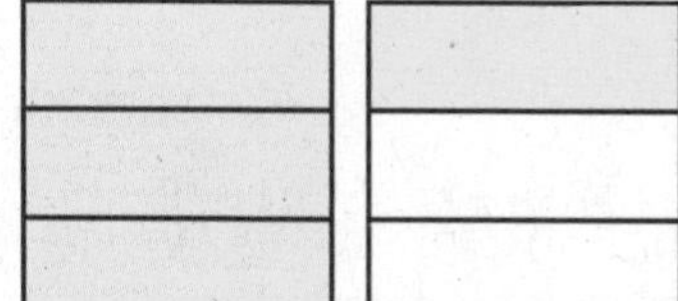

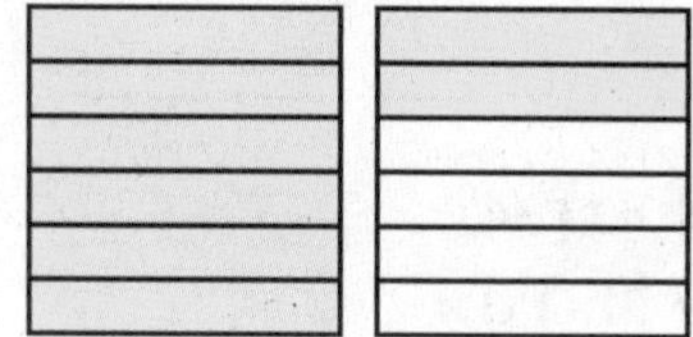

$\frac{4}{3} =$ ______

Share and Show 

1. Use the models to find equivalent fractions.

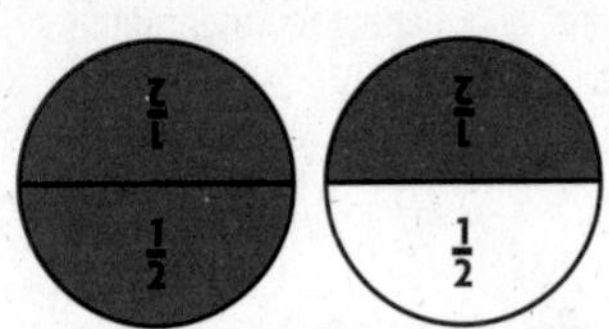
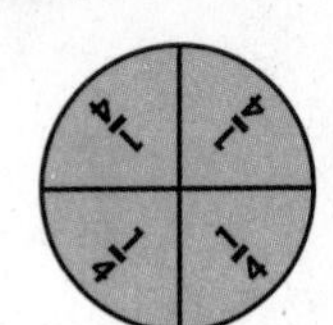
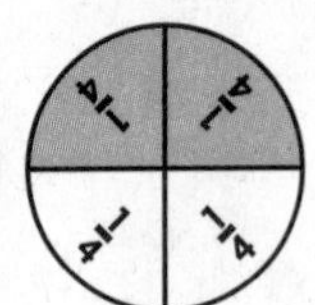

$$\frac{3}{2} = \frac{\square}{4}$$

Shade the models to find equivalent fractions.

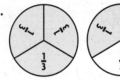

2. 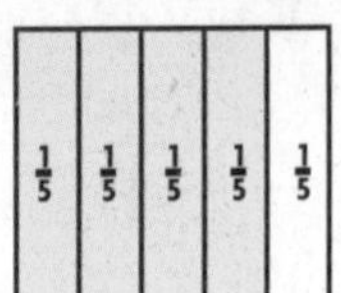

$$\frac{4}{5} = \frac{\square}{10}$$

3. 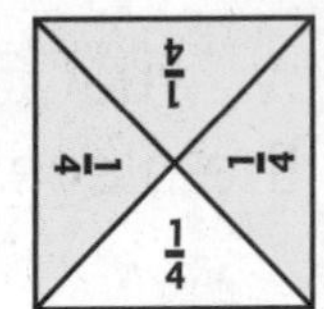 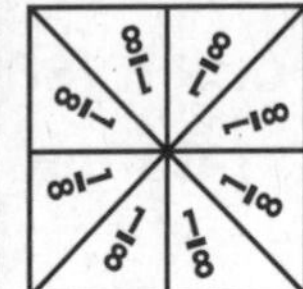

$$\frac{3}{4} = \frac{\square}{8}$$

4. 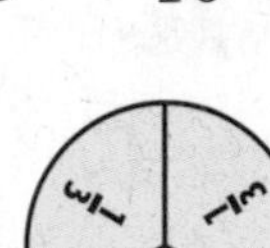 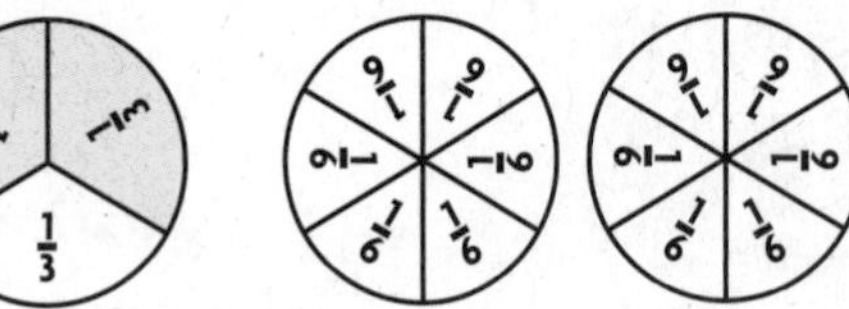

$$\frac{5}{3} = \frac{\square}{6}$$

5. 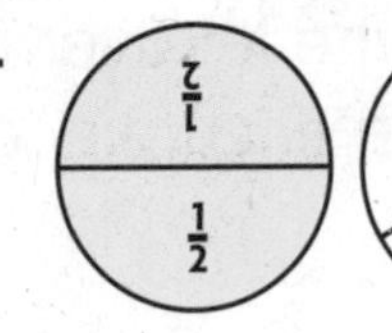 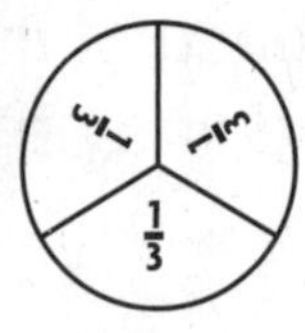 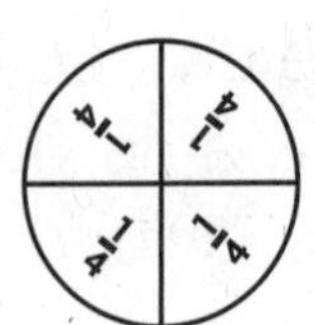

$$\frac{2}{2} = \frac{\square}{3} = \frac{4}{\square}$$

Math Talk What is another fraction that is equivalent to $\frac{2}{2}$?

6. Heidi ate $\frac{3}{6}$ of her granola bar. Molly ate $\frac{4}{8}$ of her granola bar. Which girl ate more of her granola bar? Shade the models. Explain your answer.

$\frac{1}{6}$	$\frac{1}{6}$	$\frac{1}{6}$
$\frac{1}{6}$	$\frac{1}{6}$	$\frac{1}{6}$

$\frac{1}{8}$	$\frac{1}{8}$	$\frac{1}{8}$	$\frac{1}{8}$
$\frac{1}{8}$	$\frac{1}{8}$	$\frac{1}{8}$	$\frac{1}{8}$

____

____

7. Andy swam $\frac{6}{10}$ mile in the race. Use the number line to find a fraction that is equivalent to $\frac{6}{10}$.

$$\frac{6}{10} = \frac{\square}{\square}$$

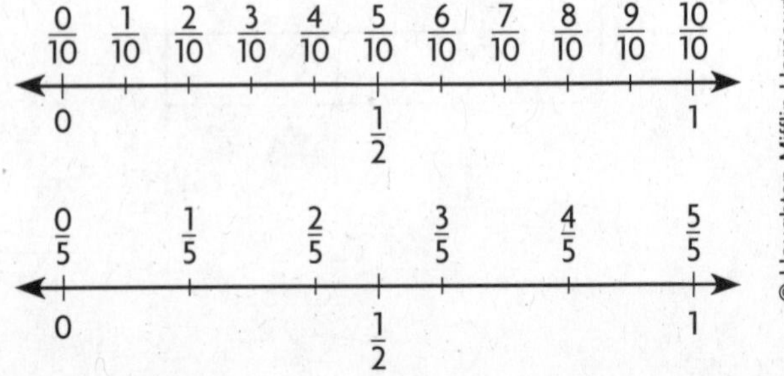

Name ______________________

On Your Own

Shade the models to find equivalent fractions.

8.

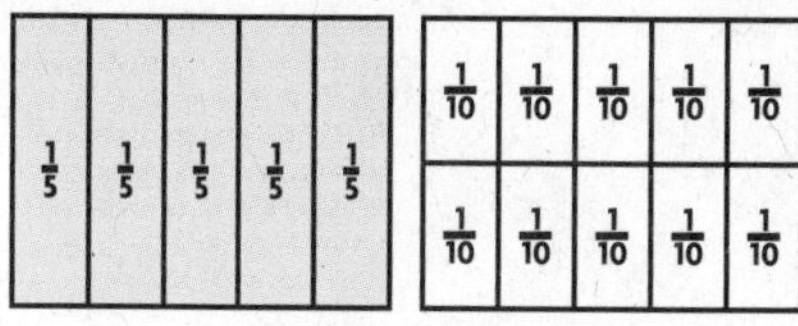

$\frac{5}{5} = \frac{\square}{10}$

9.

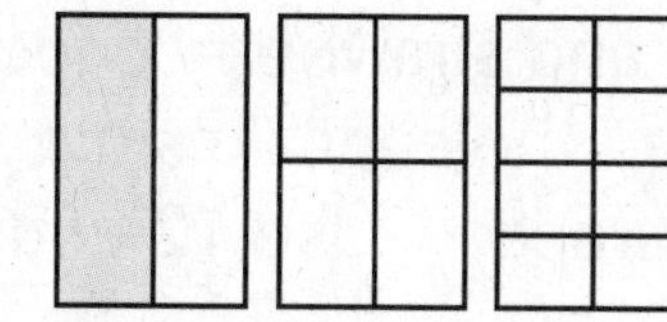

$\frac{1}{2} = \frac{2}{\square} = \frac{\square}{8}$

10.

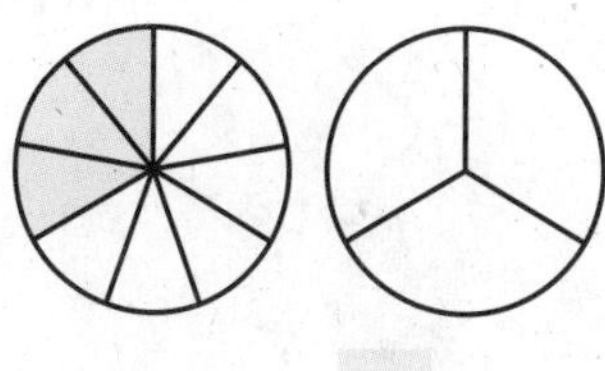

$\frac{3}{9} = \frac{\square}{3}$

11.

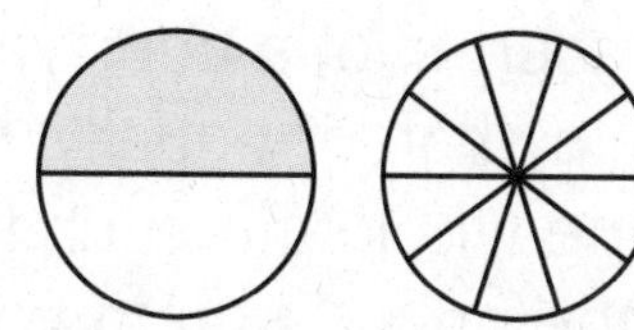

$\frac{1}{2} = \frac{5}{\square}$

12.

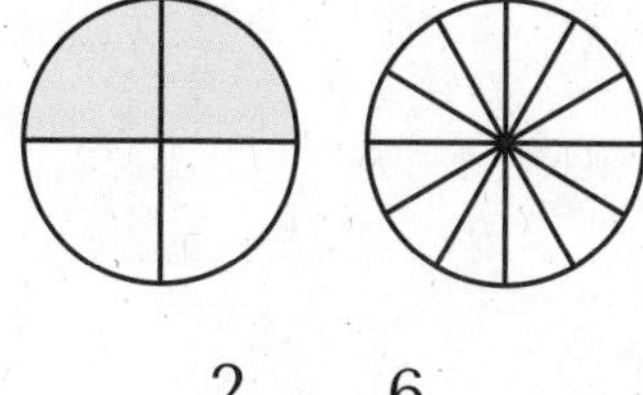

$\frac{2}{4} = \frac{6}{\square}$

13.

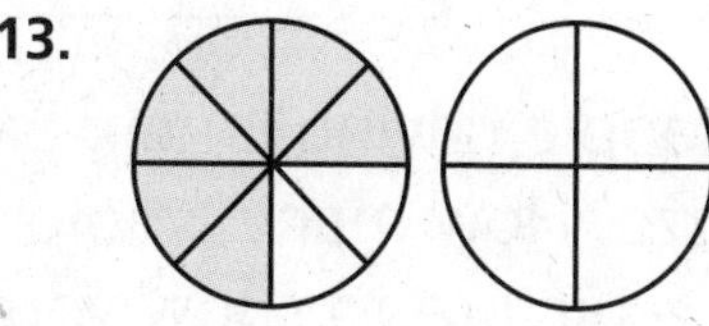

$\frac{6}{8} = \frac{\square}{4}$

14. Write the fraction that names the shaded part of each.

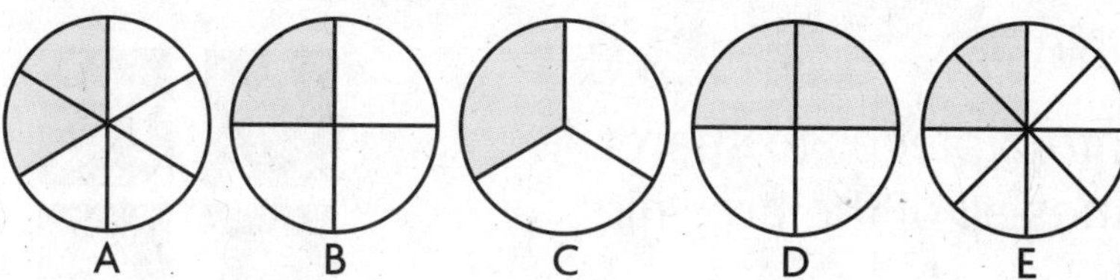

_____ _____ _____ _____ _____

Which pairs of fractions are equivalent? ______________________

15. Josh and Matt order small pizzas. Josh cuts his pizza into 3 equal pieces and eats 2 of them. Matt cuts his pizza into 6 equal pieces and eats 4 of them. Write the fractions that name the amount they each ate. Are the fractions equivalent? Draw a quick picture.

____

Problem Solving REAL WORLD

16. Chris bought 12 cupcakes. She chose 4 chocolate, 4 strawberry and 4 yellow. She and her family ate the chocolate and strawberry cupcakes for dessert. What fraction of the cupcakes did they eat? Write an equivalent fraction. Use 12 counters or draw a picture. ______________________

____

17. H.O.T. After dessert, $\frac{2}{3}$ of a cherry pie is left. Suppose 6 friends want to share it equally. What fraction names how much of the whole pie each friend will get? Use the model on the right. **Explain** your answer.

____

____

18. There are 16 people having lunch. Each person wants $\frac{1}{4}$ of a pizza. How many whole pizzas are needed? Draw a picture to show your answer. ______

19. Lucy has 5 brownies. Each brownie is cut in half. What fraction names all of the brownie halves? $\frac{\square}{2}$

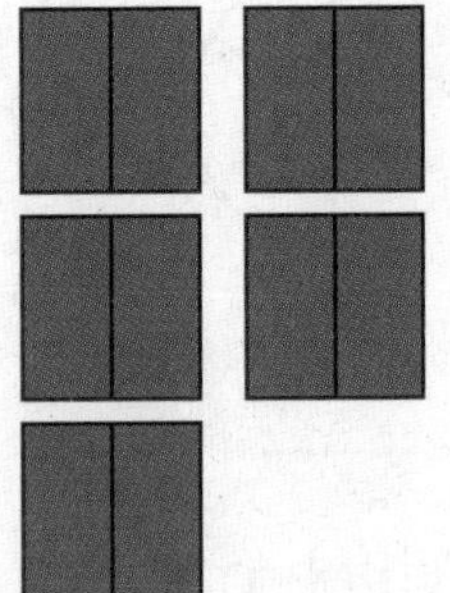

Lucy cuts each brownie half into 2 pieces to share with friends. What fraction names all of the brownie pieces now? $\frac{\square}{4}$

$\frac{\square}{2}$ and $\frac{\square}{4}$ are equivalent fractions. They both name all of the brownie pieces.

20. Test Prep Mrs. Peters made an apple pie. There is $\frac{6}{8}$ of the pie left over. Which fraction below is equal to the part of the pie that is left over?

Ⓐ $\frac{1}{2}$ Ⓑ $\frac{2}{4}$ Ⓒ $\frac{3}{4}$ Ⓓ $\frac{1}{4}$

FOR MORE PRACTICE:
Florida Benchmarks Practice Book, pp. P199–P200

Name ______________________________

Chapter Review/Test

▶ Check Vocabulary

Choose the best term from the box to complete the sentence.

Vocabulary
benchmarks
equivalent fractions
greater than

1. ______________ are two or more fractions that name the same amount. **(MA.3.A.2.4; p. 361)**

2. Numbers that are easy to work with, such as $\frac{1}{2}$ and 1, are called ______________. **(MA.3.A.2.3; p. 343)**

▶ Check Concepts

Compare. Write < or >. **(MA.3.A.2.2, MA.3.A.2.3; pp. 343–346, 347–350, 351–354)**

3. $1\frac{2}{6} \bigcirc 2\frac{2}{8}$

4. $\frac{1}{12} \bigcirc \frac{1}{8}$

5. $\frac{9}{10} \bigcirc \frac{7}{8}$

6. $1\frac{6}{10} \bigcirc 1\frac{2}{6}$

7. $\frac{4}{5} \bigcirc \frac{4}{10}$

8. $\frac{11}{12} \bigcirc \frac{7}{5}$

Order from greatest to least. **(MA.3.A.2.3; pp. 357–360)**

9. $\frac{11}{12}, \frac{8}{3}, \frac{3}{6}$

___ ◯ ___ ◯ ___

10. $\frac{1}{8}, \frac{1}{12}, \frac{1}{3}$

___ ◯ ___ ◯ ___

11. $1\frac{1}{8}, 2\frac{4}{5}, 2\frac{7}{8}$

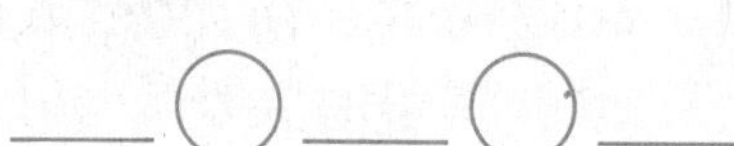

Find an equivalent fraction. **(MA.3.A.2.4; pp. 361–364, 365–368)**

12.

$\frac{4}{5} = \frac{}{}$

13.

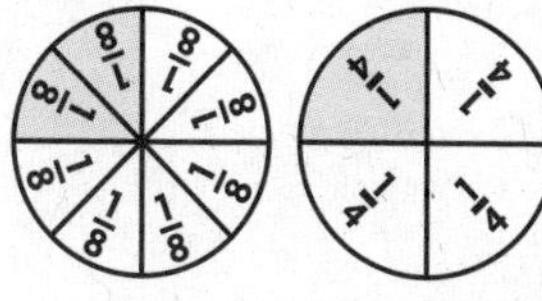

$\frac{2}{8} = \frac{}{}$

14.

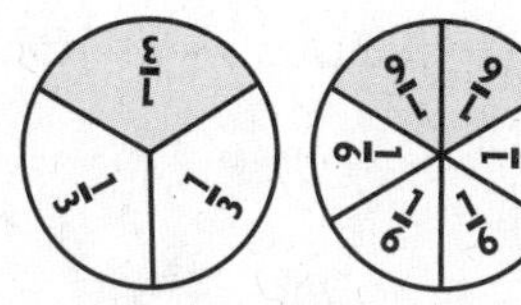

$\frac{1}{3} = \frac{}{}$

Go online **Assessment Options** Chapter Test

Fill in the bubble for the correct answer choice.

15. At the zoo, the keeper cut celery stalks into 10 equal pieces. She gave 2 of the 10 pieces to the monkeys for breakfast and 3 of the 10 pieces to the monkeys for lunch.

    Which fraction is equivalent to $\frac{5}{10}$, the amount the monkeys ate in all? **(MA.3.A.2.4; pp. 365–368)**

    Ⓐ $\frac{1}{4}$ Ⓒ $\frac{1}{2}$

    Ⓑ $\frac{1}{10}$ Ⓓ $\frac{1}{5}$

16. Kimberly and Madison are decorating the front of their book covers. Kim drew a design on $\frac{4}{5}$ of her book cover. Madison drew a design on $\frac{2}{3}$ of her book cover.

    Which number sentence shows the book cover that has more of its front covered by a design?

    (MA.3.A.2.3; pp. 351–354)

    Ⓕ $\frac{2}{3} > \frac{4}{5}$ Ⓗ $\frac{4}{5} < \frac{2}{3}$

    Ⓖ $\frac{2}{3} = \frac{4}{5}$ Ⓘ $\frac{4}{5} > \frac{2}{3}$

17. David, Maria, and Simone are shading index cards for a science project. David shaded $\frac{1}{4}$ of his index card. Maria shaded $\frac{5}{8}$ of her card, and Simone shaded $\frac{5}{6}$ of her card.

    Which shows the shaded parts of the index cards from greatest to least? **(MA.3.A.2.3; pp. 357–360)**

    Ⓐ $\frac{5}{6} > \frac{1}{4} > \frac{5}{8}$

    Ⓑ $\frac{5}{6} > \frac{5}{8} > \frac{1}{4}$

    Ⓒ $\frac{5}{8} > \frac{1}{4} > \frac{5}{6}$

    Ⓓ $\frac{1}{4} > \frac{5}{8} > \frac{5}{6}$

Name ______________________________

Fill in the bubble for the correct answer choice.

18. Marissa is decorating her book cover. She is shading $\frac{1}{4}$ of the cover blue. Which picture shows a shaded amount that is equivalent to $\frac{1}{4}$?

(MA.3.A.2.4; pp. 361–364)

Ⓕ 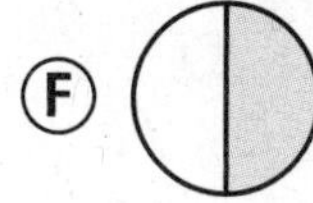

Ⓖ 

Ⓗ 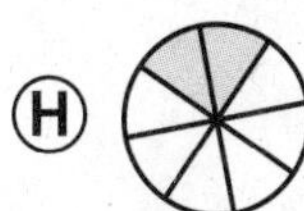

Ⓘ 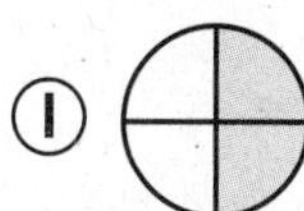

19. Olivia is shading two tiles for math class. She shades $\frac{7}{8}$ of one tile green. Then Olivia shades $\frac{5}{8}$ of the other tile yellow. Which statement about the shaded areas of the two tiles is **true**?

(MA.3.A.2.3; pp. 351–354)

Ⓐ $\frac{5}{8} > \frac{7}{8}$

Ⓑ $\frac{7}{8} > \frac{5}{8}$

Ⓒ $\frac{5}{8} = \frac{7}{8}$

Ⓓ $\frac{7}{8} < \frac{5}{8}$

20. Nicholas ran $2\frac{1}{3}$ miles on Monday, $1\frac{2}{5}$ miles on Tuesday, and $\frac{6}{4}$ miles on Wednesday. Which shows the distances he ran from least to greatest?

(MA.3.A.2.3; pp. 357–360)

Ⓕ $1\frac{2}{5} < \frac{6}{4} < 2\frac{1}{3}$

Ⓖ $\frac{6}{4} < 1\frac{2}{5} < 2\frac{1}{3}$

Ⓗ $2\frac{1}{3} > \frac{6}{4} > 1\frac{2}{5}$

Ⓘ $1\frac{2}{5} < 2\frac{1}{3} < \frac{6}{4}$

21. Tali ran $\frac{3}{4}$ mile during track practice. Which of the following is greater than $\frac{3}{4}$ mile? (MA.3.A.2.3; pp. 351–354)

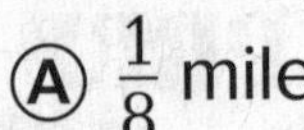

Ⓐ $\frac{1}{8}$ mile　Ⓒ $\frac{4}{8}$ mile

Ⓑ $\frac{7}{8}$ mile　Ⓓ $\frac{5}{8}$ mile

22. Bryan and Casey's mother made two pizzas. She cut one pizza into eighths and the other pizza into sixths. She placed $\frac{6}{8}$ of the first pizza in Bryan's lunch and $\frac{3}{6}$ of the second pizza in Casey's lunch.

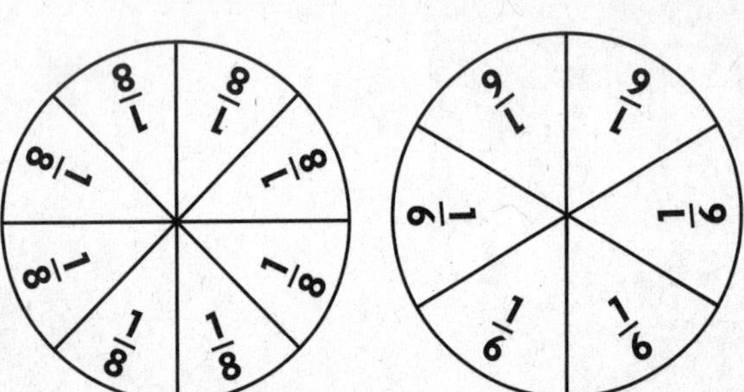

Which correctly compares the fractions of pizza?

(MA.3.A.2.3; pp. 339–342)

Ⓕ $\frac{3}{6} > \frac{6}{8}$　Ⓗ $\frac{6}{8} < \frac{3}{6}$

Ⓖ $\frac{3}{6} = \frac{6}{8}$　Ⓘ $\frac{6}{8} > \frac{3}{6}$

23. Mrs. Harrison is ordering a dozen flowers for a party. She says that $\frac{6}{12}$ of the flowers must be red and that $\frac{1}{3}$ of the flowers must be yellow.

Which number sentence about the flowers is **true**?

(MA.3.A.2.3; pp. 343–346)

Ⓐ $\frac{6}{12} > \frac{1}{3}$

Ⓑ $\frac{6}{12} = \frac{1}{3}$

Ⓒ $\frac{1}{3} > \frac{6}{12}$

Ⓓ $\frac{6}{12} < \frac{1}{3}$

Big Idea 3

Two-Dimensional Shapes

BIG IDEA Describe and analyze properties of two-dimensional shapes.

Go online

Math on Location Videos from The Futures Channel

Plane shapes form the sides and bottom of aquariums.

with Math on Location Videos

Aquarium Makers

Rectangles form the sides and bottoms of most aquariums. Other aquariums are made from rectangles with other plane shapes on the bottom.

Project

You will begin to learn about the big idea when you work on this project.

Work with a partner. Choose a shape for your aquarium. Then make a model of it. You can make one with rectangles for sides and a hexagon for the bottom. Or you can make one with rectangles for sides and a rectangle or a triangle for the bottom. Use the Important Facts to help you.

Important Facts

- Aquariums can have different shapes. Some aquariums are shaped like this:

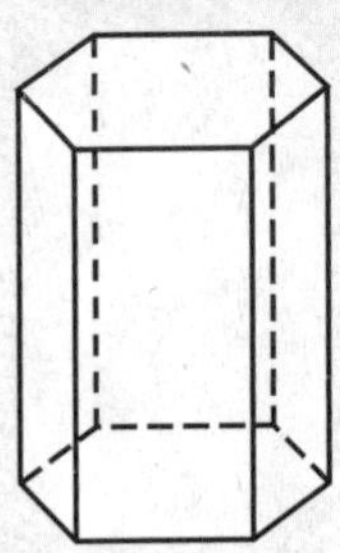

or like these:

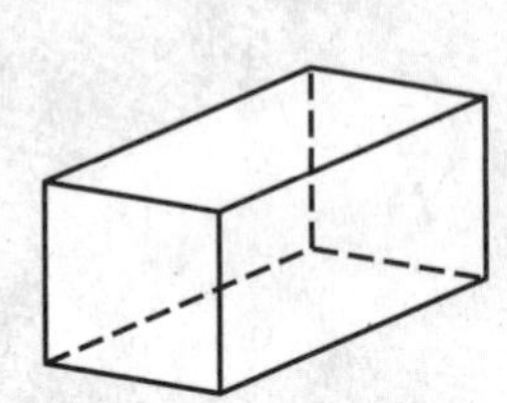

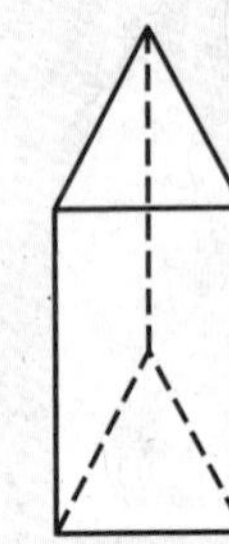

Completed by ______________________

Chapter 9

Plane Shapes

Show What You Know

Check your understanding of important skills.

Name ______________________

Plane Shapes

1. Color the triangles blue.

2. Color the rectangles red.

Identify Plane Shapes Connect the dots. Name each shape.

3. ____________

4. ____________

5. ____________

Number of Sides Write the number of sides.

6. ______ sides

7. ______ sides

Florida FUN FACT

In 1935, President Franklin Roosevelt set aside Fort Jefferson, on Dry Tortugas, and the surrounding waters as a National Park. It is located about 70 miles west of Key West.

Go online Assessment Options
Soar to Success: Math

Vocabulary Power

▶ Visualize It

Complete the tree map by using the words with a ✓.

Review Words
circle
✓ rectangle
✓ square
✓ triangle

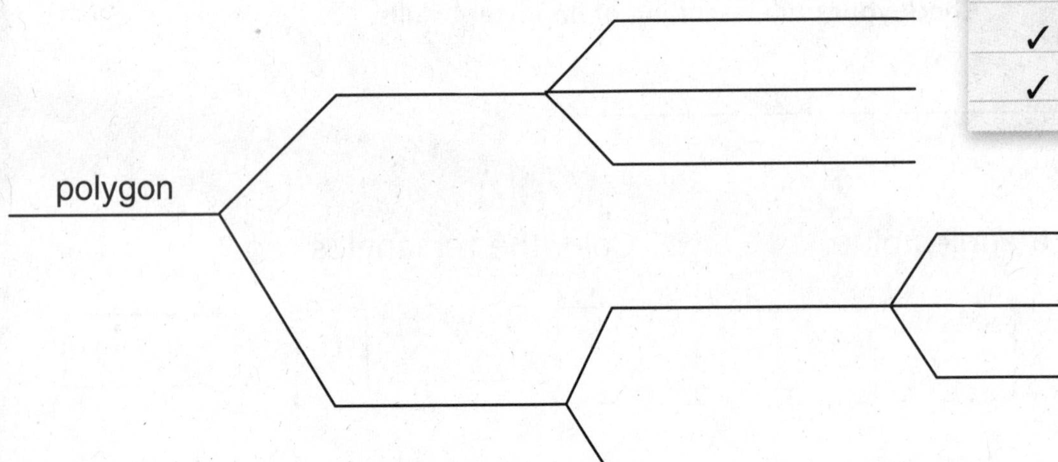

Preview Words
acute angle
✓ acute triangle
hexagon
line
obtuse angle
✓ obtuse triangle
✓ parallelogram
polygon
point
✓ quadrilateral
ray
✓ rhombus
right angle
✓ right triangle
✓ trapezoid
vertex

▶ Understand Vocabulary

Draw a line to match each word with its definition.

1. point	• A straight path that does not end and extends in both directions
2. line	• A shape formed by two rays that share an endpoint
3. ray	• An exact position or location
4. hexagon	• A part of a line, with one endpoint, that is straight and continues in one direction
5. angle	• A closed plane shape made up of straight line segments
6. polygon	• A polygon with 6 sides and 6 vertices

Go online • Student Edition • Multilingual eGlossary

Name ______________________

Describe Plane Shapes

Essential Question What are some properties of two-dimensional shapes?

MA.3.G.3.1 Describe, analyze, compare and classify two-dimensional shapes using sides and angles – including acute, obtuse, and right angles – and connect these ideas to the definition of shapes.

UNLOCK the Problem REAL WORLD

An architect draws plans for houses, stores, offices, and other buildings. Look at the shapes in the drawing at the right.

A **plane shape** is a shape on a flat surface. It is formed by curves, line segments, or both.

Use the highlighted math words below to describe plane shapes.

point
- is an exact position or location

line
- is straight
- continues in both directions
- does not end

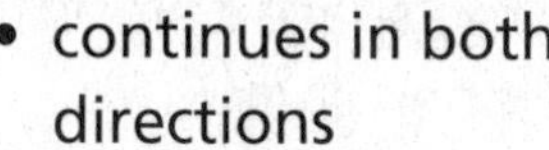

line segment
- is straight
- is part of a line
- has 2 points called endpoints

ray
- is straight
- is part of a line
- has 1 endpoint
- continues in one direction

point

An **angle** is formed by 2 rays that share an endpoint. The shared endpoint is called a **vertex**. The plural of *vertex* is *vertices*.

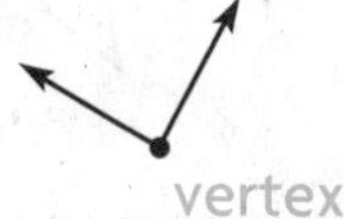

Look at this plane shape called a square. Describe the square using math words.

Think: How many line segments, angles, and vertices does a square have?

The square has _____ line segments,

_____ vertices, and _____ angles.

Try This! **Plane shapes have length and width but no thickness, so they are called 2-dimensional shapes.**

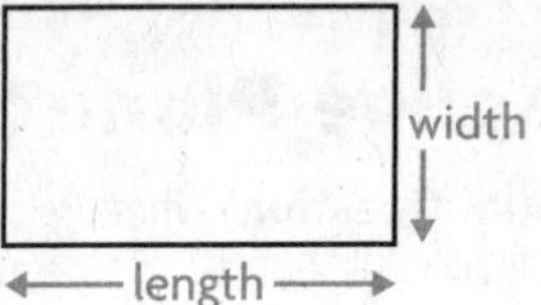

Plane shapes can be open or closed.

A **closed shape** starts and ends at the same point.

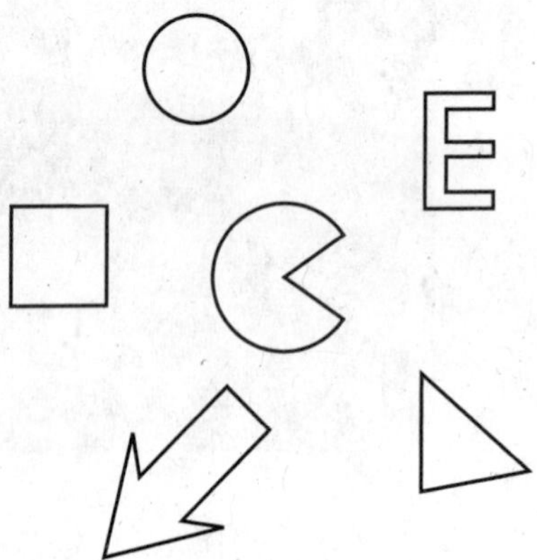

In the space below, draw more examples of closed shapes.

An **open shape** does not start and end at the same point.

In the space below, draw more examples of open shapes.

- Is the plane shape at the right a closed shape or an open shape? **Explain** how you know.

Name ______________________

Share and Show 

1. How many line segments does this shape have? ______

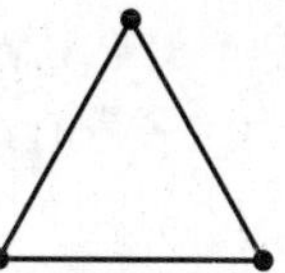

Write whether each is a *point, line, line segment,* or *ray.*

2. 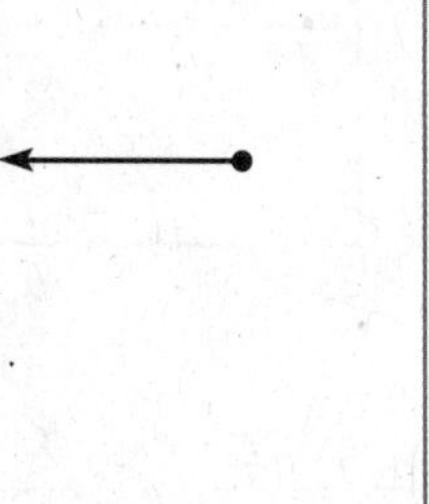 ______________

3.  ______________

4. 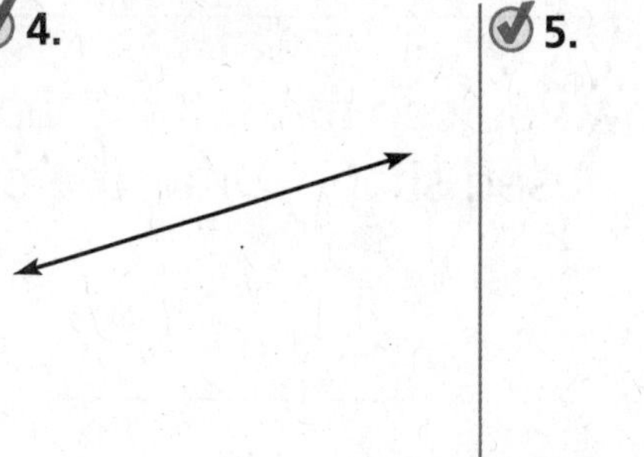 ______________

5. ______________

Math Talk Explain the difference between a ray and a line segment.

On Your Own

Write whether each is a *point, line, line segment,* or *ray.*

6. 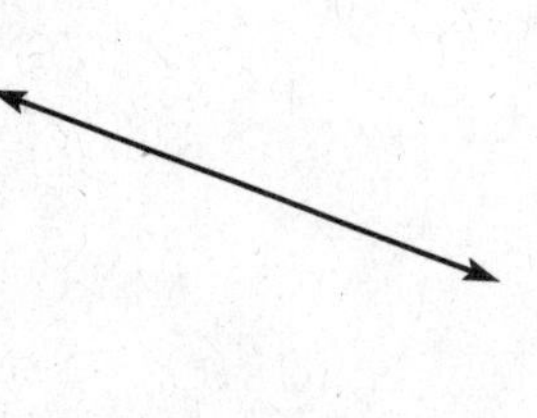 ______________

7. 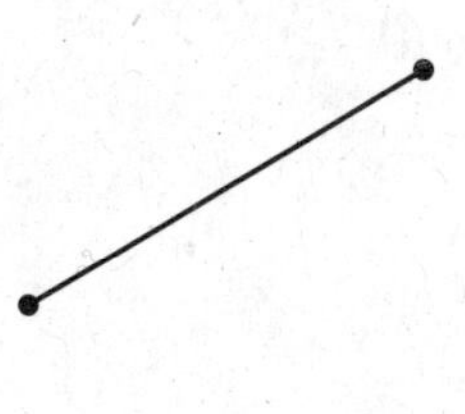 ______________

8.  ______________

9. 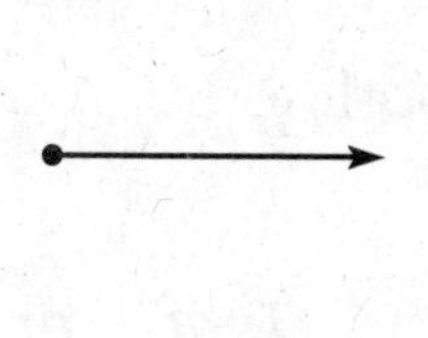 ______________

Write whether the shape is *open* or *closed.*

10.  ______________

11. 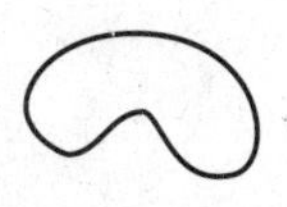 ______________

12. 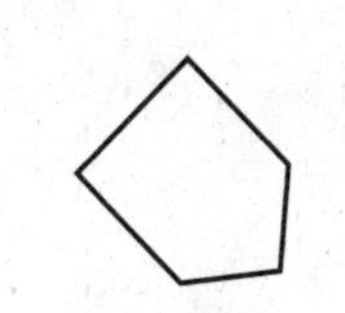 ______________

13. 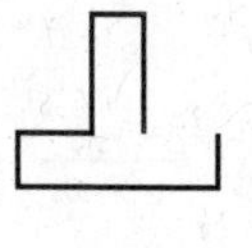 ______________

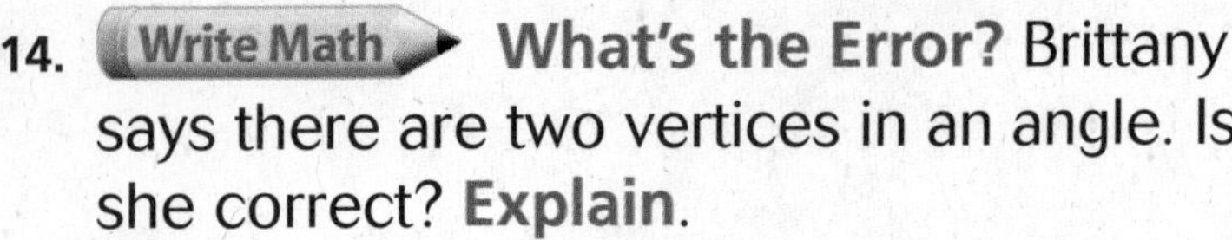

Problem Solving REAL WORLD

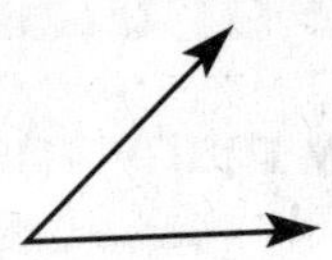

14. Write Math ▸ **What's the Error?** Brittany says there are two vertices in an angle. Is she correct? **Explain.**

____

____

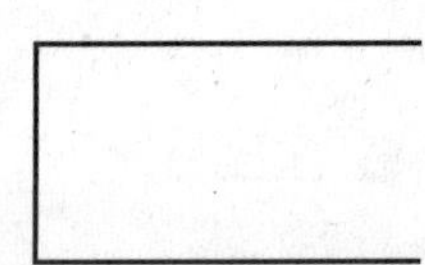

15. **Explain** how you can make the shape at the right a closed shape. Draw the closed shape.

____

16. Look at Carly's drawing at the right. What did she draw? How is it like a line? How is it different? Draw an example of each.

____

____

____

____

SHOW YOUR WORK

17. H.O.T. At the right, draw a closed shape with 5 line segments, 5 vertices, and 5 angles.

18. Test Prep Which shows a line segment?

Ⓐ 

Ⓑ 

Ⓒ 

Ⓓ 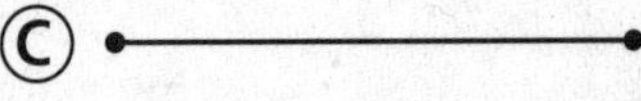

Name ____________________

Identify Polygons

Essential Question How can you tell whether a plane shape is or is not a polygon?

MA.3.G.3.1 Describe, analyze, compare and classify two-dimensional shapes using sides and angles – including acute, obtuse, and right angles – and connect these ideas to the definition of shapes.

UNLOCK the Problem REAL WORLD

A **polygon** is a closed shape made up of line segments. Each line segment of a polygon is a **side**.

Look at the small pieces of glass in this lampshade. Are some of these shapes polygons? ▶

Here is one of the plane shapes in the lampshade. It is a closed shape. It has 4 sides that are line segments. So, the shape is a polygon.

 **Write the number of sides the polygon has.**

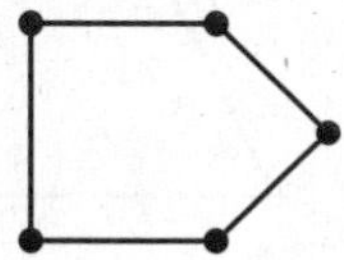

____

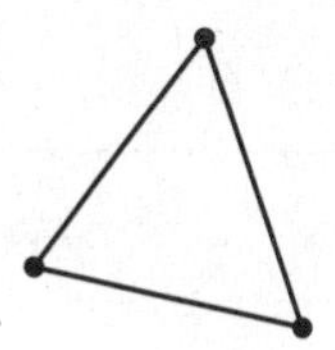

____

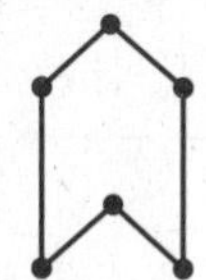

____

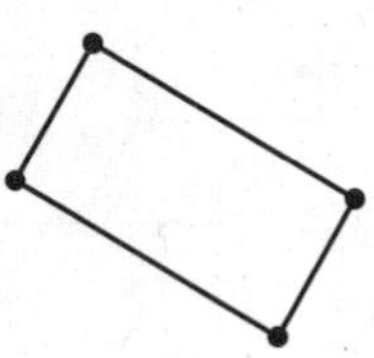

____

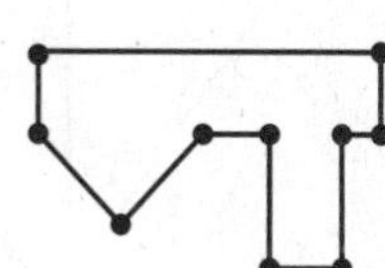

____

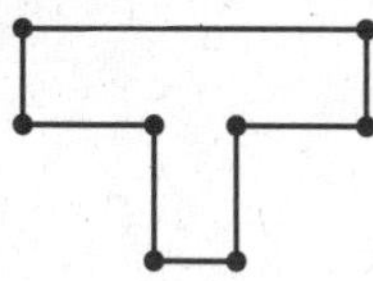

____

• Draw some shapes that are polygons.

Try This! The shapes below are not polygons. Draw a line to match each shape with its description.

The shape has curves.

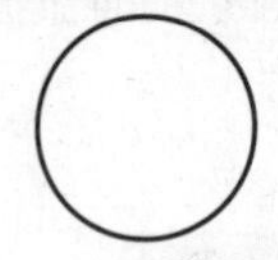

The shape is not closed.

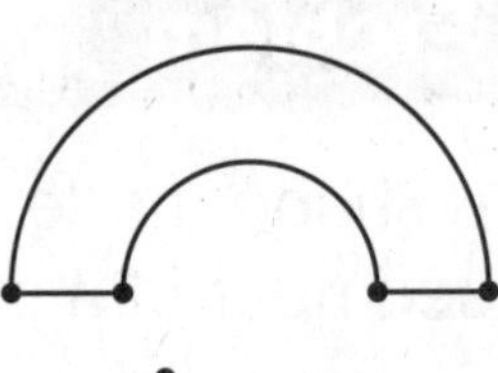

The shape has no line segments.

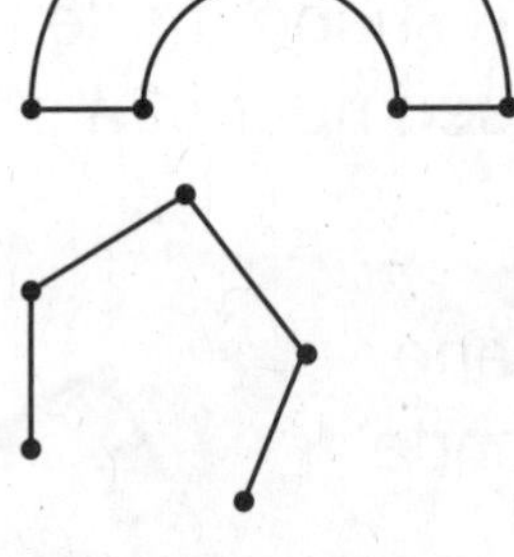

Math Talk **Explain** how you could change one of the shapes above into a polygon.

Share and Show 

1. The shape at the right is a polygon. How do you know?

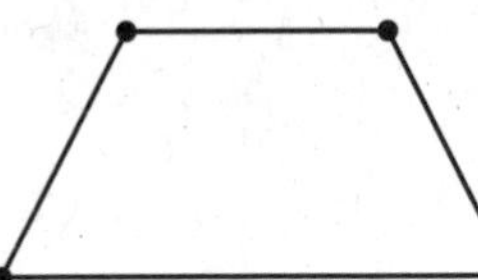

____

____

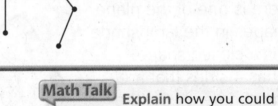

Is the shape a polygon? Write *yes* or *no*.

2. 

____

3. 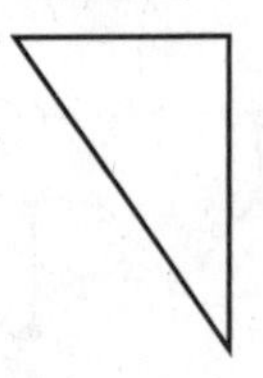

____

4. 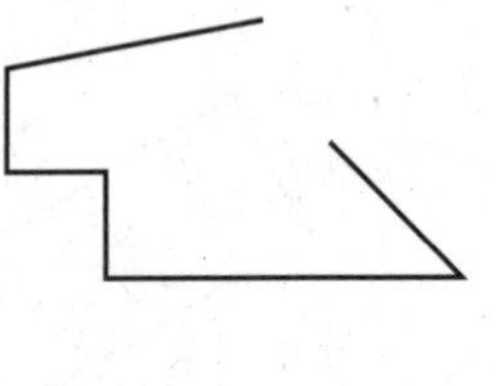

____

Write the number of sides.

5. 

____

6. 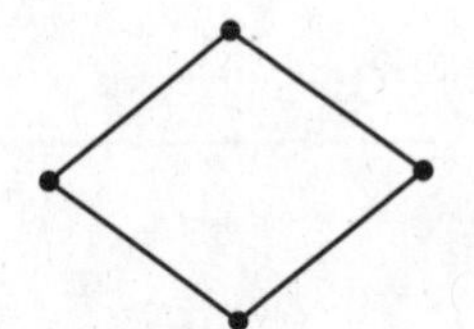

____

7. 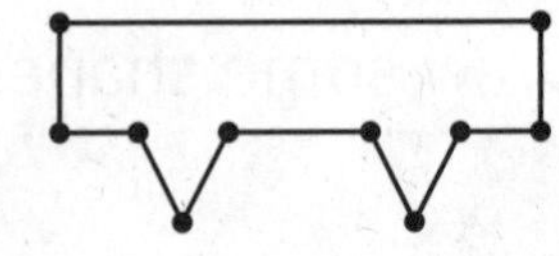

____

Name ______________________

On Your Own

Is the shape a polygon? Write *yes* or *no*.

8. 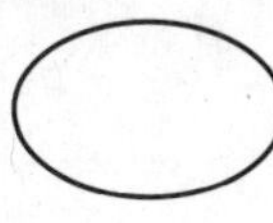 ______

9. 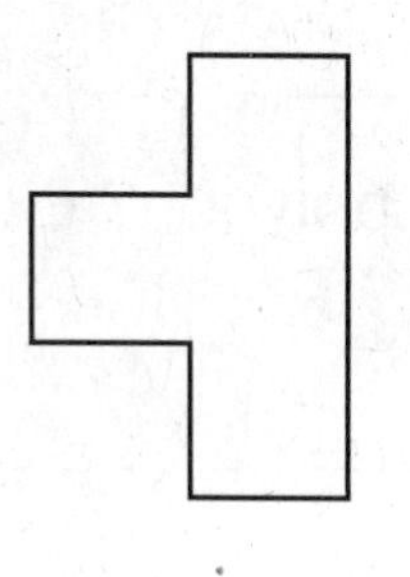 ______

10. 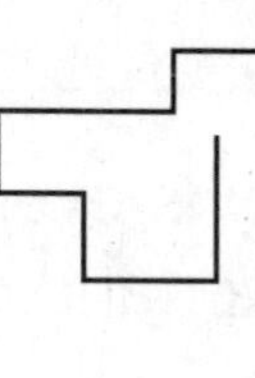 ______

Write the number of sides.

11.  ______

12. 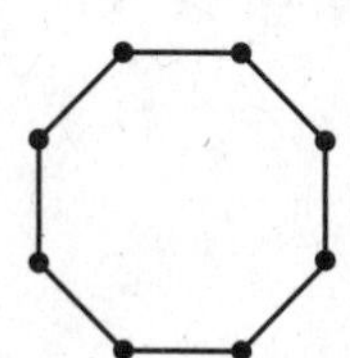 ______

13. 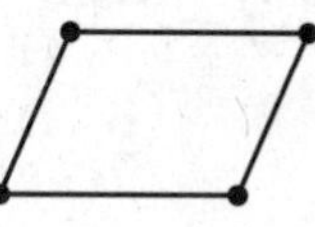 ______

Problem Solving

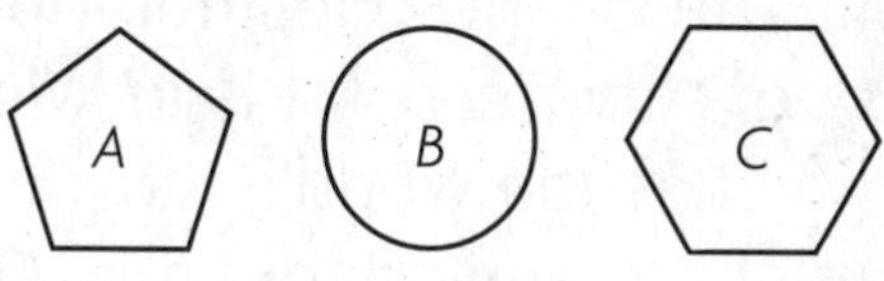

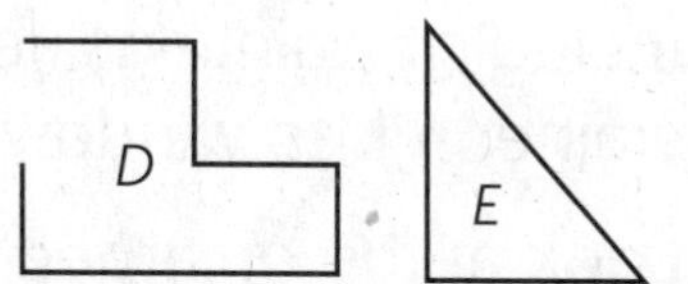

Use shapes *A–E* for 14–15.

14. **Write Math** **Sense or Nonsense?** Jake said shapes *A–E* are all polygons. Does his statement make sense? **Explain** your answer.

____

____

____

15. **Explain** how shapes *C* and *D* are alike and how they are different.

____

____

16. Is the letter at the right a polygon? **Explain** how you know.

____

____

17. H.O.T. Is every closed shape a polygon? **Explain** your answer and draw an example.

____

____

18. **Test Prep** Kevin drew the shape at the right. How many sides does the shape have?

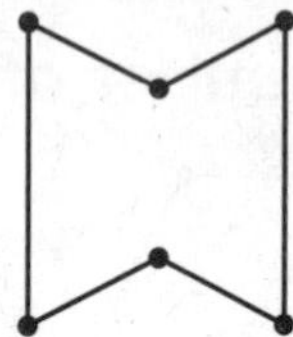

Ⓐ 4 Ⓑ 5 Ⓒ 6 Ⓓ 8

Connect to Art

Polygons

The Charles Hosmer Morse Museum of American Art is in Winter Park, Florida. It has the world's most complete collection of the artwork of Louis Comfort Tiffany, including paintings, jewelry, vases, and stained glass windows and lamps.

Look at the enlarged section of a stained glass lampshade at the right. Draw three shapes you see on the glass. Tell whether the shapes you drew are polygons. If they are polygons, write the number of sides.

19.	20.	21.

 FOR MORE PRACTICE:
Florida Benchmarks Practice Book, pp. P211–P212

Name ______________________________

Classify Polygons

Essential Question How do you describe and classify polygons?

MA.3.G.3.1 Describe, analyze, compare and classify two-dimensional shapes using sides and angles – including acute, obtuse, and right angles – and connect these ideas to the definition of shapes.

CONNECT In the last lesson, you learned that a polygon is made up of line segments. In this lesson, you will learn how to name polygons. Polygons are named by their number of sides and number of vertices.

Math Idea

A polygon that has all sides the same length and all angles the same measure is a regular polygon.

UNLOCK the Problem REAL WORLD

Some traffic signs are in the shape of polygons. A stop sign is in the shape of which polygon?

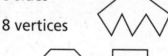

Find the shape of the stop sign.

triangle

3 sides

3 vertices

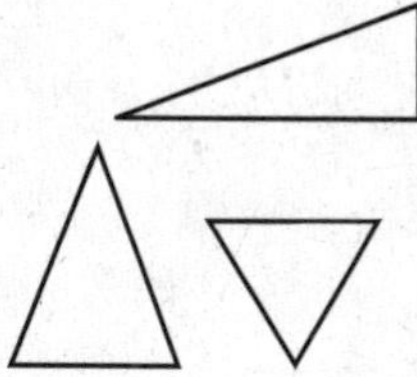

quadrilateral

4 sides

4 vertices

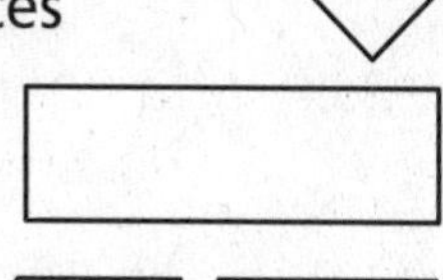

pentagon

5 sides

5 vertices

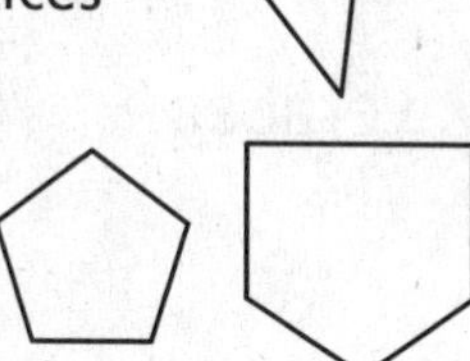

hexagon

6 sides

6 vertices

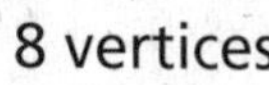

octagon

8 sides

8 vertices

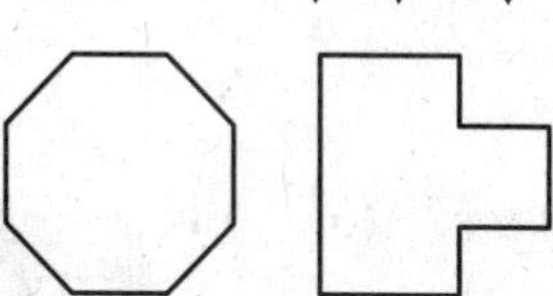

decagon

10 sides

10 vertices

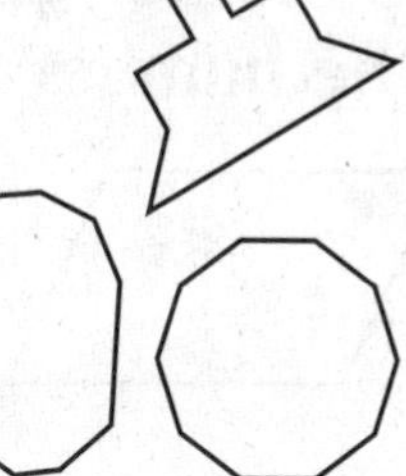

How many sides does the stop sign have? __________

How many vertices? __________

So, a stop sign is in the shape of an __________.

Math Talk Can you find objects in your classroom that represent the different polygons? **Explain.**

Share and Show 

1. How many sides and vertices does this polygon have?

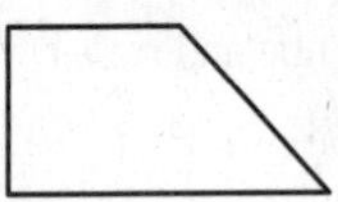

______

Name the polygon. Write the number of sides and the number of vertices.

2. 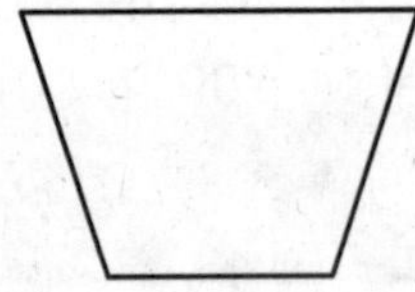

______

____ sides

____ vertices

3. 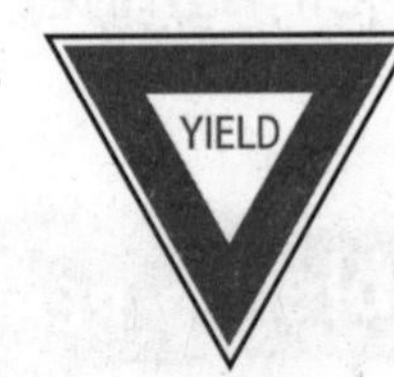

______

____ sides

____ vertices

4. 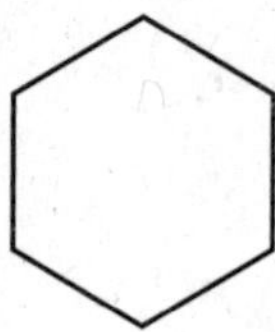

______

____ sides

____ vertices

5. 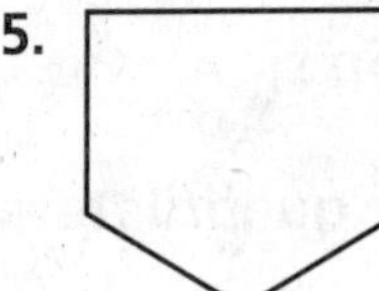

______

____ sides

____ vertices

Math Talk **Explain** why a pentagon is a polygon.

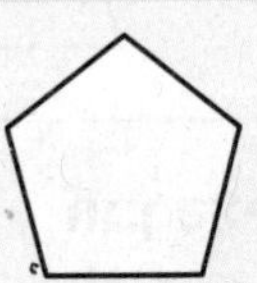

On Your Own

Name the polygon. Write the number of sides and the number of vertices.

6. 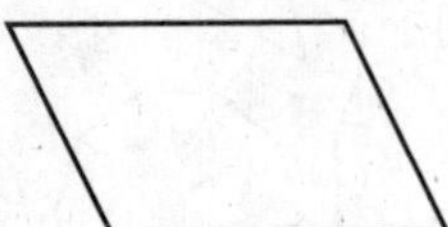

______

____ sides

____ vertices

7. 

______

____ sides

____ vertices

Name ______________________________

Problem Solving REAL WORLD

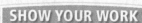

SHOW YOUR WORK

8. Scott has 15 craft sticks. He glues some sticks together to make 2 pentagons and 1 triangle. He uses 1 stick for each side. How many sticks does he have left? Draw a quick picture.

____

9. **Write Math** **What's the Error?** Eric says that the shape at the right is an octagon. Do you agree? **Explain**.

____

____

____

10. Draw a polygon with 2 fewer sides than a pentagon. Then name the polygon.

____

11. **H.O.T.** Are all quadrilaterals polygons? **Explain** your answer.

____

____

____

____

____

12. **Test Prep** Alicia drew the polygon at the right. What is the name of the polygon she drew?

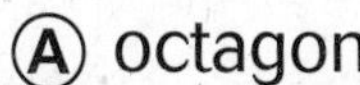

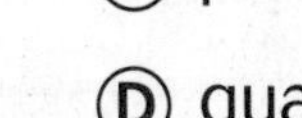

Ⓐ octagon Ⓒ pentagon

Ⓑ hexagon Ⓓ quadrilateral

Connect to Reading

Compare and Contrast

When you *compare,* you look for ways things are alike. When you *contrast,* you look for ways things are different.

Mr. Briggs drew some shapes on the board. He asked the class to tell how the shapes are alike and how they are different.

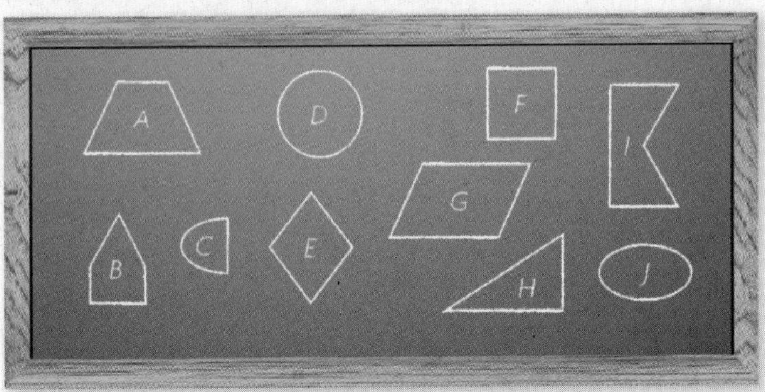

Sort the shapes according to the clues in the sentences below. Then complete the sentences.

- Shapes ______, ______, ______, and ______ all have 4 sides and 4 vertices.
- These shapes are closed. ____________________
- All four sides of shapes ______ and ______ appear to be the same length.
- These shapes have curves. ______________
- In these shapes, the sides do not appear to be the same length. ______________
- Shapes ______ and ______ do not have any straight sides.
- Shapes ______________ are polygons.
- Shapes ______________ are quadrilaterals.
- Shapes ______________ have no sides or vertices.

FOR MORE PRACTICE:
Florida Benchmarks Practice Book, pp. P213–P214

Name ________________________________

Types of Angles

Essential Question How can you describe and classify angles?

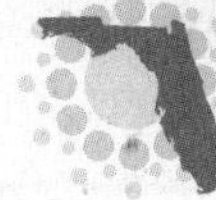

MA.3.G.3.1 Describe, analyze, compare and classify two-dimensional shapes using sides and angles – including acute, obtuse, and right angles – and connect these ideas to the definition of shapes.

Jason drew the quadrilateral at the right on dot paper. Look at the angles in the quadrilateral that Jason drew.

How many angles are there?

How can you describe the angles?

Angles have different names.

A

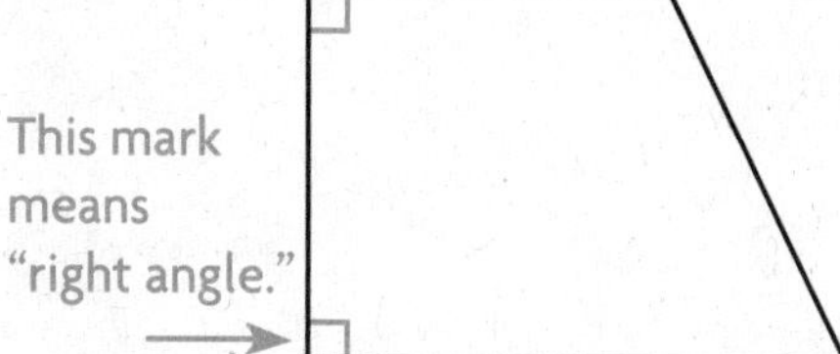

A **right angle** forms a square corner.

B

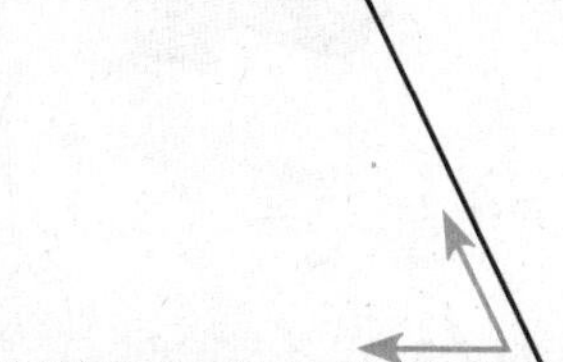

An **acute angle** is less than a right angle.

C

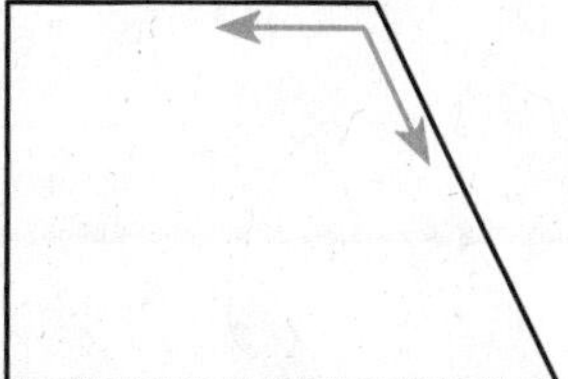

An **obtuse angle** is greater than a right angle but less than a straight angle.

D

In a **straight angle**, two rays point in opposite directions and form a line.

Look at Jason's quadrilateral.

There are ________ angles in Jason's quadrilateral.

Two are ________ angles, ________ is an ________ angle,

and ________ is an ________ angle.

- Which type of angle is not in Jason's quadrilateral? ________________

You can use the corner of a sheet of paper to tell if an angle is a right angle.

Model angles.

Materials ■ bendable straws, scissors, paper, pencil

- Cut a small slit in the shorter section of a bendable straw. Cut off the shorter section of a second straw and the bendable part. Insert the slit end of the first straw into the second straw.

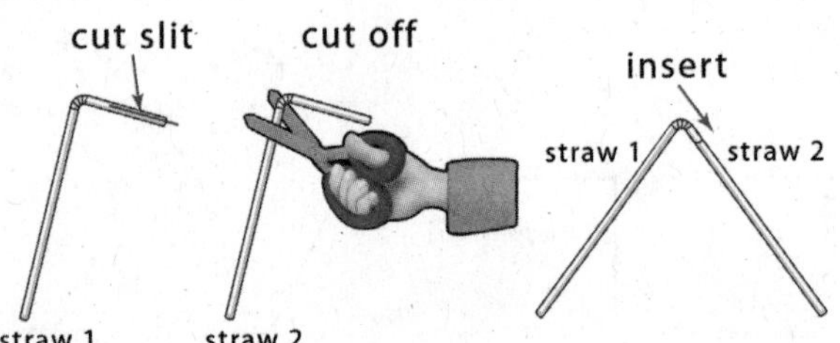

- Use the corner of a sheet of paper. The angle you made with the straw is a right angle if it matches the corner of the paper.
- Open and close the straw to make other types of angles.

In the space below, trace the angles you made with the straws. Label each *right, acute,* or *obtuse.*

Share and Show

1. How many angles are in this shape? _____

Use the corner of a sheet of paper to tell if the angle is *right, acute,* or *obtuse.*

2. 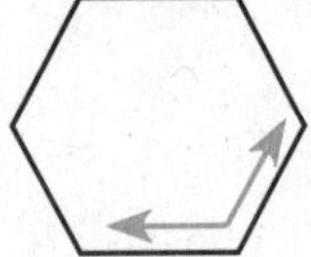

____

3. 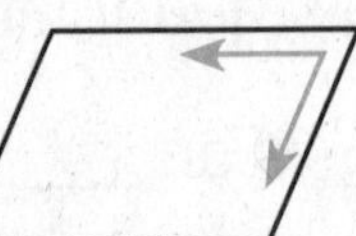

____

4. 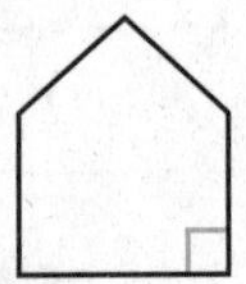

____

Name ______________________________

Write how many of each type of angle the polygon has.

5. 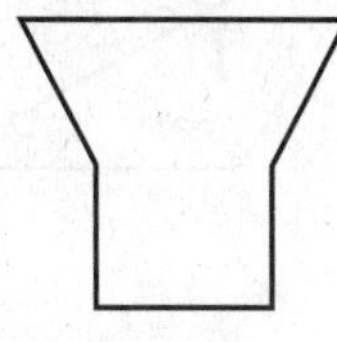

_____ right

_____ obtuse

_____ acute

6. 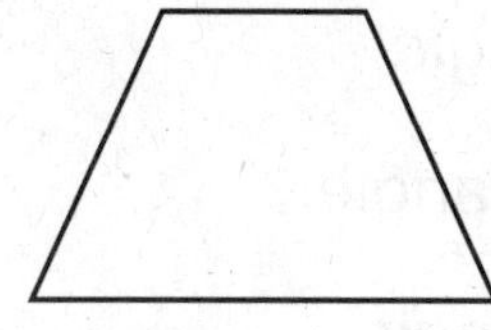

_____ right

_____ obtuse

_____ acute

7. 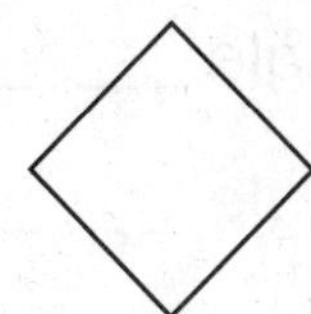

_____ right

_____ obtuse

_____ acute

Math Talk Explain what you know about the angle if it is greater than the corner of the paper.

On Your Own

Use the corner of a sheet of paper to tell if the angle is *right, acute,* or *obtuse.*

8. 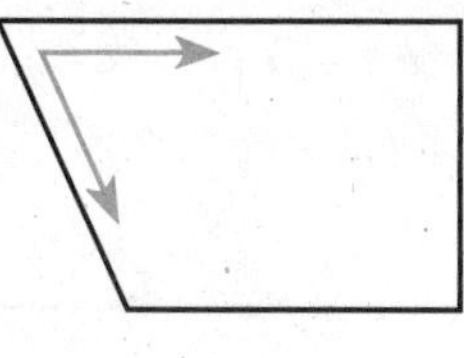

____

9. 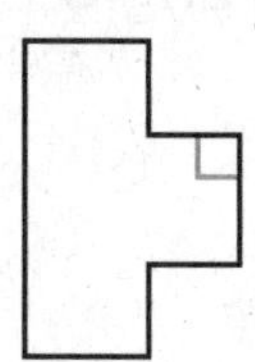

____

10. 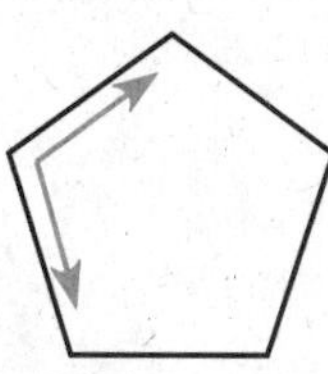

____

Write how many of each type of angle the polygon has.

11. 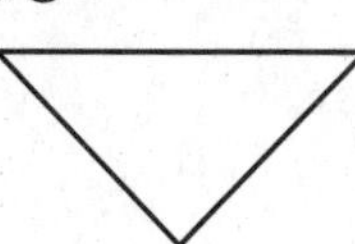

_____ right

_____ obtuse

_____ acute

12. 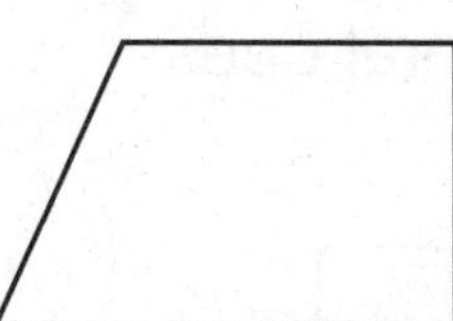

_____ right

_____ obtuse

_____ acute

13. 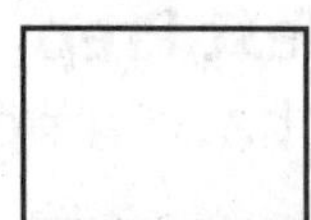

_____ right

_____ obtuse

_____ acute

Problem Solving REAL WORLD

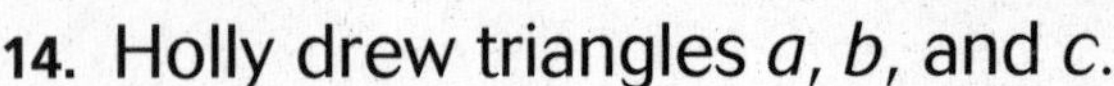

14. Holly drew triangles *a*, *b*, and *c*.

Triangle ______ has 1 right angle.

Triangle ______ has 1 obtuse angle.

Triangle ______ has 3 acute angles.

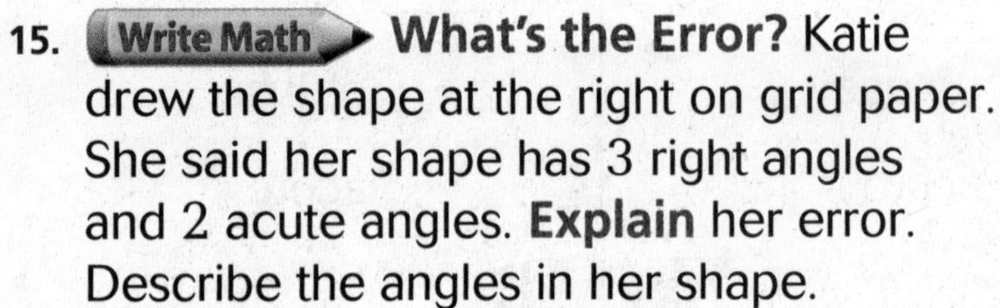

15. Write Math **What's the Error?** Katie drew the shape at the right on grid paper. She said her shape has 3 right angles and 2 acute angles. **Explain** her error. Describe the angles in her shape.

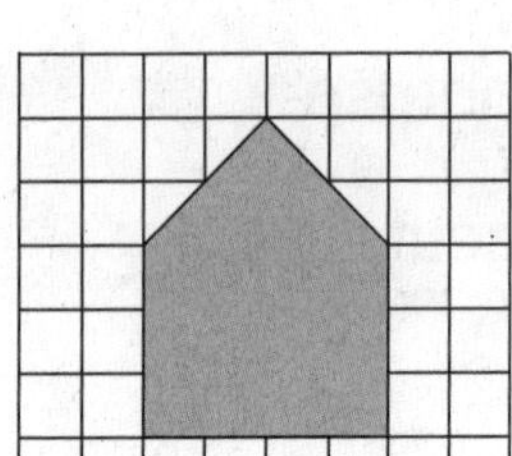

---

16. H.O.T. Write 1 capital letter that has an acute angle and 1 that has a right angle.

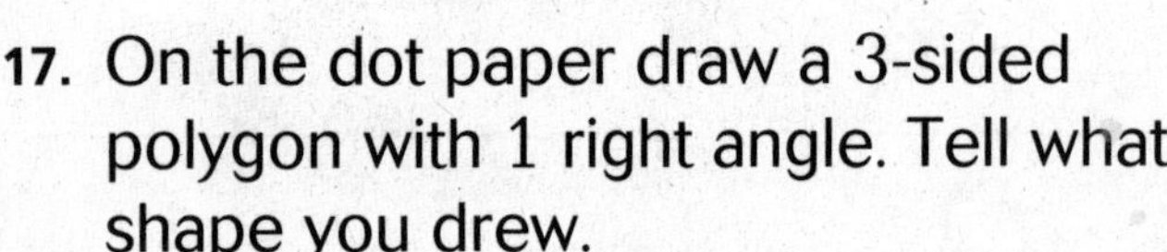

17. On the dot paper draw a 3-sided polygon with 1 right angle. Tell what shape you drew.

18. **Test Prep** Which quadrilateral does NOT have a right angle?

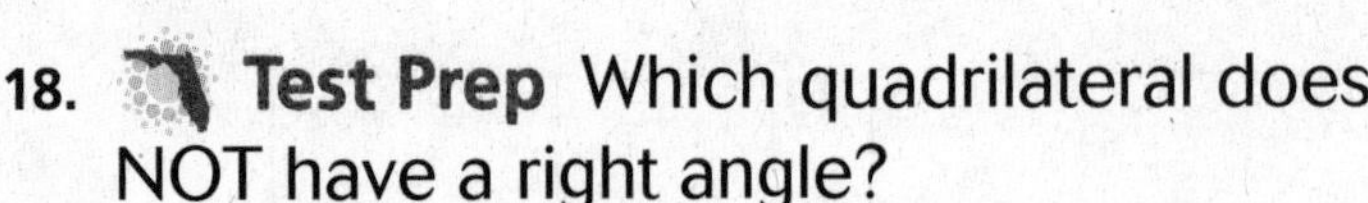

 Ⓐ 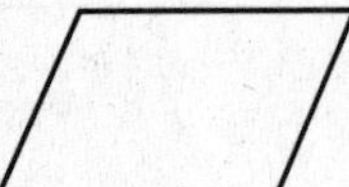

 Ⓒ 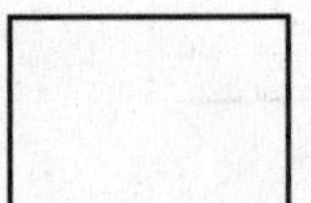

Ⓑ 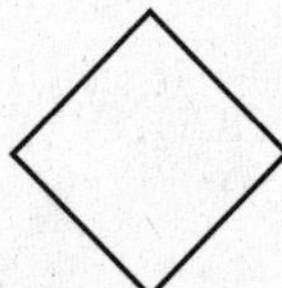

Ⓓ 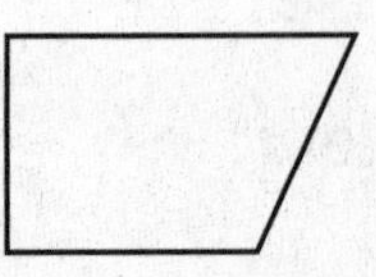

FOR MORE PRACTICE:
Florida Benchmarks Practice Book, pp. P215–P216

Name ______________________________

Describe Sides of Polygons

Essential Question How can you identify pairs of parallel sides in polygons?

MA.3.G.3.1 Describe, analyze, compare and classify two-dimensional shapes using sides and angles – including acute, obtuse, and right angles – and connect these ideas to the definition of shapes.

UNLOCK the Problem REAL WORLD

The polygon at the right is a quadrilateral. How many pairs of sides are parallel?

TYPES OF LINES	TYPES OF LINE SEGMENTS
Lines that cross or meet are **intersecting lines**. Intersecting lines form angles. 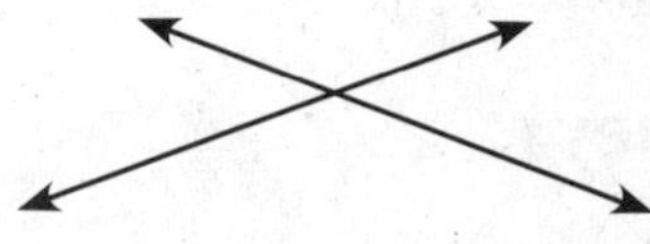	The orange and blue line segments meet and form an angle. So, they are intersecting.
Intersecting lines that cross or meet to form right angles are **perpendicular lines**. 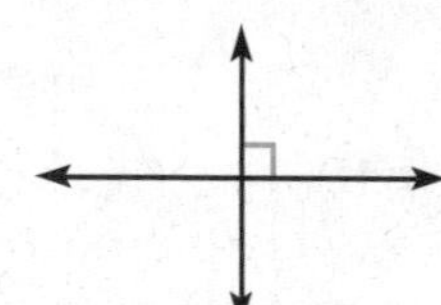	The red and blue line segments meet at a right angle. So, they are perpendicular.
Lines that appear never to cross or meet and are always the same distance apart are **parallel lines**. They do not form any angles. 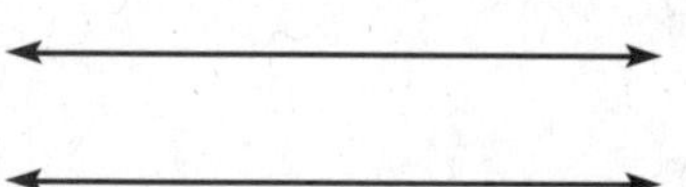	The green and blue line segments would never cross or meet. They are always the same distance apart. So, they appear to be parallel.

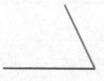

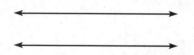

So, the quadrilateral above has ____________ of parallel sides.

Try This! Draw a quadrilateral with only 1 pair of parallel sides. Then draw a quadrilateral with 2 pairs of parallel sides. Outline each pair of parallel sides with a different color.

Share and Show 

1. Which sides appear to be parallel?

____

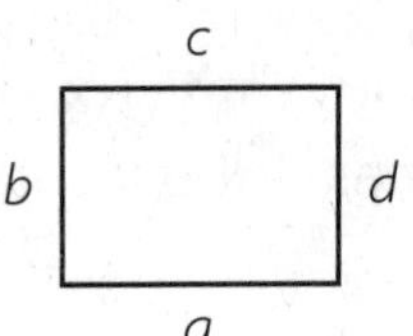

Think: Which pairs of sides appear to be the same distance apart?

Look at the green sides of each polygon. Tell if they appear to be *intersecting, perpendicular,* or *parallel*.

2. 

____

3. 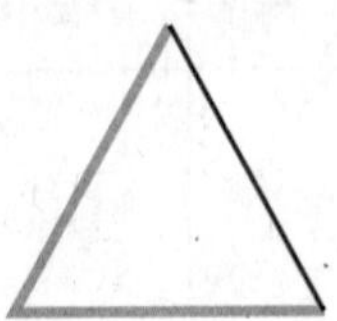

____

4. 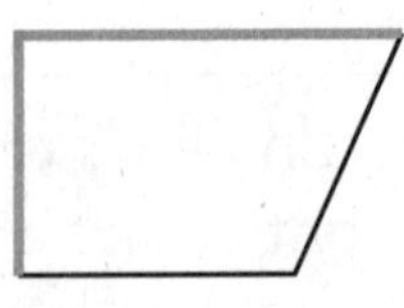

____

Math Talk **Explain** how intersecting and perpendicular lines are alike and how they are different.

On Your Own

Look at the green sides of each polygon. Tell if they appear to be *intersecting, perpendicular,* or *parallel*.

5. 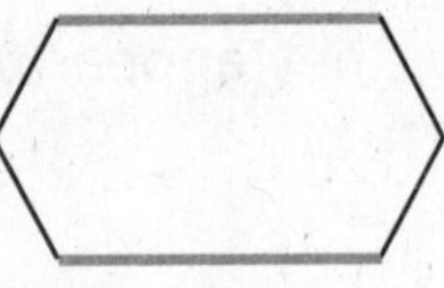

____

6. 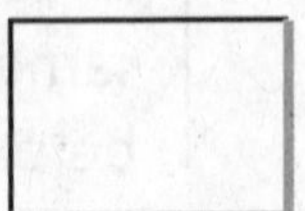

____

7. 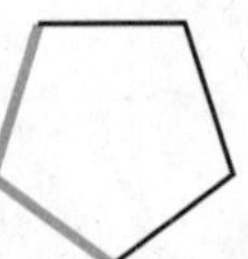

____

Name ___________________________________

Problem Solving REAL WORLD

8. Draw a quadrilateral. Describe the angles in your quadrilateral. Then tell how many pairs of parallel sides your quadrilateral has.

____

____

9. Adam drew 3 quadrilaterals. One quadrilateral had no pairs of parallel sides, one had 1 pair of parallel sides, and the other had 2 pairs of parallel sides. Draw 3 quadrilaterals that Adam could have drawn, and write the number of parallel sides for each.

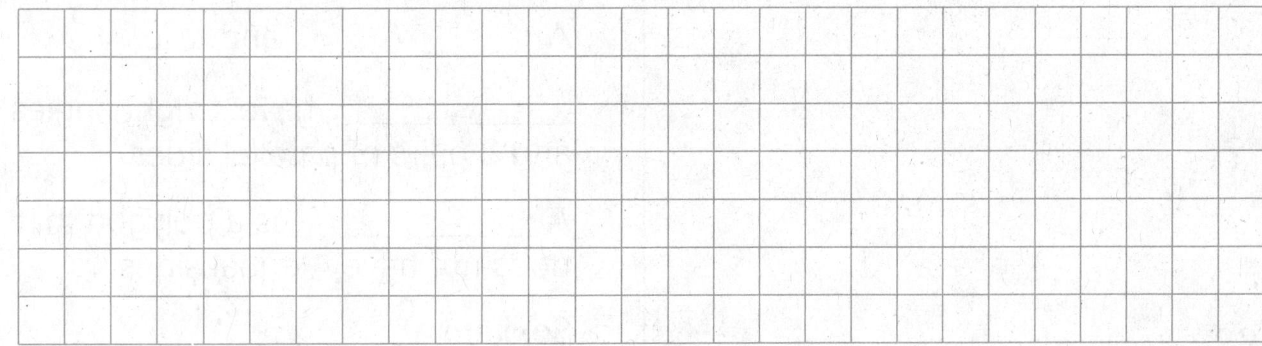

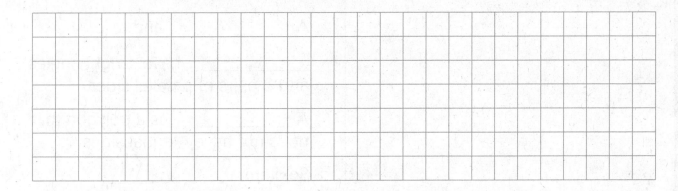

10. H.O.T. Write Math Can the same two lines be parallel, perpendicular, and intersecting at the same time? **Explain** your answer.

____

____

11. **Test Prep** How many pairs of parallel sides are in a square?

Ⓐ 0 Ⓒ 2

Ⓑ 1 Ⓓ 4

UNLOCK the Problem

12. I am a polygon. I have 2 fewer sides than a hexagon. I have 2 pairs of parallel sides and 4 right angles. My sides are not all the same length. What am I?

a. What do you need to know? ____________________

____

____

b. How will you find the answer to the riddle? ____________________

____

c. Draw to solve the riddle.

d. Complete the sentences.

A ____________ is a polygon that has 2 fewer sides than a hexagon.

A ____________ and a ____________ have 4 right angles and 2 pairs of parallel sides.

A ____________ is a polygon that does not have 4 equal sides.

So, I am a ____________.

13. What are intersecting lines that cross or meet to form right angles called?

____

14. **Test Prep** Which shape can never have parallel sides?

Ⓐ quadrilateral

Ⓑ octagon

Ⓒ triangle

Ⓓ hexagon

FOR MORE PRACTICE:
Florida Benchmarks Practice Book, pp. P217–P218

Name ___________________________________

Mid-Chapter Checkpoint

▶ Check Vocabulary

Choose the best term from the box.

Vocabulary
acute angle
angle
polygon
quadrilateral
right angle

1. An ______________ is formed by two rays that share an endpoint. (MA.3.G.3.1; pp. 377–380)
2. A ______________ is a closed shape made up of straight line segments. (MA.3.G.3.1; pp. 381–384)
3. A ______________ forms a square corner. (MA.3.G.3.1; pp. 389–392)

▶ Check Concepts and Skills

Name the polygon. Write the number of sides and the number of vertices. (MA.3.G.3.1; pp. 385–388)

4. 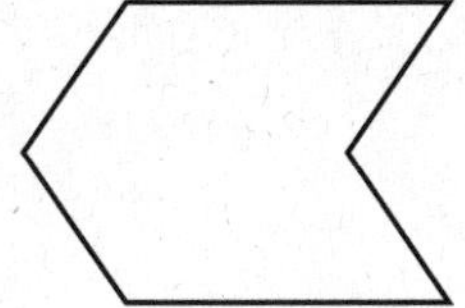

____

_____ sides

_____ vertices

5. 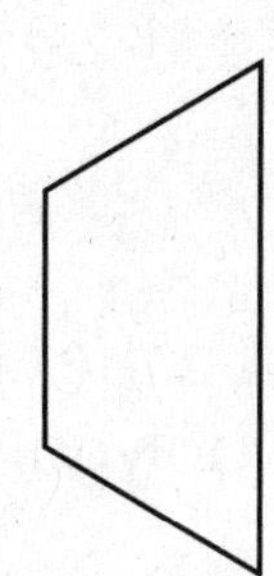

____

_____ sides

_____ vertices

6. 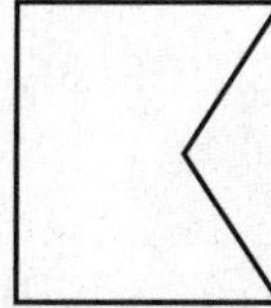

____

_____ sides

_____ vertices

Use the corner of a sheet of paper to tell if the angle is *right, acute,* or *obtuse*. (MA.3.G.3.1; pp. 389–392)

7. 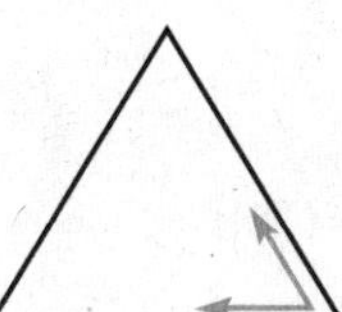

____

8. 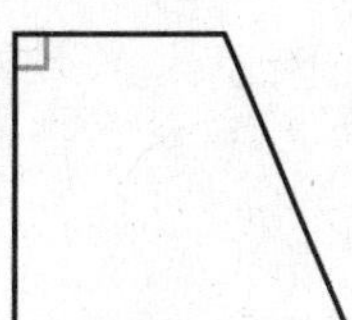

____

9. 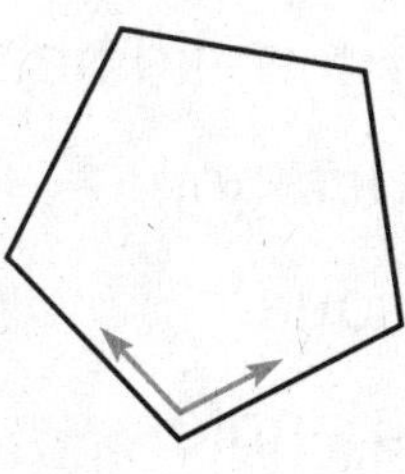

____

Name ________________________________

TEST PREP

Fill in the bubble for the correct answer choice.

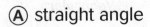

10. The hands on the clock at the right form an angle. Which best describes the angle? **(MA.3.G.3.1; pp. 389–392)**

Ⓐ straight angle

Ⓑ obtuse angle

Ⓒ right angle

Ⓓ acute angle

11. This sign tells drivers there is a steep hill ahead. How many sides and angles are in the sign? **(MA.3.G.3.1; pp. 385–388)**

Ⓕ 4 sides and 4 angles

Ⓖ 5 sides and 5 angles

Ⓗ 6 sides and 6 angles

Ⓘ 8 sides and 8 angles

12. Janine drew this picture of the front of her house. Her house is in the shape of which polygon? **(MA.3.G.3.1; pp. 385–388)**

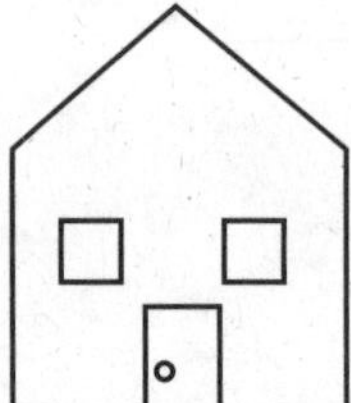

Ⓐ hexagon

Ⓑ pentagon

Ⓒ octagon

Ⓓ quadrilateral

13. Peter drew a quadrilateral with 4 sides and 4 right angles. All the sides are the same length. Which polygon did he draw? **(MA.3.G.3.1; pp. 385–388)**

Ⓕ octagon

Ⓖ square

Ⓗ triangle

Ⓘ hexagon

Name ______________________________

Classify Triangles

Essential Question What are the ways to describe, classify, and compare triangles?

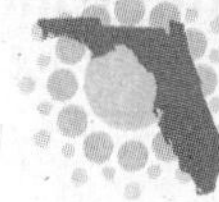

MA.3.G.3.1 Describe, analyze, compare and classify two-dimensional shapes using sides and angles – including acute, obtuse, and right angles – and connect these ideas to the definition of shapes.

UNLOCK the Problem REAL WORLD

Sailboats can be named by the type of sail they have. Most sails are in the shape of triangles.

Triangles can be named by the number of equal sides and by their angles. What are the math words you can use to describe the sail outlined on this boat?

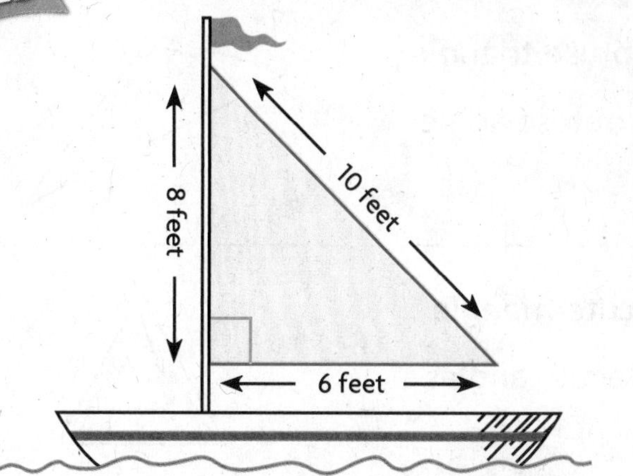

One Way Name triangles by the number of equal sides.

equilateral triangle

3 equal sides

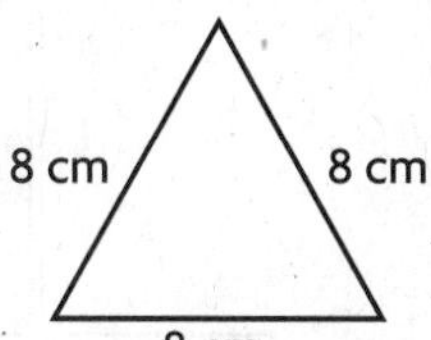

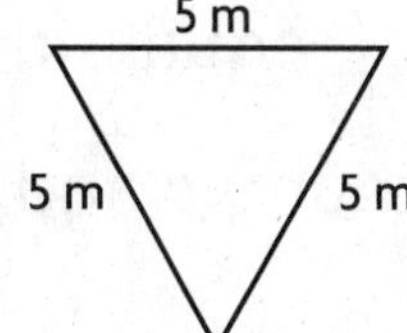

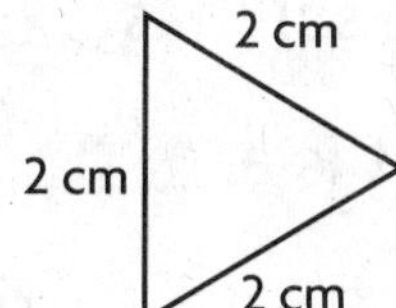

---

isosceles triangle

2 equal sides

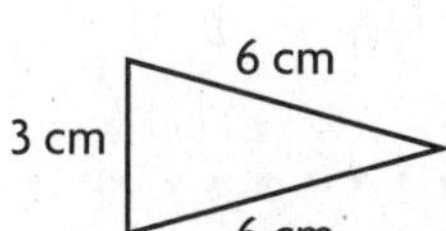

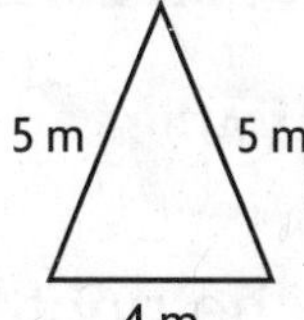

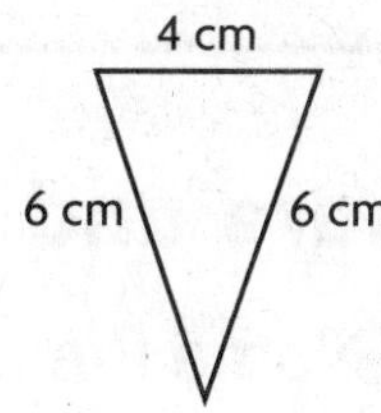

---

scalene triangle

0 equal sides

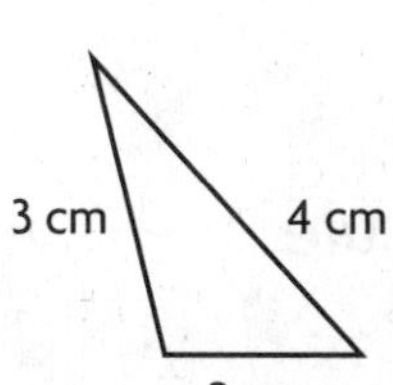

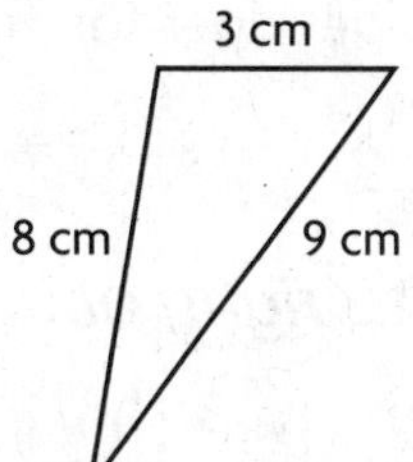

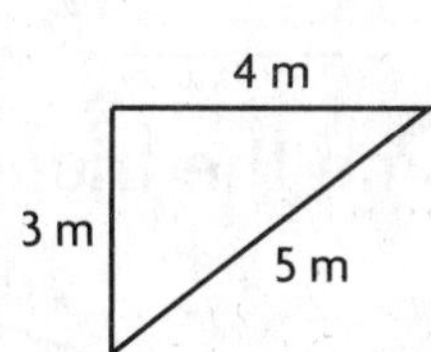

The sail above has 0 equal sides, so it is

a ______________ triangle.

Another Way Name triangles by their angles.

right triangle

1 right angle

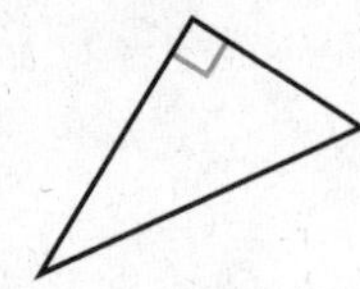
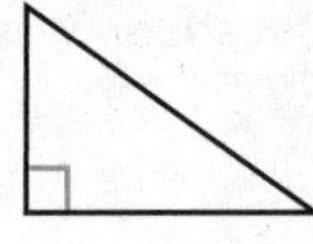

obtuse triangle

1 obtuse angle

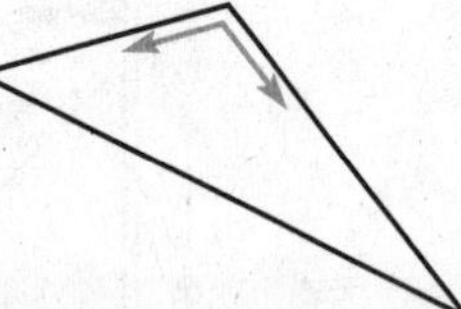
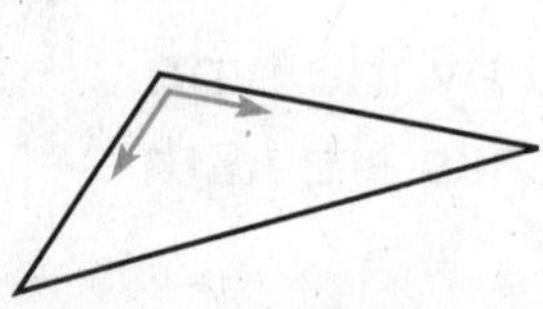
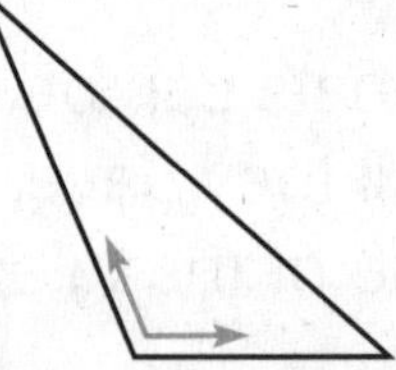

acute triangle

3 acute angles

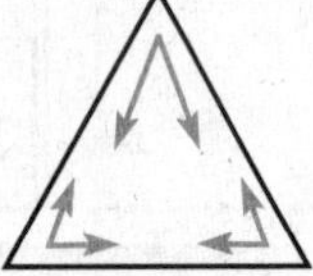
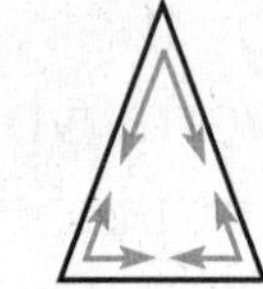
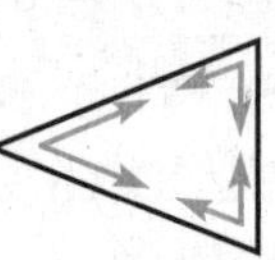

The sail has 1 right angle, so it is a

__________ triangle.

The sail has __________ equal sides,

so it is a __________ triangle and a

__________ triangle.

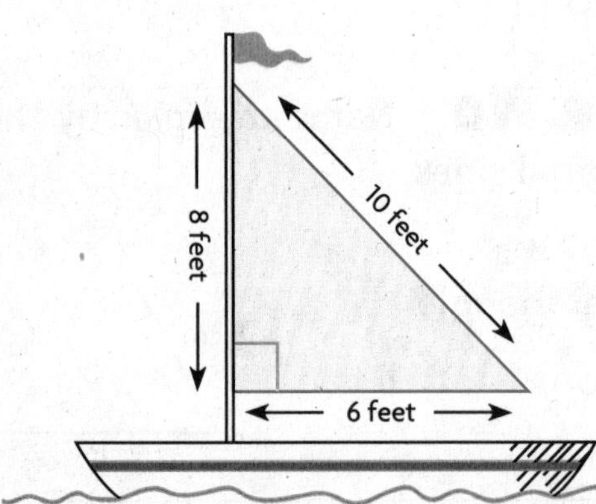

Share and Show

1. Name the triangle at the right.
   Write *equilateral, isosceles,* or *scalene*.
   Think: How many equal sides does the triangle have?

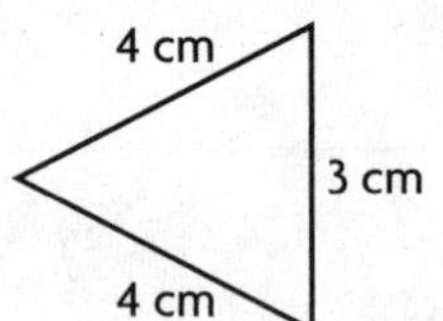

____

Name the triangle. Write *right, obtuse,* or *acute*.

2.

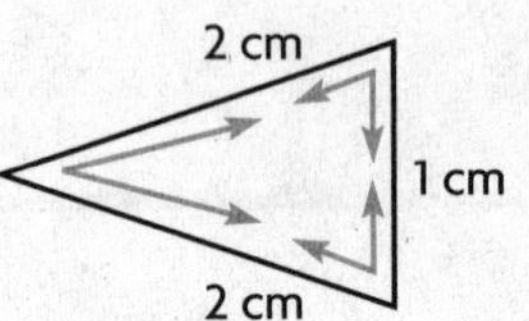

____

3.

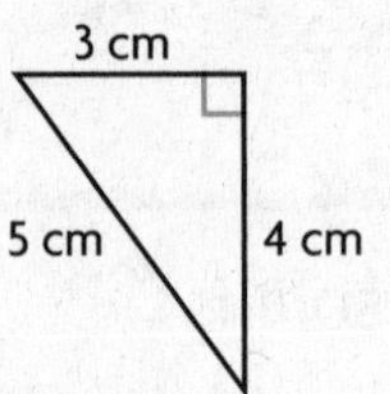

____

4.

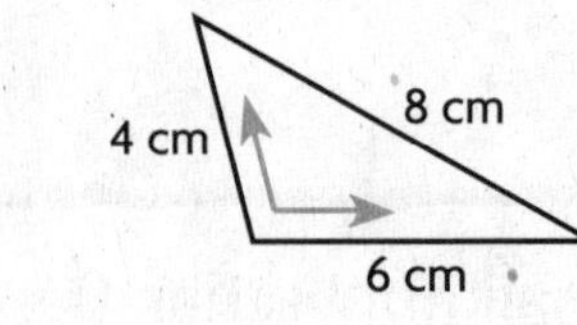

____

Name ___________________________

On Your Own

Name the triangle. Write *equilateral*, *isosceles*, or *scalene*.

5.

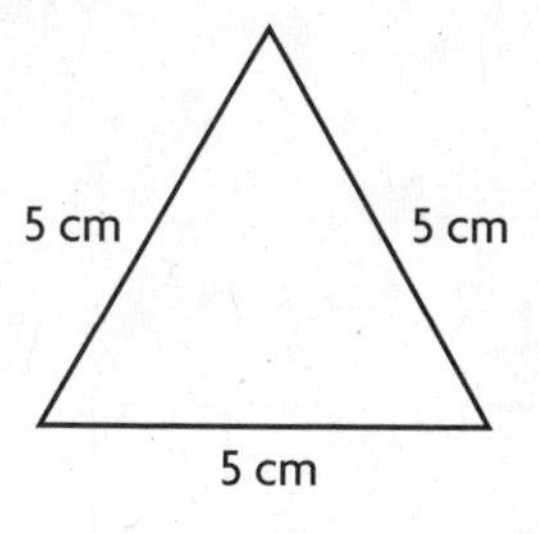

____

6.

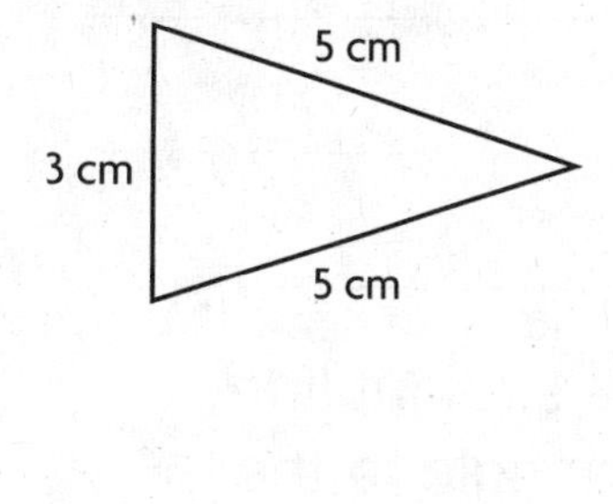

____

7.

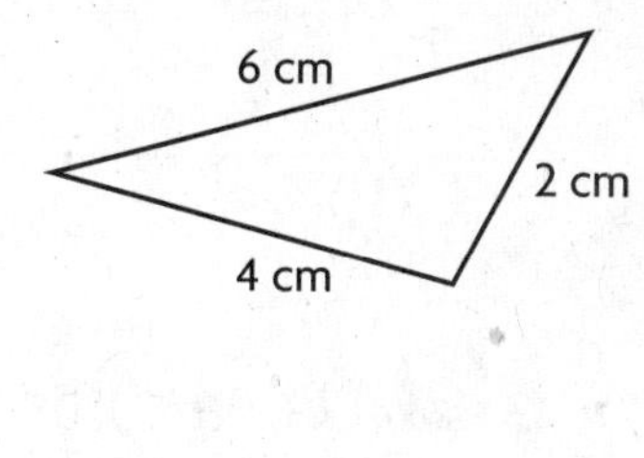

____

Name the triangle. Write *right*, *obtuse*, or *acute*.

8.

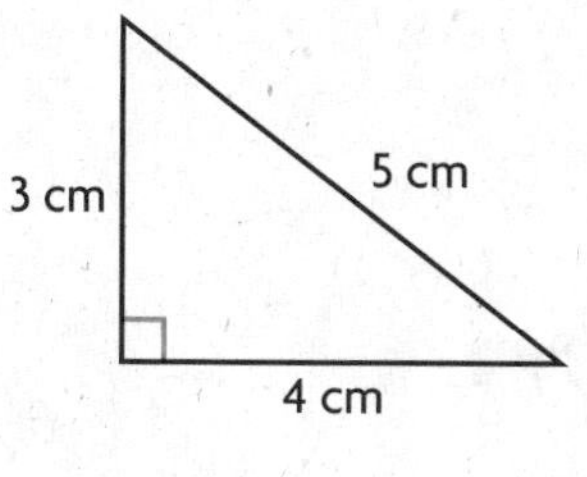

____

9.

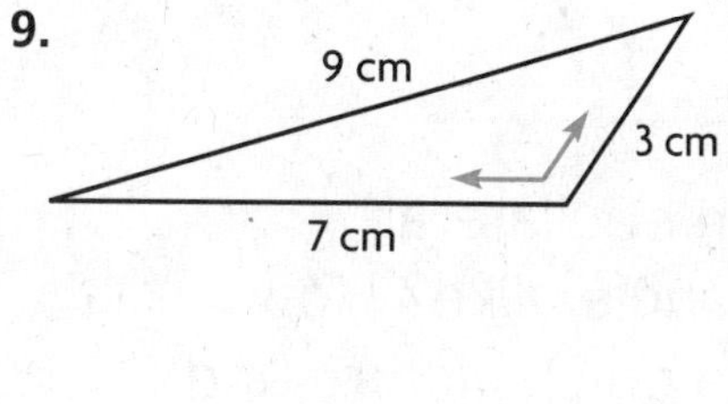

____

10.

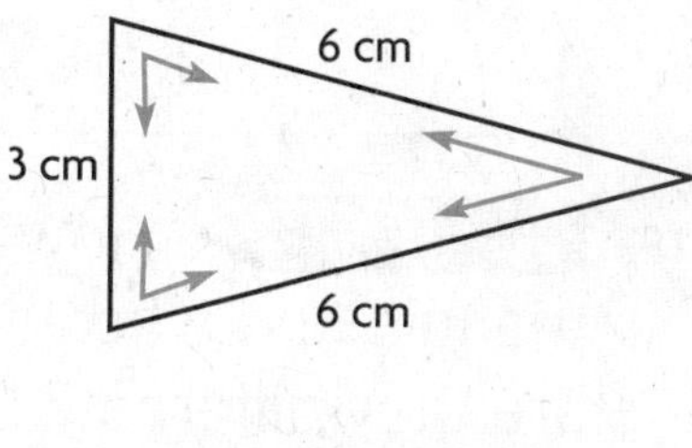

____

Math Talk **Describe** how a triangle can be both equilateral and acute.

Name the triangle by the lengths of its sides. Write *equilateral*, *isosceles*, or *scalene*.

11. 12 inches, 12 inches, 12 inches

____

12. 4 inches, 6 inches, 6 inches

____

13. 9 inches, 5 inches, 7 inches

____

14. 14 inches, 7 inches, 14 inches

____

Problem Solving REAL WORLD

15. I am a triangle. Two of my sides are 5 inches long. My third side is less than 5 inches. None of my angles are right angles. What two names do I have?

____

SHOW YOUR WORK

16. **Sense or Nonsense?** Martin said a triangle can have two sides that are parallel. Does his statement make sense? **Explain** your answer.

____

____

____

17. H.O.T. Use a ruler to draw a straight line from one corner of this rectangle to the opposite corner. What shapes are there now? What math words can you use to describe them?

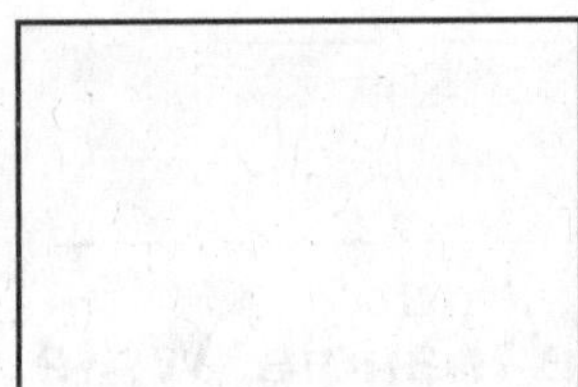

____

18. **Write Math** How are an equilateral triangle and a scalene triangle alike? How are they different? Draw a quick picture and **Explain** your answer.

____

____

____

____

19. Draw a triangle with 1 right angle and 2 equal sides. Name your triangle in two ways.

____

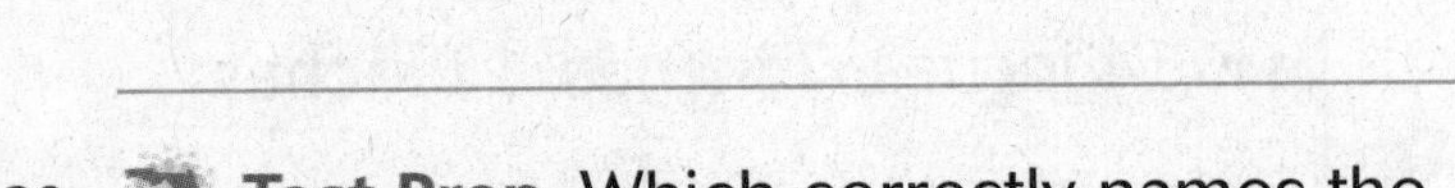

20. **Test Prep** Which correctly names the triangle below?

Ⓐ scalene and obtuse

Ⓑ isosceles and acute

Ⓒ scalene and acute

Ⓓ isosceles and obtuse

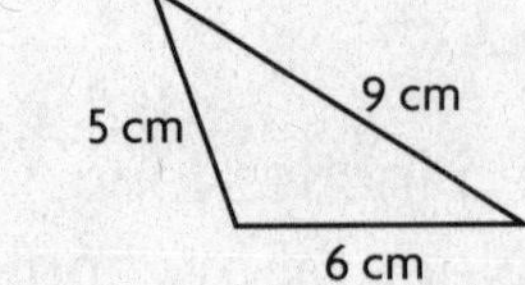

FOR MORE PRACTICE:
Florida Benchmarks Practice Book, pp. P219–P220

Name ______________________________

Classify Quadrilaterals

Essential Question How can you describe, classify, and compare quadrilaterals?

MA.3.G.3.1 Describe, analyze, compare and classify two-dimensional shapes using sides and angles – including acute, obtuse, and right angles – and connect these ideas to the definition of shapes.

UNLOCK the Problem REAL WORLD

Quadrilaterals are named by their sides and their angles.

Complete the sentences to describe the quadrilaterals.

square

- ______ pairs of parallel ______
- ______ equal ______
- ______ right angles

rectangle

- ______ pairs of parallel ______
- ______ pairs of equal ______
- ______ right angles

rhombus

- ______ pairs of parallel ______
- ______ equal ______

trapezoid

- exactly ______ pair of parallel ______
- lengths of ______ may not be the same
- sizes of ______ may not be the same

parallelogram

- ______ pairs of parallel ______
- ______ pairs of equal ______

Math Talk **Explain** why a trapezoid is not a parallelogram.

Share and Show 

Look at the quadrilateral at the right.

1. Outline each pair of parallel sides a different color.

   How many pairs of sides are parallel? ________

2. Put an X on one pair of equal sides.
   How many pairs of sides are equal? ________

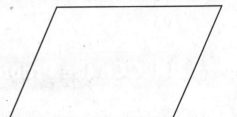

3. Name the quadrilateral. ________

Circle every name that describes the quadrilateral.

4. 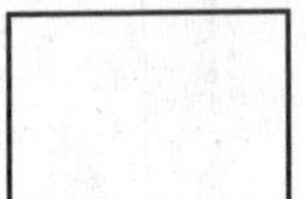

   parallelogram

   rectangle

   rhombus

   square

5. 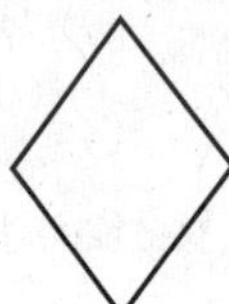

   parallelogram

   rhombus

   trapezoid

   rectangle

6. 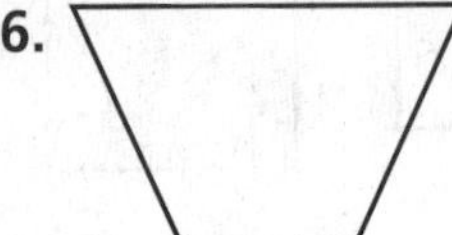

   rectangle

   rhombus

   trapezoid

   parallelogram

On Your Own

Circle every name that describes the quadrilateral.

7. 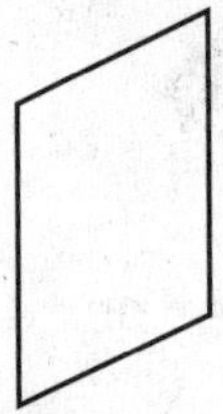

   rectangle

   trapezoid

   parallelogram

   rhombus

8. 

   rhombus

   parallelogram

   trapezoid

   square

9. 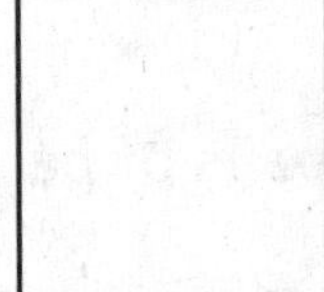

   parallelogram

   square

   rectangle

   rhombus

Math Talk **Explain** why a square is a parallelogram, a rectangle, and a rhombus.

Name ______________________________

Use the quadrilaterals at the right for 10–12.

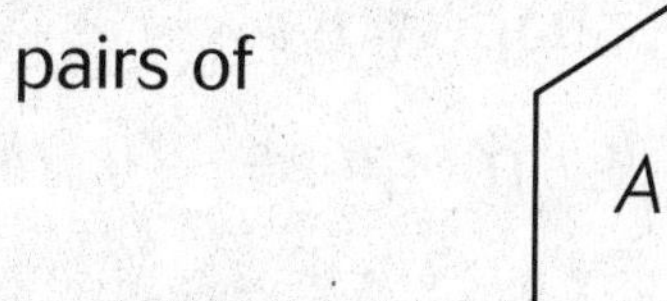

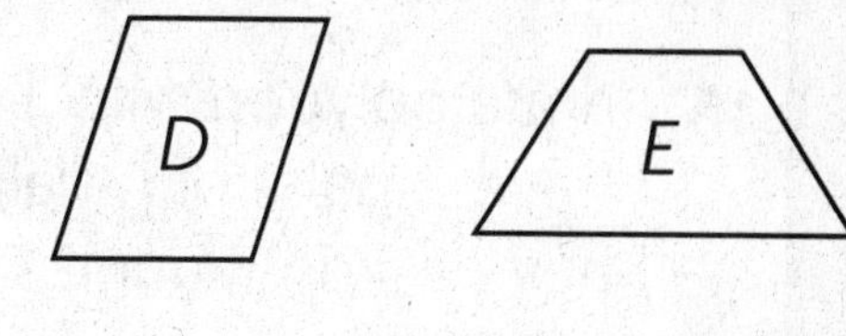

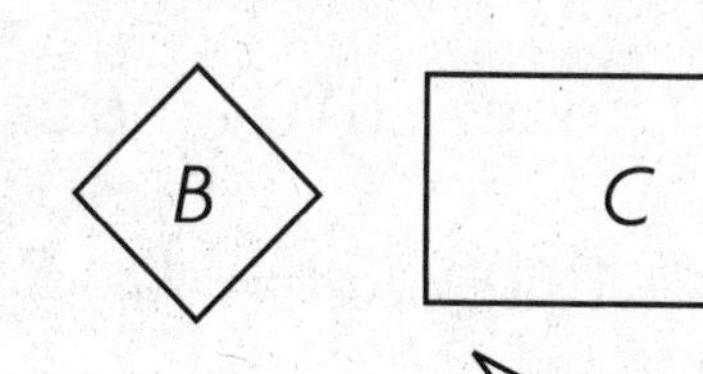

10. Which quadrilaterals have 4 right angles?

____

11. Which quadrilaterals have 2 pairs of parallel sides?

____

12. Which quadrilaterals have no right angles?

____

13. Write Math ▶ **What's the Error?** Jacki drew the shape at the right. She said it is a parallelogram because it has 2 pairs of parallel sides. Describe her error.

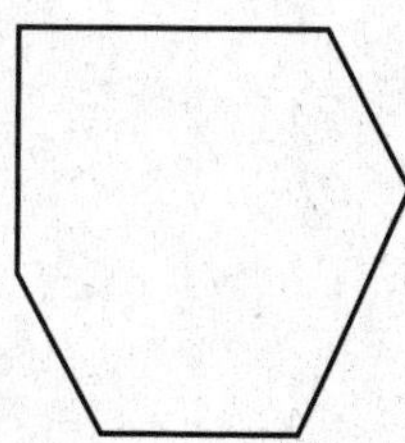

____

____

____

14. The flag for the state of Arkansas is shown at the right. How can you describe the blue and white quadrilaterals you see in the flag?

____

____

____

____

15. Circle the shape at the right that is not a quadrilateral. **Explain** your choice.

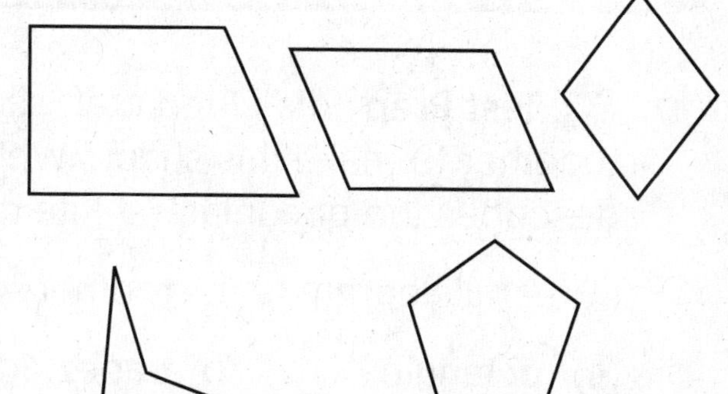

____

____

____

UNLOCK the Problem REAL WORLD

16. I am a polygon with 1 more side than a triangle.
I have 2 pairs of parallel sides and 4 equal sides.
I have no right angles. What shape am I?

Ⓐ trapezoid Ⓑ rectangle Ⓒ rhombus Ⓓ square

a. What do you need to find? ______________________

____

b. How will you use an array to solve the problem? ______________________

____

c. Draw to solve the problem.

d. Complete the sentences.

A __________ or a __________ has 1 more side than a triangle.

A __________, a __________,

and a __________ have 2 pairs of parallel sides.

A __________ and a __________ have 4 equal sides.

The shape cannot be a __________ because it has no right angles.

So, it must be a __________.

e. Fill in the bubble above to show your answer.

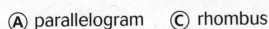

17. **Test Prep** Rita glued craft sticks together to make this shape. Which best describes the quadrilateral Rita made?

Ⓐ parallelogram Ⓒ rhombus

Ⓑ rectangle Ⓓ trapezoid

FOR MORE PRACTICE:
Florida Benchmarks Practice Book, pp. P221–P222

Name ______________________________

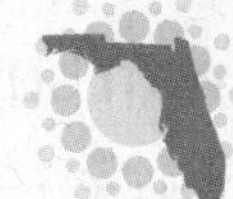

Search for Patterns · Plane Shapes

Essential Question How can you solve problems by using the strategy search for patterns?

MA.3.A.6.2 Solve non-routine problems by making a table, chart, or list and searching for patterns.

UNLOCK the Problem REAL WORLD

Sean is using square tiles to make a pattern. He made 4 rows of the pattern at the right. What rule can Sean use to find the total number of tiles he will need to make any number of rows in the pattern?

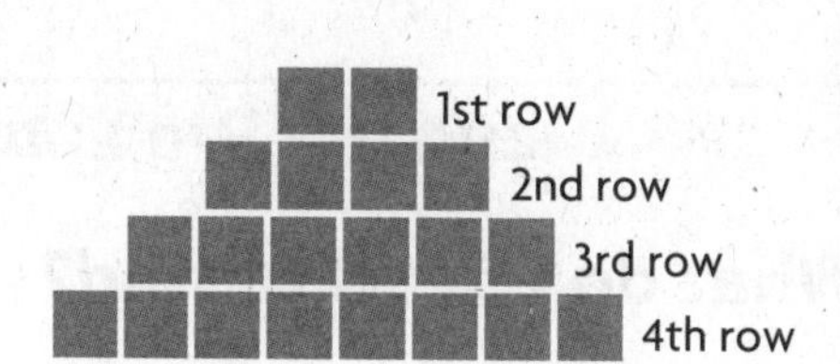

Use the graphic organizer to help you solve the problem.

Read the Problem

What do I need to find?

I need to look for __________ to find the total number of tiles in the pattern when there are any number of rows.

What information do I need to use?

I need to look at the number of tiles in each of the 4 rows. Then I need to find the total number of tiles as each row is added and look for patterns.

How will I use the information?

I will make a table to look for a pattern and find a rule.

Solve the Problem

Make a table to record the number of tiles in each row and the total number of tiles.

Row	1	2	3	4
Number of Tiles in Row	2			
Number of Tiles in All	2			

Look at the total number of tiles. You can multiply to find the total number of tiles.

Think: Row $1 \times 2 = 2$ tiles
Row $2 \times 3 = 6$ tiles
Row $3 \times 4 = 12$ tiles
Row $4 \times 5 = 20$ tiles

Sean can use this rule: Multiply the number of the row by the next greater number to find how many tiles in all he will need.

Try Another Problem

Dylan is making a pattern with square tiles.

What color is the 20th tile in his pattern?

Read the Problem	Solve the Problem
What do I need to find?	**Record the steps you used to solve the problem.**
What information do I need to use?	
How will I use the information?	

- **Explain** how you can check your work.

Math Talk **Explain** another way you could solve the problem.

Name ___________________________

Share and Show 

1. Allie uses 51 square tiles to make a pattern. The bottom 3 rows are shown. How many more rows will Allie put on the top to complete the pattern?

First, look at the picture of the tile pattern.

Next, write a rule for the pattern.

Think: There are 16 tiles in the bottom row, 13 tiles in the middle row, and 10 tiles in the top row.

The number of tiles is ___________ than the row below it.

A rule is ___________.

Then, find the number of tiles in the remaining rows.

$10 - 3 =$ ____ ____ $- 3 =$ ____ ____ $- 3 =$ ____

Add the numbers of tiles in each row:

$16 + 13 + 10 +$ ____ $+$ ____ $+$ ____ $=$ ____

Last, since the total number of tiles is correct, count the number of new rows.

So, Allie will put ___________ rows on the top to complete the pattern.

2. The towers form a pattern. How many blocks will be needed to make the 20th tower?

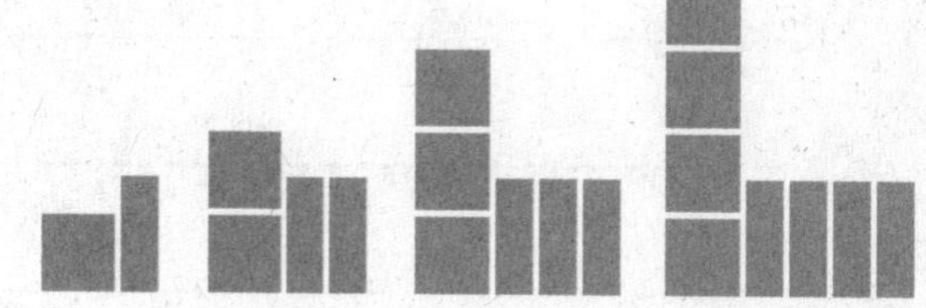

____

3. Carter has 50 counters in all. Does he have enough counters to make the next shape in his pattern? **Explain.**

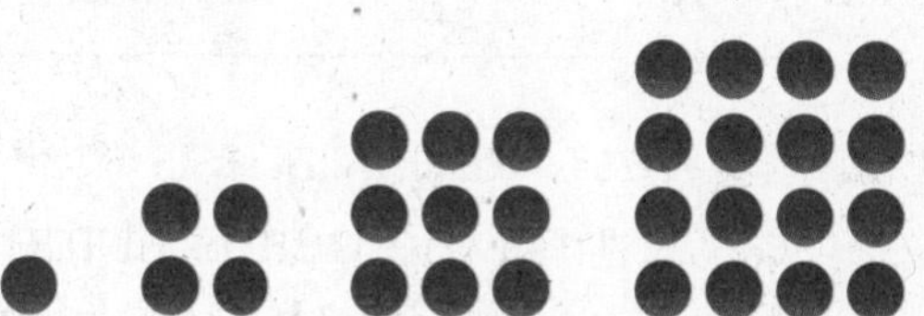

____

____

____

____

On Your Own

4. Kirsten is making a pattern with buttons. She has used 16 buttons. Of these, $\frac{3}{4}$ are blue. How many buttons are blue?

____

5. Stacy chose a square, a trapezoid, and a triangle from a bag of pattern blocks. The block she chose first did not have 4 sides. She did not choose the square last. In what order did Stacy choose the blocks?

____

6. Eric has a choice of black, tan, or blue pants. He has a red shirt and a blue shirt. How many possible combinations of pants and shirts does he have?

____

7. H.O.T. Write Math Carolyn has 9 red beads and 10 white beads. She has 5 times as many blue beads as red beads. How many beads does Carolyn have in all? **Explain** how you know.

____

____

____

____

8. **Test Prep** Maria is making a bracelet. She has strung the beads at the right. What is the next group of beads she will string?

Ⓐ 1 square, 1 star

Ⓑ 2 squares, 1 star

Ⓒ 1 square, 4 stars

Ⓓ 4 squares, 4 stars

Choose a STRATEGY

Act It Out
Use Manipulatives
Draw a Diagram
Make a Table, Chart, or List
Search for Patterns

SHOW YOUR WORK

FOR MORE PRACTICE:
Florida Benchmarks Practice Book, pp. P223–P224

Name ________________________________

Chapter Review/Test

▶ Check Vocabulary

Choose the best term from the box to complete the sentence.

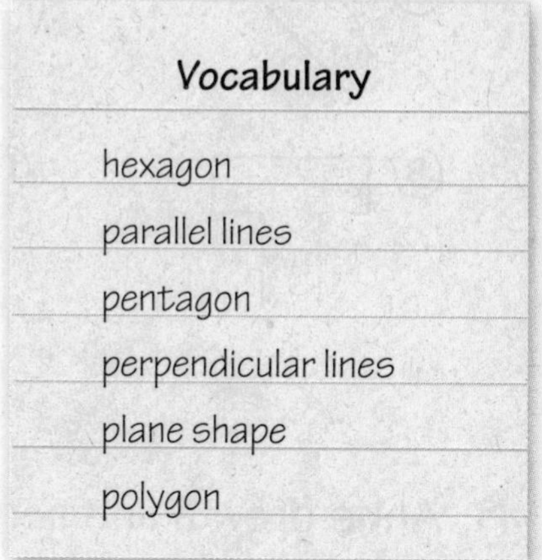

1. A ________________ has 6 sides and 6 vertices. **(MA.3.G.3.1; pp. 385–388)**

2. A ________________ is formed by curves, line segments, or both. **(MA.3.G.3.1; pp. 377–380)**

3. ________________ appear never to cross and are always the same distance apart. **(MA.3.G.3.1; pp. 393–396)**

▶ Check Concepts and Skills

Look at the green sides of each polygon. Tell if they appear to be *intersecting, perpendicular,* or *parallel*. **(MA.3.G.3.1; pp. 393–396)**

4. 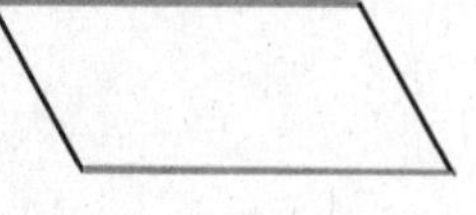

____

5. 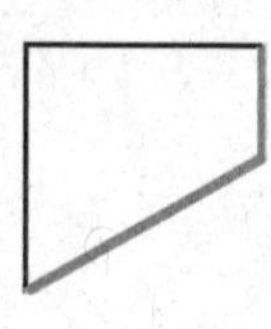

____

6. 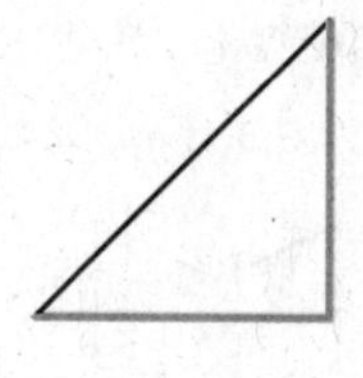

____

Circle every name that describes the quadrilateral. **(MA.3.G.3.1; pp. 403–406)**

7. 

parallelogram
rectangle
rhombus
trapezoid

8. 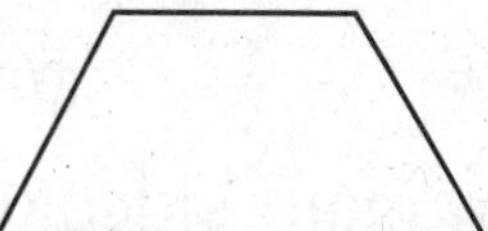

parallelogram
rhombus
trapezoid
rectangle

9. 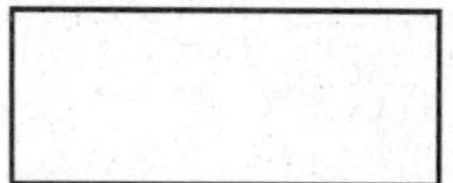

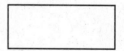

rhombus
rectangle
square
parallelogram

Go online Assessment Options
Chapter Test

Fill in the bubble for the correct answer choice.

10. Which is NOT an example of a closed shape?
[MA.3.G.3.1; pp. 377–380]

Ⓒ  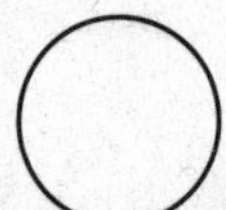

Ⓑ 

Ⓓ 

11. Anne drew a line segment. Which of these could be the shape Anne drew? [MA.3.G.3.1; pp. 377–380]

Ⓕ •

Ⓗ 

Ⓖ

Ⓘ 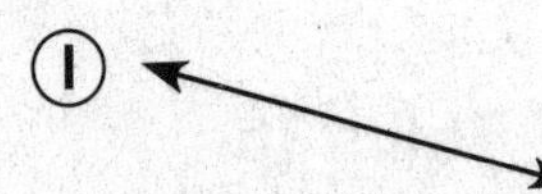

12. Which of the shapes below is NOT a polygon?
[MA.3.G.3.1; pp. 381–384]

Ⓒ 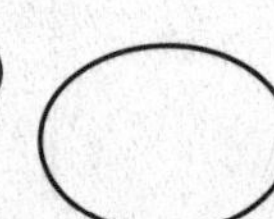

Ⓑ 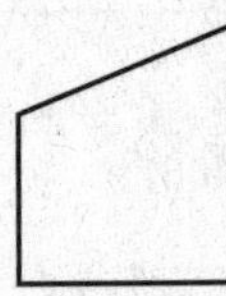

Ⓓ 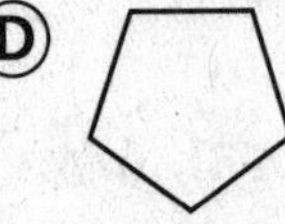

13. Sam drew the shape below. How many sides does his shape have? [MA.3.G.3.1; pp. 381–384]

Ⓕ 5

Ⓖ 6

Ⓗ 7

Ⓘ 8

Fill in the bubble for the correct answer choice.

TEST PREP

14. Philip drew a shape with 2 fewer sides than a hexagon. Which shape did he draw?
[MA.3.G.3.1; pp. 385–388]

Ⓐ triangle

Ⓑ pentagon

Ⓒ octagon

Ⓓ quadrilateral

15. Jennifer drew the polygons below. Which shape is an octagon? **[MA.3.G.3.1; pp. 385–388]**

Ⓕ 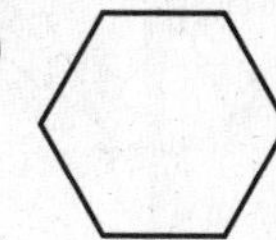

Ⓗ 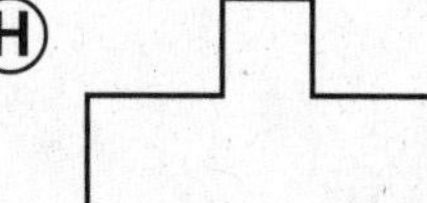

Ⓖ 

Ⓘ 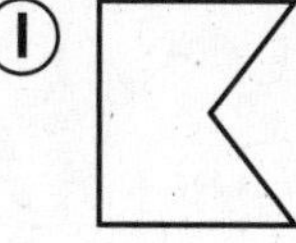

16. Which angle is less than a right angle?
[MA.3.G.3.1; pp. 389–392]

Ⓐ 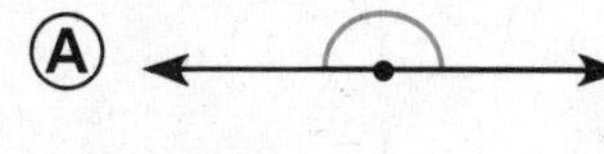

Ⓒ 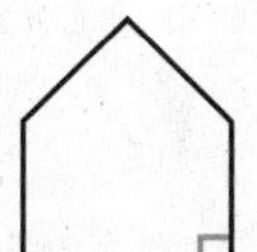

Ⓑ 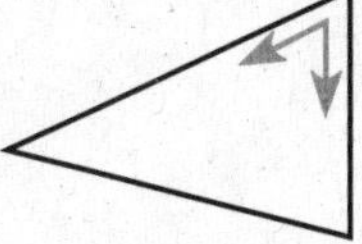

Ⓓ 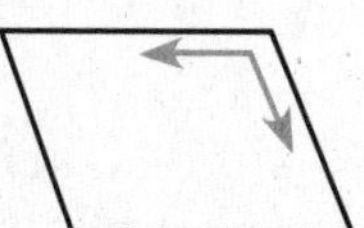

17. Which polygon below does NOT have a right angle? **[MA.3.G.3.1; pp. 389–392]**

Ⓕ 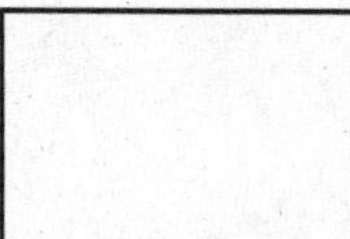

Ⓗ 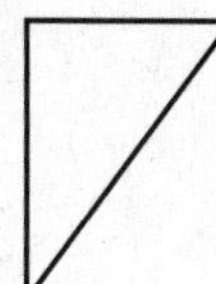

Ⓖ 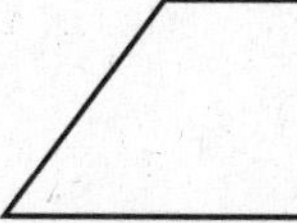

Ⓘ 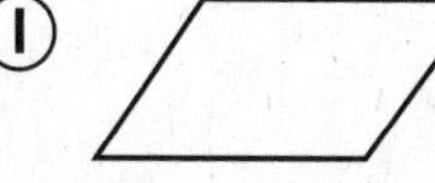

18. How many pairs of parallel sides are in the rectangle?
[MA.3.G.3.1; pp. 393–396]

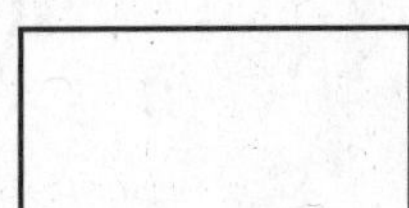

Ⓐ 1

Ⓑ 2

Ⓒ 3

Ⓓ 4

19. Mr. Reynolds drew these triangles on the board. How are triangles *A* and *D* alike? [MA.3.G.3.1; pp. 399–402]

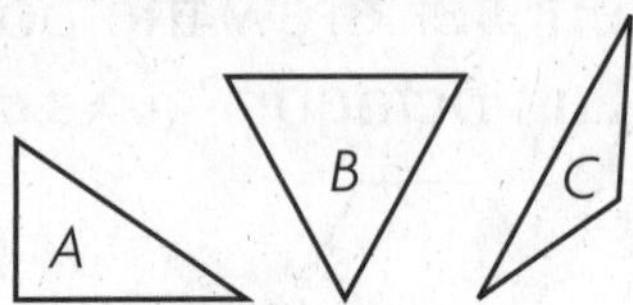

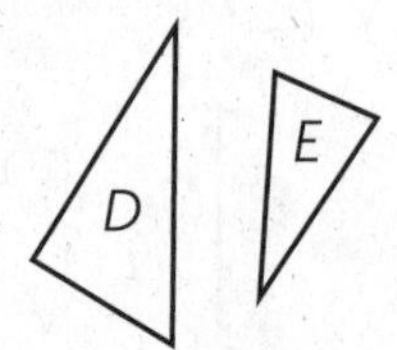

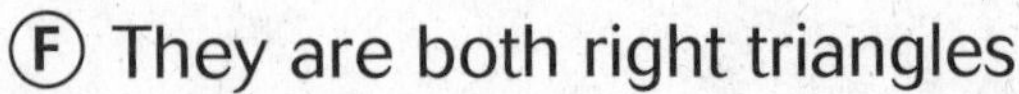
Ⓕ They are both right triangles.

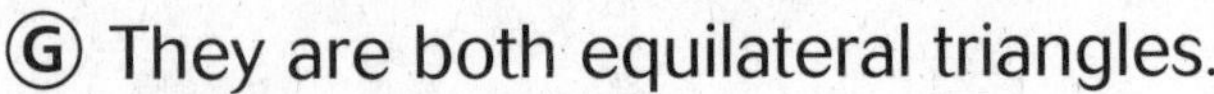
Ⓖ They are both equilateral triangles.

Ⓗ They are both acute triangles.

Ⓘ They are both obtuse triangles.

20. Which quadrilateral has only 1 pair of parallel sides?
[MA.3.G.3.1; pp. 403–406]

Ⓐ 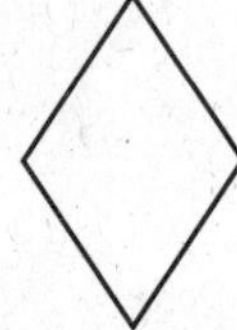

Ⓒ 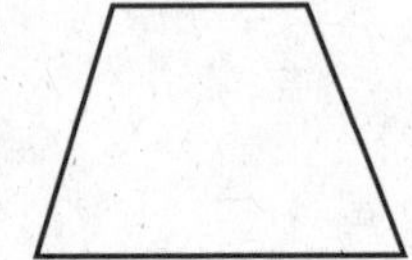

Ⓑ 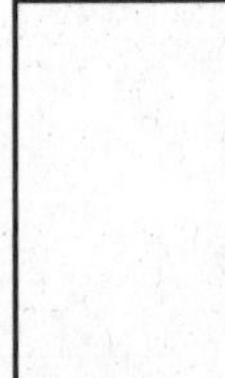

Ⓓ 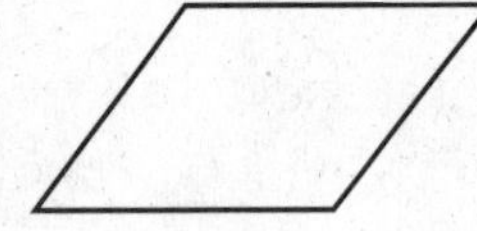

21. Select the statement that is NOT correct.
[MA.3.G.3.1; pp. 403–406]

Ⓕ All squares are rectangles.

Ⓖ All rectangles are squares.

Ⓗ All rectangles are parallelograms.

Ⓘ All parallelograms are quadrilaterals.

Chapter 10

Plane Shapes in Motion

Show What You Know

Check your understanding of important skills.

Name ______________________________

Classify Plane Shapes

Write the number of sides and the number of angles.

1. _____ sides
   _____ angles

2. _____ sides
   _____ angles

Combine Plane Shapes

Write the number of triangles needed to cover each shape.

3. _____ triangles

4. _____ triangles

5. _____ triangles

Geometric Patterns

Circle the pattern unit. Then draw the next two shapes.

6. □ △ □ △ □ △ □ △ _____ _____

Florida FUN FACT

Starfish, also called sea stars, live in Florida's coastal waters and reefs. They are known for their symmetry.

FLORIDA BENCHMARKS

Vocabulary Power

▶ Visualize It

Complete the Bubble Map by using the words with a ✓.

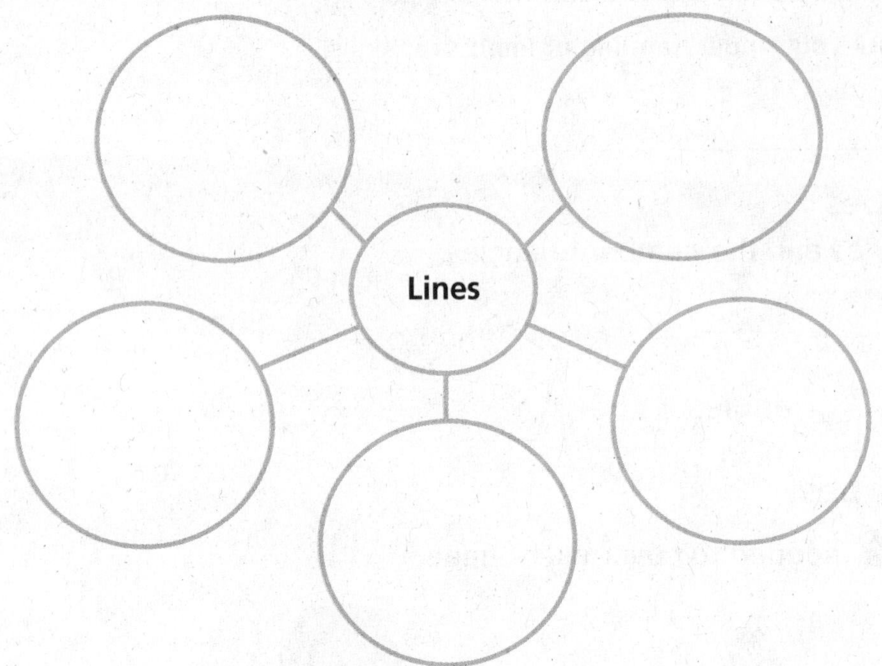

Review Words
hexagon
✓ intersecting lines
line
✓ parallel lines
✓ perpendicular lines
rhombus
square
trapezoid
triangle

Preview Words
congruent
✓ diagonal
growing pattern
✓ line of symmetry
repeating pattern
symmetry

▶ Understand Vocabulary

Write the word or words that match the description.

1. They are lines that appear never to cross or meet and are always the same distance apart.

   ____

2. Two figures that have the same size and shape are ______________________________.

3. When a figure can be folded along a line so that the two parts match exactly, it has

   ______________________________.

4. They are lines that cross or meet to form a right angle. ______________________________

Go online • Student Edition • Multilingual eGlossary

Name ______________________________

Combine Plane Shapes

Essential Question How can you combine plane shapes to make new shapes?

MA.3.G.3.2 Compose, decompose, and transform polygons to make other polygons, including concave and convex polygons with three, four, five, six, eight, or ten sides.

Investigate

Materials ■ pattern blocks

Pattern blocks can be combined to make new shapes.

A. Combine two triangle pattern blocks to make a new shape. Trace the shape.

B. Combine two blue rhombus pattern blocks to make a new shape. Trace the shape.

C. Combine the two rhombus pattern blocks another way to make a new shape. Trace the shape.

D. On your MathBoard, combine other pattern blocks to make new shapes. Trace the shapes.

When you combine shapes, the sides must be touching without overlapping.

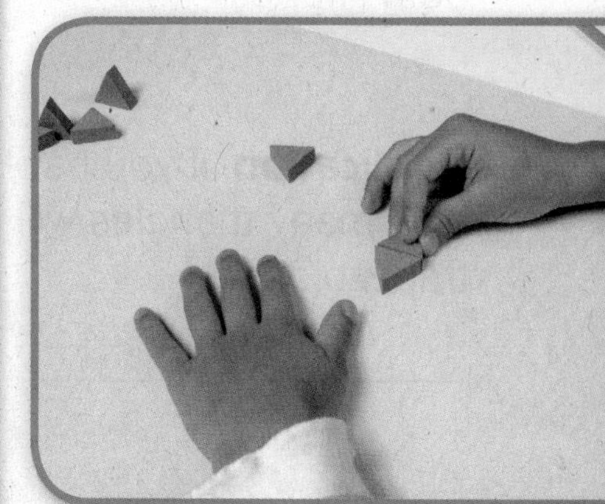

Draw Conclusions

1. Look at the new shapes you made in A, B, C, and D. Name as many of the new shapes as you can.

2. On your MathBoard, combine six triangle pattern blocks to make a hexagon. Then combine the same pattern blocks to make a different hexagon. Trace both shapes.

3. **Application** If you have 7 triangle pattern blocks, how many triangles will be left if you make 2 trapezoids?

Math Talk **Explain** how the hexagons you made in Problem 2 are alike and how they are different.

Connect

Combine different pattern blocks to make a new shape. Trace the new shape.

Name ___________________________

Share and Show 

Draw and name a new shape that can be made by combining two of the pattern block shapes shown.

1. 

____

2. 

____

3. 

____

What pattern blocks can be combined to make the shape? Trace the blocks you used.

4. 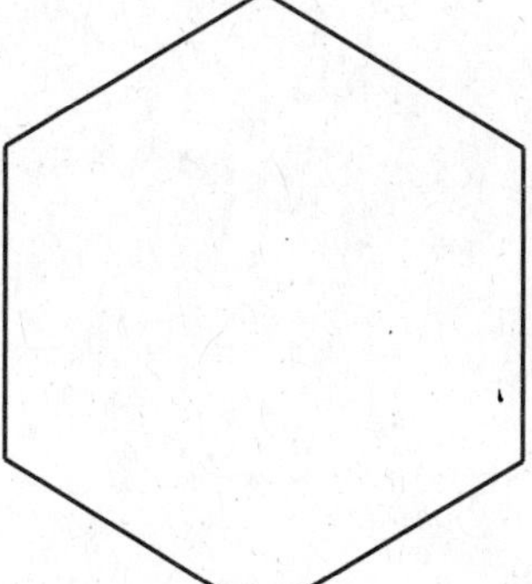

____

____

____

5. 

____

____

____

Problem Solving

6. Carter is combining blue rhombus pattern blocks. How many blocks will it take to make 3 hexagons?

SHOW YOUR WORK

7. H.O.T. Combine the pattern blocks below to make a 7-sided shape. Trace your shape. How many right angles does your shape have?

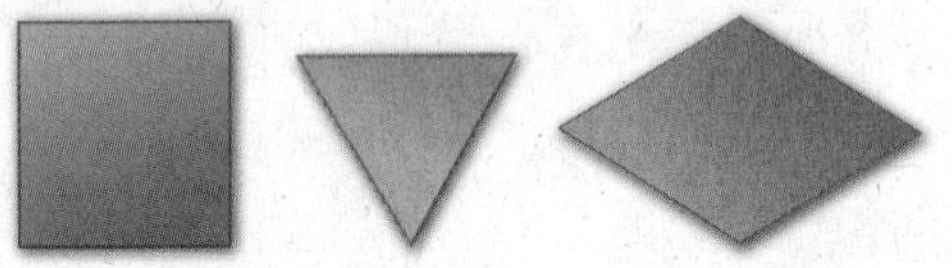

8. Write Math Use 4 triangle pattern blocks. **Explain** the different shapes you can make by combining some or all of them.

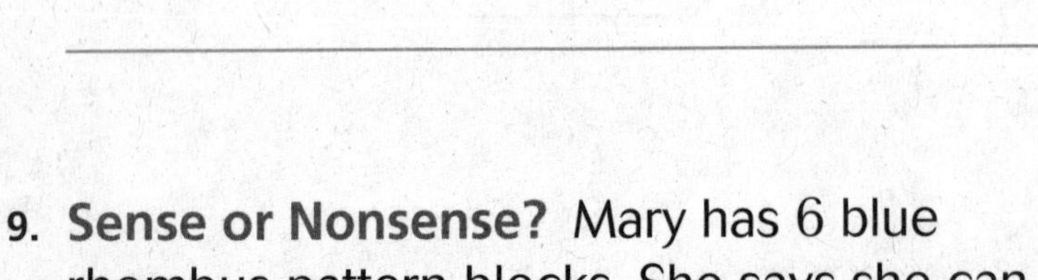

9. **Sense or Nonsense?** Mary has 6 blue rhombus pattern blocks. She says she can combine them to make 2 hexagons. Does Mary's statement make sense? Draw a picture to **explain**.

FOR MORE PRACTICE:
Florida Benchmarks Practice Book, pp. P231–P232

Name ____________________________________

Separate Plane Shapes

Essential Question How can you separate plane shapes to make new shapes?

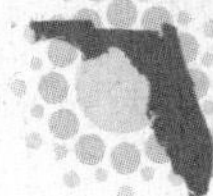

MA.3.G.3.2 Compose, decompose, and transform polygons to make other polygons, including concave and convex polygons with three, four, five, six, eight, or ten sides.

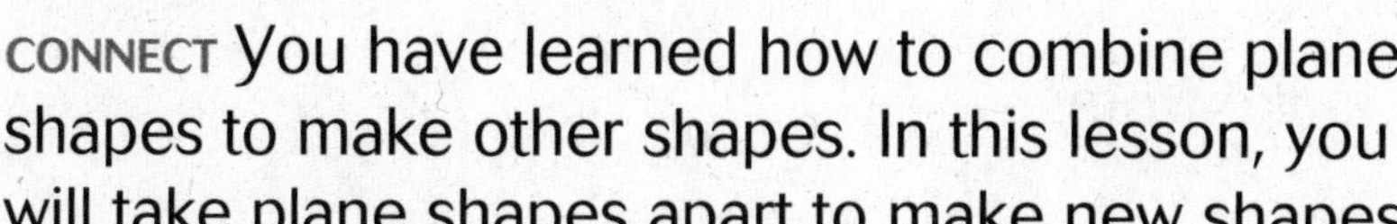

CONNECT You have learned how to combine plane shapes to make other shapes. In this lesson, you will take plane shapes apart to make new shapes.

Investigate

Materials ■ pattern blocks, scissors

You can cut plane shapes apart to make new shapes.

A. Trace a hexagon pattern block twice and cut the two shapes out. Fold one hexagon in half so that the two vertices are on the fold.

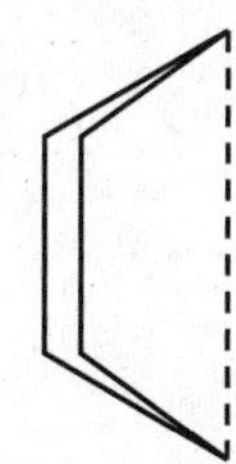

B. Cut the shape along the fold. Trace the new shapes.

C. Now, fold the other hexagon in half so that the middle of the side is on the fold. Cut the shape along the fold. Trace the new shapes.

D. Choose another pattern block. Trace it and cut the shape out. Fold the shape in half and cut it along the fold. Write the names of the new shapes.

____

____

Draw Conclusions

1. In B, what new shapes did you make from the hexagon? ______

2. In C, what new shapes did you make from the hexagon? ______

3. How can you cut apart the pentagon in C to make 2 trapezoids? Draw a picture to show your answer.

4. **Application** Trace and cut out a blue rhombus. Fold the rhombus in half two ways. What new shapes would you have if you cut the rhombus apart along both folds? Trace one of the shapes.

______

Connect

You can make new shapes by drawing diagonals in plane shapes.

A **diagonal** is a line segment that connects two vertices of a polygon that are not next to each other.

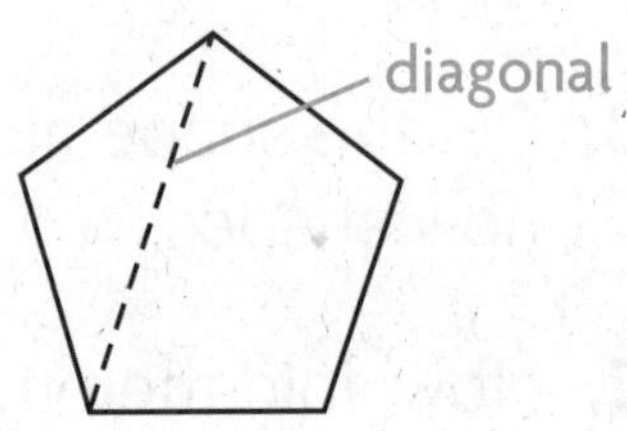

- What new shapes do you see in this pentagon?

______

Try This!

STEP 1 Trace a square pattern block and cut it out. Draw a diagonal in the square.

STEP 2 Cut the shape along the diagonal. What new shapes do you have?

______

Math Talk **Explain** what happens when you draw 2 intersecting diagonals in a shape.

Name ______________________

Share and Show 

Trace and cut out the shape. Fold the shape in half and cut along the fold. Write the name of the new shapes.

1.

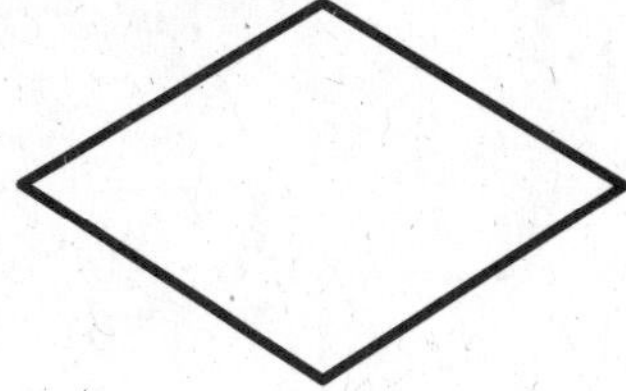

____

2.

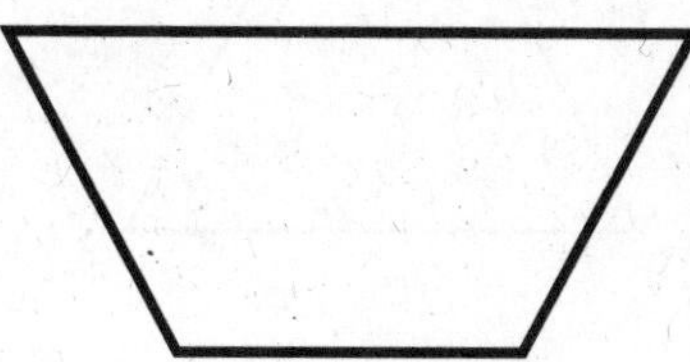

____

3.

____

4.

____

Trace and cut out the shape. Draw a diagonal and cut the shape along the diagonal. Write the names of the new shapes.

5.

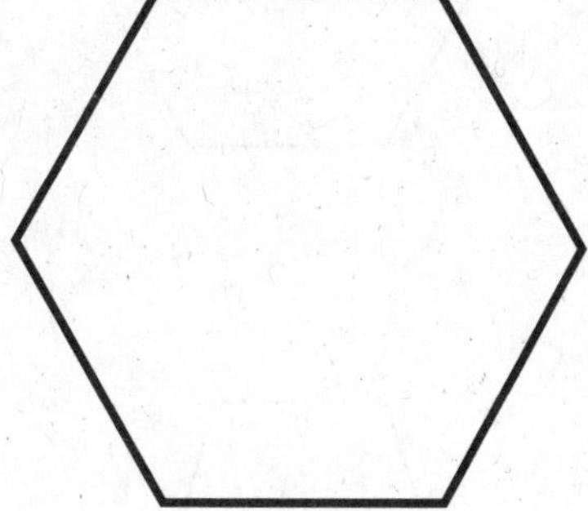

____

6.

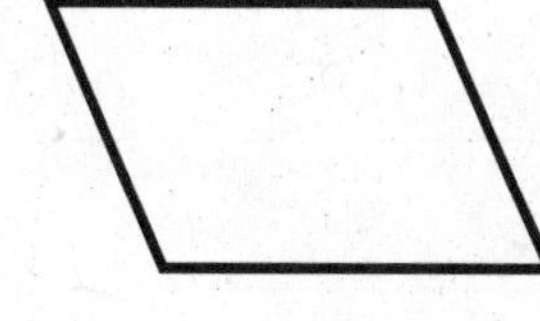

____

7.

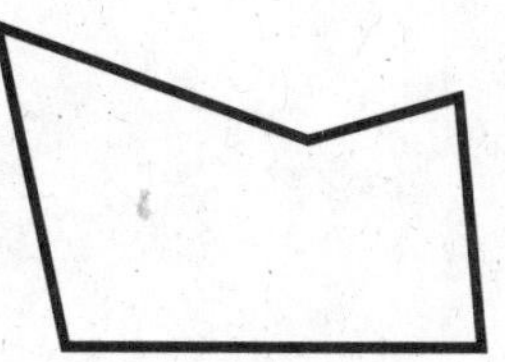

____

8.

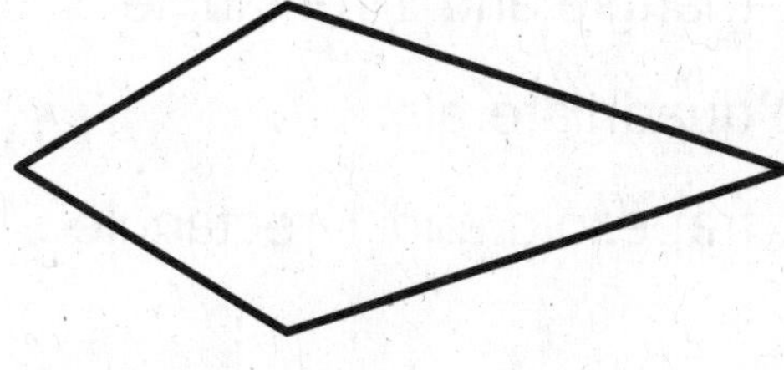

____

Problem Solving REAL WORLD

Use the polygons for 9–12.

9. Look at the polygons below. How many possible diagonals can be drawn in each?

 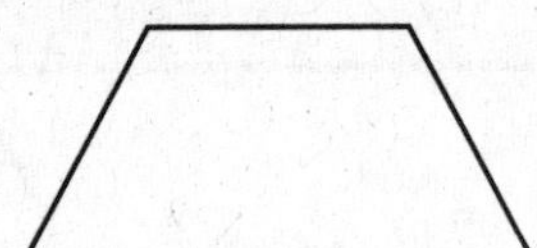 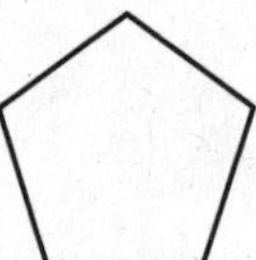 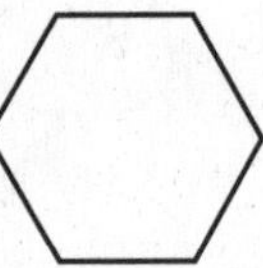

____ ____ ____ ____

10. H.O.T. Explain why you can't draw a diagonal in a triangle.

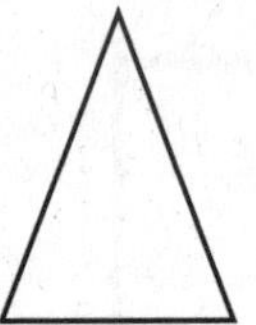

____

____

____

11. How can you make one cut in the hexagon to make a triangle and a pentagon? Show your work.

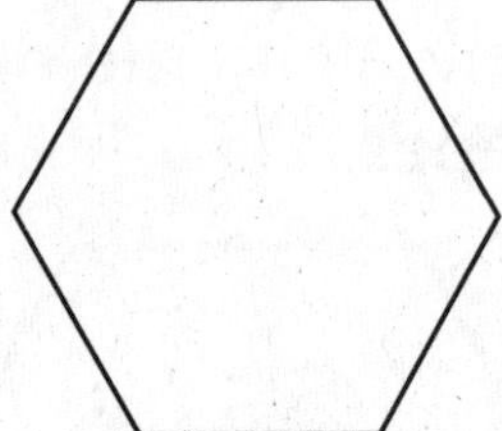

____

____

12. What new shapes do you make if you cut the pentagon at the right in half?

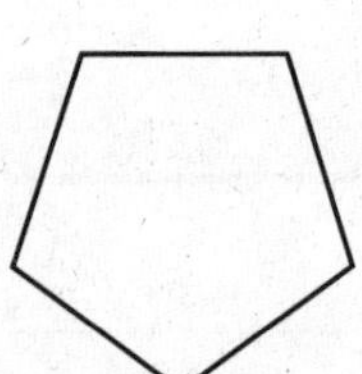

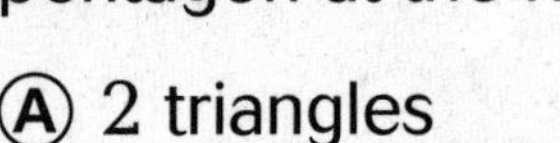

Ⓐ 2 triangles

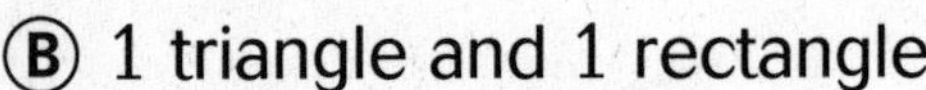

Ⓑ 1 triangle and 1 rectangle

Ⓒ 2 quadrilaterals

Ⓓ 1 trapezoid and 1 rectangle

FOR MORE PRACTICE:
Florida Benchmarks Practice Book, pp. P233–P234

Name ______________________________

Patterns with Shapes

Essential Question How can you use plane shapes to find patterns?

MA.3.A.4.1 Create, analyze, and represent patterns and relationships using words, variables, tables and graphs.

UNLOCK the Problem REAL WORLD

The part of the pattern that repeats is the **pattern unit**. When the same pattern unit is used over and over again, it makes a **repeating pattern**. Draw the next two shapes in the repeating pattern below.

 **Find the pattern unit.**

Think: What part of the pattern repeats? ______________________________

- What if there was a hexagon after each square? Draw what the pattern unit would look like.

Try This! **Find and draw the next two shapes in the growing pattern below.**

A **growing pattern** is a pattern in which the number or figure increases by the same amount each time.

Think: What rule or words can we use to describe the pattern?

The pattern is *add 2 rectangles, 1 in each row.*

Math Idea

A rule must be true for all the numbers or shapes in the pattern.

Activity

Materials ■ trapezoid pattern block

Use pattern blocks to show a pattern.

STEP 1 Trace a trapezoid pattern block and record the number of sides.

STEP 2 To the right of the trapezoid you traced, trace the pattern block again, and record the total number of sides.

STEP 3 Continue to trace until you have combined four trapezoid pattern blocks without overlapping. Record the number of sides in the new shape.

STEP 4 List the number of trapezoids and the number of sides in the table below. Describe the pattern.

____

____

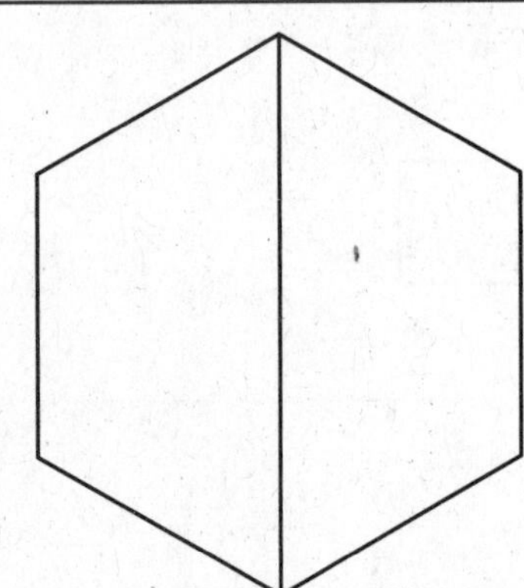

Trapezoids	Sides
1	4
2	6
3	
4	

- What if you traced and combined 7 trapezoid pattern blocks? How many sides will there be? How do you know?

____

____

Math Talk **Explain** how you know your description is correct.

Share and Show 

1. Here are 2 combined rhombuses. How many sides will 5 combined rhombuses have? _____

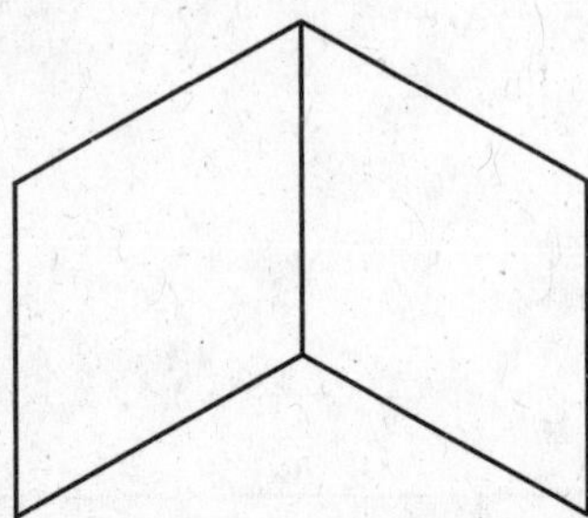

Rhombuses	Sides
1	
2	
3	
4	
5	

Name ______________________________

2. Write the pattern unit. Draw the next shape.

____

3. Describe the pattern. Draw the next shape.

____

Math Talk **Explain** how you know which is a growing pattern.

On Your Own

4. Write the pattern unit. Draw the next shape.

____

5. Describe the pattern. Draw the next shape.

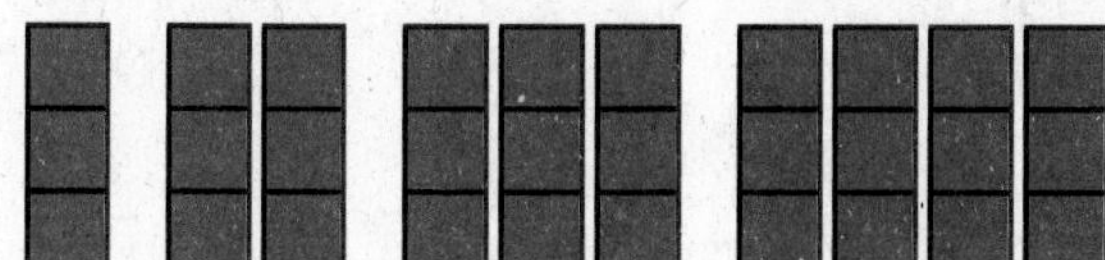

____

6.

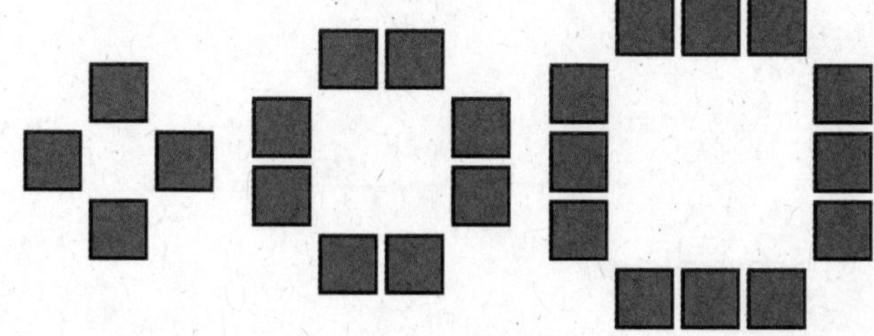

____

Problem Solving REAL WORLD

7. Tracy is looking for the missing shape in the pattern at the right.

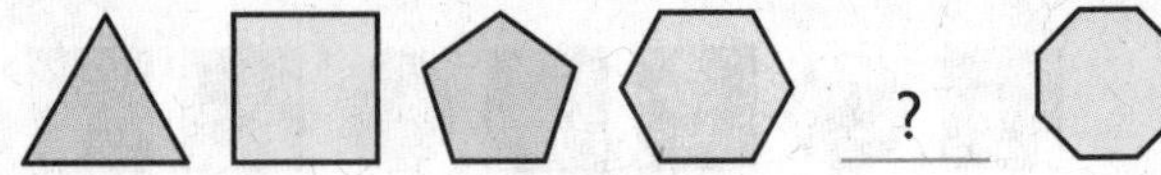

How many sides do each of the shapes have? ______

How many sides should the missing shape have? ______

How many sides will the tenth shape have? ______

Explain how you know. ______

______

8. H.O.T. On your MathBoard, trace a hexagon pattern block and write the number of sides. Right beside the first hexagon, trace three more hexagons and count and record the number of sides after each one. What is the total number of sides for the four combined hexagons? How can you describe the pattern?

______

SHOW YOUR WORK

9. Write Math Draw a pattern below. **Explain** whether your pattern is repeating or growing.

10. **Test Prep** What is a rule for the pattern below?

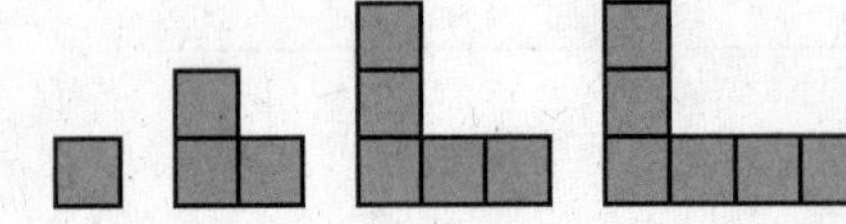

Ⓐ Add 3 squares.

Ⓑ Add 2 squares.

Ⓒ Add 1 square.

Ⓓ Subtract 1 square.

FOR MORE PRACTICE:
Florida Benchmarks Practice Book, pp. P235–P236

Name ______________________

Transform Plane Shapes

Essential Question How can you transform combined plane shapes to make new shapes?

MA.3.G.3.2 Compose, decompose, and transform polygons to make other polygons, including concave and convex polygons with three, four, five, six, eight, or ten sides.

CONNECT You have learned to combine plane shapes and take them apart to make new shapes.

How can you combine shapes in different ways to make new shapes?

Activity 1 **Materials** ■ pattern blocks ■ paper

STEP 1 Combine a trapezoid and a triangle pattern block without overlapping. Trace the shape and record the number of sides in the new shape.

______ sides

STEP 2 Now, move the triangle to a different position. Trace the shape and record the number of sides in the new shape

______ sides

Try This! Choose two more pattern blocks to combine in different ways. Trace them below. What do you notice about the number of sides?

In the next activity, you will separate a pattern block shape. Then you will move the shapes to different positions to make new shapes.

Activity 2 **Materials** ■ pattern blocks ■ paper ■ scissors

STEP 1 Trace a trapezoid pattern block on a sheet of paper. Draw a diagonal. Cut out the trapezoid and also cut along the diagonal. What are the names of the new shapes you have?

____

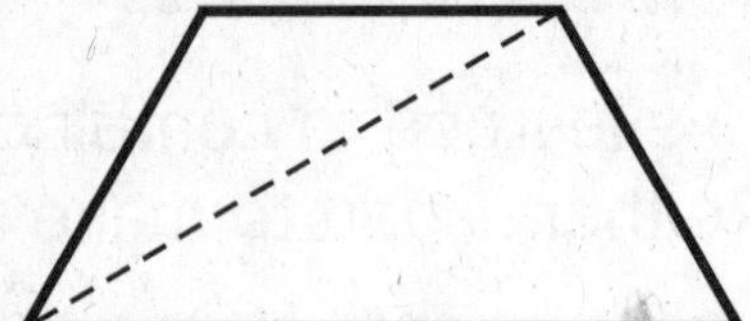

STEP 2 Move the triangles to different positions. Trace the new shape and record the number of sides.

____

STEP 3 Now, show a different way to combine the triangles. Trace the new shape and record the number of sides.

____

STEP 4 Choose another pattern block and trace it. Draw a diagonal and cut out the shapes. Move the shapes to different positions and trace the new shape.

Math Talk Since you can't draw a diagonal in a triangle, **explain** how you can separate it another way.

Name ______________________________

Share and Show 

1. Show another way you can combine a trapezoid pattern block and a triangle pattern block that is different than what you did on page 429. Write the number of sides.

____

Combine the pattern blocks two ways. Trace the shapes below and write the number of sides for each new shape.

2. trapezoid and square

3. rhombus and trapezoid

On Your Own

4. Choose two other pattern blocks. Combine them and trace the new shape below. Write the number of sides for the new shape.

Problem Solving REAL WORLD

Use pattern blocks to solve.

5. Julia traced a square pattern block and drew a diagonal. She cut out the square and cut along the diagonal. She moved one shape to a new position. What shape could she have made?

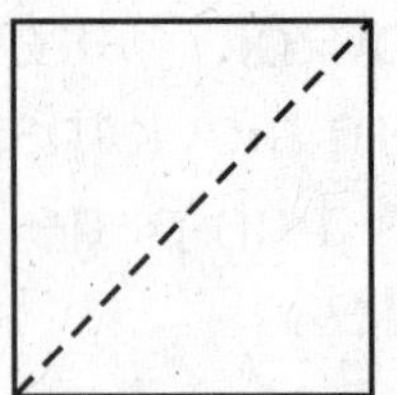

____

6. Is there more than one way you can combine a triangle pattern block and a square pattern block? Draw a quick picture to explain your answer.

____

____

7. H.O.T. To make the shape at the right, Jack cut a pattern block shape along the diagonal. Then he moved one part to a new position. Which pattern block did Jack start with?

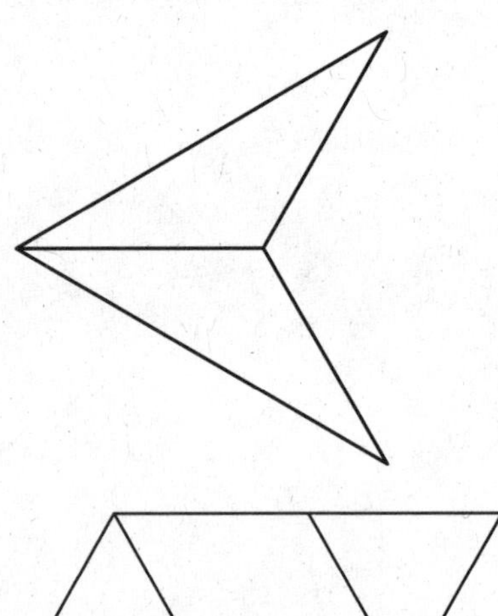

____

8. Look at the parallelogram at the right. Name the shapes you can make if you cut off one triangle and move it to a different position. Draw one new shape.

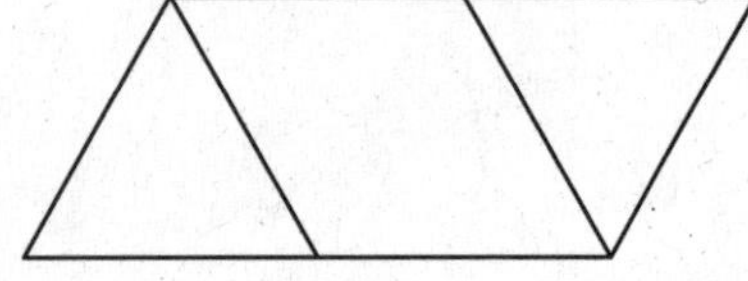

____

9. **Test Prep** Ethan drew a diagonal in a regular hexagon and cut along it to make two new shapes that were the same size and shape. What shapes did Ethan make?

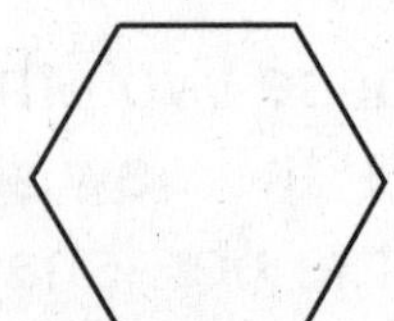

Ⓐ 2 rectangles
Ⓑ 2 trapezoids
Ⓒ 2 parallelograms
Ⓓ 2 triangles

FOR MORE PRACTICE:
Florida Benchmarks Practice Book, pp. P237–P238

Name ______________________________

Mid-Chapter Checkpoint

▶ Check Vocabulary

Choose the best term from the box.

Vocabulary
diagonal
growing pattern
pattern unit
repeating pattern

1. A ____________________ is a line segment that connects two vertices of a polygon that are not next to each other. **(MA.3.G.3.2; p. 422)**

2. A ____________________ is the part of the pattern that repeats. **(MA.3.A.4.1; p. 425)**

3. In a ____________________, the number or figure increases by the same amount each time. **(MA.3.A.4.1; p. 425)**

▶ Check Concepts

What pattern blocks can be combined to make the shape? Trace the blocks you used. **(MA.3.G.3.2; pp. 417–420)**

4. 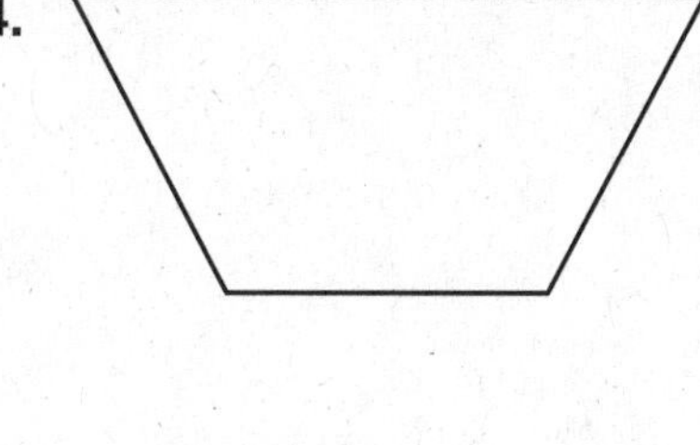

____

5. 

____

Write the pattern unit or describe the pattern. Draw the next shape. **(MA.3.A.4.1; pp. 425–428)**

6. 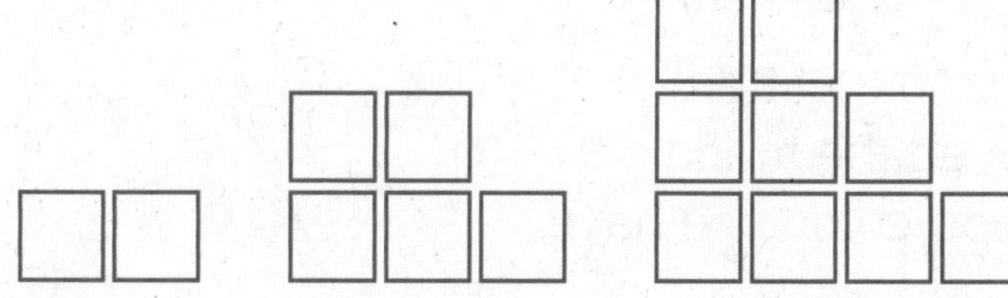

____

Fill in the bubble for the correct answer choice.

7. Morgan traced a square pattern block. She drew a diagonal and cut along it. Which shape does she have?

Ⓐ 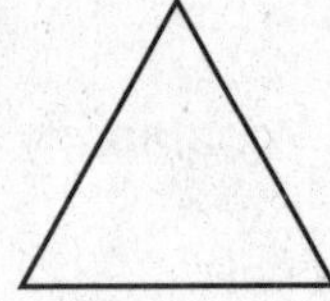

Ⓒ 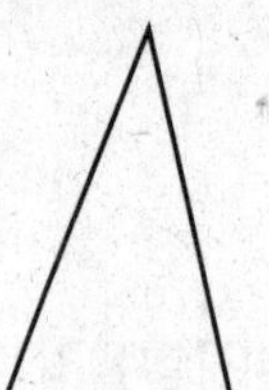

Ⓑ 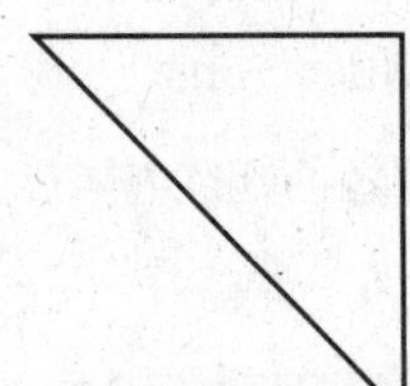

Ⓓ 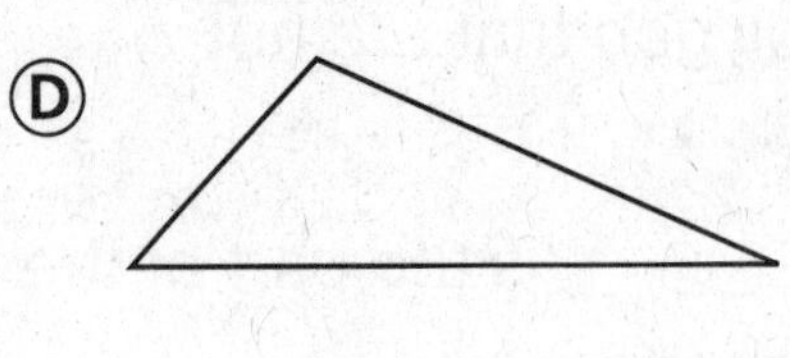

8. Which pattern block shapes are you NOT able to combine to make a hexagon?

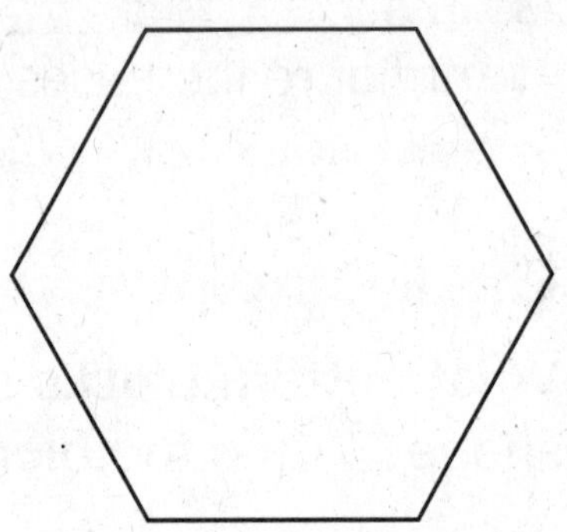

Ⓕ 6 triangles

Ⓖ 3 rhombuses

Ⓗ 2 squares

Ⓘ 2 trapezoids

9. Nick made the tile pattern below. What is a rule for his pattern?

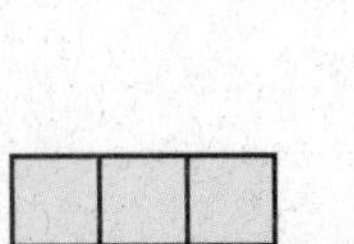
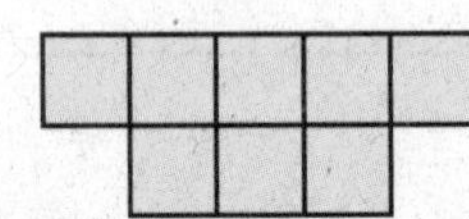
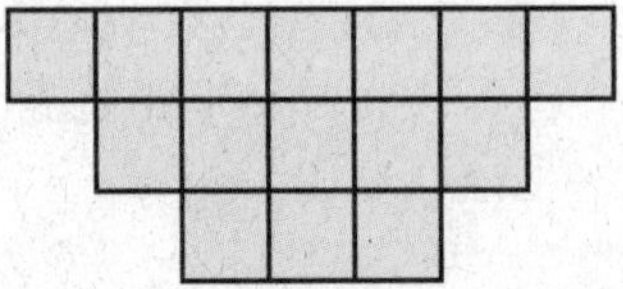

Ⓐ Add 1 row with 1 more tile.

Ⓑ Add 1 row with 2 more tiles.

Ⓒ Add 1 row with 3 more tiles.

Ⓓ Add 1 row with 4 more tiles.

10. Brittany combined trapezoid and triangle pattern blocks to make this shape. She moved the triangle to a different position. Which new shape could she have made?

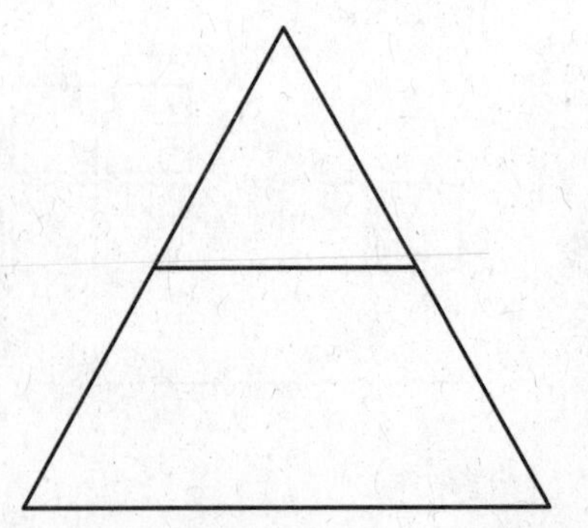

Ⓕ rectangle

Ⓖ square

Ⓗ parallelogram

Ⓘ hexagon

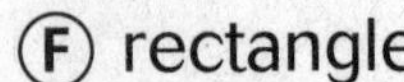

Name ____________________________

Identify Congruent Shapes

Essential Question How can you identify two-dimensional congruent shapes?

MA.3.G.3.3 Build, draw and analyze two-dimensional shapes from several orientations in order to examine and apply congruence and symmetry.

UNLOCK the Problem REAL WORLD

Shapes that have the same size and the same shape are **congruent**.

Look at the traffic signs at the right. Do the signs appear to be congruent?

Compare size and shape.

These pairs of shapes appear to be congruent.

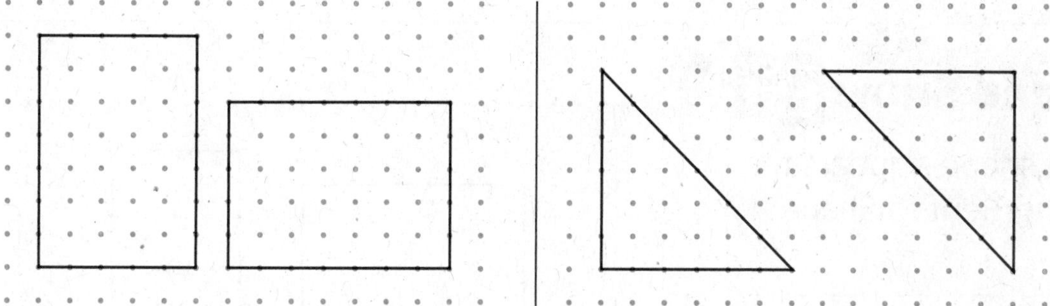

Same size, same shape

These pairs of shapes are not congruent.

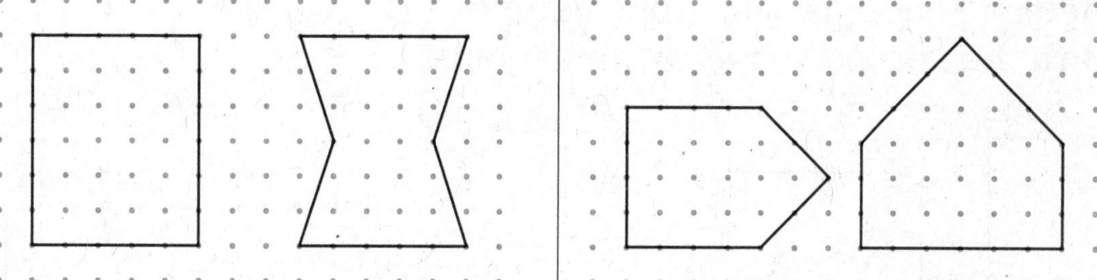

Same size, not the same shape

Same shape, not the same size

The traffic signs appear to be the same __________

and the same __________. So, they are __________.

Activity Materials ■ pattern blocks ■ paper

Trace pattern blocks to find congruent shapes.

STEP 1 Choose a pattern block. Trace the block in the space below.

STEP 2 Now, trace the same block again.

STEP 3 Compare the tracings you made.
Are the outlines the same size and shape? ___________

- Are the shapes you traced congruent? **Explain.**

____

Share and Show

1. Which shape appears to be congruent to Shape *A*?

____

Think: Which quadrilateral is the same size and shape?

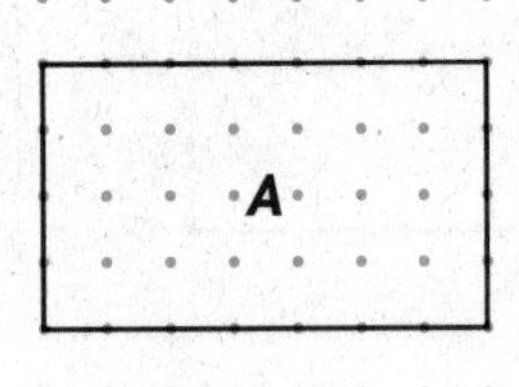

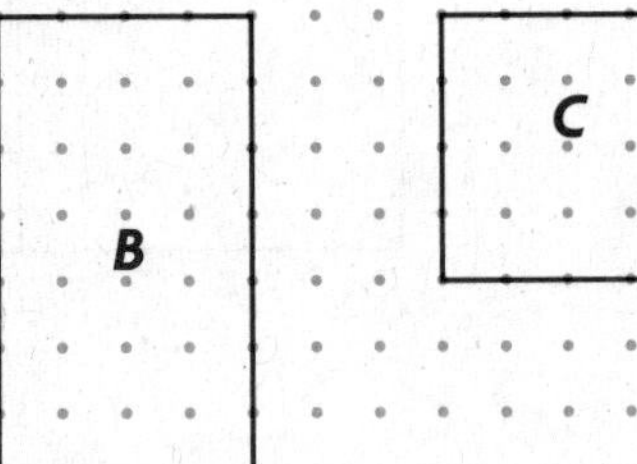

Look at the first shape. Tell if it appears to be congruent to the second shape. Write *yes* or *no*.

2.

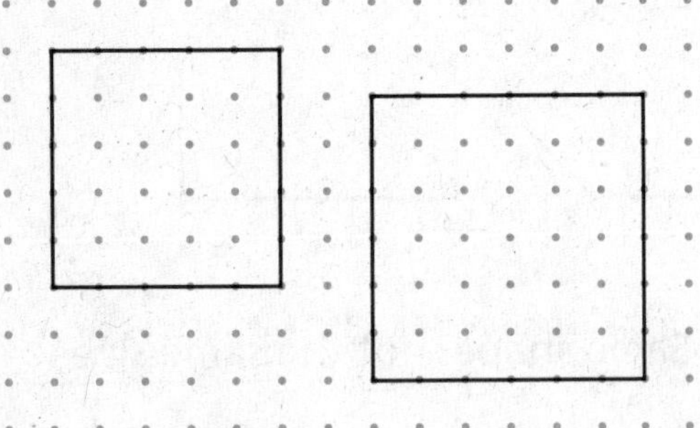

____

3.

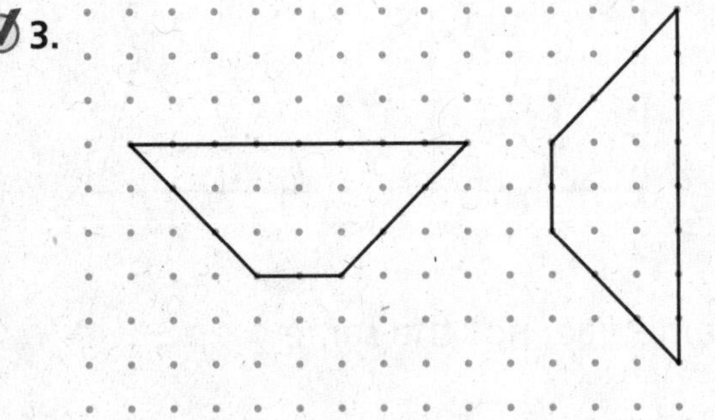

____

Math Talk **Explain** why the shapes in Exercise 3 may not appear to be congruent.

Name ______________________________

On Your Own

Look at the first shape. Tell if it appears to be congruent to the second shape. Write *yes* or *no*.

4.

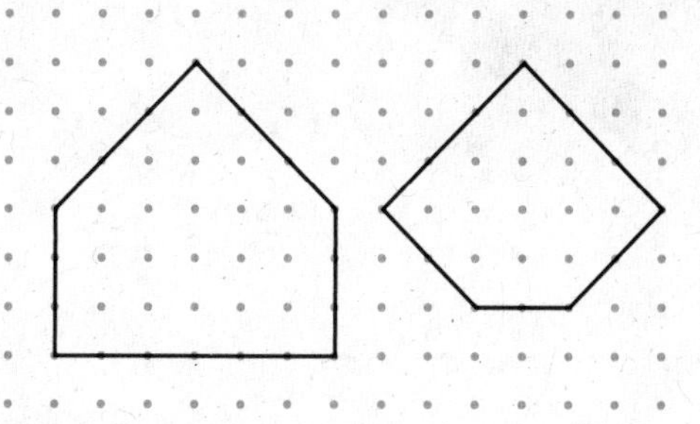

____

5.

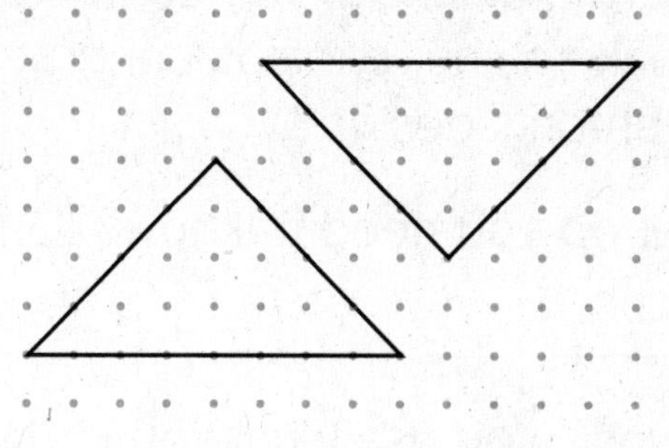

____

Solve.

6. H.O.T. What two congruent shapes can you combine to make a regular hexagon?

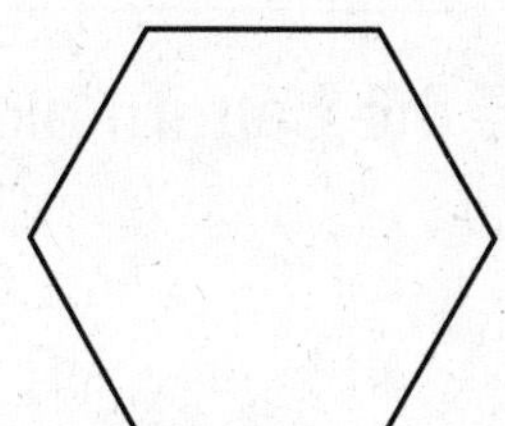

____

7. The lengths of three sides of a rectangle are 1 inch, 3 inches, and 1 inch. What is the length of the fourth side?

____

8. Write Math **What's the Error?** Isabel says that all circles are congruent. **Explain** her error.

____

____

9. **Test Prep** Which shapes appear to be congruent?

Ⓐ *W* and *X*

Ⓑ *X* and *Y*

Ⓒ *X* and *Z*

Ⓓ *W* and *Z*

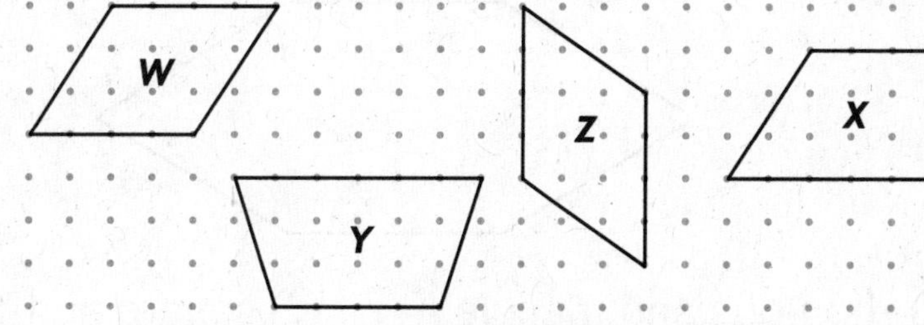

UNLOCK the Problem REAL WORLD

10. Ashton made the design at the right with pattern blocks. Which pattern blocks can you combine to make a shape that is congruent to Ashton's design?

a. What do you need to know? ______________________________

____

b. How will you use what you know about congruence to help you solve the problem? ______________________________

____

c. Trace the pattern blocks you used.

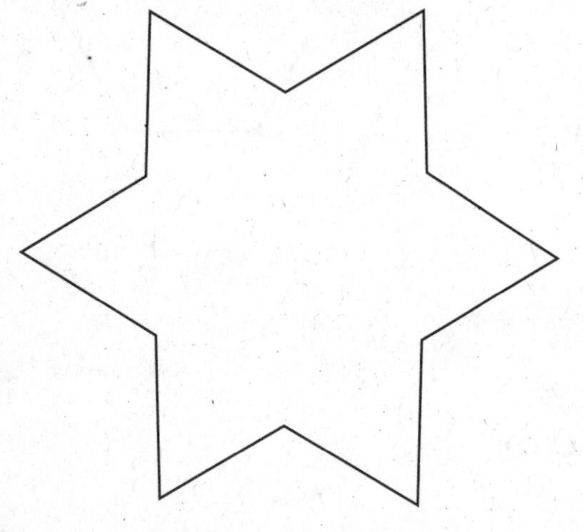

d. Complete the sentences.
Ashton's design is made up of

____ ______________,

____ ______________, and

____ ______________.

One way to make a shape that is congruent is to use

____

____

11. Test Prep Which pattern blocks can you combine to make a shape that is congruent to the shape below?

Ⓐ rhombus and triangle
Ⓑ trapezoid and rhombus
Ⓒ square and 2 triangles
Ⓓ rhombus and square

FOR MORE PRACTICE:
Florida Benchmarks Practice Book, pp. P239–P240

Name ____________________________________

Draw Congruent Shapes

Essential Question How can you draw two-dimensional congruent shapes?

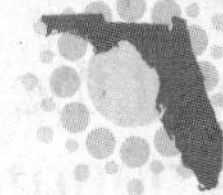

MA.3.G.3.3 Build, draw and analyze two-dimensional shapes from several orientations in order to examine and apply congruence and symmetry.

UNLOCK the Problem REAL WORLD

You know congruent shapes have the same size and the same shape.

Math Idea

On this dot paper, the space between two dots is one unit.

1 unit

1 unit

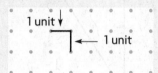

Activity Use dot paper to draw a congruent shape.

Materials ■ dot paper ■ ruler

STEP 1 Look at the rectangle. Count the number of units on each side.

STEP 2 Draw a congruent rectangle on dot paper.

Math Talk What other way can you draw a rectangle that is congruent to the rectangle in Step 1? **Explain.**

Share and Show 

1. Why do you need to count the number of units on each side to draw a congruent shape?

____

____

Use the dot paper. Draw a congruent shape.

2.

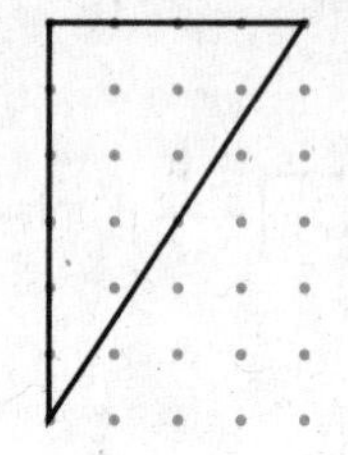

3.

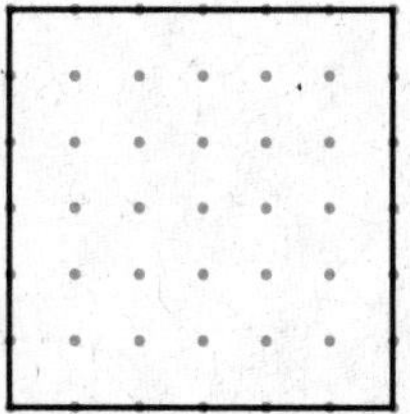

4.

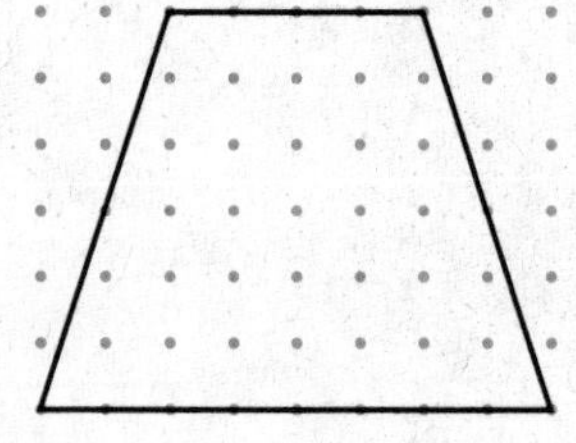

Math Talk If two quadrilaterals have line segments the same length, are the two shapes they form always congruent? **Explain.**

Name ___________________________________

On Your Own

Use the dot paper. Draw a congruent shape.

5.

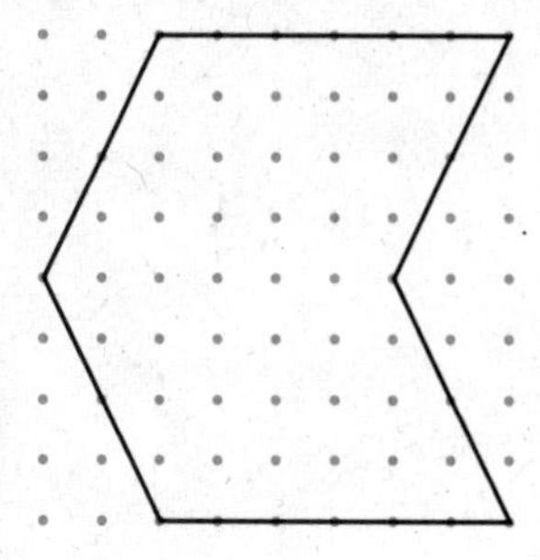

6.

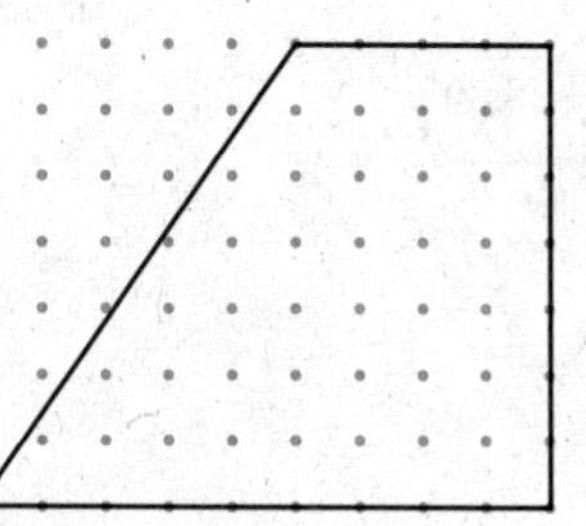

7.

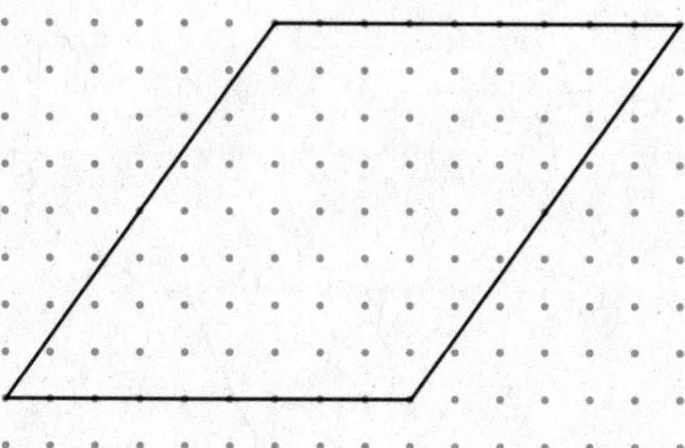

8.

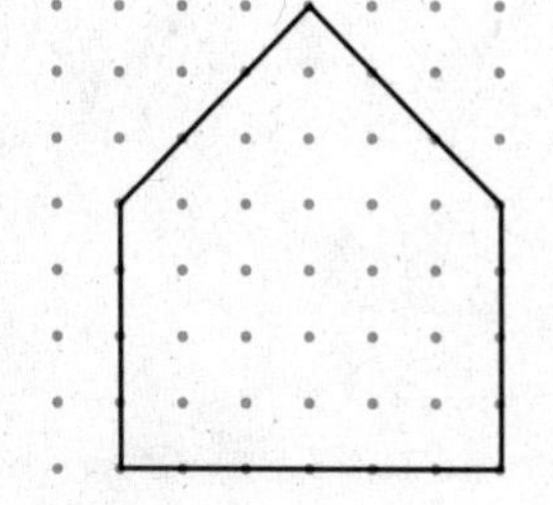

Problem Solving

9. Tanya drew the shape at the right. Draw a shape that is congruent to her shape but in a different position. Then draw a shape that is not congruent.

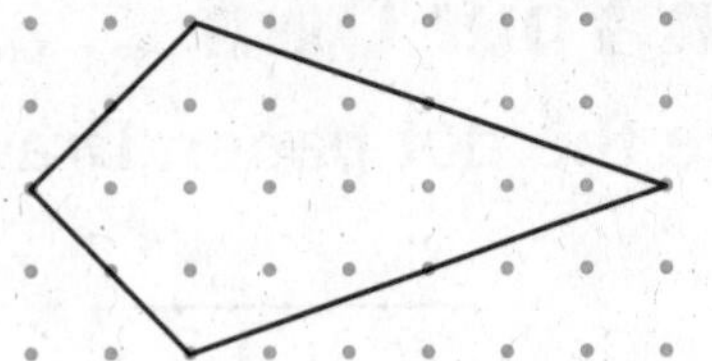

10. Write Math **What's the error?** Sam drew the triangles at the right and said they were congruent. Draw a shape that is congruent to Triangle *A* and **explain** Sam's error.

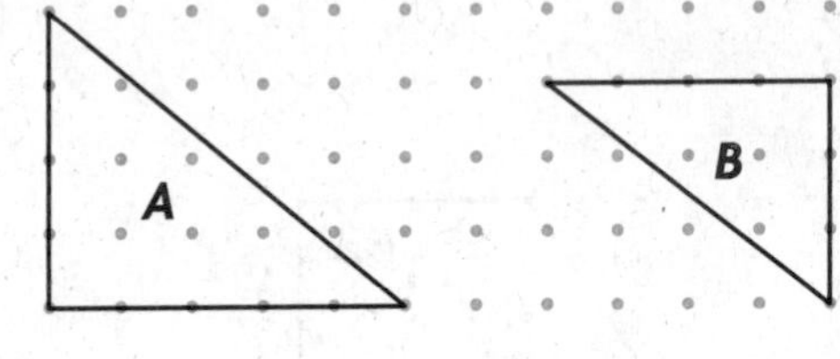

11. Test Prep Aaron drew a shape that is congruent to the one on the right. Which shape could he have drawn?

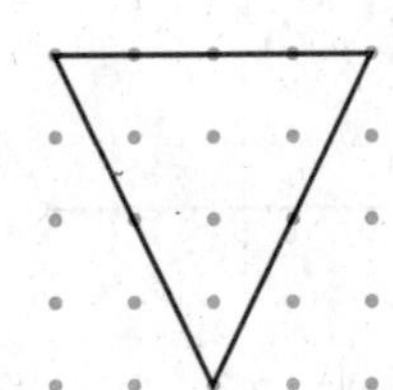

Ⓐ 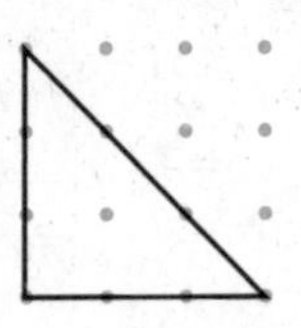

Ⓒ 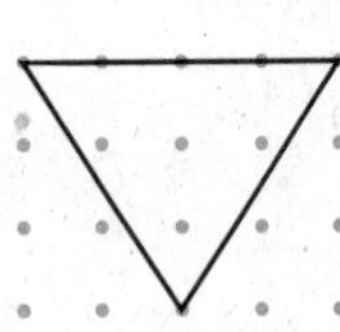

Ⓑ 

Ⓓ 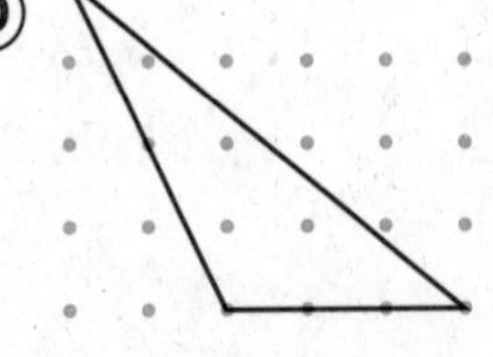

Name ____________________________________

Identify Symmetry

Essential Question How can you identify which two-dimensional shapes have symmetry?

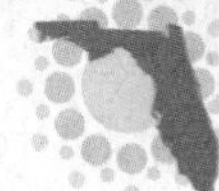

MA.3.G.3.3 Build, draw and analyze two-dimensional shapes from several orientations in order to examine and apply congruence and symmetry.

UNLOCK the Problem REAL WORLD

A shape has **symmetry** if it can be folded in half so that the halves match exactly.

A **line of symmetry** divides a shape into two congruent parts.

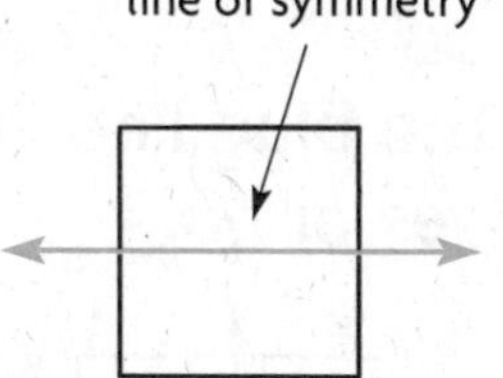

What shapes appear to have a line of symmetry?

These shapes appear to have a line of symmetry.

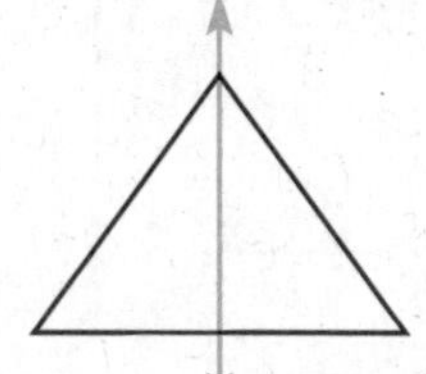
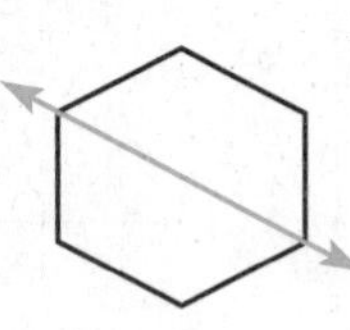
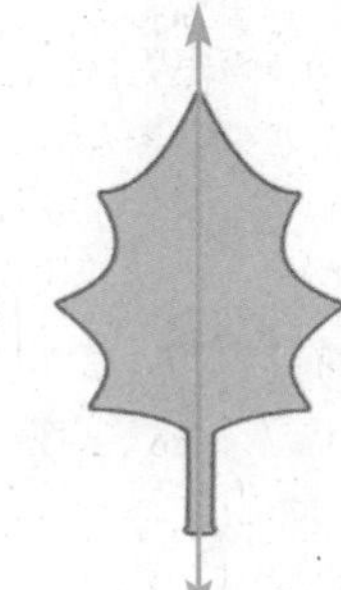

These shapes do not have a line of symmetry.

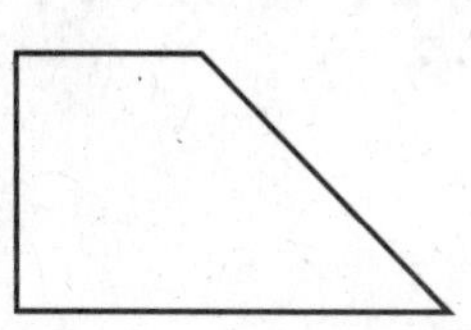
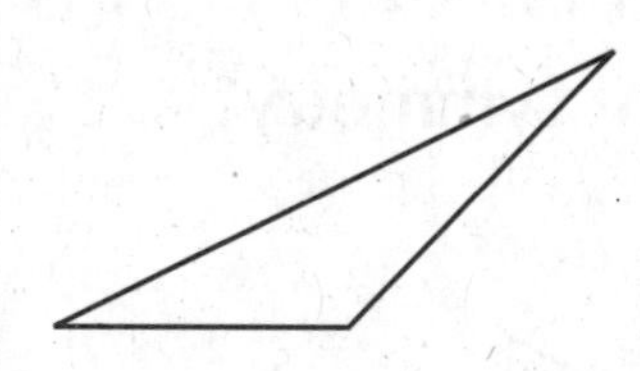

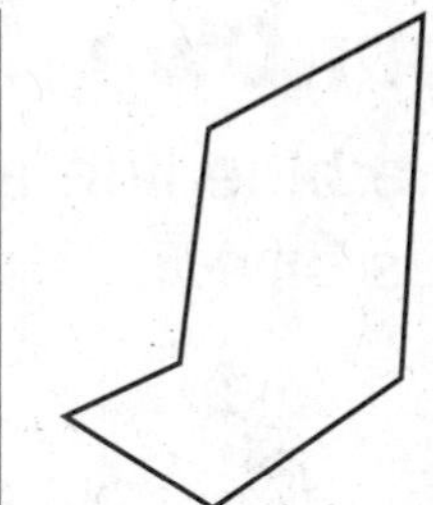

Activity Fold paper to explore symmetry.

Materials ■ paper ■ scissors ■ crayon or marker

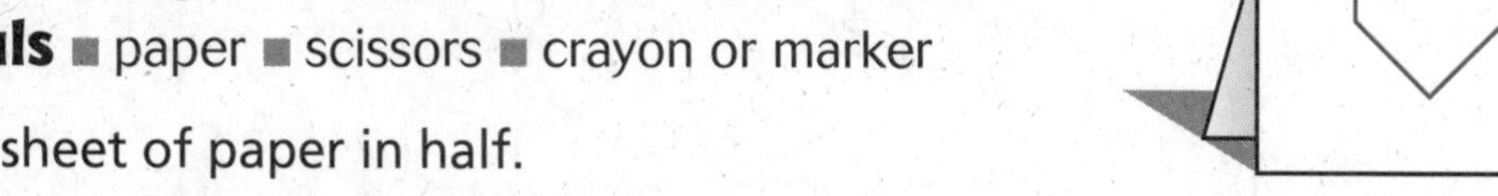

- Fold a sheet of paper in half.
- Draw a shape that begins and ends on the fold. Cut out the shape with the paper still folded.
- Unfold the shape and draw a line on the fold. The line on the fold is a line of symmetry.

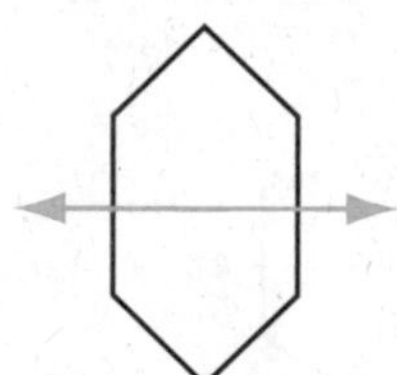

Share and Show 

1. Does the blue line appear to be a line of symmetry? **Explain** your answer.

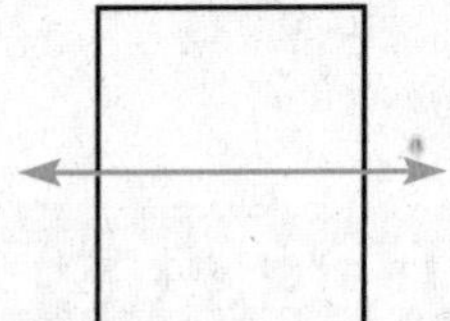

Does the blue line appear to be a line of symmetry? Write *yes* or *no*.

2. 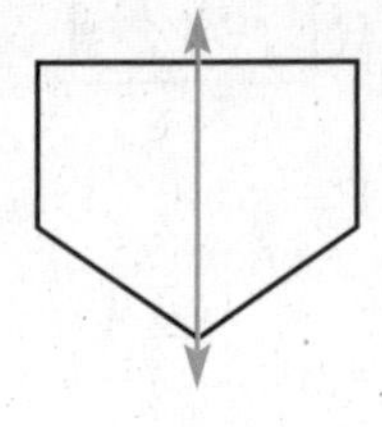

3. 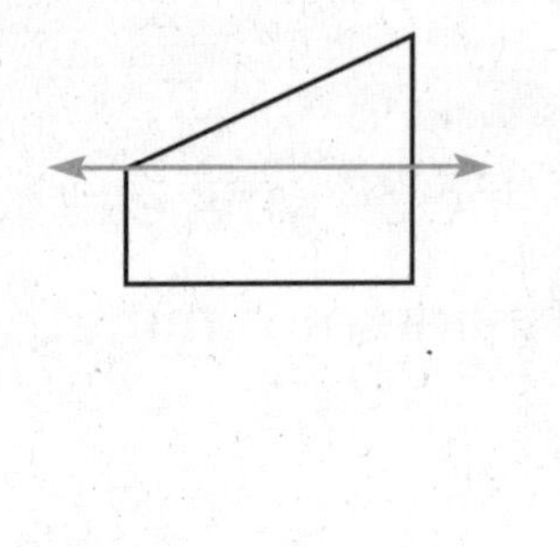

4. 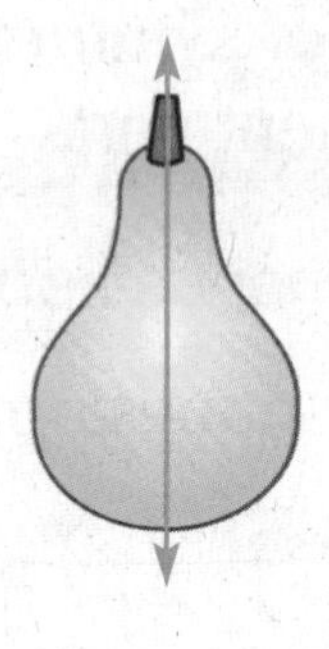

Math Talk **Explain** how you know the polygon in Exercise 3 does not have a line of symmetry.

On Your Own

Does the blue line appear to be a line of symmetry? Write *yes* or *no*.

5. 

6. 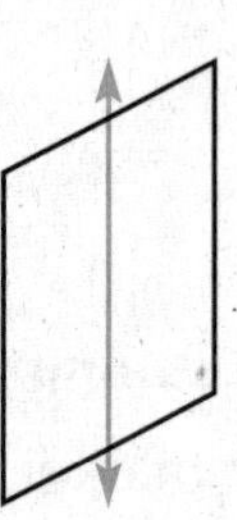

7. 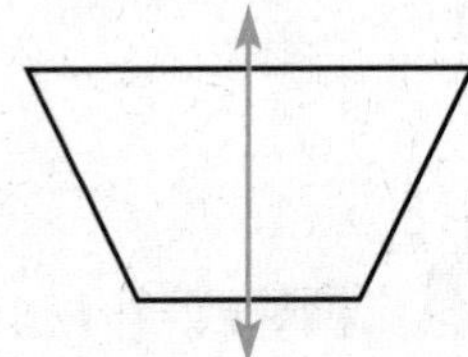

8. 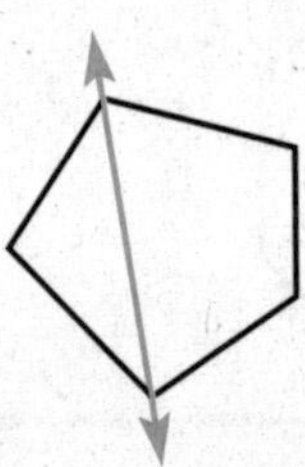

9. 

10. 

Name ___________________________

Problem Solving REAL WORLD

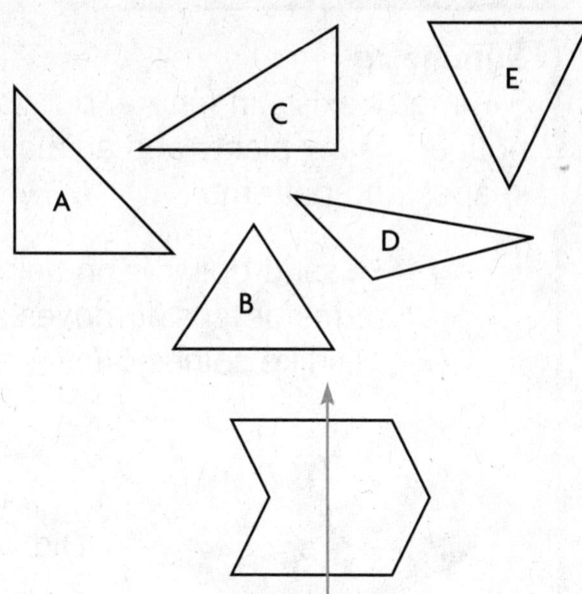

11. Michelle drew the triangles at the right. Which triangles appear to have a line of symmetry?

____

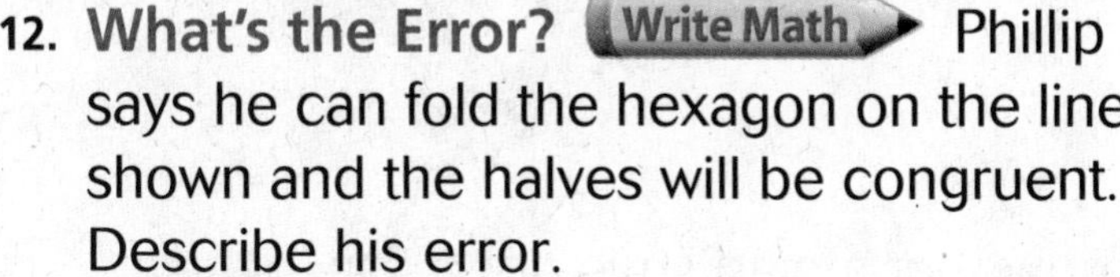

12. **What's the Error?** Write Math Phillip says he can fold the hexagon on the line shown and the halves will be congruent. Describe his error.

____

____

____

13. H.O.T. How could you finish this drawing so it has a line of symmetry?

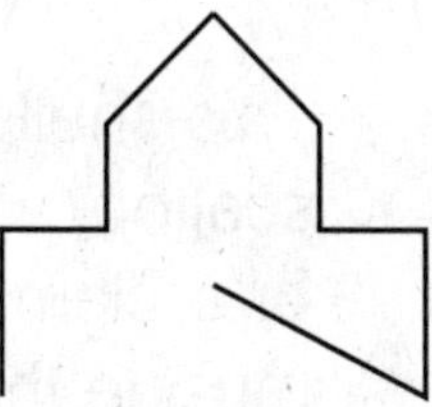

14. **Test Prep** Which shape appears to have a line of symmetry?

Ⓐ 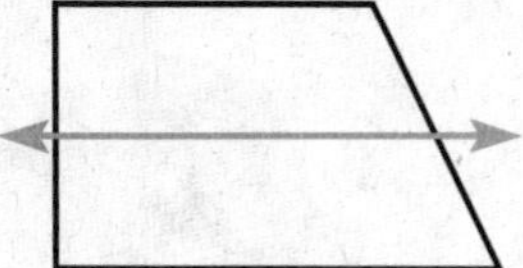

Ⓒ 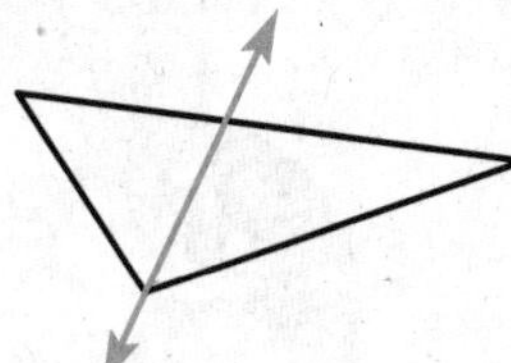

Ⓑ 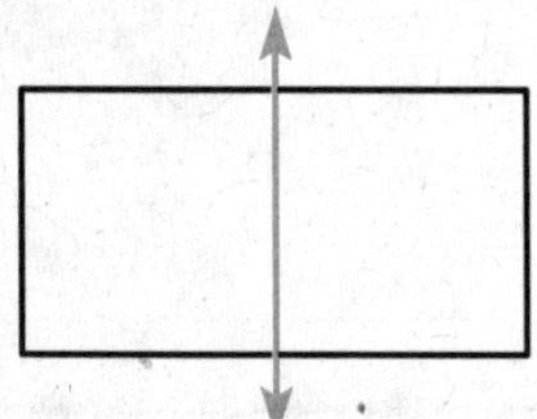

Ⓓ 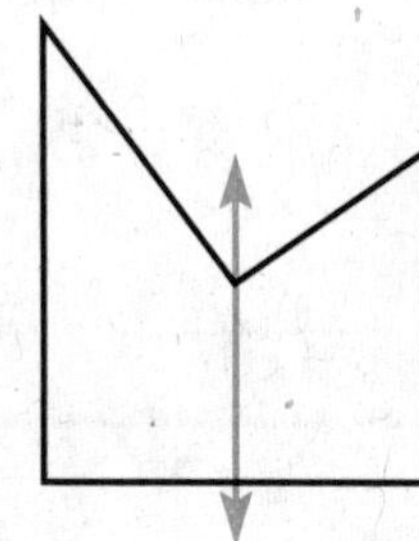

Connect to Science

Symmetry

Symmetry exists in nature, but you may not have noticed. Many plants and animals have symmetrical shapes and patterns.

A sand dollar is an animal that has no arms or legs. It moves around on tiny hairlike spines on its underside.

Did you know that a starfish is not a fish at all because it has no backbone? It uses tiny projections on the underside of its arms to move through the water.

This shell was once the home of a scallop, which is similar to an oyster or a clam. A scallop has a strong muscle that helps it swim.

Look at the objects below. Tell if the blue line appears to be a line of symmetry. Write *yes* or *no*.

15.

______

16.

______

17.

______

FOR MORE PRACTICE:
Florida Benchmarks Practice Book, pp. P243–P244

Name ______________________________

Lines of Symmetry

Essential Question Can you find more than 1 line of symmetry in some two-dimensional shapes?

MA.3.G.3.3 Build, draw and analyze two-dimensional shapes from several orientations in order to examine and apply congruence and symmetry.

UNLOCK the Problem

Some shapes appear to have 1 or more lines of symmetry. Some shapes have no lines of symmetry.

How many lines of symmetry does a square have?

Remember
A diagonal is a line segment that joins two vertices of a polygon that are not next to each other.

Activity

Materials ■ square shape

STEP 1 Fold a square in the middle of one pair of parallel sides. Do the parts match? __________

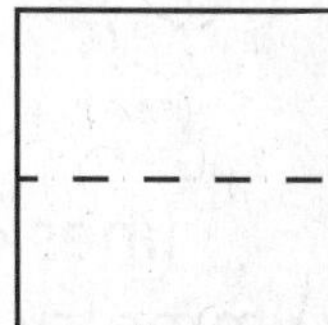

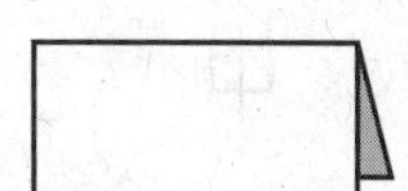

STEP 2 Fold the square in the middle of the other pair of parallel sides. Do the parts match? __________

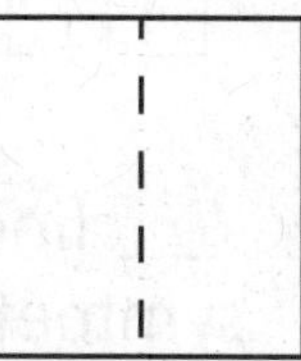

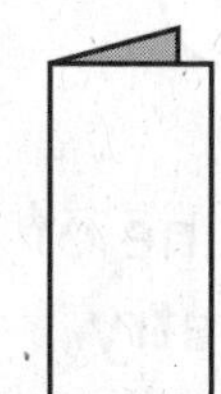

STEP 3 Fold the square along a diagonal. Do the parts match? __________

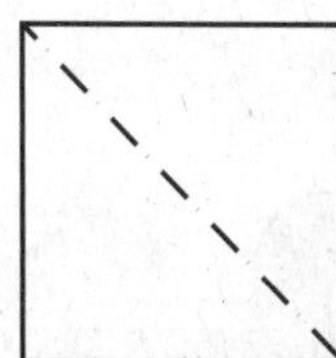

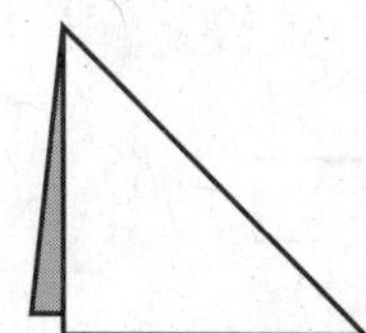

STEP 4 Fold the square along the other diagonal. Do the parts match? __________

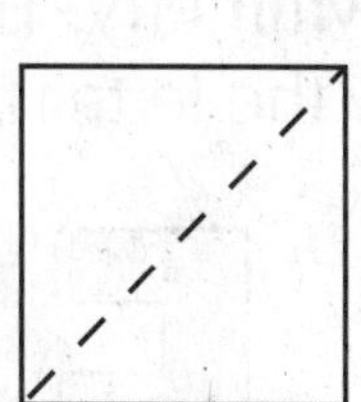

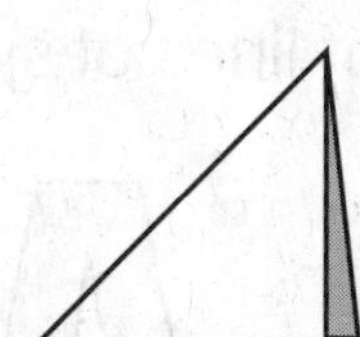

The square can be folded in the middle of both pairs of parallel sides. It can be folded along the diagonals. Since the parts match exactly, each fold is a line of

______________________________.

You have folded the square 4 different ways.

So, a square has _____ lines of symmetry.

Examples

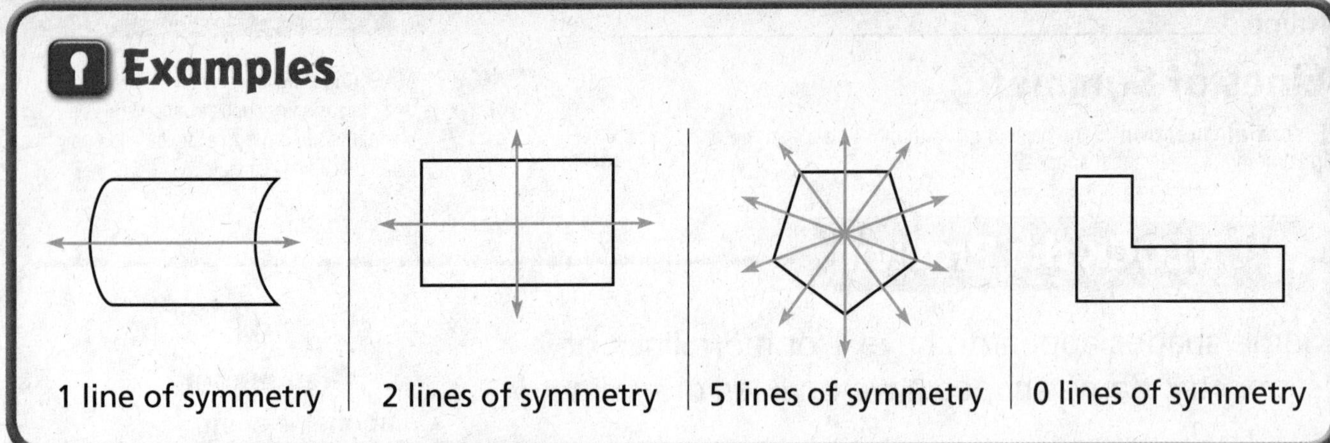

Try This! Some letters and numbers appear to have lines of symmetry.

Write the number of lines.

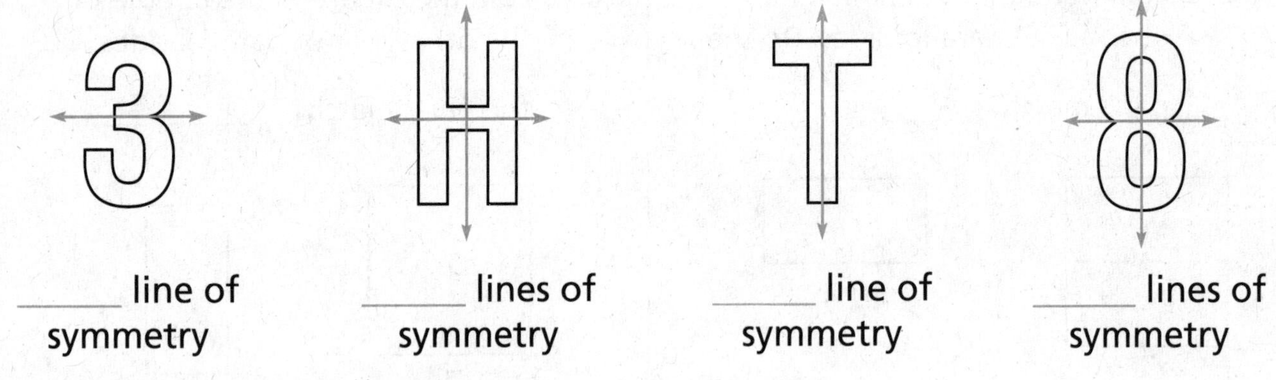

_____ line of symmetry

_____ lines of symmetry

_____ line of symmetry

_____ lines of symmetry

Share and Show 

1. These letters appear to have lines of symmetry. Draw the line or lines of symmetry. Then write the number of lines of symmetry the letter has.

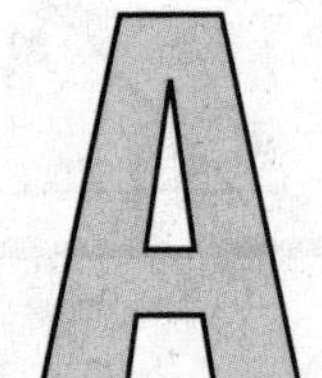

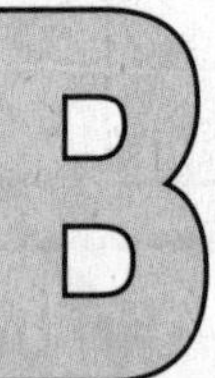

_____ _____ _____ _____

Name ___________________________

Draw the line or lines of symmetry. Then write the number of lines of symmetry the shape has.

2.

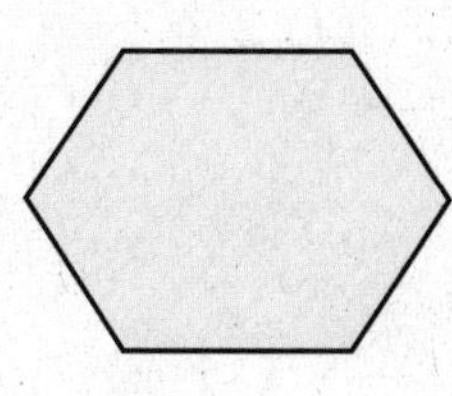

______

3.

______

4.

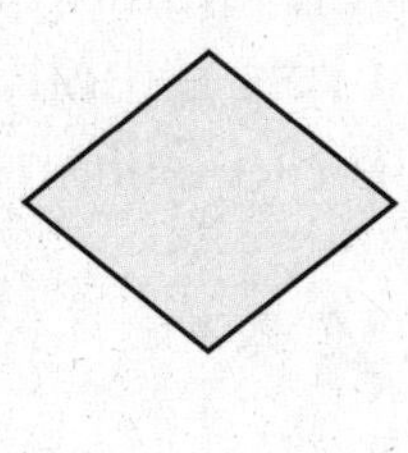

______

Math Talk **Explain** how you can find all the lines of symmetry in a rectangle.

On Your Own

Draw the line or lines of symmetry. Then write the number of lines of symmetry the shape has.

5.

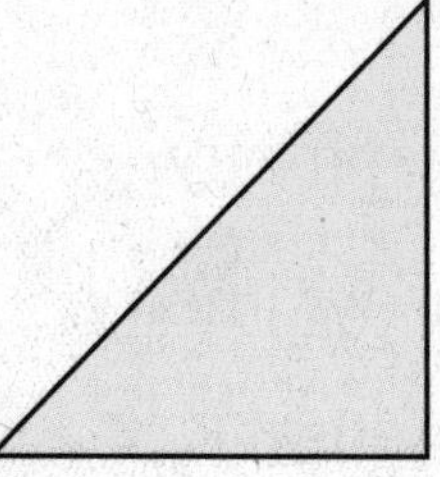

______

6.

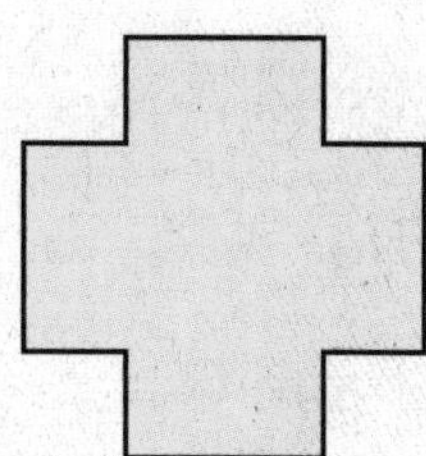

______

7.

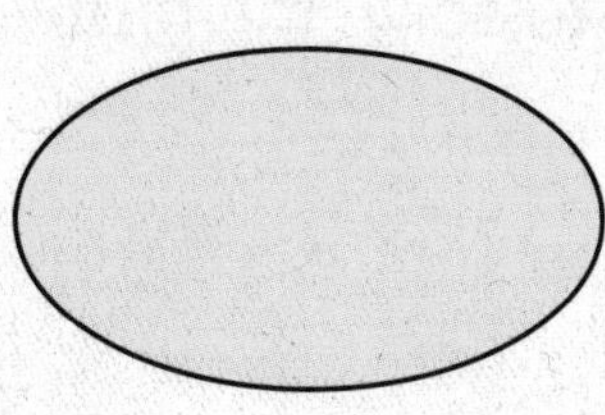

______

8.

______

9.

______

10.

______

UNLOCK the Problem

11. Gillian is making a book cover. She drew a shape on it that has exactly 2 lines of symmetry. Which shape did Gillian draw for the cover?

Ⓐ 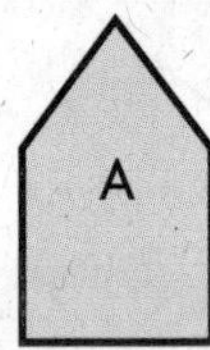

Ⓑ 

Ⓒ 

Ⓓ 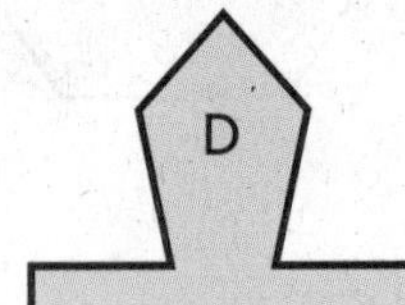

a. What do you need to know? ______________________________

b. How will you use what you know about symmetry

to help you solve the problem? ______________________________

____

____

c. Show the steps you use to solve the problem.

d. Complete the sentences.

Shape A has ____________ of symmetry.

The ____________ has 5 lines of symmetry.

Shape C has ____________ of symmetry.

____________ has 1 line of symmetry.

Gillian drew ____________ for the cover.

e. Fill in the bubble for the correct answer choice above.

12. How many lines of symmetry does this pentagon appear to have?

 Ⓕ 0

 Ⓖ 1

 Ⓗ 2

 Ⓘ 5

13. Which letters appear to have only 1 line of symmetry?

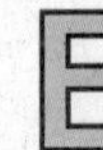

Ⓐ K and X
Ⓑ X and O
Ⓒ B and O
Ⓓ K and B

 FOR MORE PRACTICE:
Florida Benchmarks Practice Book, pp. P245–P246

Name ____________________________________

Draw Symmetric Shapes

Essential Question How can you draw two-dimensional shapes with a line of symmetry?

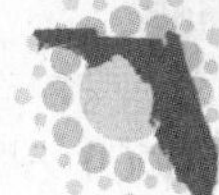

MA.3.G.3.3 Build, draw and analyze two-dimensional shapes from several orientations in order to examine and apply congruence and symmetry.

UNLOCK the Problem

CONNECT You have identified shapes that have 0, 1, or more than 1 line of symmetry. In this lesson, you will draw shapes that have 1 or more lines of symmetry.

Activity Use dot paper to draw shapes with a line of symmetry.

Materials ■ dot paper ■ ruler

STEP 1 Fold a sheet of dot paper in half, and draw any design that has a side on the fold.

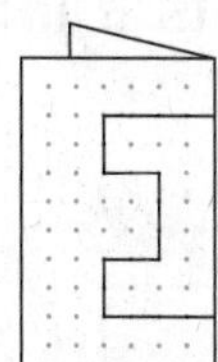

STEP 2 Unfold the paper, and complete the other half to make a shape with a line of symmetry along the fold.

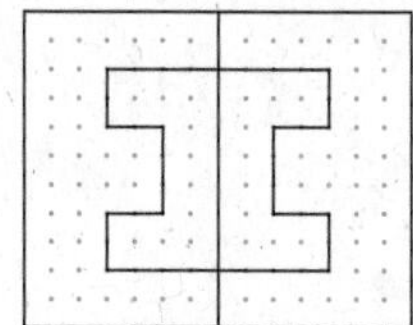

STEP 3 Draw the shape you made on the dot paper below.

- Does the shape you made have more than 1 line of symmetry? **Explain** how you can check. ____________________

____

Share and Show 

1. The dot paper shows half of a shape with a line of symmetry. Draw the other half of the shape.

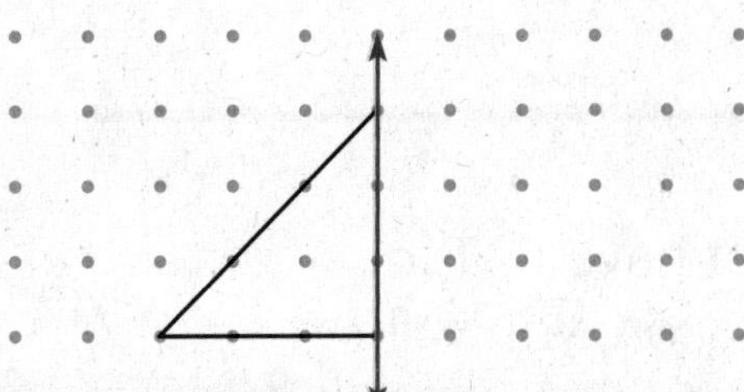

Half of each shape is drawn. Draw the other half so that the red line is a line of symmetry.

2.

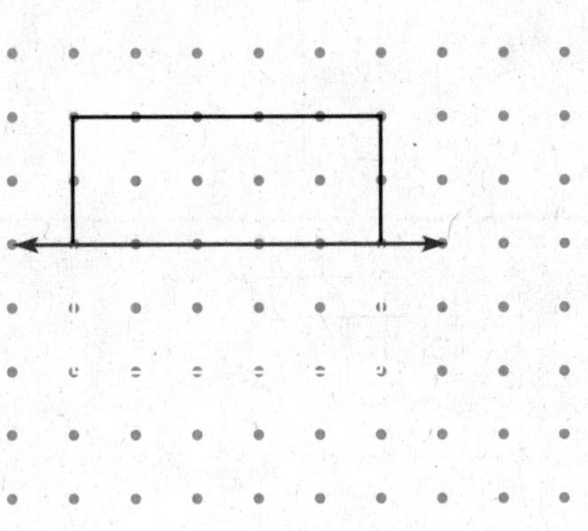

3.

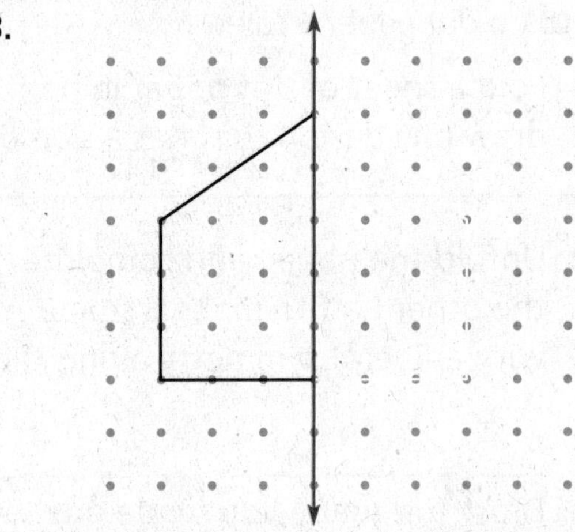

4.

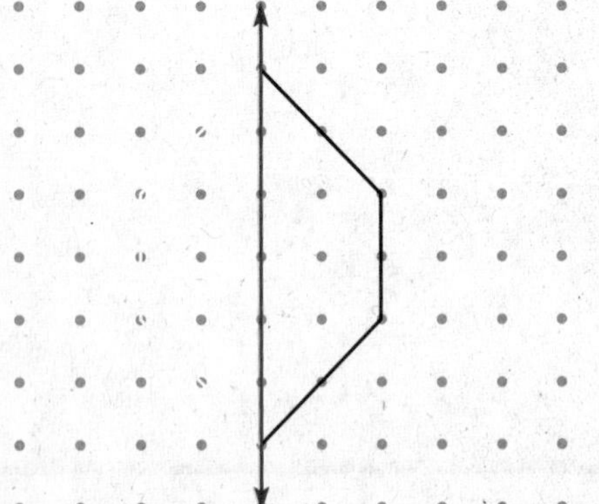

5.

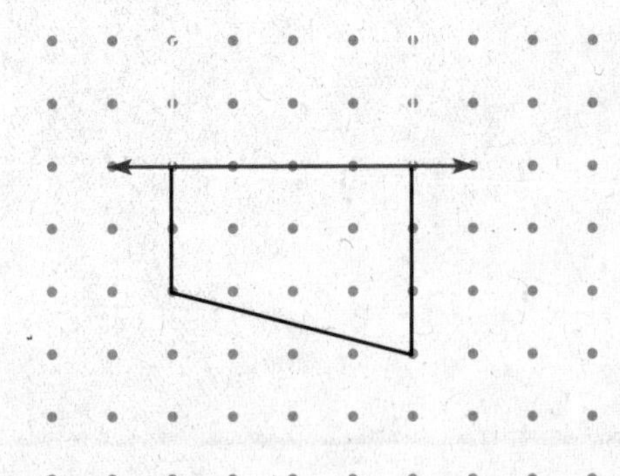

Math Talk **Explain** how you know the shape you drew in Exercise 5 has a line of symmetry.

Name ________________________________

On Your Own

Half of each shape is drawn. Draw the other half so that the red line is a line of symmetry.

6.

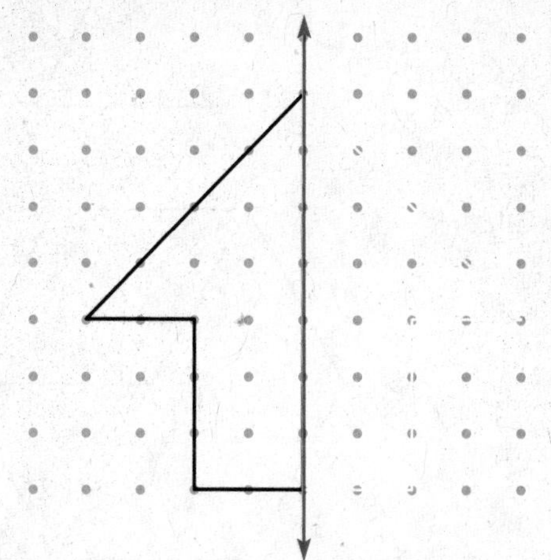

7.

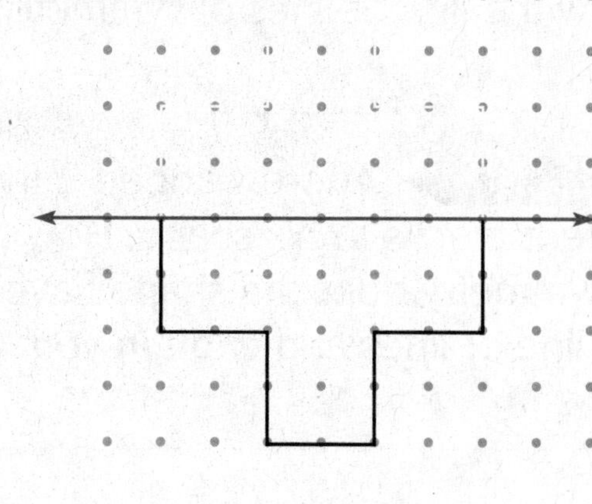

8.

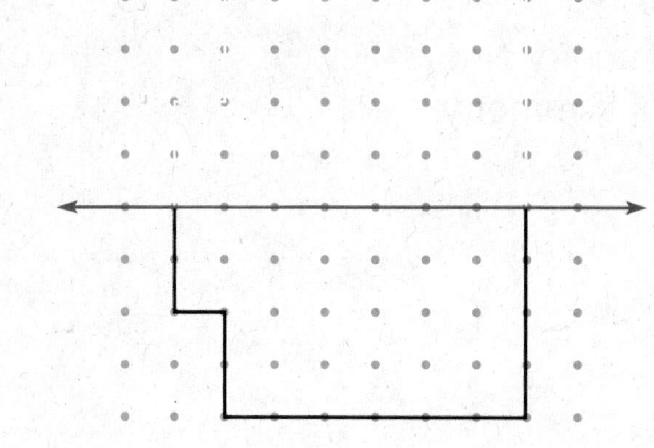

9.

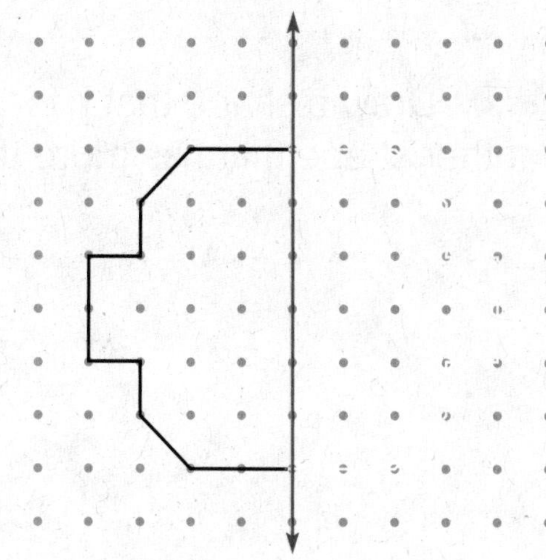

10.

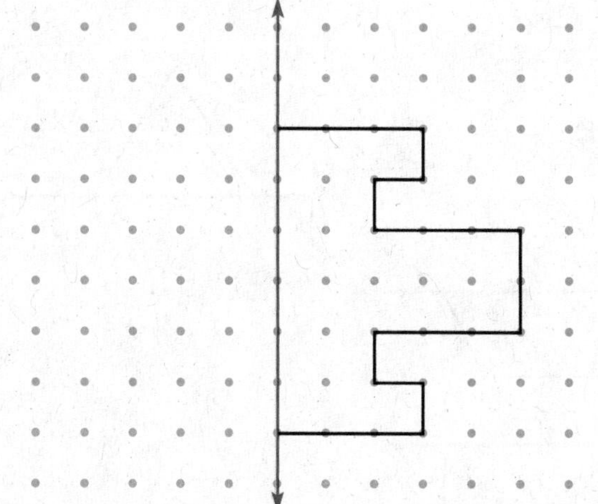

11.

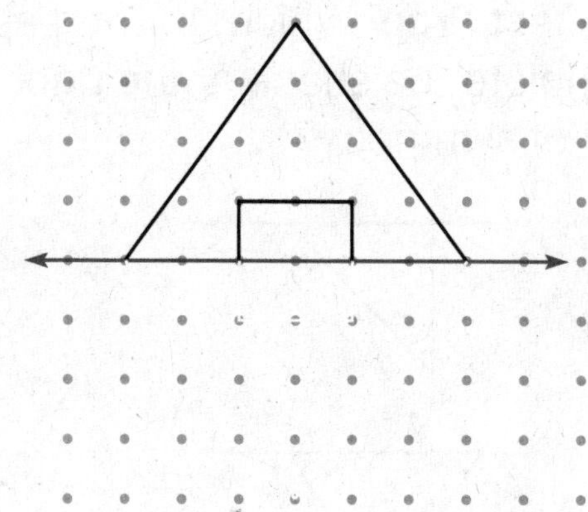

Problem Solving 

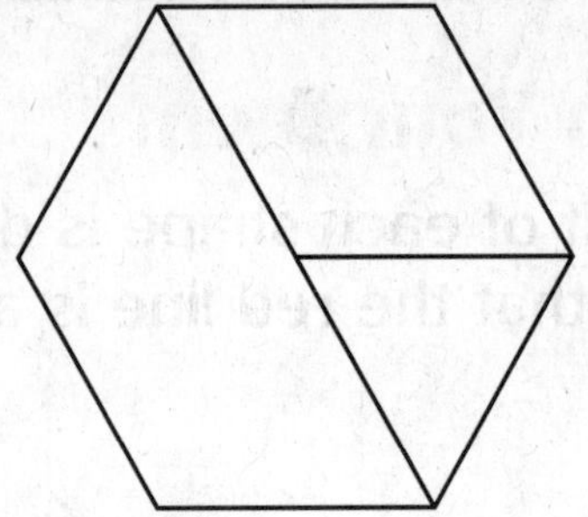

12. Andrew combined 3 pattern blocks to make the shape at the right. How many lines of symmetry does the shape appear to have? Draw the line or lines of symmetry.

____

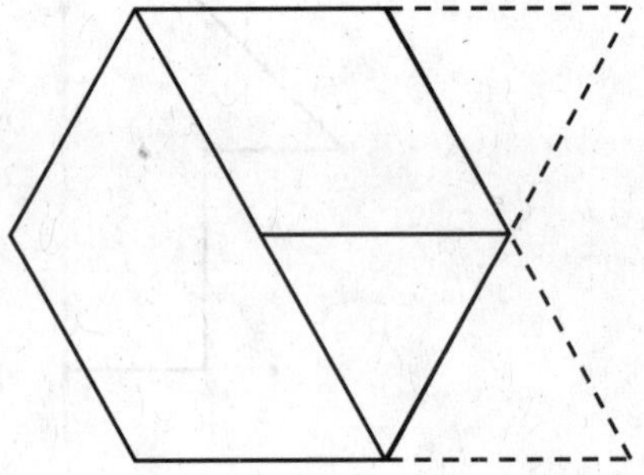

13. **Write Math** Andrew added 2 triangle pattern blocks to his shape. How many lines of symmetry does the shape have now? Draw the line or lines and **explain** your answer.

____

____

____

14. **H.O.T.** Draw a shape that has 1 line of symmetry and another shape that has more than 1 line of symmetry.

15. **Test Prep** Which drawing appears to complete the shape at the right across the line of symmetry?

Ⓐ 

Ⓒ 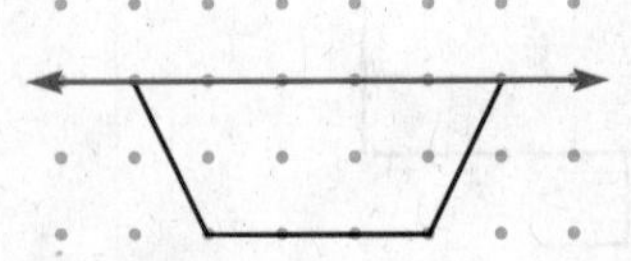

Ⓑ 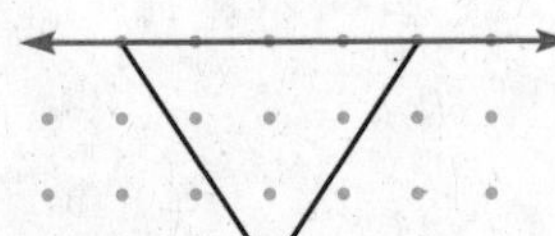

Ⓓ 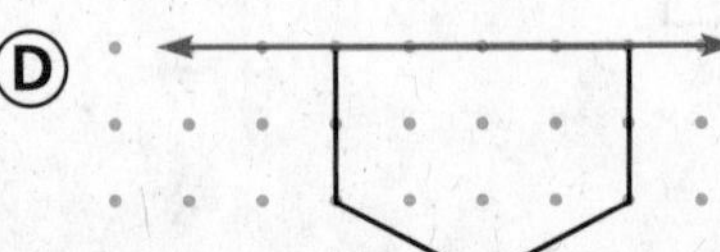

Name ______________________________

Draw a Diagram · Plane Shapes

Essential Question How can you solve problems by using the strategy draw a diagram?

MA.3.G.3.3 Build, draw and analyze two-dimensional shapes from several orientations in order to examine and apply congruence and symmetry.

UNLOCK the Problem REAL WORLD

Jenna combined and traced a square, a triangle, a trapezoid, and a blue rhombus on dot paper. She said that it was only half of the design she wanted to make. She challenged Scott to make the other half of the design so it has 2 lines of symmetry.

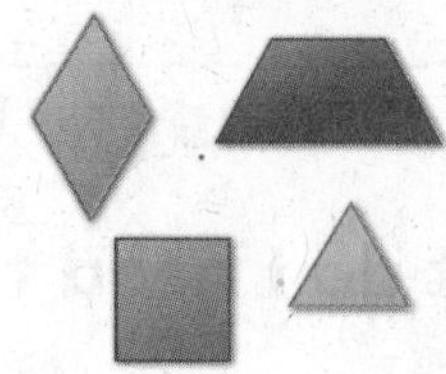

Read the Problem

What do I need to find?

how to draw the other half of the design so it has 2 lines of symmetry

What information do I need to use?

the square, triangle, trapezoid, and blue rhombus pattern block shapes

How will I use the information?

I will combine and trace the same pattern blocks on dot paper so that when the design is complete, it will have 2 lines of symmetry.

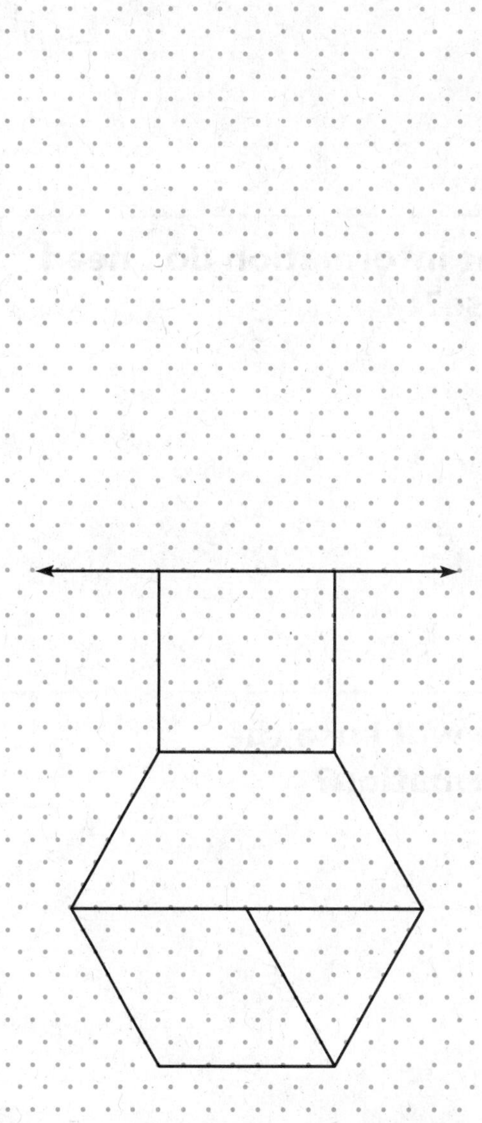

Solve the Problem

Try Another Problem

Cameron traced pattern blocks to make a design with 1 line of symmetry. The pattern blocks he used are a trapezoid, a square, and 2 triangles. How can you complete the design so it has 2 lines of symmetry?

Read the Problem	Solve the Problem
What do I need to find?	
What information do I need to use?	
How will I use the information?	

Name ______________________________

Share and Show 

1. Marlo traced 2 pattern blocks. What pattern blocks can you add so her design will have more than 1 line of symmetry?

   First, look at the picture.

   Think: What pattern block can you add so the design will have 1 line of symmetry?

   Add __________ pattern block.

   Draw the line of symmetry.

   Think: Now, what pattern blocks can you add so the design will have another line of symmetry?

   Add __________ pattern blocks.

   Last, draw the lines of symmetry.

   There are __________ lines of symmetry.

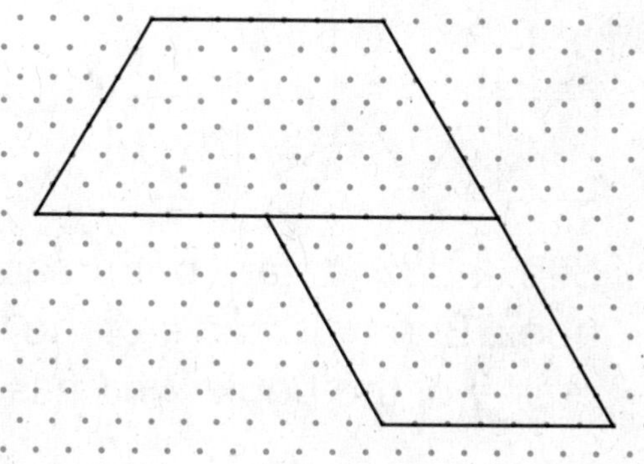

2. **What if** you add 1 square pattern block below the triangle on the bottom row? Will the design still have 3 lines of symmetry? **Explain.**

   ____

   ____

   ____

3. Add pattern blocks to the design at the right so it will have 4 lines of symmetry. Draw to show your answer. What blocks did you add?

   ____

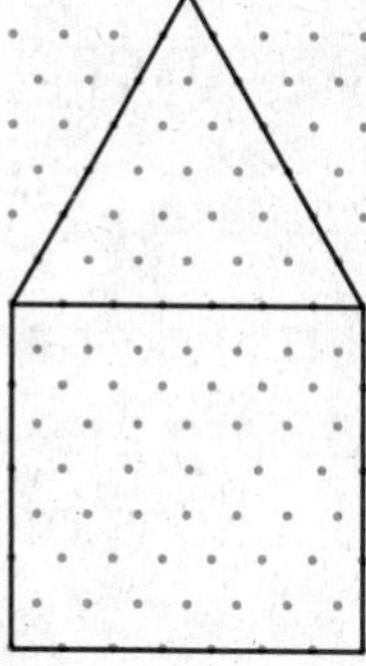

4. Draw all the lines of symmetry on the design in Problem 3.

On Your Own

Choose a STRATEGY

- Act It Out
- Use Manipulatives
- Draw a Diagram
- Make a Table, Chart, or List
- Search for Patterns

5. Lauren is younger than Alex and older than Lisa. Lisa is older than Fernando. List the children in order from youngest to oldest.

____

6. Brian is putting a border pattern around a birthday card. Draw the next two shapes in his pattern.

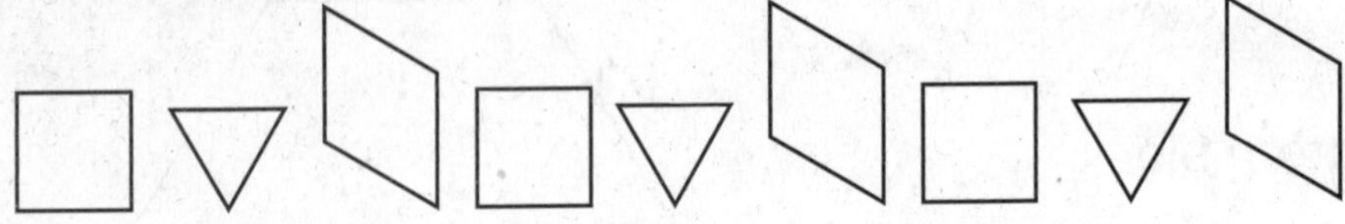

7. Ben and Marta are both reading the same book. Ben has read $\frac{2}{3}$ of the book. Marta has read $\frac{3}{4}$ of the book. Who has read more?

____

SHOW YOUR WORK

8. Helene is making a quilt with squares of fabric. There are 9 rows, with 8 squares in each row. How many squares of fabric are there in all?

____

9. There are 42 students from 6 different classes in the school spelling bee. Each class has the same number of students. How many students are from each class?

____

10. Kyle has a tan jacket and a blue jacket. His baseball caps are black, white, and blue. How many combinations of one jacket and one cap can he make?

____

FOR MORE PRACTICE:
Florida Benchmarks Practice Book, pp. P249–P250

Name ____________________

▶ Check Vocabulary

Choose the best term from the box.

Vocabulary
congruent
growing pattern
line of symmetry
repeating pattern
symmetry

1. A shape has ____________ if it can be folded along a line so that the two parts match exactly. (MA.3.G.3.3; p. 443)

2. A ____________ is a pattern in which the number or figure increases by the same amount each time. (MA.3.A.4.1; p. 425)

3. Shapes that have the same size and same shape are ____________. (MA.3.G.3.3; p. 435)

▶ Check Concepts

Look at the first shape. Tell if it appears to be congruent to the second shape. Write *yes* or *no*.
(MA.3.G.3.3; pp. 435–438)

4. 

____

5. 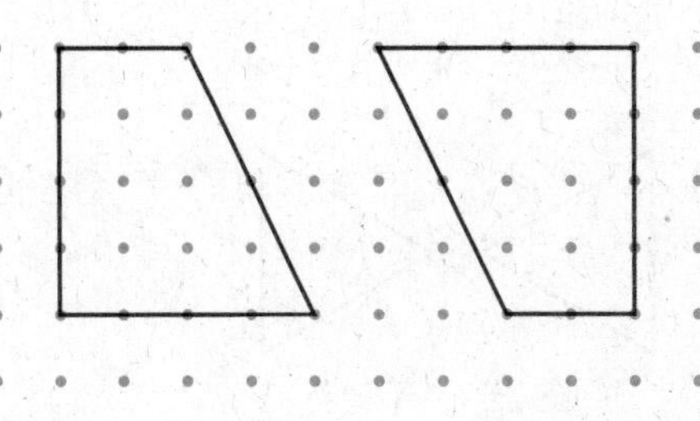

____

Does the blue line appear to be a line of symmetry? Write *yes* or *no*. (MA.3.G.3.3; pp. 443–446)

6. 

____

7. 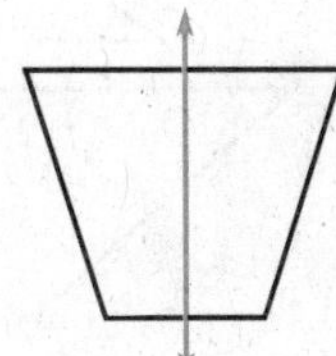

____

8. 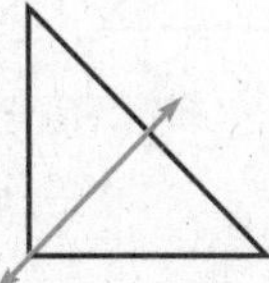

____

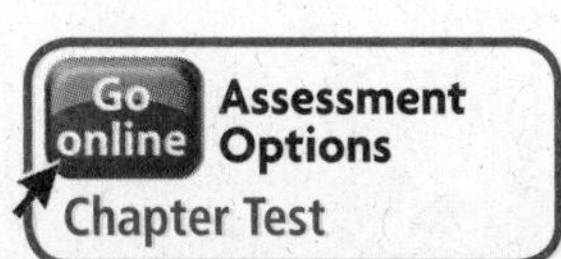

Fill in the bubble for the correct answer choice.

9. Parker combined and traced 2 pattern blocks to make this new shape at the right. Which pattern blocks did he use? (MA.3.G.3.2; pp. 417–420)

 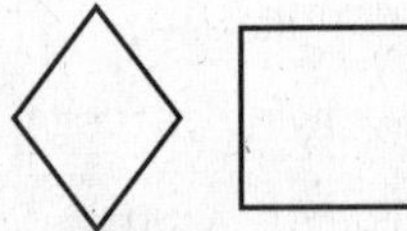

Ⓒ 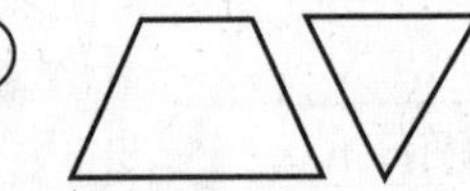

Ⓑ 

Ⓓ 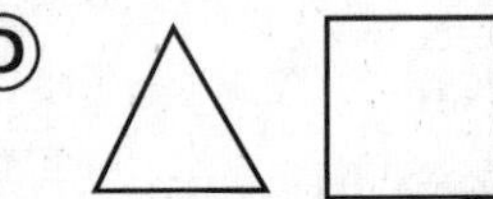

10. Deanna drew a diagonal in this rhombus. She cut out the rhombus and cut along the diagonal. Which of these could be the shapes Deanna now has? (MA.3.G.3.2; pp. 421–424)

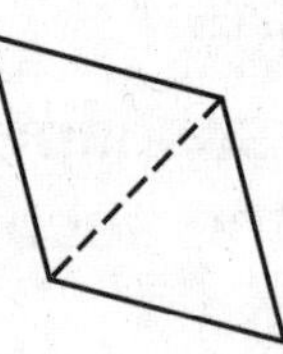

Ⓕ 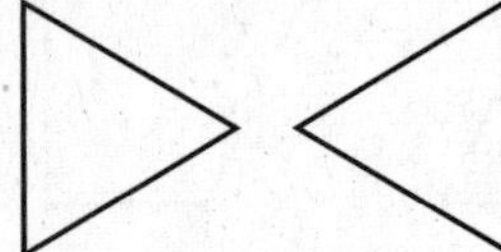

Ⓗ 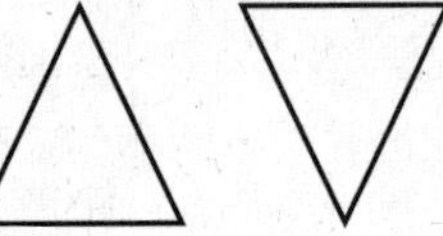

Ⓖ 

Ⓘ 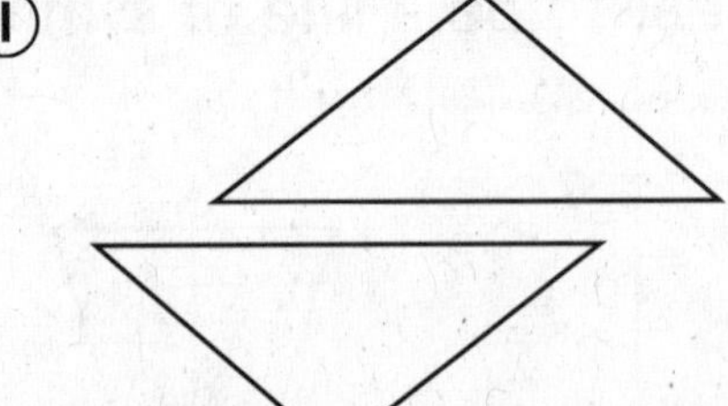

Name ___________________________

TEST PREP

Fill in the bubble for the correct answer choice.

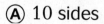

11. Colin combined rhombus pattern blocks. How many sides will 6 combined rhombuses have?

(MA.3.A.4.1; pp. 425–428)

Ⓐ 10 sides
Ⓑ 12 sides
Ⓒ 14 sides
Ⓓ 16 sides

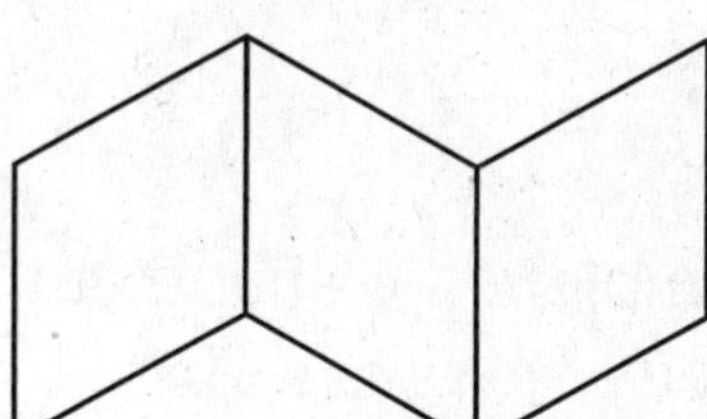

12. Samantha drew these quadrilaterals on dot paper. Which quadrilaterals appear to be congruent?

(MA.3.G.3.3; pp. 435–438)

Ⓕ *A* and *B*
Ⓖ *B* and *D*
Ⓗ *C* and *D*
Ⓘ *A* and *C*

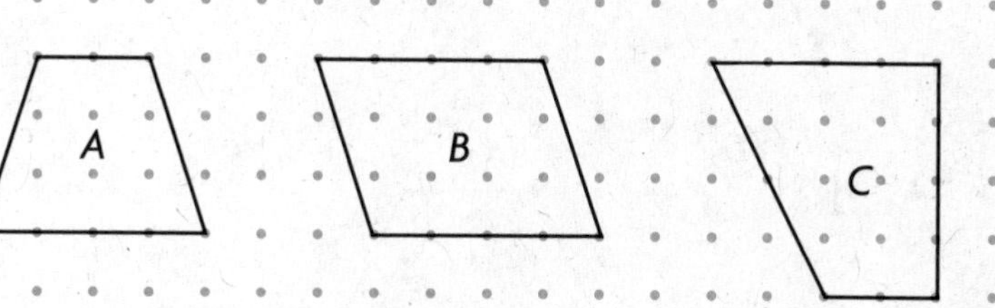

13. Doug drew 4 polygons. In which polygon does the blue line appear to be a line of symmetry?

(MA.3.G.3.3; pp. 443–446)

Ⓐ
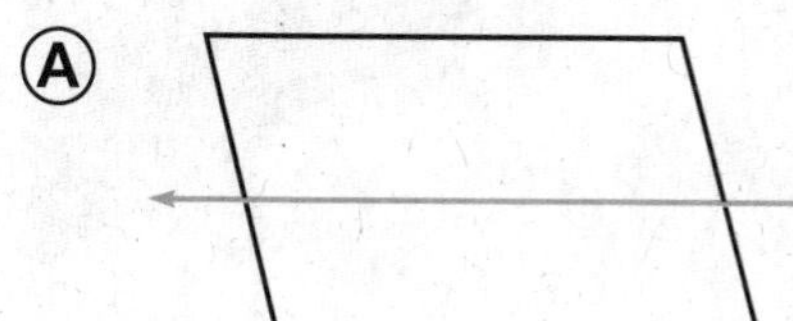

Ⓒ
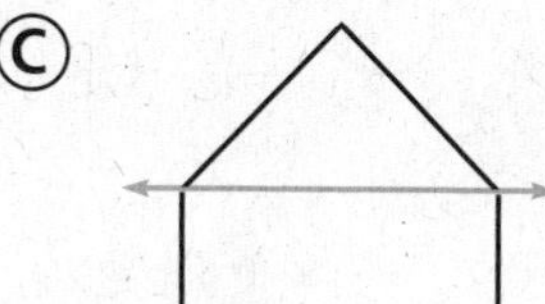

Ⓑ
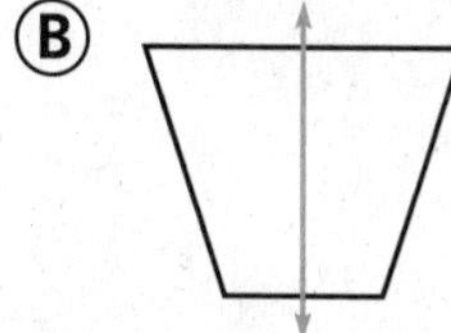

Ⓓ
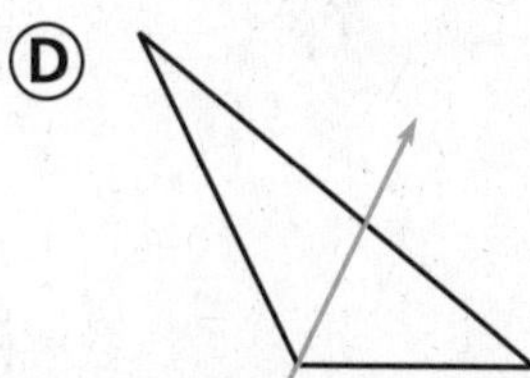

14. How many lines of symmetry can you draw in the rectangle? (MA.3.G.3.3; pp. 447–450)

Ⓕ 1 line

Ⓖ 2 lines

Ⓗ 3 lines

Ⓘ 4 lines

15. Which drawing appears to complete the shape at the right across the line of symmetry? (MA.3.G.3.3; pp. 451–454)

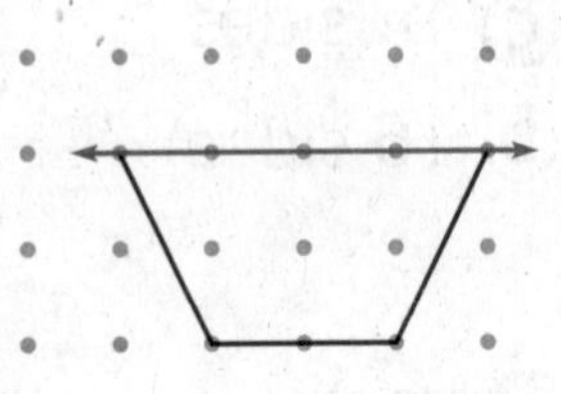

Ⓐ 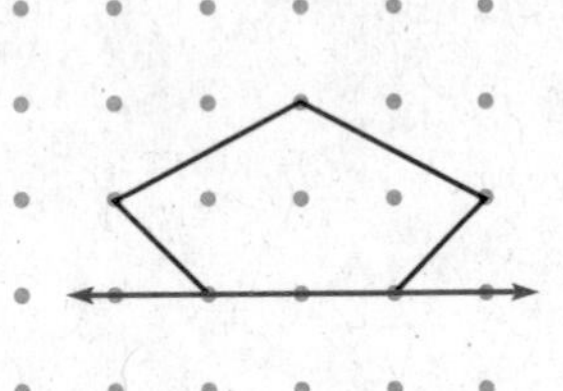

Ⓒ  

Ⓑ 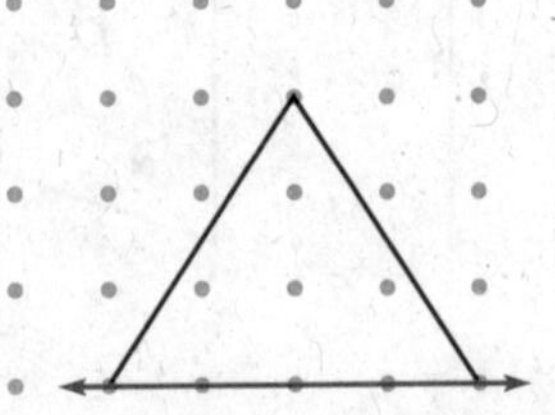

Ⓓ 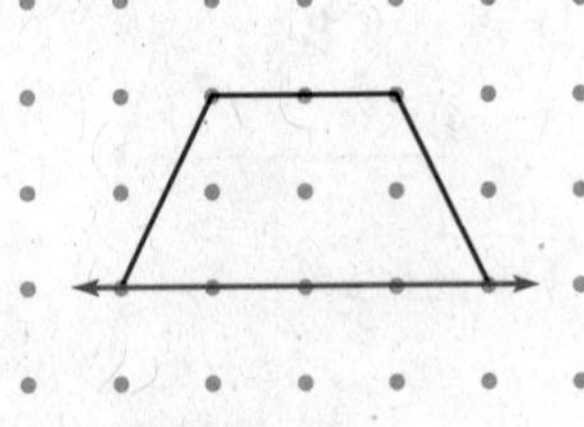

16. Yara traced pattern blocks to make a design. Which pattern block can she add so her design has 1 line of symmetry? (MA.3.G.3.3; pp. 455–458)

Ⓕ 

Ⓖ 

Ⓗ 

Ⓘ 

Chapter 11

Length and Perimeter

Show What You Know

Check your understanding of important skills.

Name ______________________________

▶ Use Nonstandard Units to Measure Length

Use paper clips to measure each.

1. 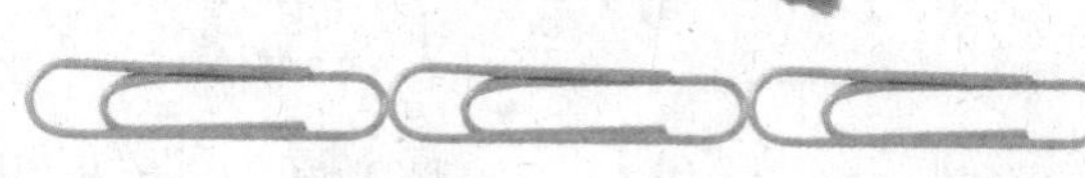

about _____ (paper clips)

2. about _____ (paper clips)

▶ Inches Use a ruler to measure the length to the nearest inch.

3. 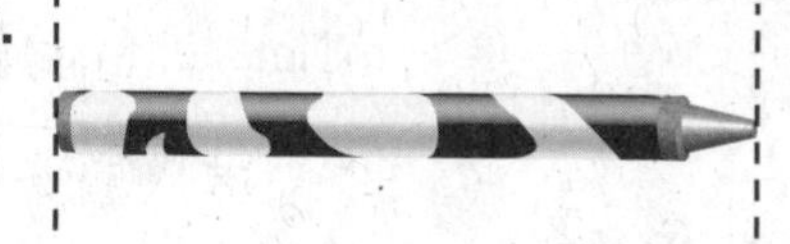

about _____ inches

4. 

about _____ inch

▶ Add 3 Numbers Write the sum.

5. $2 + 7 + 3 =$ _____
6. $3 + 5 + 2 =$ _____
7. $6 + 1 + 9 =$ _____

Florida FUN FACT

Devil's Millhopper, located near Gainesville, Florida, is a state park that was built inside a sinkhole 120 feet deep. It takes 236 steps to get to the bottom.

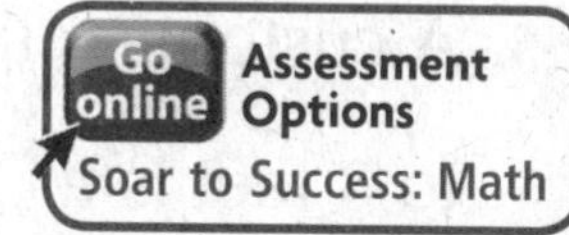

FLORIDA BENCHMARKS

Vocabulary Power

▶ Visualize It

Use the review and preview words to complete the H-diagram.

Customary Units		Metric Units
___________		___________
___________		___________
___________		___________
___________		___________
		___________

Review Words

centimeter
foot
inch
meter
yard

Preview Words

centimeter (cm)
decimeter (dm)
foot (ft)
kilometer (km)
length
meter (m)
mile (mi)
millimeter (mm)
perimeter
yard (yd)

▶ Understand Vocabulary

Complete the sentences by using the preview words.

1. The measurement of the distance between two points is the ___________.
2. The distance around a figure is the ___________.
3. A customary unit used to measure length or distance that is equal to 12 inches is a ___________.
4. A metric unit used to measure length or distance that is equal to 100 centimeters is a ___________.
5. A customary unit used to measure length that is equal to 3 feet is a ___________.

Go online • Student Edition • Multilingual eGlossary

Name ______________________________

Customary Length

Essential Question How do you know which customary unit to use to measure the length of an object or a distance?

MA.3.G.5.2 Measure objects using fractional parts of linear units such as $\frac{1}{2}$, $\frac{1}{4}$, and $\frac{1}{10}$.

UNLOCK the Problem REAL WORLD

Length is the measurement of distance between two points. Customary units used to measure length and distance are inch (in.), **foot (ft)**, **yard (yd)**, and **mile (mi)**.

Customary Units of Length
1 foot = 12 inches
1 yard = 3 feet or 36 inches
1 mile = 1,760 yards or 5,280 feet

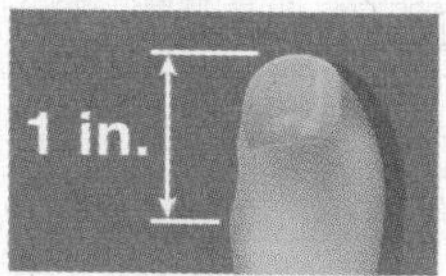

The length of your thumb from the tip to the knuckle is about 1 inch.

Name some things in your classroom that are about 1 inch long.

____

____

____

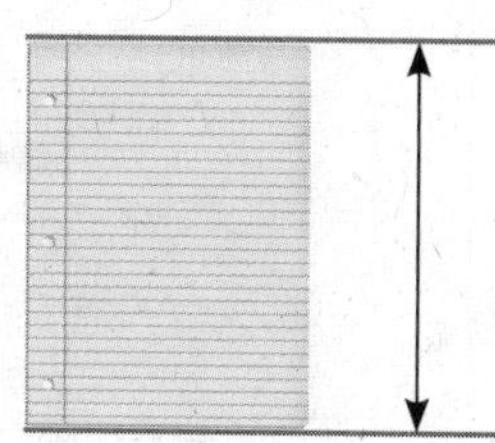

A sheet of notebook paper is about 1 foot long.

Name some things that are about 1 foot long.

____

____

____

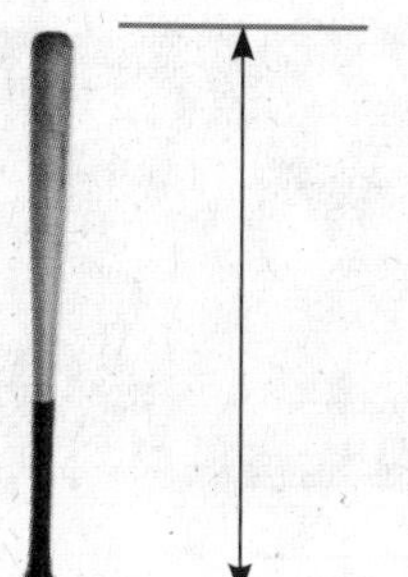

A baseball bat is about 1 yard long.

Name some things that are about 1 yard long.

____

____

____

It takes about 20 minutes to walk 1 mile.

About how long would it take you to walk home from school?

____

Is the distance greater than or less than 1 mile?

____

Math Talk Which is longer, 20 inches or 1 foot? **Explain** how you know.

Share and Show 

1. Would you measure the length of a pencil in inches or in feet? ________

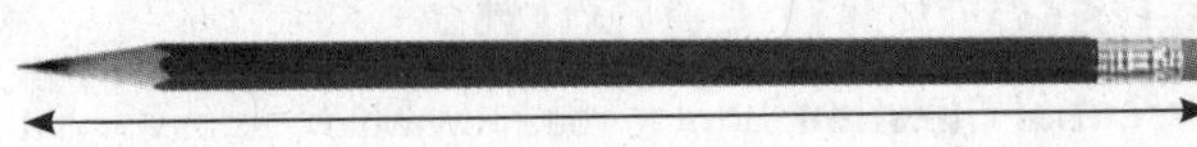

Math Talk **Explain** how you would choose the unit to measure the length of your classroom.

Choose the unit you would use to measure the length. Write *inch, foot, yard,* or *mile*.

2. 

____

✓3. 

____

✓4. 

____

On Your Own

Choose the unit you would use to measure the length. Write *inch, foot, yard,* or *mile*.

5. 

____

6. 

____

7. 

____

8. a one-dollar bill

____

9. the distance between two towns

____

10. a school bus

____

Name ______________________________

Problem Solving REAL WORLD

SHOW YOUR WORK

11. Annie is walking to her friend's house. Her friend lives three houses away. What unit best measures how far Annie will walk?

____

12. Midnight, the cat, has five newborn kittens. What unit would you use to measure the length of the newborn kittens? Would you use the same unit to measure the length of the mother, Midnight? **Explain**.

____

____

____

13. H.O.T. Andrew has a vegetable garden with 10 rows of corn and 10 rows of tomatoes. What unit of length should be used to measure the corn section of Andrew's vegetable garden?

____

14. Toni saw a giraffe at a wildlife park. What unit would be used to measure the height of the giraffe?

____

15. Write Math Madison visits her grandmother in another state. Does Madison travel 100 feet, 100 yards, or 100 miles? **Explain** your answer.

____

____

____

UNLOCK the Problem REAL WORLD

16. Mark, Karen, and Andy each measured one of the items below, using different units of measure. Mark's measure was less than Andy's. Neither Mark nor Andy used a yardstick. Which item did each person measure and what unit did he or she use?

• height of a flower • length of a desk • width of a classroom

a. What do you need to find? ______________________________

b. What clues are you given? ______________________________

____

c. Describe the steps you use to solve the problem.

d. Complete the sentences.

__________ used a yardstick

to measure the __________.

Mark's measure was __________ than Andy's. Mark measured the

__________ in __________.

Andy measured the __________

in __________.

17. Nina measured a bookshelf and said it was 2 yards wide. Carly measured the same bookshelf and said it was 2 feet wide. The bookshelf is 24 inches wide. Who is correct?

____

18. **Test Prep** Kenny uses a large piece of poster board to draw a picture. About how long is the poster board?

Ⓐ 4 inches Ⓒ 4 yards

Ⓑ 4 feet Ⓓ 4 miles

 FOR MORE PRACTICE:
Florida Benchmarks Practice Book, pp. P257–P258

Name ______________________________

Measure to the Nearest Half Inch

Essential Question How can you measure length to the nearest half inch?

MA.3.G.5.2 Measure objects using fractional parts of linear units such as $\frac{1}{2}$, $\frac{1}{4}$, and $\frac{1}{10}$.

CONNECT You already know how to measure length to the nearest inch. You can also measure an object to the nearest half inch.

UNLOCK the Problem REAL WORLD

Example 1 Use a ruler to measure the glue stick to the nearest half inch.

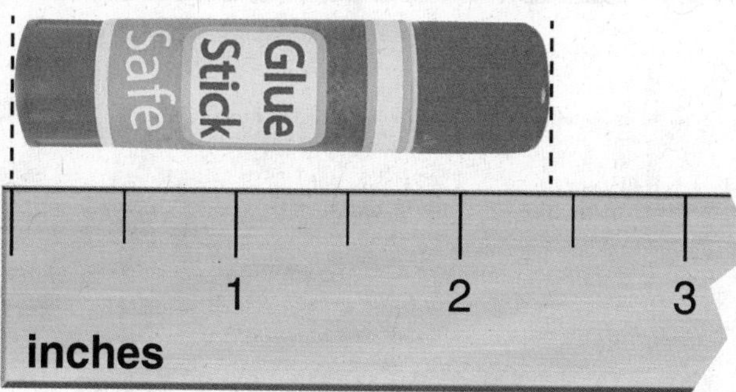

- Line up the left end of the glue stick with the zero mark on the ruler.
- The half inch mark that is closest to the right end of the glue stick is ______.

So, the length of the glue stick to the nearest half inch is ______ inches.

Example 2 Use a ruler to measure the eraser to the nearest half inch.

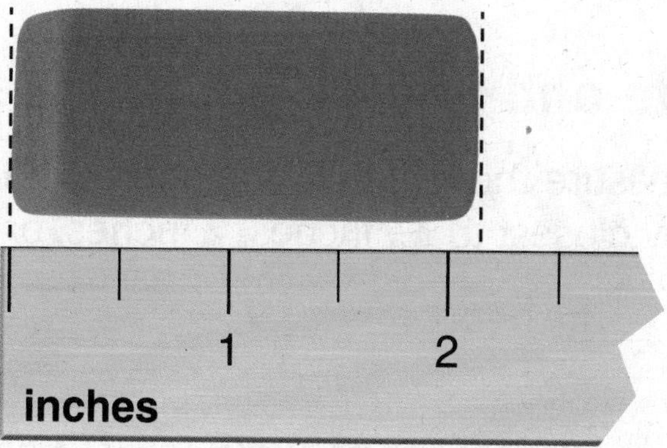

- Line up the left end of the eraser with the zero mark on the ________.
- Find the half inch mark that is closest to the ________ end of the eraser.
- The half inch mark that is closest to the right end of the eraser is ______.

So, the length of the eraser to the nearest half inch is ______ inches.

Math Talk Why would you want to measure to the nearest half inch instead of to the nearest inch?

Remember

Be sure that the left end of the object you are measuring is lined up with the zero mark on the ruler.

Try This! **How wide is your math book to the nearest half inch? Use your ruler to find the answer.**

_____ inches

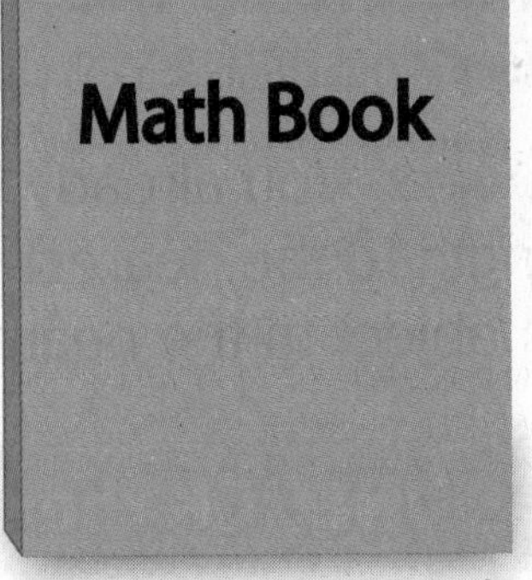

Draw a line segment 4 inches shorter than the width of your math book.

Write the length. _____ inches

Share and Show

1. Measure the length to the nearest half inch. Is the key closest to $1\frac{1}{2}$ inches, 2 inches, or $2\frac{1}{2}$ inches?

_____ inches

Measure the length to the nearest half inch.

2.

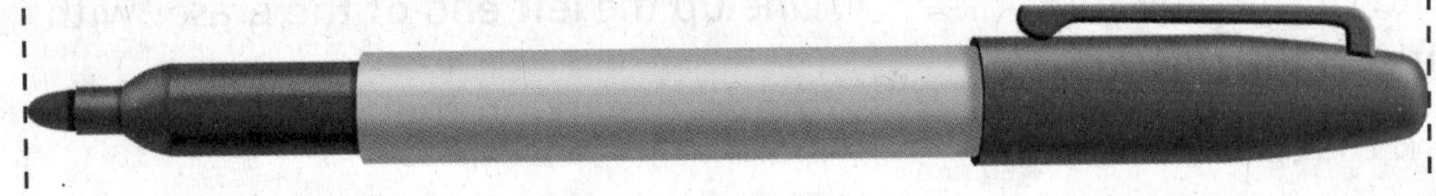

_____ inches

3.

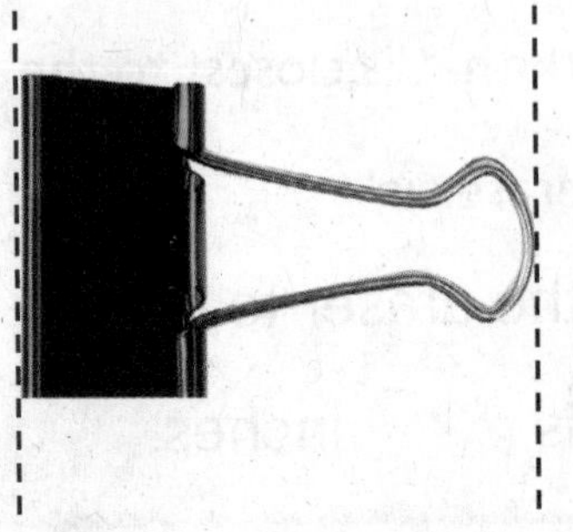

_____ inches

4.

_____ inches

Math Talk Why does measuring the shell to the nearest half inch give you a closer measurement than measuring to the nearest inch? **Explain.**

Name ______________________________

On Your Own

Measure the length to the nearest half inch.

5. 

_____ inches

6. 

_____ inches

7. 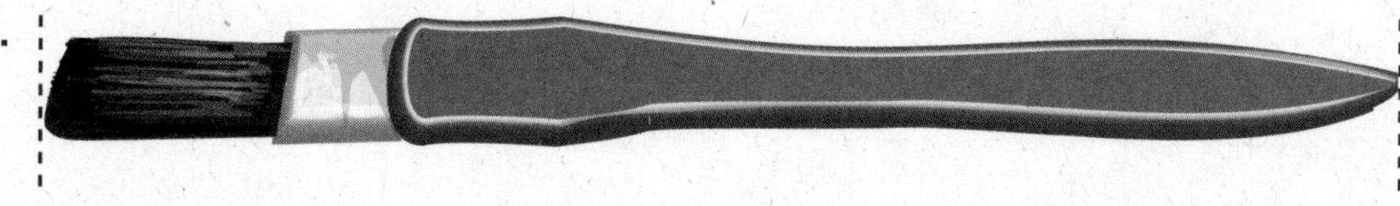

_____ inches

8. 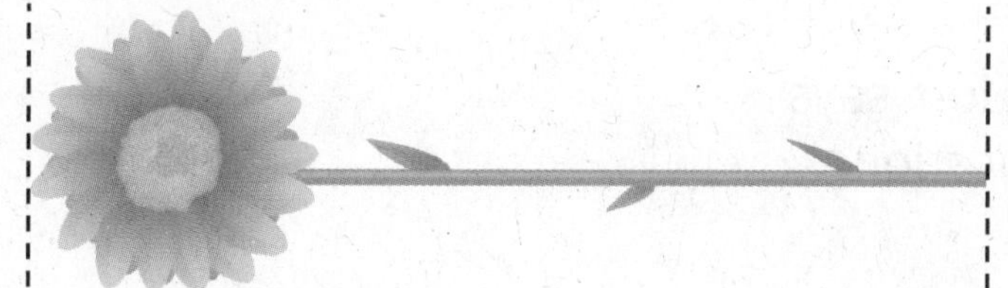

_____ inches

Use a ruler. Draw a line for each length.

9. $2\frac{1}{2}$ inches

10. $4\frac{1}{2}$ inches

Algebra **Write the next 3 numbers in the pattern.**

11. $1, 1\frac{1}{2}, 2, 2\frac{1}{2},$ _____, _____, _____

12. $9\frac{1}{2}, 8\frac{1}{2}, 7\frac{1}{2},$ _____, _____, _____

Problem Solving

SHOW YOUR WORK

13. Tara's hand is $4\frac{1}{2}$ inches wide. Between which two inch marks on the ruler is the width of Tara's hand?

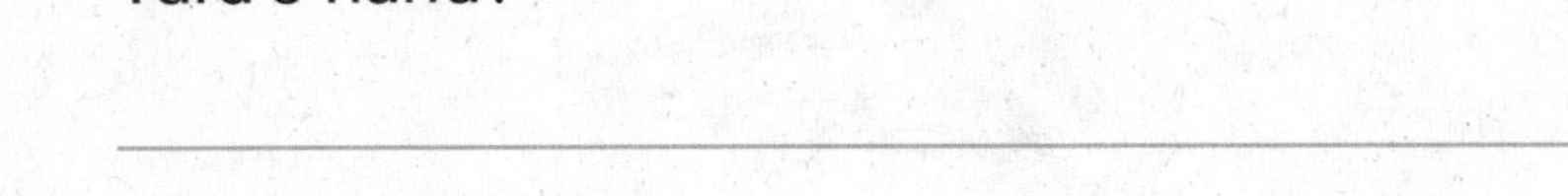

14. Find two different-sized objects in your desk. Measure the length of each object to the nearest half inch. Use < or > to compare the lengths.

Object ____________ Length ____________

Object ____________ Length ____________

15. Write Math **What's the Error?** Joni says that this piece of ribbon is $3\frac{1}{2}$ inches long. Describe her error.

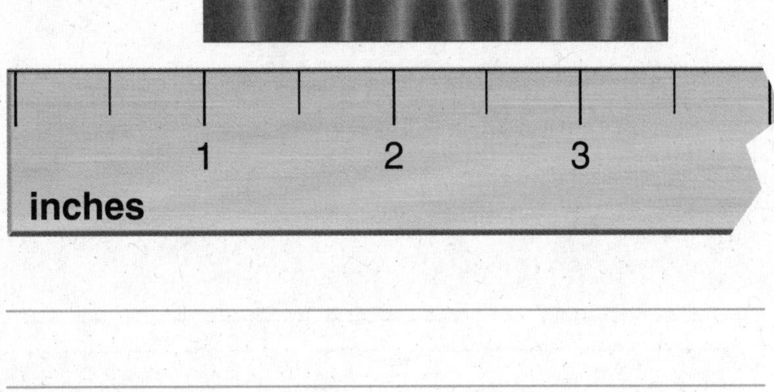

16. **Test Prep** What is the length of the pencil to the nearest half inch?

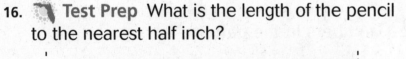

Ⓐ $3\frac{1}{2}$ inches

Ⓑ 4 inches

Ⓒ $5\frac{1}{2}$ inches

Ⓓ 6 inches

FOR MORE PRACTICE:
Florida Benchmarks Practice Book, pp. P259–P260

Name ____________________

Measure to the Nearest Quarter Inch

MA.3.G.5.2 Measure objects using fractional parts of linear units such as $\frac{1}{2}$, $\frac{1}{4}$, and $\frac{1}{10}$.

Essential Question How can you measure length to the nearest quarter inch?

CONNECT You have learned to use a ruler to measure to the nearest half inch. You can use what you know to measure to the nearest quarter inch.

UNLOCK the Problem REAL WORLD

When you measure an object to the nearest quarter inch, the measurement is closer to the actual length of the object.

How do you measure an object to the nearest quarter inch?

Activity Materials ■ inch ruler

Measure the length of the crayon to the nearest quarter inch.

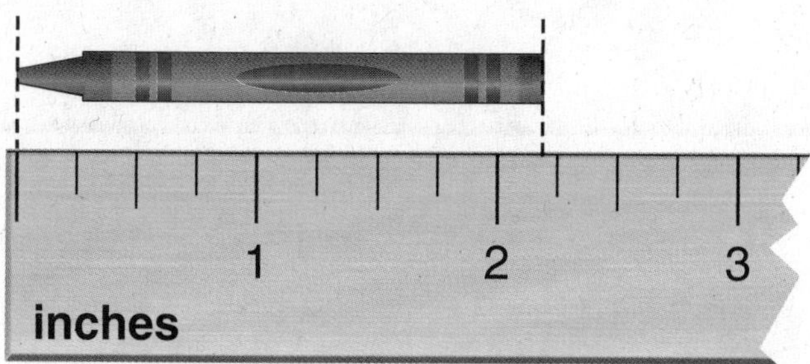

- Line up the left end of the crayon with the zero mark on the ruler.
- Find the quarter inch mark that is closest to the right end of the crayon.

The right end of the crayon is closest to

the _____ mark.

So, the length of the crayon to the nearest

quarter inch is _____ inches.

Math Idea

The quarter inch markings on a ruler divide each half inch into two equal parts and each whole inch into four equal parts.

1 $\frac{1}{4}$ $\frac{2}{4}$ $\frac{3}{4}$ 2 $\frac{1}{4}$

inches

Math Talk Can you measure an object to the nearest $\frac{1}{4}$ inch and get a measurement of $2\frac{1}{2}$ inches? **Explain.**

Try This! Measure the length of a pencil to the nearest quarter inch.

Materials ■ inch ruler ■ pencil

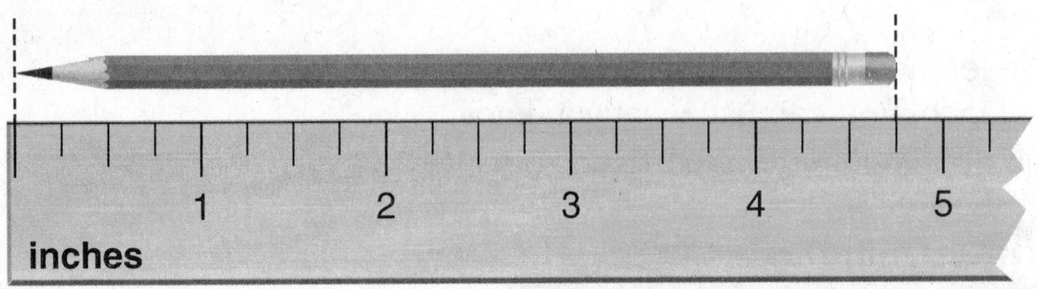

- Line up the left end of the pencil with the zero mark on the ruler.
- Find the quarter inch mark that is closest to the __________ end of the pencil.
- The length of the pencil to the nearest __________ inch is __________ inches.
- What is the length of your pencil to the nearest quarter inch? ______________

Share and Show 

1. Is the length of the nail closest to $1\frac{1}{4}$, $1\frac{1}{2}$, or $1\frac{3}{4}$ inches?

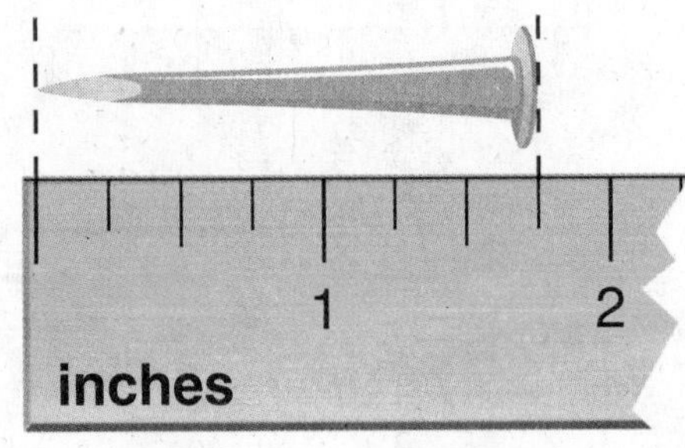

_____ inches

Measure the length to the nearest quarter inch.

2. 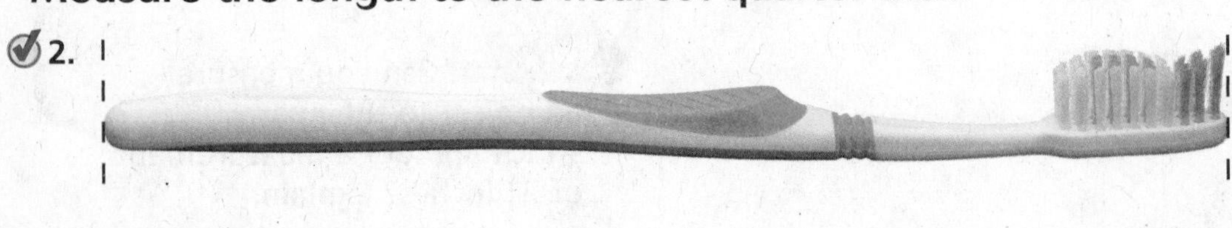

_____ inches

Name ______________________________

Measure the length to the nearest quarter inch.

3.

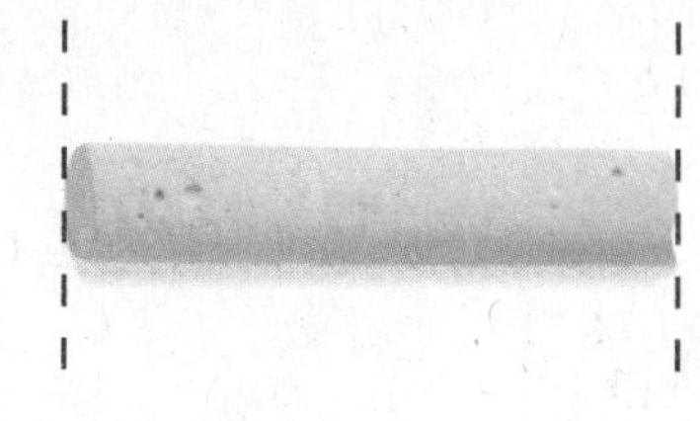

_____ inches

4.

_____ inches

Math Talk **Explain** why the length of the caterpillar to the nearest quarter inch is a whole number.

On Your Own

Measure the length to the nearest quarter inch.

5.

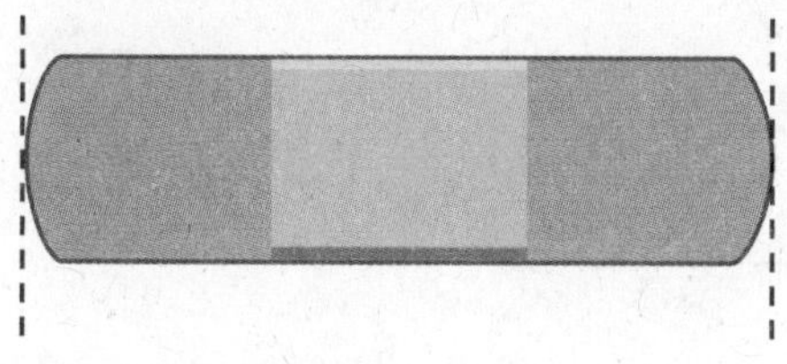

_____ inches

6.

_______ inches

7. Find an object in your desk. Name the object. Measure its length to the nearest quarter inch.

_________________ _____ inches

Use a ruler. Draw a line for each length.

8. $3\frac{3}{4}$ inches

9. $1\frac{1}{4}$ inches

10. Measure this line to the nearest quarter inch. _____ inches

Problem Solving REAL WORLD

11. Emily's comb is $8\frac{1}{4}$ inches long. Between which two inch marks is the end of the comb?

12. H.O.T. Darren is using a ruler to measure the length of a marker. He says that the length is $5\frac{3}{4}$ inches. Is he correct? **Explain** how you know.

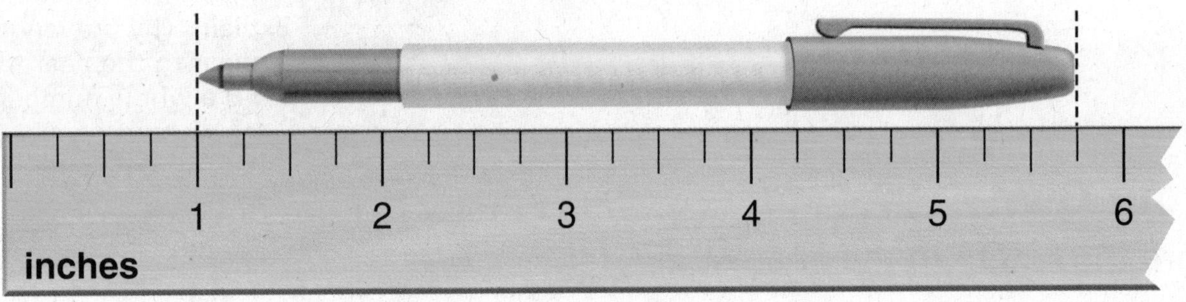

13. Test Prep What is the length of the paper clip to the nearest quarter inch?

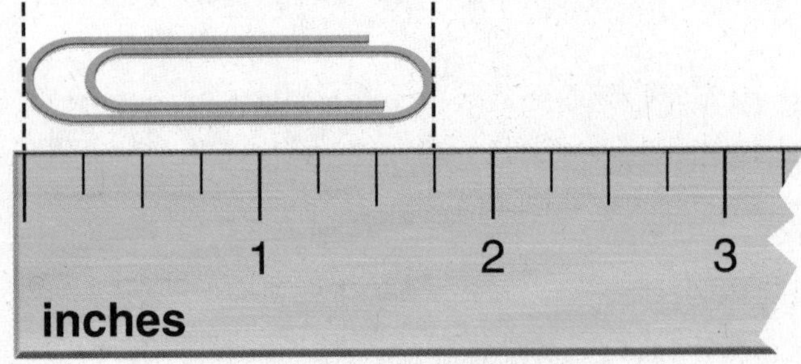

Ⓐ $1\frac{3}{4}$ inches

Ⓑ 2 inches

Ⓒ $2\frac{1}{4}$ inches

Ⓓ 3 inches

FOR MORE PRACTICE:
Florida Benchmarks Practice Book, pp. P261–P262

Name ______________________________

Metric Length

Essential Question How do you know which metric unit to use to measure the length of an object or a distance?

MA.3.G.5.2 Measure objects using fractional parts of linear units such as $\frac{1}{2}$, $\frac{1}{4}$, and $\frac{1}{10}$.

UNLOCK the Problem REAL WORLD

Length and distance can be measured using metric units such as **millimeter (mm)**, **centimeter (cm)**, **decimeter (dm)**, **meter (m)**, and **kilometer (km)**.

The thickness of a dime is about 1 millimeter.

Name two things that are about 1 millimeter wide.

____

____

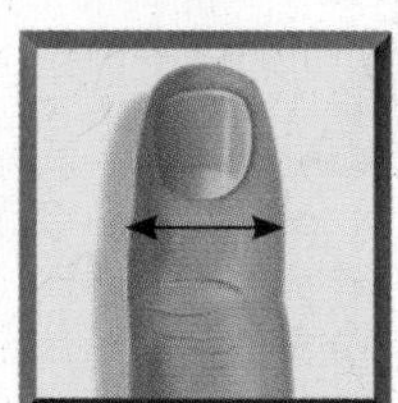

A child's finger is about 1 centimeter wide.

Name two things that are about 1 centimeter wide.

____

____

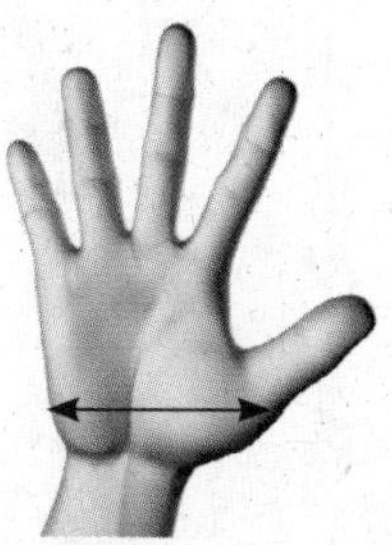

An adult's hand is about 1 decimeter wide.

Name two things that are about 1 decimeter wide.

____

____

A doorway is about 1 meter wide.

Name two things that are about 1 meter wide.

____

____

It takes about 10 minutes to walk 1 kilometer.

Name one distance you might measure in kilometers.

____

____

Math Talk Name an object in your classroom that you would measure in meters. Why wouldn't you measure this object in centimeters?

Share and Show 

1. Would you measure the length of this crayon in centimeters or in decimeters?

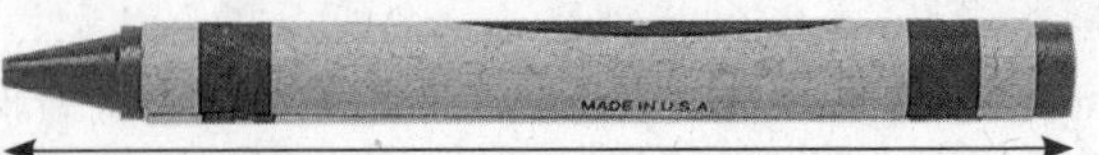

Choose the unit you would use to measure the length. Write *millimeter, centimeter, meter,* or *kilometer*.

2. 

3. 

4. 

Math Talk Why would you use centimeters to measure the width of your school picture? **Explain.**

On Your Own

Choose the unit you would use to measure the length. Write *millimeter, centimeter, meter,* or *kilometer*.

5. 

6. 

7. 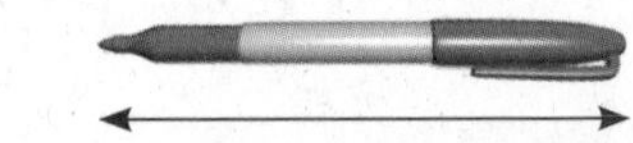

8. distance from your house to school

9. width of a bookshelf

10. thickness of a nickel

11. wingspan of a butterfly

12. height of a flagpole

13. length of a dollar bill

Name ________________________________

Problem Solving REAL WORLD

14. Brad walks from his house to the park to play basketball. It takes him 20 minutes to get to the park. Is the park 2 decimeters, 2 meters, or 2 kilometers from his house?

____

15. Carlos used erasers to measure the length of a piece of string. It was 5 erasers long. If each eraser was 4 centimeters long, how long was the string?

____

16. H.O.T. **What if** you measure your desk in centimeters and then in decimeters? Will there be more centimeters or more decimeters? **Explain.**

____

____

____

17. Write Math **What's the Error?** The plant in Stacy's room is about the same width as her front door. She says the plant is about 1 decimeter wide. Describe and correct Stacy's error.

____

____

18. **Test Prep** Which unit would you use to measure the shell?

Ⓐ centimeters Ⓒ kilometers

Ⓑ meters Ⓓ decimeters

Connect to Science

Inches and Centimeters

In the United States, the customary system of measurement, which includes inches as a unit of measure, is used more often.

inches 1 2
centimeters 1 2 3 4 5 6 7

Most other countries use the metric system of measurement. The metric system is almost always used in scientific measurement. When scientists record observations of length, they often use centimeters as the unit of measure.

You can use estimates to compare measures using inches and centimeters.

Try This!

Look at the ruler above.

Notice that 1 inch is about $2\frac{1}{2}$ centimeters.

About how many centimeters is 5 inches?

STEP 1 Make a table to compare inches and centimeters. 1 inch is about $2\frac{1}{2}$ centimeters.

inches	1	2	3	4	5	6
centimeters	$2\frac{1}{2}$	5	$7\frac{1}{2}$	10	$12\frac{1}{2}$	15

STEP 2 Find 5 inches in the table. Then find the estimated number of centimeters it is.

So, 5 inches is about ________ centimeters.

Complete each comparison.

19. 4 inches is about _____ centimeters.

20. 5 centimeters is about _____ inches.

21. $17\frac{1}{2}$ centimeters is about _____ inches.

22. 10 inches is about _____ centimeters.

FOR MORE PRACTICE:
Florida Benchmarks Practice Book, pp. P263–P264

Name ______________________________

Centimeters, Decimeters, and Meters

Essential Question How can you estimate and measure the length of your desk to the nearest centimeter, decimeter, and meter?

MA.3.G.5.2 Measure objects using fractional parts of linear units such as $\frac{1}{2}$, $\frac{1}{4}$, and $\frac{1}{10}$.

UNLOCK the Problem REAL WORLD

How can you use a centimeter ruler to measure length to the nearest centimeter and decimeter?

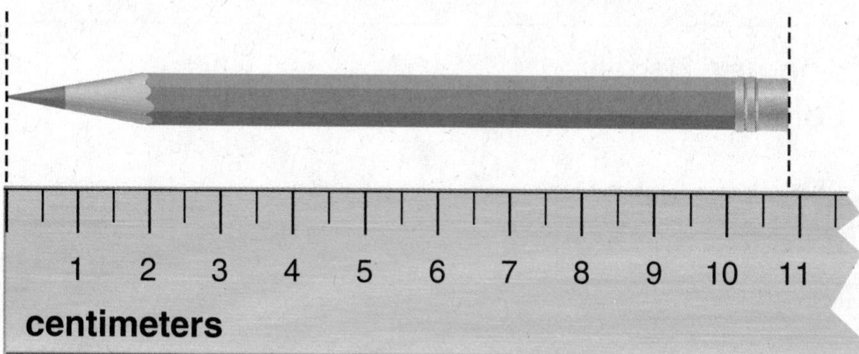

The right end of the pencil is closest to the 11-centimeter mark.

So, the pencil is __________ centimeters long, to the nearest __________, and 1 decimeter long, to the nearest __________.

Math Idea

1 decimeter = 10 centimeters

1 centimeter = $\frac{1}{10}$ decimeter

Activity 1 Materials ■ centimeter ruler

STEP 1

Choose two objects to measure. Estimate the length of each object in centimeters or decimeters. Record your estimates in the table.

STEP 2

Use a centimeter ruler to measure each object. Record your measurements in the table.

Length of Objects		
Object	Estimate	Measure

Math Talk What strategy did you use to find your estimate?

Activity 2

Materials ■ centimeter grid paper ■ tape ■ crayons

Table of Measures		
1 decimeter	=	10 centimeters
1 meter	=	100 centimeters
	=	10 decimeters
1 kilometer	=	1,000 meters

You can measure longer lengths in meters.

- Use the Table of Measures to find the number of decimeters in 1 meter.

  _____ decimeters = _____ meter

- Mark 10 decimeter strips on grid paper. Then cut out the strips. Color each decimeter strip a different color.

- Tape the decimeter strips end to end so that the edges do not overlap.

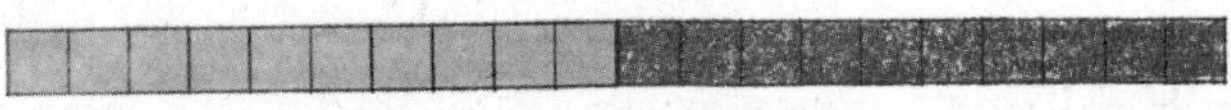

- Estimate the length of your classroom in meters. Then use your 1-meter strip to find the actual measure.

Length of Classroom	
Estimate	Measure

Share and Show

1. To the nearest centimeter, how long is this crayon? _____

Measure the length to the nearest centimeter.

2. the length of your math book

   _____ centimeters

3. the length of your shoe

   _____ centimeters

4. the length of your pencil

   _____ centimeters

5. the length of a marker

   _____ centimeters

Name ____________________

Circle the best estimate.

6. the length of a bulletin board

2 cm   2 m   2 km

7. the length of a road race

5 dm   5 m   5 km

Math Talk What fraction of a meter is a decimeter? **Explain** how you know.

On Your Own

Measure the length to the nearest centimeter.

8. the length of a piece of chalk

_____ centimeters

9. the width of your math book

_____ centimeters

10. the length of a pencil case

_____ centimeters

11. the length of an eraser

_____ centimeters

12.

_____ centimeters

13.

_____ centimeters

Circle the best estimate.

14. the length of a straw

20 cm   20 dm   20 m

15. the width of a doorway

10 cm   100 dm   1 m

16. the length of a paintbrush

15 cm   15 dm   15 m

Use a ruler. Draw a line for each length.

17. 12 centimeters

18. 9 centimeters

H.O.T. Circle the greater length.

19. 1 m 14 cm *or* 104 cm

20. 1 dm 3 cm *or* 23 cm

Problem Solving REAL WORLD

SHOW YOUR WORK

21. Dominick says that he is 1 meter 36 centimeters tall. Marie is 105 centimeters tall. Who is taller? **Explain** how you know.
Hint: 1 meter = 100 centimeters

22. H.O.T. There are three snakes in an exhibit at the zoo. Ralph is 1 meter long. Chester is 12 decimeters long. Drake is 25 centimeters long. Which snake is the longest? Which snake is the shortest? **Explain** how you found your answers.

23. Write Math **Sense or Nonsense?** Ben says that 32 centimeters is the same as 3 decimeters plus 2 centimeters. Do you agree? **Explain.**

24. **Test Prep** Julie's book is 40 centimeters long. How many decimeters is this?

Ⓐ 4,000 decimeters

Ⓑ 400 decimeters

Ⓒ 40 decimeters

Ⓓ 4 decimeters

Name ______________________________

Mid-Chapter Checkpoint

▶ Check Concepts

1. Would you measure the length of a fence in inches or in feet? (MA.3.G.5.2; pp. 465–468) ____________

2. Would you measure the length of a paper clip in centimeters or in meters? (MA.3.G.5.2; pp. 477–480)

____

Choose the unit you would use to measure the length. Write *inch, foot, yard,* or *mile*. (MA.3.G.5.2; pp. 465–468)

3. your arm ____________

4. a driveway ____________

5. your finger ____________

Measure the length to the nearest half inch.
(MA.3.G.5.2; pp. 469–472)

6. 

____

7. 

____

Choose the unit you would use to measure the length. Write *millimeter, centimeter, meter,* or *kilometer*. (MA.3.G.5.2; pp. 477–480)

8. height of a door ____________

9. a picture frame ____________

10. a robin's egg ____________

Circle the best estimate. (MA.3.G.5.2; pp. 481–484)

11. a stapler

12 cm 12 dm 12 m

12. a postage stamp

2 cm 2 dm 2 m

13. height of a tall tree

10 cm 10 dm 10 m

Fill in the bubble for the correct answer choice.

14. Alexa is drawing with a blue marker. (MA.3.G.5.2; pp. 473–476)

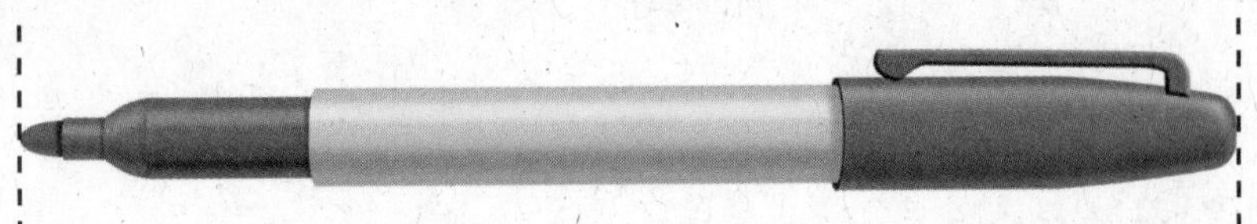

Which is closest to the length of the marker?

Ⓐ $3\frac{3}{4}$ inches

Ⓑ 4 inches

Ⓒ $4\frac{1}{4}$ inches

Ⓓ $4\frac{1}{2}$ inches

15. Which customary unit of measure would be the most appropriate for finding the distance between two cities in Florida? (MA.3.G.5.2; pp. 465–468)

Ⓕ inch

Ⓖ foot

Ⓗ yard

Ⓘ mile

16. Matthew has a science book on his desk. Which is the best estimate for the length of his book?
(MA.3.G.5.2; pp. 481–484)

Ⓐ 3 centimeters

Ⓑ 3 decimeters

Ⓒ 3 meters

Ⓓ 3 kilometers

17. Which metric unit of measure would be best for measuring the length of a grasshopper?
(MA.3.G.5.2; pp. 477–480)

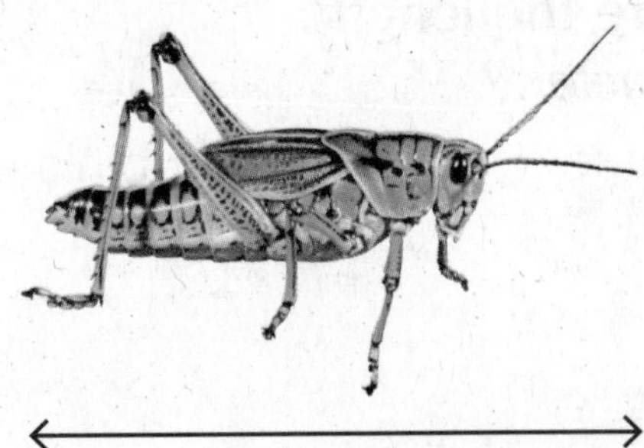

Ⓕ centimeter

Ⓖ decimeter

Ⓗ meter

Ⓘ kilometer

Name ____________________________________

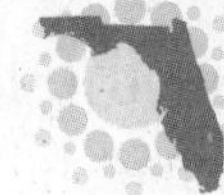

Model Perimeter

Essential Question How can you find perimeter?

MA.3.G.5.1 Select appropriate units, strategies and tools to solve problems involving perimeter.

Investigate

Perimeter is the distance around a shape.

Materials ■ geoboard ■ dot paper

You can find the perimeter of a shape on a geoboard or on dot paper by counting the number of units on each side.

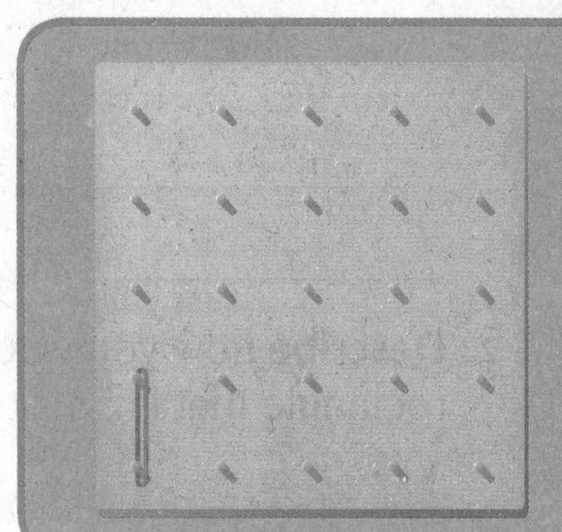

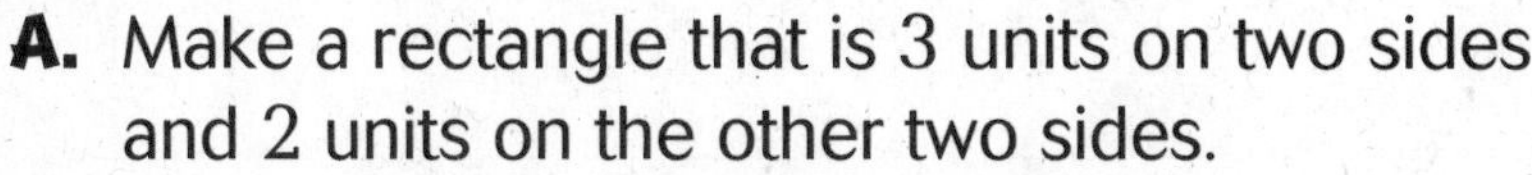

A. Make a rectangle that is 3 units on two sides and 2 units on the other two sides.

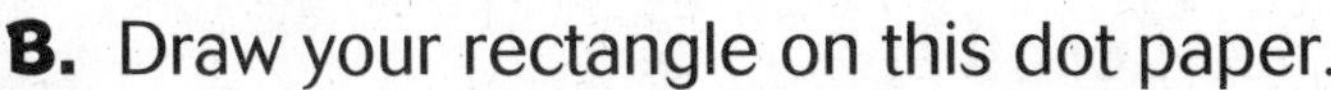

B. Draw your rectangle on this dot paper.

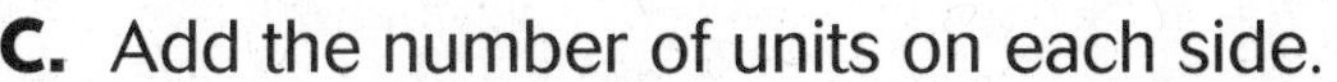

C. Add the number of units on each side.

_____ + _____ + _____ + _____ = _____

D. So, the perimeter of the rectangle is _____ units.

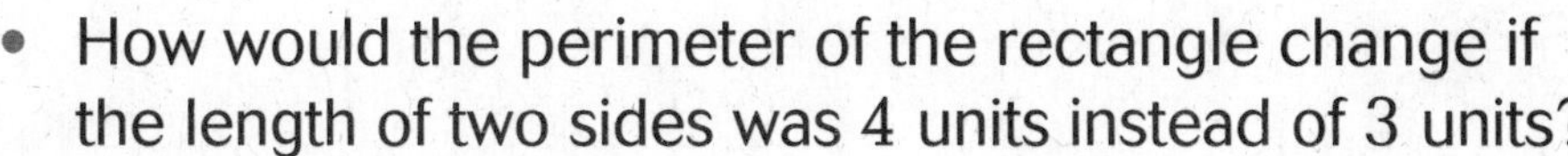

- How would the perimeter of the rectangle change if the length of two sides was 4 units instead of 3 units?

____

____

Draw Conclusions

1. **Explain** how you can find the length of the other two sides if you know the shape is a rectangle, that the length of one side is 4 units, and that the perimeter is 14 units.

____

____

____

2. **Describe** how you would find the perimeter of a rectangle that is 5 units wide and 6 units long.

____

3. **Evaluate** Jill says that finding the perimeter of a square is easier than finding the perimeter of other shapes. Do you agree? **Explain.**

____

____

Connect

You can also use grid paper to find the perimeter of shapes by counting the number of units on each side.

Start with 1 at the arrow and count all of the units to find the perimeter.

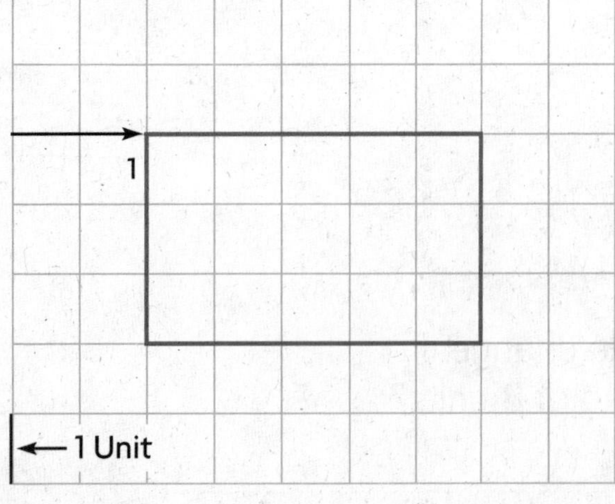

Perimeter = _____ units

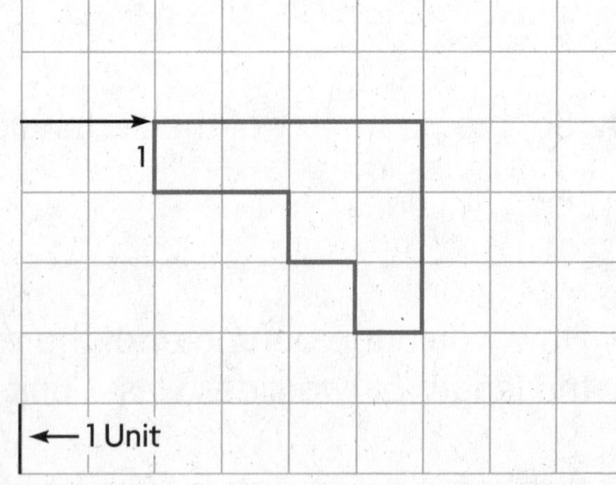

Perimeter = _____ units

Name ______________________________

Share and Show MATH BOARD

Find the perimeter of each shape. Each unit is 1 centimeter.

1.

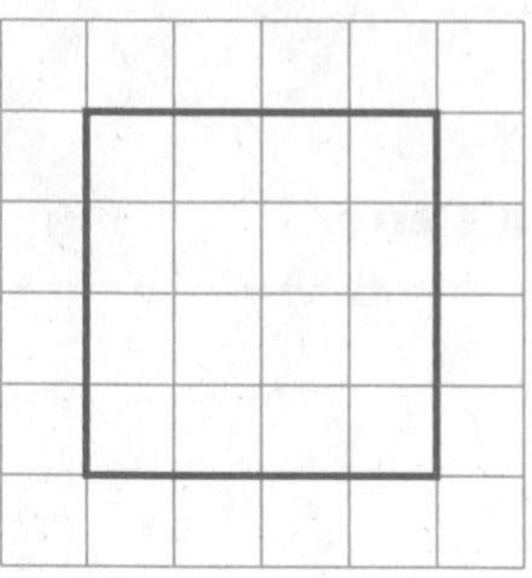

_____ centimeters

2.

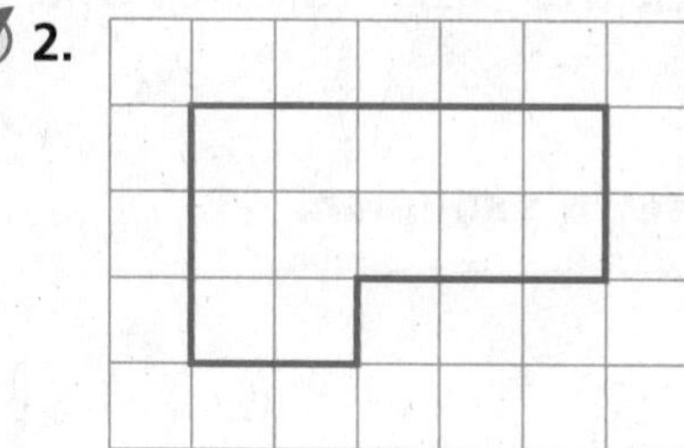

_____ centimeters

3.

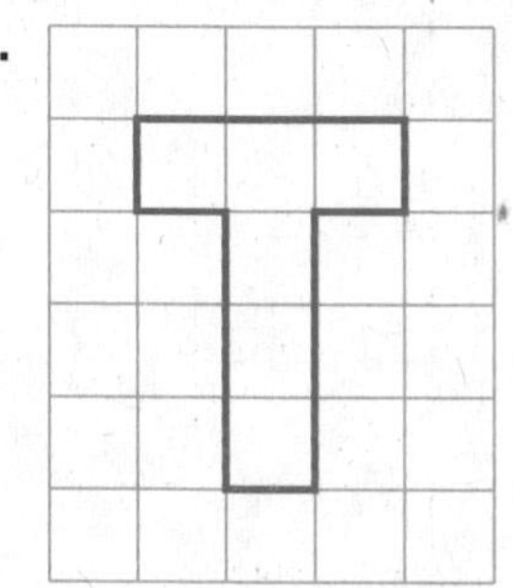

_____ centimeters

4.

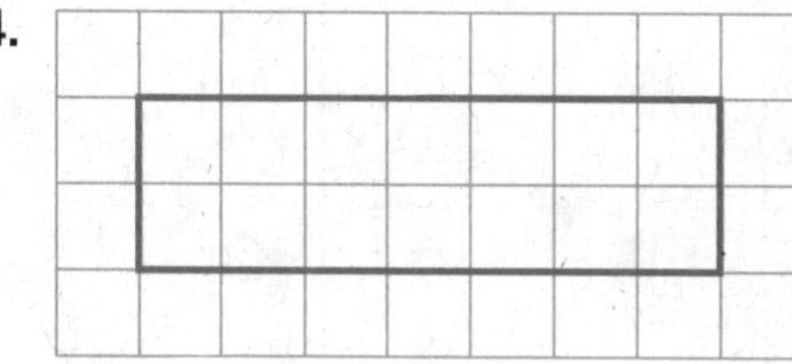

_____ centimeters

Find the perimeter.

5. A 4-sided shape with sides that measure 4 centimeters, 6 centimeters, 5 centimeters, and 1 centimeter.

_____ centimeters

6. A 4-sided shape with two sides that are 10 inches, one side that is 8 inches, and one side that is 4 inches.

_____ inches

7. Write Math **Explain** how to find the length of each side of an equilateral triangle that has a perimeter of 27 centimeters. ______________________________

____

Math Talk If a rectangle has a perimeter of 12 units, how many units wide and how many units long could it be? **Explain.**

Problem Solving

What's the Error?

Kevin is solving perimeter problems. He counts the units and says that the perimeter of this shape is 22 units.

Look at Kevin's solution.

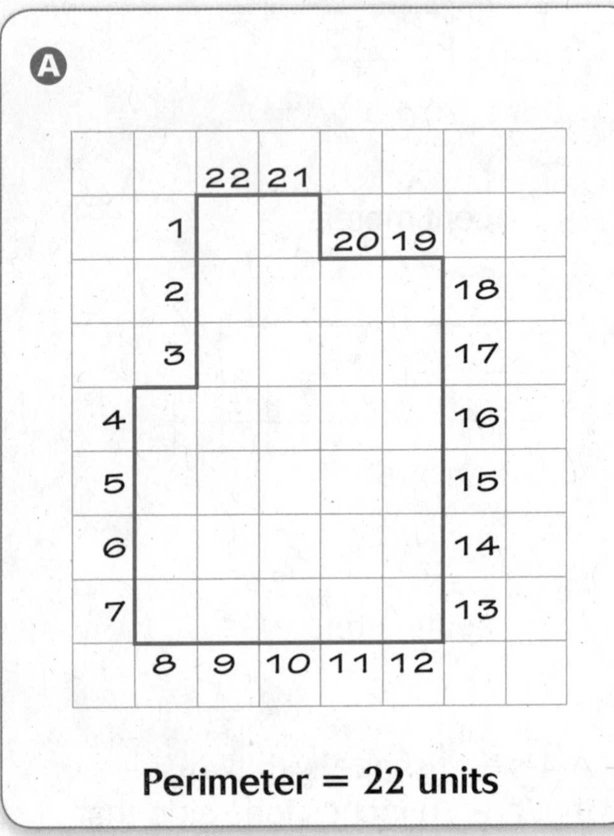

Find Kevin's error.

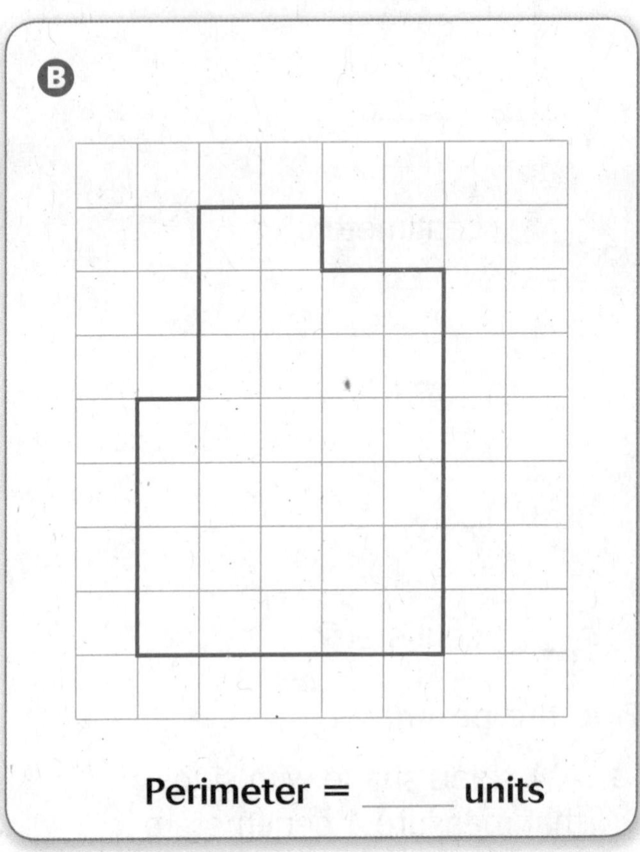

8. What is the correct perimeter of the shape above?

____

9. Describe the error Kevin made.

____

____

____

10. Circle the places in the drawing of Kevin's solution where he made an error.

FOR MORE PRACTICE:
Florida Benchmarks Practice Book, pp. P267–P268

Name ______________________________

Measure Perimeter

MA.3.G.5.1 Select appropriate units, strategies and tools to solve problems involving perimeter.

Essential Question How can you estimate and measure perimeter?

You can estimate and measure perimeter in standard units, such as inches and centimeters.

Find the perimeter of the cover of a notebook.

Activity Materials ■ inch ruler

STEP 1 Estimate the perimeter of a notebook in inches. Record your estimate. _____ inches

STEP 2 Use an inch ruler to measure the length of each side of the notebook.

STEP 3 Record and add the lengths of the sides.

_____ + _____ + _____ + _____ = _____

So, the perimeter of the notebook cover is _____ inches.

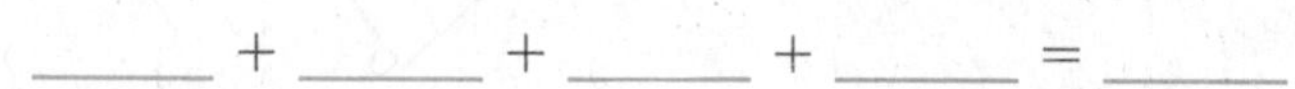

Math Talk **Explain** how your estimate compares with your measurement.

Try This! Find the perimeter.

Use an inch ruler to find the length of each side.

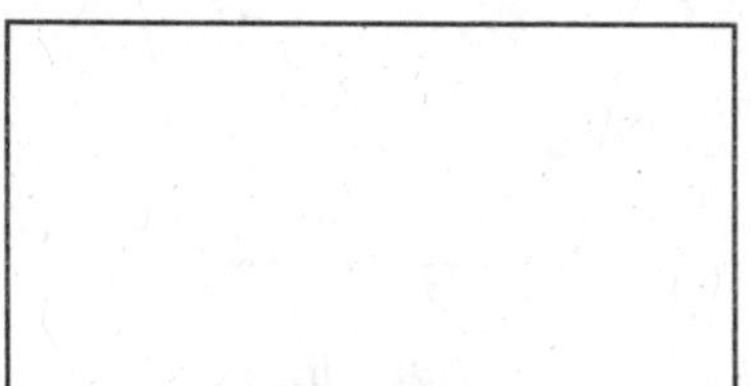

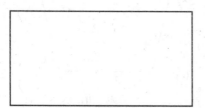

Add the lengths of the sides:

_____ + _____ + _____ + _____ = _____

The perimeter is _____ inches.

Use a centimeter ruler to find the length of each side.

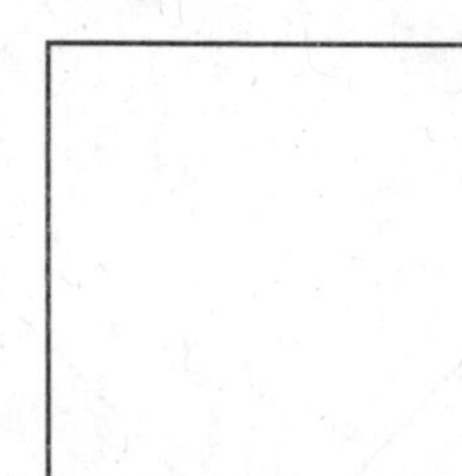

Add the lengths of the sides:

_____ + _____ + _____ + _____ = _____

The perimeter is _____ centimeters.

Share and Show 

1. Find the perimeter of the triangle in inches.

Think: How long is each side?

Math Talk **Explain** how many numbers you add together to find the perimeter of a shape.

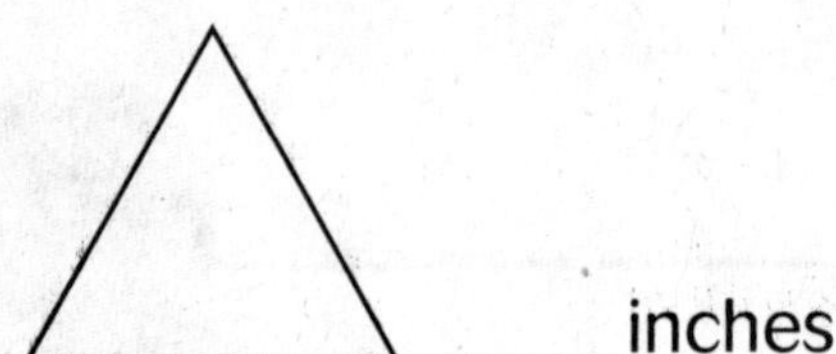

_____ inches

Use a centimeter ruler to find the perimeter.

2.

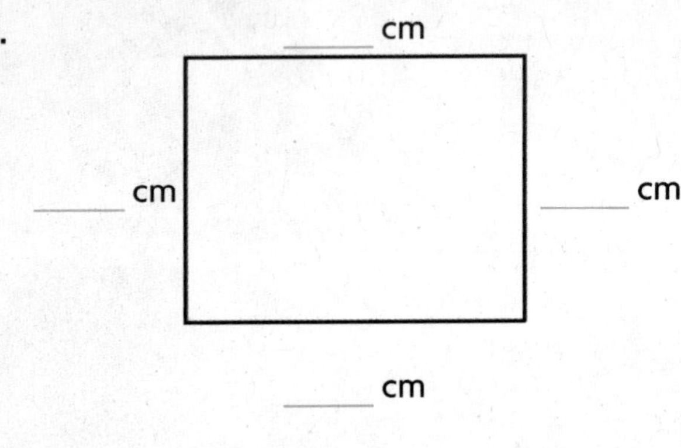

_____ centimeters

3.

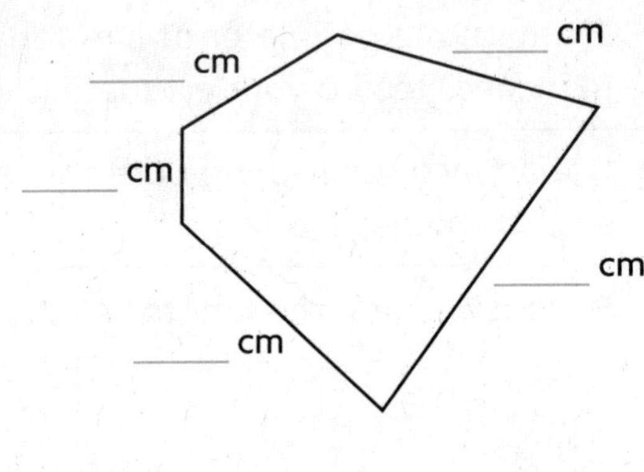

_____ centimeters

Use an inch ruler to find the perimeter.

4.

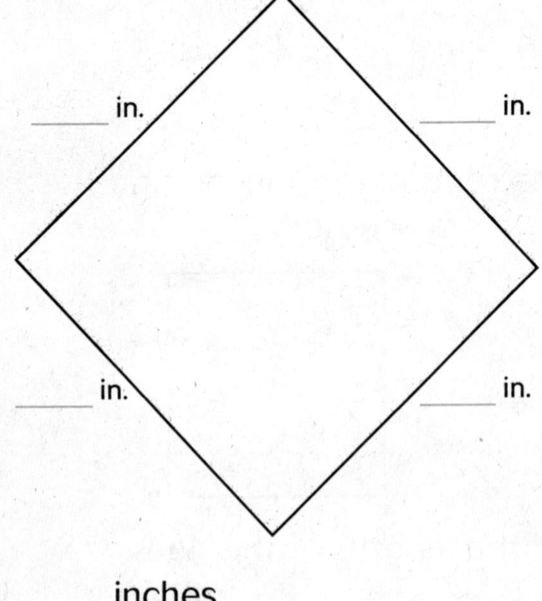

_____ inches

5.

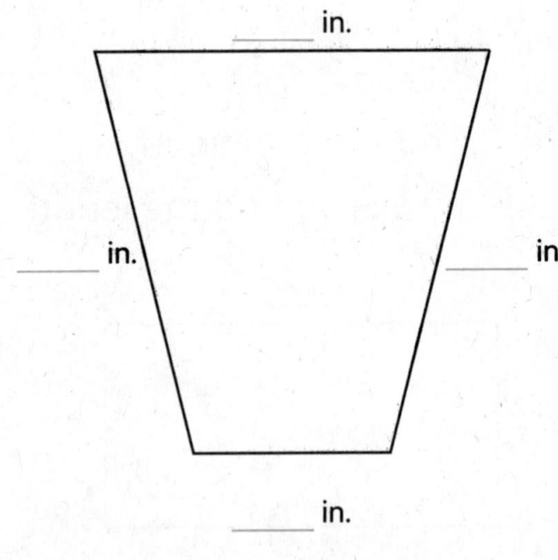

_____ inches

Name ______________________________

On Your Own

Use a centimeter ruler to find the perimeter.

6.

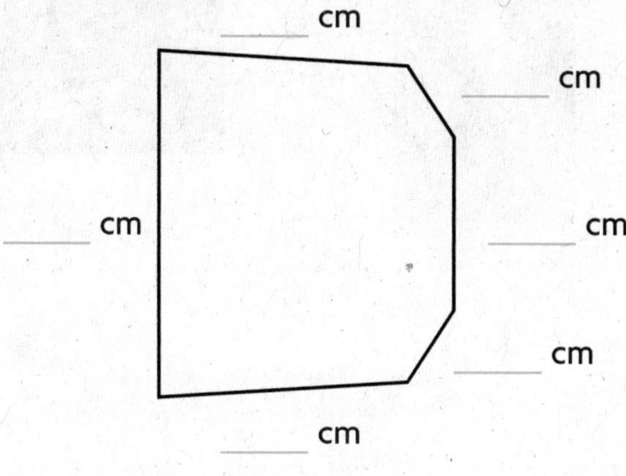

_____ centimeters

7.

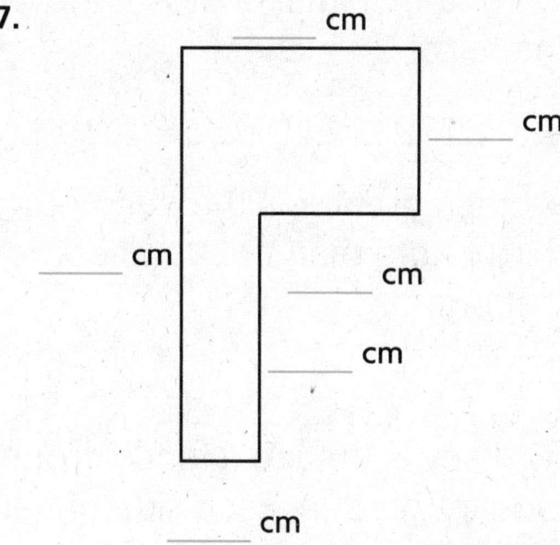

_____ centimeters

Use an inch ruler to find the perimeter.

8.

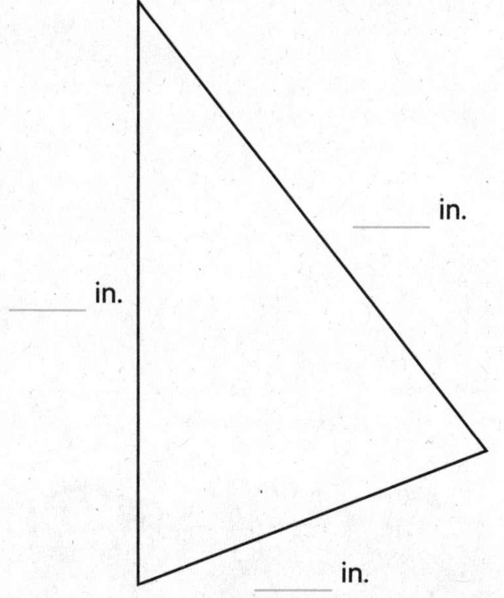

_____ inches

9.

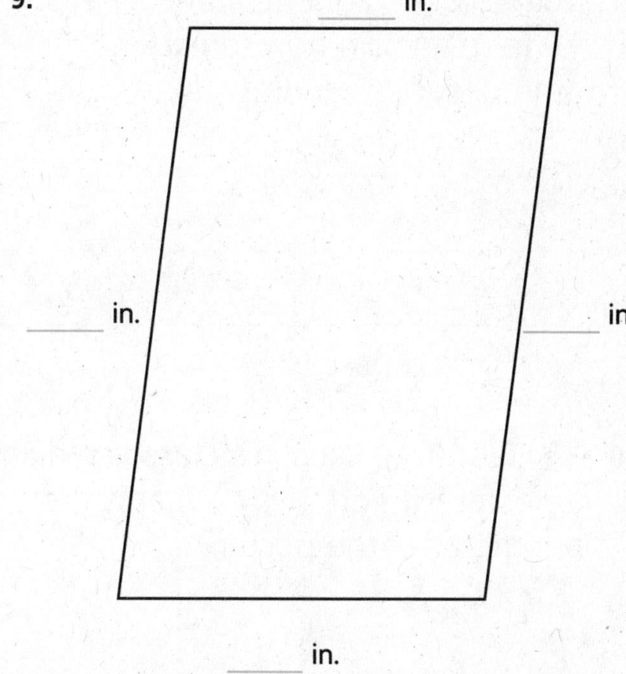

_____ inches

Problem Solving 

Use the pictures for 10–11.

10. Which of the animal photos has a perimeter of 24 inches?

____

11. How much greater is the perimeter of the bird photo than the perimeter of the cat photo?

____

SHOW YOUR WORK

12. H.O.T. Lacy is putting a fence around her square garden. Each side of her garden is 3 yards long. The fence costs \$5 for each yard. How much will the fence cost?

____

13. Write Math A rectangle has a perimeter of 28 feet. If one side is 10 feet, explain how to find the other sides.

____

____

____

____

14. **Test Prep** Austin's class is making a poster for Earth Day. What is the perimeter of the poster?

Ⓐ 24 feet

Ⓑ 28 feet

Ⓒ 30 feet

Ⓓ 32 feet

Name ______________________________

Find Perimeter

Essential Question How can you find the perimeter of a shape?

MA.3.G.5.1 Select appropriate units, strategies and tools to solve problems involving perimeter.

UNLOCK the Problem REAL WORLD

Adam is putting a rectangular frame around a picture that he made in art class. The length of the picture is 20 inches. The width of the picture is 16 inches. How many inches of frame does Adam need in all?

- Circle the numbers you will need to use.
- What are you asked to find?

____

20 in.

16 in.

16 in.

20 in.

One Way Use addition.

Perimeter = length + width + length + width

20 + 16 + 20 + 16 = _____

The perimeter is _____ inches.

So, Adam needs _____ inches of frame.

Another Way Use multiplication.

A Find Perimeter of a Rectangle

Perimeter = 2 × length + 2 × width

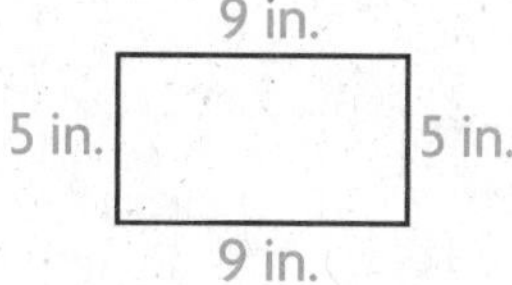

Perimeter = (2 × 9) + (2 × 5)

Perimeter = 18 + 10

Perimeter = _____

So, the perimeter is _____ inches.

B Find Perimeter of a Square

Perimeter = 4 × one side

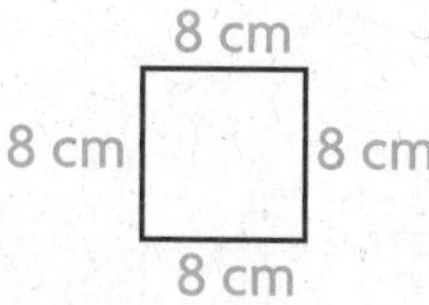

Perimeter = 4 × 8

Perimeter = _____

So, the perimeter is _____ centimeters.

Math Talk **Explain** how finding the perimeter of a square is different from finding the perimeter of a rectangle that is not a square.

Share and Show 

1. What is the perimeter of this shape?

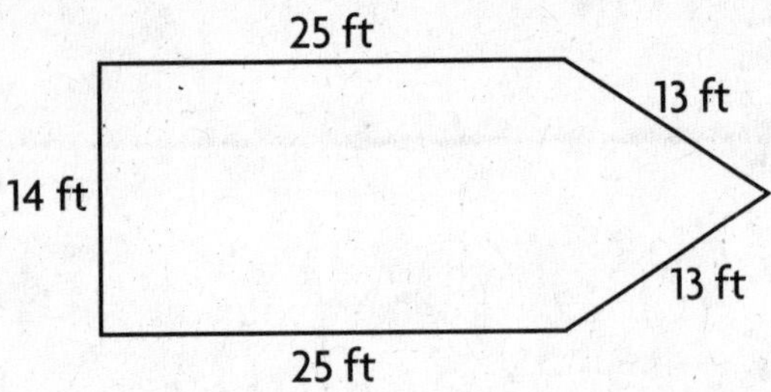

_____ + _____ + _____ + _____ + _____ = _____ feet

Find the perimeter.

2.

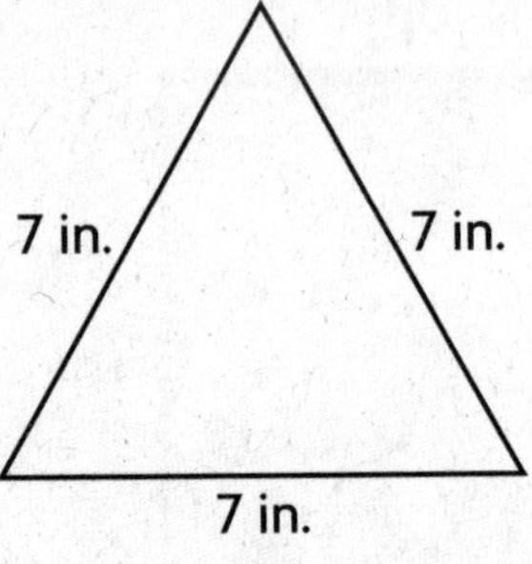

_____ inches

3.

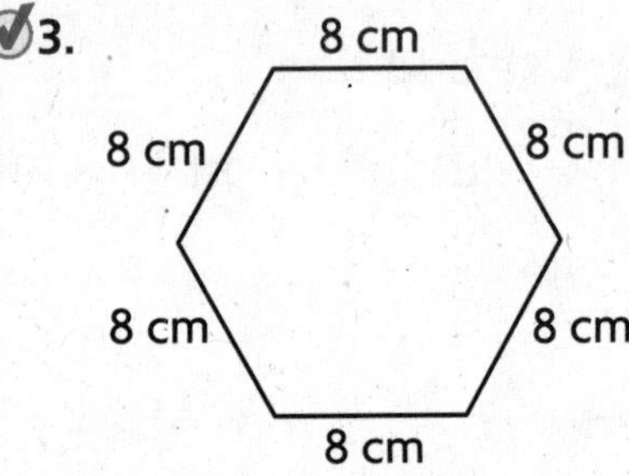

_____ centimeters

Math Talk **Explain** how you can use multiplication to find the perimeter of a hexagon with equal sides.

4.

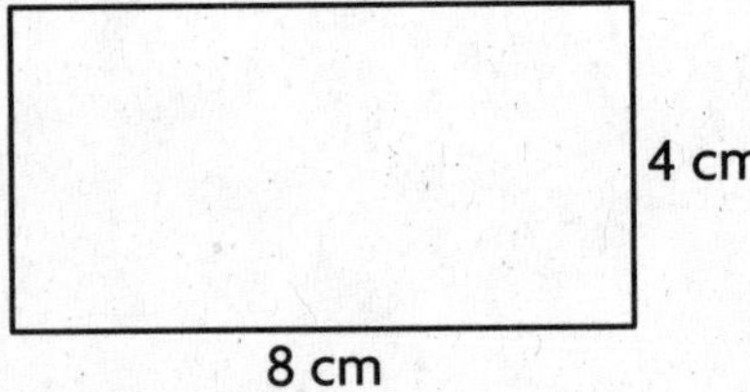

_____ centimeters

5.

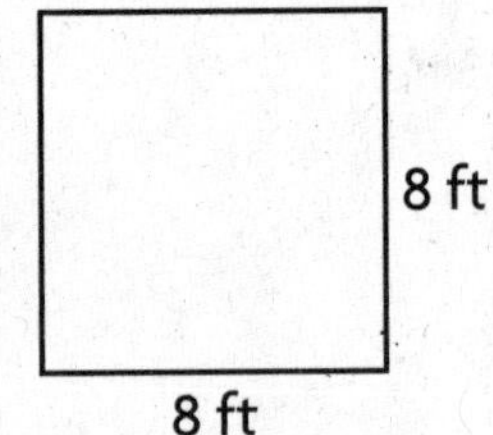

_____ feet

6.

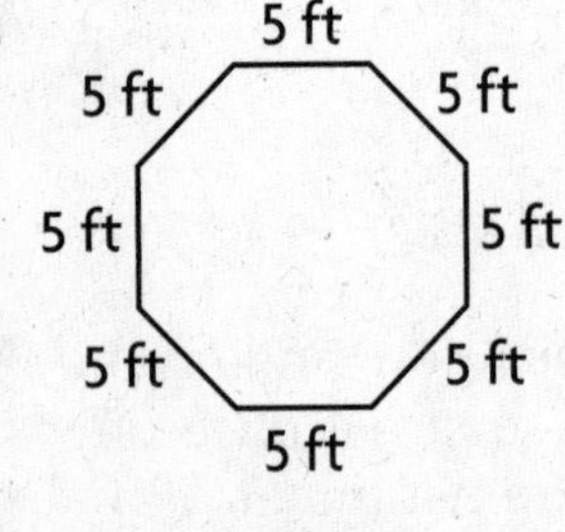

_____ feet

7.

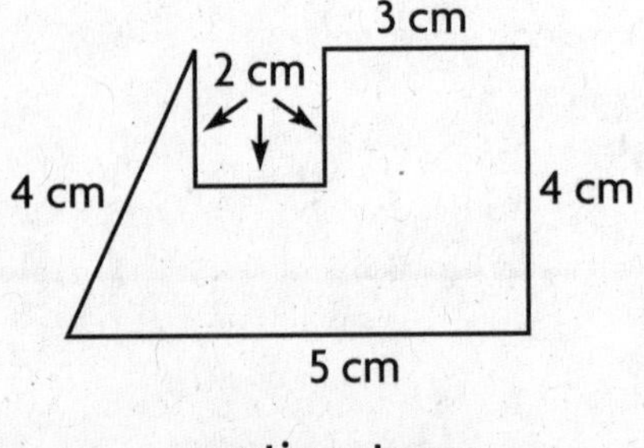

_____ centimeters

Name ______________________________

On Your Own

Find the perimeter.

8.

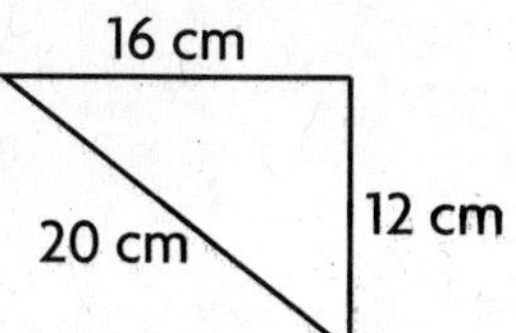

_____ centimeters

9.

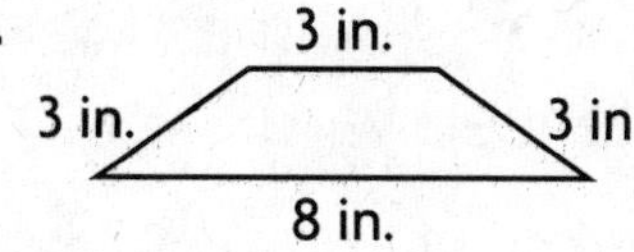

_____ inches

10.

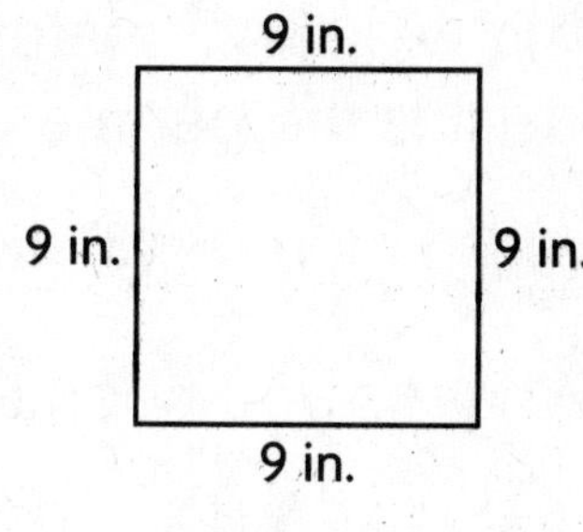

_____ inches

11.

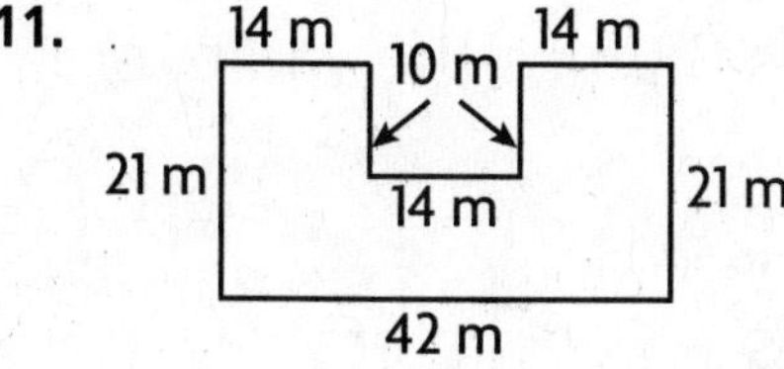

_____ meters

12.

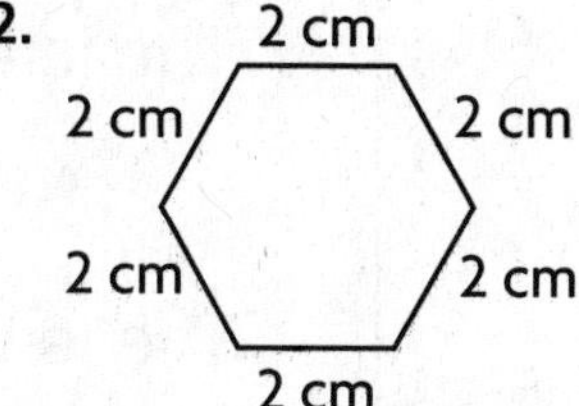

_____ centimeters

13.

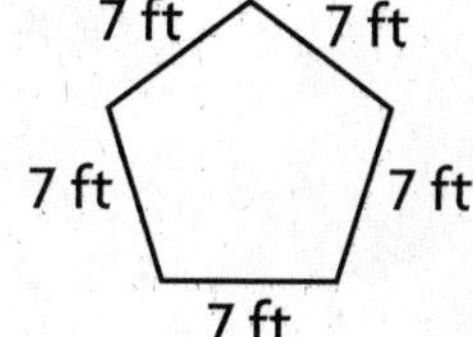

_____ feet

H.O.T. **Algebra** **Find the missing length.**

14.

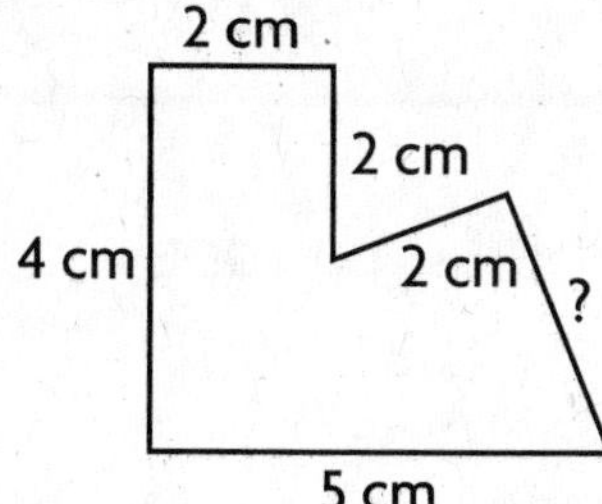

Perimeter = 18 cm

? = __________

15.

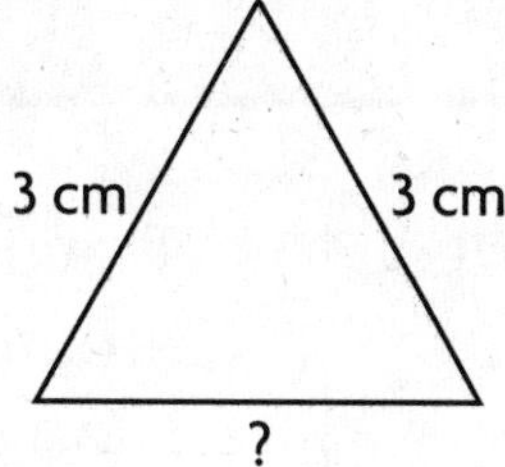

Perimeter = 9 cm

? = __________

16.

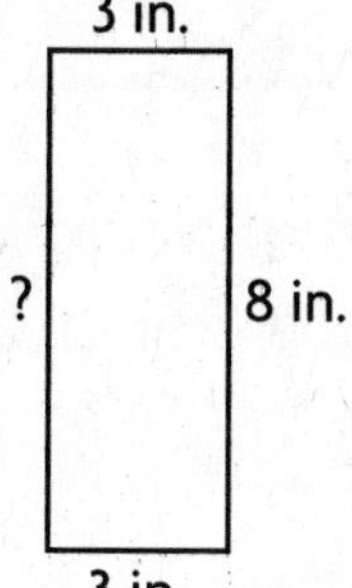

Perimeter = 22 in.

? = __________

UNLOCK the Problem REAL WORLD

17. Mr. Lewis fenced in his rectangular backyard. The width is 7 meters. The length is 3 times the width. What is the perimeter of the fenced yard?

Ⓐ 10 meters Ⓑ 14 meters Ⓒ 21 meters Ⓓ 56 meters

a. What do you need to find? ______________________

b. What operations will you use? ______________________

c. Show the steps you use to solve the problem.

d. Complete the sentences.

The width of the fenced yard is _____ meters.

The length is 3 times the width, or $3 \times$ _____.

The length is _____ meters.

So, the perimeter is _____ + _____ + _____ + _____ = _____ meters.

e. Fill in the bubble for the correct answer choice above.

18. Each side of a square is 8 feet. What is the perimeter of the square?

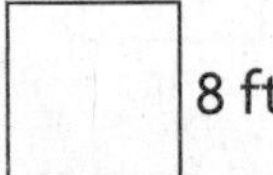

Ⓕ 12 feet Ⓗ 28 feet

Ⓖ 24 feet Ⓘ 32 feet

19. Trevor's dad is putting a rope around their garden. How much rope does his dad need?

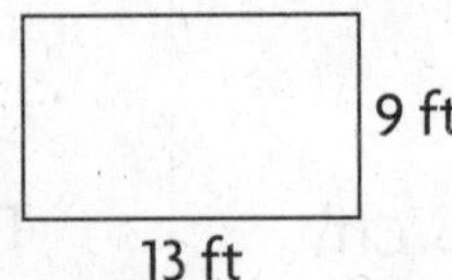

Ⓐ 28 feet Ⓒ 44 feet

Ⓑ 36 feet Ⓓ 54 feet

FOR MORE PRACTICE:
Florida Benchmarks Practice Book, pp. P271–P272

Name ______________________________

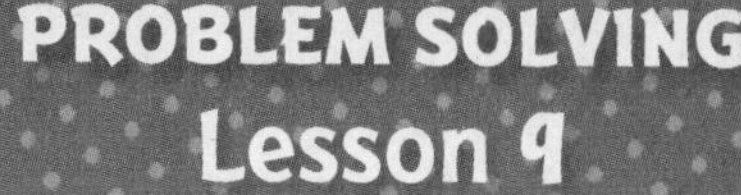

Search for Patterns · Perimeter

Essential Question How can you solve problems by finding a pattern?

MA.3.A.6.2 Solve non-routine problems by making a table, chart, or list and searching for patterns.

UNLOCK the Problem REAL WORLD

Lara is making a pattern with tiles. Suppose she continues the pattern. How many tiles will be in the fifth shape? What will be the perimeter of the fifth shape? What patterns do you see?

1 2 3

Read the Problem

What do I need to find?

The number of tiles in the ________ shape, the ________ of the ________ shape, and what patterns there are.

What information do I need to use?

I need to use the number of ________ in the shapes and the ________ of the shapes.

How will I use the information?

I will make a table to record the number of tiles in the shapes and the perimeters of the shapes. Then I will look for patterns.

Solve the Problem

Complete the table.

Shape	Number of Tiles	Perimeter (in units)
1	4	8
2	6	
3	8	
4		
5		

The number of tiles increases by ______. So, the pattern rule is ______.

The perimeter increases by ______ units. So, the pattern rule is ______.

There will be ______ tiles in the fifth shape. Its perimeter will be ______ units.

Math Talk **Explain** how knowing the pattern rule could help you find the perimeter of the tenth shape.

Try Another Problem

Jake makes a different pattern with tiles. If the pattern continues, how many tiles will be in the sixth shape? What will be the perimeter of the sixth shape? What patterns do you see?

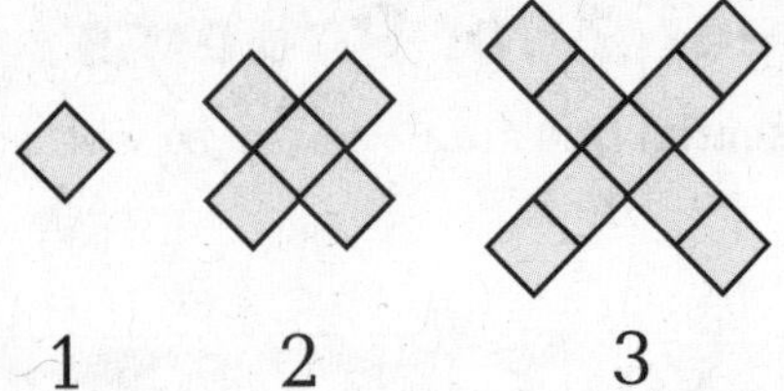

Read the Problem

What do I need to find?

What information do I need to use?

How will I use the information?

Solve the Problem

Complete the table.

Shape	Number of Tiles	Perimeter (in units)
1	1	4
2	5	12
3	9	20
4		
5		
6		

The number of tiles increases by _____. So, the pattern rule is __________.

The perimeter increases by _____ units. So, the pattern rule is __________. There will be _____ tiles in the sixth shape. Its perimeter will be _____ units.

Math Talk **Explain** how you would find the perimeter of Shape 8.

Name ______________________

Share and Show 

1. Kurt is making a pattern. He is using colored tiles. How many tiles are in Shape 5? What is the perimeter of Shape 5? What patterns do you see?

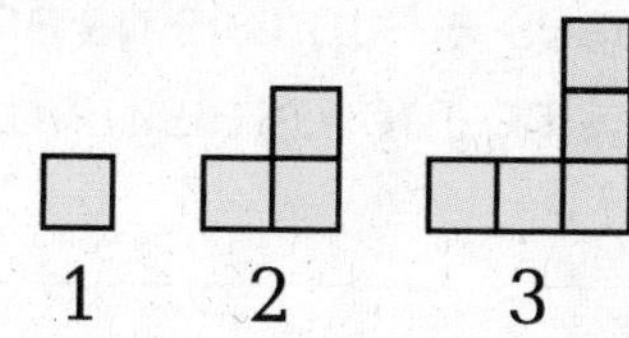

First, describe what you need to find.

____

____

Shape	Number of Tiles	Perimeter (in units)
1		
2		
3		
4		
5		

Next, complete the table. Find the number of tiles and the perimeter of the fifth shape. What patterns do you see?

The pattern rule for finding the number of tiles in Shape 5 is ____________. So, Shape 5 has _____ tiles. The pattern rule for finding the perimeter of each shape is ____________. So, the perimeter of Shape 5 is _____ units.

2. **What if** the length of one side of each tile above is 2 units? What would be the perimeter of the third shape? **Explain** how you know.

____

____

____

____

3. Holly is using regular polygons to make a growing pattern. The length of each side is 1 unit. If the pattern continues, what is the perimeter of the next shape? Describe the shape.

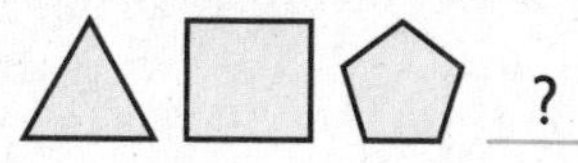

____

On Your Own

Choose a **STRATEGY**

Act It Out
Use Manipulatives
Draw a Diagram
Make a Table, Chart, or List
Search for Patterns

4. Jeni is making oatmeal raisin bread. She uses $\frac{2}{3}$ cup raisins and $\frac{1}{2}$ cup oats. Is Jeni using more raisins or more oats in her bread?

5. H.O.T. At the right is a diagram of Paula's bedroom. Her bedroom is in the shape of a rectangle. Label the lengths of the missing sides. What is the bedroom's perimeter?

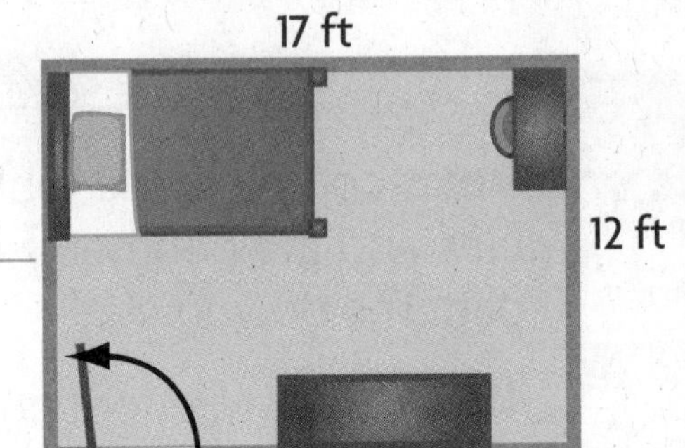

6. Write Math Richard had 31 baseball cards. His brother gave him 5 more. Richard put his cards into 4 equal piles. How many cards did Richard put in each pile? **Explain.**

7. Marie's mother tied 4 balloons to each of 6 tables at a party. Five of the balloons popped. How many balloons did not pop?

8. **Test Prep** To train for a race, James rode his bike 3 miles the first day, 7 miles the second day, and 11 miles the third day. If the pattern continued, how far did James ride the seventh day?

1	2	3	4	5	6	7
3	7	11				

Ⓐ 21 miles

Ⓑ 23 miles

Ⓒ 27 miles

Ⓓ 28 miles

FOR MORE PRACTICE:
Florida Benchmarks, Practice Book, pp. P273–P274

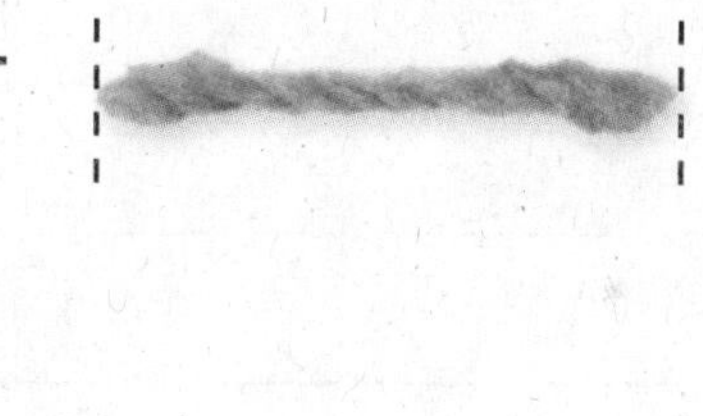

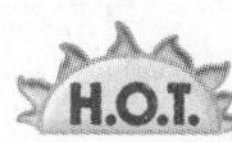

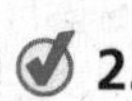

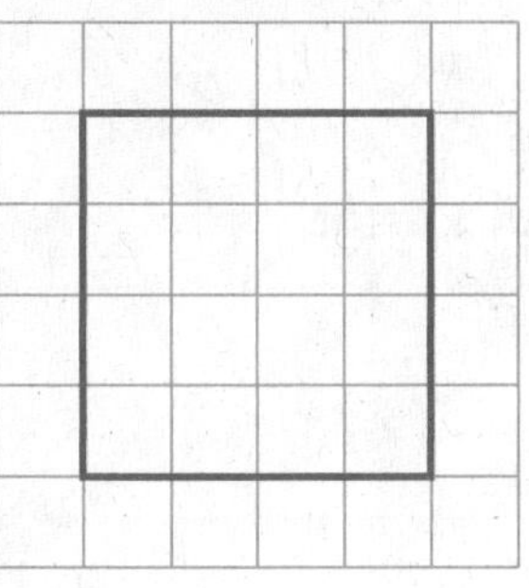

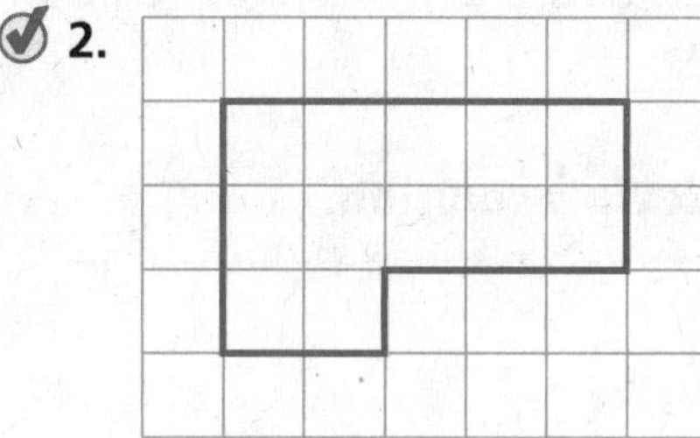

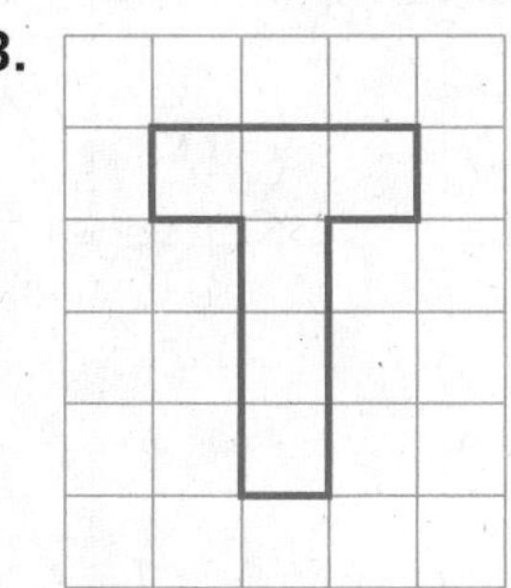

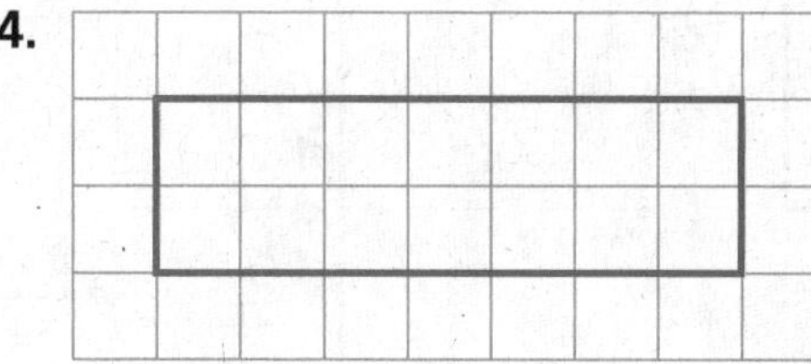

Share and Show 

1. Find the perimeter of the triangle in inches.

   Think: How long is each side?

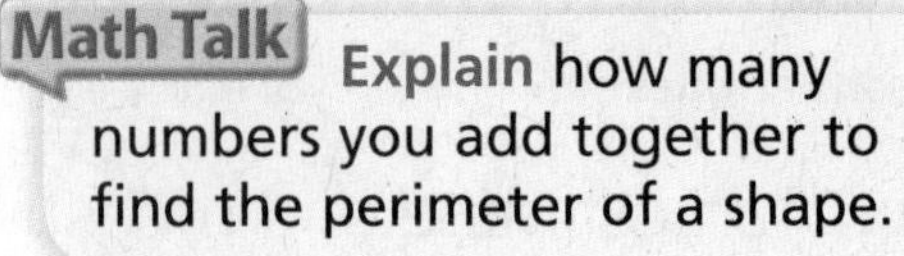

Use a centimeter ruler to find the perimeter.

2.

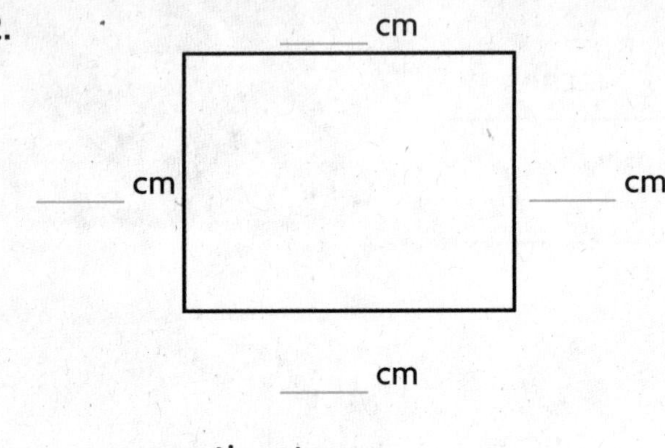

_____ centimeters

✓3.

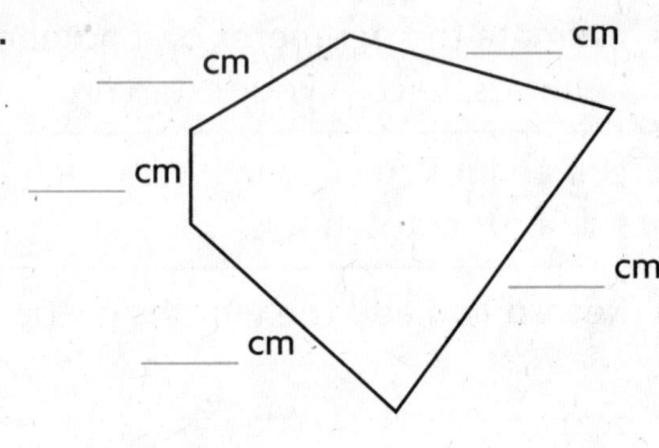

_____ centimeters

Use an inch ruler to find the perimeter.

4.

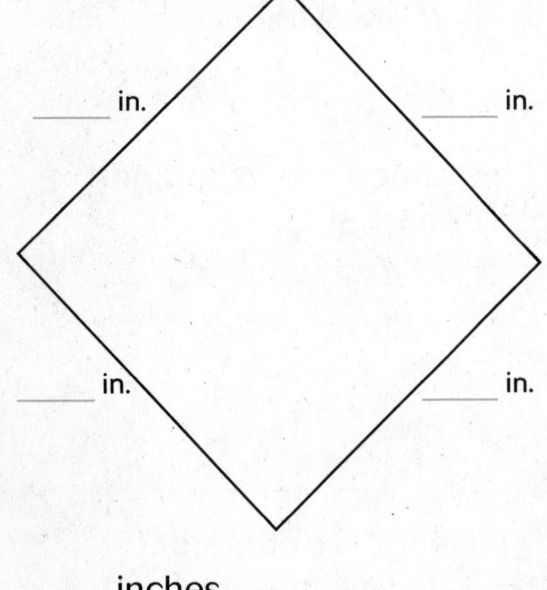

_____ inches

✓5.

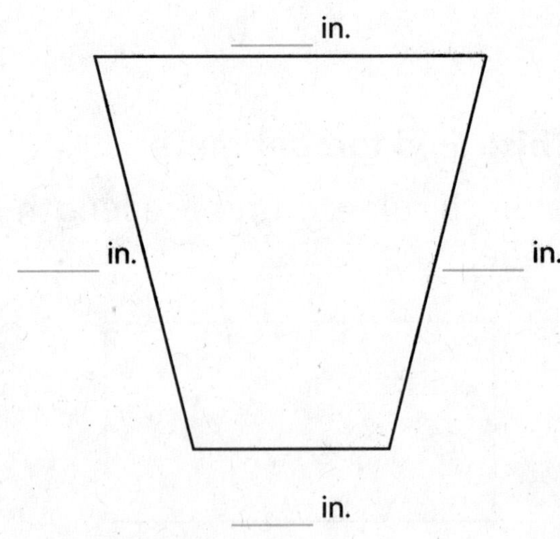

_____ inches

Problem Solving 

Use the pictures for 10–11.

10. Which of the animal photos has a perimeter of 24 inches?

____

11. How much greater is the perimeter of the bird photo than the perimeter of the cat photo?

____

SHOW YOUR WORK

12. H.O.T. Lacy is putting a fence around her square garden. Each side of her garden is 3 yards long. The fence costs $5 for each yard. How much will the fence cost?

____

13. Write Math A rectangle has a perimeter of 28 feet. If one side is 10 feet, explain how to find the other sides.

____

____

____

____

14. **Test Prep** Austin's class is making a poster for Earth Day. What is the perimeter of the poster?

Ⓐ 24 feet

Ⓑ 28 feet

Ⓒ 30 feet

Ⓓ 32 feet

 FOR MORE PRACTICE: Florida Benchmarks Practice Book, pp. P269–P270

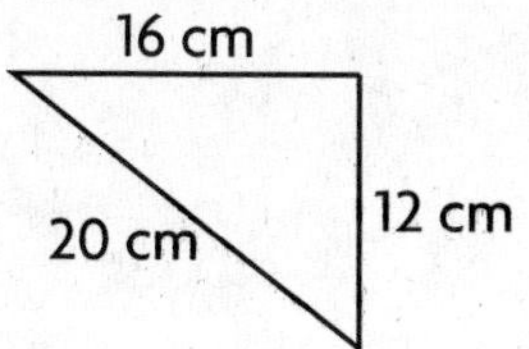

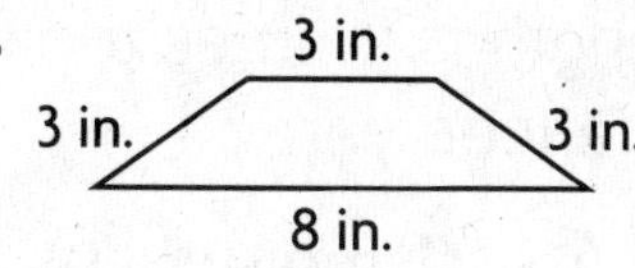

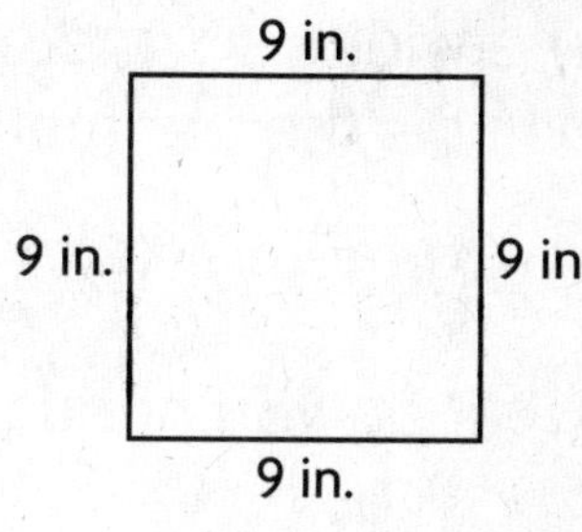

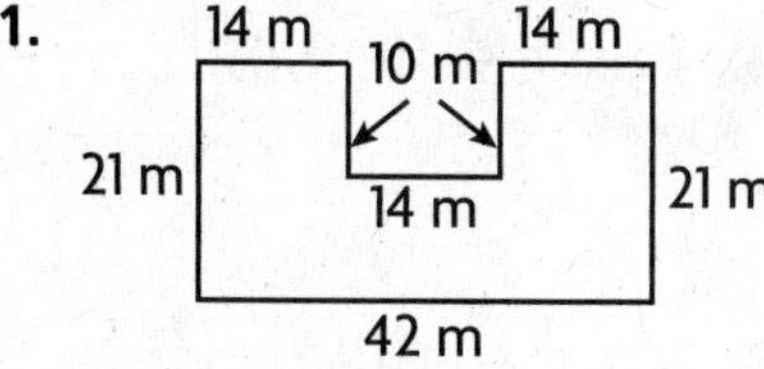

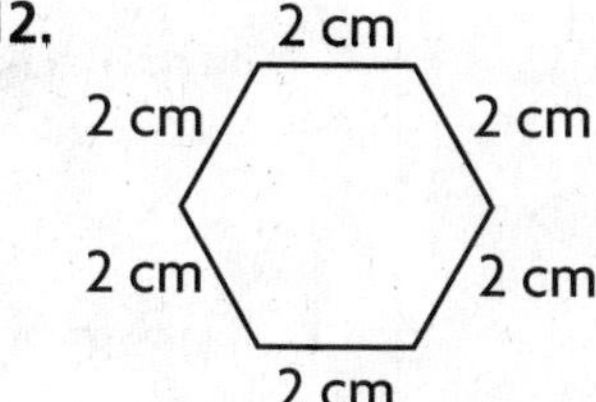

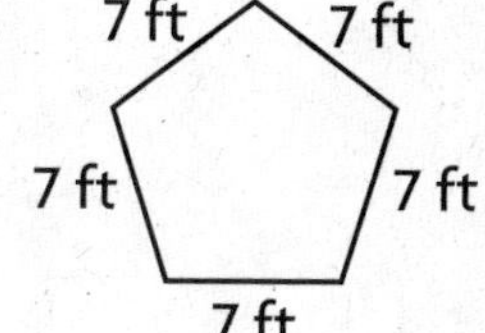

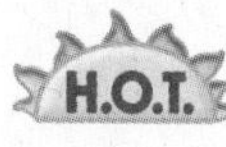

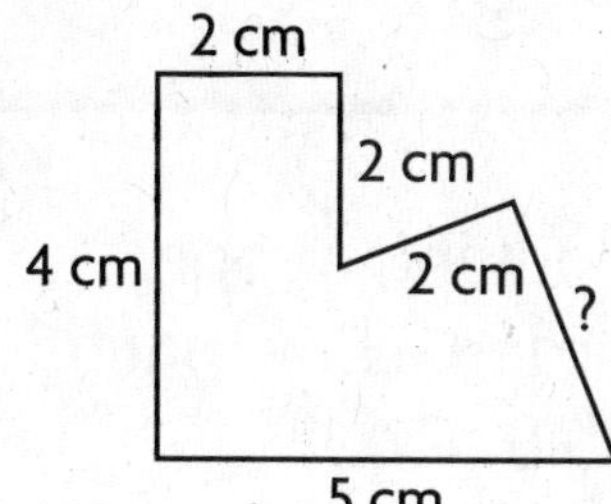

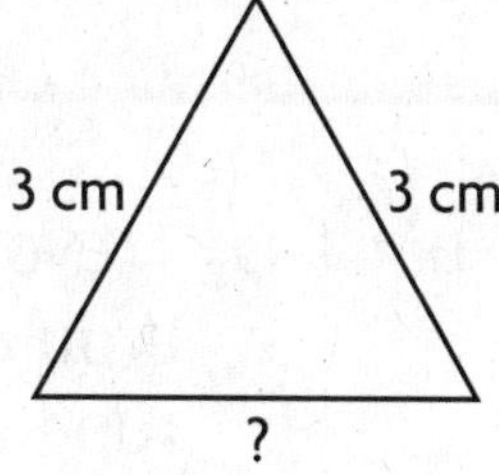

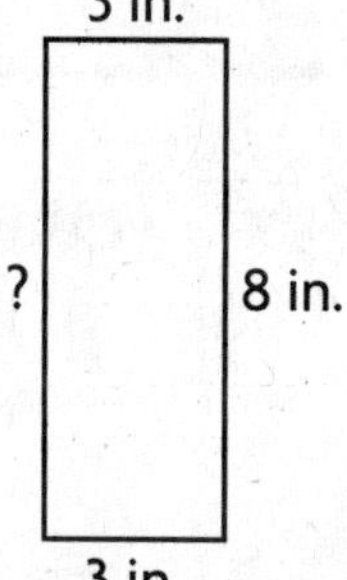

Name ___________________________

Elapsed Time in Years

Essential Question How can a time line help you find elapsed time in years?

MA.3.G.5.3 Tell time to the nearest minute and to the nearest quarter hour, and determine the amount of time elapsed.

CONNECT You learned how to use a calendar to measure days, weeks, and months. In this lesson, you will learn how to use a time line to measure **years**, **decades**, and **centuries**.

UNLOCK the Problem REAL WORLD

Julia turned 8 years old two months before she started third grade in 2010. In what year was Julia born?

- What year did Julia start third grade? ___________
- How old was Julia when she started third grade? ___________
- Circle the question.

Example 1

A time line shows the sequence, or order, of events.

Read a time line from left to right. Events on the left happened before, or earlier than, events on the right.

UNITS OF TIME
12 months = 1 year
10 years = 1 decade
10 decades = 1 century

This time line shows 10 years, or 1 ___________.
Label the missing years.

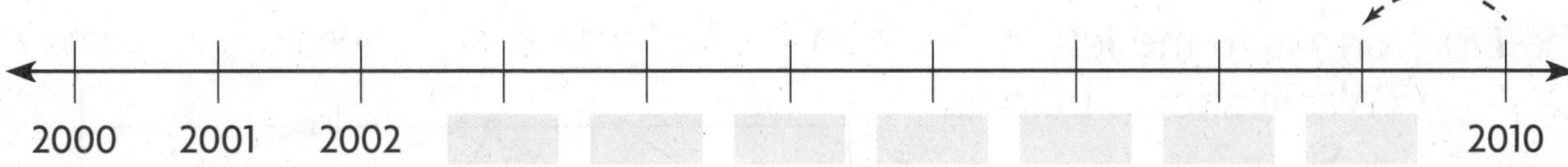

STEP 1 Circle the year Julia started third grade.

The year is ___________.

STEP 2 Draw jumps on the time line to count back 8 years to the year she was born.

Your arrows should end on the year ___________.

So, Julia was born in ___________.

Math Talk How is a time line like a number line?

Example 2

This time line shows 100 years, which is 10 decades, or 1 century. Label the missing years.

Years in Which Toys Were Introduced

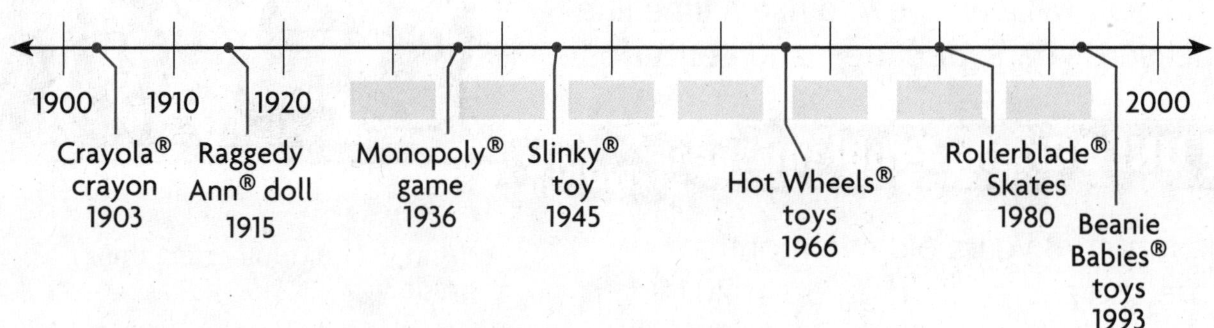

Rollerblade skates were first introduced in 1980. How many years after Hot Wheels toys were they introduced?

STEP 1 Circle the dot on the number line for Hot Wheels toys and for Rollerblade skates.

STEP 2 Draw jumps on the time line to count back.

1980 to 1970 = _____ years

1970 to 1966 = _____ years

So, Rollerblade skates were introduced _____ years after _______________.

Share and Show

Use the time line on right for 1–3.

Years in Which Movies Were First Shown

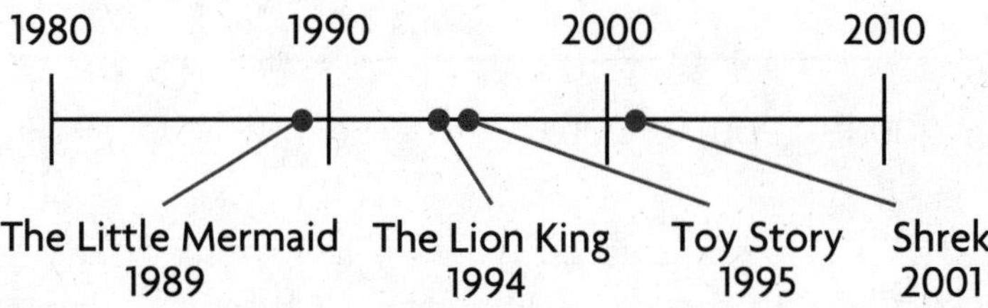

1. The *Lion King* is to the left of *Toy Story*. Was it shown before or after *Toy Story*?

____

Which movie was shown earlier? Explain how you know.

2. *The Little Mermaid* or *The Lion King*

____

3. *Shrek* or *Toy Story*

____

Math Talk *A Bug's Life* was first shown in 1998. **Explain** how you know how many years later it was introduced than *The Little Mermaid*.

Name ______________________________

On Your Own

Use the time line for 4–5.

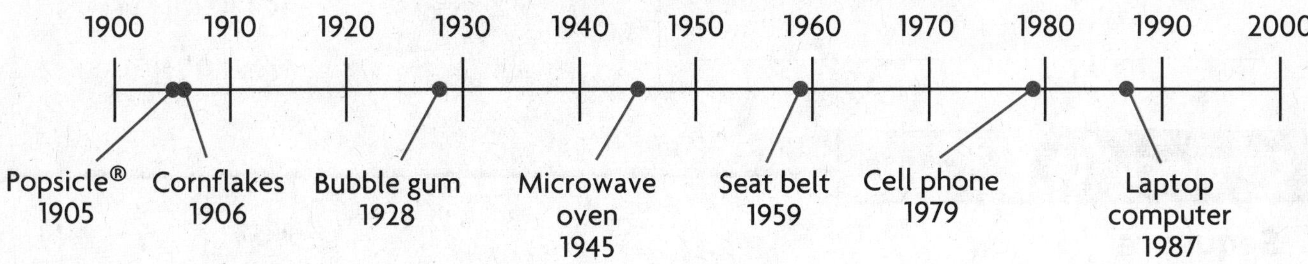

Which item was introduced earlier? Explain how you know.

4. microwave oven or cell phone

____

____

____

5. seat belt or bubble gum

____

____

____

6. H.O.T. Make a time line on a sheet of paper. Label the year you were born and the year you started third grade. Include other dates with information about you.

7. **Algebra Complete the table.**

Years	1	2	3	4	5		7	
Months	12	24	36			72		96

Problem Solving REAL WORLD

Use the time line above for 8–10.

8. Write Math **Explain** how to find how many years passed between the introduction of the microwave oven and of the laptop computer.

____

____

9. The Post-it Note® was introduced in 1974. Which other item's introduction date is closest to the date for the introduction of the Post-it Note?

____

10. **Test Prep** How many years before bubble gum was introduced was cornflakes breakfast cereal introduced?

Ⓐ 22 years
Ⓑ 44 years
Ⓒ 1906 years
Ⓓ 1928 years

Connect to Reading

Sequence

David is visiting the Sea Park. He really wants to see the Alligator Show, the Sea Turtle Exhibit, and the movie, *All About Oceans*. He would also like to see the Dolphin School exhibit and the Daring Divers. How should David plan his day?

One way to sequence information is to arrange the data in order of importance. Things that are most important should be listed first. You can also sequence information by putting things in order by time.

SEA PARK SCHEDULE

Sea Turtle Exhibit [45 minutes]
10:00 A.M.; 1:00 P.M.; 3:00 P.M.

Alligator Show [30 minutes]
9:30 A.M.; 11:30 A.M.; 2:30 P.M.

Daring Divers [20 minutes]
9:00 A.M.; 11:00 A.M.; 2:00 P.M.

All About Oceans [50 minutes]
11:00 A.M.; 12:00 P.M.; 1:00 P.M.

Dolphin School [30 minutes]
9:00 A.M.; 12:00 P.M.; 3:00 P.M.

Things I Really Want to See
Alligator Show
Sea Turtle Exhibit
All About Oceans

Things I'd Like to See
Daring Divers
Dolphin School

11. Look at the schedule. In what order should David plan to visit the exhibits that he really wants to see? Write the exhibit and the time.

____

12. Suppose David can see one other exhibit. What can he see? At what time?

____

FOR MORE PRACTICE:
Florida Benchmarks Practice Book, pp. P293–P294

Name ____________________

Chapter Review/Test

▶ Check Vocabulary

Choose the best term from the box.

Vocabulary
calendar
century
decade
elapsed time
time line
year

1. Ten years is also called a ________________. **(MA.3.G.5.3, p. 535)**

2. A ________________ shows the days, weeks, and months of a year. **(MA.3.G.5.3, p. 531)**

3. ________________ is the amount of time that passes from the start of an activity to the end of the activity. **(MA.3.G.5.3, p. 523)**

▶ Check Concepts and Skills

Write the time. **(MA.3.G.5.3, pp. 509–512, 513–516)**

4. 

____

5. 

____

6. 

____

7. 

____

Write the time for the activity. Use A.M. or P.M. **(MA.3.G.5.3, pp. 517–520]**

8. play catch

____

9. eat lunch

____

10. walk the dog

____

11. get ready for school

____

Find the elapsed time. **(MA.3.G.5.3, pp. 523–526)**

12. Start: 2:15 P.M.

End: 3:10 P.M. ________________

13. Start: 10:20 A.M.

End: 1:05 P.M. ________________

Go online Assessment Options Chapter Test

Fill in the bubble for the correct answer choice.

14. Tim arrived at the soccer game at quarter to 4. What is another way to write this time?

(MA.3.G.5.3, pp. 509–512)

Ⓐ 3:25

Ⓑ 3:45

Ⓒ 4:25

Ⓓ 4:45

15. Laura ate dinner at quarter past 6. What is another way to write this time? **(MA.3.G.5.3, pp. 509–512)**

Ⓕ 6:15

Ⓖ 6:25

Ⓗ 6:30

Ⓘ 6:45

16. The hour hand on Tony's watch is between the 7 and the 8. The minute hand is on the 7. What time is it?

(MA.3.G.5.3, pp. 513–516)

Ⓐ 6:35

Ⓑ 7:07

Ⓒ 7:35

Ⓓ 8:35

17. Morgan and her mother walked their dog after supper. At what time did they walk the dog?

(MA.3.G.5.3, pp. 517–520)

Ⓕ 12:30 P.M.

Ⓖ 6:30 A.M.

Ⓗ 7:15 A.M.

Ⓘ 7:15 P.M.

Name ______________________________

18. Jared built a model airplane. He started at 2:30 P.M. and finished 1 hour 55 minutes later. At what time did Jared finish his model airplane? **(MA.3.G.5.3, pp. 523–526)**

Ⓐ 2:55 P.M.

Ⓑ 3:30 P.M.

Ⓒ 4:25 A.M.

Ⓓ 4:25 P.M.

19. Valerie's family went out to dinner. They left at 5:45 P.M. They returned home 2 hours 25 minutes later. At what time did they return home? **(MA.3.G.5.3, pp. 523–526)**

Ⓕ 6:10 P.M.

Ⓖ 7:45 P.M.

Ⓗ 8:10 P.M.

Ⓘ 8:45 P.M.

20. Anthony spent 1 hour 35 minutes at soccer practice. He left practice at 4:15 P.M. At what time did he arrive at soccer practice? **(MA.3.G.5.3, pp. 527–530)**

Ⓐ 2:40 P.M.

Ⓑ 2:45 P.M.

Ⓒ 3:15 P.M.

Ⓓ 3:45 P.M.

Name ______________________________

21. Suppose it is September 8. Avery's ballet class begins in 2 weeks. On what date is Avery's first ballet class?
(MA.3.G.5.3, pp. 531–534)

Ⓕ September 14

Ⓖ September 22

Ⓗ September 28

Ⓘ October 6

22. Susan is going to visit her grandparents 3 weeks after school ends. School will end on May 28. On what day is Susan going to visit her grandparents?
(MA.3.G.5.3, pp. 531–534)

May

Sunday	Monday	Tuesday	Wednesday	Thursday	Friday	Saturday
				1	2	3
4	5	6	7	8	9	10
11	12	13	14	15	16	17
18	19	20	21	22	23	24
25	26	27	28	29	30	31

June

Sunday	Monday	Tuesday	Wednesday	Thursday	Friday	Saturday
1	2	3	4	5	6	7
8	9	10	11	12	13	14
15	16	17	18	19	20	21
22	23	24	25	26	27	28
29	30					

Ⓐ June 11

Ⓑ June 18

Ⓒ June 25

Ⓓ July 1

23. Alexis made a time line to show some events in the life of Fishy, her kitten. Fishy was about 3 weeks old when he started getting teeth. What other event on the time line happened at about the same time?
(MA.3.G.5.3, pp. 535–538)

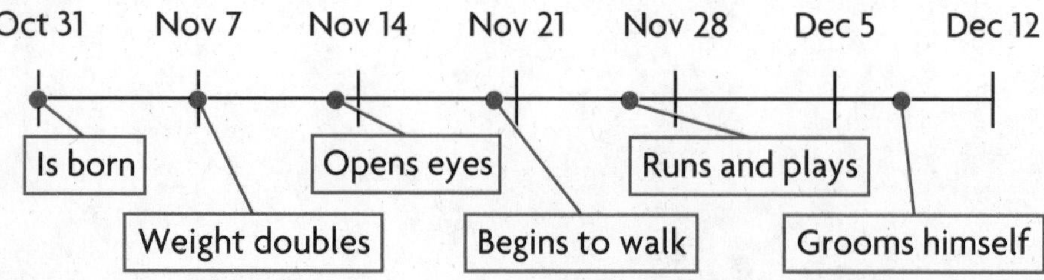

Ⓕ opens eyes

Ⓖ runs and plays

Ⓗ is born

Ⓘ begins to walk

Glossary

Pronunciation Key

a	add, map	f	fit, half	n	nice, tin	p	pit, stop	yo͞o	fuse, few
ā	ace, rate	g	go, log	ng	ring, song	r	run, poor	v	vain, eve
â(r)	care, air	h	hope, hate	o	odd, hot	s	see, pass	w	win, away
ä	palm, father	i	it, give	ō	open, so	sh	sure, rush	y	yet, yearn
b	bat, rub	ī	ice, write	ô	order, jaw	t	talk, sit	z	zest, muse
ch	check, catch	j	joy, ledge	oi	oil, boy	th	thin, both	zh	vision, pleasure
d	dog, rod	k	cool, take	ou	pout, now	t͟h	this, bathe		
e	end, pet	l	look, rule	o͝o	took, full	u	up, done		
ē	equal, tree	m	move, seem	o͞o	pool, food	û(r)	burn, term		

ə the schwa, an unstressed vowel representing the sound spelled *a* in *above*, *e* in *sicken*, *i* in *possible*, *o* in *melon*, *u* in *circus*

Other symbols:
- • separates words into syllables
- ′ indicates stress on a syllable

acute angle [ə•kyo͞ot′ ang′gəl] **ángulo agudo** An angle that has a measure less than that of a right angle (p. 389)
Example:

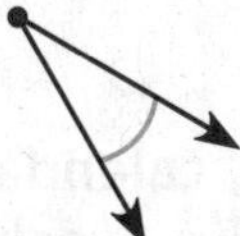

acute triangle [ə•kyo͞ot′ trī′ang•gəl] **triángulo acutángulo** A triangle that has three acute angles (p. 400)

addend [a′dend] **sumando** Any of the numbers that are added in addition
Examples: 2 + 3 = 5
↑ addend ↑ addend

addition [ə•di′shən] **suma** The process of finding the total number of items when two or more groups of items are joined; the opposite operation of subtraction

A.M. [ā•em] **a.m.** The time between midnight and noon (p. 517)

analog clock [a′nəl•og kläk] **reloj analógico** A tool for measuring time, in which hands move around a circle to show hours, minutes, and sometimes seconds (p. 509)
Example:

angle [ang′gəl] **ángulo** A shape formed by two rays that share an endpoint (p. 377)
Example:

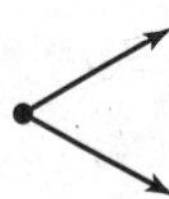

Word History

When the letter *g* is replaced with the letter *k* in the word ***angle***, the word becomes *ankle*. Both words come from the same Latin root, *angulus*, which means "a sharp bend."

array [ə•rā′] **matriz** A set of objects arranged in rows and columns (p. 131)
Example:

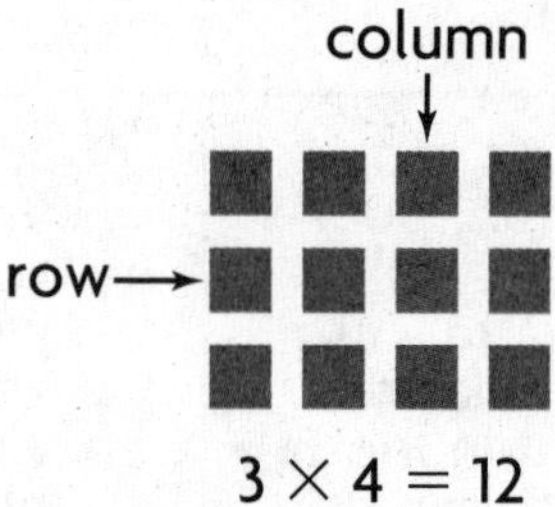

Associative Property of Addition [ə•sō′shē•ə•tiv prä′pər•tē əv ə•di′shən] **propiedad asociativa de la suma** The property that states that you can group addends in different ways and still get the same sum
Example:
$4 + (2 + 5) = 11$
$(4 + 2) + 5 = 11$

Associative Property of Multiplication [ə•sō′shē•ə•tiv prä′pər•tē əv mul•tə•plə•kā′shən] **propiedad asociativa de la multiplicación** The property that states that when the grouping of factors is changed, the product remains the same (p. 161)
Example:
$(3 \times 2) \times 4 = 24$
$3 \times (2 \times 4) = 24$

bar graph [bär graf] **gráfica de barras** A graph that uses bars to show data (p. 83)
Example:

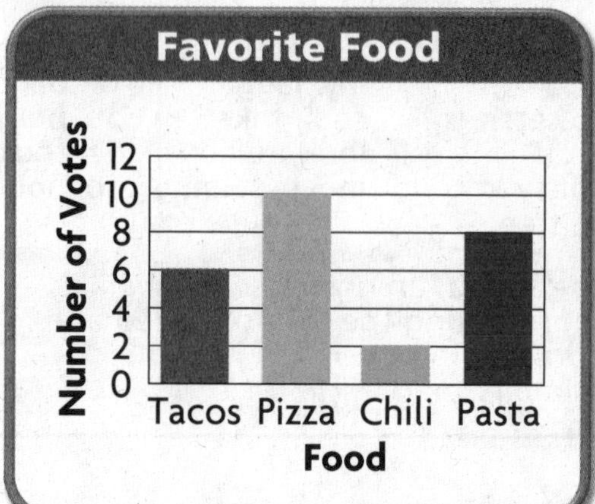

benchmark numbers [bench′märk num′bərz] **números de referencia** Numbers that are easy to work with, such as $\frac{1}{2}$ and 1 (p. 343)

calendar [ka′lən•dər] **calendario** A chart that shows the days, weeks, and months of a year (p. 531)

capacity [kə•pa′sə•tē] **capacidad** The amount a container can hold
Example:
1 half gallon = 2 quarts

cent sign (¢) [sent sīn] **simbolo de centauo** A symbol that stands for *cent* or *cents*
Example: 53¢

centimeter (cm) [sen′tə•mē•tər] **centímetro (cm)** A metric unit that is used to measure length or distance (p. 477)
Example:

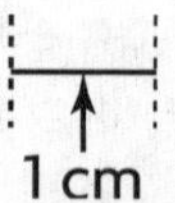

century [sen′chə•rē] **siglo** A measure of time on a calendar, equal to 100 years (p. 535)

change [chānj] **cambio** The money you get back if you have paid for an item with coins or bills that have a value greater than the cost of the item

circle [sûr′kəl] **círculo** A round closed plane shape (p. 378)

closed shape [klōzd shāp] **figura cerrada** A shape that begins and ends at the same point (p. 378)
Examples:

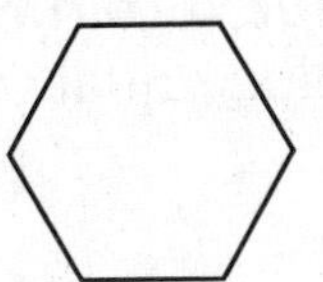

combination [kom•bə•nā′shən] **combinación** A result of joining two or more things (p. 165)

Commutative Property of Addition [kə•myo͞o′tə•tiv prä′pər•tē əv ə•di′shən] **propiedad conmutativa de la suma** The property that states that you can add two or more numbers in any order and get the same sum
Example: $6 + 7 = 13$
$7 + 6 = 13$

Commutative Property of Multiplication [kə•myo͞o′tə•tiv prä′pər•tē əv mul•tə•plə•kā′shən] **propiedad conmutativa de la multiplicación** The property that states that you can multiply two factors in any order and get the same product (p. 135)
Example: $2 \times 4 = 8$
$4 \times 2 = 8$

compare [kəm•pâr′] **comparar** To describe whether numbers are equal to, less than, or greater than each other (p. 339)

compatible numbers [kəm•pat′ə•bəl num′bərz] **números compatibles** Numbers that are easy to compute with mentally (p. 28)

cone [kōn] **cono** A three-dimensional, pointed shape that has a flat, round base
Example:

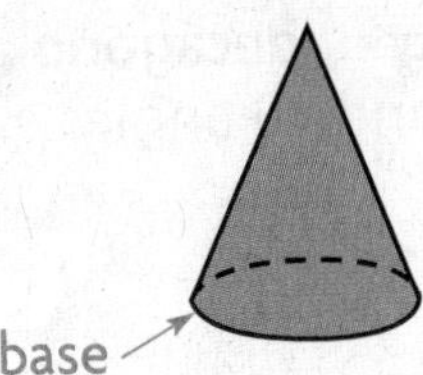

congruent [kən•gro͞o′ənt] **congruente** Shapes that have the same size and shape (p. 435)
Example:

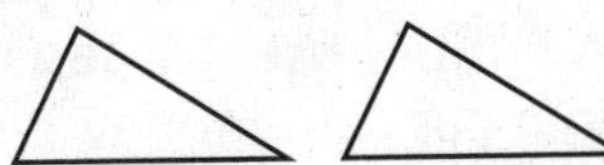

cube [kyo͞ob] **cubo** A three-dimensional shape with six congruent square faces
Example:

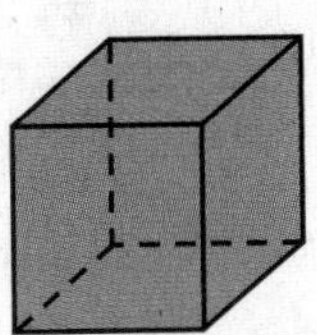

cup (c) [kup] **taza (t)** A customary unit used to measure capacity

cylinder [sil′in•dər] **cilindro** A three-dimensional object that is shaped like a can
Example:

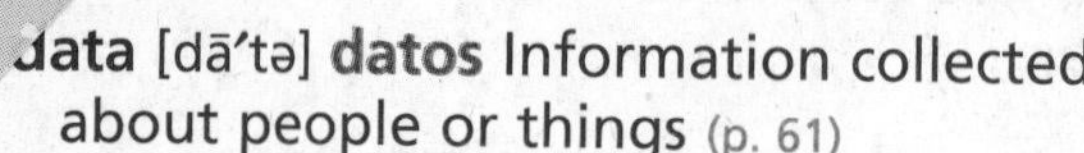

data [dā′tə] **datos** Information collected about people or things (p. 61)

decade [de′kād] **década** A measure of time, equal to 10 years (p. 535)

decagon [de′kə•gän] **decágono** A polygon with 10 sides and 10 angles (p. 385)

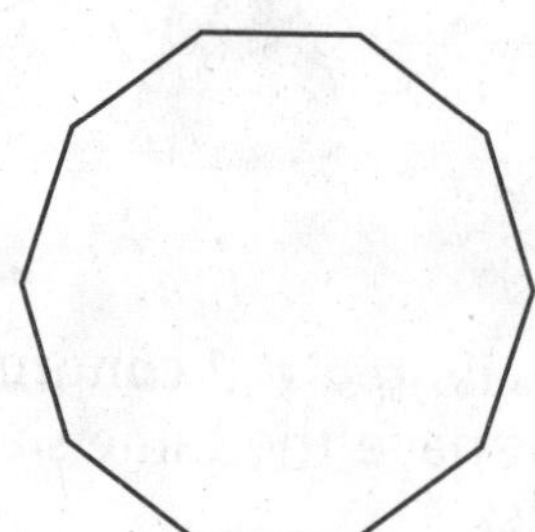

decimal point [de′sə•məl point] **punto decimal** A symbol used to separate dollars from cents in money
Example: \$4.52
↑ decimal point

decimeter (dm) [de′sə•mē•tər] **decímetro (dm)** A metric unit that is used to measure length or distance; 1 decimeter = 10 centimeters (p. 477)

denominator [di•nä′mə•nā•tər] **denominador** The part of a fraction below the line, which tells how many equal parts there are in the whole or in the group (p. 303)
Example: $\frac{3}{4}$ ← denominator

diagonal [dī•a′gə•nəl] **diagonal** A line segment that connects two vertices of a polygon that are not next to each other (p. 422)
Example:

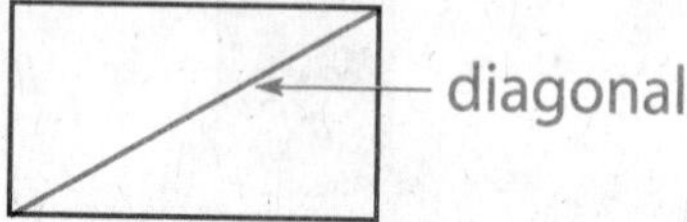

difference [di′frəns] **diferencia** The answer to a subtraction problem
Example: 6 − 4 = 2
↑ difference

digital clock [di′jə•təl kläk] **reloj digital** A clock that shows time to the minute, using digits (p. 509)
Example:

digits [di′jətz] **dígitos** The symbols 0, 1, 2, 3, 4, 5, 6, 7, 8, and 9

dime [dīm] **moneda de 10¢** A coin worth 10 cents and with a value equal to that of 10 pennies; 10¢
Example:

Distributive Property of Multiplication [di•stri′byə•tiv prä′pər•tē] **propiedad distributiva** The property that states that multiplying a sum by a number is the same as multiplying each addend by the number and then adding the products (p.169)
Example: 5 × 8 = (5 × 4) + (5 × 4)
5 × 8 = 20 + 20
5 × 8 = 40

divide [di•vīd′] **dividir** To separate into equal groups; the opposite operation of multiplication (p. 205)

dividend [di′və•dend] **dividendo** The number that is to be divided in a division problem (p. 213)
Example: 35 ÷ 5 = 7
↑ dividend

division [di•vi′zhen] **división** The process of sharing a number of items to find how many groups can be made or how many items will be in a group; the opposite operation of multiplication (p. 205)

divisor [di•vī′zər] **divisor** The number that divides the dividend (p. 213)
Example: 35 ÷ 5 = 7
↑ divisor

dollar [dol′ər] **dólar** Paper money worth 100 cents and equal to 100 pennies; $1.00
Example:

eighths [ātths] **octavos**

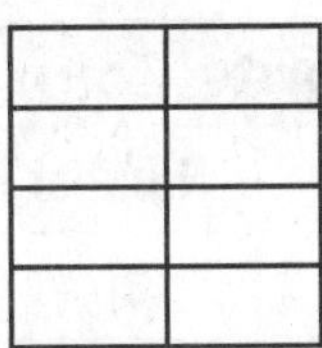

These are eighths. (p.291)

elapsed time [i•lapst′ tīm] **tiempo transcurrido** The time that passes from the start of an activity to the end of that activity (p. 523)

equal groups [ē′kwəl grüpz] **grupos iguales** Groups that have the same number of objects (p. 109)

equal parts [ē′kwəl pärts] **partes iguales** Parts that are exactly the same size (p. 291)

equal sign (=) [ē′kwəl sīn] **signo de igualdad** A symbol used to show that two numbers have the same value
Example: 384 = 384

equal to (=) [ē′kwəl too͞] **igual a** Having the same value
Example: 4 + 4 is equal to 3 + 5.

equation [i•kwā′zhən] **ecuación** A number sentence that uses the equal sign to show that two amounts are equal
Examples:
3 + 7 = 10
4 − 1 = 3
6 × 7 = 42

equilateral triangle [ē•kwə•la′tər•əl trī′ang•gəl] **triángulo equilátero** A triangle that has three equal sides and three equal angles (p. 399)
Examples:

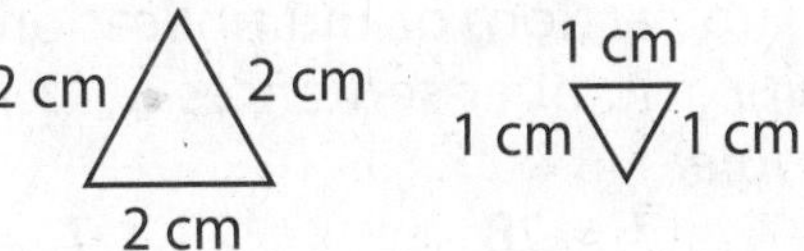

equivalent [ē•kwiv′ə•lənt] **equivalente** Two or more sets that name the same amount

equivalent fractions [ē•kwiv′ə•lənt frak′shənz] **fracciones equivalentes** Two or more fractions that name the same amount (p. 361)
Example:

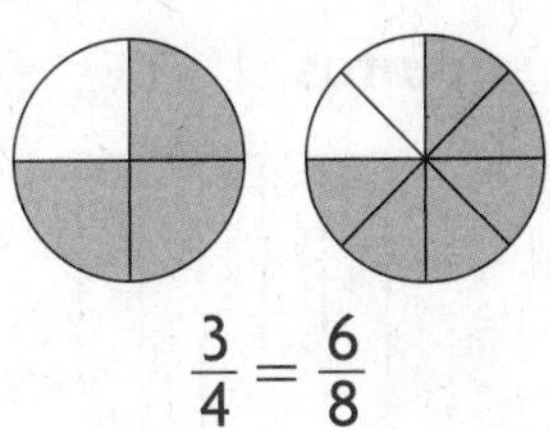

$\frac{3}{4} = \frac{6}{8}$

estimate [es′tə•māt] *verb* **estimar**: To find about how many or how much (p. 27)

estimate [es′tə•mət] *noun* **estimación**: A number close to an exact amount (p. 27)

even [ē′vən] **par** A whole number that has a 0, 2, 4, 6, or 8 in the ones place

expanded form [ik•spand′id fôrm] **forma desarrollada** A way to write numbers by showing the value of each digit (p. 17)
Example: 7,201 = 7,000 + 200 + 1

experiment [ik•sper′ə•mənt] **experimento** A test that is done in order to find out something (p. 62)

expression [ik•spre′shən] **expresión** The part of a number sentence that combines numbers and operation signs but doesn't have an equal sign
Example: 5 × 6

fact family [fakt fam′ə•lē] **familia de operaciones** A set of related addition and subtraction, or multiplication and division, number sentences (p. 239)
Example:

$4 \times 7 = 28$ $28 \div 7 = 4$
$7 \times 4 = 28$ $28 \div 4 = 7$

factor [fak′tər] **factor** A number that is multiplied by another number to find a product (p. 117)
Examples: $3 \times 8 = 24$

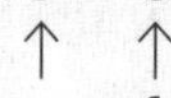

fifths [fifths] **quintos**

These are fifths.

foot (ft) [fo͝ot] **pie** A customary unit used to measure length or distance;
1 foot = 12 inches (p. 465)

fourths [fôrths] **cuartos**

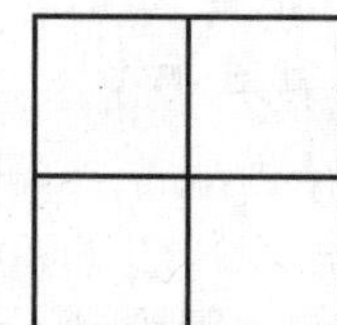

These are fourths. (p. 291)

fraction [frak′shən] **fracción** A number that names part of a whole or part of a group (p. 299)
Examples:

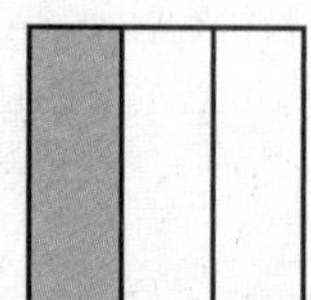

$\frac{1}{3}$

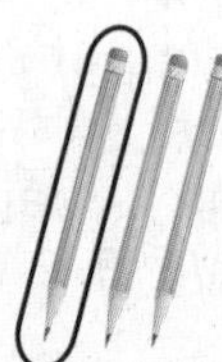

fraction greater than 1 [frak′shən grā′tər t͟han wun] **fracción mayor que 1** A number which has a numerator that is greater than its denominator (p. 309)

Word History

Often, a ***fraction*** is a part of a whole that is broken into pieces. *Fraction* comes from the Latin word *frangere*, which means "to break."

frequency table [frē′kwen•sē tā′bəl] **tabla de frecuencia** A table that uses numbers to record data (p. 61)
Example:

Favorite Color	
Color	**Number**
blue	10
red	7
green	8
yellow	4

gallon (gal) [ga′lən] **galón (gal)** A customary unit used to measure capacity;
1 gallon = 4 quarts

gram (g) [gram] **gramo (g)** A metric unit that is used to measure mass;
1 kilogram = 1,000 grams

greater than (>) [grā′tər t͟han] **mayor que** A symbol used to compare two numbers when the greater number is given first (p. 339)
Example: $6 > 4$

Grouping Property of Addition [gro͞o′ping prä′pər•tē əv ə•di′shən] **propiedad de agrupación de la suma** *See* Associative Property of Addition.

Grouping Property of Multiplication [gro͞o′ping prä′pər•tē əv mul•tə•plə•kā′shən] **propiedad de agrupación de la multiplicación** *See* Associative Property of Multiplication.

growing pattern [grō′ing pat′ərn] **patrón acumulativo** A pattern in which the counting number or the number of figures increases by the same amount each time (p. 425)

H

half dollar [haf dol′ər] **moneda de 50¢** A coin worth 50 cents and with a value equal to that of 50 pennies; 50¢
Example:

half hour [haf our] **media hora** 30 minutes (p. 509)
Example: Between 4:00 and 4:30 is one half hour.

halves [havz] **mitades**

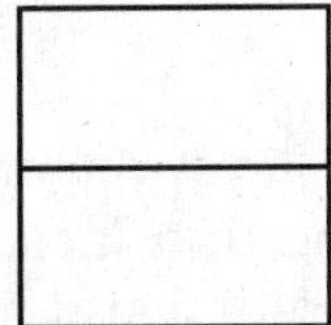

These are halves. (p. 291)

hexagon [hek′sə•gän] **hexágono** A polygon with six sides and six angles (p. 385)
Examples:

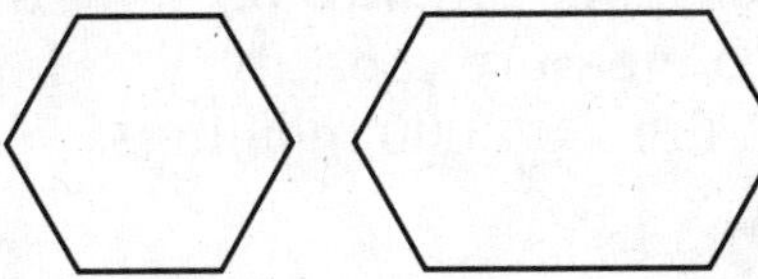

horizontal bar graph [hôr•ə•zän′təl bär graf] **gráfica de barras horizontales** A bar graph in which the bars go from left to right (p. 87)

hour (hr) [our] **hora (h)** A unit used to measure time; in one hour, the hour hand on an analog clock moves from one number to the next;
1 hour = 60 minutes (p. 509)

hour hand [our hand] **horario** The short hand on an analog clock (p. 509)

I

Identity Property of Addition [ī•den′tə•tē prä′pər•tē əv ə•di′shən] **propiedad de identidad de la suma** The property that states that when you add zero to a number, the result is that number
Example: $24 + 0 = 24$

Identity Property of Multiplication [ī•den′tə•tē prä′pər•tē əv mul•tə•plə•kā′shən] **propiedad de identidad de la multiplicación** The property that states that the product of any number and 1 is that number (p. 139)
Examples: $5 \times 1 = 5$
$1 \times 8 = 8$

inch (in.) [inch] **pulgada (pulg.)** A customary unit used to measure length or distance (p. 465)
Example:

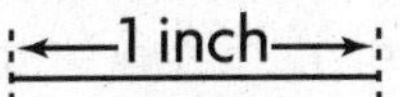

intersecting lines [in•tər•sek′ting līnz] **líneas secantes** Lines that cross (p. 393)
Example:

inverse operations [in′vûrs ä•pə•rā′shənz] **operaciones inversas** Opposite operations, or operations that undo one another, such as addition and subtraction or multiplication and division (p. 235)

isosceles triangle [ī•sä′sə•lēz trī′ang•gəl] **triángulo isósceles** A triangle that has two equal sides (p. 399)
Example:

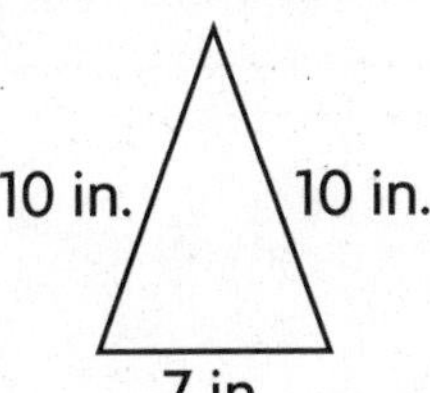

key [kē] **clave** The part of a map or graph that explains the symbols (p. 69)

kilogram (kg) [kil′ə•gram] **kilogramo (kg)** A metric unit used to measure mass; 1 kilogram = 1,000 grams

kilometer (km) [kə•lä′mə•tər] **kilómetro (km)** A metric unit used to measure length or distance;
1 kilometer = 1,000 meters (p. 477)

length [lengkth] **longitud** The measurement of the distance between two points (p. 465)

less than (<) [les t͟han] **menor que** A symbol used to compare two numbers when the lesser number is given first (p. 339)
Example: $3 < 7$

like fractions [līk frak′shənz] **fracciones semejantes** Fractions that have the same denominator (p. 351)
Example: $\frac{3}{8}$ and $\frac{7}{8}$

line [līn] **línea** A straight path extending in both directions with no endpoints (p. 377)
Example:

Word History

The word *line* comes from *linen*, a thread spun from the fibers of the flax plant. In early times, thread was held tight to mark a straight line between two points.

line of symmetry [līn əv si′mə•trē] **eje de simetría** An imaginary line on a shape about which the shape can be folded so that its two parts match exactly (p. 447)
Example:

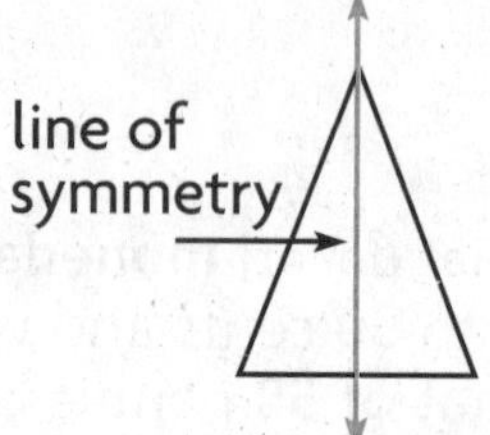

line plot [līn plöt] **diagrama de puntos** A graph that records each piece of data on a number line (p. 95)
Example:

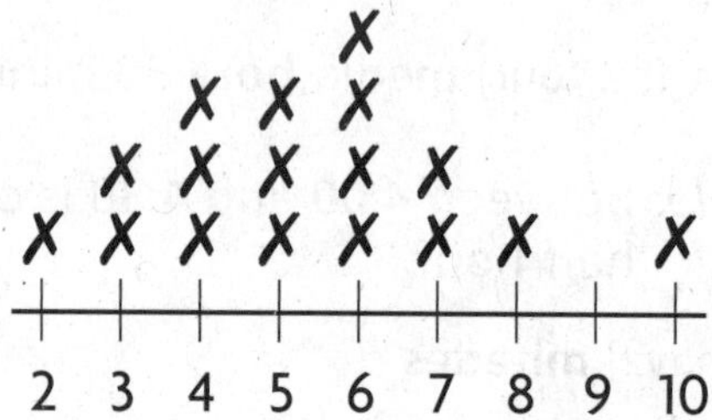

line segment [līn seg′mənt] **segmento** A part of a line that includes two points, called endpoints, and all of the points between them (p. 377)
Example:

liter (L) [lē′tər] **litro (L)** A metric unit used to measure capacity;
1 liter = 1,000 milliliters

mass [mas] **masa** The amount of matter in an object

meter (m) [mē′tər] **metro (m)** A metric unit used to measure length or distance;
1 meter = 100 centimeters (p. 477)

midnight [mid′nīt] **medianoche** 12:00 at night (p. 517)

mile (mi) [mīl] **milla (mi)** A customary unit used to measure length or distance;
1 mile = 5,280 feet (p. 465)

milliliter (mL) [mi′lə•lē•tər] **mililitro (mL)** A metric unit used to measure capacity

millimeter (mm) [mi′lə•mē•tər] **milímetro (mm)** A metric unit used to measure length or distance;
1 centimeter = 10 millimeters (p. 477)

minute (min) [mi′nət] **minuto (min)** A unit used to measure short amounts of time; in one minute, the minute hand on an analog clock moves from one mark to the next (p. 513)

minute hand [mi′nət hand] **minutero** The long hand on an analog clock (p. 509)

mixed number [mikst num′bər] **número mixto** A number represented by a whole number and a fraction (p. 309)
Example: $4\frac{1}{2}$

multiple [mul′tə•pəl] **múltiplo** A number that is the product of two counting numbers (p. 157)
Examples:

6	6	6	6	counting
× 1	× 2	× 3	× 4 ←	numbers
6	12	18	24 ←	multiples of 6

multiplication [mul•tə•plə•kā′shən] **multiplicación** The process of finding the total number of items in two or more equal groups; the opposite operation of division (p. 113)

multiply [mul′tə•plī] **multiplicar** To combine equal groups to find how many in all; the opposite operation of division (p. 113)

nickel [nik′əl] **moneda de 5¢** A coin worth 5 cents and with a value equal to that of 5 pennies; 5¢
Example:

noon [no͞on] **mediodía** 12:00 in the day (p. 517)

number line [num′bər līn] **recta numérica** A line on which numbers can be located
Example:

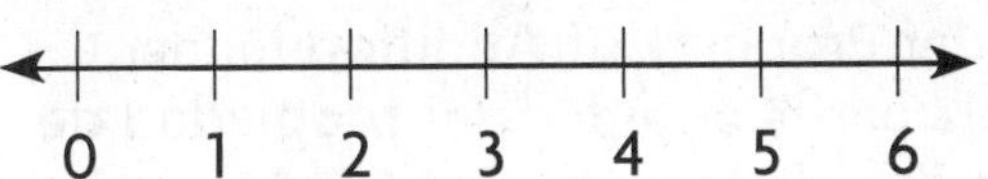

number sentence [num′bər sen′təns] **enunciado numérico** A sentence that includes numbers, operation symbols, and a greater than symbol, a less than symbol, or an equal sign
Example: $5 + 3 = 8$

numerator [no͞o′mə•rā•tər] **numerador** The part of a fraction above the line, which tells how many parts are being counted (p. 303)
Example: $\frac{3}{4}$ ← numerator

obtuse angle [əb•to͞os′ ang′gəl] **ángulo obtuso** An angle that has a measure greater than that of a right angle (p. 389)
Example:

obtuse triangle [əb•to͞os′ trī′ang•gəl] **triángulo obtusángulo** A triangle that has 1 obtuse angle (p. 400)

octagon [ok′tə•gän] **octágono** A polygon with eight sides and eight angles (p. 385)
Examples:

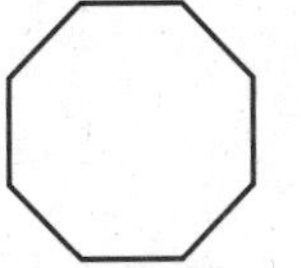
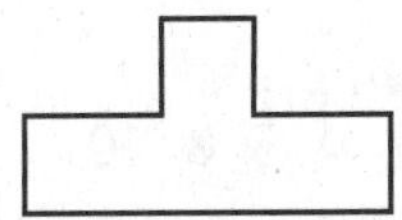

odd [od] **impar** A whole number that has a 1, 3, 5, 7, or 9 in the ones place

open shape [ō′pən shāp] **figura abierta** A shape that does not begin and end at the same point (p. 378)
Examples:

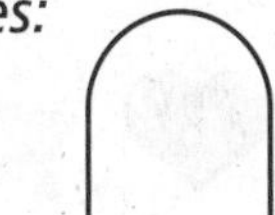
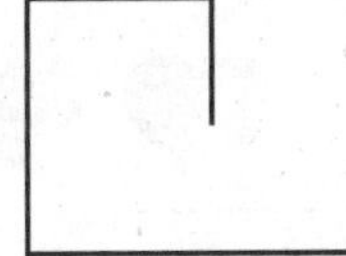

order [ôr′dər] **orden** A particular arrangement or placement of numbers or things, one after another

Order Property of Addition [ôr′dər prä′pər•tē əv ə•di′shən] **propiedad de orden de la suma** *See* Commutative Property of Addition.

Order Property of Multiplication [ôr′dər prä′pər•tē əv mul•tə•plə•kā′shən] **propiedad de orden de la multiplicación** *See* Commutative Property of Multiplication.

ounce (oz) [ouns] **onza (oz)** A customary unit used to measure weight; 1 pound = 16 ounces

parallel lines [pâr′ə•lel līnz] **líneas paralelas** Lines that never cross; lines that are always the same distance apart (p. 393)
Example:

parallelogram [pâr•ə•le′lə•gram] **paralelogramo** A quadrilateral whose opposite sides are parallel and have the same length (p. 403)
Example:

pattern [pat′ərn] **patrón** An ordered set of numbers or objects in which the order helps you predict what will come next (p. 407)
Examples:
2, 4, 6, 8, 10

pattern unit [pat′ərn yo͞o′nət] **unidad de patrón** The part of a pattern that repeats (p. 425)
Example:

pentagon [pen′tə•gän] **pentágono** A polygon with five sides and five angles (p. 385)
Example:

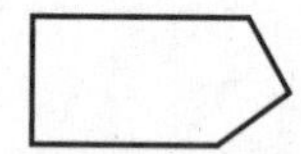

perimeter [pə•ri′mə•tər] **perímetro** The distance around a shape (p. 487)
Example:

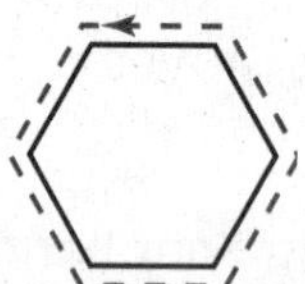

perpendicular lines [pûr•pən•di′kyə•lər līnz] **líneas perpendiculares** Lines that intersect to form right angles (p. 393)
Example:

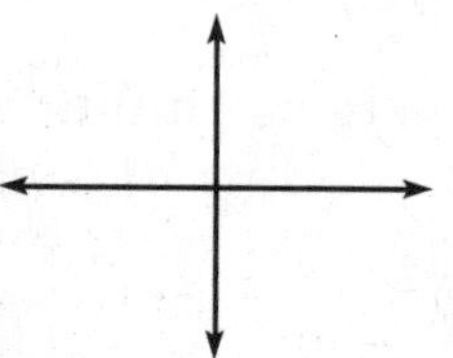

pictograph [pik′tə•graf] **pictografía** A graph that uses pictures to show and compare information (p. 69)
Example:

How We Get to School	
Walk	❊ ❊ ❊
Ride a Bike	❊ ❊ ❊ ❊
Ride a Bus	❊ ❊ ❊ ❊ ❊ ❊
Ride in a Car	❊ ❊
Key: Each ❊ = 10 students.	

pint (pt) [pīnt] **pinta (pt)** A customary unit used to measure capacity; 1 pint = 2 cups

place value [plās val′yo͞o] **valor posicional** The value of each digit in a number, based on the location of the digit (p. 9)

plane shape [plān shāp] **figura plana** A shape in a plane that is formed by curves, line segments, or both (p. 377)
Example:

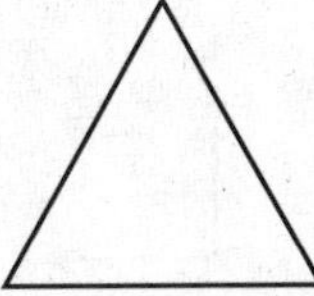

P.M. [pē•em] **p.m.** The time between noon and midnight (p. 517)

point [point] **punto** An exact position or location (p. 377)

polygon [po′lē•gän] **polígono** A closed plane shape with straight sides that are line segments (p. 381)
Examples:

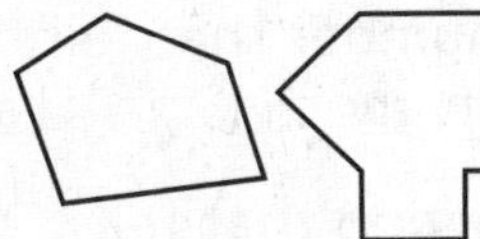

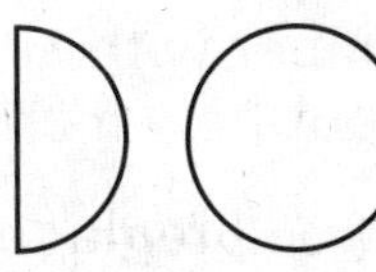

polygons   not polygons

Word History

Did you ever think that a ***polygon*** looks like a bunch of knees that are bent? This is how the term got its name. *Poly-* is from the Greek word *polys*, which means "many." The ending *-gon* is from the Greek word *gony*, which means "knee."

pound (lb) [pound] **libra (lb)** A customary unit used to measure weight; 1 pound = 16 ounces

product [prä′dəkt] **producto** The answer in a multiplication problem (p. 117)
Example: $3 \times 8 = 24$
↑ product

Q

quadrilateral [kwä•drə•la′tə•rəl] **cuadrilátero** A polygon with four sides and four angles (p. 385)
Example:

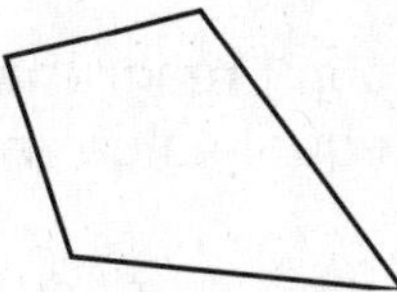

quart (qt) [kwôrt] **cuarto (ct)** A customary unit used to measure capacity; 1 quart = 2 pints

quarter [kwôr′•tər] **moneda de 25¢** A coin worth 25 cents and with a value equal to that of 25 pennies; 25¢
Example:

quarter hour [kwôr′tər our] **cuarto de hora** 15 minutes (p. 509)
Example: Between 4:00 and 4:15 is one quarter hour.

quotient [kwō′shənt] **cociente** The number, not including the remainder, that results from division (p. 213)
Example: $8 \div 4 = 2$
↑ quotient

R

ray [rā] **semirrecta** A part of a line, with one endpoint, that is straight and continues in one direction (p. 377)
Example:

rectangle [rek′tang•gəl] **rectángulo** A quadrilateral with 2 pairs of parallel sides, 2 pairs of equal sides, and 4 right angles (p. 403)
Example:

rectangular prism [rek•tang′gyə•lər pri′zəm] **prisma rectangular** A three-dimensional shape with six faces that are all rectangles
Example:

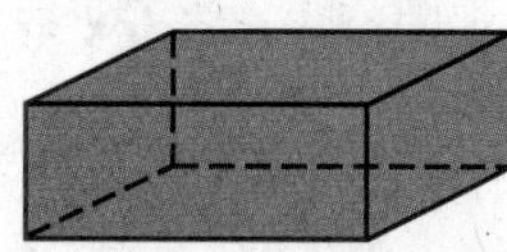

regroup [rē•grōōp′] **reagrupar** To exchange amounts of equal value to rename a number
Example: 5 + 8 = 13 ones or 1 ten 3 ones

regular polygon [reg′yə•lər pä′lə•gän] **polígono regular** A polygon that has all sides that are equal in length and all angles equal in measure (p. 385)
Examples:

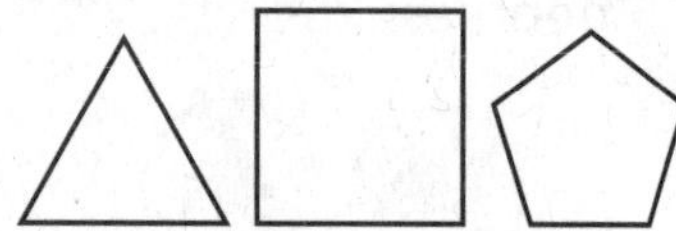

remainder [ri•mān′dər] **residuo** The amount left over when a number cannot be divided evenly (p. 272)

repeating pattern [ri•pēt′ing pat′ərn] **patrón que se repite** A pattern which uses the same pattern unit over and over again (p. 425)

results [ri•zults′] **resultados** The answers from a survey (p. 61)

rhombus [räm′bəs] **rombo** A quadrilateral with 2 pairs of parallel sides and 4 equal sides and four angles (p. 403)
Example:

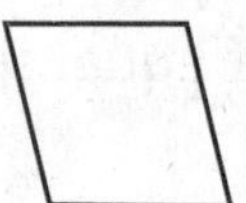

right angle [rīt ang′gəl] **ángulo recto** An angle that forms a square corner (p. 389)
Example:

right triangle [rīt trī′ang•gəl] **triángulo rectángulo** A triangle with one right angle (p. 400)
Example:

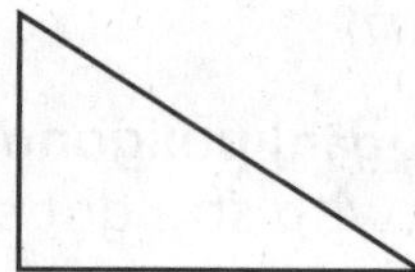

round [round] **redondear** To replace a number with another number that tells about how many or how much (p. 27)

rule [rōōl] **regla** An instruction that tells you the correct way to do something (pp. 257, 425)

scale [skāl] **escala** The numbers placed at fixed distances on a graph to help label the graph (p. 83)

scalene triangle [skā′lēn trī′ang•gəl] **triángulo escaleno** A triangle in which no sides are equal (p. 399)
Example:

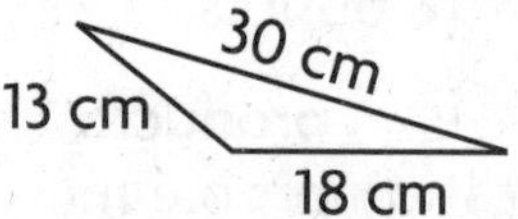

second (sec) [se′kənd] **segundo (seg)** A small unit of time;
60 seconds = 1 minute (p. 510)

sequence [sē′kwəns] **ordenar** To write events in order (p. 538)

side [sīd] **lado** A straight line segment in a polygon (p. 381)

sixths [siksths] **sextos**

These are sixths. (p. 291)

sphere [sfir] **esfera** A three-dimensional shape that has the shape of a round ball
Example:

square [skwâr] **cuadrado** A quadrilateral with 2 pairs of parallel sides, 4 equal sides, and 4 right angles (p. 403)
Example:

square pyramid [skwâr pir′ə•mid] **pirámide cuadrada** A three-dimensional, pointed shape with a flat base that is a square
Example:

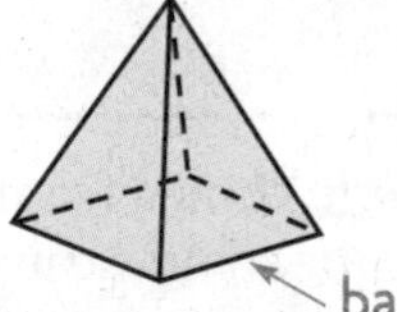

standard form [stan′dərd fôrm] **forma normal** A way to write numbers by using the digits 0–9, with each digit having a place value (p. 14)
Example: 345 ← standard form

straight angle [strāt ang′gəl] **ángulo llano** An angle in which two rays point in opposite directions so that they form a line (p. 389)
Example:

subtraction [sub•trak′shən] **resta** The process of finding how many are left when a number of items are taken away from a group of items; the process of finding the difference when two groups are compared; the opposite operation of addition

sum [sum] **suma o total** The answer to an addition problem

survey [sûr′vā] **encuesta** A method of gathering information (p. 61)

symmetry [sim′ə•trē] **simetría** A shape has symmetry if it can be folded along a line so that the two parts match exactly; one half of the shape looks like the mirror image of the other half. (p. 443)

tally table [ta′lē tā′bəl] **tabla de conteo** A table that uses tally marks to record data (p. 61)
Example:

Favorite Sport	
Sport	**Tally**
Soccer	𝍸 |||
Baseball	|||
Football	𝍸
Basketball	𝍸	

tenths [tenths] **décimos**
Example:

These are tenths.

thirds [thûrdz] **tercios**

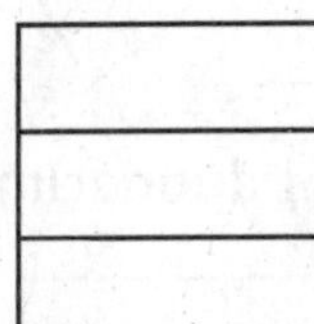

These are thirds. (p. 291)

three-dimensional shape [thrē•di•men′shən•əl shāp] **figura tridimensional** A shape that has length, width, and height
Example:

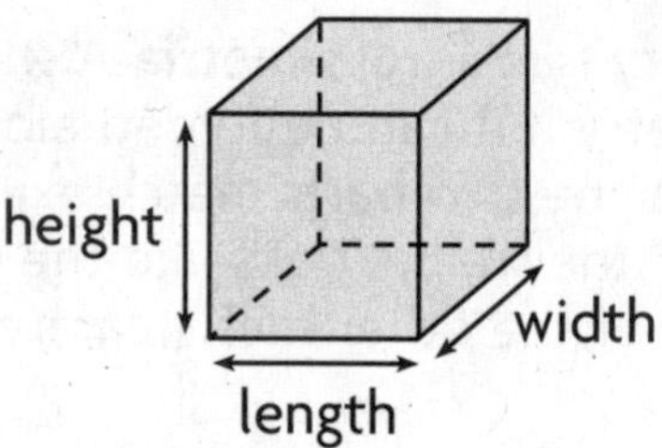

time line [tīm līn] **línea cronológica** A drawing that shows when and in what order events took place (p. 535)

trapezoid [trap′ə•zoid] **trapecio** A quadrilateral with exactly one pair of parallel sides and four angles (p. 403)
Example:

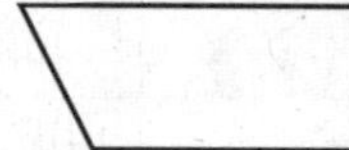

tree diagram [trē dī′ə•gram] **diagrama de árbol** An organized list that shows all possible combinations (p. 165)
Example:

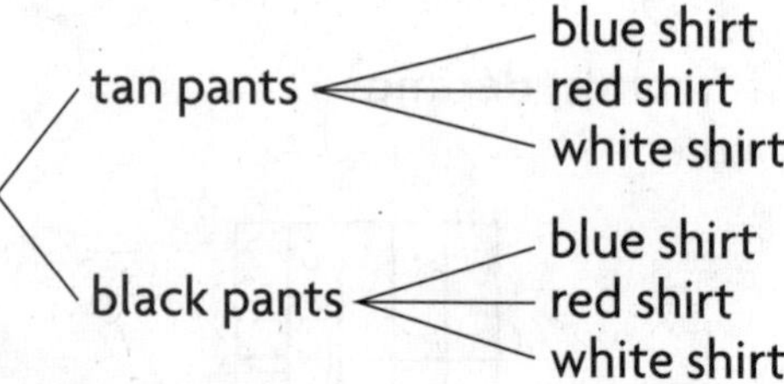

triangle [trī′ang′gəl] **triángulo** A polygon with three sides and three angles (p. 385)
Examples:

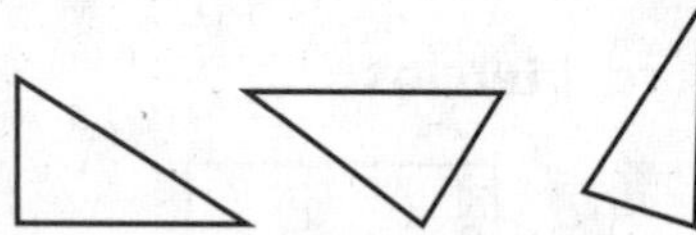

twelfths [twelftth] **duodécimos**

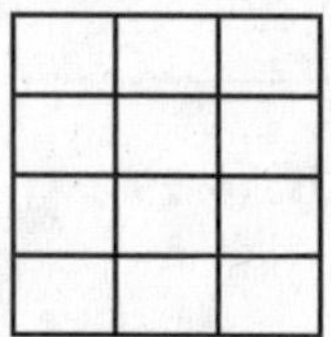

These are twelfths.

two-dimensional shape [to͞o•di•men′shən•əl shāp] **figura bidimensional** A shape that has only length and width (p. 378)
Example:

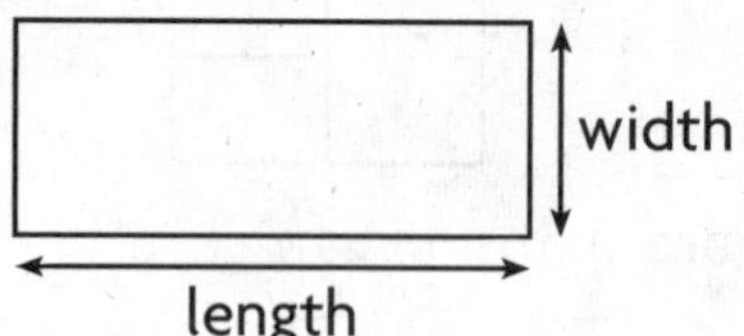

unit fraction [yo͞o′nət frak′shən] **fracción unitaria** A fraction that has 1 as its top number, or numerator (p. 299)

unlike fractions [un•līk′ frak′shənz] **fracciones no semejantes** Fractions that have different denominators (p. 351)
Example: $\frac{4}{6}$ and $\frac{3}{5}$

variable [vâr′ē•ə•bəl] **variable** A symbol or a letter that stands for an unknown number (p. 191)

Word History

The word ***variable*** comes from the Latin word *variabilis*, meaning "changeable." At first, the word applied to changes of color, as in the speckled fur of animals. Eventually, the word was used for things that involve change of any kind.

Venn diagram [ven dī′ə•gram] **diagrama de Venn** A diagram that shows relationships among sets of things
Example:

2-Digit Numbers **Even Numbers**

35 **17** **29** **12** **10** **8** **6** **4**

vertex [vûr′teks] **vértice** The point at which two rays of an angle or two (or more) line segments meet in a plane shape (p. 377)
Example:

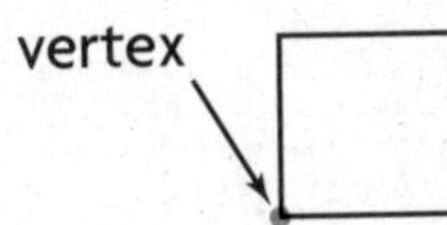

vertical bar graph [vûr′ti•kəl bär graf] **gráfica de barras verticales** A bar graph in which the bars go up from bottom to top (p. 87)

weight [wāt] **peso** The heaviness of an object

whole number [hōl num′bər] **número entero** One of the numbers 0, 1, 2, 3, 4, ... The set of whole numbers goes on without end.

word form [wûrd fôrm] **en palabras** A way to write numbers by using words (p. 14)
Example: The word form of 212 is two hundred twelve.

yard (yd) [yärd] **yarda (yd)** A customary unit used to measure length or distance; 1 yard = 3 feet (p. 465)

year (yr) [ˋyir] **año** A measure of time equal to twelve months; 1 year = 365 days (p. 535)

Zero Property of Multiplication [zē′rō prä′pər•tē əv mul•tə•plə•kā′shən] **propiedad del cero de la multiplicación** The property that states that the product of zero and any number is zero (p. 139)
Example: $0 \times 6 = 0$

Table of Measures

METRIC	CUSTOMARY
Length	
1 centimeter (cm) = 10 millimeters (mm)	
1 decimeter (dm) = 10 centimeters (cm)	1 foot (ft) = 12 inches (in.)
1 meter (m) = 100 centimeters	1 yard (yd) = 3 feet, or 36 inches
1 meter (m) = 10 decimeters	1 mile (mi) = 1,760 yards, or 5,280 feet
1 kilometer (km) = 1,000 meters	
Mass/Weight	
1 kilogram (kg) = 1,000 grams (g)	1 pound (lb) = 16 ounces (oz)
Capacity	
1 liter (L) = 1,000 milliliters (mL)	1 pint (pt) = 2 cups (c)
	1 quart (qt) = 2 pints
	1 gallon (gal) = 4 quarts

TIME	
1 minute (min) = 60 seconds (sec)	1 year (yr) = 12 months (mo), or about 52 weeks
1 hour (hr) = 60 minutes	1 year = 365 days
1 day = 24 hours	1 leap year = 366 days
1 week (wk) = 7 days	1 decade = 10 years
	1 century = 100 years

MONEY
1 penny = 1 cent (¢)
1 nickel = 5 cents
1 dime = 10 cents
1 quarter = 25 cents
1 half-dollar = 50 cents
1 dollar ($) = 100 cents

SYMBOLS
< is less than
> is greater than
= is equal to

Photo Credits

KEY: (t) top, (c) center, (b) bottom, (bg) background, (fg) foreground.

Front Cover: (bg) top-Con Tanasiuk/Design Pics/Corbis; (bg) bottom-PBNJ Productions/PBNJ Productions/Corbis; (bl) Digital Vision/Fotosearch; (br) Michael McMurrough / Alamy; Salamander-Design Pics/Fotosearch; **Spine:** Digital Vision/Fotosearch.

Back Cover: (bg) Con Tanasiuk/Design Pics/Corbis; (tr) Design Pics/Fotosearch.

Title Pages: iv (bl) DigiPro Photography & Imaging/Alamy; iv (tr) Zeno Elea/Alamy; iv (bg) Mark Downey/PhotoDisc/Getty Images; (cr) Jeffrey Coolidge/PhotoDisc/Getty Images; (c) Purestock/Getty Images; (b) Digital Vision Ltd/agefotostock; (bg) Mark Downey/PhotoDisc/Getty Images; (tc) Jeffrey Coolidge/PhotoDisc/Getty Images; (tl) Corbis.

Table of Contents: v (r) Michael Aw/PhotoDisc/Getty Images; (cr) Digital Vision/Getty Images; vi (l) PhotoDisc; (bl) Digital Stock/Corbis; vii (r) Corbis; (tr) D. Hurst/Alamy; (r) PhotoDisc; viii (bl) PhotoDisc; (l) Corbis; ix (r) Radius Images/Radius Images.

Big Idea 1: 3 (bl) Mark Conlin/Alamy; 17 Corbis; 20 Corel Stock Photo Library; 24 PhotoDisc/Getty Images; 27 (cr) Corel Stock Photo Library; 35 (tr) Hemera Technologies/JupiterImages; 36 (tr) Javier Larrea/agefotostock; 39 (tr) NASA; 42 NASA; 44 PhotoDisc/Getty Images; 46 D. Falconer/PhotoLink/PhotoDisc/Getty Images; 48 Image Club Graphics; 52 (tr) Artville; 59 (bl) Courtesy of Brevard Zoo; 62 (tr) Corbis; 69 (br) PhotoDisc/Getty Images; 73 (br) Lee Foster/Alamy; 74 (br) gary718/Shutterstock; 75 (br) Olga Lyubkina/Shutterstock; 91 (cr) Corbis; 92 (cr) Jeff Greenberg/PhotoEdit; 100 (tr) Digital Stock/Corbis ; 107 (bc) Art Wolfe/Getty Images; 110 (tr) Tatiana777/Shutterstock; 113 (tc) Corbis; 121 Eduard Stelmakh/Shutterstock; 127 (tr) PhotoDisc/Getty Images; 131 (cr) PhotoDisc/Getty Images; 146 Image Club Graphics; 151 (bc) ZTS/Shutterstock; 160 (tr) Potapov Alexander/Shutterstock; 173 (cr) Joe McDonald/Animals Animals - Earth Scenes; 176 (cr) Raul Gonzalez Perez/Photo Researchers, Inc.; 187 Geostock/PhotoDisc/Getty Images; 188 G. K. & Vikki Hart/PhotoDisc/Getty Images; 189 (tr) Annette/Shutterstock; 203 (bc) Steve Byland/Shutterstock; 205 (cr) Tom Mackie/Alamy; 208 (tr) PhotoDisc/Getty Images; 209 (br) John Pontier/Animals Animals – Earth Scenes; 213 (cr) Steve Byland/Shutterstock; 216 (tc) Ronnie Howard/Shutterstock; (tr) PhotoDisc; 217 (cr) Juniors Bildarchiv/Alamy; 220 (tr) Corbis; 231 (tr) Tim Krieger/Brand X Pictures/PictureQuest; 235 (cr) Creatas/SuperStock; 247 (bc) Andre Nantel/Shutterstock; 253 (cr) FloridaStock/Shutterstock; 264 (tr) Image Source/Getty Images; 267 (cr) PhotoDisc/Getty Images; 275 (cr) Dennis MacDonald/Alamy; 278 (tr) Corel Stock Photo Library; 279 (tr) SuperStock; 282 (cr) Richard Wong/Alamy.

Big Idea 2: 287 (cr) Coinery/Alamy; 288 (tr) Richard T. Nowitz/Corbis; 289 (bc) Stuart Pearce/agefotostock; 299 (cr) Corel Stock Photo Library; 312 (tr) ingret/Shutterstock; 321 (tr) PhotoDisc/Getty Images; 322 (tr) Jostein Hauge/Shutterstock; 329 (br) PhotoDisc/Getty Images; 337 (bc) PhotoDisc; 339 Corbis; 340 (tr) Kevin Sanchez/Cole Group/PhotoDisc/Getty Images; 351 Roy Morsch/agefotostock.

Big Idea 3: 373 agefotostock/SuperStock; 375 (bc) Cameron Davidson/Alamy; 381 (r) Christie's Images/Corbis; 415 (bl) Tom and Becky Burazin/Getty Images; 446 (bl) Corel Stock Photo Library; (tr), (cl), (cr) Siede Preis/Photodisc/Getty Images; (bc) Dee Golden/Shutterstock; (br) C Squared Studios/PhotoDisc/Getty Images; 463 (bc) Silver Image Photo Agency; 466 (cl) George Doyle & Ciaran Griffin/Getty Images; (tr) Alan Schein Photography/Corbis; (bl) PhotoDisc; (br) Alamy; 468 (cr) PhotoDisc/Getty Images ; 474 (bl) PeppPic/Shutterstock; 475 (tr) Ingram; 485 (cr) Brand X Pictures; 486 (bl) Corbis; 494 (tc) Corel Stock Photo Library; (tr) Corel Stock Photo Library; 507 (bc) Courtesy of Museum of Discovery and Science & AutoNation IMAX Theater; 509 James Gritz/PhotoDisc/Getty Images; 512 (c) Corel Stock Photo Library; 513 Leonard Lee Rue III/Photo Researchers, Inc.; 517 (cr) PhotoDisc/Getty Images; 518 Russell Illig/PhotoDisc/Getty Images; 520 (tr) Dave G. Houser/Corbis; 523 Corbis; 527 (tr) Michele Burgess/agefotostock; 528 (tr) PhotoDisc; 538 (cr) PhotoDisc.

All other photos Houghton Mifflin Harcourt libraries and photographers; Guy Jarvis, Weronica Ankarorn, Eric Camden, Don Couch, Doug Dukane, Ken Kinzie, April Riehm, and Steve Williams.